MAN, MYTH & MAGIC

VOLUME 2

Braz – Dant

EDITORIAL STAFF
Editor-in-Chief   Richard Cavendish

Editorial Board   C. A. Burland
Glyn Daniel
E. R. Dodds
Mircea Eliade
William Sargant
John Symonds
R. J. Zwi Werblowsky
R. C. Zaehner

Special Consultants   Rev. S. G. F. Brandon
Katharine M. Briggs
William Gaunt
Francis Huxley
John Lehmann

Deputy Editor   Isabel Sutherland

Assistant Editors   Frank Smyth
Malcolm Saunders
Tessa Clark
Julie Thompson
Polly Patullo

Art Editor   Valerie Kirkpatrick
Design Assistant   Andrzej Bielecki
Picture Editor   John McKenzie

REVISION STAFF
Executive Editor   Yvonne Deutch
Editorial Consultant   Paul G. Davis
Editors   Emma Fisher
Mary Lambert
Sarah Litvinoff
Designer   Caroline Dewing
Production Manager   Robert Paulley
Film Controller   David Nugent

Library of Congress Cataloging in Publication Data

Main entry under title:

Man, myth, and magic

   Bibliography: p.
   1. Occult sciences. 2. Psychical research.
I. Cavendish, Richard. II. Deutch, Yvonne.
BF1411.M25 1983   133   82-13041
ISBN 0-86307-041-8 (set)
ISBN 0-86307-043-4 (v.2)

British Library Cataloguing in Publication Data

Man, myth and magic.
   1. Mythology – Dictionaries
   2. Religion – Dictionaries
   I. Cavendish, Richard
   291.1'3'0321 BL303

   ISBN 0-86307-041-8 (set)
   ISBN 0-86307-043-4 (v.2)

Reference Edition Published 1983

© Marshall Cavendish Limited MCMLXXXIII
© B.P.C. Publishing Limited MCMLXX

Printed and Bound in Italy by L.E.G.O. S.p.a. Vicenza.

Published by Marshall Cavendish Corporation,
147 West Merrick Road,
Freeport, Long Island
N.Y. 11520

Distributed in India by Standard Literature.

MAN, MYTH & MAGIC

The Illustrated Encyclopedia
of Mythology, Religion
and the Unknown

Editor-in-Chief
Richard Cavendish

Editorial Board
C. A. Burland; Professor Glyn Daniel;
Professor E. R. Dodds; Professor Mircea Eliade;
William Sargant; John Symonds;
Professor R. J. Zwi Werblowsky;
Professor R. C. Zaehner.

New Edition edited and compiled by
Yvonne Deutch, B.A. University of Exeter;
M.A. University of Kansas, Lawrence, Kansas.

MARSHALL CAVENDISH
NEW YORK, LONDON, TORONTO

CONTENTS Volume 2

Times Newspapers

BRAZIL

Early European explorers were astonished by such customs as comperage, in which the Indians gave women to their European guests, cannibalism and the ritual execution of prisoners, and by the men's habit of piercing holes in their lips or cheeks through which protruded plugs of wood or stone

Ritual execution and religious cannibalism were encountered by early explorers among the tribes of Brazil. Today this vast country still presents complex patterns of mythological belief and strange practices

WHEN IT WAS first discovered by Europeans, the coast of Brazil was populated by a number of tribes which nearly all had the same customs and shared the Tupi language. They lived in stockaded villages, several hundred inhabitants to each house, and four houses to each village. They hunted for game in the forest, fished, farmed, and waged war on each other in a systematic way to capture prisoners who were later ritually executed and then eaten.

As the interior was explored more deeply,

quite different tribes were found. A large group of these, speaking the Ge language, roam the country during the dry season to hunt and gather food, returning to their villages and plantations during the wet season. They have a complicated social organization, being divided into clans and groups of inter-tribal marriages. Some tribes are nomadic all the year round, but in the Amazon basin there is a large group of settled tribes belonging to the Arawak and Carib cultures, whose main focus is in the Guyanas and the Caribbean. It is a vast country, and there is no single pattern of custom and belief.

The early chroniclers who encountered the Tupi-speaking tribes wrote detailed reports of the savage paradise in which

they found themselves. They tried to understand such customs as comperage, in which the Indians gave women to their European guests; the men's habit of piercing holes in their lips and cheeks, through which protruded sharp plugs of wood, stone or resin, like the fangs of jaguars; and of course cannibalism, which they put down.

The common justification of cannibalism is that by eating the flesh of an enemy warrior you absorb his manly virtues. For the Tupi, the principal virtue was that of courage, but the fact that the wives of chiefs were given the genitals of a dead prisoner shows that his sexuality was also esteemed. The virtue of courage, however, was intimately linked to the idea of revenge. The ghosts of those who had died, either naturally

325

Tupi women were even more voracious cannibals than the men and made no bones about eating a prisoner

Harald Schultz

or in wars to get prisoners, had to be placated by capturing an enemy and clubbing him ritually to death. These prisoners were first adopted into the captor's family, given a young girl as wife, and sometimes lived in captivity for 20 years before being put to death. Strangely enough to our eyes, prisoners seldom tried to escape, for to die in the land of their enemies was a sure passport to immortality in the Indian heaven.

The Great Walker

There are few overt references to cannibalism in their mythology. The main figure is called Maira and is half-way between a god and a hero. He is sometimes called the Walker, in honour of the great journeys the Tupi excelled in, and sometimes the Maker. He did not, however, create the world in its entirety, but transformed what was already in existence into an order in which human beings could live: he was thus a culture hero, giving the main rudiments of their social life to the Indians.

One myth deals with Maira in the shape of a young child who, when wandering in the woods, was met by a poor widow and her children gathering food. Thinking he was about to stop them, the children began to beat him, an act in which he encouraged them – for as the blows fell, it began to rain edible roots, fruit and vegetables, in fact all the food plants the Tupi now grow. Later, when Maira had reassumed adult form, he visited the Indians. Though wanting to give him proper homage for his generosity, the Indians also wished to be quite sure of his identity. They made him jump over three fires, in the second of which he died, his head exploding like thunder.

It is the usual fate of a culture hero to be a stranger, and to die at the hands of those he has befriended. Myths from other tribes show that the theme of the young boy producing food plants when he is beaten is allied to initiation rites, when a youth becomes a man. These rites usually deal with a number of novices at the same time. The Tupi initiation rite, however, was individualistic: a youth proved himself by executing a prisoner, after which he went into seclusion for some months, endured ordeals such as the scarification of his body, took a new name, and was then able to marry.

A jaguar was sometimes dealt with in the same way as a prisoner. An explanatory story from the Tupi-speaking Urubu tribe tells how a man avenged his brother's death by following the cannibalistic murderer to an underground village of jaguars, and killing the chief who was dressed up in his ritual feather regalia. It is this feather regalia which all men now wear, especially for ceremonial occasions, that was originally the property of the jaguar; and other beliefs show us that this jaguar is an aspect of the culture hero himself.

The feather head-dress is an image of the sun, and the hero lives in the house of the sun in the east. At night he has to pass from the west underground, when he puts on a jaguar shape, to go back to his birthplace. Often the souls of the dead are thought to accompany the daytime sun, and anyone dressing up in the feather regalia is imitating this heroic state. Significantly, the Tupi prisoner was dressed up in just this way, and various rites transformed him into something approaching a chief as well, that is, a representative of the village where he was to be executed. More particularly, he was transformed into a kind of ritual brother-in-law.

Cannibal Wives

A study of mythology shows that the jaguar is regarded as a brother-in-law throughout South America. Sex always has curious associations with eating and the killing of game, a symbolic equation that has much to do with the operation of the incest taboo. The consequence of this taboo, of course, is to stop a man marrying in his own immediate family, however that is defined. Everyone being in the same position, the simplest solution is to give your sister to another man as his wife in exchange for his sister. When such an exchange is not possible, the husband has to pay for his wife by working for his in-laws. This happened regularly among the Tupi, and such were the antagonisms created by the system that the same word did duty both for brother-in-law and for enemy. The word was 'tobajara', meaning in effect, the rival with whom you have a competition for honour. The jaguar, who rivals man in killing game, is used in myth as the figure to denote the rival in sexuality and marriage.

The enemy captive was a rival of this kind. He was given a wife by his captor and so, like any husband, had to do menial work for him. But he was unlike the usual run of husbands in that he was treated with much affection instead of with the customary disdain and avoidance, and indeed he was called 'the loved one'.

Here we may see an interesting parallel with the vegetation gods of the Middle East, dying yearly amid the laments of the women. However, the Tupi women, even the prisoner's wife herself, made no bones about eating the prisoner. They were even more voracious cannibals than the men, who saw the rite partly as an opportunity to gain prestige for themselves. Throughout the country, the ideal of men is to be hard in body and mind, to be wakeful, abstinent, capable of great physical endurance and of undergoing painful ordeals such as scarification, liquid pepper in the eyes, fasting, or being stung by the largest and most venomous wasps and ants.

The Reign of Women

This masculine ideal is set against the feminine vice of softness and sleepiness. Several mythologies tell how death came to men because they were too sleepy to answer the call of a tree whose bark regularly comes off in sheets, and which had the gift of immortality.

Masculine virtue is thus aimed at immortality and power. The lethargy, which all are afflicted with, stems from mythological times when it was the women rather than the men who had charge of things. The story is of wide occurrence in South America. Sometimes it describes how the women

Harald Schultz

Ritual costumes of the Umutina Indians of the Matto Grosso in the interior of Brazil *Left* Man wearing the skins of a jaguar and a wild cat. The jaguar plays an important part in Brazilian Indian beliefs. In some cases the hero who long ago gave a tribe its culture and social organization was a jaguar, some believe that the sun takes the form of a jaguar at night, and many of the shamans, or priests, are possessed by the jaguar spirit and turn into jaguars after death *Right* A father and his small son dance in a ceremony honouring the dead. Many Indians of Brazil believed that the ghosts of the dead needed to be placated, which was done by clubbing an enemy captive to death. Prisoners died happily because they believed that death in the country of their enemies was a sure passport to immortality in heaven

found what were to be the sacred flutes of the tribe, the representatives of the ancestors, by which means they kept the men in subjection. Nowadays the men, having successfully revolted, have the care of these instruments together with that of the entire religious apparatus and it is death for a woman or an uninitiated youth to see them.

Tupi myth also tells of this reign of women, who did all the work while the men, who had no genitals, lolled in their hammocks like children. The women satisfied their sexuality by calling a giant snake from under the ground, on whose raised head they took their pleasure. This custom continued till a young boy discovered what was happening and cut off the snake's head. The women took offence and left. It was then that Maira took charge by fashioning male members for the men out of the snake's body and sewing them in place, reserving the head for himself. Appeased in this way, the women returned, and the men took command.

This story deals with an adolescent fantasy which often goes with initiation. Tupi youths tied a piece of string around their foreskins to hide their shame, while men wore the penis sheath. The significance of this can be seen among the Bororo, where youths live in their mothers' houses until they are initiated, when they must go to the Men's House at the centre of the village. There they are given a penis sheath and are then ready for marriage. During this lengthy rite, the penis sheath is called the boy's wife, and is a substitute for the sister he cannot marry: instead he marries the daughter of the man who gives him the sheath. The myth of the reign of women plainly relates to this situation.

Battle of the Sexes

Initiation always deals with the separation of a boy from his mother, and his adoption into the society of men. Often one finds the institution of a Men's House or type of club in tribes like the Mundurucu, where men have to live with their wives' families, instead of the wife living with the husband's family: it becomes a 'home from home' where the strains of being a perpetual in-law are not felt. At the same time it is the place where the men celebrate their independence from women in religious form, with the help of masks, dances, songs, musical instruments and mysteries.

Besides the competition for honour between men there is thus a battle between the sexes. The serpent, who is the private lover of women, has to be killed by men whereupon a sound relation between the sexes can be established through marriage. The north-western tribes tell a story which is a complication of this theme. It deals with a young man suspected of being a cannibal, who is killed by his own people and turns into a palm tree. The sacred flutes, often kept under water when not needed, are carved from the trunk of this tree, and a beer made from its fruit. Whenever an important man dies, his body is burnt and the ashes mixed with the beer, which everyone then drinks in commemoration of him. It is all part of the initiation theme, for the hut where the novices are secluded is often thought of as a cannibalistic monster, serpent or water-demon, which has to be killed for the youths to emerge as newborn men.

The name of the cannibal palm-tree spirit is Jurupari, who has become one of the bogey-men throughout Brazil, for those of European and Negro descent as much as for the Indians. He is the master of the jungle, and is much feared. Among the Cashinawa tribe elements of the Jurupari myth appear in the figure of a Rolling Head, who creates the rainbow – the form taken by the great serpent when it is killed – and the moon.

The Tupi say that the moon was once a

327

Harald Schultz

man who committed incest with his sister, and the Jurupari stories may have a similar background. In any case, it is this moon man who must be ritually killed, like the Tupi prisoner, in imitation of the moon's monthly birth and death. Among the Bororo people, this moon man is the brother of the sun. Among the Arawak tribes, the sun and moon are also brothers, the sun creating useful animals and the moon harmful ones. Sometimes they are figured as the jaguar and the anteater – a dangerous animal when roused – who quarrel over who is the stronger. The jaguar says that he is, since he eats flesh while the other eats only ants, but the anteater replies that this can only be proved by an examination of their faeces. By a trick he exchanges the jaguar's excrement for his own, leaving the jaguar humiliated.

The Tupi also have a story concerning twins. Their mother is the wife of Maira who leaves her when she disbelieves in his

Above left A chief of the Kamaiura Indians in the Xingu park, wearing a ceremonial head-dress of eagle and parrot feathers. Christian missionaries have laboured for centuries to convert the Brazilian Indians and at the missionary posts outside the park tribal rituals are forbidden *Below left* Waura Indians of the Upper Xingu area in northern Brazil. Two men almost entirely concealed in huge straw masks are begging food from a woman *Above* Masked and robed figures representing dangerous spirits, which have emerged from the forest to attend the initiation of young girls, among the Tikuna Indians of the Upper Solimoes River

magical powers. Already pregnant with his child, she follows him but is seduced by Mikur the opossum, who fathers the other child on her; she then comes to a village of jaguars where she is killed, and the twins are brought up by a jaguar grandmother. When they are adult they avenge their mother by killing all the jaguars but one, who is allowed to escape by Mikur's son, and then go in search of their father. When they find him he puts them through a number of tests and ordeals, such as having to pass through the Clashing Rocks, in which Mikur's son is always killed and has to be brought back to life by his brother.

Playing Possum

There are many possible interpretations of such a myth. One certainly deals with the distinction between the mortal body and the immortal soul. The fact that the opossum's son dies and is brought back to life points to the particular manifestation of this belief in shamanism. A shaman is a man (occasionally, in South America, a woman) able to fall into trance and converse with spirits which help him or her to divine the future, diagnose disease and perform cures. The trance is likened to a death, especially that mock death known as 'playing possum', from which comes part of the significance of this animal.

Shamanism is sometimes hereditary, father training son in the techniques of the craft. More often the vocation descends on a man, after a period of psychological disorder or shock, in which he rushes into the woods

and returns unable to think or speak clearly and smelling like a corpse – opossums, it should be noted, also have an unpleasant odour. He is then trained to recognize the spirit which confronted him, usually that of a bird or animal. He acquires the ability to be possessed by it and eventually by others, the chief of which is the jaguar spirit. The shaman's equipment usually includes the gourd rattle or maraca, which to some Indians speaks with the voice of the spirits. He may use a variety of plant drugs to help him into trance, usually tobacco, together with techniques such as exaggerated over-breathing. His seances take place at night, for spirits are fearful of light, and he may put on a remarkable theatrical performance in which he talks to the spirits; they reply with shrieks, bellows, groans and roars.

The shaman, then, is a man who can separate soul from body without actually dying, and who is able to travel to the sky or below the earth in search of the souls of his patients which have been stolen away. The loss of one's soul is a common complaint amongst Indians, and often occurs when someone sees a ghost in the jungle, or the Tupi Anyang, a hostile spirit who is covered with long hair, is of a greenish colour, has no bones in his body, and performs obscene antics. But Indians may also suffer from an invasion by spirits or by disease, which must then be extracted. This the shaman does by first blowing on the afflicted part with tobacco smoke, the vehicle of spiritual power, and then sucking

Kamaiura Indian praying for the rains to stop so that the fishing season can begin. The wooden flute is the instrument through which he speaks to the gods. Among many Indians the sacred flutes represent the ancestors of the tribe, and it is death for a woman or a boy who has not yet been initiated to see them. At one time, so the story says, the women had charge of the flutes and so were able to rule the men, but the men rebelled and seized the flutes

Times Newspapers

out the disorder, which he expels with an explosive sound from his mouth. Sometimes he also produces a piece of meat, a worm, a thorn or stone as the material embodiment of the spirit or disease.

Such practices are readily connected with ideas of sorcery, which is the product of bad feeling either within a village or between two perhaps unrelated villages. The shaman of one village will be seen as a sorcerer by the inhabitants of the other, if things go ill with them, and raids are often mounted to kill him.

After death, shamans turn into were-jaguars among some tribes, into powerful but malevolent spirits among others. Often they are buried in a distant part of the jungle and the paths leading to the grave

blocked with thorn bushes, to stop the ghost from returning. But this is a common feature of funerals in Brazil. The Tupi were an exception, and buried their dead within their houses.

Celestial Jaguar

The shaman is always a powerful figure, and the Tupi shaman rivalled the chief. Several large villages might band together to form a primitive federation during war, and one of the largest of these groups was headed by a shaman. This was not merely on account of the fear he inspired, but because of his visionary powers. One of the strangest phenomena witnessed by the early colonists was the series of migrations which occurred at intervals under the leadership

of a shaman, who inspired whole populations with visions of the Land without Evil, and who took on the main attributes of the culture hero Maira in doing so.

The Land without Evil was Maira's own land, and several localities were favoured for this paradise – in the sky, in the middle of the continent, and on an island in the Atlantic. One group of Tupi searching for it inland wandered all the way up the Amazon, where they were met by Spaniards going in the opposite direction looking for El Dorado – one of history's odder coincidences. Other groups went to the shore where they built houses in which they danced day and night, singing and beating the ground with stamping tubes. These dances lasted for many days, during which everyone fasted. Their purpose was either to make the house rise magically into the sky, or to allow the dancers to become weightless – an experience induced by extreme exhaustion – and thus able to walk over the sea.

It is said that thousands of Indians died during these treks, both from starvation and from the attacks of their enemies, and that one group, having reached the Atlantic shore, performed their dance and failed to achieve the necessary exaltation, turned around and made for the Pacific. Such beliefs in a Promised Land are common today, and they are often the result of a technically advanced culture meeting a more primitive one.

Tupi myth says that Maira set fire to the world and then flooded it, as a punishment for men's ingratitude. Ge-speaking Indians still believe this may happen; one of their ceremonies, which takes place round a sun-pole, is partly intended to ward off this danger. These Indians originally lived in a part of Brazil plagued by drought and flood, so their belief is understandable. South of Brazil, however, there is the idea that a Celestial Jaguar will one day make an end to the world, and in Brazil proper many tribes think of eclipses as the swallowing of sun or moon by a jaguar, as a punishment for the sins of mankind. Tupi messianism – belief in the coming of a saviour god – is all part of this pattern: it is still concerned with the Jaguar who gave them culture, who made them compete among themselves for honour, and who must be placated if they are not to eat each other up entirely.

FRANCIS HUXLEY

Bread, one of the oldest foods of man, has at various times and places been used as a witch detector, a love charm and even as the means of locating the body of a drowned person. It was once also, curiously, considered a cure for indigestion and it is traditionally unlucky to take the last slice of bread from a plate

BREAD

BREAD, THE STAFF OF LIFE, is a synonym for food itself. We speak of 'earning our daily bread' when we mean working for our living; 'taking the bread out of someone's mouth' means to deprive him of his livelihood. Because of its vital importance from the cradle to the grave, bread has many sacred associations; it is surrounded by ceremonies and superstitions which derive from its original association with the corn spirit. At one time at the sowing of the corn, the soil was fertilized by sacrificial human blood. The spirit of the corn, sometimes represented by a human victim bound in wheatsheaves, was ritually killed at harvest time (see CORN).

This theme of the first and last fruits of the field dominates the rites of bread. In north-west India the first of the grain is formally presented to one of the family; in the Russian Volga region it was the custom for the village elder to present a portion of the first bread of the new harvest to each member of the community. A Swedish traditional rite, revealing traces of sacrifice, involves the baking of the last sheaf into a loaf shaped like a young girl.

The modern harvest loaf is highly decorative, the designs often taking the form of horns of plenty and wheatsheaves, reminiscent of the earlier plaited 'corn dollies' which were kept as good luck charms until the next harvest. In Devonshire a little grain was always cut before reaping began and was made into sheaves which were laid on the church altar. In Yorkshire the parson cut the first corn which was made into Communion bread. This had great potency as a love charm, and found a ready market among practitioners of witchcraft. Consecrated bread was frequently stolen at night from churches, allegedly for use at the Satanic Mass, a crime for which witches went to the stake in considerable numbers.

Proof of the Loaf

Bread played a prominent role in the primitive European system of trial by ordeal in which accused persons attempted to prove their innocence by eating a piece of bread and butter; if they choked they were considered guilty. In 1619 the witch Joan Flower swallowed a mouthful of bread and butter, declaring that 'she wished it might never go through her if she were guilty', and dropped dead.

The baking of bread had its special taboos. A menstruating woman was prohibited from participating in the kneading, as it was believed that her touch prevented the dough from rising. Another was the marking of a cross on the dough to prevent it from

falling into the hands of Satan. Bread baked on Good Friday was held to retain its freshness and the woman who baked it was considered highly blessed. The Russians, however, regarded all Fridays as ominous for baking, and Good Friday even more so. In Western Europe, bread baked on that day was highly valued for its therapeutic qualities; a loaf was often suspended from a cottage ceiling for a year and then replaced with a fresh loaf from the new harvest.

Household bread was equally valued both as a medicine and as a magic charm by corn-growing peoples. In Belgium stale bread placed in the cradle was thought to protect the baby; in Egypt it was considered a cure for indigestion; in Morocco it was an accepted specific against stammering.

Bread is the 'staff of life', the food which sustains man's body, and in Christian symbolism the Body of Christ, the spiritual food which sustains man's soul. The breaking of the sacred bread at the Mass, in imitation of Christ's breaking of bread at the Last Supper

The sealing of friendship, like the taking of oaths, involved the ritual eating of bread and salt. In love-making too the sharing of bread had its part to play ; French brides used to arouse the passion of the bridegrooms by sharing with them a cake called the 'Bride's Pasty'.

Bread has always symbolized domesticity and contentment. To waste bread therefore was regarded as an offence and punished in an appropriately unpleasant manner. In

every morsel of the bread she had wasted. In Britain and the United States bread thrown into the fire is said to feed the Devil.

The Sin Eater

There are a number of popular superstitions concerning the magical aspects of bread. A long hole in the loaf portends a death in the household. In the United States it is believed that an over-addiction to bread gives one a hairy chest. A curious tradition that it is unlucky to take the last slice of bread on a plate is widespread in Britain and America. For a single woman to do so means that she will remain an old maid. Also in the United States, it is bad luck to turn a loaf upside down; if one falls that way, it portends a quarrel.

Bread has also figured in the lore of sea and weather. Sailors believe that to cut a loaf and turn it upside down causes a ship to sink. In the belief that storms can be averted, bread is placed on the window-sill in Spain, facing the direction of the anticipated outbreak.

A remarkable quality formerly ascribed to bread was its power to react to the presence of a drowned body. It was believed that a loaf weighted with quicksilver and placed in the water would be irresistibly drawn towards the place where the body lay. As

Sacred bread in another form; the manna with which God miraculously fed the Israelites in the desert. Detail from *The Israelites Gathering Manna,* by Roberti, 15th century

recently as 1921 a corpse was discovered after this method had been tried at Wheelock in Cheshire.

Bread had an important function in connection with the Last Rites. Until a century ago it was not uncommon for an old man, called a Sin Eater, to be hired to take upon himself all the sins of the newly dead, in return for sixpence, a bowl of beer, and a loaf which had been in contact with a corpse. The idea behind this practice was that it would enable the soul of the dead person to proceed directly to Paradise (see SIN EATER).

FURTHER READING: Christina Hole, *English Folklore* (Scribner, 1940); Ronald Sheppard and Edward Norton, *The Story of Bread* (Fernhill, 1957).

Michael Holford/National Gallery London

BREATH

Element of Life and Soul

Breathing air into the lungs is the first action after birth – and death comes with the final breath. Since air is life, it has been identified with man's soul or spiritual essence in many religions. Learning to control breathing is therefore the basis of many Eastern paths to spiritual enlightenment

THE FIRST MAN, according to the book of Genesis, was fashioned from earth by the hand of God, who then breathed life into him through his nose – a process imagined by some commentators as being like the blowing up of a bladder. God 'breathed into his nostrils the breath of life; and man became a living being.' This connection between breath and the source of life is found in many religions and myths.

In a legend of the Australian aborigines, for instance, the god Pundjel fashioned two male figures from a mixture of clay and bark. After smoothing the bodies by a series of magical passes encompassing them from head to foot, he then lay upon them – each in turn – and blew into their mouths, their nostrils and their navels. After some time they came to life and moved about.

Similarly a commentator on the Koran says that the body of Adam was originally a clay figure which took 40 years to dry, after which God endowed it with the breath of life. The name Adam is a Hebrew word possibly coming from a root which means 'red' and so connected with the red clay of the first man's body. The red colour further connected it with blood, the 'water of life', in the sense that without blood a man dies.

According to Saturnius and Basilides (who taught at Antioch and Alexandria respectively in the 2nd century AD), the first man was made by seven evil angels, led by the god of the Jews, who said, 'Come, let us make man after our image.' They fashioned a being of enormous proportions but it could only crawl along the ground until the good supreme Creator himself endowed it with air, the divine spirit or soul. In other words, it needed to be impregnated with *pneuma* (in Greek) or *prana* (in Sanskrit) – terms which refer not to mere breath but to life-giving vital air or 'spirit'. Only after this

could the crawling creature stand upright and become truly a man.

The identity of breath and soul is established in early mythologies of widely separated peoples. In Fiji, for instance, people suffering from bronchitis or asthma were considered to run the risk of losing their souls. A magician was employed to capture the sick man's 'butterfly' (as his wavering breath was called) and secure it firmly to the body again. This he did with spells and conjurations. Also in Fiji, when the canoe of a chief was launched, a number of men were sacrificed so that their souls (or breath) might supply a wind of good luck for the sails of the craft.

In ancient times the breath of the dying was believed to re-enter the living. The Algonquins buried their dead children in frequented places so that the souls might re-enter future mothers there. A similar idea is at the root of a Roman custom which entitled the nearest relative of a dying person to inhale the final breath.

Pregnant by the Wind

Since air was life – men and animals cannot live without it, any more than without blood – it was thought possible that a woman might be impregnated by it. In Egypt the vulture, Maut, was supposed to reproduce her species by the intervention of the wind; the Virgin Mary was also said to have conceived at the impulse of a breath.

Some Arabic legends relate that Mary conceived by the breath of the angel Gabriel; in another Arabic account of the Immaculate

The Egyptian goddess Maat, who was begotten by air and first appeared as an egg, but later adopted a more conventional shape

Conception, a dove descends upon her, inspiring her with the word or breath and the word is made flesh. The angel, like the dove associated with Mary, is a winged creature whose natural element is air. The dove was the bird of breath, air or soul. It belonged to the Egyptian goddess of love, Hathor, and to other love goddesses and mother goddesses. A dove-like bird is shown enveloping a statue of Juno, the Roman queen of the sky or air, at Hierapolis in Syria; it appears in the shape of a pigeon carved in gold.

The dove, as the bird of air and the spirit of God, also stood for the Holy Ghost or Holy Spirit. In the New Testament – in the gospels of St Matthew and St Luke – it is the Holy Ghost who impregnates the Virgin Mary. St Mark and St John describe how the Holy Ghost in the form of a dove descended into Jesus when he was baptized in the river Jordan (see also DOVE).

Air was not only the substance of the divine Spirit but also the home of spirits in the plural. Angels, demons, ghosts and the fairies called 'sylphs' inhabited the air. The word 'sylph' was used for the winged air-sprites which belonged to air as one of the four elements, the basic materials of which everything in the world was thought to be made (see ELEMENTS).

These conceptions grew out of the earliest embodiments of storm, hurricane, wind, rain, night and day, which man's early reasoning likened to the various animals that surrounded him, and which he thought of in animal form. As time went by, he conceived of weird imaginary combinations of animal and bird forms which he thought peopled the storm, the darkness and the kingdoms of the four elements.

In ancient Egypt, breath or air was typified by a human-headed bird which accompanied the deceased in the underworld called Amenta. Its winged form relates it to the air, and shows its kinship with angels and other aerial beings which assumed important roles in later beliefs and customs.

Left The Fool, a card from a 19th century Tarot pack, connected with air in the sense of emptiness – the Nothing that was before anything existed, but which contained the potential existence of all things *Above right* The ancient Egyptians visualized air as a human-headed bird, which accompanied the dead to the underworld

Eliphas Levi said that if a man breathes in a certain way upon the back of a woman's neck she will automatically surrender to his will

Spirits Proud and Wrathful

Incense, representing the breath of life, is another aspect of this symbolism. It was presented to the dead together with an offering of blood, the mystical 'water of life'. The incense or breath was thought to pervade the blood, which stood for the red clay, the earth from which plants grow or the body of the first man brought to life by the breath of God. And so the double offering stood for the instilling of life into matter. The dead man could use the offered blood to make a material clothing for his spirit, so that he would be able to appear visibly on earth as a ghost.

According to some Jewish magicians, the phantoms of the dead or dying clothe themselves in a subtle aerial vapour in order to become visible to the eyes of the living. This applies to every sort of apparition, whether angels, spirits or demons. It is not, therefore, the phantom itself which is seen, but merely the subtle vapour or ghostly air which it has concentrated about itself. It may be that the fragrance of flowers and oils was used in earlier civilizations to make communication with ancestral spirits easier, by enabling them to show themselves in visible form. Smoke and perfumes served as vehicles for the temporary embodiment of demons which had been summoned up to visible appearance in the ceremonial magic of the Middle Ages.

An early Jewish treatise on magic (the *Pneumatica Kabbalistica*) alludes to 'Dwellers of the Lowest Air', as 'Spirits Proud and Wrathful, Authors of Arrogance and Fury, and the Seducers of Men'. These demons are said to require thicker and coarser odours and damp obnoxious vapours to make bodies in which the magician can see them.

An Egyptian myth is the basis of a more profound doctrine about air. The Egyptians believed that from the marriage of Chaos (matter before it was brought to life) and the Wind (the life-breath) came forth Mut or Mat in the form of an egg. Mat or Maat was the Egyptian word for both 'mother' and 'matter', and was also the name of the goddess of truth and justice.

The original egg — mother and matter, the womb in which the chick is hatched — later became the 0 or nought, which is the number of the first card in the Tarot pack. In early French packs this card is actually called *Le Mat*, the Fool.

The Fool is the first of the cards, the Origin from which all the others proceed. It stands for the Nothing before anything existed, which contained in itself the potential existence of everything; the ultimate Truth (the goddess Maat) behind all the surface phenomena of the universe. It is associated with air in the sense of a vacuum, an emptiness, and is identified with God as Pure Nothingness — having no identifiable characteristics but containing all things (see also TAROT).

The Sleeping Serpent

Breath or air as the creative spirit is also linked with the mind, the creator of ideas. In Hinduism, mind and breath (prana) are considered to be identical. Many forms of yoga involve *pranayama* (control of breathing) although far more is involved than the inhalation, retention and expiration of breath. The theory behind it is that when the process of breathing ceases to agitate the body and subsides, the mind attains absolute tranquility, freedom from thought, and the ultimate identity of itself with the object of meditation. The flow of breath having been controlled to the point where it ceases altogether, conception of mental images also ceases, and the mind becomes empty, merging into a formless radiance which is of the nature of pure bliss.

This doctrine was developed in its final and most perfect form in certain Hindu and Buddhist manuals, in which the whole of creation is regarded as illusory. Prana, the breath or life-current, is primarily used to compel the upward surge of *kundalini*, the great magical *shakti* or power residing in every individual (see KUNDALINI). She is visualized as a sleeping serpent coiled at the base of the spine. She is activated by a concentration of *citta* (mind-substance) set in motion by controlled breathing. The breath is thus a compulsive energy used to awaken the dormant cosmic power. This power is also likened to fire, fanned into activity by pranayama.

Magic powers accrue to the adept who stays the kundalini at any one of the six lotuses (*chakras*) situated at intervals along the spinal column. In the real adept, the true yogi, the fire is not arrested at any of these centres but is exalted to the highest lotus: the thousand-petalled lotus (*sahasrara*) in the region of the brain, where the goddess Kundalini unites with her lord, Shiva (pure consciousness). *Samadhi* (literally 'together with the lord') is the result.

When samadhi is stabilized and rendered permanent, it is known as liberation (*mukti*); it causes the yogi to become aware of his natural state. Liberation is not a state to be attained, for it is man's real nature. Attainment consists in removal of the ignorance which veils the true state.

There are several ways of raising kundalini. The use of breath forms the basis of *hatha yoga*, one of the major traditional forms of spiritual culture for realizing the union (*yoga*) of individual and absolute consciousness. *Ha* stands for the moon, *tha* for the sun. The solar and lunar currents circulating in the physical organism constitute the life-current (prana) which can be directed by breathing techniques. Breath and mind being one, the control of the one automatically effects the control of the other.

Mechanism of Desire

The prana is interrelated with sexual energy. Kundalini, the mystic fire, can also be expressed sexually. Mind and breath, united and rhythmically directed towards a given goal, is the basis of sexual magic. The magically-charged breath is supposed to have affinities with the mechanism of desire. According to Eliphas Levi, the 19th century occultist, if a man breathes in a certain way upon the back of a woman's neck she will automatically surrender to his will.

The ancient Hindu work *Yoga Vasishtha* contains a classic description of the awakening of the great magic power (shakti):

When the *Kundalini* is filled with *prana* she darts upwards. She then becomes erect and stiff like a stick or an excited serpent. If the various physical orifices are then closed, the body is filled with *prana* and its physical and material components are fundamentally changed.

A western counterpart of the sun, moon, fire trinity is the caduceus of Hermes. This is the prototype of the magic wand used in ceremonial magic. It comprises the twin currents of moon and sun symbolized as serpents twined about a pole or wand which terminates in a winged and luminous bulb. The breath (or prana) represented by the serpents attains perfect equilibrium and transmits its influence to the wand, which

Michael Holford

thus becomes potent to perform the will of the magician. The bulb of the wand, radiant with illumined will, is symbolical of that radiance with which the head-lotus (*sahasrara chakra*) is flooded when the risen goddess (Kundalini) unites with her lord: Shiva, the lord of Fire or Light.

Jumping like a Frog

The vagaries of kundalini when improperly or incompletely aroused have occasionally been recorded. One of the physical results of such a deviation is known as *buchari siddhi*, or 'the power of jumping like a frog'. This siddhi has been described by Aleister Crowley who observed it of his guru, Allan Bennett, one of the first to introduce Buddhism to England. One day, Bennett had been

Breath is life, in the sense that man cannot live without it. The Virgin Mary was impregnated by the Holy Spirit, often linked with the air that God blew into Adam's body to bring him to life. In El Greco's *Annunciation* the angel Gabriel, a winged being of the air, announces the event to Mary. The dove, another winged being of the air, is the symbol of the Holy Spirit

practising pranayama and his body had assumed the rigidity characteristic of certain trance conditions, causing it to jump about erratically. When it came to rest it resembled an overturned idol. He was completely oblivious that his body, galvanized by the interior power, had been rocked from its *asana* (meditation posture) and thrown

about the room to land finally in a topsy-turvy attitude several yards distant from its original position.

In the Tibetan Mystery Schools the breath plays a vital part in the process of death. The lama appointed to aid the dying makes sure that the prana is maintained in the sushumna (central canal) and not dissipated by re-entering the left or right nerve-currents. If consciousness is retained to the last, the breath or soul passes over consciously to the *bardo* (after-death plane or realm of the disembodied 'dead'). There it awaits rebirth in a form appropriate to its spiritual development. In this way, the breath, as the soul, survives the death of the physical organism (see also YOGA).

KENNETH GRANT

The search for a lost Earthly Paradise, where men of God could live in peace together, led St Brendan on an extraordinary voyage westwards. The story of his travels was one of the influences which inspired Columbus to discover America, centuries later

ST BRENDAN

THE IRISH ABBOT Brendan (c484–577) like other Celtic saints of the Dark Ages, is obscured as a human being by a cloud of legends. His chief legendary exploit was an Atlantic voyage in search of the Earthly Paradise or 'land promised to the saints'. A belief that Brendan reached an unknown country far west of Ireland was among the ideas that influenced Columbus. Modern students have maintained that the story reflects a vague Irish knowledge of America before the arrival of the Norsemen.

Whatever its factual value, the story has a place of honour in medieval romance. Versions in many European languages are proof of its popularity. The legend was sometimes counted as part of the Arthurian cycle, having grown similarly out of dark age Celtic tradition: certainly there are mythological links between St Brendan's Voyage, the Quest of the Grail, and the passing of Arthur over water to Avalon.

St Brendan, called 'the Navigator', is the patron of Kerry in south-west Ireland. His name is variously spelt. The mistaken form 'Brandan' is common, probably because of confusion with the mythical hero Bran, also a voyager (see BRAN). Brendan was born towards the close of the 5th century in or near Tralee. During a long life he founded monasteries at Ardfert in Kerry and at Clonfert in Galway. He undoubtedly went outside Ireland; his alleged visits to Wales and Brittany are quite credible and it is known that he met St Columba at Iona. St Brendan is commemorated in church dedications and place-names from Brittany to the Faroe Islands. The true extent of his travels is open to question but it appears that the legend of his voyage grew up around some venture which caused his absence from Ireland during the 530s or 40s.

Faery Lands Forlorn

The legend is not an isolated fantasy. Its gradual growth, over three or four centuries, took place against a rich background of Irish seafaring, both real and imaginary. Early in the Christian era the Irish adopted the coracle or skin-boat from the Britons, and improved it into the efficient and seaworthy curragh, made by stretching greased waterproof hides over a wooden frame. The largest curraghs could hold a crew of a dozen or more, and make long journeys propelled by oar and sail, weathering storms by lying low in the waves.

Migratory Irish monks, of whom St Brendan was only one, were using curraghs

Map of St Brendan's voyage, showing the amiable whale on which the saint and his companions landed, mistaking it for a small island

from the 5th century onward to venture farther and farther. Their main purpose was sea-pilgrimage, the search for a 'desert in the ocean', where they could live in peace and penitential remoteness from society. They were exploring the Hebrides within Brendan's lifetime; they reached Orkney in 579 AD, the Shetlands before 620, the Faroes about 670 and Iceland about 795. The Norse who colonized Iceland after 874 found the abandoned remains of an Irish monastery. There is doubtful evidence that a few reached Greenland, perhaps in flight from the Norse; and an accidental voyage to Arctic seas by a pilgrim named Cormac is recorded much earlier, almost as far back as Brendan himself.

Besides traditions about these explorations by monks, the Irish had popular sea yarns on the lines of Sinbad the Sailor. These stories (*The Voyage of Mael Duin* is the most important) describe wanderings by curragh among faery islands supposed to lie west of Erin. They have a strong flavour of pagan myth. Similar themes and episodes occur in the Brendan legend. However, the claim that it is merely a Christian version of the old type of story cannot be sustained. St Brendan's voyage has absorbed other literary elements too – classical, for instance – and in a sense it could be called a Christian Odyssey.

Allusions to the voyage begin to appear in Irish writings in the early 9th century. We are told that Brendan 'sailed the sea', 'sought the Land of Promise', 'visited wonderful islands'. A sketch of the voyage is

Insulæ Fortunatæ · *Cabo de No* · *Cabo finis terræ* · *Mauritania* · *M. Atll* · *Africa*

included in the *Life of St Machutus* (the Breton St Malo), written between 866 and 872. The two major versions, however, are in a *Life of St Brendan* dating from somewhere about 900, which is preserved in the medieval *Book of Lismore*; and the *Navigatio Sancti Brendani*, an account of the voyage alone, probably composed about 910–20.

The Friendly Whale

The main plot is fairly well defined. Brendan sails with a company of monks to look for a wonderful land in the western ocean, which is regarded as a retreat, as an isle of the blest, and sometimes as the lost Earthly Paradise. He discovers a whole series of islands, witnesses many marvels,

and celebrates Easter on the back of a whale. After years of peril on the high seas he attains his goal and returns safely.

While the *Lismore* version is far from negligible, all serious study of the legend must be based on the *Navigatio*. This is a prose Latin work, entertaining and skilful, written in Ireland by an unknown but gifted Irishman. It is not, of course, evidence as to anything Brendan actually did, for this is in the realm of legend. The problem is whether the *Navigatio* reflects a real Irish knowledge of Atlantic geography and particularly of America before the Norse 'Vinland' voyages. Such knowledge, if present, might or might not have been derived in some way from the historical Brendan; that question remains a purely speculative one.

In its *Navigatio* form the story is as follows. St Brendan is visited at Ardfert by another monk named Barinthus, who has been to the 'land promised to the saints' over the western ocean, though he is uncertain of the route. Brendan decides to go in quest of it. Choosing 14 companions, he builds a great curragh, and sails from a creek near the foot of Brandon Mountain. Veering winds bear the boat hundreds of miles off course to a steep rocky island with a single landing place.

After a spell ashore, the monks go on to another island inhabited by large sheep and by a mysterious person called 'the procurator', who helps and advises them. Landing on what appears to be a nearby islet, they find they are on the back of a whale. Brendan afterwards tames the beast and induces it to help them. They cross a narrow sound to an island on the west of the Island of Sheep; this is the Paradise of Birds.

In due course they go on to another island where the disciples of the Irish saint Ailbe live; to an island with a poisonous spring; to a region of calm where the sea is like a 'thick curdled mass'; to a very different stretch of sea, cold and stormy, where monsters threaten them; to a flat flowery island almost level with the waves; to an island with fragrant air, vividly green grass, and fruits described as huge grapes.

They pass a translucent sea where they can watch the fishes far below, and, on another day, a vast crystal column among the waves. From here they sail north to a rugged island covered with slag, where giants are working at a colossal smithy, surrounded by fire and fumes. After this comes a remote northern mountain with black cliffs and smoke pouring from the summit, and then, far to the south of it, a precipitous islet with an Irish hermit living in a cave near the top.

Most of these adventures have fairy-tale elements, yet there are many strangely exact statements of compass bearing and distance, the latter expressed in the Norse manner as 'so many days' sail'. Brendan does not touch on all the islands in one impossible tour, but in a series of forays, returning periodically to the Island of Sheep as a base. His final, successful expedition from there takes 40 days. He passes through a thick fog into light, and at last beholds the promised land. It is sunny and fruitful. The explorers traverse it for weeks without coming to a farther shore. A man whom they meet on a river bank – doubtless a disguised angel – tells them to turn back. Some day God will restore this lost Paradise to all Christian men, but in the meantime it must stay hidden, or known only to a few as a haven from persecution. So the monks leave, and reach Erin again without mishap.

Chronologically, Brendan's exploits

Irish monks, like St Brendan, were using coracles from the 5th century onward to venture farther and farther. Their main purpose was sea-pilgrimage, the search for a 'desert in the ocean', where they could live in peace and penitential remoteness from society. St Brendan's voyage may have unknowingly taken him to America centuries before Columbus

seem to extend from 539 to 551 or thereabouts. However, he is only actually engaged on them for a total of seven years. The *Navigatio* (or at any rate the surviving imperfect text) fails to explain the discrepancy. But the *Lismore* version, which preserves some independent scraps of tradition, says that Brendan returned to Ireland at one stage, and after an interval set out again in a wooden ship instead of a curragh. Besides splitting the voyage into two instalments, the same source adds further details to the more northerly-sounding episodes, such as encounters with small dark imps and with a 'sea-cat' which seems to have been a walrus.

Based on a Map

How should the *Navigatio* be construed? In some sections at least, the author is undoubtedly giving glimpses of actual places, seen through a haze of folklore or poetic imagery. Thus the northern island of giant smiths is generally acknowledged to be Iceland. The smithy is a volcano, perhaps Hekla, to which the author has transferred a standard classical myth about Etna and its Cyclopean forge, found in Virgil and Aeschylus. Again, the Island of Sheep is almost certainly Strömö in the Faroes. The name 'Faroes' is derived from a Danish word for sheep, and the animals, said to have been imported by the first Irish settlers, are a staple of the economy. The Paradise of Birds is Vagar, across the sound west of Strömö. Vagar still swarms with wild-fowl of many species. Both sheep and birds are mentioned in a description of the Faroes by the Irish geographer Dicuil, written in 825.

Other clues are less clear, but they are plentiful, and, when taken together, forceful. Granted that the *Navigatio* is fiction woven round a popular hero, to that extent resembling a romance like *Mael Duin*; nevertheless it appears, as *Mael Duin* emphatically does not, to be based on a map or something like one. As to the extent of this map, opinions differ. But a survey of writers who have studied the legend shows that there are arguments for including not only the Faroes and Iceland, but also St Kilda, Rockall, Jan Mayen, southern Greenland, the Newfoundland Banks and iceberg zone, Madeira, the Azores, the Sargasso Sea, and parts of the West Indies, the Bahamas and mainland America.

Such a map would not be as utterly incredible as it sounds. A well-read Irishman in the early 10th century could have put most of it together from classical and later geographers, from the Irish monastic tradition, and from reports of Viking voyages. But if the author of the *Navigatio* was painstaking and learned enough to put together such a map, what were his sources for references to America?

At present there is no answer. Some evidence does exist for pre-Norse Atlantic crossings, which might have been described in oral traditions or lost documents. But the data are hard to interpret, and point to a period much earlier than the Irish seafaring. It is safe to conclude that the *Navigatio* does reflect a knowledge of Atlantic geography;

A monk at Brandon Hill on the coast of Kerry, Ireland. From its foot the saint set out on his voyage in search of the Earthly Paradise or 'land promised to the saints'. The story has a historical background in Irish seafaring

Daily Telegraph Colour Library

that it also reflects pre-Norse ideas about land on the far side; that these ideas may have a fragmentary factual basis; but that if they do, we can still only guess at the source of information. While the proved Irish achievement is astonishing, there is no good reason to think that America itself was discovered by St Brendan or by any Irishman of the Dark Ages. The problem merges into the broader problem of early trans-Atlantic contacts.

The Shifting Island

Whatever geography the *Navigatio* contains is lost to sight in the later romantic adaptations, where the whole story is jumbled and made more fantastic. Brendan's fame spread through medieval Europe, but no idea of a map went with it. The sole persistent belief was that the saint discovered one otherwise unknown island in the western ocean — a warm, supremely fertile place. 'St Brendan's Isle' was not thought of as the Earthly Paradise (which medieval Christians pictured in Asia, and could not take seriously anywhere else), but as something more like the island of giant grapes supposed to have been visited during the quest.

This at least was believed in literally. St Brendan's Isle appears on a number of medieval maps, usually to the south-west of Europe. It moves farther and farther out with the progress of exploration. In the Hereford map of 1275 it lies among the Canaries. The Dulcert chart (1339) shifts it towards Madeira. Pizigani (1367), Beccarui (1426, 1435), and others transplant it to the region of Azores. A few years later, after the Portuguese discovery of the Azores themselves, Bianco marks 'St Brandan's or the Fortunate Isles' as two groups farther westward still. Behaim's map, published in 1492 just before Columbus sailed, shows a huge St Brandan's Isle near the actual location of the South American coast.

Columbus himself is said to have made inquiries in Galway where Brendan finally settled, and to have taken a Galway seaman on his first voyage. His son testifies to the effect the legend had on him. Certainly he knew more about it than some of the mapmakers. He spoke of St Brendan's islands — in the plural — and of the trans-Atlantic Paradise, which he was prepared to accept because it buttressed his concept of circumnavigation. Later, in fact, Columbus argued that Paradise was to be found up the Orinoco river, and that he had reached its approaches, like Brendan before him, by sailing westward.

GEOFFREY ASHE

FURTHER READING: Geoffrey Ashe, *Land to the West: St. Brendan's Voyage to America* (Viking Press, 1962); Tim Severin, *Brendan Voyage* (McGraw-Hill, 1978); George A. Little, *Brendan the Navigator* (Gill & Son, Dublin, 1945).

Beauty and horror, compassion and cruelty are the keynotes of the work of the painter Pieter Breughel the Elder. Together with the intimately observed detail of the everyday life of his time is a preoccupation with the theme of the oppressor and the oppressed. The innocent are ever at the mercy of the powerful; the peasants dance, but there is a scaffold in the background

BREUGHEL

PIETER BREUGHEL the Elder, the greatest of a family dynasty of painters and one of the greatest of all European artists, possessed an extraordinary range of vision. His work shows profound comment on human affairs and presents a marvellous panorama of the visible world. At the same time, like Hieronymus Bosch, he gives spectral shape to sin, death and the conception of hell with all its attendant demons and monstrosities.

In the paintings illustrating the parables of the Gospel and common proverbs of his time, he comments philosophically on human failings. In other works there is an urgent sense of the tragedy of his own time, a dark period in the history of the Netherlands which was at that time unhappily dominated by Spain. He conveys in his paintings of biblical themes, even if in cryptic and covert fashion, his reaction to the miseries of a land harried by the persecution of a foreign ruler and the warring fanaticisms of religion and politics.

In Breughel's magnificent landscapes and the figures that people them, there is a new feeling for the relationship of man to his environment. And from the illustrations of parables and proverbs given contemporary guise it was but a short step to his superb portrayal of the everyday life of his time. Patriotic sympathy animates the masterpieces in which he observes his rustic fellow-countrymen and women — in the farthest remove from an alien court – at the marriage feast and in the lumbering peasant dance that symbolizes their temporary respite from toil and care.

Little is known about his life, except that he died in 1569 aged about 45. Neither his birthplace nor his exact date of birth are known for certain. It is assumed that he came from a village called Brueghel or Brögel, either in Dutch Brabant or in the present Limburg province of Belgium — perhaps the existing Brögl near the little town of Brée. It is a reasonable guess that he was born about 1525 since it is known that he was admitted to the Antwerp Guild of St Luke as fully fledged painter in 1557. The nickname he acquired 'Peasant Breughel' seems to apply rather to his subjects than to his origin. It is recorded, however, that he was the pupil of Pieter Coeck van Aelst, painter, designer and architect, whose daughter Breughel eventually married. Pieter Coeck died in 1550 and soon after Breughel went to work for the Antwerp engraver and print publisher, Jerome Cock. He made a journey to Italy, possibly to gather material on Cock's behalf.

The journey and the period afterwards

Giraudon

Death mows all down before him in a setting of battle, torture and execution: detail from *The Triumph of Death*, painted in 1568, the year in which the Spanish army, sent to put down the revolt in the Netherlands, entered Brussels in triumph

spent with Cock were both of great influence on Breughel's development. Unlike so many Dutch and Flemish artists of the period he showed no sign of wishing to emulate the works of the Italian Renaissance masters he saw at Rome. But there can be no doubt of the vivid impression left on his mind by the varieties of landscape he encountered on his extensive tour: the awesomeness of Alpine heights, the spreading vistas of lake, river and plain, the southern coasts.

King Carnival

Such were the subjects he drew, and Cock engraved, on Breughel's return to Antwerp. Cock, who had a shop near the Antwerp Bourse, was a pioneer of graphic reproduction. He catered for taste at various levels with engravings of landscapes, moral themes and fantastic subjects in the style of Hieronymus Bosch (see BOSCH). In all of these Breughel had a hand and he became so intimate with the work of Bosch that he might be called the heir of his imagination. One of Breughel's signed drawings, the satirically symbolic *Big Fishes eat Little Ones* (Albertina, Vienna) was near enough to the style of the earlier master to be engraved and published under Bosch's name. The subjects Breughel penned for

the engraver reappear, marvellously elaborated, in the paintings he produced independently from about 1557 until shortly before his death in Brussels in 1569. Marvellous indeed is the product of these years, both in the number of masterpieces, and in the immense amount of workmanship and thought they represent. They are the distillation of the beauty and also the horror that an inspired artist could perceive in the conditions of the time.

A cosmic, worldwide vision appears in the early landscapes of c 1557: they are not views of one place but a universe seen in vast perspective of shimmering water, towering mountains, distant cities and dense woods. The *Landscape with the Temptation of St Anthony* (National Gallery of Art,

One of man's most destructive failings, his futile attempts to grasp power which is beyond him, is reflected in *The Tower of Babel*

Washington) combines such a prospect with details reminiscent of Bosch, an aerial armada of evil spirits, misshapen semi-human forms and gnomes. Another of these world-landscapes is the setting for *The Fall of Icarus* (Royal Museum, Brussels) c 1558, with its great ocean and beautifully painted ship in full sail. Icarus has sunk into the sea, only one leg showing above the surface and Breughel seems to comment not only on the vanity of his attempt to fly but on the insignificance of individual calamity and the indifference of the world towards it, as represented by the ploughman and the

shepherd who are taking no notice.

In *The Tower of Babel* (Kunsthistorisches Museum, Vienna) the stupendous building seems another reflection on the vanity of human ambition. The popular print market demanded proverbial philosophy and this was provided for by the large-scale pictures, teeming with life and incident, of 1559–60. In *The World Turned Upside Down* (Gemälde-Galerie, Berlin-Dahlem) he illustrates nearly a hundred maxims and popular sayings, forming a huge anthology of reference to human folly. An inn sign with a globe and an inverted cross sums up the picture's meaning. One figure 'runs his head against the wall' another 'cries over spilt milk'. In the centre is a young woman with an aged husband; she 'hangs a blue

cape round him' in allusion to a popular expression meaning to be unfaithful.

The Battle between Carnival and Lent (Kunsthistorisches Museum, Vienna) is another amazing compendium of figures, gay with the colour of pageantry beloved by his countrymen but pointing the contrast between festivity and the quiet of the religious and contemplative life with a wealth of ingenious detail. The protagonists are King Carnival, a gross fellow perched on a wine barrel with a spit impaling a pig's head for weapon, confronted by Lent in the form of a lean old woman with a wooden shovel to which — symbol of meagre fare — are affixed two herrings.

A World in Flames

But the mood of Breughel's art now changed; it became more intense, reflecting the disquiet of the times. Calvinism was spreading like wildfire through the Netherlands. The efforts of Philip II of Spain to put down the heresy grew more and more ferocious. Numerous executions, the arbitrary powers given to the Inquisition, and the presence of Spanish troops outraged popular feeling. Antwerp, like other cities in the 1560s, was ripe for revolt. Breughel moved to Brussels

Previous page The archangel Michael and the heavenly host routing the gibbering monsters of evil in *The Fall of the Rebel Angels*
Below 'In its rendering of the pathos of physical disability, it also suggests the plight of imperfect humanity, constantly liable to be led astray': *The Blind Leading the Blind*

in 1563 after his marriage, supposedly to be rid of a prior and embarrassing liaison. Although Brussels was the court centre, he found the same spirit of unrest and menace in the city.

Patronized by the court, his sympathies were nevertheless with the common people and his paintings offer many clues to this feeling of kinship. In *Monkeys* (Berlin) 1562, the sad creatures chained at a prison-like embrasure with a distant view of Antwerp behind them seem to symbolize the captivity of a people. It is not merely fanciful to see the hated foreign mercenaries in the disguise of biblical warriors in *The Battle of the Israelites and Philistines* (Vienna) 1562. To express his depth of feeling he again had recourse to the manner of Bosch. *The Fall of the Rebel Angels* represents the defeat of evil ideas and intentions in the shape of gibbering monsters. *Dulle Griet* (Mayor van den Bergh Museum, Antwerp) 1564 shows 'Mad Meg', a hell-raising fury, sweeping through a demonic chaos full of nameless hybrids and grotesques such as Bosch had conceived, against the background of a world in flames.

Breughel was a witness of these years of wild popular outbursts and savage reprisal, and left his testimony for posterity. *The Numbering of Bethlehem* (Brussels) 1566, shows a door-to-door inquisition such as many a snowbound Flemish village must have witnessed. *The Conversion of St Paul* (Vienna) 1567, might also be taken to denote, rather than its ostensible subject, the approach of the dread Duke of Alva,

riding with his troops from Lombardy through an Alpine pass, with a commission to put down revolt in the Netherlands by every means. *The Massacre of the Innocents* (Vienna) c 1567, is just such a cruel scene as Breughel might have witnessed.

These pictures are the more pointed for the contemporary dress and surroundings they depict. It remained for Breughel to distil the essence of the contemporary situation in the great *Triumph of Death* (Prado, Madrid) c 1568. Transcending the grotesque the painting is grimly direct in its symbolism. Death in skeleton shape mows all down before him in a lurid setting of flaming towns and sinking ships. 1568 was the year in which the Duke of Alva entered Brussels in triumph. The great artist finally produced a work of sombre reflection in *The Magpie on the Gallows* (Landesmuseum, Darmstadt) with its peasants dancing in the shadow of the scaffold.

In famous works of his later years, Breughel exercised the magic purely of an art perfected in design, colour and human understanding, manifest in those incomparable masterpieces at Vienna, the *Hunters in the Snow*, *The Wedding Banquet* and *The Peasant Dance*. Yet the sense of parable remained with him. There is no more touching a picture than his *Blind leading the Blind*, painted in the year before he died. In its rendering of the pathos of physical disability, it also suggests the plight of imperfect humanity, constantly liable to be led astray.

WILLIAM GAUNT

Brer Rabbit

Hero of the 'Uncle Remus' stories, published between 1880 and 1906 by the American journalist Joel Chandler Harris: the stories are based on folk tales brought from Africa by Negro slaves and probably influenced by the Great Rabbit of Algonquin Indian mythology; Brer Rabbit is a mischievous 'trickster' who cleverly outwits his enemies, especially the malicious Brer Fox.

" De ashes flew'd up so, dat Brer Fox, he tuck'n had a sneezin' spell."

Editions du Chalet

Breviary

Book which contains the services or 'divine office' of the Roman Catholic Church for each day of the year, and each section of the day, as distinct from the service of the Mass (contained in the missal) and those of baptism, marriage and other sacraments (in the Rituale Romanum); revised in 1960, the breviary contains psalms, lessons from the Bible, hymns and prayers, including those used on each saint's day.

BRIDGES

THE FUNCTION OF A BRIDGE, an artificial structure which overcomes a natural barrier, and links two places that are naturally apart, is the key to the important role of bridges in religious customs and beliefs. Since the natural barrier was usually a river, which to the primitive mind was a living thing and regarded as a god or a spirit, the building of the bridge might affront a deity, who had to be appeased by sacrifices.

The most notable rites of this type took place in ancient Rome. There the oldest bridge over the river Tiber was the Pons Sublicius, which was made entirely of wood, the use of metal being taboo. On this bridge, annually on the Ides (the 15th) of May, a curious ritual was performed. Puppets made of bullrushes to represent old men, bound hand and foot, and called *Argei*, were flung into the river by the Vestal Virgins.

The exact meaning of this ritual has been much debated but the most probable conclusion is that the rites were propitiatory, the Argei being substitutes for human sacrifices made to the river god in compensation for the bridge.

The purpose of a bridge in providing a link between two naturally separated places seems also to have inspired the idea of a bridge between the lands of the living and the dead. This idea is common to many religions; the earliest instance is in the *Gathas* of Zoroaster (c 570 BC). The bridge is called the *Cinvato paratu*, the 'Bridge of the Separator'. The references to it are very obscure but there is reason for thinking that already in ancient Iranian doctrine it was believed that the dead had to face the ordeal of crossing a bridge controlled by a grim deity. In later Iranian religion this ordeal took the form of a judgement, which determined the fate of the dead.

A fateful bridge, called *al-Sirat* also occurs in Islamic teaching. The ordeal is described as follows: 'The believer will pass over it, swift as sight, or as lightning, or as wind, or as a race-horse. Such will escape, safe and sound; others will be torn (by hooks), others will fall fainting in the fires of Hell, and it will continue until the last passes or is carried away.'

BRIGIT

BRIGIT WAS the daughter of the powerful tribal god, the Dagda, according to early Irish literary tales. Her name, meaning 'the Powerful One' or 'Queen', links her with the North British Brigantia, 'the High One', with whom she may originally have been identical. Brigantia was goddess of the Celtic tribe of the Brigantes, who occupied what are now roughly the six northern counties of England. Dedications to this deity are also known from the Continent, and it seems probable that her spheres of influence must have been closely similar to those of her Irish counterpart.

The evidence suggests that the two goddesses are in fact fundamentally the same deity, but venerated according to local preferences and requirements in different Celtic regions. In Brigit and Brigantia we are dealing with powerful pagan Celtic religious ideas: the influence of these deities was widespread in Celtic areas, and their cult enduring. In British art Brigantia is associated with Minerva (see ATHENE). Caesar, in his observations about certain Celtic divinities, remarks: 'About these gods they hold nearly the same views as other people do . . . that Minerva first instituted the arts and crafts.'

Brigit of Ireland is essentially a patroness of craftsmen and their crafts. Brigantia is not only likened to Minerva but figures also in Roman times as a nymph goddess, who presided over springs to which healing powers were probably attributed. Brigit was similarly concerned with medicine and healing of all kinds, and many wells of different virtues were named after her successor in Christian times, St Brigit of Kildare. It thus seems very probable that Brigantia of North Britain and Brigit of pagan Ireland shared the same origins.

Brigit also shows a close affinity with certain Celtic goddesses portrayed in groups of three in the art of Roman Gaul and Britain. She figures in Irish traditions as one of three sisters all named Brigit. It is almost certain that this is a purely literary attempt to explain the pagan Celtic idea of a single god or goddess depicted in triple form in order to emphasize his or her divine powers. This threefold character would then link Brigit with the portrayals of the triple goddesses of Gaul and Britain; these mother goddesses were worshipped in the Roman Empire by men of all nations. The Celts regarded the number three as being especially magical and powerful, and for this reason they often gave their deities attributes or characteristics with this number, such as three heads.

Brigit of Ireland is also deeply concerned

National Museum of Antiquities of Scotland, Edinburgh

Roman statue of Brigantia, the northern English equivalent of the Irish goddess Brigit. She holds the spear of the Roman Minerva and the globe of rulership, with wings of victory sprouting from her shoulders: 3rd century AD, from Birrens, Dumfriesshire

St Brigid of Ireland, the pagan goddess in her Christian form, associated with fertility, childbirth and healing

with fertility and childbirth and this further links her with the groups of three mother goddesses with their symbols of plenty and maternity. In the literature of early Ireland, Brigit was the goddess of poetry and wisdom. One of her sisters (or other manifestations of herself) was the patron goddess of medicine; the third Brigit was responsible for the well-being of the smiths.

It is probable that the old calendar festival of *Imbolc* (1 February), which seemingly celebrated the start of the milk season of the ewes, was connected with rites in honour of Brigit. This would emphasize her concern with fertility, both human and animal. *Imbolc* corresponds to the feast of St Brigit in the Christian calendar.

There seems to be little real doubt that the widespread and popular cult of the pagan goddess Brigit was replaced in Christian times by the cult of the saint, doubtless identical with the goddess in more than name. The worship of this Christian Brigit, with her curative and fertility associations, was as widespread and persistent as would be expected in the light of the earlier cult.

Brigit of Kildare was the first Christian of this name to be recorded. At Kildare a sacred fire was kept permanently burning. It was tended by 19 nuns in turn, and by St Brigit herself on the 20th day. No male was ever allowed to come near it or to breathe upon it. This suggests that we are dealing with a survival in a Christian context of a pagan cult exclusive to women, such as we know to have existed in Celtic Europe.

Midwife to the Virgin

Like her pagan predecessor, St Brigit was widely invoked and loved. She too was especially associated with fertility and childbirth; dedications to her are numerous in the Celtic-speaking regions of the British Isles. Her cult has persisted down to modern times. In the Catholic islands of western Scotland she was traditionally known as the Virgin Mary's midwife; in this role she achieved a popularity superior even to that of the Virgin Mary herself. She was credited with many miracles and indeed was referred to as 'the Mary of the Gaels'. Brigit was invoked by women in labour, and by the midwife, before delivery began — practices which carry back down the centuries to the pagan goddess conferring ease of birth and prosperous fertility.

Her feast day, *La Feill Bhride* (1 February) was attended by tremendous local celebrations and elaborate ritual which had to be carried out correctly if St Brigit was to be pleased and generous. She was the symbol of the stirring of life again after the dead months of winter. Her pagan origins are emphasized by the fact that if she were thought to be displeased, a sacrifice of a clearly non-Christian nature was made to her. A cockerel was buried alive near the point where three streams met, reflecting perhaps her ancient threefold character. Incense was then burned on the hearth of the family concerned.

FURTHER READING: A. Ross, *Pagan Celtic Britain* (Columbia Univ. Press, 1968).

'Brittany is poetry' wrote a French poet in the 12th century and this ruggedly beautiful region is rich in poetic legend. Lancelot of the Lake spent his childhood here; Merlin the Wizard fell in love here; and it was here that Tristan and Isolde were reunited before death. But besides its romantic associations, Brittany also has its darker side. Ankou, the terrifying spirit of death, is still believed to stalk the countryside and even today the practice of sorcery survives

BRITTANY

BRITTANY FORMS PART of the area of western France also known as Armorica. Her people are Celts and have close affinities with other Celtic people such as the Welsh, the Cornish and the Irish. Nearly a million Frenchmen still speak the Celtic language Breton or *brezhoneg,* from which Welsh and Gaelic are descended. This indicates the extent to which the Bretons, like the Welsh, have preserved their national individuality. Like all Celts, the Breton people have a love of freedom and a fierce attachment to the traditions of their birthplace.

Brittany was peopled in distant times by a race who have left huge stone monuments, tombs and circles of stone. The Gauls who occupied the area during the Roman Empire were driven out by a mass migration from Britain in the 5th and 6th centuries, at the decline of the Empire. The

Ankou, Reaper of Death

He is tall and of a fearsome thinness – sometimes a skeleton wrapped in a shroud. He is whitehaired, his locks falling over his shoulders, and wears a flat broad-brimmed hat of the type still popular in the remoter parts of the country...

Still he makes his nightly journeys, reaping his rich harvest of human lives. Often he is represented as carrying upon his shoulder a scythe which is sharpened with a human bone, sometimes a sword, sometimes as at La Roche-Maurice a lance, and sometimes as at Noyal-Pontivy a club. And because of the long journeys he must take, he is provided with a cart, covered in a shroud, the axles of which may be heard creaking on dark nights. Well may they creak, for never a spot of grease do they see, so incessantly is the cart in use. This cart is drawn by a team which varies according to the district in which it finds itself; in the Morbihan by two oxen and a lean horse, in Finistère and the Côtes-du-Nord by two and occasionally by three horses one behind the other, the shaft-horse sleek and well-fed, the others little more than skeletons.

If the Ankou journeys alone he walks beside his horses; but if he takes with him his servants he stands in the cart using his scythe to right and left with terrible effect while they, skeleton forms like their master, wearing the same flat Breton hat, and dressed in black, lead the team and pile the bodies of the dead into the cart. And of those who die upon the night of St Sylvester it is said that they must draw of their own strength the cart of the Ankou instead of resting in it on the journey to their Maker.

W. Branch Johnson
Folktales of Brittany

---

invaders from the British Isles gave their newly gained territory the name of their homeland – whence the name Brittany. From the time of the arrival of the Bretons up to the 10th century, it was ruled by kings and later by sovereign dukes. In 1532, Brittany lost its independence, but remained virtually a separate state until 1789, the date when it was annexed to France. It was after the French Revolution that the region was divided up into its present five departments: Finistère, Morbihan, Côtes du Nord, Ille et Vilaine and Loire Atlantique.

The Bridge of the Secret

The Bretons played an important part in the formation and spread of the Arthurian legends (see ARTHUR). Their travelling entertainers had a high reputation in the Middle Ages; the poetess Marie de France, who borrowed from them the themes of her lays, wrote in the 12th century: 'Brittany is poetry'. Many heroes of the stories of the Round Table were Bretons. Lancelot of the Lake, who was brought up by the fairy Vivien, spent his childhood in the forest of Broceliande near Paimpont which still exists today. He took his name from the nearby lake where the fairy had her palace. The Bridge of the Secret, where Lancelot and Queen Guinevere pledged their love, can also still be seen. (See also LANCELOT.)

In the same forest is the Fountain of Youth, whose waters are believed to have powers of rejuvenation, and the Fountain of Barenton, sacred to the Druids and still the symbol of Celtic poetry. It was there that Merlin the Wizard met Vivien and fell in love with her. The Garden of Joy, not far away, was their trysting-place. The water of Barenton also possesses allegedly miraculous powers: when it is poured on the Stone of Merlin nearby it lets loose storms and causes other natural phenomena. At one time the population of the neighbouring town of Concoret (Morbihan) used to go there in procession and the priest would dip

'The guardian saints of Brittany are a curious collection, numbering over 500 in all. Some are minor local gods or early Breton chiefs. Some, who have lasted for centuries and are still acknowledged, are barely tolerated by the Roman Catholic Church.' Included among them is St Gwenole who founded the abbey at Landévennec, now in ruins

the foot of the cross in the spring, to bring rain in dry years.

It was also in Brittany that part of the story of Tristan took place (see TRISTAN). The hero's uncle, King Mark of Cornwall, took his name from that of an ancient Celtic horse god (horse in Breton is *marc'h*). Strange legends are still current about Mark in the region of Douarnenez and in Penmarc'h. The latter place name means 'the horse's head'.

Tristan of Leon after his love affair with Mark's wife, the Irish Isolde, retired to Brittany. There he married another Isolde, the daughter of the king of Carhaix in western Finistère. When mortally wounded, he asked to be taken to await the boat which was bringing his first love back to him, it was to the headland of Penmarc'h that he was taken; it was there that the two lovers died, facing the sea which unites all Celts.

The Scythe of Ankou

For the past 150 years, scholars of folklore have been collecting a rich store of folktales, stories and narrative songs of a remarkable diversity. Some of them include characters from far earlier times and have connections with pre-Christian beliefs. Others tell of miracles and fabulous feats ascribed to national saints. Others help to explain some local feature such as a strange hollow in the ground or a huge stone monument.

The major theme which constantly recurs is that of death and the afterlife. It is a theme which permeates the peninsula completely. A seemingly divine person known as Ankou is at one and the same time the provider and the master. Awe-inspiring, omnipotent, Ankou is the true ruler of the world. In popular imagination he appears to be supreme, since everyone eventually obeys him: the Virgin Mary and even Jesus Christ himself have submitted to him.

Ankou has various guises. Each parish has its own version, which changes moreover, because the last person to die in the year has to play the role of Ankou during the whole of the following year. He is represented as a skeleton, or as a man without a nose and with empty eye-sockets. He often has a hat with a wide brim which hides his face and prevents people from recognizing him at first. In pictures he usually carries a scythe handled the wrong way up. Ankou uses it to kill those people he has marked out, but instead of using it in the normal way of reapers, he throws it in front of him, cutting edge first. To travel along the pot-holed roads, he rides on a cart with creaking axles. Two acolytes escort him; one holding the horse's bridle, and the other opening the gates and doors.

This funeral carriage, called *Karrig an Ankou*, Ankou's Chariot, often appears in the narratives. To hear it is a bad omen: it means that there will be a death in the parish. For the homecoming reveller who encounters it around midnight, it is a terrifying experience. Ankou inspires dread and it is rare ever to escape him. The unfortunate man will only have a short space of time to put his affairs in order. He will be seized by a fierce fever and then it will be just a matter of days before death.

At Death's Door

Another aspect of death is represented by the world of *Anaon*. This word describes both the sinners who have not yet been freed of their ties with life here on earth, similar to the Catholic souls in purgatory, and the spirit who presides over their domain. The land of Anaon corresponds to the pagan hell, where cold reigns instead of fire, as in medieval Christian tradition. Dwellers in Anaon communicate with the living who can not only help Anaon, but also fight against him. Certain rites can permit a soul to be rescued from this frozen torment: a Mass or a series of Masses, special pilgrimages, appropriate exorcisms.

Signs of Anaon are found everywhere as his land overlaps that of the living in some ways; it includes, for example, some place in the countryside where a dead person lived sinfully. There are also territories on earth which belong to Anaon. These are very old sacred places, dedicated since prehistory to the gods of death and the afterlife. The sinners, often drowned sailors, gather at the approaches to Pointe du Raz and the Ile de Sein. The kingdom of Anaon, known as the Marsh of Hells (*Yeun Ellez*) is situated in the Armorican peninsula, between Brasparts and La Feuillée. Bounded on three sides by wild hills, where sandstone juts from the heath in sharp spines, it was thought to be the door to the underworld.

It is here that the living come to rid themselves of troublesome ghosts. For an exorcism of this sort, it was necessary to

have the help of a priest well-versed in this kind of service. Dressed in his surplice and holding his stole in his hand, he went to the haunted place. There he took off his shoes to become, according to the ritual, *beleg betek an douar*, 'priest to the earth'.

A bitter struggle followed which could last for hours, even days, during which the exorcist would attempt to put his stole on the ghost's neck. When he had succeeded in doing this and had pronounced the magic words, the dead person was transformed into a black dog. A man was then chosen by the priest to take the animal, following a prescribed route, from presbytery to presbytery, to the boundary of Yeun Ellez. Then the priest of one of the nearby parishes led the sinister animal to the marsh. Barefoot, he led it to *Youdig*, where hell opens its gates, and made it disappear for ever.

Long-range Murder

It was also believed that it was possible to induce the death of another. This could be done by forming the figure of a baby in wax *(bugel koar)* for a woman to keep hidden next to her belly for nine months. After this, a priest would baptize it in the presence of godparents; it was then sufficient to prick the effigy several times in the heart, the stomach and the brain to kill the person it was supposed to represent, who would go into a 'decline'.

Another way of causing an enemy's death consisted of going to see certain old women who, in return for a suitable reward, would dedicate a person to St Yves, patron of

According to legend, the standing stones of Carnac were an army of pagans who pursued St Cornely; to escape them he turned them to stone. In fact they are part of a huge burial ground, probably dating from c 2000 BC, and including stone tombs, stone circles and grave mounds

---

The Legend of Carnac

St Cornely, we are told, pursued by an army of pagans, fled towards the sea. Finding no boat at hand, and on the point of being taken, he transformed his pursuers into stones, the present monoliths. The Saint had made his flight to the coast in a bullock-cart, and perhaps for this reason he is now regarded as the patron of cattle. Should a bullock fall sick, his owner purchases an image of St Cornely and hangs it up in the stable until the animal recovers. The church at Carnac contains a series of fresco paintings which outline events in the life of the Saint, and in the churchyard there is a representation of the holy man between two bullocks. The head of St Cornely is said to be preserved with the edifice as a relic. On the 13th of September is held at Carnac the festival of the 'Benediction of the Beasts', which is celebrated in honour of St Cornely. The cattle of the district are brought to the vicinity of the church and blessed by the priests — should sufficient monetary encouragement be forthcoming.

Lewis Spence
Legends and Romances of Brittany

Brittany. St Yves was renowned as a judge of the highest integrity, able to give fair judgement between two enemies. By calling the man you dislike your sworn enemy, you could ask St Yves to give judgement between the two of you. As the penalty of this rite is death for one or the other of you, it is advisable to be sure that your own deeds will stand scrutiny before practising it.

Quite often, death is linked with the idea of transformation: the exorcism of Anaon ends in changing a dead person into an animal. This also happens in other circumstances. The spirits which populate the countryside, such as the *Spontailh* from Carnac or the malicious *Martine* from Coglès, assume a great variety of aspects to baffle humans.

Magicians and fairies, of course, have similar powers, either over themselves or over other people. According to a legend associated with the Ile du Lok a bad fairy used to seduce men and then turn her lovers into fish to stock her fish-pond. At Loudéac the story used to be told of a green serpent, who had once been a handsome young prince, but who was turned into a snake by a white female cat.

The Well of the Sea

There are innumerable legends and customs attached to the stone formations of Brittany. Traditionally, the upright standing stones are believed to be human beings who have been petrified as punishment or as an act of vengeance. The region is particularly rich in megaliths and other stone monuments, which still exist beside the Christian crosses which were erected many centuries later. The megaliths of Saint-Just and those on the peninsula of Crozon form a chequer pattern.

The most impressive monuments stand in rows. Those at Carnac consist of some 3000 upright stones side by side, with a considerable number of dolmens (stone tombs),. stone circles and burial mounds enclosing masonry. The stones of Carnac, according to tradition, were once an army before being transformed into rock by St Cornely to stop them pursuing him. The legend surrounding the stones of Plouhinec is that they hide treasures which can be seen once a year, when the stones go to drink at the River Etel. The curious onlooker, however, runs the risk of being crushed to death by the stones rushing back. The monument of Kerloas in Plouarzel has two projections: one is believed to confer male children on the man who rubs himself on it; while the other gives power over her husband to the woman who does similarly. The rock called *Ar Gazeg Ven* (the stone mare) at Locronan has the reputation of making the woman who sits on it fertile.

Other stones are legendarily connected with water. The standing stone of the Ile d'Un, on the Grand-Lieu Lake, together with the stone of Saint-Samson on the bank of the River Rance, are the bungs which hold back underground waters and prevent a flood. The worship of springs is also a marked characteristic of Breton belief; it seems probable that the ancient Bretons believed in the existence of a vast ocean under the earth which gushed out at springs and ran over in rivers. It was thought necessary to provide against its overflowing at certain places which were known to be the most dangerous.

Sometimes, indeed, it was believed that the waters broke loose and destroyed whole cities; Brittany has many of these submerged cities. The Grand-Lieu lake covers one: there are also Etier de Langon, the bay of Mont-Saint-Michel, that of St Brieuc close to Erquy and above all that of Douarnenez under whose waters reposes the famous Ville d'Ys. The destruction of this town is sometimes attributed by legend to the sudden opening of the Well of the Sea, releasing underground waters, rather than to the natural encroachment of the sea over the coast. It is believed that the person responsible for this catastrophe was the Princess Ahes or Dahud, who took the keys to the well from her sleeping father at the request of her lover, the Devil. She was an ancient Armorican goddess of water.

There are still people who are considered to have special powers in connection with springs. The clergy have Christianized them by putting them under the protection of a local saint, with whom they share their healing power. Sometimes, this has resulted in a curious synthesis of Christian and pagan practice. At St-Jean-du-Doigt, for instance, the parish priests go in procession every year, in order to renew the healing qualities of the spring, and dip a relic in the water. This relic, the finger joint of St John the Baptist, has given its name to the place.

The sacred springs are reputed to cure a wide variety of afflictions, including eye troubles, infectious illnesses, chest complaints, fevers, rheumatism and toothache. They also have powers of divination. The garment of a sick child, placed on the surface of the water, is said to tell the outcome of his illness. If it floats, he will recover, but if it sinks, he will die. Offerings are made to encourage a favourable prognostication; they usually take the form of coins, nails or pins which are thrown into the spring.

Christian and Pagan

The guardian saints of Brittany are a curious collection, numbering over 500 in all. Some are minor local gods or early Breton chiefs. Some, who have lasted for centuries and are still acknowledged, are barely tolerated by the Roman Catholic Church. The most illustrious are the Seven Saints, who created the seven bishoprics of Brittany. They are Kaourintin, Pol, Brieg, Samsun, Malo, Patern and Tugdual. Also worth mentioning are Gwenole, who founded the abbey at Landévennec, and Ronan the hermit of Locronan.

St Anne, the patroness of Brittany, is traditionally called *mamm goz ar Vretoned*, the grandmother or ancient mother of the Bretons. She has the same name as a Celtic goddess, Ana, thought by the ancient Irish to be the mother of gods; a fact which probably accounts for the high honour in which she is held. A legend established around the very ancient sanctuary of Ste-Anna-la-Palud has it that St Anne may have been a Breton, coming from the same part of the country as the submerged Ville d'Ys. She was married in Judaea and after the death of her husband returned to Armorica, where Jesus came to visit her. This is obviously a memory of the earlier, native Anne, later taken over by the Christian Church.

The religious history of Brittany, in fact, shows a constant struggle between the old religion and the new. In the 17th century, the power of the Church was at such a low ebb that it was necessary to organize missions to revive it. Paganism ruled, especially in the interior of the peninsula, and many priests themselves shared their services between the two forms of worship.

Modern Sorcerers

The sorcerer of ancient times still flourishes today under the modern name of healer, despite the annoyance of priests and doctors. Many people still believe that the cause of an illness is the 'Evil Eye'; it is therefore more a question of lifting a spell than of nursing a patient. There are whole families who share these special gifts but in other cases the gift is held by just one member of the family. The daughter who is born after six sons, with no other daughters in between, for instance, is said to be endowed with special powers; a child who is taken onto holy ground before being baptized is able to foresee the future; the person who can suffocate a living mole can give milk to cows and women. Some acts of sorcery are still performed, Black Masses are celebrated and there are occasional attempts at bewitching. The works of Agrippa, the 16th century occult writer, are still talked about, particularly when someone has been persuaded to tell of supernatural experiences of which they have been victims or witnesses.

Since the end of the First World War, however, ideas have progressed and many old customs have disappeared. The modern face of Brittany differs from that at the beginning of the century. But it is a bit like those creatures in legends which transform themselves: behind the facade, the people are still the same, one of whose characteristics is a lively, sparkling and extravagant imagination: this is Brittany's most attractive side, and the means by which she remains the magician of the western world.

G. LE SCOUËZEC

FURTHER READING: G. Massignon ed, *Folktales of France* (University of Chicago Press, 1968).

Brocken

Highest peak of the Harz Mountains in Saxony (now in East Germany), long famous as the place where witches held their revels on Walpurgis Night, the eve of 1 May; scene of the witches' sabbath in Goethe's *Faust*: the Brocken Bow or Brocken Spectre is the giant shadow cast on clouds or fog below him by someone standing on a hilltop, so named because the phenomenon is supposed to occur frequently on the Brocken.
See GERMAN WITCHCRAFT.

Witches were believed to travel on eggshells, bunches of straw and even wisps of grass. The broomstick, however, is the vehicle popularly associated with the witch – oddly, since it is also the emblem of the virtuous housewife

BROOMSTICK

THE HUMBLE BROOMSTICK has played an intriguing part in the social, sexual and psychic life of mankind. In popular belief witches invariably fly through the air on broomsticks, though in fact the number of witches who confessed to doing so is remarkably small.

Brooms were originally made of a stalk of the broom plant with a bunch of leaves at the head. As an indoor, domestic implement, the broom became a symbol of woman. The equivalent symbol for man is the pitchfork, and in many medieval pictures of witches' gatherings the women hold brooms and the men or the devils hold pitchforks. In some parts of England until quite recently a woman would prop up a broom outside her door when she went out, or she might push the broom up the chimney with its end sticking out at the top, as a sign that she was out. But perhaps originally her purpose was to guard her home by being symbolically present there in the form of the broom, for the 17th century Scottish witch Isabel Gowdie (see GOWDIE) said that before leaving to go to the witches' sabbath, a woman would put her broom on the bed to represent her to her husband. The witch would say, 'I lay down this besom in the Devil's name; let it not stir till I come again.'

In the Middle Ages it was believed that witches travelled on an infinite variety of flying objects, including animals, hobby horses, shovels, eggshells, bunches of straw and wisps of grass, or without any visible means of support at all. A forked stick was a particularly popular witch-vehicle.

She Ambled and Galloped
A famous Irish witch of the early 14th century, Alice Kyteler (see KYTELER), was said to own a staff 'on which she ambled and galloped through thick and thin, when and in what manner she listed, after having greased it with the ointment which was found in her possession.' There is no clear

indication here of flying through the air, though the mention of the ointment suggests it. According to an anonymous tract from Savoy, *Errores Gazariorum*, written c1450, a stick anointed with flying ointment was presented to every witch on her initiation. The earliest known case of a witch confessing to flying on a broom was in 1453, when Guillaume Edelin of St Germain-en-Laye, near Paris, stated that he had done so. A witch of Savoy, tried in 1477, said that the Devil gave her a stick 18 inches long and a jar of ointment. She would grease the stick and, putting it between her legs, say 'Go, in the Devil's name, go!': and at once she was carried through the air to the sabbath.

A hundred years later, in 1563, Martin Tulouff of Guernsey said that he saw his aged mother straddle a broomstick and whisk up the chimney and out of the house on it, saying as she went, 'Go in the name of the Devil and Lucifer over rocks and thorns.' In 1598 Claudine Boban and her mother, witches of the province of Franche-Comté in eastern France, also spoke of flying up the chimney on a stick. The belief that witches usually left their houses by way of the chimney became firmly embedded in popular tradition, in spite of the rarity

Broomsticks are popularly associated with witches. A modern witch with broomstick and black cat, and *(below)* her traditional predecessor, flying to the witches' meeting on her broom. The belief that witches flew on broomsticks was probably partly based on the fact that they used them in ritual dances

with which it appears in witches' own confessions: there may be some connection with the custom, mentioned earlier, of pushing a broom up the chimney to indicate the housewife's absence.

The lawyer and witch-hunter Jean Bodin, in his *Démonomanie* of 1580, maintained that witches flew on either a broom or a black ram but that it was only the woman's spirit that flew through the air, while her body remained at home to perplex investigators. There is evidence that the 'flying' of witches was a dream or hallucinatory experience, and most witches said that they went to their meetings in the ordinary way, on foot or on horseback.

It is also possible that the belief that witches flew on broomsticks was partly based on the fact that they danced with a stick between their legs, jumping high in the air. This may explain the curious statement of a Somerset woman named Julian Cox at her trial in 1664, that 'one evening she walked out about a mile from her own house, and there came riding towards her three persons upon three broomsticks, born up about a yard and a half from the ground.' Two of the three persons she knew, the third 'came in the shape of a black man'.

Freedom of the Air
An effective form of defence against aerial witches was considered to be a peal of church bells. Stronger methods were sometimes used: in Slav countries people used to fire muskets at the clouds, screaming as they did so, 'Curse, curse Herodius, thy mother is a heathen damned of God', while others bestrewed the ground with scythes and billhooks, edge upwards to ensure that there should be no soft landing for the witches.

Towards the end of the 18th century the whole question of the flying of witches was thrashed out in an English court of law. The judge, Lord Mansfield, delivered his famous judgement: that he knew of no law of England that prohibited flying and that, as far as he was concerned, anyone so inclined was perfectly free to do so. It remains a mystery, therefore, why from the moment of its sanction by British law, flying by British witches appears to have stopped almost immediately, except for isolated reports of East Anglian witches skimming church spires on flying hurdles throughout the next 50 years.

Broomstick Wedding
Once grounded, the broomstick survived only as one of the props in the Mummers' play, in the now extinct broomstick dance of the Fen country, and in the long discarded comic dance of the weird sisters in *Macbeth*. Its eclipse appears so complete that only 150 years ago Collin de Plancy wrote in his *Dictionary of Demonology*: 'The idiots who imagined that sorcerers and demons celebrated the Sabbath also argued that witches travelled to the Sabbath on broomsticks. Nowadays everyone knows there are no sorcerers and no one rides on broomsticks.'

A rite which survived, however, in Wales and among gypsies, was the old custom of the broomstick wedding. The happy couple solemnized their union by leaping from the

street into their new home over a broom placed in the doorway. This had to be done before witnesses and without dislodging the broom. At any time within a year the marriage could be dissolved by reversing the process, the couple jumping backwards out of the house over the broom, again before witnesses and without touching the broom.

For a single girl to step over a broomstick, however, was a most unfortunate omen for it meant that she would be a mother before she became a wife. Lighthearted wags used to delight in putting broomsticks in the paths of unsuspecting virgins. It was also very unlucky to make a broom in May, by long tradition an antifertility month and unsuitable for weddings, or during the 12 days of Christmas. It was disastrous to sweep dust out of the front door, which meant dispersing all the luck of the house. On the other hand, in India, a sweeper's broom is still often tied to the mast of a ship, as a charm to 'sweep' storms away; in the symbolic manner of the great Dutch Admiral Van Tromp, who hoisted a broom at his masthead as a sign of his intention to sweep English ships off the seas.

In England since the Second World War the witch's broomstick has regained significance with the revival of witchcraft itself. The ritual importance of 'wand, riding-pole or broomstick' is stressed in the manuals of the modern witch covens.

Man, it seems, finds it impossible to escape from the dreams of his childhood. perhaps influenced by the nursery rhyme of the old woman who ascended in a basket to brush the cobwebs from the clouds with her broom. But it is still surprising that an object specifically designed for sweeping the floor should also be in fantasy a vehicle on which to swoop through the skies.

FURTHER READING: M. A. Murray, *The Witch-Cult in Western Europe* (Oxford University Press, rep. 1967); Charles A. Hoyt, *Witchcraft* (Southern Illinois University Press, 1981); M. Summers, *History of Witchcraft and Demonology* (Routledge & Kegan Paul, London, rep. 1973).

A few witches confessed to leaving their houses by way of the chimney, mounted on a broomstick, and it quickly became part of the traditional popular beliefs about witches: detail from David Tenier's *Scène de Sorcière*

Giraudon

Burned at the stake as a heretic, Giordano Bruno was one of the most original thinkers of his time

GIORDANO BRUNO

GIORDANO BRUNO, philosopher and mathematician, was born in 1548 in the little Italian town of Nola near Naples. A lifetime of enforced wandering through Europe, during which he formulated revolutionary ideas concerning the workings of the universe, resulted in hostile accusations by the Church at Rome. In 1592 he was prosecuted and imprisoned by the Inquisition and in 1600 was burned as a heretic at the stake.

At the age of 17, Bruno entered the principal Dominican monastery in Naples. Here he soon became acquainted with the writings of classical authors such as Aristotle, Virgil and Plato. He undoubtedly read and questioned the works of Ptolemy, the Alexandrian astronomer, whose geocentric theory of planetary movement, explaining the earth to be the immovable centre of the universe, had been accepted for over 1300 years. Here too he was soon noted for his remarkable powers of memory, so much so that he was summoned to Rome by Pope Pius V to discuss his system of mnemonics or memory training.

Bruno's preoccupation with the writings of Erasmus, and his love of disputing accepted beliefs soon led him into trouble. Hearing that an indictment had been drawn up against him, he fled from the monastery, at the same time abandoning his monastic habit. This hasty decision had far-reaching consequences; it cut him off from any hope of reconciliation with the Church.

On the Run

In 1579, in the course of the wandering life to which he was henceforth condemned, Bruno reached Calvinist Geneva. Here he was persuaded by the Marchese de Vico to abandon the monastic habit for good. His hopes of liberty and security were shattered when he indiscreetly exposed 20 mistakes, which he declared had been made in a single lecture by one of the most prominent local professors.

Threatened with reprisals, Bruno made his way to Paris, supporting himself by teaching. His lectures were so successful that King Henri III sent for him to discover whether his marvellous memory was natural or was achieved with the aid of magic. Bruno based his memory devices on those expounded by Raymond Lull, the 13th century Spanish mystic philosopher; they involved the use of geometric symbols, figures, circles and tables (see LULL).

In spite of royal patronage Bruno felt obliged to move on at the approach of the religious wars in France, and decided to go to England. The atmosphere in Elizabethan London was sympathetic to refugees from all over Europe, and especially to Italians. These years (1583–85), which were spent in comparative safety at the house of the French Ambassador, Michel de Castelnau, were to be his most rewarding. He was introduced to the fashionable circles of intellectuals; he met and discussed his ideas with such eminent scholars of the day as Sir Philip Sidney and Sir Fulke Greville. Indeed, his stay in England was marred by only one unpleasant incident, during a short visit to Oxford, where the dons evidently took exception to his theories and to his bombastic manner. Bruno, angered by his reception referred to his critics as 'the herald of the idol of Obscurity and the bailiff of the goddess of Presumption'.

The Infinite Universe

Ever since leaving Naples Bruno had supported himself by writing, lecturing and publishing. Now in London, encouraged by de Castelnau and others, he began to put his unorthodox views on cosmology and philosophy down on paper. In his work *Ash Wednesday Supper* of 1584, Bruno introduces his readers to the Copernican theory of the universe; he states, contrary to accepted Church tradition, that the sun is the centre of the cosmos. For centuries it had been believed that the universe consisted of a *finite* series of concentric spheres with the earth, motionless, at its centre. Bruno was one of the earliest to realize that the universe must be of infinite extent, incorporating innumerable worlds, and he expounds this fully in his book entitled *On the Infinite*

Universe and Worlds published later in 1584.

Bruno maintains that just as men regard the earth as the central point of the universe, about which everything revolves, so too beings on other worlds such as the sun and the moon believe that they are the focal point of their universe.

He divides the worlds into two categories, the suns and the earths or planets; each dependent on the other for its existence. The earths rotate round the suns, but the suns too are continually moving. Behind all movement he envisaged a world soul or spirit, manifesting itself even in inanimate objects such as plants and stones. The individual soul, Bruno believed, could through wisdom, reason and love, rise higher and higher to eventual unity with God.

Bruno was also interested in the magical arts. He compared them to a sword which can be used ill in the hands of a wicked person, but which, correctly manipulated by

Giordano Bruno was burned alive at Rome in 1600 as 'an impertinent and pertinacious heretic': his scepticism about religion and his belief in magic both contributed to his condemnation

Mansell Collection

a God-fearing man, can produce much good. He lists ten different kinds of magic which can be employed to this end. They include natural and sympathetic magic, as well as invocation of the dead (necromancy) and of demonic powers. He advocates mathematical magic, involving the use of figures, characters, words and numbers.

A very impractical man, Bruno was quite incapable of foreseeing the conclusions which would be drawn from his bold statements, especially by his enemies. He worked quickly and his pupil Eglin has left us a description of him 'standing on one leg and dictating as fast as the pen could follow'. He published no less than 61 books on philosophy, the art of memory, geometry and other subjects.

Leaving England in 1585, he spent the next six years visiting European centres of learning, and in particular those in Germany. Finally in 1591 he accepted an invitation from a Venetian nobleman named Giovanni Mocenigo to go to Venice and instruct him in 'the art of memory and invention'. Whether Mocenigo intended to lure Bruno into a trap or whether he was merely dissatisfied with his teaching, is uncertain; but in 1592 he denounced him to the Inquisition and Bruno was put in the jail of the Holy Office on a charge of heresy.

Burnt at the Stake

Although he had never given any overt sign of intending to break with the Church, it had been said of him even in tolerant England, that he was a man of no religion. Indeed one of the minor charges against him was that he had published extravagant praises of the heretic ruler, Queen Elizabeth I. From very early on, however, he had sought to be reconciled to the Church, on condition that he did not have to return to the monastic life.

In 1593 Bruno was transferred to the dungeons of the Inquisition at Rome. Refusing to retract any of his philosophical opinions, he was finally condemned as 'an impenitent and pertinacious heretic' and was publicly burned at the stake in the Campo dei Fiori (Square of Flowers) at Rome on 17 February 1600.

FURTHER READING: F. A. Yates, *Giordano Bruno and the Hermetic Tradition* (University of Chicago Press, 1964).

Brut

Or Brute, or Brutus, legendary descendant of Aeneas: expelled from Rome with his followers, he conquered the island of Albion, which took its name of Britain from him, and subsequent British kings were descended from him; the story was told in Geoffrey of Monmouth's *History of the Kings of Britain*, c1135, and was generally accepted as true until the 17th century.
See ARTHUR.

Buddha

Siddhartha Gautama, the founder of Buddhism, born c 563 BC in what is now Nepal, the son of a chieftain of the Sakya clan; as a young man he left his home and family to become a wandering holy man, and received spiritual illumination while meditating under a bo-tree; he continued to travel about, teaching and gathering disciples, and was called Buddha (the enlightened one), Bhagava (the lord), Tathagata (truth-finder) and Sakyamuni (wise man of the Sakyas); he died at the age of 80 in c 483 BC.
See BUDDHISM: GAUTAMA BUDDHA

Z.F.A.

BUDDHISM

Buddhism

Gerald Cubitt

Arising in India five centuries before the birth of Christianity, Buddhism dominated its native land for 15 centuries, and in due course prevailed in Central Asia, the Far East and Southeast Asia. It has exhibited astonishing power to propagate itself, and less ability to hold its gains. No other religion has prevailed, as Buddhism did in China, in a major civilization other than its native one, and in recent decades Buddhism has even achieved a modest foothold in the West

BUDDHISM DENIES THAT there is a personal world-creator, yet it affirms men's capacity to meet and become superhuman saints, saviours endowed with vast wisdom and compassion. It denies that there is an immortal soul, but affirms that there is personal continuity from life to life through many rebirths until liberation is attained. Permitting wide liberties of thought and practice to individuals and groups, Buddhism exhibits sharp sectarian differences. Yet all kinds of Buddhists are agreed that the supreme goal is Enlightenment, and that in this world-age the way and the goal were discovered and proclaimed by Siddhartha Gautama, the Sage of the Sakya tribe.

Gautama, the Buddha or 'enlightened one', preached his first sermon near Benares in c 530 BC. When he died 45 years later, he left a flourishing community of hundreds of monks and thousands of lay followers. As his successor he nominated, not a disciple but the *Dharma*, his 'truth' or 'doctrine'. These teachings were transmitted orally

and were not written down until the 2nd century BC. By this time the teachings had been edited and amplified but the marvellous memories of the professional reciters, and the zeal of the various Buddhist sects to prevent each other from adulterating the scriptures, kept changes within bounds.

Buddhism's essential aim is to achieve enlightenment or liberation, Nirvana, which is liberation from the remorseless round of birth, death and rebirth. Unless a man achieves liberation, he is reborn over and over again, 'transmigrating' from one existence to another. Faced with this prospect of never-ending reincarnation, a man might react by pursuing worldly pleasures or, at the other extreme, by asceticism and the attempt to set himself apart from all worldly things.

Gautama in his first sermon proclaimed a Middle Way between vulgar pleasure-seeking and futile self-denial. This Way, leading to enlightenment and Nirvana, is the Holy Eightfold Path: right views, intention, speech, action, livelihood, effort, mindfulness and concentration. He declared the Four Holy Truths: that life is fraught with suffering; that the source of suffering is craving for sensual pleasure, for afterlife and for annihilation; that there is an end of suffering when craving ceases; and that there is a path which leads to this ending, the Holy Eightfold Path.

The five mendicants who heard this sermon experienced a spiritual awakening. That the words themselves were not the sole cause of this is plain, for readers usually

Previous page **Buddha, 'the enlightened one', is the title of Siddhartha Gautama, founder of this family of religions and philosophies whose essential aim is to liberate all things from the endless cycle of birth, death and rebirth, the prison in which Indian thought sees man enchained: from Katmandu in Nepal**
Buddhism grew up originally in India, though few traces of it remained there after c 1200 AD, but it still has a powerful influence in the Far East. The temple of the Emerald Buddha at Bangkok, Thailand *(left)* is one of the great shrines in Southeast Asia. Buddhists believe in many demons and spirits, like this guardian spirit *(right)* in the same temple

do not attain the first degree of sainthood upon perusing them. The early account mentions the Buddha's tremendous personal charisma, the thorough readiness of his listeners, and the solemn way in which he imparted this gnosis.

Meditation on suffering is not recommended out of any penchant for melancholy, but because it kills lust and arouses compassion, quells wishful illusions and liberates energy. Transmigration, the round of birth and death, is fraught with suffering because living beings constantly re-condemn themselves to this predicament by their worldly desires. In early India it was axiomatic that you become what you desire. Cessation, the ending of suffering, is Nirvana. It is a happy state in this life, consequent upon the extinction of ignorance and craving, and an indescribable state after the death of the liberated saint, the *arhant*.

Reverence for Life

Buddhists, as is well known, regard the difference between human beings and animals as unimportant, and equal compassion should, in any case, be extended to all. Scrupulous respect for the life and dignity, for the rights and wishes of all living beings is a Bodhisattva's first and most elementary duty. During a debate with the Saskya Pandita which the Venerable Tsong-kha-pa had in about AD 1400 his opponent, probably absent-mindedly, crushed a louse between his nails. Tsong-kha-pa interrupted him, exclaiming, 'While we are here debating these abstruse metaphysical subtleties, I hear the laments of a fellow-creature rising to the sky!' The Saskya Pandita was so much taken aback by this reproof that his hat fell off, he left the tent in confusion, and victory remained with Tsong-kha-pa and his 'Yellow Church'. Likewise, it is quite usual for Bodhisattvas to sacrifice their own lives for animals. When he was a prince of Benares, the Bodhisattva who subsequently became the Buddha Gautama, threw himself down in front of a tigress who had given birth to five cubs and was exhausted from hunger and thirst. 'But she did nothing to him. The Bodhisattva noticed that she was too weak to move. As a merciful man he had taken no sword with him. He therefore cut his throat with a sharp piece of bamboo and fell down near the tigress. She noticed his body all covered with blood, and in no time ate up all the flesh and blood, leaving only the bones.' On another celebrated occasion, as King Sibi, the Bodhisattva ransomed a pigeon by giving a pound of his own flesh to the hawk who had caught it. This fellow-feeling for all living beings, whoever they may be, is much akin to Dr Schweitzer's 'reverence for life' . . . Even the bacteria had already been thought of by the Buddhist monks, who took special precautions against harming the invisible creatures who were said to abound in water and in the air.

E. Conze 'Buddhism: the Mahayana'
in *The Concise Encyclopedia of Living Faiths*

The Three Trainings

Another formula for the Path is the 'three trainings' of morality, concentration and wisdom. Morality here means abstention from specific wrong acts. The five basic precepts observed by Buddhist laymen and monks alike are: not taking life, not taking what is not given, not engaging in sexual misconduct, not telling untruths, and not drinking liquor. The monk also undertakes to observe a code of over 200 rules of restraint. Particular importance attaches to not harming human or animal life, and most of the other precepts serve that objective.

The chief roads to concentration are the four 'abodes of mindfulness': contemplating the body, the feelings, mental states and dharmas (doctrines). You watch your breath go in and out; you are mindful of your actions, whether walking, standing, sitting or lying down; you reflect on the body as consisting of 32 parts and of the four elements of earth, water, fire and wind; and you imagine the successive stages of the body's decomposition after death. As for feelings, you note pleasure, pain and neutral feeling, whether of body or of mind. States of mind are to be watched, noting lust, hate, folly, concentration or distraction. The meditator on dharmas notes what hindrances are present in him. He is aware of the presence or absence of the factors of enlightenment, namely mindfulness, dharma-investigation, vigour, rapture, tranquility, concentration and equanimity. He contemplates the Four Holy Truths until he really understands them.

Concentration is characterized by single-mindedness. After passing through the preliminary stages, the meditator attains the first trance, which is filled with rapture and happiness. In the second trance rapture gives place to serenity and clear awareness. By the time the fourth trance is reached, the meditator is beyond pleasure and pain, beyond joy and grief; he dwells in equanimity and pure awareness.

Three grades of wisdom are distinguished, the lowest based on hearing the doctrine, the next on thinking about what has been heard, and the highest on meditative trances. Morality provides a base for concentration, which in turn supports wisdom, and through wisdom the mind is freed from the 'outflows' — sensual desire, becoming (living again and again) and wrong views. Extinguishing the outflows, one becomes a saint (arhant), attains Nirvana, and is freed from further births.

Psychic Powers

Prominent among the fruits of meditation are the six super-knowledges: magic powers (such as flying, walking on water, changing one's form and projecting a mind-made body), clairaudience (the ability to hear sounds not actually present), mind-reading, memory of former lives, clairvoyance, and extinction of the outflows. The first five are mundane. They are reached through concentration, and may be attained by non-Buddhists. The sixth is supramundane, reached through insight, and attained only by arhants.

The early tradition regarded the mundane super-knowledges with ambivalence. The great saints, including the Buddha himself, went on shaman-style journeys to the paradises and hells, received communications from spirits through clairaudience and clairvoyance, read the minds of their students in order to select the the appropriate teaching or meditative practice for them, and remembered their own and others' former lives. They also foretold the future, 'saw' human events that were going on at a great distance, and subdued demons.

On the other hand, monks were forbidden to exhibit their psychic powers to ordinary people, because this cheapened the spiritual attainments. They were to refrain from reciting spells and from interpreting dreams, omens and the stars. Similarly, the super-knowledges were not to be used for worldly purposes, because this would conduce to worldly greed. Yet the literature of Indian Buddhism is full of tales in which a saint used his paranormal powers to rescue someone from worldly distress. This tension between worldly engagement and Nirvana-oriented disengagement characterizes the entire history of Buddhism.

The Earning of Merit

So far it might seem that the early Buddhist ethic was merely one of abstention, and that the goals of the religious life were entirely ascetic and unworldly. This is not the case. Donation was a cardinal virtue for both laity and monks. The laymen earned merit by giving material requisites to monks and nuns, and by helping the sick and the needy.

Merit is a sort of spiritual currency, that can be spent on a happy next life in a paradise, or turned over to the benefit of a deceased relative, or invested in further spiritual progress. The monk was not rich in material goods but he was supposed to be rich in Dharma (Doctrine), which he donated by teaching it. He also earned merit just by living the monastic life, and like the layman he often devoted his merit to the well-being of deceased relations.

Another merit-earning activity is worship (*puja*). In the household life, puja means honouring your parents, guests, teachers and other worthy persons. In a sacred context, it means making the same ritual gestures of reverence and hospitality: bowing with palms pressed together, kowtowing, touching the honoured one's feet, circumambulation, chanting salutations and verses of praise, and offering food, water, lights, incense, flowers, cloth and precious substances. Today in the Theravada countries of Sri Lanka and Southeast Asia, footwashing is performed for holy guests, images are bathed, and worthy persons are splashed with water on New Year's Day.

The Three Jewels

The most worshipful entities are the Buddha, the Dharma (Doctrine) and the Sangha (Community). These are the three Jewels or Treasures. The Sangha has four divisions: monks, nuns, laymen and laywomen. But in common use the word means chiefly the community of monks. You become a Buddhist by declaring, 'I go to the Buddha-refuge, I go to the Dharma-refuge, I go to the Sangha-refuge.' Here the third refuge is the community of holy persons, not all of whom are monks, just as not all monks are saints.

The early teaching sets forth a simple series of stages on the path. The primary division is between worldlings and saints. The worldling who has taken the refuges is a faith-follower, one who pursues the truth and accepts the doctrine on the authority of another. There are four grades of holy person or saint. The *stream-winner* is certain not to fall into a bad rebirth and not to relapse until he attains enlightenment. This stage is attainable through morality and perfect faith in Buddha, Dharma and Sangha. In no more than seven births the

You become a Buddhist by saying, 'I go to the Buddha-refuge, I go to the Dharma-refuge, I go to the Sangha-refuge': the Dharma being the true doctrine and the Sangha the community of holy persons, including monks and laymen. The monks vow to observe a code of more than 200 moral rules but the five basic rules, applying to laymen as well as monks, are not to take human or animal life, not to take what is not given, not to engage in sexual misconduct, not to tell lies, and not to drink intoxicants
Right A young boy, regally dressed, sits with the women of his family before taking the vows which will make him a Buddhist monk
Facing page The boy's head is shaved *(above)*. This is a mark of the renunciation of the worldly life in many different societies: Christian monks, for instance, have 'tonsures' or shaved patches on their heads. Later *(below)* the boy takes the saffron-yellow robe of a monk and vows to keep it holy as long as he breathes

stream-winner will attain sainthood. The *once-returner*, free from the fetters of lust and ill-will, will attain sainthood in his next human rebirth. The *non-returner* gets rid of all his fetters in this life, and then is reborn in a high heaven where he reaches Nirvana. The arhant extinguishes all the outflows and in this very life realizes liberation of mind through wisdom.

In the earlier layers of the early scriptures, Buddha is little more than the first arhant among equals. His uniqueness consists of having reached full enlightenment without having a master in this life. In later parts of the early canon, the Buddha is exalted far above his holy disciples. Whereas the earlier texts ascribe to him only the three great cognitions (memory of his former lives, cosmic vision and knowledge that his outflows were extinguished), later Pali texts claim he was omniscient.

Gautama was probably never considered to be the only Buddha. The Pali texts speak of a series of six former Buddhas, whom Gautama remembers through his own super-knowledge, and of the future Buddha, Maitreya, who is now a Bodhisattva (Buddha-to-be).

What is Nirvana?

Is Nirvana annihilation or eternal existence, the cessation of all thought and feeling or perfect beatitude? The early texts give enigmatic answers. They say that there is an unborn, unbecome, unmade, unconditioned; and then they define the unconditioned as destruction of lust, hatred and

folly. Whether the Buddha exists after death ranks as an undeclared point, along with whether the world is eternal, whether the world is infinite, and whether the soul and the body are the same. The Buddha refused to admit that the Buddha exists after death, or does not exist, or both exists and does not exist, or neither exists nor does not exist. To each of these statements he answered, 'This does not fit the case.' Then he likened the Buddha after death to a fire which has gone out; it has not gone north, south, east or west. The Buddha, he says, is deep and immeasurable like the great ocean. Since the Nirvana-realm is unique, analogies are inadequate, and the prudent teacher guards against treating them as descriptions. The only adequate indication of Nirvana is instruction on how to experience it.

Early Buddhism rejected the Upanishadic concept of a world-soul *(brahman, atman)*, the material and efficient cause of all things (see BRAHMAN). Nirvana is not a stuff out of which the world is made, and its attainment is not a reversion of the soul to its unmanifested state. The Buddha denied that there is an atman or self, in the sense of an unchanging substance which serves as host to changing and transient properties. He treated all phenomena as processes and declared a Middle Path between the eternalist extreme of being ('what is, always is') and the annihilationist extreme of non-being ('then it was real, now it's extinct'). The action of cause and effect is not a modification of substances, but dependent

co-arising: 'When A exists, then B comes into being; when A does not exist, B does not come into being.' Relations are real, substances are not.

Transmigration is not the re-embodiment of a soul, but the passing over of a consciousness, consisting of the seeds of good and evil deeds *(karma)* committed during this life and previous lives. It is likened to the flame passing from one candle to another, or a poem passing from the teacher's mind to the pupil's. The transmigrant consciousness finds a species and a family in conformity with its moral legacy.

The world of transmigration *(samsara)* consists of three realms: the *desire-realm* (comprising the subterranean hells, the animal world, the ghost world. the human world, the demon world and the lower god worlds); the *form-realm* (the higher god worlds); and the *formless realm*, inhabited by beings who as contemplatives in this life achieved the trance-planes of endless space, endless consciousness, nothing-at-all, and neither-perception-nor-non-perception.

Buddhist cult practice implements the conviction that all living beings are members of one cosmic family. Merit is transferred to the account of beings in hell, to alleviate their sufferings and hasten their release. Animals are given sanctuary in temple precincts, hunting and butchering are considered immoral, and veterinary treatment is provided as a pious act. Offerings of merit, rice-cakes and water are made to the ghosts of departed relatives on the anniversaries of their deaths, and to all the ghosts on the

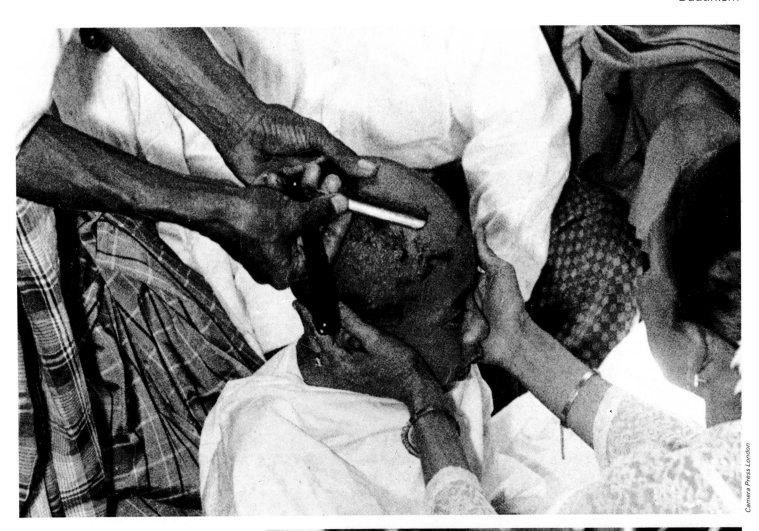

15th day of the seventh month. Offerings are made to numerous gods, godlings and demons. In return, the gods grant worldly blessings such as children, riches and freedom from danger and disease. The two great Indo-Aryan gods of the 6th century BC entered early Buddhism, Indra as protector and Brahma as inspirer of the Dharma. Rebirth in Brahma's heaven is obtained through the four contemplations known as 'Brahma-dwellings': friendly love, compassion, sympathetic joy and equanimity. In general, the early Buddhist approach to spirits was to subdue them through Dharma, then treat them with friendly respect rather than with terror or aversion.

The Converted Emperor

During the second century AN (after the Nirvana of Gautama in or about 483 BC), the Buddhist monastic order split into two sects, the Sthaviras (Elders) and the Mahasanghikas (members of the Great Assembly). The former restricted their assembly to arhants, and denied that a layman could become an arhant, thus excluding laymen from their councils. The latter admitted laymen and non-arhants to their meetings, which consequently were called 'great'. The Elders were an ecclesiastical establishment, enhancing the status of the cleric and the arhant. The Mahasanghikas made less of arhantship, and exalted Buddha even more than the Elders did. They maintained that he is supermundane, does not reside among men, has an infinite body, has boundless power, and is endowed with endless life. He

sends out apparition-bodies throughout the whole cosmos, and through them works ceaselessly for the salvation of all living beings.

In or about 274 BC Asoka came to the throne of the Maura Empire. After consolidating his power and expanding his territory, he was stricken with remorse at the bloodshed and destruction he had wrought in the course of conquest, and became a Buddhist convert. He went on pilgrimages, gave up hunting, frequented the company of monks, and spent some time in retreat. Then he proclaimed a policy of Dharma-conquest rather than military conquest, and appointed special Dharma-commissioners to oversee the execution of his policy. He commended

tolerance between sects and urged all to concentrate on the common essence of Dharma. But he promoted the growth of Buddhism and other ascetic sects, and by sending missionary monks to foreign countries he gave Buddhism tremendous impetus.

During Asoka's reign, the sect of Vibhajyavadins (Distinctionists) split off from the school of the Elders. The Vibhajyavadins themselves soon split into several sects. Their strongholds were in western India (present-day Madhya Pradesh and Maharashtra). An archaic Vibhajyavadin sect which called itself simply Theravada (the Doctrine of the Elders) passed through the south of India to Ceylon in the late 3rd century BC. After many vicissitudes and

Buddhist worshippers put flowers in the hats of these statues, burn incense to them and periodically give them new clothes. Worship earns merit, which can be spent in a happy next life in a paradise before another rebirth on earth, or which can be used to alleviate the sufferings of a dead relative in one of the numerous hells

recurrent encroachment by Hinduism, other Buddhist sects and Christianity, it is still there (see SINHALESE BUDDHISM). In the 5th and 6th centuries AD, there were Theravada centres on the Madras coast, from which the sect spread to Burma. Today it prevails in Burma, Thailand, Laos and Cambodia as well as Ceylon.

About four centuries AN there arose a

The coming Buddha saves people from danger, receives confessions of sins, and comes to the dying to lead them to his paradise

movement calling itself the Bodhisattvayana or Mahayana (great course or vehicle), in contrast to the Hinayana – inferior course or vehicle. Initially it was probably not a separate sect but just a new way of stating some typical Mahasanghika doctrines: that the phenomena of the world are illusory and empty, that the true Buddha is transworldly, that the Buddhas who appear in the world are his phantom-bodies, that they exist simultaneously in many world-realms, and that the saving activity of the Buddhas never ceases.

The idea of the Bodhisattva – the one who is on the path of becoming Buddha – was acknowledged by all the Hinayana sects, but most used the term only to designate Gautama before he attained enlightenment. Mahayana proclaimed that the Bodhisattva-yana is the course which all devotees should follow. It taught a path along which even the humblest could set out, and it assured him of help from an array of celestial Bodhisattvas and Buddhas.

The Bodhisattva Career

We know from stone reliefs that stories of the Buddha's former lives were popular by the 2nd century BC. These tales celebrate a series of virtues called 'perfections'. The idea of the perfections was developed by the Elder sects, and Mahayana adopted the idea and made it the heart of the Bodhisattva path, which it recommended not just for admiration but for practice by all devotees, whether male or female, monastic or lay.

The Bodhisattva path begins with the awakening of the aspiration for supreme, perfect enlightenment. This momentous act requires the accumulation of much merit and wisdom, and the aid of good spiritual friends. It also has great results. It cancels bad karma, prevents bad rebirths and leads to good ones.

Having awakened his aspiration, the Bodhisattva cultivates good qualities, does good to others, and meditates on the aims of his career. In due course he makes a set of vows, resolving to save living beings and often specifying that when he becomes a Buddha his Buddha-land will have such-and-such amenities and advantages.

Then the Bodhisattva proceeds to practise six virtues until they become perfections. *Donation* means giving one's goods, the Dharma, and even one's life and body, to those who have need of them. It is a perfection when the giver has no thought of reward, and is spontaneous and unselfconscious about the act. *Morality* consists of observing the precepts, transferring the resultant merit to the account of others, and encouraging others to do the same. *Patience* means enduring hardship and injury from others, and accepting difficult and unpalatable doctrines. *Vigour* is unflagging energy and zeal in overcoming vice and cultivating virtue. *Meditation* consists of practising the trances, concentrations and attainments without accepting the worldly advantages these can procure. *Wisdom* is the queen of the perfections, since it consists in the direct realization of the truth of emptiness (see SUNYAVADA), which quells all fictions and 'thought-constructions' and thus renders the other five virtues perfect.

When the Bodhisattva masters the six perfections, he achieves the non-relapsing state and is not bound to rebirths by his karma, but chooses at will where he is going to be reborn in order to benefit living beings. Eventually he becomes a Buddha, unless he has vowed to remain a Bodhisattva until all living beings attain enlightenment.

The celestial Bodhisattvas in the Mahayana pantheon are Great Beings who have achieved the non-relapsing stage and sovereignty over the realms of transmigration. Most of them are probably descended from the deities of North Indian popular religion in the last five centuries BC, and they have taken over the attributes and functions of the great gods Indra and Brahma. They occupy subordinate positions in the early Mahayana Sutras, but become more and more prominent after 200 AD, until they surpass the Buddhas themselves.

The Buddha to Come

Devotion to Maitreya, the coming Buddha, is common to both Hinayana and Mahayana. He will be born at Benares in the distant future when human virtue and prosperity have increased immensely. Meanwhile he is staying in the Tusita Heaven, where the devout may be reborn if they earnestly pray for it, particularly at the moment of death. There they will pass the interlude in celestial bliss, listening to Maitreya's discourses. And when he comes to earth again, they will accompany him. As a high god Maitreya is powerful, and as a Bodhisattva

he is compassionate, so worshippers can expect a response to their prayers. He is the inspirer of Buddhist teachers, appearing to them in dreams or trances, consoling them when they are in doubt or frustration. He also saves people from danger, receives confessions of sins, and comes to the dying to lead them to his paradise.

Manjusri is said to have become a non-relapsing Bodhisattva 64 myriads of aeons ago. Because he vowed not to hurry to enlightenment but to remain in samsara as long as a single living being is unsaved, his Buddhahood is not imminent. He was born in Gautama's time as a Brahmin and lived 450 years. Merely hearing his name deducts many ages from one's time in transmigration and worshipping him guarantees good rebirth. If you recite a certain Sutra and chant his name, he will appear to you in seven days, in a dream if you have bad karma, otherwise in a waking vision. He is the embodiment of Wisdom, and in art is shown riding a lion, holding a sword in his hand.

Another Great Being is Avalokitesvara who appears in multifarious forms in order to help and save living beings – as a Buddha, as a Bodhisattva, as an arhant, or as a Hindu god. The merit from devotion to him is equal to that from worshipping a vast number of Buddhas. He grants boons to those who call him to mind and recite his name. He saves them from evil passions, grants a son or daughter (as she chooses) to a supplicant woman, and saves those who think of him from fire, shipwreck, robbers, execution, prison, witchcraft, demons, wild beasts, snakes and thunderbolts. His cult burgeoned during the 4th century AD, and by the 7th he was the most popular divinity in the Indian Buddhist pantheon.

We have seen how the Mahasanghikas idealized the Buddha, and treated the historical Gautama as one of numerous apparitions projected by the eternal, supermundane Buddha. They also believed, as against the Elders, that many Buddhas exist in the universe at the same time, each reigning over a Buddha-field or Buddha-land.

From the beginning, there was an apparent contradiction between Gautama's various roles. The Lotus Sutra, completed c 200 AD, declares that he did not really enter Nirvana at the end of his 80 years on earth, but only

Serenity in stone: faces of Bodhisattvas, saints who are on the path to becoming Buddhas, at the Bayon Temple in Angkor Thom, Cambodia, built in the 12th century by the Emperor Jayavarman VII, a supporter of Buddhism in an area where Hinduism and Buddhism co-existed and influenced each other, as they had earlier done in India

gave the appearance of doing so, to shock and invigorate people who would otherwise have taken his presence for granted. In reality, he is always active, teaching and helping all living beings in this and all other worlds. The Buddha of the Lotus Sutra is a marvellous and ever-present teacher, but he does not relieve the pupils of the necessity to make an effort, gain merit and accumulate wisdom. In India, Gautama always remained the most popular of the celestial Buddhas.

Vairocana, 'Descendant of the Sun', began as an epithet of Gautama but became one of the chief Buddhas in the Avatamsaka Sutra (c 300 AD). Aksobhya, 'the Unshakable', was popular in the first two centuries AD. He presides over a Buddhafield in the Eastern Direction where people who do good deeds or hear his name can attain birth. Amitabha, 'Unlimited Light', (also called Amitayus, 'Unlimited Lifespan' and the Amida of Japan – see AMIDA) presides over a paradise in the Western Direction called 'the Happy Land'. All beings who go to Amitabha's land unfailingly attain enlightenment. To obtain rebirth in the Happy Land one must have a minimum of good conduct, must hear the name of Amitabha, and must fix one's ·intent on going there. There are no hells, animals, ghosts or women in that land. All material requisites come just by wishing for them. Fragrant jewel-flowers shower down from jewel-trees, and the clouds play continual sweet music. And the beings there hear whatever Dharma-discourse they wish to hear. The cult of Amitabha was never as

popular in India as that of Sakyamuni, but it enjoyed tremendous fortune in China.

Tantric Buddhism, or Vajrayana, 'the Thunderbolt Vehicle', arose c 600 AD, after a long period of incubation. The Tantric centuries equalled in glory any other period in Indian Buddhist history. They produced great art and architecture, profound scholarship, and a remarkable line of holy men. Just as Mahayana revitalized a tradition that was falling prey to academic hair-splitting and complacency, so Vajrayana revived spiritual zeal and accomplishment at a time when the Bodhisattva ideal was more celebrated in academic analyses than realized in practice.

Revival in India

From the 7th to the 12th centuries, Vajrayana flourished in Bihar and Bengal. The great monastic universities of Nalanda and Vikramasila taught the whole range of Buddhist, Hindu and secular learning to thousands of students, including Chinese, Tibetans and Southeast Asians. But Moslem invaders destroyed organized Buddhism in the Ganges valley, sacking Nalanda in 1198 and again several times over the next decades. It survived as a folk cult for two or three centuries, then vanished from the Ganges area.

Vajrayana also prospered in the sub-Himalayan valleys, in Swat, Gilgit, Kashmir, Katmandu. It was exterminated by Moslem rulers only in the 15th century. It survives to this day in the Katmandu Valley.

It is doubtful whether Buddhism ever had

much strength in the Tamil country in southern India, except in a few towns such as Conjeeveram, a great centre of learning where there was still a Theravada community even in the 15th century. West India and the Deccan were Buddhist strongholds to the end of the 7th century but the last Buddhist monuments in Maharashtra date from the 5th century, and thereafter Hinduism dominated the whole region. Probably Brahmin advisers at the courts were more skilful at winning the princes' favour than were the Buddhist monks. Buddhism flourishes best in strong nation-states (as in Sri Lanka, Burma and China in the T'ang period). The loosely structured feudal society of the Rajput period favoured the equally loosely organized Hinduism.

While it is not true that Hinduism absorbed all the best from Buddhism, it still assimilated and perpetuated a great deal. The strong emphasis on compassion in devotional Hinduism owes much to Buddhist inspiration. The later Vedanta schools (see VEDANTA) are indebted to Buddhism in many important respects. Samkara's Vedanta supplanted Buddhism by borrowing not only philosophy but monasticism from it, and Samkara is with good reason called a Buddhist in disguise.

Modern India has rediscovered its Buddhist heritage with pride. A few caste Hindus and millions of former untouchables have been converted to Buddhism and for every convert, there are many more Indians who study Buddhist doctrine with approval, go on pilgrimage to the Buddhist holy places, and see the religious universalism of the Buddha as a forerunner of the egalitarian democracy India is now striving to develop. Asoka's ideal of Dharma-victory still lives, and its symbol, the Wheel of the Dharma, stands in the centre of India's flag. (See also CHINA; GAUTAMA BUDDHA; JAPAN; NIRVANA; TANTRISM; TIBET; ZEN.)

RICHARD H. ROBINSON

FURTHER READING: R. H. Robinson, *The Buddhist Religion* (Dickenson, 1969); E. Conze, *Buddhism, its Essence and Development* (Cassirer, Oxford, England, 1951); N. W. Ross, *Buddhism: A Way of Life and Thought* (Knopf, 1980); *Buddhist Thought in India* (Univ. of Michigan Press, 1967).

Buffalo
The American bison, on whom Plains Indians depended for survival; a major supernatural power in their myths, such as Buffalo Old Man and Old Woman in Kiowa or Apache tales; great buffalo dances as of Mandans, with full head-dresses from buffalo heads and mime of herd movement, used to lure herds for hunters; associated with rain, buffalo was prayed to by Sioux and others when rain was needed.
See GREAT PLAINS INDIANS.

Our ancestors believed that there was more to building a house than bricks and mortar. Rituals designed to ensure the prosperity of the building and its occupants included the burial of human beings — sometimes small children — beneath the foundations

BUILDERS' RITES

BEFORE A BUILDING of any type could be erected, it was necessary to propitiate the powers of Nature, because the order of Nature was being interfered with, and particularly the spirit of the earth on which the building would rest. Through every stage of the construction, from the initial selection of the site until the final completion of the roof-top, there followed a succession of magical rites.

In the choice of a site the spirit world was consulted and the entrails of animals examined for signs and portents. A sign of the intentions of the gods might be manifested through Nature itself. In the legend of the foundation of Mexico City, for instance, we are told how a group of Indians, observing an eagle holding a serpent in its talons, recognized this as an intimation from the gods that the city should be established on that spot (see AZTECS).

It was the custom in Ireland in the last century to stick a new spade into the earth and only if it had not been removed overnight by the fairies did building operations begin. Another Irish custom, equally bizarre, was that of throwing a hat into the air during a gale and building the house where it happened to fall, since such a site was considered likely to be sheltered from adverse winds. After the land was surveyed, it would be blessed by the priest or magician and thus made safe for occupation.

The orientation of a building with the sun was of immense symbolic importance. The Temple of Solomon, for instance, had entrance towers facing towards the east, and the Holy of Holies was at the west. The

Symbols to propitiate spirits and ensure a building's stability: an inscribed brick and 'tet' pillar, a symbol of stability, discovered in the foundations of an Egyptian building (above); European builder's mark of a circle and two mallets on a foundation stone (right)

altar of a Christian church is usually at the east end. This ancient association with the sun was deliberately flouted by Sir Walter Mildmay, in Puritan abhorrence of superstition, when he built the original Emmanuel College Chapel at Cambridge facing north and south rather than east-west.

To endow a new building with good fortune and to secure it against the assaults of evil spirits, bread and salt were laid in the foundations. It remained the custom as late as the 17th century to build a bottle of water and a piece of bread into the walls of English cottages, as charms to secure the occupant from want.

It was once common practice to sacrifice a human being to the Earth deity and it was believed that no building would stand unless its foundations were laid in blood. In the old royal city of Mandalay, men were buried alive under the gates. In Siam victims were crushed to death in a pit. The custom survived into comparatively modern times among some primitive peoples; for instance, in 1881, the King of Ashanti (now a region of Ghana) mixed the blood of 200 maidens with the mortar when building a new palace. The survival of the custom in the West until Christian times is suggested by the discovery of skeletons in the foundations of old churches, as at Darrington, in Yorkshire, in 1895 when the church walls were found to be resting on a human skull. It is probable that the recurring stories of nuns and monks immured alive are based upon distorted traditions of this character. The legend that St Columba buried St Ronan beneath the foundations of his monastery to propitiate the guardian spirits of the soil may well have a similar basis. In the English fen-lands, traditionally, those who caused flooding by neglecting to keep up the sea walls would be used as living foundations when the walls were rebuilt.

Such practices were followed not merely as a form of psychic insurance for the durability of a building but with the additional aim of providing a ghostly guardian who would prevent the intrusion of hostile spirits, since it was assumed that a human being so sacrificed would haunt the site for ever. An example of this superstition came to light in 1966 with the discovery of the skeletons of babies who had been ritually entombed in the Roman fortress at Reculver, Kent. The tradition persists that the site is haunted by the sobbing ghost of 'a child that had been buried alive by the Romans'.

Shadows for Sale
These rites were replaced over the years by forms of sacrifice less offensive to sophisticated religious taste. A human shadow was used instead of the living person, in places as far apart as the British Isles and Rumania; there were even 'shadow traders' who secretly measured a man's shadow and buried the measurements beneath the foundations.

Puppets or domestic animals later replaced the human being as objects of sacrifice, the blood being poured into the foundations. In the early 1960s during restoration work at Lauderdale House in Highgate, London, workmen found part of a goblet, two shoes and four mummified chickens which had been built into the chimney breast in the late 16th century. More recently a mummified cat was found immured in a cottage wall at Cricksea, Essex, where it had been buried alive to protect the house against fire. Coins are frequently discovered cemented into the brickwork of old chimneys; it has been suggested that the motive was to provide 'ransom money for the person who ought to have been there'.

The custom of placing documents beneath foundation stones is extremely ancient. It is recorded that Chaldean kings, interested in antiquity, used to tunnel into the ruins of old palaces for the foundation records deposited by their predecessors. Closer to our modern rites were those performed at Crowland Abbey, Lincolnshire, in 1112 when the Abbot laid the first cornerstone while the citizens submitted written offerings of either money or unpaid labour.

The actual materials used in the work of construction were ritualistically important, particularly in relation to ancient tree worship. This tradition survived among the Ozarks hillmen of the United States in the custom of transferring some of the timbers from an older building to a new one. An English superstition asserts that it is courting trouble if a builder uses tomb-stones instead of bricks.

In Africa and the East, building operations were often festive occasions, as were those brought to the United States by the early European settlers. No ceremony could have been more light-hearted than the erection of a cottage in Donegal, which used to be a communal undertaking with the neighbours carrying wood and stones to the site to the music of a hired fiddler. Among some primitives, building operations could be far from joyful, however; the Bapedi tribe of South Africa, for example, had to maintain a state of absolute continence during the work of construction, and any departure from such restraint, it was thought, would impair the soundness of the completed building.

Topping Out

Within the house the hearth was regarded as a domestic shrine and the door as a barrier against spirits, the latter bearing magical inscriptions. At Alatri in Italy phallic symbols were carved on the lintel of a postern or passage in the walls of the citadel. In the Channel Islands, however, house builders considerately provided roof ledges upon which witches could rest while on the way to their destinations.

From classical times to the present the completion of a building has been celebrated as a feast. In ancient Rome the contractor, having erected a state or religious building, offered thanks to the Bona Dea, a fertility

Foetuses of dogs and llamas on sale in Bolivia: they bring good luck if buried under the foundations of a new building. This belief is probably a survival of the earlier custom of killing an animal or a human being to provide a spirit-guardian for a building

goddess, who then became its protectress.

The once universal 'topping out' ceremony, in which a barrel of beer was drunk while a tree or wreath was attached to the roof of a completed building, survives today only in attenuated form. It is still observed occasionally, however, as in 1963 when a green bough was nailed to the newly completed dome of Smithfield Poultry Market, 'as a means of warding off evil spirits'. The topping out ceremony in its original splendour can still be seen in Germany where a bush like a Christmas tree is placed in position after the last timber of the house has been put on. In one such ceremony one of the carpenters gives thanks to God, 'the highest builder in Heaven'. Healths are drunk, after which the glasses are thrown to the ground to prevent bad luck.

Little else of the potent magic of the building trade has survived in the modern world. And yet public buildings and bridges are still ritually opened, and the first sod of a new site turned with a new spade, or the first mortar laid with a shiny trowel. And there is still the ceremonial laying of the foundation stone, with its inscribed tribute to local dignitaries.

(See also HOUSE.)

ERIC MAPLE

FURTHER READING: L. Sprague de Camp, *The Ancient Engineers* (Doubleday); R. Thonger, *A Calendar of German Customs* (Dufour, 1968); N. Wymer, *English Town Crafts* (C. River Books, 1976); E. E. Evans, *Irish Folkways* (Routledge, 1966).

Symbol of virility, fertility and power, the bull was the focus of many cults in ancient times from India to the Mediterranean. In Crete, young men and women literally 'took the bull by the horns' in order to extract these sacred qualities. The modern bullfight originated in beliefs which date back thousands of years

BULL

CONTEMPORARY MAN in Western society has but one basic interest in bulls – their role in the production of beef. For most of us, even this knowledge is quite indirect since in urban society we rarely encounter bulls except piecemeal in the butcher's. It is natural then if we do not know of the lengthy, intensive and dramatic involvement of our ancestors with these creatures, or realize that millions of people in the world today still closely relate their lives to them.

The story of men and bulls begins in the Paleolithic or Old Stone Age. Man was a hunter, and some of the most widespread and frequently hunted animals were various types of wild cattle. Those best known to ancient man in Europe and the Near East were a species now called *bos primigenius*, *urus*, or aurochs – a huge, savage creature with shaggy hair and long, curving horns, from which Spanish fighting cattle are descended. Of all the animals hunted by our forefathers, the aurochs were probably the most valuable. Not only were they a plentiful source of meat but their bones were used for spear points, harpoons and fishhooks, and their skins were fashioned into clothing, boats and tents.

Wild cattle are herding animals, the aurochs herd consisting of a number of cows and calves dominated by a single fierce bull. Consequently, he who would successfully hunt the aurochs had first to kill this dangerous paramount bull. And ancient bulls, like their modern descendants, were powerful, swift, sharp-horned creatures. Standing six feet high or more at the shoulders, they were assuredly a most difficult animal to kill. These ancient bull hunts, these Stone Age *corridas*, must certainly have been savage, bloody affairs in which members of both species perished. Thus, while the aurochs was one of early man's primary benefactors, he was a dangerous and unwilling one; a benefactor who produced profound awe and fear in the hearts of those who hunted.

Art for Meat's Sake

A measure of these emotions is discernible in much of the cave art of south-west Europe (see CAVE ART). Produced from about 40,000 years ago and extending through the Magdalenian culture period, altogether some 25,000 years, it is with few exceptions an art of animals. In much cave art, such as at Altamira in Spain and at Lascaux in France, wild bulls and cows predominate. Scholars agree that for the most part it is magical art; this theory that it was 'art for meat's sake' has been adduced from two kinds of evidence, the art itself and its location. As to the art, not only does it concern animals, but the animals are repeatedly

The kings of Crete were apparently revered as incarnations of the bull god of the island, and bulls played an important part in Cretan religion: ritual vase from Cnossus in the form of a bull's head, used for making offerings of oil or wine

drawn pierced with spears and darts, with traps set before them, headless, disembowelled, dying. Clearly these drawings were part of sympathetic magical rituals based on the belief that the image of an animal is in some way connected with the real animal.

The location of the drawings also demonstrates their magical nature. In virtually every case they are found not in cave mouths or on rocks in the open, but deep within subterranean caverns, far removed from the areas of day-to-day living. We must assume that this artistic secretiveness was not born of modesty but of fear of discovery and retaliation by the very animals which man sought to kill.

The Supreme Bull

During early Neolithic times, when cattle were domesticated, a new dimension was added to the relationship of man and bull. Precisely how this happened is not known, but it was a tremendous forward stride for humankind. It released man from the bondage of the hunting culture. No longer was he a virtual slave to the arbitrary movements of wild animal herds. Now he could keep a ready supply of meat and later milk on hand at all times.

Perhaps the most interesting aspect of animal domestication, however, was that it appears to have been directly responsible for our ancestors' first learning that sexual activity is connected with pregnancy. While he had undoubtedly witnessed copulation among animals through the years, there is no evidence that man saw the relationship between the exuberant sexuality of the bull and the subsequent calving of the cow, or in his own sexual activity and the child-bearing of his women.

Once animals began to be domesticated, however, proximity and daily observation allowed him to perceive the cause and effect relationship in procreation. Further, when Neolithic man made this discovery, bulls came to assume a new value in his eyes. Still a symbol of boundless strength and power, bulls were then esteemed for their sexuality as well, for it was obvious that a single animal could impregnate an entire herd.

During this time man also learned the rudiments of agriculture – that seeds when sown would produce plants. But it was many years before the value of breaking the earth became known and before the plough was invented. For most of this period, cattle-raising and agriculture were separate spheres of activity. Cattle were for meat and milk; grain was for bread and beer. Late in the Neolithic Age, however, man saw a relationship between his cattle and his crops. He believed that the great fertility of the bull could influence the successful growth of grain. As a cattle-raiser he knew the tremendous fertilizing power of the bull. From this it was but a step to believe that the fertility of the bull could be as efficacious for grain as it was for cattle.

One of the first recorded hymns shows clearly that praise is given to 'the great bull, the supreme bull which treads the holy pasturage – planting corn and making fields luxuriant'. This is not homage to the earth

Egyptian bronze statue of the sacred Apis bull, fathered by a ray of moonlight and after death embalmed and buried like a king

Roger Wood Studio

or to seeds, but to the bull for his aid in walking among the plants and causing them to grow by emanating fertility. The plough plays only an incidental part; it opens the earth to receive the fertile force.

Exalted Overpowering Ox

Historians agree that all the first great civilizations of the Tigris-Euphrates region and those of the Nile and the Indus rivers were built upon the broad, firm base of stockbreeding and agriculture. In the hunting cultures, all able-bodied men hunted; there was little division of labour or specialized tasks not involving the hunt. With animal domestication and planting, however, one man's effort could feed several other men, whose time and labour were then released for other pursuits. In time the inevitable enrichment of culture thus effected resulted in the first civilizations.

During this period, the bull continued to play a central role in man's life, as the obvious inseminator of herds and the imagined fertilizer of the fields; both archeological relics and records of early civilizations relate repeatedly to the bull. In the analysis of these materials, however, a most surprising fact emerges: one or more of the central gods in the religions of each of these peoples was a bull god. Hymns and prayers to these deities indicate that as

---

The Bull in Heliopolis

An Egyptian hymn to the great bull god:

Hymn to Amen-Ra, the Bull in Heliopolis,
president of all the gods,
beneficent god, beloved one,
the giver of the warmth of life to all beautiful cattle,
Hail to thee, Amen-Ra,
Lord of the thrones of . . . Thebes,
   Bull of his mother,
   Chief of his fields . . .
   Lord of the sky,
eldest son of the earth,
lord of the things which exist,
establisher of things,
establisher of all things,

One in his times among the gods,
Beautiful Bull of the company of the gods,
   father of the gods,
   maker of men,
   creator of beasts and cattle,
lord of the things which exist,
creator of the staff of life,
master of the herbage whereon cattle live,
   Form made by Ptah,
   beautiful child,
   beloved one.

From E. A. W. Budge *The Gods of the Egyptians*

well as being a symbol of great strength and fertility, the bull was believed to be directly responsible for thunder, storms, rain, floods, in fact for water in any form. Other evidence, especially from Egypt, links the bull god with the sun and the moon.

Throughout ancient Sumeria, a bull god called Enlil was worshipped as god of the storm and supreme god of fertility. It was through his power that there was water, the fields were green, and all things grew. Mankind itself drew life and sustenance from him. Praising Enlil as their father, the 'exalted overpowering ox', 'Lord of the world of life', 'powerful chief of the gods', the Sumerians of about 3000 BC addressed him with stirring invocations.

Similarly, in ancient India, a wealth of evidence indicates a bull-oriented religion among the earliest inhabitants of the Indus valley. The Aryans who conquered them, moreover, c 1500 BC, left an eloquent literary testimony concerning bull worship. Hundreds of hymns by these people, originally passed on orally from generation to generation, were ultimately written down and compose a sacred Hindu literary work known as the *Rig-Veda*. The Aryans worshipped a number of bull gods – Dyaus, Parjanya, Rudra, Indra and Agni – and many of the *Rig-Veda* hymns are devoted to them.

The archeological testimony from Egypt is even more compelling. Not only do we know that the people worshipped a variety of bull gods, but that two cults, those of Apis and Mnevis, were probably the oldest, most widespread and enduring of all Egyptian religious sects. The worship of both bull gods was quite similar. Each was considered to be a god of fertility and strength, each had celestial aspects, and each had elaborate connections with other gods. Each god was believed to have an earthly manifestation, Apis being immaculately conceived by the impregnation of a special cow by a ray of moonlight, while Mnevis was the incarnation of the sun-god Amon-Re. Upon the death of each divine bull, it was embalmed like a king and interred in large tombs which were known as Serapea.

An additional association between men and bulls appeared in both early Mesopotamia and Egypt; kings related themselves to bulls and bull gods. Thus in Sumeria the great Sargon called himself the *patesi* or 'tenant farmer' of Enlil. King Rimush acknowledged that he was appointed by Enlil. And Naram-Sin, who wore the horns of bulls into battle, presented captive kings to Enlil in recognition of the bull god's sovereignty. This close association between king and god in Sumeria had many interesting facets. Both bull god and king came to share the title 'Wild Bull'. Sargon was so called, and the seal of his servant shows a man watering a bull. Kings wore bull-horned head-dresses as a symbol of their divine appointment and power. And to make the interrelation complete, there arose the custom of placing long, curled beards upon images of the bull god. This practice, probably ritualistic in origin, was rooted in the conception common in Mesopotamia that the beard was a sign of strength and masculinity. Consequently, only Sumerian kings were allowed to grow long beards.

The relationship in Egypt between kings and bull gods was even closer. Narmer-Menes, the king who forcibly united Upper and Lower Egypt into a single kingdom not long before 3000 BC, worshipped Apis and spread the gospel of the bull god throughout the land. Moreover, either his adroitness or his simplicity led him actually to conceive of himself as a bull. In either case, at a very early date bull worship in Egypt became identified with king worship.

Since bull worship was such a characteristic feature of all the earliest civilizations, it was inevitable that many of the other culture centres throughout the Mediterranean, facing similar problems and holding similar values, would sooner or later focus attention on the bull. Thus in Crete, in Greece and in Rome, man's relations with bulls reflected both his Near Eastern heritage and his own particular cultural needs.

In Crete, for example, while the bull god was primarily connected with the sun and fertility, he was likewise linked with the force, the deep-throated roar, and the destructiveness of earthquakes, which were common to the island. Crete also developed the first public, ritualized bullfights. In Greece, the bull became the focus for socially approved rites of sexual abandon which evolved directly into Greek theatre. And in Rome, as the foremost rival of Christianity for centuries, Mithraism introduced the ritualistic washing away of sins and purification of the body with a bath in the blood dripping from a dying bull.

The Minotaur's Prey

Cretan kings, called Minos, were supreme in both the spiritual and material lives of their subjects, like the kings of Egypt. Apparently revered as the incarnation of the island bull god, Minos stands at the centre of all Cretan legends and myths. As natural leader of the bull cult, the king was the focus of activity during celebrations.

Stories of Minos and of the ceremonies and practices of Cretan bull worship spread widely about the Mediterranean. Eventually many of them became part of the mythology of neighbouring groups in the Aegean area, such as the Greeks. There is, for example, the Greek legend of Europa and the Bull in which the maiden Europa was seduced and taken across the sea to Crete by the god Zeus in the form of a bull. Here she gave birth to Minos, who later became the bull-god-king of the island.

Another early Greek myth refers to Minos as the tyrant who ruled over Crete and who demanded tribute from Athens every nine years in the form of seven young men and seven maidens. On arrival in Crete, these youths were taken into a giant maze and released. Here they became the prey of a ferocious man-bull or Minotaur who roamed the confines of the maze in search of such human tribute. This Minotaur was the result of the union between Pasiphae, wife of Minos, and a bull with which she had become enamoured. By concealing herself within a wooden cow, constructed for her by the master craftsman Daedalus, she had seduced the bull. The man-bull creature that she bore was imprisoned by Minos in a

Left Spanish bullfighting is a descendant of the Cretan bull games and, more remotely, of the hunting of savage wild bulls by prehistoric man. The bullfight is not a sport but a ritual combat of human courage and skill against brute force: in the writings of Ernest Hemingway and other modern authors it has acquired its own heroic aura of the terror of death and the pride of victory
Right Cretan bull-leaping, from a fresco at Cnossus; each dancer grasped the charging bull's horns, which were regarded as the focus of its life-giving power, was hurled up into the air, turned a somersault on the bull's back and landed on his feet on the ground

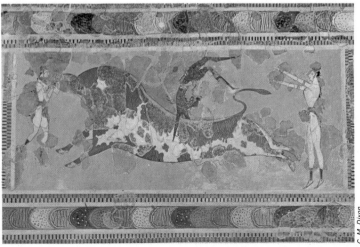

labyrinth at Cnossus, and it was here that the young Athenians met their end. Long did Athens live in fear of Crete and its Minotaur until one of her heroes, Theseus, entered the labyrinth, and slew the beast.

Scholars have interpreted the myth with the aid of other myths and have concluded that it is an account, albeit garbled and distorted, of early bull cult practices. These included three major groups of ritualistic observances: fertility dances, bullfights or bull fertility rites, and sacrifices.

Bull Dancers of Crete

Each spring, just at the time when all nature revived, Minos held the spectacular island corrida, or running of the bulls. Every phase of these great rituals, from the chase and capture of the wild bulls to their final death in the arena, appears in hundreds of Cretan art forms. From this evidence we know that these were great fertility rites which were performed in an effort to impregnate the land with new life. This impregnation was accomplished at the arena in two ways: by horn grappling and by bull sacrifice.

The Cretans, like the ancient Sumerians, considered the horns of a bull to be the focus, the concentrated essence of the bull's strength and fertility. At the corrida it was the magic, fertile horns of the wild bull which became the centre of religious interest. The initial part of the Cretan bullfight was consequently composed of a series of ritual actions designed to procure a portion of this tremendous power for the benefit of mankind. To do this, specially trained male and female athletes went into the arena unarmed. Standing before the onslaught of a bull, the sacred performers had neither cape nor sword, and in fact did nothing until the beast was almost upon them. Then by grasping the horns of the charging bull a split second before the lowered head snapped upward in a mighty toss, the athlete was catapulted into the air. Performing a forward somersault in mid-air, he landed with his feet on the back of the bull or on the ground.

That the feat was extremely dangerous is obvious. There are, in fact, numerous Cretan depictions of athletes trapped under the hoofs and caught between the horns of

Michael Holford

raging bulls. The aim of this and other horn-grasping methods was non-lethal contact with the horns of the sacred bull. With every grasping, every swing, every toss, the bull cult devotees believed that their champions were absorbing strength and fertility for the ultimate benefit of all men.

The Cretan obsession with male virility is further evidenced by the numerous images of bulls showing erect phalli found at Cnossus. An even more striking indication of Cretan pride in male sexuality is the fact that all female performers in the bullring wore a breechcloth bunched together toward the front to give the appearance of the male organ. In the spring then, as the warming sun quickened the land, Cnossus held its sacred bullring ceremonies designed to

fructify the earth and its creatures with the exuberant sexuality of the bull.

The spread of the bull cult from Crete was inevitable. Assimilating elements from bull religions all over the Near East and Africa, Cretans used them in creating many spectacular bull rituals of their own, and in turn spread these throughout the Mediterranean world. These practices were usually modified by those who adopted them, but many of them took root around the shores of the Mediterranean and became the hybrid systems of bull ritual that were to develop into the modern Spanish bullfight.

JACK CONRAD

FURTHER READING: J. R. Conrad, *The Horn and the Sword* (Dutton, 1957). See

Wandering in the desert after their escape from Egypt, the Israelites demanded visible gods to lead them. They melted down their golden ear-rings to make a statue of a bull-calf (Exodus, chapter 32): *The Worship of the Golden Calf,* **by Filippo Lippi**

also F. Altheim, *A History of Roman Religion* (Dutton, 1938); L. Cottrell, *The Bull of Minos* (Evans, London, 1953); Sir A. Evans, *The Palace of Minos* (Biblo and Tannen, 1921); E. E. Evans-Pritchard, *The Nuer* (Oxford University Press, 1969); H. Frankfort, *Before Philosophy* (Penguin, London, 1949); W. K. C. Guthrie, *The Greeks and Their Gods* (Beacon Press, 1968); L. Spence, *Myths and Legends of Ancient Egypt* (Harrap, London, 1949).

BURIAL
In the Shadow of Death

The disposal of the dead nowadays is approached with brisk, professional efficiency; burial rites are becoming increasingly impersonal. Yet underlying our aseptic attitude, the age-old emotions of mourning for our loved ones and fear of their returning to haunt us still persist

VERY FEW PEOPLE want to die. Very few admit that they will, and almost everyone everywhere has hoped that survival can somehow be contrived if enough trouble is taken. The trouble can be taken by the hoper himself, behaving well enough in life to earn immortality; or even, if he is lucky in his religion, by repentance on his deathbed. Or his survivors may propitiate someone or something on his behalf.

Life after death can also be thought of in two ways. The spirit may survive, bodiless, or reborn in a new human, a tree, an animal, or an ancestor figure. Or the body itself may be resurrected in the flesh for the spirit to inhabit. Most funeral customs are the result of one of these two ways of thinking, and the most elaborate rites have come from the conviction that the reborn spirit will need in its future life all that it had on earth, so that if it is to settle comfortably it must be as rich as possible, often at great cost to the living.

At the funeral of a king in Scythia, for instance, slaves and horses were killed and buried with him, while the Egyptians of the Middle Kingdom were content to bury the great with wooden and clay models of their slaves, houses, animals and boats. In China all the possessions, including whole armies, navies, and air forces, were traditionally fashioned out of paper and burnt at the funeral. Through the centuries the importance accorded to death has declined, a sensible shift from human sacrifice through wood to paper.

Two opposite motives lie behind burial customs all through history: one is affection for the dead and the other is fear of them. Fear causes burial in a sealed container, a coffin six feet underground, a mound or a jar. Affection provides something red, to give blood and so 'new life' to the corpse, as in this South American burial *(left)*: or food and useful articles for the dead man to use in the afterlife, like the beaker in this reconstruction of a prehistoric burial at Shrewton in Wiltshire *(right)*

Not all customs have been elaborate, but all successful religions have included in their rituals the means for ensuring some form of life beyond death. On the other hand, no religion has managed to demonstrate what *does* happen after death, and so there are also rituals to protect the living if anything goes wrong, preventing the furious ghost, unable to find a new body or paradise or whatever, from haunting his careless kin. Terror of the unsettled spirits of the dead dies very hard; food may be put out for them, or their names made taboo so that they are not inadvertently summoned. Graveyards are still shunned at night, fingers are crossed, and very few people are prepared to deny the existence of ghosts with complete confidence.

The Trappings of Fear

Over thousands of years, the world's customs have become such a tangle of facts, faiths, superstitions and rationalizations that it is hard to be sure of the real meaning of any particular custom. However, the customs themselves, all rooted in the ancient and continuing hopes and fears, follow a consistent pattern. We have a common daydream of sudden wealth: 'What would you do if you won the Pools?' We would be reborn, of course, a trip round the world, everything new, a new life. Usually, as losers, we make do with an occasional new suitcase, but our clothes are clean and we have a new face-flannel for a holiday. Similarly with the dead, the body is washed, straightened and wrapped in new cloth for

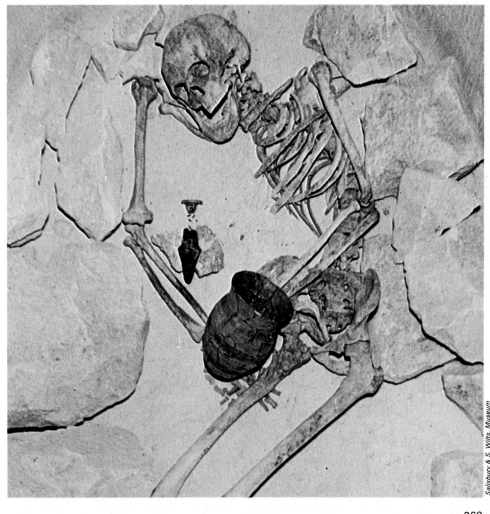

Axel Poignant

its new state, and it probably goes in a new box, in a new hole, six feet deep.

With all this there will be prayers to help the spirit leave the body and to comfort it in the afterlife; some religions, including Christianity, pass the responsibility on to God, and neither tell the dead what to do nor give him ghostly possessions. But the love-hate ambivalence of all family relationships persists in death; gold, blood, hair, memorial plaques, flowers, ashes in a debased baroque urn on the mantelshelf – whichever we use, our motives are obscure and dark, coloured by superstition in the most rational of us, twitched back from the edge of common sense by a little nudge of fear. Hygiene and honour may seem to compel us, but the washing, anointing, parcelling-up, shutting in a box, burying deep and pinning down with a heavy stone may also be seen to come from fright.

The Business of Burial

A state funeral in England or America still has much pageantry; troops slow-marching with reversed rifles to bands playing the Dead March in *Saul*, black crepe muffling the drums, the coffin on a horse-drawn gun carriage, and the mournful notes of the 'Last Post'; but state funerals are rare.

When the average Englishman dies at home, the funeral is organized by an undertaker, who is called in as soon as possible. Some people still keep the body in the house, and then one of the family, or a nurse, may lay it out before he comes. The corpse is stripped, straightened, washed, and dressed in clean or new nightdress or pyjamas, the eyes and mouth are closed, the hands folded on the breast, the hair brushed and combed, and a clean sheet is put over the body, turned down to show the face. If the undertaker's assistant comes to do the laying-out, he will also pin on a square like a nappy after the washing, shave a noticeable beard, and arrange the corpse, using bandages for arms and legs, to look as if it is asleep with the head a little on one side. He has been taught to step back at intervals to see that the effect is 'natural'. (If there is a delay before the funeral in hot weather, the corpse may be embalmed. It is not eviscerated; the blood is simply drawn off through a vein in the arm-pit and replaced with a formalin-based embalming fluid.) The corpse is then put into the coffin and covered with a shroud to match the pillow and lining, if the family prefers this to ordinary clothes.

In some parts of Britain, relatives and close friends traditionally came to see the corpse and at night one of the family would sit up with it, with candles at head and feet, but this is now rare, and viewing is becoming rare too. More and more people prefer not to keep the body in the house at all, but have the undertaker's men lay it out and take it straight back to his shop, where there are special rooms for visiting if required.

The coffin is made of wood. Most undertakers now sell caskets as well as coffins, an American fashion for a rectangular box instead of the traditional tapered shape.

Notices of the funeral are sent out privately and to the newspapers, and as soon

Other people's methods of disposing of their dead usually seem bizarre *Above* In Sicily corpses were placed on shelves in the catacombs; a similar method is used in some of the modern American mausoleums *Right* In Nigeria the bodies of criminals are denied proper tribal burial and are thrown onto a platform and left to disintegrate *Far right* In the East Indies a widow might be buried alive with her dead husband, to accompany him in the otherworld: an 18th century engraving

as the arrangements can be made and the family gathered, the corpse is buried. The hearse is a powerful, black car like an estate-wagon, much more expensive than most people have in life, and either it is driven to the house with the coffin already in it, or it arrives empty and the undertaker's bearers carry the coffin out, on their shoulders in the south, down at arm's length by the handles in the north. All over the coffin and on the roof of the hearse (and sometimes in a special car as well) are the flowers, often made up into wreaths and crosses as in the 19th century, but mostly now in sheaves, large flat arrangements tied with bows and bagged in cellophane. The hearse drives very slowly to the church or the cemetery chapel, followed by the matching cars of the undertaker's fleet, containing the mourners.

When they arrive at the church, the coffin is carried in and set on draped trestles before the altar for the burial service. Then it is taken to the grave, already dug, and lowered in. The words of committal are read by the priest, and the mourners may throw a

Mansell Collection

Radio Times Hulton Picture Library

little earth onto the coffin before they leave. Later the grave is filled by the cemetery staff, and the flowers are put on top of it.

Some months later, there may be a memorial service which strangers can attend if the family feels the dead to have been very loved or distinguished, and in any case when the grave has settled a memorial stone, slab ('mousetrap' in the trade), or curb may be put up with name, dates of birth and death, and a remembering or loving message. In the last century, these stones were often large and fanciful; now the authorities in charge have clamped down on size and style, and also encourage lawn cemeteries, plain fields with little bronze plaques let flat into the ground so that the grass can easily be cut with a motor-mower. Graves may be visited, and flowers placed or planted, but not many people visit their family graves regularly.

Cosmetics for the Corpse

During the 19th century, funerals were much more complicated than this, and hung over the family for at least a year, during which it was almost compulsory to wear black. The periods of mourning for different degrees of blood relationship were exactly laid down and exactly followed; a widow might wear black for the rest of her life. Now, some old-fashioned people wear dark clothes for the funeral, and men may wear a black tie or an armband for a little while, but that is all. The English see less and less necessity for 'a good funeral' and for the outward rites of grief and mourning.

In the United States of America, however, where funerals were once deliberately simple, the undertakers, who call themselves 'funeral directors' with more conviction than they do in England, have steadily increased the possibilities of big spending on funerals, both as status symbols and as 'grief-therapy', and though mourning clothes are as unfashionable as they are in England, everything else is more elaborate. The undertaker plays a more prominent part throughout. The corpse is almost always embalmed, the face and hands are carefully painted, hair tinted and waved, and spectacles set in place. A complete new outfit (dress or suit, underclothing, hose, shoes) is put on, though nothing shows below the waist, and an artistic arrangement made in a rich wooden or metal casket, lined with ruched and tucked velvet. It is set up in a bower of flowers in an interior-decorated reposing room at the funeral home, where friends often visit the glamorous corpse for several days before the funeral.

The emphasis, exactly as in Ancient Egypt, is on eternal preservation. No 'grave goods' are supplied, but the undertaker does everything he can to foster the belief that the incomplete embalming, the forever metal casket, and the concrete vault that may be bought to enclose it, will prevent decomposition.

Black Crepe and Plumes

The Roman Catholic countries of Europe and South America have neither simplified their burial customs, as in England, nor changed their slant as in the United States, but rather cling to the old black-and-baroque fashions of the 18th and 19th centuries. Mourning is still extensively worn, and there are sometimes horse-drawn hearses with black plumes and velvet caparisons. The motor-hearses have richly carved and gilded decorations, and there are longer processions and more flowers. Graves are still regularly visited.

Roman Catholics also preserve the custom of having a portrait of the dead person at the tomb, an ancient and widespread practice that produced superb portraits and ancestor figures. Some of the most interesting were carried on royal coffins in medieval England and France. The corpse was formerly carried exposed on top of the coffin so that all might see that the king was dead, but later it was put inside and was replaced by a portrait statue, robed and crowned. The few which survive may be seen in Westminster Abbey. The modern pictures for the average man are a very dim reminder, small sepia photographs set in the tombstone.

Primitive man lived in tiny communities in an enormous world with long hours of darkness. There is less room for fear in our shrunken, bright, and crowded world. Millions of us are hardly conscious of night at all, the unknown is receding into space, and our funeral customs, already diluted from primitive rituals, are going the way of all religious ceremony, becoming more and more alike, less and less urgent.

BARBARA JONES

The Symbolism of Funeral Rites

Men have lost their reason in nothing so much as their religion, wherein stones and clouts make martyrs; and, since the religion of one seems madness unto another, to afford an account or rationale of old Rites requires no rigid Reader. That they kindled the pyre aversely, or turning their face from it, was an handsome Symbol of unwilling ministration; that they washed their bones with wine and milk, that the mother wrapped them in linen and dried them in her bosom, the first fostering part, and place of their nourishment; that they opened their eyes towards heaven, before they kindled the fire, as the place of their hopes or original, were no improper Ceremonies . . . that in strewing their tombs the *Romans* affected the Rose, the Greeks *Amaranthus* and myrtle; that the Funeral pyre consisted of sweet fuel Cypress, Fir, Larix, Yew, and Trees perpetually verdant, lay silent expressions of their surviving hopes. Wherein Christians who deck their Coffins with Bays, have found a more elegant Emblem. For that he seeming dead will restore itself from the root, and its dry and exuccous leaves resume their verdure again; which, if we mistake not, we have also observed in furze. Whether the planting of yew in Churchyards hold not its original from ancient Funeral rites, or as an Emblem of Resurrection, from its perpetual verdure, may also admit conjecture . . .

That they buried their dead on their backs, or in a supine position, seems agreeable unto profound sleep, and common posture of dying; contrary to the most natural way of birth; Nor unlike our pendulous posture, in the doubtful state of the womb . . .

That they carried them out of the world with their feet forward, not inconsonant unto reason: as contrary unto the native posture of man, and his production first into it. And also agreeable unto their opinions, while they bid adieu unto the world, not to look again upon it; whereas *Mahometans* who think to return to a delightful life again, are carried forth with their heads forward . . .

Sir Thomas Browne *Urn Burial* (1658)

The Origins of Burial

The deliberate burial of the dead is one of man's earliest cultural achievements. It was first associated with the culture of Neanderthal man, towards the close of the Middle Stone Age. In the later Stone Age when present-day man made his appearance, some 40,000 years ago, there was a great outburst of magical, artistic activity, evidence of which can be found in the cave art of southern France (see CAVE ART). At the same time, there was a greater elaboration both of graves and grave goods; objects were placed beside the corpse and the bones of the dead were sometimes coloured with red ochre. In living cultures, where it is possible to establish the meanings of such customs, the red of the ochre is often associated with blood, a basic element in life itself. In these same societies the burial of the grave goods implies their continued use by the dead though in a different form from life on earth. It therefore seems probable that by the time of the Upper Paleolithic Age, the period of cave art, man had some idea of continuity after death, of another world, a land of the dead, of which the Christian heaven and hell is but a dualistic expression.

The basic logical requirement of such a conception is the development of a dualistic view of man's nature, which is seen as split into flesh and spirit, mind and matter, body and soul. Of these two elements, one dies with the body, one lives on after death. So that life and death are not two completely opposed states: the spirit interpenetrates death and peoples the otherworld with the living dead.

The significance of the appearance of elaborate burial customs and artistic achievements in the Upper Paleolithic Age is greater than at first appears. For their existence suggests that by this time man had developed a means of elaborating concepts and ideas, a language such as we know today. The development of language from a more elementary sign system, such

Marking the resting place of the dead with imperishable stone, as a perpetual memorial and a symbol of eternal life, occurs in burials ancient and modern *Right* Tombstones in a London cemetery *Left* Prehistoric dolmen or 'chamber tomb' in Ireland, probably once wholly or partly covered with earth

C. M. Dixon

Jim Bamber

as animals possess, was undoubtedly the greatest technological advance in the history of man. It is the feature that most clearly separates contemporary man from the apes.

Thinking is not confined to the users of language, but there can be no doubt that the development of thought and its use as a major instrument of human growth is dependent upon the invention of a communication system of this kind. One of the first signs of this advance in the technology of communications is the appearance of burial customs which suggest that man had developed a set of ideas which divided his nature into body and soul, and his universe into earth and heaven, or this world and the next. The belief in immortality, as the famous anthropologist Malinowski pointed out, is one of the principal sources of religious inspiration.

A Cemetery in the Belly
The burial customs we know from direct observation and written record, rather than from digging into the past, display a number of striking similarities, as well as a wide range of variation in other respects. The variations are in specific customs such as methods of disposal. Burial in the earth (inhumation) is only one such method. Other forms include burial in caves and in mounds or tumuli, obvious forerunners of the Egyptian pyramids and the mausoleums of Europe, by which the important dead are singled out for exceptional treatment. Water burial is practised by seafaring peoples not only out of necessity but also as a way of honouring the great. In Scandinavian legend the corpse of the slain Balder, with his wife and horse, and the gift of Odin's ring Draupnir, was laid in his ship upon a funeral pyre and launched blazing out to sea (see BALDER). Elsewhere, as among the LoDagaa of northern Ghana, burial in a river or its bank is a method of cleansing the community of someone who has died a 'bad death'.

The placing of the dead in trees or on scaffolds is found in many parts of the world and is especially associated with the Zoroastrian religion, practised by the Parsee community of Bombay. Their holy book, the *Zend-Avesta,* proclaims a punishment of a thousand stripes for a person who shall bury in the earth the corpse of dog or

man, and not disinter it before the end of the second year. For only such a treatment can secure the proper ascent of the dead to the other world. (See PARSEES.)

The Sioux and other American Plains Indians also buried their dead on platforms, and sat for days beneath them to keep the dead company. This may have been partly to protect the body against wild animals; for the same purpose other nomadic tribes used cremation. Eastern Indians often practised a secondary burial – disinterring a corpse, scraping the bones clean, tying them into a skin and burying the bundle – sometimes in a pot, to be kept near the family. Plains Indians would often employ a symbolic second burial, cutting a lock of hair from the deceased, wrapping it in skins and keeping it as a sacred possession.

Cannibalism, in those relatively rare parts of the world where it was practised, was sometimes a recognized means of disposing of the dead and was an obligation on the surviving relatives. The meat of the funeral feast is 'nothing less than the corpse of the departed kinsman'. Of inhabitants of the eastern highlands of New Guinea it has been remarked that 'their cemeteries are their bellies'. Certainly this mode of disposal of the dead, the consumption of one generation by the next, is a striking way of conquering death.

Methods of disposing of the dead vary from people to people. But they may also vary within a particular group. We have already seen how important leaders may be accorded special treatment; 'sinners' or despised categories of persons may be differentiated in the same way, especially those who have died a 'bad death'; for example, suicides, witches and those killed by drowning or by lightning, young children who have not yet been fully incorporated into the society and, in Africa, women who have died in childbirth. In each of these cases, whether intentionally or unintentionally, something is wrong.

In Europe, until recent times, certain Christian sects refused to bury unbaptized children and suicides in 'holy ground', while the blood-guilty were interred at a crossroads with a stake in the heart. The last crossroads burial in England took place outside Lord's cricket ground in 1823. And in 1811, in the neighbourhood of Shoreditch, a corpse was arrested for debt, a survival of

The urge to defy the transitoriness of human life by erecting a permanent monument to the dead we love runs very deep *Above* Etruscan sarcophagus at Rome, commemorating a married couple *Right* Perhaps the most magnificent tomb ever built, the Taj Mahal at Agra, India, where the bodies of Shah Jahan and his favourite wife lie side by side in the vault beneath the dome

the procedure whereby the body of a debtor could be legally deprived of a proper burial until his creditors had been repaid.

Love and Fear
The dead are treated in different ways not only for reasons of status, but also as a sanction upon those who remain behind. The earthly system of rewards and punishments is often projected onto the dead, and their destination after death may depend on the way in which they are buried. Only a full burial will ensure proper despatch to the other world; a partial performance may mean that the dead man becomes not a sanctified ancestor but an unsanctified ghost hanging around his earthly dwelling, haunting those who survive in an attempt to get his grievances put right.

The attempt to put oneself at a distance from the ghost is a constant theme of funeral customs everywhere. It is the task of the living to set the dead on the path to the other world, the last journey from which there is no return. For this purpose, the dead may be provided (as in rural Greece) with a coin for the ferryman who rows them across the river of death, with food to sustain them on the way, and with property to use when they get there. This property may include slaves, slaughtered on the tomb, or wives, burnt on the funeral pyre, or the more humble possessions of the deceased, his clothes, his weapons or his drinking vessels.

The general trend towards actions of this kind, which are implicit in the body-soul division, is illustrated by a report from Lincolnshire at the turn of the century. A widow had placed her husband's mug and jug on his grave, having first broken them both. Explaining her actions to the rector, she said, 'I was that moidered with crying that I clean forgot to put 'em in t'coffin . . . So I goes and does t'next best. I deads 'em both over his grave, and says I to mysen,

Burial in the earth is only one method of disposing of the dead . . . others include burial in caves and mounds, forerunners of the Egyptian pyramids, the mausoleums of Europe, and monumental tombs

Gerald Cubitt

The Bishop Orders His Tomb

And so, about this tomb of mine. I fought
With tooth and nail to save my niche, ye know:
– Old Gandolf cozened me, despite my care;
Shrewd was the snatch from out the corner South
He graced his carrion with, God curse the same!
Yet still my niche is not so cramped but thence
One sees the pulpit o' the epistle side,
And somewhat of the choir, those silent seats,
And up into the aery dome where live
The angels, and a sunbeam's sure to lurk:
And I shall fill my slab of basalt there,
And 'neath my tabernacle take my rest,

With those nine columns round me, two and two,
The odd one at my feet . . .
Peach-blossom marble all, the rare, the ripe
As fresh-poured red wine of a mighty pulse
– Old Gandolf with his paltry onion-stone,
Put me where I may look at him! . . .
And then how I shall lie through centuries,
And hear the blessed mutter of the mass,
And see God made and eaten all day long,
And feel the steady candle-flame, and taste
Good strong thick stupefying incense-smoke! . . .

Robert Browning
The Bishop Orders His Tomb in St Praxed's Church

my old man, he set a vast of store, he did, by yon mug and jug, and when their ghoastes gets over on yon side he'll holler out, "Yon's mine, hand 'em over to me," and I'd like to see them as would stop him a-having of them an' all.'

In simpler hunting societies such as those of North America, where the social investment in property was small, a man's possessions were usually destroyed after his death. As the accumulation of capital goods becomes a more prominent feature of society, so grave goods become more nominal, tokens and toys being substituted for the real thing. Eventually expenditure on the dead is seen as neglect of the living, and strong efforts are made to cut down on such 'unnecessary' expenses.

The destruction of a man's property provides a clear instance of the double attitude that lies behind many aspects of funeral ceremonies. Sidney Hartland commented (in his article on 'Death and Disposal of the Dead' in *Hasting's Encyclopedia of Religion and Ethics):* 'Throughout the rites and observances attendant on death, two motives – two principles – are found struggling for the mastery. On the one hand, there is the fear of death and of the dead, which produces the horror of the corpse, the fear of defilement, and the overlapping desire to ban the ghost. On the other hand, there is the affection, real or simulated, for the deceased, which bewails his departure and is unwilling to let him go.' The corpse is thus both loved and feared.

Above Grave in Botswana, southern Africa, with flowers, cup and saucer and other objects, which are modern descendants of the offerings made all over the world to show love and respect for the dead, and at the same time to placate an angry ghost *Below* Funeral procession with wreaths and mourners in Sicily, a survival of the twin attempts to honour the dead and formally cut him off from the world

No moment in most people's lives attracts the ceremonial with which they are honoured after death. Roman Catholic countries have retained elaborate funeral customs, including the solemn and sinister horse-drawn hearse *(left)*. Protestant burials *(right)* have generally become simpler, though in the United States there has been a return to embalming and the monumental style of ancient Egypt

To take a cue from Freud, the double-edged attitude towards the dead, seen in so many funeral customs, is a projection of the love and hate that mark the relations we have with our nearest and dearest. Significantly it is often the closest kin, the dead man's heirs and widow, who are seen as being in the greatest danger from the ghost; it is they who have to be provided with the strongest protection from his revenging spirit. So it is they too who often have to undergo the severest ordeals during the course of these ceremonies, since they are the ones who have most to gain (and most to lose) from his death.

The funeral ceremony is not only a matter of disposing of the dead and despatching him to the other world, but also of filling his place in the land of the living and redistributing his rights and duties over people and property.

The transition from life to death is the major 'rite of passage' through which all must go, and the great change in status from living to dead cannot be performed just with a nod of the head. The process has to be a gradual one and the burial service is customarily followed, at a suitably discreet interval, by a second funeral, an obituary service, in which the close kin are released from mourning, the dead are despatched to their final abode, and their life on earth is summed up in what is the equivalent of a funeral oration.

Reaction to death mellows in the course of the funeral and one of the functions of such ceremonies is to relieve the bereaved of anxiety and grief, as well as to reconcile the community to the loss of one of their number, for death constitutes a distinct threat to those who remain behind. But such a threat can never be totally set aside. The idea of continuity after death is itself an aspect of the refusal to accept the reality of death. So too perhaps is the idea that death, except for the old, is 'unnatural'. In most pre-industrial societies a specific supernatural cause was assigned for every event. Hence the frequent ordeals, centring upon the corpse, that occurred during the funerals, in an attempt to find out who killed the dead man. In one form or another, accusations of witchcraft or of sins against the supernatural powers were a constant accompaniment to funerals.

The Loss of Eternal Life

One striking illustration of this attempt to reject its inevitability is to be found in the tales of the origin of death. The biblical story of Adam, Eve and the apple has its parallels in other stories that attribute the coming of death to man's disobedience. But often what is remarkable is the triviality of the offence man has committed. Another set of stories, found in all parts of the world, contrasts the mortality of man and the waxing and waning of the moon. In one version God sends messengers to convey the news of immortality to man, and of death to the moon; the message to man gets delayed or reversed, with the result that he loses the gift of eternal life. But the manner in which this was lost is almost accidental, rather than a matter of deliberate planning. It is as if the chance introduction of death left open the possibility that the present state of affairs could be reversed.

It is doubtful if, in any society, men have placed much hope in such an outcome or much weight on tales of this kind. If an explanation of death was required, to meet the enquiries of children or the fears of the old, then these stories were ready to hand. In their actions, as distinct from their formal 'beliefs', most people display a more practical attitude towards death. It is the elaborate funeral ceremonies that enable small face-to-face communities to meet the shock that the loss of a member inevitably brings. In our more impersonal society, the impact of death (unless of a national figure) is very localized; even close kin are shielded from immediate contact by specialist undertakers. But in simpler societies, funerals are often the most elaborate ceremonies in the whole ritual calendar, the occasions on which a community gets together to dispose of the dead, redistribute his roles and property, and at the same time set its fears at rest by demonstrating the solidarity of the living in the face of loss and bereavement.

(See also CREMATION; CULT OF THE DEAD.)

JACK GOODY

FURTHER READING: E. Bendann, *Death Customs* (Humanities, 1970); Jack Goody, *Death, Property and the Ancestors* (Stanford University Press, 1962); Barbara Jones, *Design for Death* (Bobbs-Merrill, 1967).

Burning

Cremation ranks second, in antiquity and popularity, only to earth burial as a way of disposing of the dead: burning an animal was a way of offering it to a god, the rising smell and smoke being thought to carry the essence of the beast up to the god: the belief that burning a substance releases its 'soul' or 'essence' is found in alchemy: in Europe heretics and witches were burned to death. See CREMATION; FIRE; SACRIFICE; SUTTEE.

British Museum

They have been called 'the harmless people' but this has not protected them against the injuries inflicted by civilisation, or against the harm they fear from natural forces and ghosts

BUSHMEN

ONLY A FEW THOUSAND Bushmen today continue to live as their ancestors lived in South Africa. Less than two centuries ago their people were ruthlessly killed off by the Dutch, and within living memory European settlers used to hunt down the 'wild' Bushmen, his women and children, as though they were game. Their numbers have been further reduced by many tribesmen leaving their old hunting grounds to become 'tamed' by working for white settlers. The remaining representatives of the Bushman race are mostly found in the Kalahari Desert in the south-west.

To understand Bushman beliefs, with their emphasis on Nature worship, magic and taboo, we must take into account that the Bushmen are a Stone Age people, in terms of their intellectual and cultural development. They have no written language, no codified laws or system of government, no agriculture and no settled communities.

Until they came into contact with Europeans, the Bushmen lived almost exactly the same sort of life that primitive men lived thousands of years ago. They wore no clothes except a pouch to cover their genitals and, occasionally, a cloak of animal skins. Wholly nomadic, they existed by hunting and root-gathering. Their needs were so simple that their language was, and is, extremely rudimentary, not far removed in sound from the utterances of animals – the so-called 'Click' language which early travellers likened to the clucking of turkeys. Understandably, their intellectual potential was limited to an awareness of basic natural phenomena, leading to a reverence for the life-giving rain, for rivers and harmless animals, and a dread of storms, drought and the fiercer wild beasts.

This aboriginal African race has only vague ideas of religion and no organized form of worship. They see the world around them as divided into forces of good and evil, and they do what they can to show their gratitude to the former and to placate the latter. Incapable of building temples or even of making idols, they pay homage to the spirit world by means of dances, music and incantations. They rely on myths for an interpretation of such phenomena as birth, death, the origin of the world, the nature of an afterlife, and the role of the supernatural in the affairs of men.

The Great Captain

Some tribes speak of a god called Tsui-Goab who is a combination of legendary super-chief, folk hero and lord of the skies. But Bushmen do not worship or pray to him or any other deity in a formal manner, for they have nothing resembling a temple or shrine. The nearest they come to a concept of God in the Christian sense is their vague belief in a 'Lord', or 'Great Captain' who is bigger and stronger than any mortal man and who lives in a two-storey house in the sky. The Captain, his wife and his numerous children live on the ground floor of this mansion while the upper storey is occupied by the souls of the dead. The Captain's house appears to be a glorified version of the Bushman's hut, and his diet is a banquet of the Bushman's favourite food – honey, locusts, bluebottles, butterflies and ant eggs. The souls of the dead do nothing and eat nothing, which implies that this divine chieftain has no particular interest in mere mortals.

More powerful in some Bushmen's eyes is Gaunab, the equivalent of the Devil, the embodiment of evil responsible for all the calamities that afflict mankind, including storms, thunderbolts, lightning and drought. To people whose day-to-day existence is constantly threatened by sudden danger, the forces of evil are bound to seem stronger than those of good, and this is why so many Bushman religious beliefs strike Western observers as vague and inconsistent. Much more important to men who live so close to Nature are the realities of their daily life. Rain is undoubtedly their principal concern and most of their rites and ceremonies are conducted to placate the rain spirit.

Walling up a Ghost

Living in a state of constant watchfulness, particularly at night, Bushmen are more aware of ghosts than they are of gods, and the ghosts of dead people are closer to them than some deity who lives far away in the sky. The reason for this is that primitive people do not accept the Western concept of death as an ending of life due to known causes. In their view, a person does not die, but is spirited away in mysterious and sometimes sinister circumstances. The one who has thus gone remains somewhere in the offing as a ghost. He might have died because malignant spirits entered his body and made him sick; or sorcerers might have carried him off by magical spells. Even a very old man refuses to believe that death is inevitable in the course of Nature: he will argue that he has enemies who will bewitch him with their powerful medicine. In a curious way he may be right, since his actual fate, when he is too old and decrepit to hunt, could well be to be abandoned, to die ultimately of starvation or as the prey of wild beasts.

The graves of dead Bushmen show this fear of ghosts, for they try to make sure that the deceased's spirit does not come forth to harm them by placing heavy stones on the corpse and then piling up a mound over the grave. And in order to protect themselves from supernatural spirits, whether of dead people or of hostile gods like Gaunab, the Bushmen have their magicians and witch-doctors, like every other pagan group in Africa. Some magicians are men, some women. Some are benefactors, others malefactors. All have special powers, perhaps to make rain, perhaps to control the movement of animals, perhaps to cure the sick.

Messages from Bones

Bushmen witch-doctors are individuals recognized as having heightened powers of perception, who become the principal social and medical advisers of the group. They are, among other things, soothsayers and can predict such things as the weather or the probable success or failure of a hunting expedition. In addition, every Bushman acts as his own soothsayer by means of his 'bones', or fragments of animal bone marked with special signs. He consults them on every important occasion and 'reads' them according to fixed laws that are based on their positions and conjunctions.

The Bushmen of southern Africa have preserved the religious beliefs of the Stone Age. A Bushman in trance, communicating with spirits *(above)* and a ritual dance round a fire *(below)*

Jurgen Schadeberg

Jurgen Schadeberg

Important functions of the magician are to make rain, to ensure a plentiful supply of game for the hunters, to protect the group from evil spirits. Some magicians specialize in various traditional cures, based largely on herbs and a primitive form of blood-letting. Naturally their medicine is of a very simple kind but they cope with a great many diseases by massage, herbal compresses and a process of extracting the 'evil medicine' by sucking the part affected and spitting out the poison or foreign body which is causing the sickness.

The Bushman's knowledge of the properties of herbs, natural salves and lotions is sometimes surprising, as is shown by their use of urine as a sterilising agent. Urine is, in fact, virtually bacteria-free and has been used in the West as a disinfectant in battle-field conditions. This treatment, as used by the Bushmen, was first described by a Dutchman, Johannes Gulielmus de Greven-brok, in 1695:

> A very frequent remedy is to turn the patient on his back and on his front and make water on him. They do not allow even his face to escape a bath of urine. Some even take a sea-shell or tortoise-shell, fill it with water discharged by one man, mix it with a powder from a certain plant, and administer it to the sick man. They do not attach any healing property to the water of women; the women themselves think it injurious to them.

To what extent a magical element is present in this type of doctoring is difficult to say. Certainly neither the Bushmen nor their relations, the Hottentots, indulge in as much mumbo-jumbo and fetishism as the Bantu and the Negroes of Equatorial Africa.

Puberty Rites

One of the principal duties of the magician is to preside over the puberty ceremonies. For the boys, the initiation consists of living in isolation in a special camp for about a month. During the first few days they are roughly handled by the magician and half-starved: their only food is a little water and raw roots or berries. After the first few days of hardship, the boys are allowed to dance the tribal dances, wearing ostrich feathers and the beaks of white storks. On one of the nights of the dance, a female demon called Hishe appears in their midst and is driven away by the magician. Hishe is variously

described as an old hag; a small creature with red eyes, wings and claws; a lion walking upright; or a hermaphrodite. She is obviously a hobgoblin invented by the magicians to frighten the boys during initiation, for if they overcome their fear, they are considered to be men. Similarly the initiates are given a hunting test when each lad is required to show his skill in stalking and shooting an animal. Those who pass these tests are branded by the magician, who cuts the boys between the eyebrows and shoulder-blades with incisions about half an inch long. This cicatrization ends the rites and announces that the boy has become a man, with a man's rights and responsibilities.

Among one group in the eastern Kalahari, coming of age involves circumcision. The boys are operated on at the age of 12, being brought forward one by one to the medicine-man who pulls the boy's foreskin as far over the glans as possible before cutting it off with one slash of a ceremonial stone knife. The boys are given two or three weeks' convalescence, for the operation is a very severe one. Many of the boys faint, some have been known to die from loss of blood, but none cry out, as this is considered unmanly.

The same aura of magic surrounds the puberty rites prescribed for the girls. The ceremony begins with the first menstruation, when the girl is in a state of taboo. She is shut up in a tiny hut and is seen only by her mother until her menstrual flow ceases. The severest penalties attach to a man who sees a girl at this time and there are many legends recounting how a man who looked on a girl during her first period was transformed into a stone. For her part, a girl who was foolish enough to defy the taboo might find herself turned into a frog. Once her puberty rites are ended, however, a feast is held in her honour. The feast is followed by a dance of all the women and girls of the clan, with only two of the older men present.

As soon as a wife is pregnant, she is again in a state of taboo. She may not eat certain foods; no one may pass behind her back; and no man may be present at the birth. In the case of the first child, delivery is in a hut, under the floor of which the afterbirth is carefully buried in case some magician should use it to bewitch the mother or her child. For subsequent births, the woman simply goes to a secluded place, has her baby, and returns to the camp.

Twin births are considered unlucky, and one of the infants, usually the girl, is buried alive, though it is doubtful whether this practice still continues. The justification for it was based on the difficulty of a woman carrying two babies on the march, let alone suckling them both.

The Painted Rocks

The Bushmen have a large body of folklore and myths, mainly about the heavenly bodies and animals. Some of the stars and planets are regarded as semi-divine, and there is considerable evidence of moon worship.

Supernatural properties are attributed to certain animals and insects, notably the mantis which no Bushman would kill. The mantis is the central character of a great many Bushman legends and is endowed with human attributes, including the power of speech. He has his favourite animals, especially the eland, the cow antelope and the gemsbok, or South African antelope, which he protects on behalf of the hunters. The mantis is regarded as the Bushman's best friend in the animal world.

Perhaps the most remarkable aspect of Bushman culture is their skill as artists. The rocks all over South Africa are covered with their paintings, many of which belong in the front rank of prehistoric art. Some anthropologists interpret these pictures as mystical in origin and purpose – a manifestation of a fertility cult or of sympathetic magic. According to this theory, the artist drew the portrait of those animals the hunters wished to kill. Other students of Bushman art prefer the simpler explanation that these paintings, some of them obviously of raids by Negro tribes from the north, were simply records of historical events.

The whole subject of Bushman art remains something of a mystery, for some paintings are undoubtedly many thousands of years old while others are quite recent, only ending with the arrival of the white men. Today, Bushmen have lost all skill and desire to paint the rocks and they cannot even interpret the work of their ancestors.

JAMES WELLARD

FURTHER READING: A. Jackson, *The Bushmen of South Africa* (Oxford Univ. Press, 1957); E. Thomas, *The Harmless People* (Knopf, 1959).

Butterfly

Symbol of the soul and of attraction to the light: in Europe, North America and the Pacific it was widely believed that the soul has the form of a butterfly, which gave the creature uncanny and sometimes ominous connotations; in northern Europe to see one flying at night was a warning of death, and some said that the soul-butterfly's ability to leave the body in sleep accounts for dreams; medieval angels were sometimes depicted with butterfly's wings and fairies are often shown with them.
See INSECTS.

Tom Scott

Buzzard

Scavenger bird, associated in much mythology with cleanliness and so with curative powers; Pueblo Indians used its feathers in curing rituals, and to 'sweep away' evil; American superstition says a buzzard feather worn behind the ear will prevent rheumatism, buzzard grease will cure smallpox; also associated with death in the Old South, where beliefs say that witches sometimes take buzzard form, and that a buzzard shadow will do harm if it passes over you.
See BIRDS.

CABALA

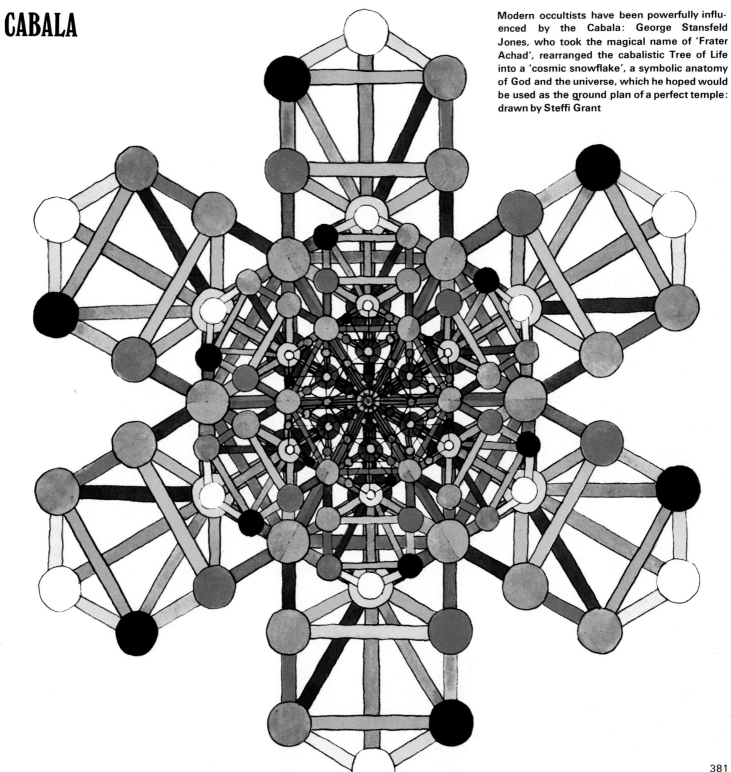

Modern occultists have been powerfully influenced by the Cabala: George Stansfeld Jones, who took the magical name of 'Frater Achad', rearranged the cabalistic Tree of Life into a 'cosmic snowflake', a symbolic anatomy of God and the universe, which he hoped would be used as the ground plan of a perfect temple: drawn by Steffi Grant

Eventually used as a term for almost 'any mixture of occultism, Hermetism, Rosicrucianism, exotic theosophy and general infatuation with secret lore', the Cabala was originally a body of Jewish doctrines about the nature of God and the vital role of man in God's universe

THE CABALA, strictly speaking, is a system of Jewish mystical thought which originated in southern France and Spain in the 12th and 13th centuries. Yet even for the founders and early masters of this school, Cabala was but one among many terms (true knowledge, inner knowledge, knowledge of the mysteries, hidden wisdom) used to designate their secret lore, and it was only later that Cabala became the term generally used. Later the word was used for Jewish mysticism and occultism in general, and later still Christian Cabalists gave it an even wider meaning.

Cabala or Cabbala or Qabbalah are among the English spellings of a Hebrew word whose more correct transliteration is Kabbalah and whose meaning is 'receiving' or 'that which is received'. By the 2nd and 3rd centuries AD, the word had the technical sense of 'tradition', and especially of tradition handed down by word of mouth, as

The Cabala's central doctrine deals with the unfolding of the hidden and unknowable God into the 'fullness' of the manifest God, known by his works. A diagram of the universe by the 17th century author Robert Fludd, with the links between the hidden God and the world

distinct from the written Scriptures. At this date it still had no 'secret' or mystical connotations but referred to acknowledged legal, ceremonial and religious traditions.

The origins of Jewish mysticism are obscure. Many of the prophetic, visionary or apocalyptic passages in the Old Testament played a considerable role in subsequent mystical lore (see DANIEL; EZEKIEL), but there is no justification for viewing these as part of a continuous mystical or esoteric (hidden or secret) tradition. The earliest fully articulated mystical system that is accessible to the historian of Judaism is the Merkabah or 'throne' mysticism (see THRONE) that flourished from the 4th to the 10th centuries in Palestine and Babylonia. No doubt this mystical tradition, or parts

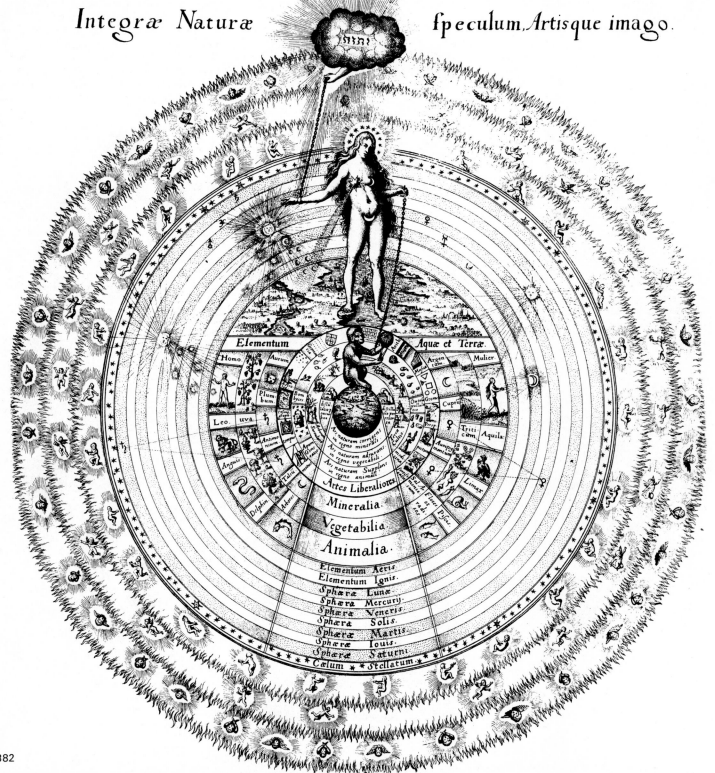

of it, goes back to the early Rabbinic period (2nd to 3rd centuries), and beyond that to still earlier currents and trends. The Mediterranean world of late antiquity with its mingling of Gnosticism, Neoplatonism, magic and speculations about angels, demons and divine powers, created a climate in which mystical lore could develop.

Some Jewish writings which were not included in the Old Testament (the *Book of Enoch*, for example, and the *Testaments of the Patriarchs*) suggest the existence of groups which cultivated esoteric doctrines and mystical disciplines. In the 1st century AD the Jewish philosopher Philo of Alexandria describes in his *De Vita Contemplativa* a Jewish sect leading a contemplative and semi-monastic life. There is evidence that the Essenes, held by most scholars to be identical with the Dead Sea or Qumran sect whose writings were found in and since 1948 near Jericho (see DEAD SEA SCROLLS), possessed a secret lore. It seems to have consisted mainly of angelology and magic, and there is no reason to assume any continuity of Essene doctrines and the forms of mysticism cultivated in rabbinic and other circles.

At any rate, the Mishna (a 2nd century rabbinic collection of religious law) attests the existence of two subjects that should not be taught in public and which, therefore, were considered as esoteric disciplines intended for initiates only. These subjects were 'the work of creation' (based on Genesis, chapter 1) and 'the work of the chariot' (the mysteries of the Divine Throne, based on Ezekiel, chapter 1). The precise nature and contents of these mystical disciplines is a matter for conjecture but it seems certain that some of the early rabbis practised an ecstatic contemplation which culminated in the vision of the Throne of Glory, the Merkabah.

In the later *Hekhaloth* texts, the ascent of the soul to heaven and the 'perils of the soul' encountered during these ascents are described realistically and convincingly enough. Like all forms of mysticism involving the rising of the soul to heaven, Merkabah mysticism ramifies into theories about the structure of the universe, because the ascent takes place in a spatially conceived cosmos, divided into higher and lower worlds, spheres and heavenly palaces; into angelology and demonology, because the various cosmic spheres had their angelic guardians and powers; and into magic, because the adept had to use special words and mystic signs to force his passage and subdue the angelic or demonic powers barring his progress. Esoteric speculations and ecstatic experiences of this kind were probably tinged with Gnostic elements (see GNOSTICISM). They were viewed with misgivings and suspected of being apt to lead weaker spirits into heresy.

The characteristic feature of Merkabah mysticism was its emphasis on the transcendent, mysteriously awesome and truly numinous aspect of the deity. The experience of loving communion with God, so common in later mysticism, is absent here. The initiate rises through spheres, worlds, heavens and celestial mansions or 'palaces' *(hekhaloth)* guarded by all sorts of terrifying angelic beings until at last, if he be worthy, he stands in awe and trembling before the supreme vision of the Divine Splendour.

Creation and Splendour

The *Sefer Yetsirah* or 'Book of Creation' which was written at some time between the 3rd and 6th centuries in Palestine or Babylonia, and which came to enjoy great prestige in the subsequent history of Jewish mysticism, stands completely outside the Merkabah tradition. Its theory of the universe derives the world from 32 elements, which are the first ten numbers and the 22 letters of the Hebrew alphabet. The book is obscure, perhaps deliberately, but its doctrine of ten *sefiroth* (which here means numbers) and its emphasis on letter mysticism clearly influenced the later Cabala. All reality is a reality of the letters, which are the ultimate elements of which the cosmos is constructed. This conception easily links on the one hand with the cabalistic doctrine of the cosmic process as an unfolding of the mystical name of God (that is, of the Hebrew letters constituting his name), and on the other hand with the theory and practice of magic which seeks to manipulate reality by means of these letters (see ALPHABET).

From Palestine and Babylonia some of these esoteric and magical texts and traditions spread to the Jews of Spain, Italy and France, and led to the formation of the German 'Hasidism' which flourished in the 12th and 13th centuries. The mysticism of the German Hasidism was a mixture of parts of the Merkabah tradition (but without its ecstatic practice), magical elements, ideas derived from the *Sefer Yetsirah*, and philosophical doctrines. The practical emphasis was on piety, humility and self-effacement, on penitential and ascetic discipline, and on the practice of devotional contemplation — particularly at prayer — in the form of meditation on the Hebrew letters and their numerical values. In due course German Hasidism merged with the new Cabala that developed in the 12th and 13th centuries, at first in Provence, in southern France, and subsequently also in northern Spain.

It is precisely this new system of mystical theosophy (or 'knowledge of God'), and its continuation into the 16th century and beyond, which constitutes the Cabala in the strict sense of the term. Its origins still need further clarification, for it is evident that many different influences coalesced in its emergence: Gnostic and Merkabah traditions, elements deriving from other oriental sources, and philosophical theories of various kinds.

It is a curious fact that the Cabala should have developed in the same area and at the same time that saw the flowering of Provençal culture and the sudden and violent efflorescence of the Cathar heresy (see CATHARS). There is no reason to doubt the existence of cultural contacts but there are few, if any, definite and specific similarities. Cabalists and Cathars can both be said to have held Gnostic doctrines, but there is nothing to suggest either a common source or direct influence of one movement on the other.

The principal work of Spanish Cabala, the *Zohar* or 'Book of Splendour' was written in the years after 1280 AD. The *Zohar* draws on many of the cabalistic doctrines and traditions which had evolved by them, but there is no reason to consider it the work of an 'editor' who merely combined ancient sources or texts. The author, Moses de Leon of Guadalajara, wrote the work in a peculiar imitation-Aramaic. The *Zohar* in due course became the classical main text for the Cabalists. Subsequent cabalistic works, whether expounding similar or different doctrines, could not affect the prestige and central position of the *Zohar*. Even the completely new cabalistic system evolved by Isaac Luria in the 16th century pretended to be a profounder interpretation of the mysteries of the *Zohar*.

The Abyss of Nothingness

The backbone of the cabalistic system is its doctrine of the deity, which distinguishes between the inaccessible and unknowable *deus absconditus* (the hidden god) on the one hand, and the self-revealing dynamic God of religious experience on the other. Of the former not even existence can be predicted. He, or rather 'It', is the paradoxical fullness of the great divine Nothing. The Cabalists called it *En Sof*, literally the 'infinite'.

En Sof is so hidden in the abyss of its Nothingness that it is not even mentioned in the Bible, let alone addressed in prayer or accessible in contemplation. Scripture, God's word, is by definition nothing but the revelation, that is, the self-manifestation, of God. An existing God means a manifest, revealed and related God. The process of manifestation is the process by which God 'comes into being' (at least in the perspective of the being to which he relates).

The text of the Bible, when read superficially, seems to describe the creation of the world and God's first dealings with it, but the Cabalist pierces through this outward layer of meaning to an inner, hidden level which is, to him, the ultimately significant one. What Scripture tells is the process of Divine becoming and of the inner Divine life. For in the depths of the Divine hiddenness, turned in upon itself, there occurs a primordial, initial wrench by which it begins to turn outwards, to unfold, to exist. Here existence is a process of extraversion in the introverted En Sof.

This initial movement is described in a highly mystical passage in the *Zohar* as the concentration or crystallization of energy in one luminous point (or rather a point 'dark with luminosity') which bursts the closed confines of En Sof. The process of 'emanation' has started. Cabalistic writings use the term emanation rather than creation, and where the Bible says 'create' they interpret it in the sense of 'emanate'.

An emanation is something which has 'flowed out' from its source, as distinct from something which has been created, made by a Maker. A theory of emanation from God is a way of providing links between the many different phenomena of the world and the spiritual One, in which all things have their source. But the Cabalists use the theory of emanation not so much for this

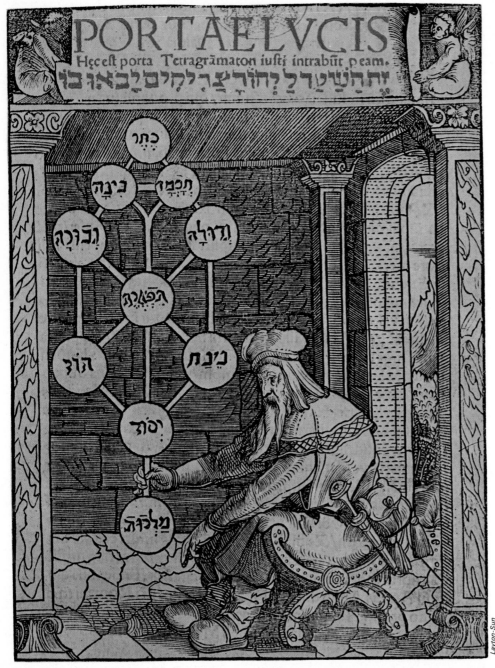

The Tree of Life, from *Portae Lucis* (1516) by Paul Ricci, a Jew turned Christian who taught at Pavia University. The ten spheres of the Tree are the sefiroth, which are aspects of God, the stages of the process of the hidden God's unfoldment and, to magicians, centres of power which man can grasp and use, as Ricci himself explained in saying that the lore of the Cabala teaches us how 'to attain more easily and beyond the use of Nature to the glories of the Eternal Father and our prerogatives in this world, which resemble them'

purpose but rather to account for the procession of the fullness of the Divine Being from the Hiddenness of the Divine Non-Being or Nothingness.

The Ten Sefiroth

The *pleroma* or dynamic 'fullness' of the Life Divine is described as a complex organism consisting of ten emanations, potencies or focal points, called sefiroth. These potencies are not ten gods, but ten aspects, stages or manifestations of the Living Deity. The 'World of Emanation' or 'World of the Sefiroth' is not the universe but the godhead in its 'existent' aspect. The dynamic interrelation of the ten sefiroth pictured in the three lines of the sefirotic Tree (the right side is male, the left female, and the middle line mediates between them and harmonizes them) make up the dramatic inner-life of the godhead which, in spite of its complexities, is essentially one.

Orthodox critics held the dualism between the hidden and the manifest God, as well as the doctrine of sefiroth, to be departures from strict Jewish monotheism. The Cabalists, who had some of the greatest luminaries of orthodox Jewish learning in their camp, replied that they were speaking of a profound mystery, and that the mystical understanding of the Divine Unity was precisely their main concern. In fact, the emphasis on this essential Unity grew more insistent as by the sheer inherent power of the cabalistic symbolism the various sefiroth became more and more personified.

The Cabala's picture of the divine totality as an emanated 'fullness' of ten sefiroth is reminiscent of the great Gnostic systems of earlier centuries. But whereas the Gnostic pleroma or 'fullness', the realm of the divine, consisted of hundreds of divine *aeons* or powers, the cabalistic 'World of the Sefiroth' is reduced to a manageable ten. Moreover the Gnostic aeons are a rather chaotic and disorderly lot: they ascend and descend in almost anarchic freedom, whereas the cabalistic sefiroth are ordered in a strict hierarchy.

The notion of the cosmos as a series of descending emanations from a divine source is a familiar Neoplatonic motif (see NEOPLATONISM). Medieval Arab philosophy was markedly Neoplatonic and there is definite evidence of specific Neoplatonic influences on the early Spanish Cabalists. The classical doctrine of the sefiroth is therefore an intriguing combination of Gnostic and Neoplatonic motifs. The cosmos as a hierarchical structure of successive emanations – this is Neoplatonic. But the idea that this emanated cosmos is divine or, to be more exact, constitutes the fullness of the divine realm and that the entities making it up are divine forces, is thoroughly Gnostic.

The Four Worlds

What happens after the tenth sefirah, what are the relations between the Divine Being shown in the sefirotic Tree and the actual universe in which we live? Some Cabalists seem to have thought of further emanations which finally produce our material universe. In that case there would be no break at all but a gradual, imperceptible descent from the godhead into the material world. As against this radical Neoplatonism, other Cabalists tended to hold to the traditional doctrine of creation as a discontinuous act. This could be done by letting the process of emanation stop with the tenth sefirah. God, the complex of sefiroth, then proceeds to create the universe out of nothing.

Later cabalistic cosmology spoke of four worlds. These are, in descending order; *Asiluth*, the divine world of the sefiroth; *Beriah*, the sub-divine sphere, the world of the Divine Throne and the angels; *Yesirah*, the world of the heavenly spheres down to that of the moon; and finally *Asiyyah*, the sub-lunar universe. This fourfold division is prefigured in the realm of the sefiroth, since the sefirotic Tree can be divided into four tiers corresponding to the four 'worlds'. The image of the sefirotic realm as a tree already occurs in the first cabalistic text to have survived, the 12th century *Bahir*. The tree is, of course, growing downwards and its roots are above.

While each of the sefiroth has a considerable range of symbolism and imagery, some are more important than others. The fifth sefirah, 'Power' or 'Stern Judgement', also appears as the source from which destructive evil and the demonic powers emanate. In fact, the problem of evil and the possibility of its being originally a part, albeit a fallen part, of the divine totality are recurring themes in cabalistic speculation.

Of special importance, however, in cabalistic thinking and practice is the relation between the sixth sefirah, Tifereth (the 'Beauty', also the 'Compassion' of God) and the tenth sefirah, which is called Malkhuth or Shekhinah. Tifereth is the central sefirah; it functions as the hub and pivot of the whole system. In the dynamic give-and-take of the sefiroth, Tifereth receives the power and influx of the higher potencies and, harmonizing them, passes them on to the lower ones. It embodies the creative dynamism of the sefirotic Tree and is conceived exclusively in male symbols: king, sun, bridegroom, heaven. Standing at the lower end of the sefirotic cluster is Malkhuth. As the last of the divine manifestations, it is the point at which the Divine (the world of Asiluth followed, according to the teaching of later Cabalism, by the three lower worlds of Beriah, Yesirah and Asiyyah) contacts the Non-Divine.

Standing at the lowest, receiving end of the system, Malkhuth is the receptive womb, the moon, the bride and the queen. It is only in relation to the lower worlds that Malkhuth, as that aspect of the deity which is nearest to them, acquires active, creative or even ruling characteristics. Then the royal aspect of her Queenship is emphasized and the bride is also the mother.

The Sacred Marriage

It is the frankly erotic imagery in the description of the relations between Tifereth and Malkhuth which is one of the most striking features of the cabalistic symbolism of the *Zohar*. The supreme and central mystery of the Cabala is the Holy Union or 'sacred marriage' between the two aspects of the Divine, or in other words the unification of God. The greatest catastrophe that the Cabalist can imagine is the destruction of the unity within the godhead, the separation of the Shekhinah from her husband. This was precisely the tragic consequence of Adam's sin in Eden (see FIRST MAN).

It is thus really the fate of God that is at the core of religion, and man's efforts, both in good works and in mystical contemplation, should be directed to the one end of promoting the wholeness of God, the union of male and female within the divine 'fullness'. The gravity of sin is due to man's capacity to disrupt the Divine union; man's greatness consists of his capacity to restore the lost union.

The biblical notion of man as the image of God was thus absorbed into the cabalistic doctrine, according to which the human frame reveals the same structure as the mystical Divine frame of the ten sefiroth. Since the tenth sefirah, Shekhinah, is also the mystical archetype of Israel, the sefirotic symbolism could easily absorb the Rabbinic tradition (originally developed by way of commentary on the Song of Solomon) which regarded Israel as God's bride.

An interesting consequence of this symbolism is the relative absence of erotic elements in the mystical life of the individual Cabalists. Erotic symbolism is limited to the sphere of the inner-divine and has little or no place in man's relation with God. The Cabalist knows no lover who ravishes him, and the kind of experiences recorded in Christian and Sufi mystical literature are

foreign to him. The meditative ascent to the Shekhinah and beyond aims at a communion (and not at mystical union) with God, that would promote the mystical union *within* God. It is Israel's task to promote this end by contemplative efforts and a holy life.

The Breaking of the Vessels

Classical Spanish Cabala was an esoteric doctrine, reserved for an elite of initiates. After the expulsion of the Jews from Spain in 1492 the religious ferment among the refugees who settled in North Africa, Italy and the eastern Mediterranean, caused the Cabala to spread to wider circles and to become the dominant form of popular piety, as regards theological doctrines and devotional (especially ascetic and penitential)

Diagram of the Tree of Life, showing the ten spheres, the emanations through which God revealed himself: 1 Kether, the supreme crown of God, also called Ayin, 'nothing' 2 Hokhmah, the wisdom of God, also 'the father' or Reshith, 'the beginning' 3 Binah, the understanding or intelligence of God, also 'the mother' 4 Hesed, the love or mercy of God 5 Din or Geburah, the power and stern judgement of God 6 Tifereth, the beauty, glory or compassion of God 7 Netsah, the lasting endurance of God 8 Hod, the majesty of God 9 Yesod, the foundation or basis of all active forces in God 10 Malkhuth, the kingdom of God, also called Shekhinah, Israel, the bride of God. The right-hand column headed by Hokhmah is male, the left-hand column is female, and the central pillar balances and unifies them

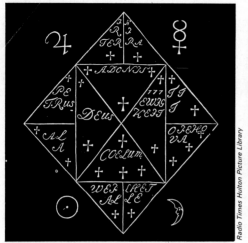

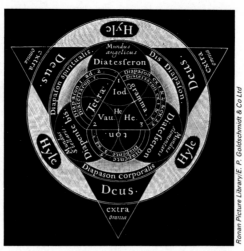

the whole cosmos. In fact, God himself is involved in the fall. Every stone and every plant shelters a fallen divine spark which yearns to return to its origin and, as it were, cries out for salvation.

Lurianic Cabala soon became the dominant form of Jewish piety and provided the theological background of the 17th century Messianic movement connected with the person of Sabbatai Zevi. The doctrines of this movement soon developed into a mystical heresy which rendered the Cabala suspect. The 18th century mystical revival initiated by Israel Baal Shem Tov and known as Hasidism encountered violent opposition, partly because it was associated, in the eyes of its critics, with the aftermath of the Sabbatian movement and its Cabala.

The Christian Cabala

Under the influence of the Cabala many doctrines and practices established themselves in Judaism which would otherwise have been less influential. Thus the belief in transmigration of souls did not really become an established and widespread doctrine until it was taken up by the Cabala. Medieval Cabala also absorbed much of the earlier magical tradition, part of which was international in character and part of which bore specifically Jewish traits.

Christian interest in the Cabala developed in the 15th century and its beginnings were closely connected with the Neoplatonic tendencies of the Medicean Academy at Florence. This interest was at first specifically Christian, attempting to prove that doctrines about the nature of Christ were the true and secret meaning of the Jewish Cabala. Moreover, it was argued that the Cabala contained the original revelation of mankind, and hence the term came to mean Platonic, Orphic and Pythagorean occultism in general, rather than specific Jewish doctrines as expounded in Hebrew texts.

The first generations of Christian Cabalists, often instructed by Jewish teachers, possessed some sound though fragmentary knowledge of the subject (Pico della Mirandola and Reuchlin are examples), but most authors used Latin translations only and not the original texts. From the 17th century onwards, ignorance steadily increased until the term Cabala became a euphemism for any mixture of occultism, Hermetism, Rosicrucianism, exotic theosophy and general infatuation with secret lore: as illustrated, for example, by W. Wynn Westcott's claim (in his *Introduction to the Study of the Kabbalah*, 1926) to have taught cabalistic doctrines which had never been published before and were not to be found in any Hebrew book.

Another cabalistic trend was in evidence in 17th century England, a combination in different proportions of natural philosophy, alchemy and Neoplatonism in the writings of Thomas Vaughan, Robert Fludd and the Cambridge Platonists, such as Henry More. This Cabala, unlike Jewish esotericism, was essentially a form of natural philosophy which combined what Fludd called 'theosophical and philosophical truths' and for which 'Mosaicall Philosophy' and Hermetism meant the same things. Hence Henry

In magic the cabalistic preoccupation with letters and names of God, as containers of secret knowledge and objects of mystical speculation, turned into the attempt to use them as sources of power. *Top left* Diagram believed to give the magician control of all evil spirits *Top right* The harmony of God, the universe and man, by Robert Fludd. At the centre, Iod He Vau He are the Hebrew letters of the supreme name of God, also called the Tetragrammaton or name of four letters *Below* Hung round the neck before sunrise on a Sunday, these symbols would make the wearer invisible

practice. A major cabalistic renaissance took place in the 16th century in Safed (Upper Galilee) where a group of scholars and mystics, mainly of Spanish origin, had settled. By far the most influential of them was Isaac Luria, whose teachings form a weird and curious mythology of a strangely Gnostic character.

In the beginning God was All in All. In order that creation (which means, that which is not God) might be, God had to empty space by withdrawing or 'retracting' his all-pervading presence. This is the mystery of the *Tsimtsum* ('retraction'). Into this newly created vacuum God wanted to infuse his carefully veiled light, thus bringing into being a created cosmos. But the channels or pipes through which the

creative light-essence of God poured into creation-in-the-making could not contain the Divine light. They collapsed and broke in the *Shevirath ha-kelim*, 'the breaking of the vessels', and the divine sparks fell into chaos, a prey to demonic powers.

Here a Gnostic type of primeval catastrophe or fall is assumed in the very heart of God's creation, even before Adam's fall. Since then the history of the world, including the creation of man, is the drama of the struggle for restoration *(tikkun)* with its ups and downs, its progress and setbacks. The two major setbacks were the fall of Adam and the destruction of the Temple.

The decisive idea at the bottom of the system was that it was not only Israel which was in exile and in need of salvation, but

More's bland assertion that the Platonists had 'more of that Cabala than the Jews themselves have at this day'. From this type of literature some cabalistic elements subsequently percolated into the symbolism of 18th century Freemasonry.

Some non-Jewish mystics, including Jacob Boehme, possessed an innate affinity with the cabalistic mode of thought, and their writings exhibit remarkable similarities which do not necessarily prove acquaintance with the doctrines of Jewish theosophy. Among writers whose intuitive insight into cabalistic motives and doctrines more than offset their ignorance in linguistic and historical matters, are Franz von Baader in Germany and A. E. Waite (*The Holy Kabbalah*, 1930) in England.

The term Cabala did not only mean theosophy and mystical philosophy. Soon after the word had penetrated the European languages it was used as synonymous with magic and from the 17th century it could also mean a plot, intrigue or clique. (The interpretation of the noun 'Cabal' as composed of the initial letters of the names of several of Charles II's advisers was never meant as anything but a pun). Cabalistic magic was mainly a matter of permuting and combining Hebrew letters and their numerical values, magic squares, anagrams and the like. These mathematico-mystical operations, known as *gematria* and expounded by Cornelius Agrippa in his *Occult Philosophy*, and by many others, could serve practical as well as theoretical ends: magical purposes on the one hand and mystical interpretation of Scripture on the other. In a wider and more popular sense cabalistic magic could mean the most diverse kinds of occult practice and divination.

Scientific study of the Cabala did not begin until the 19th century. It has made considerable progress in the 20th especially since Professor Scholem's researches have placed it on a sound linguistic and historical footing.

R. J. ZWI WERBLOWSKY

Cabala and Modern Magic

Stemming from its influence on Christian occultists of the Renaissance, the Cabala has powerfully affected modern magicians, including Eliphas Levi in the 19th century and Aleister Crowley in the 20th. The Tree of Life is seen as a diagram of the way in which the universe 'emanated' or came into existence from the One, the unity believed to exist behind all things. Conversely, it is also seen as a diagram of the way in which man can unite himself with or become the One, by 'rising through the spheres', spiritually climbing the ladder of the ten sefiroth to reach God.

The 22 major trumps of the Tarot pack are connected with the 22 Paths, which link the sefiroth together and provide mystical pathways along which the magician travels. This travelling is performed not in the ordinary physical body but in the astral body, and there is a complicated system of correspondences which help to guide the magician on his way (see CORRESPONDENCES; PATHS). As he rises through the spheres, the magician masters and controls

the powerful force of each individual sefirah.

This is, in effect, a statement of the magical belief that the adept of the occult arts must experience and master all things in order to achieve supreme perfection and power, for the Tree of the ten sefiroth is believed to be a cosmic diagram, the basic pattern which shows how the universe is arranged and how its phenomena are connected. It is also a statement of the belief that man is a miniature replica of the universe and God, and that he is capable of spiritually expanding himself to become God.

The Cabala, and Jewish magic in general, has also influenced magicians in their use of 'names of power', many of which were originally names or titles of the god of the Old Testament and the gods of the ancient world.

Human mental abilities classified in terms of God and the universe: from Robert Fludd's *Utriusque Cosmi*

These names are believed to be reservoirs of power, which the magician taps by using them.

(See also ALPHABET; GEMATRIA; GRIMOIRES; NAMES.)

FURTHER READING: G. G. Scholem, *Major Trends in Jewish Mysticism* (Schocken, 1969) and *On the Kabbalah and Its Symbolism* (Schocken, 1969). For the magical side, see W. E. Butler, *Magic and the Qabalah* (Llewellyn Pubns.); R. Cavendish, *The Black Arts* (Capricorn, 1968).

Cactus

The spiny desert plant, important in south-western American Indian rituals; among the Pueblos, Zuni chiefs are installed with rites that include whipping with cacti, which ensures good fortune; Zuni Cactus Societies use cactus flagellation to test endurance; Hopis place pieces of cactus at the corners of a new house to 'root' it to the earth; many south-western tribes use hallucinogenic drugs from cacti in mystic ceremonies.
See DRUGS; PUEBLO INDIANS.

Caduceus

Latin word for a herald's staff of office, associated with the Greek god Hermes, the messenger of the gods: in its oldest form possibly an olive branch with two prongs at the top, entwined with ribbons; later it was a wand with two snakes twined round it and sometimes with wings at the top of the staff: in alchemy a symbol of the uniting of opposites: more generally, it has been interpreted as an emblem of power (the wand) combined with wisdom (the snakes): also used as a symbol of healing.

The meteoric career of the magician Cagliostro, who achieved a European reputation only to meet with disaster, has remained one of history's enigmas. Attempting to combine Catholicism, Freemasonry and magic he aroused exasperated opposition and met his death at the hands of the Inquisition

CAGLIOSTRO

SHOWMAN, PHILANTHROPIST and genuine seeker after supernatural knowledge, Count Alessandro Cagliostro was one of the most extraordinary figures of 18th century Europe. Born Giuseppe Balsamo in 1743, as a young man he took the name of his godmother, Countess Cagliostro, to whom he was related on his mother's side. The family belonged to the lesser and impoverished Sicilian nobility. At the age of 23 he went to Malta, where he was received with open arms by the Grand Master of the Order of The Knights of Malta. The Grand Master, who was skilled in alchemy and a Rosicrucian, introduced him to occultism and encouraged him to take an interest in alchemy.

Arriving in London in 1776 with his young wife Serafina, Cagliostro was welcomed by the Freemasons, whose members at that time included some celebrated personalities, and was officially admitted to their Society. At this time, Cagliostro was obsessed by the idea of the Philosopher's Stone. He experimented with manufacturing powders and with transmuting metals and making precious stones. He spent hours bent over tables of Pythagoras and in studying cabalistic numbers. He also gained a reputation for predicting the winning numbers in a lottery; after three successful predictions, the news spread like wildfire. So many people came clamouring for his help that he had to close his doors and resolved never to play the lottery again.

Deeply interested in the theosophical theories of Emmanuel Swedenborg (see SWEDENBORG), Cagliostro introduced them to the Freemasons' lodges. He also taught the art of conjuring up spirits. After becoming involved in several disreputable incidents which were apparently engineered by his detractors, with a view to getting him out of the way so that they could steal his cabalistic and alchemical secrets, Cagliostro decided to leave London. Travelling under the sponsorship of the Grand Lodge of England, Cagliostro made a series of visits to one European lodge after another, including the Hague, Brussels, Liège, Nuremberg and Leipzig. His fame grew and he was received by Frederick II of Prussia and also by Prince Stanislas of Poland. He is also said to have met the Comte de Saint-Germain, the fashionable magician of the court of Louis XV in France.

Cagliostro's chief aim at this time was to establish the identity of Freemasonry, magic and religion, by going back to the Cabala sources and the Templar tradition (see KNIGHTS TEMPLAR). He had been brought up a Roman Catholic, had become interested in magic and had been initiated into Freemasonry. Feeling that there was an affinity between all three, he attempted to bring about a mystic fusion. The Bible, he said, was full of magic, from the miraculous powers of Moses to the secrets of King Solomon, from the prophets' visions to the witch of Endor, who made the ghost of the dead Samuel appear before King Saul. He believed that this heavenly magic, as revealed in the Scriptures, could be rediscovered with divine help, and that God could be perceived in the secrets of Nature, so marvellously revealed in the alchemist's laboratory. Putting his discoveries to the test, Cagliostro carried out feats of clairvoyance and necromancy, the summoning up of ghosts, and had success in curing certain illnesses.

The Egyptian Rite

The motives of this extraordinary man have often been maligned through misunderstanding – a confusion increased perhaps by his showmanship, his love of mystery and his curious habit of travelling under assumed names. He was not, as many suspected, out to make money; he was rich in any case. Nor had he any desire for titles. He was, in fact, a genuine philanthropist and believed that a man's first duty was to work for the good of others, to alleviate their sufferings, to free them and give them happiness. The services he gave were always free and he made many gifts to charity. He was a man naturally endowed with a gift of intuition and the teachings he gained from his initiators further developed his apparently supernatural powers.

In 1779 he visited Courland, a sovereign principality under the protection of Prussia, settling in Mittau which was then a centre of occultism and magic. Cagliostro began to carry out supernatural experiments and to use a method of clairvoyance which he discovered in an Egyptian papyrus. The 'Egyptian rite' involved hypnotizing a child, after due ceremonies of purification and preparation, and causing him to see visions and utter prophecies. In his ritual ceremonies he made circles in the air with a symbolic sword and invoked archangels to intercede for him with God. On one occasion he succeeded in invoking the Archangel Michael, whom the child saw clearly, dressed in a long white robe.

The Queen's Necklace

As a healer, too, he became renowned, practising healing by the laying on of hands and by other methods. He used an approach which was far in advance of his time in that he started from the viewpoint of the patient's personality and problems, which he seems to have perceived through clairvoyance. He combined this psychological approach with the use of very simple remedies, and had some remarkable cures to his credit. While in France, he became the friend of Cardinal de Rohan, who had long wished to meet the man whose reputation had aroused his respect. The Cardinal persuaded him to treat his uncle, the Marshal de Soubise, who was desperately ill. Three days after Cagliostro began to treat his patient, the Marshal rallied, though previously at death's door.

Up to 1785, Cagliostro seemed to have a glorious future ahead of him. The Ministers of France and the Freemasons showered him with flattering awards and he mingled with important and influential people. Yet some quality in his personality seemed to invite disaster, hostility and slander. The medical profession in particular were jealous of his success and created trouble at every opportunity. A valet-secretary dismissed for stealing revenged himself by spreading lies which soon gained currency. A certain Polish baroness who had at one time admired him became vindictive and started spreading evil stories about him. He had also aroused the antagonism of some of the Catholic clergy who did not approve of his 'miracles', seeing in them a threat to the authority of the Church.

Cagliostro's downfall was precipitated

when he was accused of being involved in the resounding scandal of the affair of Marie Antoinette's necklace. The French Queen badly wanted a sumptuous necklace of diamonds and pearls, which Cardinal de Rohan was eager to give her as he hoped to get back into favour with Louis XVI. In August 1785 a dangerous adventuress, Comtesse de Valois la Motte, was entrusted with taking the jewel-case containing the necklace to the queen, but kept it for herself. When the swindle was discovered, the thief accused Cagliostro, who was arrested and imprisoned in the Bastille. He was eventually cleared but was ordered to leave France.

Incensed by the unjust treatment at the hands of the French authorities, Cagliostro made his way to London where he endangered his position still further with the publication of his *Letter to the French People* in 1786. In it he condemned the absolute power of the French monarchy and prophesied accurately that the Bastille would be stormed and the governor put to death.

He wandered unhappily about Europe, and decided to go to Rome. Armed with credentials from several bishops he asked the Vatican for permission to visit Rome and this was granted. As soon as he arrived, in 1789, Pope Pius VI decided that his presence was a provocation and informed the Office of the Inquisition, who made a merciless report.

Cagliostro was arrested and underwent a lengthy trial. He was charged with imposture, heresy and sacrilege, to which were added accusations of fraud, lying and false pretences. He was said to be an adept in the most demonic sorcery and to be involved in political conspiracies to overthrow royalty. His personal life was also impugned and he was accused of having been a heavy drinker and a womanizer.

Cagliostro was sentenced to death but the Pope commuted this to a sentence of life imprisonment, which was to be the equivalent of prolonged torture. Taken to the fortress of San Leo, near Urbino, he died there on 6 August 1795, strangled, it is said, by his jailer. His burial place is unknown.

F. RIBADEAU DUMAS

FURTHER READING: F. Ribadeau Dumas, *Cagliostro – Scoundrel or Saint?* (Orion Press, 1967); Vincente Huidobro, *Cagliostro* (Gordon Press, 1974).

Portrait of Count Cagliostro, a famous 18th century magician and wonder-worker: said to have succeeded in conjuring up angels, he was imprisoned by the Pope and died in the dungeons of the Inquisition

Calumet

From the Latin for 'reed', the name given to the long-stemmed pipes of American Indians, and to the ceremonies themselves, in which the pipes passed among participants and onlookers, the smoke rising as an offering to the gods for peace and prosperity; Plains Indians used the ceremony to underline peace pacts, to celebrate victories, to welcome guests.
See TOBACCO.

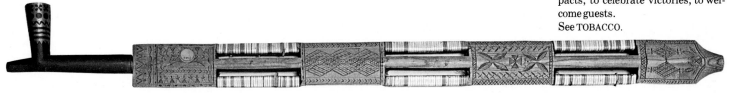

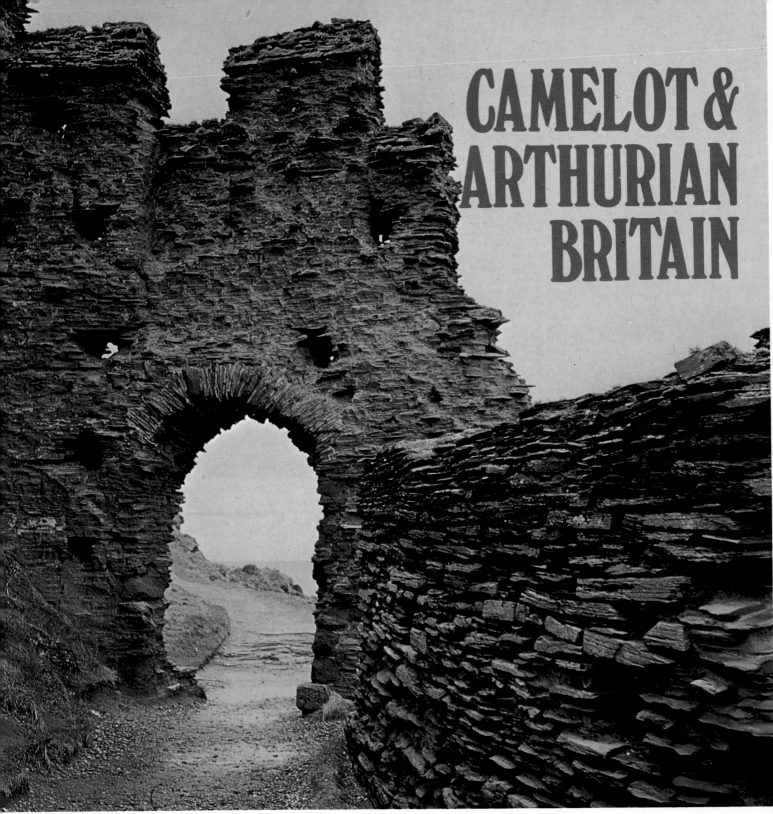

Chèze-Brown

CAMELOT & ARTHURIAN BRITAIN

Where was Camelot, the king's capital in the Arthurian legends? Recent archeological discoveries suggest that Cadbury Castle in Somerset has the strongest claim to be the 'real' Camelot

CAMELOT WAS THE CAPITAL of King Arthur where, according to legend, he reigned over the Britons before the Saxon conquest. It is not located on any authentic early map. However, *cam* and *camel* do occur as elements in British place-names of pre-Saxon origin.

The oldest known stories of Arthur never refer to Camelot, as such. The King first holds court there explicitly in the romance *Lancelot*, written by Chrétien de Troyes between 1160 and 1180. Three centuries later Malory makes it the chief city of the

realm, where the Round Table is housed. He sometimes equates it with Winchester, yet in one passage of his work it seems to be north of Carlisle. Tennyson never attempts to localize Camelot: in the *Idylls of the King*, it is symbolic, in the poet's own words 'of the gradual growth of human beliefs and institutions, and of the spiritual development of man.' The name in fact has tended to become evocative rather than geographical. Thus the conversion of T. H. White's Arthur cycle into a musical involved an almost inevitable change of title from *The Once and Future King* to *Camelot*.

Local legends and antiquarian guesswork have proposed several sites for this elusive city. One is Colchester, the Roman Camulodunum. Another theory places it near

One theory places Camelot near Tintagel in Cornwall, where according to legend King Arthur was born. The medieval castle stands near the remains of a Celtic monastery dating from about the time of the real Arthur

Tintagel, Arthur's reputed Cornish birthplace, in a district which contains the River Camel and Camelford. However, the candidate with the strongest claim to a genuine underlying tradition is Cadbury Castle in Somerset.

The 'Castle' is an earthwork fort of the pre-Roman Iron Age on an isolated hill 500 feet high, which looks over the Vale of Avalon to Glastonbury Tor in the distance. The ramparts surround an enclosure of 18 acres on top of the hill. The village of Queen

From Land's End to the Grampians

The salient point about the mass of Arthurian oddments is the grandiose geography. Nobody else except the Devil is renowned through so much of Britain. From Land's End to the Grampian foothills, Arthur's name 'cleaves to cairn and cromlech.' We hear of the Cornish fortress at Kelliwic; of a Cornish hill called Bann Arthur and a stream called the River of Arthur's Kitchen; of Cadbury and its noble shades; of the lake Llyn Berfog in Merioneth, where Arthur slew a monster, and his horse left a hoof-print on the rock; of a cave by Marchlyn Mawr in Carnarvon, where his treasure lies hidden (woe to any intruder who touches it); of a cave at Caerleon, and another near Snowdon, where his warriors lie asleep till he needs them; of still another cave in the Eildon hills, close to Melrose Abbey, where some say he is sleeping himself; of the mount outside Edinburgh called Arthur's Seat; of Arthur's Stone, and Arthur's Fold, as far north as Perth; and many more such places. Arthur seems to be everywhere.

The first natural deduction is that Arthur really was everywhere: that he flashed from end to end of his crumbling country on that terrible armoured charger, rallying the faint-hearts, reconciling the factions, and pouncing on the bewildered heathen, with Kay and Bedivere riding beside him. And the second deduction . . . is that the man who bequeathed such a towering legend was no ordinary human being. Even if most of the Arthur stories were borrowed or fabricated, it is still necessary to explain why they should ever have been attached to Arthur. Even if the bards vested him with the attributes of a god, the question still remains: Why him in particular? To which there is no adequate answer but the readiest one – because he deserved it.

Geoffrey Ashe, *King Arthur's Avalon.*

Camel – once simply Camel – is fairly close, as is the River Cam. The antiquary John Leland, in the reign of Henry VIII, speaks of local people referring to the hill-fort as 'Camalat' and as the home of Arthur. Folklore of immemorial age has clustered round it. A well inside the ramparts is called King Arthur's Well, and the summit plateau King Arthur's Palace. The King is said to lie asleep in a cave and at midsummer the ghostly hoof-beats of his knights can be heard.

To say that this place or any other *is* Camelot invites the question, what meaning can be attached to such an identification? At Cadbury Castle there can never have been a medieval city of the kind imagined by Malory. Here, the issue has been raised more insistently by the work of the Camelot Research Committee, which in 1966 began to excavate the hill. Since then traces have been found of several human occupations extending over a long time. Crucial to the Camelot problem are the proofs that about the first quarter of the 6th century AD, Arthur's presumed period, the hill was in fact the stronghold of a wealthy and powerful British ruler, who imported luxuries from the eastern Mediterranean, put up at least one substantial building on the piece of ground called King Arthur's Palace, and refurbished the defences by superimposing a huge drystone rampart of Celtic type, for which there are no known contemporary parallels anywhere else in Britain.

Interpreted in the light of other archeological findings, these results at least suggest an acceptable meaning for the phrase 'Arthurian Britain', and for Camelot as a reality around which legends have grown, as they did around the considerably smaller citadel of Troy.

The Real Camelot

Whatever the precise truth about the real Arthur, he symbolizes an historical fact which is no longer disputed. The British Celts, having lived under the rule of Rome and received a degree of Roman civilization, rallied against the first Anglo-Saxon invaders and threw them back. During the first half of the 6th century, the Britons were generally in the ascendant throughout most of what is now England, and in the Scottish Lowlands. During a large part of this time they enjoyed relative peace and prosperity. Arthur appears to have been the British commander to whom the main credit was due. He may or may not have had some royal title, but his legendary reign is based far more on his exploits as a war-leader and on the period of peace which his victories secured.

Cadbury Castle, easily the largest and most formidable of the known British strongholds of that period, fits logically into the picture as the headquarters of the greatest British leader. In that sense it could be the 'real Camelot' of the 'real Arthur'.

Furthermore, its archeological context includes other places that figure in the Arthurian legend. Thus at Tintagel in Cornwall, while there is no sign of the pre-Norman castle where Arthur was allegedly born, the

Arthur feasting in Camelot, his capital city in the later legends and the place where the Round Table was housed: from a manuscript in the British Museum

British Museum

famous headland is now known to have been inhabited in his time. Its occupants were British monks, and the imported pottery used by their community has supplied key clues to the dating and interpretation of other sites, including Cadbury itself.

At a second Iron Age hill-fort, Castle Dore in Cornwall, traces have been found of 6th century resettlement by a west country chieftain. He built a timber hall, and may have been the original of King Mark in the Tristan romance. Further hill-top dwellings have been discovered in Wales, and also on Glastonbury Tor. The Tor seems to have been the home of a certain Melwas, who appears in an early tale of Arthur and later becomes 'Meleagant' or 'Mellyagraunce'.

Knights of the Round Table

The historical questions most usually prompted by the romances may be summed up under two headings: the Round Table and the Holy Grail. In other words, can we make anything historically of Arthur's court on its secular side (meaning chiefly the order of knighthood) and on its religious side (meaning chiefly the motif of a Christian mystery which was peculiar to Britain)?

Under the first heading, one popular theory accounts for the armoured riders of Camelot by maintaining that the real Arthur turned the tide against the Saxons with a cavalry force, a personal corps of mounted men which was the basis of the legend. It is a fact that heavy mailed cavalry was developed by Rome in the last phases of the Western Empire, and may possibly have been seen in Britain early in the 5th century, a remembered model for imitation. It is also a fact that the Saxons were not horsemen, and might well have been routed by mounted Britons.

For the cavalry theory there is still no direct evidence. But research has done much to trace the outline of an actual British nobility in the Dark Ages. From the results of excavation, coupled with clues in early Welsh poetry, it is possible to form a convincing picture of warriors fighting under Arthur's command and, perhaps, assembling in his Cadbury headquarters.

These 'knights', who undoubtedly did fight against the heathen, had little of the panoply of the Middle Ages. They went to war in thick leather tunics and breeches with coats of mail, and carried long-bladed

Philip Rahtz

The place with the strongest claim to be the original Camelot is Cadbury Castle, a pre-Roman earthwork on an isolated hill in Somerset, not far from Glastonbury which itself has an important role in the legends of Arthur and the Grail. Investigations by the Camelot Research Committee have found evidence that in the early 6th century AD, the period of the real Arthur, Cadbury was in fact the stronghold of a powerful chieftain, who may have been Arthur himself

Left Traces of several different human occupations over a long period of time have been found at Cadbury: Saxon masonry

Below Uncovering stone defences at Cadbury, in 1966

Right Aerial view of Cadbury, perhaps the headquarters from which Arthur's cavalry rode against the invading Saxons

Philip Rahtz

N. Barrington

In this early society, a key place was occupied by bards. Poet-sages of legend like Merlin and Taliesin have real if shadowy originals

swords, spears and round whitewashed shields. They had horses and rode across country, whether or not they actually fought in the saddle. They were Christians, at least in name, and attended divine service before a battle. Their civilian garb was colourful if probably simple, and they wore gold ornaments and jewellery.

In this early society, with its curious mingling of barbarism and sophistication, a key place was occupied by bards. A great chieftain's title depended partly on the appropriate bard's knowledge of his ancestry. The loyalty of his vassals depended on the bard's success in keeping them convinced of his prowess, wisdom, and generosity. Poet-sages of legend like Merlin and Taliesin have real if shadowy originals. It is because of

these highly respected figures – mainly in the north – that the tradition of Arthur himself, and of a British heroic age associated with him, was handed down to supply the material of medieval romance.

The Celts and the Grail

As to the religious question, little can be said with certainty about the beliefs underlying the Grail theme itself. But Arthurian Britain and the neighbouring Celtic lands were undoubtedly a scene of Christian activity. Some of it had the restless, journeying quality which the Grail stories reflect, and some was peculiar enough to accord with the strange atmosphere of these stories, if not with the imagery in detail.

The higher social classes in Britain were

largely Christianized before the end of Roman rule, and produced such eminent figures as St Patrick. The halting of the Saxon advance in Arthur's time enabled a series of apostles, chiefly Welsh, to preside over a much wider flowering of Christian culture both in Britain and in Ireland. Ireland in particular became the most cultured western land of the Dark Ages and owed a vast debt to the British saints after Patrick.

This Celtic Church of the British Isles was almost out of touch with the Christianity of the Continent, and had a character of its own. It was based on monasteries rather than dioceses; its ruling ecclesiastics were abbots rather than bishops; and the monks, not the secular clergy, set the tone. A Welsh tradition suggests that the three

393

Previous page Arthur's entry into Camelot, from a 14th century romance; British Museum **Left** The battle of Camlann in which Arthur was mortally wounded by the treacherous Mordred: from the 15th century St Alban's Chronicle. The real Arthur's warriors were not feudal knights but fought in leather tunics and breeches with coats of mail, and carried spears, swords and round whitewashed shields

Arthur and the Welsh

As an imaginative conception, Arthurian Britain has gone through two phases. The early Welsh tradition looked backward to a glorified 'Island of Britain' where Arthur and other heroes had flourished. Geographically, England was then 'Logria', and the 'Cymry' or Welsh had dominion over it. Then the Cymry lost Logria, and Wales alone preserved the remnants of Arthurian splendour. But some day, it was prophesied, Arthur would come back as a Celtic Messiah and subdue the English.

This view was more or less adopted by Geoffrey of Monmouth when, in the 1130s, he wrote his *History of the Kings of Britain* which did so much to plant an exaggerated and glamorized Arthurian realm in the minds of readers outside Wales. However, with the popularization of the theme by non-Celtic romancers, Arthur ceased to be a purely regional hero. England's Plantagenet sovereigns claimed to possess his birthplace, his chief cities and his grave, and to be his rightful successors in the lordship of all Britain. Edward I displayed Arthur's alleged remains at Glastonbury to prove that Arthur would never return to aid the Welsh.

Both aspects of Arthur were adroitly united by Henry Tudor. He stressed his own Welsh ancestry, and marched to overthrow Richard III under the standard of the Red Dragon. When he became king as Henry VII, he allowed his propagandists to construe the event as fulfilling the prophecy of Arthur's return – meaning, now, not that the Welsh had conquered the English, but that a true 'British' prince had saved the whole land from civil war and restored its ancient Arthurian glory.

The great poetic exponent of this Tudor myth is Edmund Spenser who, in *The Faerie Queene*, portrays the England of Elizabeth I as the magnificent kingdom of the Britons restored. The same motif recurs elsewhere in Elizabethan and Stuart literature, and as late as 1757 in Gray's poem *The Bard*. (See also ARTHUR; GRAIL.)

GEOFFREY ASHE

FURTHER READING: Most aspects of this subject are surveyed in *The Quest for Arthur's Britain* (Granada Publishing Ltd., 1980), edited by Geoffrey Ashe, which includes chapters by the principal archeologists concerned, and a full bibliography.

chief religious centres of Arthurian Britain were Amesbury, Glastonbury, and Llantwit Major in South Wales. All three had monasteries, none was the seat of a bishop.

The Celtic monks of Britain and Ireland were freer than their brethren abroad. They wandered widely and they were more democratic in outlook. Women were held in higher esteem than among Continental Christians, because the importance of the monks made nuns important as well. The ascetic contempt for worldly goods was adverse to some of the arts. Sculpture, for instance, was reduced to decoration, and there was no significant church architecture. However, in literature and scholarship the Irish at least excelled, and the one British monk of the 6th century whose writings survive, Gildas, was fairly well-read and wrote in Latin.

In the less Romanized western parts of Britain, and in Ireland, the Church did not have to contend – as formerly on the Continent – with a powerful and entrenched pagan priesthood. Even the Irish Druids were not very dangerous. Hence, the old religion was not viewed as Satanic in the same way, and the Celts preserved much mythology and speculation of a kind which went into eclipse elsewhere. The trend was encouraged by the fact that they could safely possess apocryphal Christian books which the Continental hierarchy forbade to the faithful.

The writings of Celtic monks include bizarre doctrines about angels and formulae for intercourse with the spirit world. St Brigit is spoken of as a reincarnation of the Virgin Mary and, in some obscure sense, as a priestess. Pagan beings reappear in Christian contexts, not as devils but as heroes. Among them is the god Bran, a deity of the Celts both British and Irish (see BRAN). He occurs in some of the early legends of Arthur; as a ruler of Britain in the Welsh *Mabinogion*; as an Atlantic seafarer in an early Irish tale; and eventually in the Grail stories themselves, as Brons, a companion of Joseph of Arimathea. Pagan myth, Christian legend and classical scholarship combine in the saga of St Brendan's Voyage (see BRENDAN), which has links of its own with the Grail Quest.

Celtic Christianity was never heretical in any clearly defined way. But it communicated an odd flavour, a 'sense of something else'. The Celts were brought into conformity with Rome by the Synod of Whitby in 663, at a time when their missionaries, reversing the earlier movement westward, had deeply influenced the Anglo-Saxons.

The violence of the Whitby debate testifies to the feeling of the Roman clerics that they were confronting something baffling. There is no good reason to think that the Grail stories reflect anything specific that happened among Arthur's people, but the medieval authors who regarded that milieu as a proper setting for strange Christian mysteries were following a sound instinct. If Cadbury Castle was indeed Camelot, its closeness to Glastonbury, that Celtic sanctuary where the Grail legend has hovered for so long, may be more than coincidence.

CAMISARDS

THE NAME CAMISARDS was given to the Calvinist peasantry of the Cévennes and Bas-Languedoc regions of southern France, who at the beginning of the 18th century waged partisan warfare against the armies of Louis XIV. The word Camisard derives from *camisa*, meaning 'shirt' in the local dialect. It has been suggested that the Camisards may have changed their shirts frequently, to symbolize purity. According to another explanation, however, it was their custom of wearing white shirts over their ordinary clothing at night, as a distinguishing mark which could be thrown away during pursuit, which gained them their name.

The wars of religion which ravaged France during the 16th century had been terminated in 1598 by the Edict of Nantes, which gave the Calvinists, or Huguenots, freedom of conscience; the right to hold public worship in certain specified localities; and full civil rights, including the right to hold official positions. But these concessions were much resented by the Roman Catholic clergy, and were often called in question during the 17th century. In 1685 Louis XIV formally revoked the edict and thereby deprived his Protestant subjects of all religious and civil liberty.

The revocation came as a terrible shock to the Protestants, for the Edict of Nantes had been declared perpetual and irrevocable by three monarchs, including Louis XIV himself. Since it seemed impossible that they could be delivered from oppression by political means, Protestants turned for reassurance to the apocalyptic passages in the Bible. In this they were encouraged by Pierre Jurieu, a Protestant pastor who published a series of violently controversial tracts in which he interpreted the present situation in terms of prophecies taken from the Book of Revelation, and foretold the overthrow of Roman Catholicism in 1689. Circulating secretly in France, these works exerted a powerful fascination on Protestant minds. Their effect was intensified by the increasingly severe persecution to which the Protestants were now subjected. Driven from their churches and deprived of their pastors, they began to hold clandestine meetings in wild country places.

The Little Prophets

Excitement was particularly intense in the south of France, which already in the later Middle Ages had produced various religious movements of a markedly 'enthusiastic' nature (see ENTHUSIASM) and a more or less anti-Catholic tendency. Now a pupil of Jurieu, Du Serre, disseminated the apocalyptic message in the Dauphiné region, and trained young children as propagandists. These 'little prophets', headed by a girl known as 'the fair Isabel', went from village to village announcing that the reign of Antichrist had begun, and would shortly be terminated by the Second Coming of Christ. Adults listened and were soon gripped by an infectious enthusiasm. Those who had gone over to Roman Catholicism stopped attending Mass. In the presence of

the ecstatic children whole crowds would fall into convulsions, accompanied by uncontrollable sobbing.

It was in the mountains of the Cévennes, however, amongst the small farmers, cloth and silk weavers, and vine dressers, that the new faith flourished most vigorously and was most vigorously repressed. From 1686 onwards troops were quartered on these people for the winter, without compensation or any attempt at a fair distribution of the burden.

In reality these so-called *dragonnades* were imposed from Paris and were fully approved by the king; but the victims looked elsewhere for the cause of their woes. Profoundly royalist, they never blamed the king, but on the contrary prayed daily for his

well-being. Their hatred was reserved for the local authorities: the administrator of Languedoc, Nicolas Lamoignon de Basville; the local military commander, the Comte de Broglie; the priests and missionaries. And the local authorities, for their part, became ardent persecutors when, following the successful English revolution of 1688, the existence of a Protestant minority in France seemed to threaten the security of the realm.

'Fanaticism Reborn', an attack on the outrages perpetrated by the Camisards, French Protestant revolutionaries who believed that the Last Judgement was imminent, that bullets fired against them would turn to water, and that they were guided by mysterious lights in the sky

Bullets Turned to Water

The revolt of the Camisards broke out on the night of 24 July 1702. A band of some 40 Cévenols stormed the house of Abbé Du Chayla at Pont-de-Montvert and released seven Protestants who were held captive there. These men had been tortured. The abbé himself flogged them daily and he also forced them to sleep bolt upright, their feet squeezed in the middle of a great beam. The Cévenols killed the abbé, after which they went through the land killing many more priests and burning churches.

In the campaign that followed, the Camisards, as they were now called, operated in armed bands which took it in turn to fight. The men would take up arms to attack a Catholic village or castle; after which they would return to civilian life for a time. It is likely that the number involved never exceeded 4000, or the number under arms at any one time 1500. But these small, temporary units were supported by a population of some 200,000, and they operated in a wooded, mountainous, almost savage country, which they knew perfectly.

In addition, they fought in the absolute certainty of divine support. The ecstatic and visionary experiences which had marked the movement from the beginning continued in time of war. The Camisards were guided to places of safety by mysterious lights in the sky; supernatural voices consoled them; bullets fired at them turned to water. Children and women, shaking all over, encouraged them with prophecies of the Second Coming and the Last Judgement. All this

enabled them to carry on a campaign which immobilized a large number of regular troops, at one time as many as 60,000.

The Camisards fought under a number of leaders. There was Esprit Séguier, who immediately after the killing of Abbé Du Chayla tried to organize a general massacre of the Catholic clergy; he was soon captured and burned alive. There was an old soldier named Laporte, who called himself 'Colonel of the Children of God' and named his camp 'the Camp of the Eternal'. There were other old soldiers, and some wool-carders, forest-rangers, blacksmiths, bakers — all of them people of lowly origin, but inspired by fanatical faith and often by visionary experiences.

Fire and Sword

The most remarkable leader was undoubtedly Jean Cavalier (1681–1740). His father, an illiterate peasant, had been forced by persecution to become a Roman Catholic; but the boy Jean was secretly brought up by his mother as a Protestant. He became a shepherd and then a baker's boy, until at the age of 20 he went to Calvinist Geneva for a year. Returning at the beginning of the revolt, he joined the Camisards and soon showed extraordinary military talents. He imposed rigorous discipline on his forces, but also inspired them with immense faith and courage; with the result that he was able to hold in check not only the Comte de Broglie but also three French marshals.

The struggle nevertheless ended in the defeat of the Camisards. Marshal Montrevel adopted a harsh policy of extermination,

burning hundreds of villages and putting most of the inhabitants to the sword. The chances of long-term resistance faded as the Governor, Basville, drove roads through the hitherto impassable country. Marshal Villars offered, instead, a chance of reconciliation; and in 1704 peace was negotiated between the Marshal, representing Louis XIV, and Jean Cavalier. During the negotiations Cavalier, who was still only 23 years old, conducted himself not as a defeated rebel but as an equal and honourable adversary.

The terms obtained by Cavalier for the Protestants included liberty of conscience and the right of assembly outside walled towns. But they were denied the right to have churches of their own, and for this reason the treaty was rejected by most of the Camisards, while Cavalier himself was repudiated as a traitor to the cause. The fortunes of the Camisards now rapidly deteriorated. By 1705 all serious military activity had ceased and the remaining leaders had either submitted or had been killed.

Thereafter the most vocal witnesses for the movement were a handful of refugees in London, who attracted lively curiosity by their ecstasies and prophecies, and also by an attempt to resurrect a dead body in St Paul's churchyard. The end of the war between France and England, in 1711, deprived the Cévenols of the last hope of support from abroad. In 1715 Louis XIV announced, by medals and a proclamation, the extinction of the Camisard heresy.

NORMAN COHN

Camphor

Substance obtained from the wood of a laurel (Laurus camphora) and believed in Europe to preserve chastity if carried on the person, perhaps because of the Greek story of Daphne, who kept her virginity by turning into a laurel tree (see APOLLO): in Malaya those who hunt for camphor speak a special language and make offerings to the camphor spirit.

Micheal Holford

Canaanites

Early inhabitants of Palestine and Syria, before the Israelite invasions; they were absorbed by the Hebrews and their beliefs and rituals influenced Jewish religion. See ASTARTE; BAAL; PHOENI–CIANS; SYRIA AND PALESTINE.

CANCER

ACCORDING TO THE traditional system, people who come under Cancer, the fourth sign of the zodiac, are those whose birth dates fall between 22 June and 23 July. Cancer is held to be ruled by the Moon, an aspect of the Great Mother, and in recent times astrologers have tended to overstress the sentimental, maternal aspect of this sign. Although the Moon shines with reflected light, this does not mean that Cancerians live for and through others.

In earlier times, it was the hard shell of the crab, emblem of this sign, which was emphasized and the typical Cancerian is often thick-skinned rather than sensitive.

The Moon's influence inclines those born under this sign to be ambitious, unstable, easily corrupted and changeable in their opinions and loyalties. They are likely to be employed in public affairs but not to remain in any one line of business, having a tendency to roam.

A Cancerian often succeeds as an author or journalist, for he is interested to know what people think, and can gauge how much they are prepared to be told, unlike Capricorn, who may think they ought to be told the truth whether they like it or not. It is typical of Cancer to have produced one of the best-known news agencies in the world (Reuter), and also one of the most famous newspaper magnates (Lord Northcliffe).

Belying his reputation as a sensitive

and sentimental sign, Cancer is often thick-skinned, and will think no worse of you for telling him a few home truths. Tact is not usually one of his virtues, but this is because he thinks he knows the facts and presumes that everyone else is equally interested in having them publicized. Unlike Leo, who imposes himself on any situation and insists on seeing it his way, Cancer is content to float with the popular tide.

Being fond of drama, he plays up any situation, and is easily led to say a little more than a strict interpretation of the facts would warrant. He is probably the source of various stories which are too good not to be true, or at any rate too good not to be told. Cancer's stories, though not always strictly accurate, are rarely unconvincing.

CANDLE

A CHILD'S birthday cake, with a candle on it for each year of his life, points straight to one facet of the symbolism of candles. A lighted candle, as a single source of light, a single fragment of the universe's store of light, stands for an individual person's life as a single fragment of life in the world.

Among Jewish communities in medieval Europe a way of seeing into the future was to put a lighted candle in a place shielded from draughts during the ten days before Yom Kippur, the Day of Atonement, the period which was by tradition the time when each man's fate for the coming year was settled in heaven. If the candle went out, the person it represented would not see the year out. If it burned down to the end, he could expect one more year of life at least.

It was an old Jewish custom to light a candle for a dead man, a practice also adopted by Christians, and which may have its roots in the idea of giving the ghost the light of life in the darkness of the tomb. Jews lit candles by the bedside of a dying man to keep demons away, for demons are creatures of darkness and fear light, and a candle burned for a week in the room where someone had died.

At the Jewish Feast of Dedication or Feast of Lights (Hanukkah) one candle is lighted on the first evening, two on the second, and so on for the eight days of the festival. This feast, celebrated in late December at the same time as the Christian Christmas festivities, may once have been a midwinter ritual at which fire and light were kindled to assist the reviving life of the sun. But it now commemorates the rededication of the Temple at Jerusalem to the worship of the Jewish God in 165 BC, after it had been profaned by the Syrian king Antiochus IV Epiphanes (see ANTICHRIST).

The Eyes of the Lord

On the last day of Hanukkah a passage from the Bible is read (Numbers, chapter 8) which refers to one of the great symbols of Judaism, the Menorah, the seven-branched golden candlestick or lampstand said to stand six feet high, which Antiochus removed from the Temple and destroyed. A new one was made to replace it. The Menorah is first mentioned in the book of Exodus (chapters 25 and 37) where God instructs Moses to have it made. It appears again in the vision of the prophet Zechariah (chapter 4) who saw 'a lampstand all of gold, with a bowl on top of it, and seven lamps on it'. An angel told him that 'these seven are the eyes of the Lord, which range through the whole earth.'

The 'eyes' have been interpreted as the seven planets, watching the earth from the sky, with the implication that the Jewish God claimed the powers of the planetary gods of Mesopotamia. Alternatively, or additionally, the seven lamps may have symbolized the creation of the world in seven days. The last Menorah, which stood in the Temple at the time of Christ, was carried off to Rome by the Emperor Titus, who destroyed the Temple in 70 AD. It is shown on his triumphal arch at Rome.

The 4th century African Christian writer Lactantius commented sardonically that the heathen kindled lights to God as if he was in darkness, and suggested that if they contemplated the sun in the heaven they would see that God had no need of their candles. But in fact Christians themselves used candles, not only to give light at their services, but to carry in funeral processions, to burn at the tombs of the dead and to kindle before the relics of the saints.

The tendency to connect candles with the dead, and with their ghosts, also occurs in the West. A guttering candle warns that the life of someone in the house is flickering to its close, and if a candle burns blue, a ghost is near. American belief says that a candle left to burn in an empty room will cause a relative's death. Another omen of death is a corpse candle or fetch candle, the mysterious light which hovers in the air and moves away from you if you follow it (see WILL-O'-THE-WISP). The magical burglar's implement called the Hand of Glory is the hand of a dead man and it holds a candle made of his fat. The light of this candle carries so strong an aura of the petrifying stillness

Though some early Christian writers scorned the pagan use of candles in ritual, Christians themselves quickly began to carry candles in funeral processions and light them for saints: interior of a Roman Catholic church at Chichicastenango in Guatemala

of death that it prevents anyone who sees it from moving (see HAND).

Candles for Lucifer

Candles have a role in the superstitions of love as well as of death. In rural America, a girl may test her boyfriend's fidelity by lighting a candle outdoors near his house. If the flame bends towards her, or towards her lover's house, all is well. If not, the young man is faithless. But in American belief a candle can help to reclaim his affections. The girl needs merely to thrust two pins through the wick of a burning candle. This simple ritual may symbolize a 'pinning down' of his love.

Witches presented candles to the Devil at their meetings, suitably enough, since one of

his names is Lucifer, 'lightbearer'. In some cases they lit them from a candle which he bore in his hand or on his head. In 1594 in Puy-de-Dôme, in the hill country of southern France, Jane Bosdeau's lover took her to a witch meeting where 'there appeared a great black goat with a candle between his horns.' All the witches lighted candles from it and then danced around him in a circle. In 1590 the North Berwick witches met in a church and he who took the part of the Devil, in a black gown and a black hat, preached to them from the pulpit, round which were lights 'like great black candles'.

In 1679, when the Police Commissioner of Paris investigated the activities of a widow known as La Voisin, fortune teller, abortionist and supplier of poisons and

black magical ceremonies, a chapel was discovered in her house. Its walls were draped in black and on the altar stood black candles. There were also candles made of human fat, provided by one of La Voisin's lovers, a public executioner. It was La Voisin who arranged the Masses said for Madame de Montespan (see BLACK MASS), in which a woman lay naked on the altar, her arms stretched out in the form of a cross and with black candles in her hands.

A Light in Darkness

For modern witches the eve of 2 February is one of their four main festivals, harking back to old pagan ceremonies in Europe at this time of year, involving the kindling of fires and torches, apparently to drive away the winter darkness and prepare the way for the coming of spring. The Christian festival of Candlemas on 2 February commemorates the Purification of the Virgin Mary, when she took the baby Jesus to the Temple and was told that he would grow up to be 'a light to lighten the gentiles'. Candles were associated with it by the 5th century in Jerusalem and a procession with lighted candles became and remains part of the Roman Catholic ritual.

In the Highlands of Scotland on the eve of 1 February, the day of St Bride or St Bridget, who was originally a pagan goddess (see BRIGIT), a bed was placed near the door and one of the household went out, came back in again and said, 'Bridget, Bridget, come in, thy bed is ready.' One or more candles were lit to burn by the bed all night. The purpose was apparently to welcome the goddess who would soon bring the spring, with the candles standing for the light which would dispel the winter dark. Similarly, the candles on a Christmas tree suggest the birth of the 'Light of the World' in the middle of winter.

The symbolism of creating light in darkness also lies behind the use of candles in magical rituals. In a recent book, *Magical Ritual Methods*, W. G. Gray says that most formal rituals begin with the kindling of a fire or light and that 'lighting candles should never be done indifferently or with lack of attention.' At first the room should be in total darkness.

The darkness is banished by lighting the candle which is a sign of the power entrusted to man, the power with which 'we can make Suns on earth, and it endows us with minor Godship . . . so we light the taper, which becomes a Rod, and slowly stand upright . . . When we were entirely in the dark, we were afraid to move from the safety of our stone shelter, but now as Light-Bearers we can move anywhere we will, bearing the precious gift wheresoever it may be needed.'

In which connection it may be worth recalling that the sin for which the original Light-Bearer was hurled from heaven, we are told, was pride.
(See also FIRE; LIGHT.)

Axel Poignant

Candles are often connected with the dead, and the candle flame with the ghosts of the dead, shimmering in darkness. Sicilian fishermen burn ornate candles to their patron saint to obtain his blessing and protection

In the remote Essex village of Canewdon, there are still old people who remember how witches could be seen riding to their meeting place on moonlit nights

CANEWDON

'THE WITCH COUNTRY' is the name given locally to the parish of Canewdon in Essex; the village is renowned for many miles around and is a legend in its own right. Although today it is rapidly becoming urbanized, it was within living memory isolated both geographically and socially, due to its remote situation on the fringe of the Essex marshlands and to its reputation as a centre of witchcraft.

According to an old tradition, as long as the church tower stands there must always be six witches in Canewdon under a master of witches: 'three in silk and three in cotton, one being the parson's wife, one the butcher's wife and one the baker's wife.' When the last witch dies, the legend says, the tower is doomed to fall; conversely when the tower falls, the last witch will die. That this tradition survived until well into the 20th century is verified by innumerable written and oral accounts, as is the custom performed until recently in which the village children danced seven times around the church as a precaution against witchcraft.

There are still old villagers even today who prefer not to pass near the crossroads at night. It is said that a witch was once buried there with a stake driven through her heart, and her headless ghost has been known to emerge as a shadowy cloud from the churchyard and make its way along the road leading to the distant river.

Another well-known Canewdon legend is that of the witch who rowed across the local river in a stolen church bell, using feathers as oars. Her unwieldly craft capsized and the tolling of the bell has on rare occasions been heard from deep beneath the water. On the river's edge there was once a barren patch long known as the witches' field, where the witches were believed to meet to renew their powers. The very old still tell how on moonlit nights the witches could be seen riding to their rendezvous on the river bank.

The Witch Master
The last 'Master of Witches' was George Pickingale, a farm labourer who died in 1909, passing on his powers to his son, in whose hands they apparently atrophied, for little more is heard of them. Pickingale was reputed to possess the power to summon the local witches by means of a wooden whistle, and to halt farm machinery with one glance from his fierce and somewhat glassy eyes. He was adept at charming warts and was occasionally called in to arbitrate in a wages dispute. The more superstitious villagers up to a decade ago remembered how he would sit idly smoking his pipe while a bevy of imps worked for him.

Pickingale blended the qualities of both the black and the white magician. In his capacity of village wise man, his aid was sought for social purposes, but he exploited

A Canewdon villager with the church tower in the background. According to an old tradition, as long as the tower stands, there will always be seven witches in Canewdon, and the village is the centre of many stories of witches

Transworld Feature Syndicate

his reputation as a wizard to the full, coercing neighbours into drawing water for him from the village well, and using the threat of black magic to secure forced tributes of beer. Following his death at the age of 93, his cottage long remained untenanted, possibly from fear of his familiars, 'the little old white mice', which were said to haunt the premises, peering out of the darkness with red staring eyes.

Almost as remarkable, and far more dangerous, were the powers accredited to the last six witches of Canewdon who must have lived in the 1880s, and who were doubtless perfectly innocent victims of parochial vindictiveness. According to statements recorded during a survey carried out between 1958 and 1961, these were described as follows. Mrs W was a cripple who cast spells and was loathed for her venomous temper. Mrs K used to fix passers-by with her glaring eyes, and prevented them from entering church. Mrs L was an eccentric who inflicted plagues of lice upon those who offended her. Another Mrs L betrayed herself as a witch by refusing to step over a doormat under which a steel knife had been laid. Mrs C was a woman renowned for bewitching waggonwheels and known to possess imps. Mrs M was a not unkind woman but one who occasionally

terrified her neighbours by materializing spectrally at their bedsides in the dead of night, peering fiercely from beneath a poke bonnet.

The activities of these sinister women were embodied in a wealth of macabre legends, no doubt passed down the generations for centuries and attached to one bevy of suspects after another.

The White Mice
The Canewdon witches had the power of the Evil Eye and a single glance could immobilize a victim for hours on end, or even bring traffic to a halt. I am indebted to Mr Witcutt, late Rector of Foulness Island for the following anecdote. A waggoner had refused to buy beer for a Canewdon woman and afterwards his horses were unable to move. He used the whip on them but they would not budge. His mate said, 'No use hitting the horses, mate, hit the wheels. It's the old girl in there.' And he hit the wheels and she emerged from them screaming, with the marks of the whip on her face. The belief that a witch could transform herself into a wheel was once very general.

Canewdon must have been one of the last places in the British Isles where the witches' familiar survived in folk belief, although cases did occur in mid-19th century Norfolk and Suffolk. The familiar peculiar to the Canewdon witches — the white mouse — is only rarely referred to in the witch trials of the 17th century, but the legends in which these animals were mentioned indicate that not only were they the repositories of the witches' power but that they were passed down the generations from one witch to her successor. At the close of the last century several of the legends of Canewdon began to reflect the rapid decline in the belief in witchcraft. An old woman suffering on her deathbed found it impossible to die until she had passed on her powers. She finally gave a low whistle and a number of white mice emerged from a box. She was then able to die in peace.

According to another legend, white mice refused to leave the body of a dead witch, and could only be disposed of by nailing them in the coffin with their mistress. A significant legend from the same area describes the burning of the imps as the sole means of breaking the grim entail.

Canewdon was obviously the ideal place for an intensive witch-hunt and there are traditions of suspected witches having been ducked in the village pond. Fortunately for potential victims of spells the local people were adepts in white magic, their domestic charms against witchcraft consisting in the main of knives and scissors placed under doormats. The village layer-out of the dead, a notable seer, was also available in cases requiring the help of the specialist, largely because of her skill in the preparation of 'witch bottles'. These were bottles containing the hair, blood and urine of a victim of witchcraft which were boiled on the cottage hearth at midnight in order to betray the witch by 'drawing her' to the scene of her crimes. By the turn of the present century jam-jars containing urine had replaced the elaborate brew of earlier years.

The Head at the Window

A once common legend relates to the perpetual pursuit of the parish priest of Canewdon by Satan, whom the former always managed to elude since the Devil invariably entangled his tail in the hedgerows of the narrow winding lanes. An old farm known as the Tile Barn, which once stood on neighbouring Wallasea Island on the fringes of the parish, was long believed to be haunted by an invisible entity which made known its presence by emanating an ice-cold atmosphere; on one occasion a black head complete with horns was observed peering from an upper window.

The overall effect of this body of traditions tended to reduce the number of visitors to Canewdon to a minimum, as well as to endow local humour with the somewhat macabre flavour for which it has become renowned. A popular story which is no doubt still told today concerns an observation made by a villager who, upon learning that a child had been born with a full set of teeth, muttered, 'My God! we'll have werewolves here next.'

Many strange superstitions have persisted in the Essex marshlands which, until comparatively recent times, were the homes of fever-ridden, narrow-minded and somewhat belligerent country labourers and fishermen. It was not difficult to believe, at Canewdon, that a headless ghost walked nightly along the river wall or that the local sweep, who was extremely tall and thin and never removed the soot from his face, had some affinity with the Devil. This type of tradition was not, of course, peculiar to Canewdon but the importance of the Canewdon story comes from the light it sheds on the superstitious beliefs of another age, treasured in the folk memories of unlettered labourers in a remote corner of the English countryside.

There is perhaps nothing quite like Canewdon in the annals of witch belief, for it provides the modern investigator with a window into a dark, forgotten world.

ERIC MAPLE

FURTHER READING: T. R. Revesz, *Witches* (Raintree Pubs., 1977); Eric Maple, *The Dark World of Witches* (A. S. Barnes, 1964).

Cannibalism

The eating of human flesh by men: frequently a way of acquiring the strength, skill or other qualities of the victim; sometimes a form of burial, sometimes a way of protecting yourself against the ghost of a man you have killed, sometimes part of the initiation of a shaman or medicine-man; a human victim might be identified with a god and eaten to bring the god into the bodies of his worshippers.
See FOOD; SABBATH; SACRIFICE; VAMPIRES; WEREWOLVES.

Mary Evans Picture Library

Canonization

Formal recognition that a man or woman is a saint: in the Roman Catholic Church the process, in which the pope is the final judge, may take many years; if the candidate's reputation for sanctity survives the first steps in the procedure he is known as 'the Venerable'; at a later stage he is beatified and called 'the Blessed'; recognition of sainthood then depends on establishing that miracles have been obtained through appeals to the Blessed since the beatification.
See SAINTS.

CAPRICORN

THE TRADITIONAL ZODIAC places those born between 22 December and 20 January under the sign of Capricorn, the sea-goat. The tenth sign of the zodiac is derived from the Babylonian god Ea, who was the god of the region described in the Bible as 'the waters under the earth'. Ea was a very different character from Saturn, who has been the astrological ruler of Capricorn for the last 2000 years and was the most dreaded of the planets. Saturn represents restriction, limitation and control. Because of Saturn's influence, the Capricornian is often represented as a hard-working, humble, rather dreary person who never ventures to take a risk and constantly expects things to go wrong.

Fortunately for those born under this sign, however, this gloomy view of the Capricorn character is an unbalanced one. It is true that he has a tendency to be over-serious, pessimistic and emotionally inhibited; but he has other qualities derived from his planet which are often turned to good account. Chief of these is an economical streak. This urge towards economy does not often take the form of meanness, though Capricornians commonly feel that the gods keep them a little short so that there is not much that they can afford to give away.

Capricorn people typically are clear-headed, self-critical in youth, and set high standards for themselves. Among artists, typical Capricornian composers include Mozart and Schubert. When Mozart showed one of his scores to the Emperor of Austria, the Emperor remarked: 'What a terrible lot of notes, Mr Mozart', to which the composer replied, 'No more than are necessary, your Majesty'. To this day we admire the clean, economical style of Mozart, who never wrote a superfluous note.

As writers, Capricorn subjects display the same economy and their brevity often leads to wit. They say what they have to say in the fewest possible words, and are far more likely to provide too little explanation of their meaning than too much. Some Capricornians would even say that it is from pure laziness that they write no unnecessary words, but the elegant concise precision of Francis Bacon's *Essays* was not due to laziness. The same qualities make Capricornians effective as public speakers; their speeches are usually shrewd and to the point. When involved in argument or controversy, they do not bother to leap to their own defence but draw their opponents on to commit themselves and to build up a complicated structure of argument. Capricorn then demolishes the basis of his opponent's case and brings it crashing to the ground.

Capricorn, in short, tries as far as possible to produce the maximum effect with the minimum expense of effort and energy. There is never anything superfluous about Capricorn; in whatever sphere he chooses, he always knows when and where to draw the line and his theories are invariably safely founded on rock.

British Museum

CARDS

Does the history of our past and future lives lie ready and waiting in a pack of cards? Card readers believe that cards contain a wealth of occult meaning, which enables them to tell us our fortunes

READING THE PAST, the present and the future by means of a pack of ordinary playing cards or by the more elaborate and larger pack known as the Tarot, is one of the most popular methods of divination. The use of symbolically decorated cards for fortune telling probably preceded their use in games of chance, and later replaced the more primitive forms of divination, such as the throwing down of a bundle of arrows or sticks, or the inspection of entrails. Often the clairvoyant or the gypsy resorts to additional methods, gazing into a crystal ball or into a bowl of water, to confirm the reading already taken from the cards.

Cards have been made of bark, bamboo, ivory, skin or linen as well as of pasteboard and nowadays of plastic. The designs have been variously painted by hand, hand-printed from blocks, engraved or lithographed. Among the fine examples of cards to be seen in the national museums and private collections there are many variations in design. German packs, for instance, use different emblems for the 'pips' from those common in France and England.

The origin of our modern packs is still a matter of dispute and there are almost as many theories propounded by occultists and historians to choose from as there are addicts

of the cards. Cards were known as early as 969 AD in China and according to a Hindu legend they were invented in India by a Maharajah's wife to cure her husband of the nervous habit of pulling his beard, by keeping his hands occupied. Others claim that the ancestors of our modern cards were imported into Europe by the gypsies, who had originally brought them from Egypt. References to the Tarot cards are found as early as 1299 in Italy. A 14th century manuscript shows a king and two courtiers playing cards, and the pips are arranged in the same way as they are today.

The Devil's Pack Book

The decorative and colourful Tarot cards, from which our more simplified standard packs are thought to be descended, are still used in Mediterranean countries in a game called *tarocchi*. A complete Tarot pack consists of 78 cards, divided into four suits: Cups, Wands, Coins and Swords. Each suit has 14 cards, comprising the numerals one to ten, and four trumps or court cards — King, Queen, Knight or Chevalier, and Valet or Jack, named after the picture of a blazoned or coated figure of a court personage. Sometimes the court cards represent ancient and contemporary heroes, and they have even been known to commemorate political events.

In addition to the four suits of the Tarot there are 22 major trumps, which are called the Major Arcana, because they are believed to contain hidden occult mysteries. These picture cards with their unusual design and

such bizarre titles as the 'Hanged Man' and 'Death', are of great significance when used for fortune telling.

The standard pack of today, though bearing some resemblance to the ancient Tarot, consists of only 52 cards, divided into four suits, two red and two black: Hearts, Clubs, Diamonds and Spades. The Knight of the Tarot is omitted from the standard pack, leaving only three court cards in each suit. Some packs, those of Spain for example, did not include the Queen as it was thought unseemly to represent a woman in the Devil's Pack Book, as cards were often called. In France, on the other hand, the Queens sometimes exposed their voluptuous breasts, and there were sets of naked ladies to satisfy the tastes of licentious gamblers.

How to Tell Your Fortune

Every card reader has his or her favourite method for laying out the cards. Often two methods are used one after another, if greater clarification is needed or if there are additional questions which require more precise answers. When using the standard pack, it is necessary to start with a simple interpretation of each of the 52 cards and later to gain an understanding of all they mean, by themselves and in different combinations with other cards.

Of course, there are variations in the interpretation of each card but a general consistency is apparent if different authorities are consulted. In addition, every card is given a qualified or extended meaning and a 'dark' or 'light' significance when modified

People of fair complexion and stainless character; a symbol of love from the erotic to the spiritual; aristocrats and clergymen

Dark complexioned and of a frank and open disposition; hard workers and astute businessmen

Medium colouring and of equable temperament: thrifty and dependable, they often succeed as farmers or craftsmen

People of sombre appearance who are born leaders; often soldiers and politicians

by other cards in close proximity. The following, an easy method for beginners to practise, is known as the Wheel of Fortune.

The fortune teller chooses from the standard pack the court card that most resembles the client. In the case of a married woman of fair complexion, the Queen of Hearts would be taken and placed face upwards in the centre of the table, between the reader and the client. Having shuffled the rest of the pack thoroughly so that no 'influences' remain attached to the cards from any previous contact, the fortune teller hands them to the client, instructing her to shuffle them herself and to put her thoughts concerning her hopes and fears, her wishes and questions, into them. She is then asked to cut the cards into three random packs with her left hand – said to be that of the Devil – and to place these face downwards on the table. A good reader may say, 'this is a naughty superstition and you must not believe a word of it', a phrase which in no way deters the client from drinking in every word uttered, but it is to be hoped that it salves the reader's conscience.

The fortune teller then turns each pack face upwards and gains a general indication from the three top cards that are now exposed. Suppose the cards revealed are the King of Clubs, the Seven of Hearts and the Ten of Spades. A brief interpretation might read thus: 'A man, well-placed, powerful and possibly in the Consular Service, is bringing you good luck; I think he has a gift for you. He tells you that you must make your home anew in some far-away place. I think it must be your husband, Madame.'

If the fortune teller receives a positive response from the client, she gathers the three packs together again, reshuffles them and deals 9 packs of 3 cards each, face downwards (see diagram opposite), while saying: 'three above you (1), three below you (2), three behind you (3), three before you (4), three for your house and home (5), three for your hopes and fears (6), three for what you don't expect (7), three for what you do expect (8), and three for what is sure to come to pass (9).'

Under each heading the following indications might be expected as pack by pack is turned face upwards by the reader and each card has its significance revealed:
1 *Above you* This pack represents both the blessings and the evils that are being

Standard

Germanic

Tarot

Other names or possible origins

| Grails, chalices, crystals or mirrors | Batons, sticks or rods of power | Patons, seals, pentacles, 'lots' or precious stones | Arrows, daggers or magical weapons |

THE NUMERALS

	Hearts	Diamonds	Clubs	Spades
1	Love; marriage	An engagement	Conquest	A death
2	Friendship	Trouble	Enterprise	Treachery
3	Pleasure	Social activities	A kind gesture	Separation
4	Change	A legacy	Gaiety	Peace
5	An inheritance	A rendezvous	A lawsuit	A funeral
6	Originality	Forgiveness	Good news	A stroke of luck
7	Good fortune	Money	Success	Prudence
8	Company	Prosperity	Deception	Quarrels
9	A wish	A loss	Anticipation	Suffering
10	Home	Financial gain	Travel	Deprivation

Many people are alarmed when the Ace of Spades, known popularly as the Death Card, appears...

experienced at the present time, 'hanging over one's head'. They will be material, psychological and spiritual.

2 *Below you* Both the good and the bad things that one is responsible for oneself. All that is under control.

3 *Behind you* Joyful and sad times in the past.

4 *Before you* A description of coming events in the near future.

5 *Your house and home* A description of how these are now and how they will be in the future.

6 *Your hopes and fears* These will be described, confirmed or refuted.

7 *What you don't expect* Good or bad news and the turn of events to come.

8 *What you do expect* A clarification of the client's own often vague thoughts and wishes or fears about the future.

9 *What is sure to come to pass* A final and, it is to be hoped, rousing prediction for both the near and the distant future of the client.

To conclude, the fortune teller makes a summary of the whole Wheel of Fortune so that events and the people appearing as these come about are clearly impressed on the client's mind. To clarify further if necessary, or to answer any special questions arising out of the reading, the client may draw three cards at random out of the discard pack which, when placed face upwards, will give the divinatory answer.

Many people are alarmed when the Ace of Spades, known popularly as the Death Card, appears and the fortune teller should take great care to interpret this in a way that will dispel the fears of the client and bring reassurance and hope.

The Greater Trumps

The curiously decorated collection of 78 cards which form the Tarot pack are *the* cards for fortune telling and are said to reveal the hidden mysteries of the universe. Every true adept of the cards should acquire a pack of Tarots, of which there are many different versions, although basically their symbolism is the same. There are several variations in establishing the sequence of the 22 major trumps or Major Arcana and many different symbols have been used. The French Tarot of Marseilles is perhaps the most faithful to the originals, while those depicted by the occultists Oswald Wirth and

KING   A mature, generous man of good position; an aristocrat

QUEEN   A fine woman of noble lineage

KNAVE   A charming but unfaithful young man who brings news

KING   A distinguished and powerful man; possibly a diplomat

QUEEN   A woman of gentle birth and strong character

KNAVE   A dashing young man who is given to extravagance

KING   A man of forceful character; possibly a soldier

QUEEN   A seductive and treacherous woman; a temptress

KNAVE   A serious-minded youth who may prove a formidable opponent

KING   A man of affairs, rich and worldly; often a business tycoon

QUEEN   A rich and beautiful woman, elegant and sophisticated

KNAVE   A gifted young man who will succeed in life

A. E. Waite stress the Rosicrucian, cabalistic, Grail and Cathar aspects.

Adaptations of the Tarot in the last century presented the symbolism in naturalistically engraved pictures, often with a text added to facilitate their reading by the uninitiated fortune teller. Eliphas Levi and other occultists link the Major Arcana with the Hebrew alphabet and Arnold Usshar links them with runic letters.

For the collector, nothing can be more fascinating than to go in search of ancient and modern packs with local variations in shape and design. Those of Naples, Trieste and from as far away as Russia and Mexico are enchanting, while those from Germany and neighbouring countries are hard in design and mechanically crude in printing.

The Tree of Cards

A simple reading, using the Tarot cards, can be made by applying the same interpretation of the numerals and court cards as outlined for the standard pack. The addition of the Chevalier or Knight gives an extra court card for clarifying a prediction.

For a more detailed analysis the fortune teller lays out the cards according to a pattern based on the Tree of Life of the Cabala (see diagram on following page). This reading is performed only once for a general indication, but more comprehensive results are obtained if the process is repeated three times, first for the past, second for the present, and third for the future.

The fortune teller shuffles the full pack well, and after the client has also shuffled, the reader makes ten packs of seven cards each and lays them face downwards in the order shown in the diagram. Proceeding from pack to pack, the cards are turned face upwards and each card read separately, then in conjunction with the other packs, and finally the whole revealed Tree of cards is read as an unfolding 'story' woven into an integrated whole. Each individual pack can be interpreted in the following way: pack 1 relates to that which is divine; pack 2 to fatherhood; pack 3 to motherhood; pack 4 to compassion; pack 5 to strength or conquest; pack 6 to sacrifice; pack 7 to love; pack 8 to the arts and crafts; pack 9 to health; pack 10 to worldly matters.

It will be seen that the packs have the pattern of a tree with a central trunk and two supporting branches. Seen from the reader's

LE MAT.
The Fool
Folly
Everyman
on the
Life-Path

I — **LE BATELEUR.**
The Juggler
or the Magus
A gamble
Choice on the
Life-Path

II — **JUNON.**
Pope Joan or
Juno
Wisdom
Woman, the
mysterious

III — **L'IMPERATRICE.**
The Empress
Action
Woman, the
intuitive

IIII — **L'EMPEREUR.**
The Emperor
Will
Man, the
intelligent

V — **JUPITER.**
The Pope or
Jupiter
Inspiration
Man, the
creative

VI — **L'AMOUREUX.**
The Lovers
Love
The Great
Choice

VII — **LE CHARIOT**
The Chariot
Travel
Providence
guides

VIII — **LA JUSTICE.**
Justice
A decision
'As a man
sows...'

VIIII — **L'ERMITE.**
The Hermit
Sagacity
Hidden
knowledge

X — **LA ROUE DE FORTUNE.**
Wheel of
Fortune
Destiny
The Wheel
of the Law

XI — **LA FORCE.**
Strength
Courage
'Know
thyself'

XII — **LE PENDU.**
The Hanged
Man
Catastrophe
Saint or
sinner?

XIII — **LA MORT.**
Death
Inevitability
The Great
Initiation

XIIII — **TEMPERANCE.**
Temperance
Moderation
The Middle
Path

XV — **LE DIABLE.**
The Devil
Temptation
The Great
Secret

XVI — **LA MAISON DE DIEU**
Tower struck
by lightning
Change
Renunciation

XVII. — **L'ÉTOILE.**
The Star
Hope
Glory of the
Adept

XVIII — **LA LUNE.**
The Moon
Danger
The Great
Portal

XVIIII — **LE SOLEIL.**
The Sun
Happiness
Transcendent
Glory

XX — **LE JUGEMENT.**
The Day of
Judgement
Progress
The final
assessment

XXI — **LE MONDE.**
The World
Gain
Spiritual
attainment

THE TAROT
THE 22 CARDS OF THE MAJOR ARCANA

viewpoint, the central pillar represents Harmony, the left hand branch Discipline and the right hand Love. Furthermore, the packs form three triangles on the Tree: at the top, an upright one, below this two downward pointing ones. The first triangle is that of the Spirit, the second that of Reason and the third that of Intuition. The lowest pack (10) at the foot of the Tree symbolizes the Earth. The discard pack may be used for clarification or for qualifying if necessary. Some study of the Cabala is essential for this method of divination (see CABALA).

Besides the indication obtained from the numerals and court cards of the Minor Arcana, the 22 trumps of the Major Arcana enable the fortune teller to elaborate on the reading. With the Hanged Man, for example,

number 12 of the major trumps, the image is of a youth hanging upside down by one leg from a gibbet. The positive prediction is of self-sacrifice; the negative of treachery.

Among the gypsies, the Master subjects his disciple to a trance-initiation in which the disciple experiences for himself the symbolism of each trump card. In the case of the Hanged Man the experience is of being offered as a human sacrifice, of being tortured and dismembered, of a separation between the astral and the physical body. The 'shade' of the disciple seems to wander, hopelessly lost, in the underworld where he faces the negation 'God is not'. Only if his love for, and faith in, the Master is so strong that he can still, in the darkness, feel identity with him, will he be reborn to live more fully

on the earth above him. In identifying himself with the Master he comes to understand and experience the yearly and continuous death and rebirth of the sacrificed God. In this resurrection, 'God is'.

A Tale of the Tarot
A delightful though improbable story is told about the origin of the Tarot cards. When the civilization of Egypt with its temple libraries of occult lore was about to be destroyed by invading barbarians, the priest-initiates gathered together to discuss how best to preserve their ancient wisdom for posterity. In spite of much head-scratching, no bright idea was forthcoming until one initiate proposed that it should be memorized by the most virtuous and most

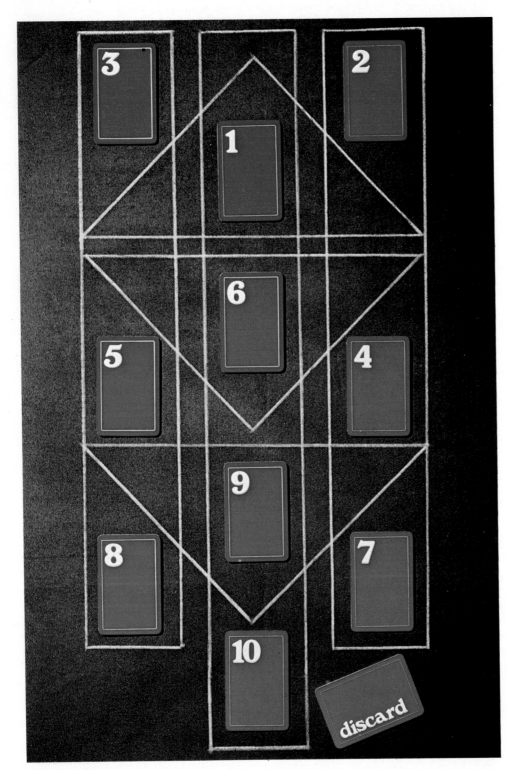

The Seed of the Future

Telling fortunes with the cards can be an amusing pastime. It can also be a deeply serious method of divination and spiritual awakening when practised by one with the gift of far-seeing as well as a profound knowledge of occult symbolism. The daily practice of taking a single card and meditating on it, thus bringing its meaning to life, is one which is highly recommended.

All this inevitably leads us to question the validity of card-reading, to wonder whether there is really 'anything in' the cards, whether messages conveyed by the random fall of shuffled cards can be rationally explained. The devotee of the art naturally has no doubts about this. But it necessitates a belief that there is no random element in anything we do; that the seemingly chance arrangement of cards is, in reality, 'designed' by the unconscious mind of the subject (see FATE).

Belief in clairvoyant powers is also a requirement. Some would attempt to explain these powers as a form of telepathic communication that spans or is outside time and space. The subject's mental processes are transferred to the symbols on the cards, which the reader is able to re-translate or interpret. The stored memories in the subject's unconscious uncover the past, immediate preoccupations give the present. If both the past and the present are made known to the conscious or waking mind, the future will almost inevitably unfold itself.

In other words, the future lies hidden like a seed in the earth, ready to sprout, grow and flower. To the seer, the flower may be known from its seed, the future is the child of the past. The symbols on the cards correspond to the archetypal images, the basic factors which lie deep in the collective unconscious of every man. When these living archetypes 'click' with their counterparts on the cards, they make themselves known by means of the intuition and speak through the lips of the seer. Destiny is in the hands of the archetypes.

(See also DIVINATION; TAROT.)

BASIL IVAN RAKOCZI

FURTHER READING: Papus, *The Tarot of the Bohemians* (Wilshire Book Co.); Brian Innes, *Tarot* (Arco, 1978); Basil Ivan Rakoczi, *The Painted Caravan* (Brucher, London, 1954).

learned among them, and that he should be smuggled out of the land in the hope that he could found a new College of the Mysteries in some more propitious place.

An excellent suggestion, no doubt, but not one initiate present was found worthy of the task. Not one possessed the required memory capacity, nor dared to submit himself to the test of utter virtue. All had been contaminated by the flesh one way or another. The conference was at a standstill, the enemy all but thundering at the gates. 'I have it', an aged priest cried out at last. 'Virtue is all but non-existent in this evil world of ours and certainly is not appreciated by barbarian hordes. Let us appeal to vice, which is forever triumphant among mortal men. Let us hastily inscribe under glyph and symbol upon a pack of easily concealed papyrus cards, our stored wisdom of the ages. We will then confide these cards to any passing rogue or vagabond, explaining that they are to be used for games of chance or hazard, in fact for gambling. Then we will speed him on his way, knowing that he will cheat all he meets by this cunning method and thus, unknowingly, save the wisdom for a more enlightened day.'

A passing gypsy, hoping for a little loot, gleefully pocketed the cards. Down the ages the wisdom travelled, passed from hand to hand, copied from one pack to another, an instrument for gain or loss, to be seen in every tavern of the world to this day. So the wisdom has remained for us to unveil, sheltered by the chicanery of tricksters.

These cults of the Pacific, which attempt to bring ships or aeroplanes loaded with cargo to the natives by magical means, are a reaction to white domination and an attempt to escape it. They are also an attempt to realize a dream

CARGO CULTS

AMONG THE STRANGEST religious manifestations of this century are the so-called cargo cults, which have occurred in great numbers among the native peoples of Melanesia, a group of islands scattered in the Pacific. Even contrasted with other bizarre religions, cargo cults have been regarded as having strange doctrines, odd practices and, most puzzling of all, a remarkable resilience in the face of defeat.

Apocalyptic religions which predict the end of the world and the salvation of only a few do exist in our society, especially in the United States, but they are relatively rare. Their membership is always small compared to the size of the community in which they exist, or the membership of established religions. But historically, such cults are by no means rare and have not always been confined to small minorities.

At the time of the great plagues in the Middle Ages, cults proclaiming that this was the end of the world sprang up, calling for everything to be put aside in an attempt to gain salvation — the method by which this was to be achieved depending upon the cult. Religions preaching that the end of the world is near have also been quite common in Jewish culture, and some scholars claim to have identified as many as 50 such cults about the time of Christ. It has even been argued that Christianity itself was one.

The main features of these cults, which set them apart from more orthodox religions, are: the key role of a leader, prophet or messiah; their simultaneous vision of imminent doom and redemption (apocalypse and millennium); the energy and speed with which the religion grows up and then disintegrates; and the radical nature of the measures imposed by the prophet on those who wish to be saved.

Buying President Johnson

The cargo cults are generally thought to have started, sometime around the 1880s, in Fiji, and since then the pattern has remained roughly the same. Out of nowhere, as it were, a prophet appears and predicts imminent salvation, which may take the form of the islanders' ancestors returning on a ship; a ship that is also loaded with consumer goods like refrigerators, radio sets, desks, furniture, and other items like canned food and even jeeps. The prophet orders various kinds of ritual observances, including such activities as building a warehouse or a jetty (to receive the ship and its goods) or houses for the returning ancestors; the destruction of property or livestock; sexual

Member of a cargo cult sitting by a red cross in the hope of bringing back the Red Cross planes which flew medical supplies to the Pacific islands during the war

abstinence; or throwing money into the sea.

When the day of doom arrives and nothing happens, the prophet may try to slip away, leaving the disillusioned people to return to as normal a life as is possible after what they have done, or he stays and tries to explain what happened, or did not happen. Cultists do not seem to notice that a new cult is very similar indeed to the ones which previously failed.

Although not all these elements are present in any particular cult, there are a number of common factors. There is always at least one prophet, sometimes several. They are usually men, though women do occasionally appear in this role. The description 'cargo cults' also indicates that the idea of ship's cargo — in the sense of western

trading goods as they are known to the Melanesian islanders — is almost universally present. Occasionally the cargo is expected to arrive in an aeroplane, and the natives try to build a primitive airstrip.

In some cults, the participants have tried to use their money to buy President Roosevelt or, more recently President Johnson, presumably because these men symbolize powerful magic, and owning them would transfer this power to the Melanesians. Other cults have rejected white men.

Whatever the details, there is a general pattern to these cults which justifies their classification as a special type of millenarian religion (the 'millennium' being the time of happiness expected to follow the end of the present world). Scholars seem to have taken

some time to realize that belief in imminent redemption is a common feature of human religion, and that cults of this kind are therefore not unique. Originally, it seems, they were interpreted as some kind of collective madness or irrationality. There have been district administrators who have taken the attitude: 'Why don't the natives stop it and pull themselves together?' And indeed, it must have been very puzzling for a colonial official to walk up to a village and find it organized as a crude parody of a European police compound, with the local inhabitants wearing scraps of western costume and checking 'passes', at the village 'gate'. Inside they would be sitting at tables, surrounded by toy imitations of paper and writing equipment.

David Attenborough

Communist Plots?

A more sinister interpretation given to the cults, based purely on the misunderstanding of a phrase ('Masinga Rule', the name of a cult), is that they were some sort of Marxist plot. There are articles in the journal of the civil servants of the Melanesian region which argue that the cargo cults are a cloak for Communist or Marxist penetration, taking the form they do simply in order to bamboozle officials into not recognizing them for what they are. A variant of this theory — this time coming not from conservative colonial officials but from left-wing social scientists — is that the cults are a form of colonial rebellion in religious disguise.

There is certainly more in this than in any of the previous theories and it is true

that in some of the cults there is explicit rejection of, and discontent with, the white power structure. It is clear that some of the prophet leaders were using the only weapon they had to hand, in order to organize the people and canalize their energies against the colonial regime. But one of the bewildering features of these cults is the enormous number of theories which have been advanced in addition to those already mentioned.

Fundamentally, these cults can be explained as attempts to organize social change, made in religious guise. The Melanesians live in fairly simple small-scale societies in relatively fertile areas of the world. There is no population problem and no pressure on the land and game resources. However, for the last 150 years these islands have been

slowly penetrated by traders, colonizers and missionaries. The natives have been used as labourers by the planters and traders, and have been introduced to such consumer goods as clothes, axes, lamps and the like. They have been administered by white officials under laws which bore very little relation to their tribal customs, and in languages which they did not understand. They have been coaxed or pressured into accepting white men's religions.

The most important lesson that the Melanesians have learned from this is that the white men are powerful people who have warehouses full of the most marvellous goods and clothing, which they will give in exchange only for money, not for the goods, and obligations of kinship which govern transactions in native society. White men know how to organize people into police forces and church congregations and sanitary villages. White men claim to know about another world where the ancestors are waiting and where all will be bliss and peace if only their rituals are observed.

What can the native reaction possibly be to all this? Their basic way of life has been disrupted. Some of the functions of their political organization have been usurped by white men, and their system of religion has been challenged by a very powerful one which promises much more than they ever envisaged. There are a number of reactions. They would like to *be* white men. Or they would like white men to be more like them, to join them rather than to rule them. Or they would like to *replace* white men and even reverse roles. Or they would like to take from white men what they have, and drive them out. Now these sound like the slogans of a colonial rebellion, or of Negro rioters in the United States. And indeed, this is where fruitful comparison can be found.

The Only Outlet

But why should the reaction to these feelings be of a religious character? The main reason is that the society in which the Melanesian lives is a traditional one, based mainly on locality and kinship ties. In such a society the roles played by individuals are clearly defined, and there are traditional institutions which are not able to adapt and respond to the new features of the situation. The kinship system is sustained by all kinds of other factors in the society but it begins to give way in the face of wage labour, when people are no longer dependent on relatives for their livelihood or for their next meal. They no longer have to live where they can

Federico Patellani

David Attenborough

Inhabitants of an island in the New Hebrides believe that a white leader, Jon Frum, will arrive bringing 'cargo' in an immense scarlet plane, and will drive the white man from the island with the help of an army which waits for him in the crater of a volcano. Cult rituals involve erecting scarlet crosses and gates *Far left* Shrine with a white-faced figure representing Jon Frum, and an image of the plane that will bring him to the island *Above left* Scarlet cross on a runway built by the cult *Left* Gates and lines of sticks making a magical airstrip on the fields of volcanic ash surrounding the volcano

continually renew their kinship ties. They no longer feel that the pleasure of their elders and of their ancestors is a necessary part of their own good fortune. In other words, the traditional social organization is not very adaptable to the new situation.

The white man has merely superimposed his way of life on native society. He has not taught the Melanesians how to reorganize themselves in order to meet their new problems. The only new organization which he *has* offered to black society is Christianity. The traders do not offer opportunities for the Melanesians to become traders and employers and planters in their own right. The colonial regimes have not, on the whole, done more than bring them into the lowest levels of administration, as village headmen or police auxiliaries.

Secrets of the White Men

The Churches, however, have encouraged participation by the Melanesians, at the highest levels they are capable of reaching, if necessary at the very top. What is more important, they have encouraged the formation of native churches in which no white men participate. The Melanesians have therefore, in a sense, penetrated the secrets of the religious organization of the white man, and have learned more about organization from religion than from any other aspect of white society, economic or political. Therefore it is logical that they should turn to a religious form of organization in order to handle the impact of white society, and

fulfil those expectations which they have been given by its members, but which white society will satisfy only on its own terms.

But this penetration of religion can lead to further frustration, which perhaps explains why so many of the cults have Christian elements. Although the Melanesians have adopted Christianity, they find that the rest of the white man's treasure is not forthcoming. Clearly, he is keeping secret some of his most powerful religious magic, especially the formula for evoking those ships or aeroplanes full of cargo which appear out of the blue. Hence the persistence: if one prophet failed to find the formula, perhaps the next one will.

Cargo cults, therefore, have as their aim the realization of some Melanesian dreams. The people want to come to terms with that white society which is at once promising so much, and exciting them so much, yet wreaking such havoc on their society. This coming to terms can be by incorporation, or absorption, or rebellion, or rejection. The prophets are an example of how political and social leadership can take a religious form.

The cargo cult ideology is, of course, a confused mixture of traditional beliefs, half-understood Christian ideas, and a rather garbled version of what the outside world is really like. More is not to be expected from people whose picture of the world touches ours only at a tangent.

Part of the trouble is that each of these fragmented Melanesian societies has a different language, spoken by perhaps only a

few thousand people. As most of these languages have no written form, communication takes place mainly through the rather inadequate resources of pidgin English, becoming considerably garbled in the process.

The cults have a pretty clear aim. The Melanesians are in a very curious and difficult situation. Their actions in, for example, slaughtering their pigs in order to prepare for the impending millennium may at first seem idiotic. On closer examination, they show just how desperately these people desire fulfilment of their wishes.

I. C. JARVIE

FURTHER READING: For a general work on millennarianism see S. Thrupp, *Millennial Dreams in Action* (Humanities, 1962); for undigested but widely scattered material, see C. Lanternari, *The Religions of the Oppressed* (Knopf, 1963); for a thorough survey of the literature on cargo cults up to 1957, with a Marxist interpretation, see Peter Worsley, *The Trumpet Shall Sound* (Schocken, 1968); for a sensitive treatment of the subject and a close look at one area, see K. O. L. Burridge, *Mambu* (Barnes and Noble, 1960); for a brilliant explanation and interpretation of cults in one area, see Peter Lawrence, *Road Belong Cargo* (Humanities, 1967); for a discussion of the problems that cults raise and the prerequisites of an explanation of them, see I. C. Jarvie, *The Revolution in Anthropology* (Regnery-Gateway, 1969).

Springing from ritual practices that can be traced back to before 3400 BC, ring and chain dances have developed in ways as different as our Christmas carol and the dances of witches

CAROLE

A CAROLE is a circle of dancers holding hands or opening into a linked chain. The word comes from the Greek *choros*, originally used to describe singing and dancing on a circular threshing floor at the antique festival of Dionysus, which afterwards became the circle of the chorus in the Greek theatre. The Ezvones, the crack Greek guards, dance the Kalamatianos, a modern ring and chain, the skirts of their uniforms swirling as they move, while the Trata, the maidens' dance at Megara in Greece, on Easter Tuesday, is an open chain.

But ring and chain dances are known all over the world, and spring from ritual practices in use long before their appearance in Greece. The Greeks themselves sought the origin of the ring and chain in the dance led by Theseus, in imitation of the windings of the labyrinth in which he had slain the

Jacqueline MacKay

Witches at their Sabbaths traditionally performed the ring and chain dance moving to the left, against the sun; angels were believed to dance the carole in heaven. *Left* **Modern witches performing a ring dance** *Right* **Angels dancing in the gardens of Paradise: detail from** *The Last Judgement* **by Fra Angelico**

man-beast, the Minotaur. But the dance existed long before Theseus was thought of.

A Bronze Age vase from the Lac de Bourget in Savoy, shows a chain of four people holding hands. The famous Liria vase of c300 BC shows a chain of four women and three men, all holding hands, led by two pipers. And a chain dance is painted on the famous François vase in the Etrurian Museum, Florence.

Earlier still, archeological finds dated c2600 BC, in Elam (a country in what is now Iran), show women holding hands in a chain, while yet earlier, on a rock drawing in a valley north of Luxor in Egypt, seven girls hold hands in a chain. These are the 'feather head-dress people' who were in Egypt before 3400 BC.

The Dreaded Carmagnole

In present-day Bulgaria the C of *chorus* has been dropped and the Hora circle can embrace a whole village community; in Rumania the Hora is danced as a sign of entry into manhood by the boys, and of readiness for marriage by the girls. It is also a test of character, the circle dissolving instantly if a badly behaved person tries to join it. In Yugoslavia, it may expand to take as many as 500 dancers. Here it has become Kolo, the Wheel. Some variations are danced without music, to the rhythmic thud of feet.

Provence has the Farandole, an open carole, which the Provencals believe was introduced by the Greek colonists when they founded Marseilles, but they do not know

enough of their own history, for the dance can be traced much further back. The Farandole is a carole which is in fact danced all along the Mediterranean coasts of both France and Spain. In Spain the closed ring is called the Sardana and the open chain the Contrapás. The Farandole winds up the French Catalan valleys to the tune called Carmagnole, a tune dreaded in Revolutionary days when the people took their chain dance to Paris. It continued there and on its home ground into the time of Napoleon, when a Bonapartist general was caught and killed in the coils of a Carmagnole-Farandole danced in the streets of Toulon.

In Spain the dance appears in Andorra as the Bal Plá, starting as a closed ring, and finishing in a Farandole which fills the

Giraudon

village square. The carnival season in the French district of Aude ends with a Galop Infernal, an infernal Farandole indeed, rushing through the streets.

The Basque country has the Dantza Khorda, the String dance, the first and last men carrying bouquets as insignia of office. The Spanish Basques over the frontier have their Aurésku, a ceremonial chain dance for festival days, and we find it again in Asturias as Dantza Prima.

Working its way north the carole is found in Switzerland under its early name, Coraule, in the Gruyere country; north again in the Walloon region of Belgium as Coródes, Longue Dance and Cramignon, accompanied by singing, the leader carrying a bouquet as in the Basque country. The carole passes into the Netherlands, again as the Cramignon, where the captain of the Young Men's Society leads the chain in and out of houses and inns, a bouquet in one hand. Further north still the chain wound its way in Danish castles and courts to singing:

There danced the maidens with hair unbound,
It was the King's daughters sang the Round.

Today in the Faroe Islands the islanders begin a ring to enliven long, winter nights, one man singing, more and more joining in, until the ring must break into a chain which develops twists and curves.

Sweden prizes the Long Dance around flaming tar barrels on Easter Eve or around the Midsummer pole. To keep warm, the dancers may continue for hours, the line running from farm to farm. Norway also cherishes the song-dance, often in circular form, and Iceland possesses similar ballad-chains, while Finland carols in long chains and big rings around the Midsummer pole.

The Holly and the Ivy

England has nearly lost the chain but has kept the ring in the various 'church clippings' (as at Painswick), in such country dances as Gathering Peascods and Sellenger's Round, danced on moonlit nights about Maypoles. Both forms have descended to children in various singing games, such as Round the Mulberry Bush or Looby Loo, while In and Out the Windows is a single-file children's version of the celebrated Helston Furry Dance. This form gave rise to the processional 'contra' dance, called 'contry' in the United States and often confused with forms of country dancing.

Country dancing, better known as 'square dancing', recently had a new vogue in America. It descends from the chain dance through intermediate stages such as the Kentuckian 'running sets', performed in squares or circles of four or more couples. Modern square dancing demands an expert caller, who guides the sets of dancers through often complex and intricate chain figures.

The medieval carole was the most popular dance for over three centuries. We hear of it again and again — of holiday makers borrowing finery 'in Carol to go', of noble ladies and gallants, country folk and Church dignitaries, all carolling in castles, on village greens and in cathedrals. Paintings show chains in beautiful gardens, and in heaven, formed by angels who are sometimes welcoming a new soul into the paradise ring. Yet, as always happened when a dance became over-popular, it was censured by the Church and disallowed by the priests who punished the dancers. Carolling was forbidden until Mass was over, for the churchyard was used as a dancing ground. In the 14th century we hear of the accursed dancers of Kolbigk in Germany setting their chain in motion on Christmas morning while Mass was still being celebrated. By some unseen power they were condemned to encircle the church for a year without respite.

From the 16th century onwards dancing gave way to singing in churches, resulting in our present use of the word 'carol' for sung seasonal verse, like our widely popular Christmas carols.

Witches at their sabbaths always enjoyed dancing, and used both ring and chain. The ring was said to have been performed facing outwards and moved widdershins, that is, to the left and against the direction of the sun, therefore adversely influencing the fertility of crops, since witches were thought to do all the harm they could. The chain was led by the chief or priest of the witch coven, who moved off so quickly that there had to be a 'rear man' to beat up the laggards. Those who fell out had to limp home alone.

VIOLET ALFORD

FURTHER READING: V. Alford and R. Gallop, *The Traditional Dance* (Methuen, London, 1935); C. Sachs, *World History of the Dance* (Norton, 1963).

Carthage

City on the North African coast, near modern Tunis, a Phoenician colony which in time became a leading power in the western Mediterranean, until its destruction by the Romans in 146 BC: the Carthaginians sacrificed children to their gods, the most important of whom were Baal Hammon and the fertility goddess Tanit.
See PHOENICIANS.

Layton-Sun

Cartomancy

The art of telling fortunes by Tarot cards or by ordinary playing cards; from Italian *carta*, 'card', and Greek *manteia*, 'divination'.
See CARDS.

CASANOVA

PERHAPS THE GREATEST confidence trickster who ever lived, whose innumerable love affairs have made his name a byword for lechery, Giacomo Casanova was born at Venice in 1725. By turns secretary to a cardinal, soldier, and violinist in an orchestra, in 1755 he was sent to prison, accused of being a Freemason and a magician. He escaped from prison and travelled about Europe, hobnobbing with the great.

Claiming to be an adept of the Cabala and an initiate of the mysteries of the Rosy Cross (see ROSICRUCIANS), Casanova swindled a large number of the credulous rich who believed in his occult powers. To some extent, it seems, he believed in them himself. The most remarkable of his victims was his 'divine madwoman', Mme la Marquise d'Urfé, an aging Parisian widow who wanted to be reborn as a man.

For this purpose it was necessary to find a maiden, who must be the daughter of a Rosicrucian adept and who would be magically impregnated with a male child by Casanova himself. When the child was born, he would be handed over to Mme d'Urfé, who would kiss him on the mouth passing her soul into him with her breath. Her corpse would then be disposed of and Casanova was to look after the little boy, who would contain the spirit of Mme d'Urfe.

The 'maiden' chosen was in fact a whore and despite Casanova's best efforts she failed to conceive. In this emergency, on Casanova's instructions, Mme d'Urfé wrote letters to the moon asking for guidance. The moon's replies, written in silver ink on green paper, appeared from nowhere floating on the water in Mme d'Urfé's bathtub. Eventually the first plan was dropped and Casanova tried to impregnate Mme d'Urfé herself with a male child, without success.

Mme d'Urfé died soon afterwards, from an overdose of an occult remedy called the Panacea. Casanova died in 1798 after writing his memoirs, in which he said that when he thought of his victims he stood astonished at his own moderation.

FURTHER READING: John Masters, *Casanova* (Michael Joseph, 1969).

In Hindu India your behaviour in previous lives determines your social status in this one. The caste system remains an important factor in the life of a modern state

CASTE

CASTE IS A TERM applied to social units which rank in a hierarchic order and within which there is a minimum of social mobility. The word caste appeared first as *casta*, a term by which the Portuguese travellers of the 15th century referred to the divisions of Indian society. Although some modern sociologists speak of 'caste-like' categories, with reference to the rigid sections of societies divided along lines of colour, race or class, caste in the narrow sense of the term is a system that is confined to Indian culture.

Unlike the classes of Western societies and the racial elements of such societies as the United States and South Africa, the Indian castes have their roots in a system of ideas which claims religious sanction for the division of humanity into a number of inherently different groups. This is an essential part of the Hindu outlook and the system of castes is thus a religious as well as a social phenomenon.

It is based on the idea that men are born with different spiritual qualities which result largely from their actions in previous existences, and that the qualities of members of one caste are essentially different

Camera Press London

from those of members of others. Membership of a caste is seen as a spiritual condition which remains unchangeable during a lifetime, though merit or demerit acquired in one life can affect a man's or woman's status in a future rebirth. The idea of reincarnation is inseparable from the religious foundations of the caste system.

In ancient India the caste system in its present complex form had not yet developed, but the social order reflected in the Vedic hymns, the oldest part of the sacred Sanskrit literature, involved a division of society into categories or estates: the so-called *varna* (literally 'colours'). Though this fourfold division of society was to become the framework for the rank-order of castes, it was very different from the castes of modern India. The order of varna consisted of four categories, the highest being that of Brahmins (priests). Below them ranked the Kshatriyas (warriors), next came the Vaisyas (merchants and husbandmen) and the lowest were the Sudras (menial artisans, labourers and servants).

A creation myth contained in a Vedic

The highest ranking groups in ancient India were the Brahmins (priests) and the Kshatriyas (warriors), who were called 'twice-born' because they went through a special initiation ceremony which was regarded as a second birth. Spiritual power was reserved to the priests, political power to the warriors. *Left* **Brahmin outside a temple in southern India** *Below* **Kshatriyas in battle, from the Hindu epic, the** *Mahabharata*

hymn ascribes this division of humanity to the very beginning of the present world-age. Purusha, an original divine being whose immense body filled the whole universe, was sacrificed by the gods in such a manner that the parts of his body transformed themselves into the various elements of the creation: his mouth turned into the first Brahmin, his arms into Kshatriya warriors, and the lower parts of his body into Vaisyas and Sudras.

The Twice-Born

In Vedic times there was still some mobility between these four categories and marriages between Brahmins and Kshatriyas were not unusual. The members of the three higher ranks were described as 'twice-born', because young males of these groups underwent an initiation rite, regarded as a 'second birth', which admitted them to the religious life. The Sudras, the lowest order, were excluded from most ritual activities and they were not allowed to study the sacred Vedic texts.

The system of varna was codified in one of the earliest Indian law books, the code of Manu, which specified the functions of the members of the four categories and regulated relations between them. This codification coincided with a hardening of the divisions of Hindu society and the mobility between the varna disappeared. The differentiation in the rights and duties of the members of the four estates became more pronounced. Manu laid down that all actions should be judged according to the status of the doer, and men of high status were not only accorded many privileges but also had obligations. A higher standard of behaviour was expected from them than from men of low birth, and those of high status who were guilty of certain offences were to be punished more severely than men of lower rank who had committed identical crimes.

The laws of Manu also determined the relations between Brahmins and Kshatriyas, priests and secular rulers. Whereas in ancient times Indian princes had the right to perform religious functions, Kshatriyas were now deprived of all their religious prerogatives, such as the right to conduct sacrifices, and were subordinated to the spiritual power of Brahmin priests (see also BRAHMAN). But the supremacy of the Brahmins' spiritual power was never expressed in the political sphere, and in this the Kshatriyas ruled supreme.

The fourfold division of society into the hierarchically ranked varna extended over the whole of India, and provided a model for the structure of Hindu society. From about 300 BC onwards numerous castes or *jati* developed within the varna framework. These were social groups whose members married only among themselves. This is one of the most characteristic features of the system. Each caste is a closed social group with distinctive customs and ritual practices, strict dietary rules and occupational preferences. From birth the individual is provided with a fixed social milieu, from which no vicissitude of fate can remove him, unless he violates the rules of his caste to such a degree that he is either temporarily or permanently excommunicated or 'outcasted'. His caste determines his choice of partner in marriage, and frequently his occupation, acts as his trade union and prescribes his religious practices. Most castes are subdivided, and it is within the local sub-caste that a man or woman generally finds most social contacts.

While each caste and sub-caste is a largely self-contained unit, there is a pronounced interdependence of castes, which render each other numerous services in both the religious and economic spheres. For instance, Brahmins act as family priests for all individuals belonging to the twice-born castes, while members of many lower castes have their prescribed roles in the ritual practices of a village community. Economically, because of the occupational specialization of castes in traditional Indian society, no one group can dispense with the services of the other social groups.

The Pure and the Impure

But despite this interdependence, there are strict rules limiting the relations between members of castes of different status. Basic to the system is the belief in the unequal degree of ritual purity attaching to the various groups. Hindus hold that certain types of contact, such as eating with a member of a lower caste or even accepting water from his hands, defiles a man of higher status and the avoidance of such polluting contacts and the maintenance of ritual purity is a constant preoccupation with Indians of high caste. Many occasions expose a man or woman to pollution.

There is, in addition, the underlying belief that impurity prevails over purity. While the purity of persons of high caste is diminished by contact with members of the lower groups, the latter do not enhance their purity if they are touched by a high-caste person.

Conformity to every detail of the rules which regulate the conduct of caste-members is considered the supreme virtue in a Hindu. A violation of the rules, even if committed accidentally, may result in dire consequences. Thus a Brahmin who unknowingly partakes of the food cooked by a person of low status loses his ritual purity and with it his own caste status.

Hindu society sees the individual not so much as an independent agent, guided in his conduct by the promptings of his own conscience, but as the member of a tightly organized community whose actions affect not only his own status but also that of those closest to him. For an individual's wrong conduct can cause a chain reaction. By incurring pollution, a man in turn pollutes the innocent members of his household, and may affect even kinsmen and friends who, ignorant of his lowered ritual status, accept food prepared in his house. Because the pollution that results from certain offences against caste rules is automatic and contagious, no group can afford to permit freedom to the individual in the regulation of his life.

Caste members are therefore critical of deviations from the narrow path of orthodox behaviour on the part of other individuals in the group, and even close kinsmen will disown a family member who has lost status by contact with a person of lower caste. The breach of a rule, such as the taboo on the eating of certain types of meat, or the ban on sexual congress with lower caste partners, is regarded as a social offence as well as a sin.

The Untouchables

Actions permissible for members of one caste are wrong for those of another, and instead of a universally applicable moral code there are as many different standards of behaviour as there are castes.

The lowest castes, including artisans doing polluting work such as tanning, leather working and scavenging, are everywhere regarded as 'untouchable', and bodily contact or even proximity to them pollutes members of clean castes. Though public discrimination against untouchables is now illegal, they still form an under-privileged class, which in many parts of India comprises a large percentage of the population.

Castes and sub-castes have elaborate organizations with caste councils and caste headmen, and these exert a considerable degree of discipline over the members. The importance of this system in the social structure of India can hardly be exaggerated: the overwhelming majority of the Hindu population takes the hierarchy of castes for granted, and considers it part of a world order closely integrated with orthodox Hindu religion.

Religious reformers through the ages have attempted to abolish these social distinctions, but they have had no lasting effect, and sects which preached the equality of man ended up as closed groups similar to castes — and are now regarded as such by the rest of Hindu society. However, although the caste system has made for a static and conservative society, it has at the same time facilitated the integration of many groups of different origin, each of which has retained many of its social and religious practices and traditions. In this way the cultural independence of small groups has been respected even though they are incorporated into the greater Indian society.

Throughout the centuries the system of castes has provided a basis, and an ideological justification, for the coexistence of different ethnic and cultural groups as well as for the mutual tolerance of a great number of communities with distinct religious and social customs.

Despite official attempts to create an egalitarian society in which caste privileges have no legally recognized place, the continued persistence of castes as distinct social units within Indian society can be predicted with a high degree of probability. In recent years the religious aspects of the system have somewhat receded into the background, but the castes have gained a new function as political pressure groups, whose cohesion and strength are rooted in the traditional solidarity of their members. Thus an ancient social order, derived originally from mythological and religious concepts, survives in a changed form in the public life of a modern state.

CHRISTOPH VON FÜRER-HAIMENDORF

CAT

Worshipped as a goddess or feared as an agent of the Devil, sacrificed to evil spirits or cherished for its powers of healing – the fortunes of the cat have fluctuated throughout history

DURING THE THOUSANDS of years in which the cat has lived among human beings it has been venerated at one period as a deity, and at other times cursed as a demon. In parts of ancient Egypt where the cat was regarded as sacred to the cat-headed goddess Bast, spiritual ruler of the city of Bubastis (now Tell Basta) to the east of the Nile Delta, to kill one might be punishable by death. Diodorus Siculus, the Greek historian, described how a Roman who committed this crime was murdered by a mob despite the pleadings of high Egyptian officials. If a cat died, from any cause whatever, its owner went into mourning, shaving his eyebrows and performing elaborate funeral rites. Cat cemeteries were established on the banks of the Nile, where the sacred animals were mummified and then laid to rest, together with vast quantities of cat mascots and bronze cat effigies.

The cat was invested with this aura of holiness elsewhere in the ancient world. The Roman goddess Diana sometimes assumed the shape of a cat, and the chariot

The cat is traditionally connected with the moon, which waxes and wanes and disappears from the sky like Lewis Carroll's Cheshire Cat in *Alice in Wonderland*, which slowly appears and vanishes again, leaving behind a smile that eventually disappears too

of Freyja, the Scandinavian fertility goddess, was drawn by cats. This reverence was due not so much to the animal's importance as the guardian of the granaries against mice (as in ancient Egypt) or to its role as the traditional enemy of the serpent, but to the beauty of its eyes which were strangely reminiscent of the moon.

In her *Cult of the Cat*, Patricia Dale-Green says, 'Like the moon it (the cat) comes to life at night, escaping from humanity and wandering over the housetops with its eyes beaming out through the darkness.' Many people believed the cat was the child of the moon and it was said that 'the moon brought forth the cat'. This curious link has been regarded as due to 'the changeableness of the pupils of the eye, which in the daytime is a mere narrow line, dilatable at night to a luminous globe.' From the magic of their eyes arose the belief that cats were seers with strong mediumistic powers. In the East the cat is said to bear away the souls of the dead, and in some parts of West Africa Negroes accept that the human soul passes into the body of a cat at death.

An Italian legend tells of a cat that gave birth to her kittens beneath the very manger in which Christ was born. But the cat was not destined to be venerated in Christian Europe, for the Church with its violent repudiation of paganism succeeded in reducing the status of this once sacred animal to that of a devil.

The gods of one religion almost invariably become the devils of the next but there has

Isobel Grierson was sent to the stake after evidence had been given that she entered the house of Adam Clark at Prestonpans in the likeness of a cat

rarely been so dramatic a fall from grace as that of the once holy cat. During the persecution of the heretical sect of the Cathars the belief was fostered that these heretics had worshipped the Devil in feline form, and the stage was set for the cat's unwitting participation in the witchcraft tragedy.

In the Middle Ages the English scholar Gervase of Tilbury stated a popular belief when he wrote, '. . . women have been seen and wounded in the shape of cats by persons who were secretly on the watch and . . . the next day the women have shown wounds and loss of limbs.' In 1718, towards the end of the witchcraft mania in the British Isles, William Montgomery of Caithness, driven berserk by a vast crowd of cats which gossiped outside his house in human language, attacked them, hatchet in hand, killing two and wounding others. On the following day, two old women were found dead in bed while another had an unexplained gash in her leg, proof positive that they had changed shape during the night. Earlier, in 1607, also in Scotland, there was the classic case of Isobel Grierson, who was sent to the stake after evidence had been given that she entered the house of Adam Clark at Prestonpans in the likeness of a cat, accompanied by other cats.

The Fear of Cats

Jane Wenham, the last person to be tried for witchcraft in England, was accused of assuming the form of a cat to terrify her victims. At the height of the witchcraft delusion it was generally assumed that a witch could take the shape of a cat only nine times, presumably because of the belief that a cat had nine lives.

More often, cats were given the comparatively minor role of witches' familiars. The villain of one of the first important trials of English witches, in 1566, was a white spotted cat called Sathan, which fed on its mistress's blood. The cruelties inflicted upon a cat caught in the mesh of witchcraft could

Facing page Satan incarnate : in medieval times a black cat was widely believed to be an embodiment of the Devil *Right* The cat was sacred to the Egyptian goddess Bast. Cemeteries containing the bodies of mummified sacred cats have been discovered with bronze statues of cats, like this one which is dated to c 600 BC

be dreadful, for the wretched animal was likely to be burned alive, both in England and on the Continent.

Some people have an intense fear of cats, and in the 17th century Increase Mather, the celebrated New England Puritan divine, observed, 'There are some who, if a cat accidentally comes into a room, though they neither see of it nor are told of it will presently be in a sweat and ready to die away.' It was generally assumed that if a cat was allowed near a corpse it would steal the soul, and the dead person would then become a

vampire. Vampire cats were common in Japan, but were easily recognizable as they had two tails.

One superstition, hardly extinct today, held that cats crept into the cradle to suck the breath of young babies. Nursemaids stood permanent guard against these attacks.

In parts of Europe where many of the old pagan ceremonies were preserved relatively unchanged, a cat often personified the spirit of the corn. At Briançon in France a cat ceremonially garbed in ribbons, flowers and corn ears presided at the harvest, while near Amiens one of these animals was ritually killed when the last sheaves of corn were cut. It was customary to roast cats alive to drive away evil spirits at the European Easter and Shrove Tuesday fire ceremonies. In the English Guy Fawkes celebrations sacks of living cats were placed on the bonfires.

Cat sacrifice in modified form continued into comparatively modern times, usually to protect a building against fire. Less than ten years ago the mummified bodies of a cat and her kittens were found plastered into a cottage wall at Cricksea in Essex, and are now on exhibition at a local museum.

Until the close of the 18th century black cats were burned alive in the Highlands of Scotland, in a ceremony called Taigheirin, to secure from the gods the gift of second sight; and the Irish Hellfire Club is said to have celebrated one of its orgies by igniting a huge tomcat.

Almost as unfortunate was any kitten born in the month of May. Rarely a good hunter, it would bring home glow-worms and snakes instead of mice and, because of this, was usually drowned. Needless to say its 'melancholy disposition' made it easily recognizable.

Lore of the Black Cat

Legendary lore has had a particularly dramatic influence on feline fortunes. In Britain the 'blackberry' cat's reputation for devilment and mischief is due solely to the fact that it is born at the end of the blackberry season, this being the time of year when, according to an old tradition, Satan was thrown out of heaven into a blackberry bush (which he then defiled with his urine and spittle).

The sins of the blackberry cat pale into insignificance when compared with those of

Michael Busselle

William MacQuitty

419

Cats have always aroused strong human emotions, some people adoring them and others detesting them. Both reactions appear in folklore and nursery rhymes, where the cat may play an attractive role, as in 'Puss in Boots' or 'The Cat and the Fiddle' (*below*): or it may be a creature of evil and the companion of witches (*right*). One of the witches executed at Lincoln in 1618 said that she saw her mother's familiar spirit, 'the cat Rutterkin, leap on her shoulder and suck her neck.' Three other witches who were involved are shown (*bottom*) with their familiars, a kitten, an owl, a mouse and a dog

Radio Times Hulton Picture Library

Radio Times Hulton Picture Library

Mansell Collection

the black cat which, in the United States and most of Europe is regarded as the embodiment of the Devil himself. In Britain, it is the white cat who plays this role. The brindled cat was notorious in England as the familiar of the witch, hence the witches' cry in *Macbeth*, 'Thrice the brinded cat hath mewed', while the black cat, generally speaking, symbolizes magic minus malice.

Even today cat lore, particularly the correct approach to the black variety, is extremely complicated. The black cat should be gently stroked along the spine and never chased away, or it will take the luck of the home with it. To come across such an animal out of doors is highly favourable in most parts of Britain, but in Yorkshire as in the United States it is unlucky; at the

same time it is lucky to own a black cat. Many Americans believe it is unlucky if the cat crosses their path from left to right.

One supernatural skill attributed to these animals is their ability to forecast the weather. When cats scamper wildly it means wind; when they wash their ears, rain; and when they sit with their backs to the fire, frost or storms. The Indonesians believe that it is possible to produce rain by pouring water over a cat.

Observers in the past have tried to rationalize the weather-forecasting element in the feline make-up. An early attempt suggested that 'the moisture which is in the air before the rain, insinuating itself into the fur of this animal, moves her to smooth the same and cover the body with it so that she

may feel less the inconvenience of Winter, as on the contrary she opens her fur in Summer that she may better receive the refreshing of the moist season.'

The cat has always been credited with that most important function of divinity, the art of healing. The instrument for this is its tail which will cure a 'queff' or stye, if drawn downwards over the eye, while the following charm is recited:

I poke thee. I don't poke thee.
　I poke the queff that's under the eye.
　O qualyway, O qualyway.

'Tail cure' is equally effective in the treatment of warts, whitloes and the itch. Cat-skin properly dried and applied to the face is believed to relieve toothache, and in the

Cat and Mouse

Cats and mice are often associated in legends concerned with the beginning of the world. According to one legend, not only did rodents precede cats but their existence was the reason for the cat's creation. At the time of the Flood, we are told, there were no cats. Noah (showing, one would have thought, extraordinary lack of foresight) took pairs of rats and mice into the Ark, with the result that it was soon over-run with vermin. Noah asked the lion, as king of the beasts, to do something about the situation. The lion sneezed, and from his nostrils appeared a pair of cats, which soon reduced the rodent population.

It has also been said that God created the cat, but that the mouse was Satan's creation; and the Devil's mouse did its best to destroy life once and for all by nibbling a hole in Noah's Ark. Fortunately it was caught by God's cat, and the hole was closed by a frog who crept into it.

Patricia Dale-Green *Cult of the Cat*

17th century a whole cat boiled in olive oil was thought to make a first-class dressing for wounds. If a disease resisted ordinary methods of treatment it was at one time customary to transfer it to the family cat, by dousing the animal with the patient's washing water and driving it from the house. When any member of the family was ill, the cat's every movement might be scrutinized for signs and portents. Its leaving home was an omen of death, and if the sick person dreamed of cats or a cat fight it was a sign that death was near.

It was noticed that cats were extremely sensitive to the presence of an unburied body in the house, and that they left home immediately someone died, returning only after the funeral. A cat that stood its ground but was caught leaping over the coffin was always killed at once, as such behaviour was thought to bode ill for the prospects of the departed in the hereafter.

Prophetic Sneezes

When signs of sickness first showed themselves in the family cat, its every sneeze was awaited with the keenest interest. A single sneeze, near a bride on her wedding morning, forecast a happy marriage, but on other occasions it might portend rain. Three sneezes in succession were a warning that the whole household would go down with colds in the near future.

It was a rule in many households that a sick or dying cat be put out of the house, to prevent death from spreading through the family. When moving house in the north-east of England it was traditional to abandon the family cat in order to preserve the luck.

Seamen were invariably kind to a cat, believing that it brought luck to any ship it boarded. In addition cats were infallible weather guides and were thought to be invaluable when a ship was becalmed, as a wind could be raised by placing a cat under a pot on the deck. To throw a cat overboard, particularly if it were black and without a single white hair, was unthinkable since this could cause a storm.

Actors also welcome cats, regarding their presence as a good omen, and they believe that kicking a cat causes the worst possible luck. But if a cat runs across the stage during a performance, it is thought to be an extremely ominous sign.

A great many cat superstitions and fears have survived in the United States. The lore of the Old South tends to see the cat as a devil, a witch, a witch's imp – but at the same time its whiskers were often used in 'conjure' magic and charms. Southern belief also says that if you kick a cat you will get rheumatism, and if you drown a cat the Devil will get you. Yet a broth made from boiling a black cat was believed to cure consumption. The attitudes in lore from the North were equally complicated. The New Englander long believed that he could tell time from a cat's eyes, for the pupils supposedly contracted at low tide, dilated at high tide. Pennsylvanians boiled black cats to keep the Devil at bay; Ozarkians, afraid to kill a cat, might chop off its paw and throw it out of the house.

Cats have played altogether happier roles in fairy tales. We are indebted to Aesop and others for the fable in which the mice solemnly debated who was to bell the cat, and for centuries children in northern Europe have listened with delight to the remarkable tale of Dildrum the cat who flew up the chimney to become King of Catland; while Puss in Boots has long been a national institution.

In the story of Puss in Boots, which has several European versions, the hero is usually a young man whose only inheritance is a cat. This cat, however, is really a prince who has been bewitched. A creature of marvellous ingenuity, the cat convinces the king that his master is a wealthy nobleman, provides the young man with great estates and splendid clothes, and wins him a beautiful princess, the king's daughter, for a wife. When asked what it wants for a reward, the cat insists on having its head cut off and when this is reluctantly done, the bewitched prince is restored to his normal human form.

In modern times although the cat has not yet recovered its lost status as a goddess, there have been other compensations. Television stardom has come its way and it would sometimes appear that the entire economic life of the nation is geared to the production of its food. Yet, quite unspoiled, the cat remains serene, civilized, god-like and utterly mysterious.

ERIC MAPLE

FURTHER READING: Patricia Dale-Green, *Cult of the Cat* (Houghton, Mifflin, 1963).

Catacombs

Large underground burying places, used by the early Christians: the fact that many martyrs were buried in them made them popular with Christians who wanted to rest near the martyrs: the most famous are those in Rome, which consist of an extensive network of narrow passages with shelves cut in the walls on which the bodies were placed; there are also small rooms for family burials and larger ones in which services were held.

Caterpillar

Larva of a butterfly or moth, in Europe often believed to be created by the Devil or by witches with the Devil's assistance; in parts of the United States the appearance of a black one is a sign of a hard winter ahead; in England carrying a caterpillar about with you is supposed to ward off fevers.

The attempt to suppress these heretics, who believed in chastity, poverty and simple piety, led to the founding of the Inquisition and the first crusade ever to be fought inside Europe

CATHARS

THE CATHARS, also known as the Albigenses (from the town of Albi, north-east of Toulouse), were a powerful religious sect which flourished in the 12th and 13th centuries, chiefly in southern France and northern Italy. In their own eyes, they were the only true Christians, and nearer than the Roman Catholic Church to the tradition of the early Christians, both in the life of chastity, poverty and simple piety which they lived and preached, and in their organization and ritual. But their theology, based on a dualistic belief in an evil principle in the universe which limited God's power, was heretical; and the fact that they were well organized, and that their zealous missionaries gained many converts posed a serious threat to the Church of Rome, whose authority and sacraments they rejected and whose hierarchy they condemned.

For more than 50 years the Roman Church tolerated Catharism, which first appeared in western Europe about the year 1140. During these years, Catharism spread so rapidly that divisions and differences developed inside the movement itself. But by the turn of the century the Church felt compelled to act against the heresy, and in 1208 Pope Innocent III declared a Crusade against the Cathars, which led to a merciless war lasting 20 years.

After the Treaty of Meaux in 1229, which ended the war, the Cathars carried on an underground struggle against the Inquisition, which was instituted by Pope Gregory IX for the express purpose of rooting out the heresy (see HERESY). The massacre of some 200 Cathars at Montségur in the Pyrenees in 1244 was a disaster from which the movement never recovered.

From Eastern Roots

The origins of Catharism lie in the old beliefs of Gnosticism and Manicheism, which grew up outside Europe, and the heresy reached France and Italy from the Balkans and Asia Minor. Their name, derived from the Greek word for 'pure', shows that the contemporaries of the Cathars regarded them as in some way connected with the Eastern Orthodox branch of Christianity. Their fundamental dualism, as well as many points of detail in their practices and beliefs, prove that the Cathars were originally a western offshoot of the Bogomils (see BOGOMILS).

Between the 4th and the 10th centuries, the Western Church had been free from any serious heretical movements but in the 11th century, with the revival of trade, signs of religious agitation began to appear.

In the 12th century this religious ferment gathered force and, as one authority on medieval Europe puts it, 'Europe was swarming with hermits, wandering preachers and foot-loose monks.' The mood of the age

was favourable to Catharism but the specific factors behind its rapid spread are uncertain. The eastern doctrines on which it was based probably filtered in from the East at first along the trade routes, so that it may have reached Lombardy in northern Italy first, and from there penetrated France and the Rhineland. This process was probably hastened by the persecution of the Bogomils in Constantinople in 1110 and 1140.

Already by this time we hear that in the south-west of France the Cathars were so well established that the Roman Catholic churches were empty. The Cathars were now apparently an organized Church with their own hierarchy, ritual and system of doctrine. By 1149 they had their first bishop in the north of France. In 1167 the Bogomil

Bishop Nicetas came from Constantinople to visit Lombardy and southern France. He summoned a Council of Cathar bishops and ministers at St Felix de Caraman, near Toulouse, apparently to assert the true Bogomil faith and to establish new bishoprics. By the end of the 12th century no less

Below Long and rigorous training prepared the 'perfect', the initiates who formed the elite of the Cathar sect, to suffer torture and death rather than betray their faith: two condemned Cathars awaiting execution, from a painting by P. Berruguete *Right* St Dominic, who preached with great fervour against the Cathars, watches the burning of heretical books: 'good' books rise, untouched, from the fire. Painting by P. Berruguete

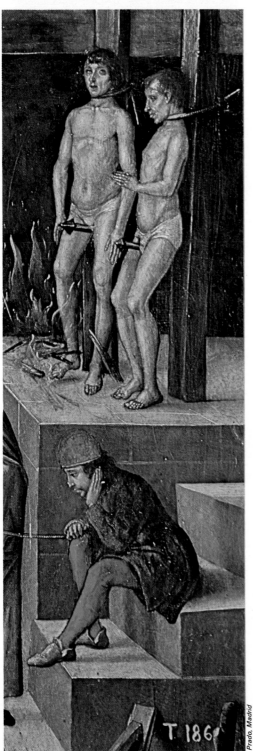

than 11 Cathar bishoprics had been established, five in France and six in Italy.

The Cathars were not confined to France and Italy. By c 1150 they were established in Germany, particularly around Cologne, and in 1162 a German-led Cathar mission arrived in England. They were branded on the forehead and expelled from the country.

The Monster of Chaos

The Cathar philosophy was based on dualism, the belief that two opposed powers or principles are active in the universe. Most of the Cathars seem to have regarded the evil principle as weaker, or somehow less real, than the good. Yet the good principle, or God, was not all-powerful. He suffered the hostility of an evil power which he had not himself created or willed, and his power was limited in other ways. 'Without doubt, God cannot lie,' said Jean de Lugio, a leading Cathar apologist, when challenged to give an example of something that God cannot do.

The evil being, which was sometimes known as the Monster of Chaos, in some way partook of the nature of man, fish, bird and beast. But at the same time, it was a spirit 'which had no beginning'. The being had various physical forms: matter, chaos, darkness, Lucifer and Satan. According to the usual Cathar view, Satan had created the material world and the flesh, and man's task was to liberate his spirit, the good part of him, from its material envelope. The material world would eventually pass away altogether. God's creation of celestial and eternal things was contrasted with Satan's creation of what was material and transitory. The evil principle, however, was eternal — only its effects would perish in time.

Christ as a Phantom

The Cathar teaching about Christ has survived mainly in its negative aspects. Christ appeared in our world merely as a phantom. His mission was to teach the doctrine of salvation set out in the gospels and to warn mankind that the god of the Old Testament was really a demon who had created the material world.

Christ's true mission, however, had been accomplished elsewhere, in 'superior worlds', and his crucifixion in this world was fictitious. Some Cathars said that the crucifixion was an image of torture inflicted in another world on the demon who had created the world. The Cathars condemned the cult of the cross and, like the Bogomils, maintained that the cross had been made of the wood of the tree of knowledge of good and evil in the Garden of Eden. The Cathars were accused of denying that Christ was the son of the Virgin Mary, and in the eyes of their contemporaries the most scandalous part of their doctrine was the denial that the human body is resurrected after death.

There were two classes of Cathars, the 'perfect' (*Perfecti*) also known as 'bons-hommes' or 'ancients', and the 'believers'. The 'perfect' formed the hierarchy of the Cathar Church, and the 'believers' were the rank and file. The 'perfect' underwent a long and rigorous initiation which culminated in a religious ceremony, the *consolamentum*, which was the Cathar equivalent of the Christian baptism, confirmation and ordination of a priest, all rolled into one.

The consolamentum was conducted before a large audience in a room which had a table in the middle, spread with a spotless white cloth, on which lay a copy of the New Testament. A Cathar 'ancient' addressed the candidate in a series of special formulas. The candidate confessed his sins and renounced this world and its works, ending with a solemn promise to give himself to God and to the gospel, never to lie or swear an oath, never again to touch a woman, to eat only vegetables and fish, and never to travel or pass the night or take food without a companion of the same sex.

The training the 'perfect' received prepared them to endure torture rather than betray their faith, and history shows that many of them went willingly to atrocious deaths. Their enemies accused them of being favourably disposed towards suicide.

Not every Cathar felt able to take the vows of sexual abstinence and extreme asceticism that were required of the 'perfect', and many waited until they were on their death-beds before receiving the consolamentum, which then took the place of the Christian rite of extreme unction. There were, however, other religious ceremonies, such as the *apparelliamentum*, a monthly public confession of sins before one of the 'perfect', and simple services at which the Lord's Prayer was recited and hymns sung.

Although the austere renunciation of the material world, and particularly of meat, wine and sexual intercourse, was a way of life to which only a minority could commit themselves, the Cathar faith was evidently one which exercised a great fascination on the men and women of the time.

It took more than a century of war and persecution after Pope Innocent III declared a crusade against the Cathars to put the heresy down. Nor did the Cathars disappear without trace. Apart from the fact that the Albigensian Crusade altered the course of French history, and that the Inquisition left a permanent mark in the consciousness of southern Europe, later religious movements have been influenced by Catharism, and as late as the Second World War there was a neo-Catharist sect in Toulouse.
(See also BLACK MASS; SABBATH.)

DAVID PHILLIPS

The Albigensian Crusade

By the 12th century the troubadour culture of poetry and song, come from no one knows where, flourished among the aristocracy of southern France. By its side flourished the austere Cathar faith often practised by the aristocrats themselves.

In 1174 the Cistercian St Bernard preached against the Cathars in Toulouse, and their bons-hommes were forced to leave the city; but not for long. In 1204 Pope Innocent III told the King of France that Count Raymond VI of Toulouse must be deposed and a good Catholic installed in his stead, but Philip Augustus of France took no action. The next year a monk, Dominic Guzman of Caluérega, assailed the heretics in a new missionary style. Like the Cathar

Perfecti, he went barefoot and simply dressed to preach to the masses.

The Pope appointed officials called Legates to Languedoc, that part of southern France lying to the west of the Rhône and to the east of the Bordeaux country. In 1207 they asked Count Raymond to join a league of southern barons, pledged to hunt down the heretics. When he refused, he was excommunicated and it was announced that whoever killed the Count would earn a blessing. On 15 January 1208, one of Raymond's squires assassinated the Papal Legate Peter of Castelnau at St Gilles on the banks of the Rhône.

For two days the Pope could not speak for rage. On 10 March 1208 he called for a crusade against the heretics who were 'worse than the very Saracen'.

The King of France refused to engage himself. But many knights of northern France were attracted by this novel crusade, the first inside Europe. In the statutory 40 days of crusading they could gain salvation without crossing the seas; their sins would be remitted and the goods of the heretics would be at their disposal.

So in the spring of 1209, some 20,000 knights with a huge band of foot soldiers, including the dreaded *routiers* or mercenaries, came down the Rhône and assembled at Lyons, whence the crusade set forth on 24 June, St John's Day. Raymond VI, an adroit opportunist, did penance at St Gilles barefoot and in his shirt, then hastened to join the crusade at Valence. He hoped not only to save his own lands but also to rid himself of Roger Trencavel, a powerful rival. Trencavel met the crusade at Montpellier and offered to make submission. This refused, he left for Carcassonne through Béziers, taking with him to apparent safety Bézier's best-known heretics and Jews.

The crusaders, moving south, invested Béziers on 21 July and prepared for a long siege. But after an ill-advised sally by the defenders the city fell into their hands next day. Over 20,000 people were massacred, including all who had taken refuge in the Church of the Madeleine. It is said that when the Papal Legate, Arnald-Amalric of Cîteaux, was asked how heretics should be distinguished from true believers, he replied, 'Kill them all. God will look after his own.'

Terrorized, cities and towns surrendered to the advancing crusaders. Only Carcassonne where they arrived on 1 August, prepared to hold out. Under safe-conduct Trencavel went to the crusader camp to negotiate, and against all honourable usage was taken prisoner; he died in captivity soon after. Bereft of its lord, Carcassonne surrendered after only 15 days' siege to the most determined and brutal of the invaders, Simon de Montfort (father of the Simon de Montfort famous in English history).

Because the Cathars renounced the Roman Catholic Church and their Catholic baptism, the sect was believed to be in league with the Devil, and was accused of encouraging debauchery and unnatural vice: illustration of Cathar atrocities, from Collin de Plancy's Dictionnaire Infernal

Prudently refused by greater northern lords, the Trencavel lands were assigned to Montfort. By September the 40 official days of crusading were over and most of the knights went home. But Montfort stayed in Languedoc and began a ruthless pursuit of the bons-hommes, who at first retreated to hill fortresses in the Minervois and Corbières regions. They held out for months during the burning summer of 1210, but were eventually forced to surrender for lack of food and water. When they did, those who refused to recant perished in huge bonfires.

Massacre at Montségur

Montfort's ambitions grew. He sought to be Count of Toulouse. The crusade had become a defensive war of south against north, with King Pedro II of Aragon and the Count of Foix rallying to Raymond of Toulouse. But in 1213 Pedro was killed at the battle of Muret, a decisive victory for Montfort. Raymond was excommunicated again. The Council of Montpellier awarded Toulouse to Montfort, and in May 1215 the city fell into his hands. Its walls were razed and its treasures plundered. Montfort's greed and brutality appalled even the Pope.

In April 1216 Raymond VI and his son returned to Languedoc from exile and were welcomed as liberators. Raymond retook Toulouse and massacred the French garrison. Montfort besieged the city for nine months, then was killed by a stone fired — it is said by women — from inside the walls.

But the triumph was short-lived. In 1222 Raymond VI died. In 1226 the Council of Bourges excommunicated his successor, Raymond VII, who had won back Simon de Montfort's conquests from Montfort's son Amaury. Amaury ceded his rights to the King of France and a new crusading army under Louis VIII came down the Rhône and retook all Languedoc except Toulouse. The country was systematically ravaged. Raymond VII yielded in 1229, and promised to rid the country of heretics and to marry his young daughter to the King of France's brother. When she died without children, in 1271, Languedoc, a ruined country with its fine civilization destroyed, was formally attached to the Crown of France.

Meanwhile, the extirpation of the Cathars had continued. The Order of Preaching Friars founded by Dominic Guzman had been entrusted with the work of the Inquisition in Languedoc, and terrorized the population. The last open resistance of the Cathars was at Montségur, their holy fortress on a hill where, between 1243 and 1244, they held out for ten months. When at last they surrendered, enormous pyres surrounded by palisades consumed the 200 Perfecti who refused to renounce their faith. Legend has it that their treasure of gold and holy books still lies hidden at Montségur.

MARGHANITA LASKI

FURTHER READING: F. Heer, *The Medieval World: Europe 1100–1350* (NAL, 1964); J. Sumption, *Albigensian Crusade* (Merrimack Bk. Serv., 1978); S. Runciman, *The Medieval Manichee* (Cambridge Univ. Press, 1947); Z. Oldenbourg, *Massacre at Montségur* (Funk and Wagnall, 1968).

St Catherine of Siena was notorious for the trances into which she repeatedly fell, at one time appearing to be dead for four hours. She believed that she had mystically married Christ and mystically died with him

ST CATHERINE

BORN ON 25 MARCH 1347, Catherine of Siena was the 23rd child of a dyer named Jacomo Benincasa. A mystic who showed all the signs of religious fanaticism, she was driven by her convictions to attempt to change the pattern of European history.

In the 14th century, religion and politics were inextricably entangled, and the Pope was nominal ruler of the Western world. Although rising nationalism had not yet broken the unity of Christendom, there was almost always fighting somewhere between Christian states. In this situation, a religious fanatic was able to exert a powerful influence on events.

At the time of Catherine's birth, the Pope ruled from Avignon in France, and French influence was supreme in the Church. Rome and the Papal States were in ruins. Led mainly by Florence, the cities of Tuscany, including Siena, maintained a precarious independence. Throughout Catherine's short life, the four scourges of mankind — war, famine, plague and heresy — constantly threatened life, and frequently took it.

Catherine's biographer, Raimondo of Capua, tells us that at the age of five she was already extremely devout, and that at about that time she had her first vision, in which she saw Christ enthroned above St Dominic's Church in Siena, attended by Sts Peter, Paul and John the Evangelist. When she was seven or so, she decided to become a hermit, but heavenly voices counselled against this. By the time she was 12, Catherine had considered and rejected marriage and the convent, the vocations then commonly open to women, but had pledged herself to perpetual virginity. Nevertheless, because she had for a short time been tempted to try and win a husband, she was later hag-ridden with guilt, accusing herself of vanity and frequently beating herself until the blood ran. She took Mary Magdalene, the Penitent, as her 'mother and mistress'.

At 16, following another vision, she became a tertiary among the Daughters of Penance of St Dominic's Order of Preachers. As a tertiary, she was not expected to enter a convent but she was bound to say certain prayers, to attend certain services regularly and to take a Dominican as her confessor and spiritual adviser. But the friar into whose hands she was put did not demand enough from her. She voluntarily shut herself up in her room at her father's house, and over the next three years accused herself of entertaining the foulest temptations.

Tomb of St Catherine of Siena in Rome: she died at 34; believing herself to be tormented by demons. Although she was buried at Rome, her head was cut off and taken to Siena, where it remains to this day

On Shrove Tuesday 1366, when she was almost 19, the vigils and pains of her adolescence were rewarded by a vision in which she was betrothed to the only husband she could accept, Christ himself.

Married to Christ

She experienced the vision in the room she used as her cell. A ring, set with a diamond symbolizing faith, and surrounded by four pearls signifying purity of intention, thought, word and deed, was placed on her finger by Christ himself. The witnesses were his Mother, Sts John, Paul and Dominic, and King David the Psalmist. Christ said to her, 'Behold, I hereby espouse thee to myself in faith, which shall adorn thee from this time forward evermore . . . until . . . thou shalt celebrate with me in heaven the eternal wedding-feast.'

After this experience Catherine was driven by inner promptings, which she described in concrete terms of voices and visions, to leave her room. She became well known in Siena, partly for her charity towards the sick and poor, but more for the trances into which she repeatedly fell, especially after receiving Holy Communion. At such times she was totally insensitive and her limbs became stiff and cold. Asked what happened at such moments, she could say only that she was so full of Christ that her senses stopped working. Whether explained in her own terms or in those of the morbid psychology of hysteria, these trances remain a remarkable example of religious ecstasy.

Her catatonic fits reached their climax

Left When she was almost 19 St Catherine experienced a vision in which she was betrothed to Christ, depicted here as an infant *Above* St Catherine of Siena, showing on her hands the stigmata: they were invisible until after her death, and she explained this by saying she had begged Christ not to let them show on her body while she was alive

one day in August 1370, when Catherine's followers, a very mixed school of disciples, heard that she had died. She lay as though dead for four hours, then wept, it is said, for two days. Afterwards she explained, 'I saw the hidden things of God, and now I am forced back into the prison of the body.'

Even in the 14th century, talk of mystical marriage and mystical death aroused criticism. By May 1374, Catherine had become so notorious that she was summoned to appear before the General Chapter of her Order at Florence to answer charges, record of which has unfortunately not survived. The hearing brought her wider notoriety – and a new confessor, Father Raimondo of Capua, later the Dominican Prior-General and her first biographer.

In the summer of 1374 there was an outbreak of plague in Tuscany and the members of the school of mystics who called Catherine 'Mother' nursed the sick and comforted the dying. Catherine had been calling for a crusade to free the Holy Places in Palestine from the Mohammedans, but forgot the need for a holy war while the plague lasted. The winter of 1375, however, found her in Pisa, moving crowds to religious fervour by her very presence, and preaching the crusade at every opportunity. Her enthusiasm was matched by that of the new pope, Gregory XI. Catherine wrote not only to him, but also to many of the rulers of Europe, stressing the need for war. But when it came, it was to Tuscany, not to the East.

Before the outbreak of the war, Catherine,

still at Pisa, underwent yet another major mystical experience when on 1 April 1375 she received the stigmata, the wounds inflicted on Christ on the cross. No one saw the five wounds until after her death, and she explained their invisibility by saying that she had especially requested it: 'I saw the Lord on the Cross . . . I saw five rays the colour of blood directed at my hands, my feet and my heart. Understanding this mystery, I suddenly cried out, "O Lord my God, I beg thee do not let these wounds show on the outside of my body."'

Believing that she was mystically married to her Saviour, had mystically died with him, and was continually sharing his sufferings, Catherine plunged into the troubled events of her last five years of life.

In Tuscany, the plague of 1374 had left near-hysteria and famine in its wake. The Council of Eight at Florence, angry at the Papal States' refusal to supply corn at realistic prices, made an alliance with Milan; permitted the sacking of the churches and monasteries of Florence; added the word *Libertas* in letters of silver to the blood-red banner of the city; and declared war on the papacy.

Catherine who habitually called the Pope 'Christ-on-earth' immediately embraced the cause of Gregory XI. For several months she was able to keep Pisa and Lucca out of the war, but Florentine successes soon nullified her influence. She then began to preach peace to Gregory XI. 'It is better to let the gold of temporal things go than the gold of spiritual things . . . smite them rather with the staff of benignity, love and peace than with the staff of war . . . Peace, then, peace! for the love of Christ crucified!' She told the Council of Eight in Florence, 'Realise then, my sweet sons, that whosoever rebels is like a rotting limb on the body of Christ and our Father Christ-on-earth, and will fall into the company of the dead . . .'

Soon she was in Florence using her eloquence and her influential friends to persuade the Eight to send her to Avignon as a member of the city's peace delegation to the Pope. At Avignon in 1376, she was repudiated by the Florentine delegation, but stayed on at the papal court, trying to persuade Gregory that true peace could come only if he would return to Italy and reform the Church. It was, in fact, his intention to restore the Roman papacy, but an earlier attempt by his predecessor, Urban V, had ended ignominiously, and Gregory had to choose his moment carefully. He judged it had come late in 1376, after Catherine's return to Italy. It is difficult to judge how much influence she actually had on his decision to return to Rome. Her admirers gave her most of the credit, but it is possible to argue that she was pleading only for what was diplomatically the obvious next move. Within two years, she was in an agony of confusion over the wisdom of her part in it.

She had told the Pope, 'Do not come (to Italy) with armed force. The magic wand of justice must be wielded by the hand of love', but it took a massacre of mercenaries at Cesena, as well as the triumphal return of the Pope to Rome, to smash the Tuscan League and bring the Florentines to a genuine peace conference. Before terms were made, Gregory had died, in March 1378.

The Terror of the Demons

The new Pope, Urban VI, was bombarded with advice from Siena. After hearing that in his zeal for reform the Pope had threatened and struck cardinals and made enemies of such powerful neighbours as Queen Joanna of Naples, Catherine began to warn him, 'Justice without mercy may appear more like injustice . . . Do your business with moderation and a tranquil heart. For the love of Christ crucified, soften a little the sudden movements of your temper'. But Urban was temperamentally incapable of taking such advice, and in September 1370 his cardinals repudiated him by electing Cardinal Robert of Geneva as anti-pope. Robert ruled from Avignon as Clement VII, supported by France and her European allies. This division, known as the Great Schism, lasted for 40 years. Catherine wrote to Urban, 'these devils incarnate have not elected a Christ on earth, but an antichrist to you who are Christ-on-earth.' The Pope commanded her to come to Rome. Before obeying, she spent a week in Siena dictating her most famous spiritual work, now known as *The Dialogues of St Catherine*, then went to Rome, to spend the rest of her life fighting for Urban's recognition as Christ-on-earth.

On 30 January 1380, Catherine suffered a stroke, remaining unconscious for some hours. In a letter written a fortnight later she attributed her attack to 'the terror of the demons . . . roused to rage' against her by her reforming work. Her description of her life at this time is worth quoting. 'At the hour of tierce I rise from Mass, and you would see a dead woman going to St Peter's . . . I remain there praying until nearly the vesper-hour . . . My body remains without food or even a drop of water, with physical torments of a sweetness I have never before endured.'

Nor could she long endure them now. Her 'demons' blamed her for the schism, arguing that if she had not persuaded Gregory to leave Avignon, the Church would not have split. She complained that the whole weight of the Barque of Peter lay on her shoulders. The burden broke her. She was struck by paralysis and before the end of March she already looked like a mummified corpse. But she did not die until Sunday, 29 April.

Catherine was buried in the Minerva Church at Rome, but her head was removed and carried to Siena, where it may still be seen, perhaps one of the most repulsive, although one of the most venerated, of Christian relics. She was canonized in 1461.
J. HOLLAND SMITH

FURTHER READING: Alice Curtayne, *Saint Catherine of Siena* (Tan Books, 1980); English versions of the saint's principal works are V. D. Scudder, *St Catherine As Seen in her Letters* (Dent, London, 1905); A. Thorold, *The Dialogue of the Seraphic Virgin, Catherine of Siena* (Tan Books, 1976).

Jim Bamber

Cat's Cradle
European and American children's game with string, a simple version of the elaborate string figures of some primitive peoples; in the Congo a cradle of string is made to encourage the sun to rest, and shine less fiercely; the Eskimo, on the other hand, uses the cradle to catch the sun and to delay the coming of winter.
See STRING.

By courtesy of the Wellcome Trustees

Caul
Portion of the amnion, or thin membrane enveloping the foetus, which covers the head of some newly born children: an omen of good fortune with powerful magical properties; it protects sailors from drowning, presumably because it was thought to keep the foetus from drowning in the womb; if sold, the caul carries its magic with it and a case of a sailor trying to buy one is known from as late as 1944.
See BIRTH.

The early Celts sacrificed human beings by drowning or suffocating them in cauldrons. In contrast, legend tells of magic vessels that revived the dead or gave the gift of poetry to those who drank from them

CAULDRON

THAT THE CAULDRON was an object of sacred and ritual significance in early Celtic societies has been established by finds of ritual cauldrons dating back to the Celtic Iron Age and earlier; and by medieval Irish and Welsh tales of sacred cauldrons, which do much to prove the truth of, and elaborate on, theories founded upon archeological discoveries. The pagan Celts, believing that hospitality had an almost religious significance, seem to have looked on the cauldron as being symbolic of this quality, for in this vessel food for the welcoming feast was cooked. It was therefore an important utensil in the king's household, and cauldrons were no doubt prized possessions wherever they could be afforded, from simple pottery vessels to the great elaborate decorated metal cauldrons described in legends.

As a symbol of plenty, the cauldron was connected with fertility. Food, and as a result life, came from the cauldron. Certain mythological cauldrons were allegedly capable of reviving the dead. Others were believed to contain a liquid that could confer poetic inspiration on those who drank it, a fitting belief for people as dedicated to poetry as the Celts. Certain sacred cauldrons were considered to be inexhaustible – no matter how much was taken from them they were never empty. So it is not surprising to find that the cauldron was an important attribute of the typical Celtic all-purpose tribal god, father of his people, such as the Dagda of Ireland.

Two of the most important cauldrons still in existence were found in Jutland, Denmark. The better-known one was discovered in a bog at Gundestrup. It is a large silver bowl onto which eight outer plates and five inner ones were originally fixed. These, and another on the inner bottom of the bowl, are all beautifully decorated, the inner ones with representations of what must be cult scenes, the outer ones with busts of Celtic gods and goddesses. This vessel, which seems to have been deliberately dismantled before being put in the bog, is a very important discovery, for it illustrates both the part played by the cauldron in Celtic ritual, and certain aspects of Celtic religious practice before the impact of Roman influence.

The other cauldron was found at Bra, where it had been broken into pieces before being placed in a small pit. Like the Gundestrup cauldron, the Bra vessel had presumably been deposited as an offering to some specific deity or supernatural force. It was originally a large bronze cauldron, decorated about the rim with ox heads and owl masks, two creatures sacred to the Celts.

Filled with Blood

Another most impressive piece of evidence for the use of the cauldron in a religious context comes from Vix in France, where a Greek *krater* (cauldron) of bronze dating to about 500 BC, was found in the richly appointed grave of a Celtic princess. A griffon-cauldron with a tripod has also been found, associated with a burial at Ste Colombe nearby. These vessels were imported from the Mediterranean region, and were no doubt buried in the belief that they would be useful in the great otherworld feast beyond the grave. One of the most enduring and persistent Celtic concepts of the otherworld is that hospitality and feasting were of prime importance, and gave never-ending pleasure and satisfaction (see CELTS).

We know from classical writings that the early Celts sacrificed human beings by drowning them in cauldrons or vats. The Cimbri, for example, who can be regarded as a Celto-Germanic tribe, slaughtered human victims over a cauldron which became filled with their blood. Sacrifices were made to the great god Teutates, a war god of the Gauls, by suffocating human victims in a cauldron, and one of the most important features of the Gundestrup cauldron is a scene which is generally thought to depict some such ritual actually in progress. A male figure, presumably the deity himself, holds a man by the feet over the mouth of a large vessel. This scene could perhaps be interpreted equally well as the act of throwing a dead warrior into the sacred cauldron of regeneration, with the god giving life back, not taking it away. But as the victim is being held over the vessel, and is not totally immersed in it, as was necessary in the cauldron of regeneration, the first interpretation is probably the correct one.

Beer for Immortality

Celtic literature contains convincing parallels to this earlier material, and also some new information. Several of the Irish and Welsh deities were believed to possess huge magic cauldrons, and the stealing of the otherworld cauldron by the semi-divine hero is a dominant theme in the early tales. The five *bruidne* (feasting halls) of ancient Irish tradition each had a magical cauldron which cooked the correct amount of food for all comers, no matter how great the company. Other Celtic deities also had wonderful cauldrons, such as the one used

National Museum, Denmark

The Gundestrup cauldron: the scene on the inner panel shows a male figure holding a man over a large vessel, and is generally thought to depict the ritual sacrifice of a human victim to the war god. The figures on the outer panels represent Celtic deities

by Goibniu, the smith god, to brew his beer for his otherworld feast. All who partook of Goibniu's feast became immortal.

The Irish god Mider, King of the Gaelic underworld and the owner of three malevolent cranes and wonderful otherworld cows, likewise owned a cauldron of this kind. Cu Chulainn one of the greatest heroes of Celtic myths, and the god Cu Roi stole it from Mider's dwelling and the vessel became Cu Roi's after a struggle. Welsh tradition has it that Pwyll, Lord of Annwfn, the otherworld, had a magic cauldron in his possession, which King Arthur and his men made an expedition to steal (see ARTHUR).

The Welsh Bran the Blessed (see BRAN) also owned a wonderful cauldron of regeneration which had been given to him by a giant and his wife after their escape from the King of Ireland, who had attempted to destroy them. The Irish king had seen them come from the Lake of the Cauldron, the monstrous man carrying the magic vessel on his back, and accompanied by his huge wife. Their violent and anti-social behaviour had displeased the Irish who had threatened to dethrone the king if he did not get rid of them. This grotesque couple are clearly deities, who are often described as appearing as huge and ugly people, doing

mischief to mankind. The cauldron is evidently a sacred otherworld vessel.

A cauldron known as the *Coire Sainta* is described in a 9th century Irish glossary.

A name for a cauldron of covetousness which was made by the artists. Thus it is. It has nine chains out of it, though it is not larger than the head of a large *cingit* (obscure). There is a hole at the end of every chain, with nine artists standing round it, while the company sang, each with the point of his spear fixed in the hole of the chain that was next him. And whosoever gave one of them a gift, it was into the cauldron he put it; whence it was called the Cauldron of Covetousness.

This appositely describes a venerated cauldron, associated with the arts, into which actual offerings were made.

The literary tradition, then, confirms the archeological evidence concerning the role of the cauldron in early Celtic mythology and ritual. Confused though much of the literary evidence has now become, it is clear that the theme of the magic otherworld cauldron, the sacred vessel of the god or goddess, runs all through the early literature of the Celts. The giving of the cauldron to a mortal, or its theft by the hero, is the focal point of several of the early legends.

The great decorated cauldrons of Iron Age Europe, and the ritual attending their final deposition on bogs or in pools, were no doubt associated with similar legends and beliefs, and with grim sacrifices that are merely hinted at in legends.
(See also GRAIL.)

Foto Hinz

CAVE ART

The Magic World of Prehistoric Man

That many prehistoric cave paintings were connected with ritual magic to ensure fertility and success in hunting has long been accepted, but new theories suggest that a richer and more complex system of sexual symbolism may be involved

CAVE AND ROCK ART is found all over the world and has been practised from the earliest times until the present day. The most immediate problem which it raises is the question of dating. There are no scientific methods of analysis which yield absolute dates that can be applied either to the paints used or to the incised and engraved lines on a rock. In the vast majority of cases it is impossible to tie rock art down to a particular period and therefore quite

impossible even to begin to enquire into its significance.

Fortunately, for some groups of rock art at least, the situation is not so desperate, for representations can be associated with particular groups of people, either on the basis of their associated archeological remains or on the basis of stylistic analogies between the rock art and pottery or metal decorations, or because certain extinct animals are represented, or because items of equipment shown in the rock art can be equated with actual (and datable) equipment found in excavations.

All archeological investigation suffers from the same disadvantage, that it can be assumed that the material recovered in excavations is only partial and that the

Among the most remarkable Stone Age paintings are those in the caves at Lascaux in France, like this one of a cow and a horse. Animals were probably represented to give men magical control over them

sample known is biased. For financial reasons, it is rare for any site to be fully excavated, and the sites actually investigated represent only a minute fraction of those known to exist. For the majority of prehistoric periods, therefore, it is impossible to know very much about the total artistic output of a particular culture. However, it is lucky that at many different periods in the past, and in many different areas of the world, artists chose large, static and imperishable rock surfaces as their canvasses.

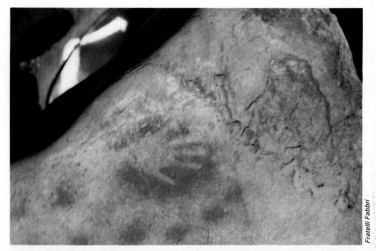

Above left The outline of a human hand in a cave at Pech-Merle in France: red ochre was probably applied to a hand placed on the wall through a blowpipe, either as a powder or in the form of a thick liquid. It has been suggested that these hands, which can also be seen *(above right)* in this painting of horses in the Pech-Merle complex of caves, may have been protection against the Evil Eye *Above* These late Paleolithic paintings found in the Levanzo cave on the island of Egadi near Sicily, include representations of fish and human figures

One of the regions where rock art has received the most extensive study is Europe. Some of the rock art of Europe can be definitely dated to the Paleolithic or Old Stone Age period. Other examples can be dated, on the basis of detailed parallels with weapons and tools found in excavations, to specific periods between 2,000 and 450 BC; others again can be assigned to particular cultures because of the inscriptions found on them. Many works, however, such as the grouped lines and abstract designs in Fontainebleau forest near Paris are still undatable.

Those examples of European cave and rock art that can be assigned some kind of date are principally found in areas which suggest that they were executed by people who were unable to practise agriculture in the plains and were forced to live by hunting, fishing and stock breeding in forested zones, in mountainous regions and in narrow valleys. Alternatively, it can be argued that the artists were those people who were put in charge of the flocks and herds, and who had to search for fodder and water in the higher areas for part of the year; or again that the artists were those who were posted to the higher areas for purposes of defence.

These rock carvings and paintings, except those of Paleolithic date, share certain features in common. Most of them were executed on rock surfaces which were (and still are) open to the air and which are visible in daylight. There are very few examples indeed of European art *inside* caves which can be dated to the post-Paleolithic periods, though notable exceptions include some of the Sicilian caves which contain paintings and engravings of probable Mesolithic and Neolithic date, certain caves in the Balkans which were possibly cult centres in later prehistoric times, and certain Cretan caves which may have been sanctuaries in historic times. The majority of these exposed rock surfaces contain 'scenes' showing domestic activities or hunting or war. Most of them include recognizable artefacts such as tools, weapons or houses. Most of them include depictions of humans which are basically 'stick figures'. These figures, engaged in various recognizable domestic and aggressive activities, differ markedly in content and character from another group of

In some caves, paintings and engravings can only be reached after several hours of scrambling, climbing and crawling

prehistoric works of art which, although also executed on rocks, include virtually no obvious cases of identifiable scenes and which, in the vast majority of cases, are situated within the dark galleries of caves. These are representations which can be dated to the Upper Paleolithic period (c 30,000–10,000 BC).

The Old Stone Age Caves

The Paleolithic cave art so far discovered is centred on south-western France and northern Spain with important, more or less isolated and restricted, examples in southern Spain, Portugal, Sicily and eastern France. In other parts of Europe where caves also exist, deliberate search for Paleolithic cave art has failed to find any examples. Only in eastern Europe, in the Urals and in Turkey, has a possibly related cave and rock art been discovered.

The Upper Paleolithic period coincided with the last major advance of ice sheets over Europe, and with the long period of their slow and irregular retreat which was punctuated by several fresh advances. As a result, although the climate was generally cold, it was not uniformly so during the whole of the period. The changes in climate affected the relative abundance of wild animals and hence the livelihood of the Upper Paleolithic peoples. They lived by hunting, fishing, fowling and gathering; they practised no agriculture and no animal husbandry. They camped beneath rock shelters and in the entrances of caves, but they sometimes erected tents or built huts of wood and stone. They did not, as far as is known, actually live in the depths of caves, much beyond the reach of daylight.

Upper Paleolithic tools and weapons were made of flint or similar rock, and of bone, antler and ivory; perishable materials such as wood and vegetable fibres were almost certainly also used. Spears tipped with various types of stone, bone or antler points were used for hunting, and harpoons with detachable heads for fishing. The quarry consisted mostly of the mammals of the Arctic steppe; horse, bison, reindeer, mammoth, woolly rhinoceros, hare and ibex. In the milder phases, and south of the Pyrenees, woodland animals were hunted: notably wild oxen, deer and wild boar. Various wild fowl and also fish are found amongst food debris.

By and large these are the animals which are found depicted on the walls of caves (and some rock shelters) as well as some carnivores, such as cave lion, wolf and bear. Besides animals, Paleolithic cave art features a varied series of signs, symbols or designs of no obvious significance, as well as some human figures and a few imaginary creatures. Vegetation and landscape are absent. Unlike the rock art of later ages, Paleolithic cave art does not include obvious representational scenes. There are (with one exception) no identifiable activities such as war, hunting or dancing, and there are no 'stick figures'. The images most commonly occur in an apparently haphazard way on the rock surfaces, with little obvious relation to each other, either in their positioning, relative size or orientation. The animal species which are shown together would not normally have been seen together in reality. In many cases a figure may be entirely or partially covered by another.

The Artists' Technique

Paleolithic cave art includes paintings, engravings, low-relief sculptures and clay modellings, as well as various combinations of these techniques. The paints used were all made of natural earth pigments which occur in the areas of the caves: red and yellow ochres and black manganese oxide. Greens, blues and white are not found in Paleolithic art. 'Crayons' of ochre have been found in the habitation debris of several sites, and caches of ochre are not uncommon in the decorated caves. Grinding stones were used for powdering the ochre. For paintings such as the 'negative' hand stencils of Gargas in the Pyrenees, it seems that the paint may have been applied in dry powder or thick liquid form through a blow-pipe directed at a hand placed on the rock; this produced a clear outline of the hand with a gradual fading of the colour around. There is clear evidence of the use of liquid paint, for in a few instances there are obvious drip lines running from the paintings. It is also likely that paint was sometimes applied as a paste mixed with fat or clay.

Engravings were produced by several different techniques. Many fine engravings were made with a specialized tool with a narrow chisel-shaped edge, known as a burin. By making a very shallow incision in

the rock, the thin weathered outer zone was removed, and the unweathered rock, generally of a paler colour, was revealed underneath. Some engravings, pecked out with flint picks, are deeply outlined; these are generally of early date. These simple engravings were probably the technical predecessors of the finely modelled low-relief sculptures, for these were executed in the same way with flint picks; they are sometimes outlined by a deeply hollowed-out groove. The sculptured surfaces were subsequently smoothed over, for tool marks are not usually discernible. Traces of red ochre paint can still be seen on some examples but these low-relief sculptures are nearly all in daylight, in rock shelters or very close to the entrances of caves, and their surfaces are generally greatly weathered. Deeper inside caves there are many examples of combined engraving and painting.

Another engraving technique made use of especially weathered cave wall surfaces and the thin clay films on some cave walls because it was possible to make tracings with the fingers or soft sticks on such soft surfaces. Clay floors of caves were also decorated but these have only survived in exceptional conditions, either under overhangs or in parts of the caves which were difficult of access. Most of these floor representations are engravings but some superb clay modellings are also known.

Some of the decorated caves are large and deep, with the decorations extending for a considerable distance underground. In some caves, paintings and engravings can only be reached after several hours of scrambling, climbing and crawling. In most caves, however, decorations usually start either within the entrance region of the cave or very near to it, and were therefore associated with the living areas in the cave mouths. Inhabited rock shelters were also sometimes embellished with the images placed on surrounding walls and overhanging rock, or on blocks of stone arranged against the wall around the living area.

Dating and Meaning

Two major points of interest for Paleolithic art, as for all rock art, are dating and significance. The meaning of superimposed representations is of the utmost importance for both these points. There is no longer any doubt about the general Paleolithic time

Michael Holford

scale during which this cave art was executed, and it has occasionally been possible to pinpoint a particular work of art within a particular Upper Paleolithic culture. Numerous schemes have been proposed which attempt to assess the relative chronology of the styles adopted during the 20,000 years of Paleolithic artistic activity. Most of these schemes depend on an assumed single or double cycle of development, from the simple to the complicated, or from the crude to the sophisticated, and also on the obvious point that an image superimposed on another must necessarily have been executed at a later period.

Most research workers dealing with prehistoric rock art have always assumed that superimposed art reflects a significant lapse of time between the first representation and the second, and that this practice indicates a lack of interest in aesthetic effect on the part of the second artist. Only recently has it been recognized that the time-span between the representation of two superimposed images may only have been a matter of a few minutes, and that the practice may have been a prehistoric artistic convention, or technique, indicating a deliberate association between representations. If this view turns out to be correct, major revisions of proposed schemes of relative dating will be necessary.

Hunting, Fertility and Magic

Long before anyone had suggested that superpositioning, the placing of one image over another, might have been a convention

for showing association, it had been generally accepted that cave art had a magical or ritual significance. Much Paleolithic art is found deep in the caves, beyond the reach of daylight, and this suggested that this period of art reflected more than mere enjoyment of art for its own sake. It seemed obvious that man's overwhelming preoccupation in Paleolithic times must have been the search for food. Ritual and magic would be used to ensure success in the hunt, and Paleolithic art was interpreted as an example of imitative magic. The hunters believed that they could gain magical power over their quarry, either by representing it on a cave wall or floor, or by enacting a ritual hunt in front of a representation of the quarry.

Many of the animals represented in cave art were those whose remains were found among the food debris of Paleolithic man. The majority of the other animals depicted, the carnivores and other dangerous beasts, would have constituted a threat to Paleolithic man's existence and would also have been hunted by him. Many of the signs and symbols of cave art, some of which are distributed around and on the animals, but many of which occur singly or grouped together on panels, were taken to be representations of darts, the throwing of stones, clubs or traps; they were thus brought into the general hunting interpretation. Marks on some of the animals were taken to signify wounds.

As more and more discoveries of decorated caves became known, this interpretation

Left On the ceiling of a cave at Altamira in Spain a herd of bison were painted in red, yellow and black pigment *Above right* A painting in the lowest of the Lascaux caves, showing a wounded bison, a dead or wounded man, and a bird perched on a stake. It may be a memorial to a dead hunter, or it may show a priest in trance before a bison which is to be sacrificed, the bird being the priest's soul or spirit watching over him *Below right* Black bull, from Lascaux

was modified to some extent. A fertility element was recognized, as well as the hunting element. It was suggested that depictions of humans, and of certain food animals which were shown without wounds, were intended to increase the numbers of the available food quarry and to increase the human population itself.

This interpretation is still generally accepted, though it has been severely criticized in the last decade. For example, there is a striking absence of correlation between the relative frequency of animals represented in the art — a frequency which varies considerably from cave to cave, and from region to region within any one cave — and the relative frequencies of the same animals in actual Paleolithic food debris. In addition, many of the so-called weapons cannot really be equated with actual artefact types, and it is difficult to see why, on numerous occasions, such weapons should have been shown in isolation or even, in some cases, as missing the quarry. It is an important fact of Paleolithic art statistics that the majority of representations are

Foto Hinz

Foto Hinz

The Value of Magic

The representations may have played a part in the rites by which young men were initiated as fully adult members of society. To judge by analogy with what is known, for example, of Australian aboriginal art, it seems highly unlikely that rock-paintings or engravings were sufficient in themselves. A much more likely probability is that they formed part of a complex of activities which certainly included dancing and may also have included miming.

. . . in primitive society no clear distinction is drawn between economic, religious or magical activities, or, to put it in more abstract terms, between ritual and what we would regard as practical activities. This same consideration applies with more or less force to cave art as a whole, and, if the psychological effect of the ritual (including the production of cave art) is taken into account, who is to say that the ice age hunters were wrong? When as much depended on luck as it did in hunting, an activity in which man was matched with only primitive weapons directly against the beasts, magical rites that had the effect of increasing confidence and heightening solidarity were evidently of the utmost practical value. The value of a rite, or rather its efficacy, depends after all on the response it evokes.

Grahame Clark and Stuart Piggott
Prehistoric Societies

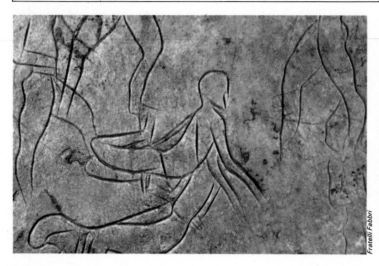

Fratelli Fabbri

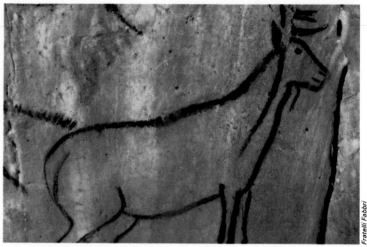

Fratelli Fabbri

shown with no wounds and with no 'weapons' about to strike them.

It is also worth noting that modern hunting and gathering communities are in no way preoccupied with the quest for food, as is assumed for the prehistoric hunters. Many such communities have the time, skill and sophistication for considerable artistic work which is in no way associated with the simple search for food. There is nothing to suggest that Upper Paleolithic hunting was more difficult than that of many hunting peoples today, and it is reasonable to examine the possibility that Paleolithic art was the result of a more sophisticated activity than simple imitative magic.

Sexual Symbolism

Recent French work, notably that of Professor Leroi-Gourhan, has started from the theory that superpositioning indicates the artist's deliberate association of representations. The content of Paleolithic art appears, at first sight, to differ fundamentally from other rock art in its absence of scenes and recognizable economic or domestic activities. Previously this has been taken, in combination with the existence of superpositions and the apparently random placing of images on cave walls, to indicate haphazard activity by individual artists. But if the new theory is right, Paleolithic art is concerned with the planned association of grouped representations.

To Leroi-Gourhan, the distribution of different animal species within a cave suggests an organized sanctuary or holy place,

Left **Acrobats apparently performing a ritual dance are the central figures in this group of engravings in Addaura, Sicily, which also shows men hunting: these are the two dominant themes in cave art in this region. The human figures are depicted with an attention to detail that is unusual in Paleolithic art** *Right* **Outlines of animals, two among scores found deep in the Niaux caves in France**

where sexual symbols – previously thought to represent weapons, traps and wounds – are placed in association with, or close to, certain animal species which themselves symbolize either the male or female element. In short, 'Paleolithic representations are concerned with an extremely rich and complex system, much richer and much more complex than . . . previously suspected.'

Studies of cave and rock art are in many ways still in their infancy. Most investigations have centred on establishing principles of dating, on the rather naive assumption that artistic work will inevitably proceed from the simple to the more complex, and in the belief that superpositioning signifies no more than a difference in time between two representations. More and more rock art is discovered each year and interpretation of all this material has been held up by the acceptance of general, all-embracing explanations of its purpose and meaning.

However detailed and extensive the research on style and dating of a particular art complex, in virtually no case do we yet know why the artists chose rock surfaces for their canvasses. It is time that investigation

into the significance and function of different groups of art entered a new phase. The clues to unravelling their meaning must lie in detailed investigation of localities, with special attention to features such as visibility and orientation and in detailed consideration of content. Any reasonable interpretation of Paleolithic cave art must, for example, attempt to account for the extreme rarity of human images and the absence of vegetation and scenery.

It is still much too early to be able to say whether there is one single common denominator, beyond the use of the same material, behind all cave and rock art. It is even too early to say whether the choice of exposed surfaces, on the one hand, and the use of dark areas, on the other, represents a major difference in intent and significance between rock and cave art or simply reflects a difference in date and in the conditions of life of the peoples involved.
(For African rock art, see ROCK PAINTINGS.)
PETER J. UCKO

FURTHER READING: For a comprehensive review of the different interpretations, see P. J. Ucko and R. Rosenfeld, *Palaeolithic Cave Art* (McGraw-Hill, 1967) and for A. Leroi-Gourhan's theories, see his *Treasures of Prehistoric Art* (Abrams, 1967) which is finely illustrated, as is P. Graziosi, *Palaeolithic Art* (McGraw-Hill, 1960). See also A. Laming, *Lascaux* (Penguin); Ann Sieveking, *Cave Artists* (Thames and Hudson, 1979).

CAVES

FROM THE DAWN of human culture caves have been used as dwellings, sanctuaries and tombs, and in fact the use of caves can be traced back long before the appearance of *homo sapiens* in the archeological record. About 300,000 BC the so-called Peking Man, a remote predecessor of modern man, lived in the Choukoutien caves near Peking. Skeletal remains found in these caves seem to indicate the practice of ritual cannibalism. Another notable instance of the pre-human use of caves was discovered in the Guattari cave on Monte Circeo, Italy, dating from the Mousterian period (c 100,000 BC). There a 'human' skull had been deposited, surrounded by a ring of stones, apparently evidence of some magical rite.

Some of the most impressive evidence of the ritual use of caves comes from the Upper Paleolithic period (c 30,000–10,000 BC), when true man had displaced his sub-human ancestors. In south-western France and the Pyrenean area of Spain figures of animals, including bison, reindeer, horses, mammoths and the woolly rhinoceros, were depicted on the walls and roofs of caves. Many of these animals are represented as pregnant or wounded with darts. This cave art is generally regarded by modern scholars as magical in intent, being designed to promote the fertility of the beasts which men hunted for food, or to ensure success in hunting them (see CAVE ART). There is also evidence that ritual practices were performed in the caves and some of them appear to have been holy places. The most notable example is the cave of the Trois Frères at Ariège in France, where a strange half-human, half-animal figure dominates an inner cavern.

There are many examples of the ritual use of caves in later times. It is difficult to determine why they were originally chosen for sanctuaries but it seems that the mysterious nature of most caves may have been the decisive factor. Often, they were probably regarded as entrances to the underworld.

The following examples give some idea of the various types of cave sanctuaries and their wide geographical distribution. The famous temple at Abu-Simbel in Egypt, built by order of Rameses II in the 13th century BC, and dedicated to the gods Re-Harmakhis (the Rising Sun), Amun, and the Pharaoh himself, is an artificial cave. It is designed so that the rising sun shines through the entrance, to illumine the divine figures in the inner sanctuary.

Ancient Crete had many cave sanctuaries, connected with the cult of the Mother Goddess. Possibly, the cave suggested the womb of the Earth Mother. Several of these caves were associated with the birth of Zeus. The cave of the Sibyl at Cumae, described by Virgil, was famous for its oracle. In India there are magnificent cave temples at

Karli, Ajanta and Ellora, held sacred by both Buddhists and Hindus. At Tun-Huang in China are the caves of the Thousand Buddhas, so-called from the multitudes of images of Buddha which they contain.

Caves were often associated with the birth of a god or a divine hero, as in the case of Zeus in Crete. In Rome the Lupercal cave sheltered the infant Romulus and Remus. Mithra was born from a rock and worshipped in caves. The birthplace of Christ at Bethlehem is a cave. Caves, natural or artificial, have also provided tombs for the dead, often acquiring special sanctity from those buried in them. The most notable example is the cave tomb of Christ in Jerusalem, over which the Church of the Holy Sepulchre was built.

Company in Death

The men of the last ice age buried their dead evidently believing in a physical afterlife . . . the dead were often buried in the dwelling caves where they had lived, so that they might remain in familiar surroundings. Grave pits were carefully dug in cave floors, and the corpse deposited either in a 'sleeping position' – on its side, on its back – or crouching. A protective layer of stones was then placed around and over the grave . . . In Predmost, Moravia, Czechoslovakia, a mass grave was found to contain at least 14 skeletons, protected by a layer of stones. Apparently the dead were to keep one another company.

Johannes Maringer *The Gods of Prehistoric Man*

Early Christian monks sought solitude for contemplation in the desert and in caves: the Goreme cave monastery in Cappadocia, Asia Minor, used by early Christian hermits and still in use today

Sonia Halliday

Although he had scarcely any formal education, Edgar Cayce became a doctor when in a trance state, and treated some 30,000 patients before his death in 1945. He also developed his own occult philosophy

EDGAR CAYCE

THE MIRACLE WORKER has always occupied a prominent position in unorthodox medicine, dealing with diseases considered incurable by more conventional doctors. Possibly the greatest occult diagnostician of modern times was Edgar Cayce (pronounced Casey) of Hopkinsville, Kentucky, known as 'the Man of Miracles' who died in 1945, at the age of 67 and whose early experiences had much in common with those of earlier mystics. As a child Cayce is said to have spoken with an angel, and to have seen visions of his dead grandfather. He was a shy, reserved boy with deep religious feelings, and although he never completed his schooling, he had a great love for reading, and went to work in a bookshop.

Cayce was only 16 when he first became aware of his power to heal. Lying in bed, after being hit in the back by a baseball, he suddenly ordered his mother to apply a poultice to the spot. She did so and by morning he had recovered completely, but could remember absolutely nothing of what had taken place. Not long after this experience he contracted a throat disease which threatened to reduce his voice to a permanent whisper. In despair he turned to a hypnotist for help but was incapable of entering the deep sleep that was necessary for this kind of treatment. But another hypnotist, Al Layne, helped him on this occasion and also played an important part in Cayce's development as a healer. Cayce put himself to sleep in Layne's presence and suddenly, speaking in a clear voice, said, 'Yes, we can see the body.' He prescribed the treatment necessary to restore circulation to the affected nerves of his throat, and Layne ordered the circulation to respond accordingly. A few minutes later Cayce woke up, completely healed.

Edgar Cayce's reputation as a healer soon began to attract the sick and suffering to him from every direction. They were all desperate for treatment, and the young man was often exhausted by his efforts to relieve ailments which had generally been given up as incurable by doctors. Much of Cayce's treatment was based on diagnosing spinal lesions as the cause of the disorder, and called for osteopathy and homoeopathy. Indeed, during most of the healing sessions he had the assistance of an osteopath. Cayce invariably went into a trance state which was followed by the diagnosis, starting with the words, 'Yes, we see the body.' The hypnotist Layne assisted in these operations, especially in the early days, but later a medical man was also present.

Typical of the cases passing through Cayce's hands was that of a woman crippled by arthritis and abandoned as incurable by her doctors. The treatment, prescribed during the trance state, involved dieting, exercises and massage, and was fully successful in restoring the use of her limbs.

On another occasion he diagnosed a disorder affecting the wife of a doctor as pregnancy accompanied by a bowel disorder, after her own physician had declared her to be suffering from an abdominal tumour. Cayce proved accurate and the 'tumour' was soon resolved by a successful delivery.

Bed Bug Juice

Whenever possible Cayce tried to arrange for his patients to be treated by a qualified physician, but he often met with deeply entrenched opposition from the ranks of orthodox medicine. It was, however, a member of the medical profession, Dr Wesley Ketchum, a homoeopath, who vindicated Cayce's methods of treatment. Dr Ketchum was suffering from an illness that he had diagnosed as appendicitis, but being determined to put Cayce's skill to the test he asked for a reading, and was told that a spinal disorder was the cause of the trouble, and that he ought to consult an osteopath. Ketchum did this and was freed from discomfort. Convinced of the truth of Cayce's claims, he examined his records and submitted a highly favourable report to the American Society of Clinical Research at Boston. This was followed by an article in the *New York Times* of 9 October 1910 which brought Edgar Cayce's achievements

Edgar Cayce, the 'Man of Miracles': a psychic healer of great power, he was said to have spoken with an angel as a child. He was also clairvoyant, and once identified a murderer while in a trance state

Neville Spearman Publishers

as a healer to the attention of the nation.

The hordes of sick who now flocked to Cayce for treatment made it necessary to form an organization to carry out his work and the Association of National Investigators was created. A fully-staffed hospital was established at Virginia Beach, Virginia, and Cayce worked there. In 1931 this organization was succeeded by the Association for Research and Enlightenment, which accumulated records of the many thousands of medical cases he had treated.

Quite apart from the homoeopathic and osteopathic techniques he employed, Cayce appears, on occasion, to have used forms of 'backwoods' therapy which were hardly likely to endear him to orthodox doctors. Remedies like bed bug juice for dropsy or oil of smoke for a leg sore had long been out of favour with a profession that tended to write off most folk medicine as quackery. Nor did his other ventures, into what was popularly known among doctors as 'Gas Pipe Therapy', enhance his reputation in medical circles. An example of this is described in Martin Gardner's *Fads and Fallacies in the Name of Science*. 'One of his readings advised attaching the copper anode of a battery to the third dorsal plexus centre, and the nickel anode first to the left ankle, then to the right ankle.' Cayce also marketed a number of patent medicines, including Ipsab for pyorrhoea and Tim for haemorrhoids, and various devices for treating the sick with electricity and radio-activity.

The New Tomorrow

Apart from his powers as a psychic healer, Cayce was clairvoyant, and on one occasion discovered the identity of a murderer while in a trance. But he was accused of complicity in the crime by an unimaginative police officer in charge of the case, and after this he refused to carry out any further experiments in psychic detection. His aid was also frequently sought by relatives of those listed as missing in the First World War, an ordeal that he found particularly harrowing.

Like many others in the field of fringe medicine, Cayce created his own occult philosophy, much of which had developed from questions submitted to him while in a trance state. This credo seems to combine many of the elements of Theosophy, Christianity and Pyramidology, no doubt the result of Cayce's extensive reading in his youth. A journal called *The New Tomorrow*, published by his followers, increased Cayce's influence in occultist circles, as did his pamphlet *Auras* published in 1945. In this Cayce disclosed his ability to see the human aura (see DOUBLE) and predicted that colour therapy would eventually become an approved form of medicine.

When he died in 1945, worn out by a lifetime of dedication to the sick, and by the strains of both poverty and persistent medical opposition, Cayce left records of no less than 30,000 cases that he had treated over a period of 43 years. The Cayce Foundation of America continues to honour the name of a man who has been described as possibly the most remarkable healer that has lived.

CELTS

In this world the Celts practised human sacrifice, by drowning stabbing and burning; their otherworld was a place of magic, of deities in many shapes, of enchantments, sacred animals and divine heroes, a world of secrets and hints and elusive symbols

THE EARLY CELTS were composed of a number of different racial elements, and at the height of their power they occupied huge tracts of Europe, from the Atlantic in the west to the Black Sea in the east, from Denmark in the north to the Mediterranean in the south. But in spite of the decentralized nature of Celtic society and the many geographical and tribal differences that must be taken into consideration, there is an impressive uniformity of religious idiom throughout the known Celtic world which allows us to think in terms of Celtic *religion* even though there is little evidence of a formal religious system.

Archeologists have identified people whose material culture is what we recognize to be Celtic, as early as 600 BC. It is almost certain that these people were Celtic-speaking but we have no written records at this stage to verify this supposition. It is extremely likely that their predecessors — people whose culture is known to archeologists as *Urnfield*, a late bronze-using people — also spoke Celtic. The evidence of names helps us here, the distribution of Urnfield remains coinciding in certain instances with very early Celtic place-names.

Pagan Celtic motifs entered Celtic Christian art: a Celtic cross at Glencolumbkille in Ireland, a site associated with St Columba

C. M. Dixon

C. M. Dixon

C. M. Dixon

The great wine flagons found in graves, together with drinking vessels and joints of pork, testify to a continuing belief in the otherworld as a place of revelry

This first phase of Celtic culture is known as *Hallstatt*, a name derived from the extensive cemetery which was found at Hallstatt, near Salzburg in Austria, in the 19th century. Some 2500 graves were investigated, and their contents, together with discoveries made in the salt mines from which the people derived their wealth, tell us much about Celtic society at this period. The people grew rich through mining and trading the salt, a most valuable commodity in the ancient world. The chieftains used iron instead of bronze for their weapons, thereby improving their chances in warfare, and the technological superiority of the metal ensured a career of rapid expansion and conquest. These Hallstatt Celts were composed of the old indigenous Urnfield people combined with intrusive racial elements from the Asian steppes and more easterly regions. New skills in horse-rearing and management introduced from these areas, combined with better weapons and perhaps innovations in methods of warfare, helped the Hallstatt warriors to establish supremacy over a wide area.

The graves and their furnishings tell us not only about certain material aspects of society, but also hint at spiritual attitudes. The burials were elaborate, being under a mound, in a wooden chamber usually made of oak. They were furnished with richly decorated weapons and personal ornaments, many of them bearing symbols which we know from later evidence to have had a religious significance. Horse trappings, drinking vessels and joints of meat were provided for the otherworld feast, that great Celtic celebration beyond the grave. All these features point to powerful beliefs about the nature of personal survival after

Many pagan Celtic monuments were later Christianized *Above* Stone figures of the 8th or 9th century, possibly hidden in the structure of a 12th century church because of their pagan affiliations: in Co Fermanagh, Ireland *Below left* Christian cross obscuring the earlier Celtic inscriptions on an Irish memorial stone: the old inscriptions give the name and descent of the dead man, probably to help keep him alive in the afterworld *Below right* The 'Bishop's Stone' at Killadeas: the south side of the stone shows a Christian abbot with bell and crozier; the west is probably a representation of a pagan Celtic head

death, and are motifs which are repeated again and again in later Celtic history. The bodies of the wealthy dead were laid out, burnt or unburnt, on four-wheeled wagons.

Chariots of the Dead
The second stage in the history of the early Celts is known to archeologists as *La Tène*, from the site on Lake Neuchâtel in Switzerland, where a great deposit of metalwork and other material was discovered in the 19th century. A wooden pier had been constructed over the water and the many articles had been thrown in, presumably as offerings to a specific god or to a plurality of deities and forces.

These articles were recognized to be Celtic but they differed from those of the Hallstatt phase. New art styles had come into existence, showing amongst other things strong classical influences, and there was clear evidence of wider trade and cultural contacts and technological developments. One of the most impressive changes in the still elaborately equipped graves is the presence of the light two-wheeled war chariot, which had replaced the four-wheeled wagon of the Hallstatt burials. This chariot is one of the most characteristic pieces of war equipment of the Celts. Archeology knows of it, the classical writers describe it, it is represented in art and it plays a prominent role in certain of the early Irish tales.

The new art style of La Tène shows a much wider contact with Etruria and the Mediterranean world than before. The great wine flagons found in the graves, together with fire dogs, drinking vessels and joints of pork — the favourite feasting food of the Celts — all testify to a continuing belief in the otherworld as a place of revelry, not gloom, in which equipment and provisions of this kind would be needed.

Each of the numerous Celtic tribes had its own ruler, its 'men of art', its laws and its customs; and in spite of the inevitable regional and temporal differences which give local variations, there is a fundamental similarity which is remarkable. In Gaul, kings had been replaced by chieftains by the time Julius Caesar invaded the country in the 1st century BC. In Ireland, the custom of kingship remained, the king being of supreme importance to society. He was regarded as semi-sacred, the earthly

manifestation and voice of the god. A good king ensured prosperity and fertility, good weather, rich harvests, freedom from plague and invasion, the general well-being of his people — as did the god himself. If the king was unsuitable in character or physically blemished, the supernatural forces were believed to show their dislike and displeasure by bringing disease and famine on mankind and blight on the earth.

Caesar describes the structure of Celtic society in his *De Bello Gallico* (book 6). 'Throughout Gaul there are two classes of men of some dignity and importance. The common people are nearly regarded as slaves: they possess no initiative and their views are never invited on any question. Most of them, being weighed down by debt or by heavy taxes or by the injustice of the more powerful, hand themselves over into slavery to the upper classes, who have all the same legal rights against these men that a master has towards his slave. Of the two distinguished classes, one is that of the Druids, the other that of the Knights. The Druids are concerned with the worship of the gods, they look after public and private sacrifice and they expound religious matters. . . The Knights take part in war whenever there is need and war is declared. . . The greater their rank and resources, the more dependents and clients do they possess.'

This same threefold division of society is found in pagan Ireland, with the king of a district, great or small, and the various grades of freemen constituting the aristocracy, the Druids (priests) and the poets and lawyers likewise occupying a privileged position in society.

The Celts, speaking two different forms of the language, which are known as P-Celtic (spoken in Gaul and Britain) and Q-Celtic (spoken in Ireland, but traces also exist on the Continent) were thus loosely linked by common origins and language, common religious traditions and a close similarity of laws and systems of learning.

Unwritten Secrets
The Celts themselves did not commit their religious traditions to writing and it is necessary to use a variety of sources of information to discover the nature of the religion and mythology of the pagan Celtic peoples. They were not illiterate, for we know that some of them used Greek for their

business transactions. However, they regarded their laws, their genealogies and their history in the same sacred light as their religion. All these disciplines were required to be handed down orally from master to pupil, from priest to acolyte. It took some 20 years of intensive application to assimilate and master the secrets of Druidic lore. The oral tradition is fundamental to the Celtic temperament; a deep respect for it has continued down to the present day in the Celtic-speaking areas of Europe (Brittany, Wales, Ireland, Scotland, the Isle of Man).

For information about Celtic religion on the continent of Europe, and to a lesser extent in Britain, there are the written comments of Greek and Roman authors, interested in noting the habits and customs of the barbarian peoples of Europe. From Roman times there are the sculptured monuments on which native gods, goddesses and cult symbols are figured, often in Roman guise, accompanied by a dedication to a native deity. There are inscriptions and native coins which often bear Celtic names and magical symbols, and there is the evidence of place-names.

Over and above this, the native literatures of Wales and Ireland, the oldest in Europe outside the classical world, form a great repository of mythology and pre-Christian practices. Although written down only in Christian times, the persistence and longevity of the oral tradition was such that we can be quite confident that there is a genuine core of true mythology to be found underneath the embellishments of the storytellers, the censorship of the Church, and the motifs borrowed from classical and Scandinavian sources.

All the evidence for pagan Celtic religion,

fragmentary and varied as it is, emphasizes the fact that the Celts were deeply conscious of religion. The inhabitants of the physical world and those of the otherworld – that gay land beyond the grave – were in constant communication with each other. There is nothing to show that the virtuous attained the otherworld after death for ethical reasons; nor is there any hint of a gloomy otherworld. The land of the gods could be entered in life by the clever, aggressive hero, by means of treachery or force. Or it could be attained by mortals through the invitation of an immortal being, who usually had amorous intentions. But for the Celt there was, and could be, no rigid division between the two territories.

At times, as on *Samain*, (1 November) the great religious feast of the Celts, which was a season of gloom and portent and sacrifice, the inhabitants of the otherworld became hostile and dangerous. They played tricks on mankind and caused panic and destruction. They had then to be appeased, and their powers turned once more in a direction favourable to mortals.

Wells Filled with Bones

The Celts did not as a rule build formal temples, in the manner of the Mediterranean world, but they did have clearly defined sanctuaries, which included structures of some sort, as well as making use of such natural features as hill-tops, open plains in the vicinity of sacred trees, groves, springs and wells, where we know that they gathered for the performance of ritual. These were places which had been made sacred by the cult legend of some deity, whose name is often enshrined in local place-names. The burial mound where the divine ancestor was interred, according to

tradition, and which was often considered to be an entrance to the otherworld, was sometimes a focal point for ritual. The simple earthen enclosure formed by a bank and a ditch, and containing perhaps some wooden or wickerwork structure in which cult images were housed: the burial place of some eminent person: a sacred pit filled with ritually smashed pottery and the bones of sacrificed humans and animals: a stone platform for sacrifice: all these are to be found in archeological contexts.

Again, the ritual shafts and wells found on the continent of Europe and in Britain, filled with layers of objects which include dogs' heads, human bones and skulls, bracelets, ritually bent weapons, smashed pottery and intact vessels, and often with traces of buildings which stood near them or enclosed them – these also seem to have served as temples for the pagan Celts. Apart from one or two examples which are outside the main stream of Celtic tradition, there is little evidence for the construction of elaborate stone temples until the time came when they were built in Celtic areas under the sway of Rome. Roman and native deities alike were then worshipped, and classical and Celtic religious symbols were displayed in such temples.

The Celts have always tended to express things in an oblique fashion, abhorring direct statement, and this can be seen to operate very strongly in their religious idiom. They preferred the subtle allusion, the hint, the symbol: so that the sophisticated, obvious temple and the life-like portraits of the classical gods were alien to their way of thought and not easy for them to accept. Under the influence of Rome, however, such things were built and fashioned in accordance with Roman custom. But the

more subtle rites and symbols continued to exist in the background, appearing from time to time in native pottery or sculpture, in crude idols, in obscure hints and references in the Irish and Welsh written sources.

These people, then, carried out their rites and enacted their myths at prominent natural features or in sacred enclosures, beside wells, or near deeply-dug shafts and pits. Apart from gatherings within individual tribal communities, to commemorate some event concerned with a local god or goddess, there were the great Celtic calendar festivals, which were often celebrated on a plain beside a grave mound, or on a hill-top.

There were four main festivals in the Celtic year. *Imbolc* (1 February), a feast about which we have little detailed information, marked the coming of the ewes into milk. In Ireland this feast was sacred to Saint Brigit of Kildare, who no doubt took it over from her pagan predecessor, the goddess Brigit (see BRIGIT). *Beltane* (1 May) was a fire festival, traces of which have persisted to the present day in Celtic areas. Cattle about to be taken to the summer grazings were first driven through purificatory fires by the Druids.

Lugnasad (1 August) was sacred to the god Lugus, whose cult was widespread. It was a festival to mark the harvesting of the crops. Finally, the great feast of the year was *Samain*, celebrated on 1 November and the night before it: the barriers were down between mortal and immortal, visible and invisible, and sacrifice and correct performance of ritual were practised to keep the sinister gods at bay. Markets were held, games were played, law courts sat and public poetic recitations were given, while racing and feasting added zest to the gatherings which sometimes lasted for several days. During the festival any breach of the public peace was punishable by death. (See also ALL HALLOWS' EVE.)

The Druids

These feasts, and other more local celebrations, were held at the main sacred site of each tribe or region. The priests who officiated at these gatherings, the intercessors between the mortal and the divine, were extremely powerful. Some of them at least were known as Druids. There is evidence that there were priests other than Druids

but we know little about them. The name Druid seems to mean 'knowledge of the oak', and this would be appropriate in a society which held the oak in special awe. Maximus of Tyre, a philosopher of the 2nd century AD, reports that the Celts worshipped Zeus in the form of a tall oak tree.

Our knowledge of the Druids is scrappy and of unequal value. Modern lore about these priests stems only from antiquarianism, not from ancient testimony. In spite of the fragmentary nature of the real evidence it is clear that the Druids constituted a powerful and influential priesthood in some Celtic regions at least. They performed the sacrifices, read the omens, and appeased the gods by performing the rites correctly.

The Irish Druids figure as magicians,

teachers, shape-shifters (those with the ability to change form) and even buffoons, but whether this reflects their true role in early Irish society, or merely the fancies of later Christian writers, must remain in question. Their origins are shrouded in antiquity and there is no reason at all to suppose that they were newcomers, originating with the Celts themselves. Their order may have had a longer ancestry in Europe. (See DRUIDS.)

Death in a Sea of Flame

The Celts practised human sacrifice. The Romans considered this ritual to be barbarous and caused it to be discontinued. They also struck a lethal blow at the Druids, whose power and political influence was a

To the Celts horns were a powerful symbol of virility and divine power. They not only gave their gods horns but enhanced their chances of success in battle by wearing horned helmets: bronze horned mask from Norfolk

British Museum

threat to the success of Roman campaigns in the Celtic areas. Caesar, referring to the practice of human sacrifice, describes the great images of interwoven branches which were filled with men and set alight, 'and the men die in a sea of flame'.

Three fierce Celtic gods, Teutates, Esus and Taranis, are mentioned by the Roman poet Lucan. A commentator on Lucan says that people sacrificed to Teutates were drowned or suffocated in a vat; those sacrificed to Esus were stabbed and then hung up in a tree; Taranis favoured burning. There is little definite in the Irish texts to demonstrate the nature of human sacrifices in that country, but it is certain that they were practised there also.

There are many dark hints and allusions which suggest that the motif of the triple death (by drowning, stabbing and burning) was more than a literary convention, and echoed the tradition of sacrifices to the three great Gaulish gods. Several stories contain the motif of the tricking of the hero and his company into a house, the door of which is secured while they are feasted and made drunk. The building is then set on fire, and all perish in the conflagration or escape through the heroism and supernatural strength of the hero. There are hints of ritual drowning in tubs or wells, numerous examples of foundation sacrifices, even in Christian contexts, and episodes in the early stories which point to the sacrifice of infants.

Animals were certainly ritually killed and

the bull-sacrifice *(tarb-feis)* was an integral feature of the inauguration of a new king, a ceremony of deep religious significance in early Irish society. Bull-hides were used by the Druids to sleep on while they had their omen-giving dreams, having first chewed some of the flesh of a cat, a dog and a red pig, and consulted their 'idol gods'.

The All-Purpose God

It is extremely difficult to find any orderly pantheon in the Celtic gods and goddesses known to us, or any clear-cut division into deities of specific functions or departments. However, the knowledge that the structure of Celtic society was of a semi-sacred nature, that the king was regarded as the visible agent of the god — sometimes his son,

A Magic Kiss

One day Niall, son of Eochu Muigmedon King of Ireland, went hunting with his four brothers. They came across a hideous old woman guarding a well. 'She was as black as coal. Her hair was like a wild horse's tail. Her foul teeth were visible from ear to ear and were such as would sever a branch of green oak. Her eyes were black, her nose crooked and spread. Her body was scrawny, spotted and diseased. Her shins were bent. Her knees and ankles were thick, her shoulders broad, her nails were green.' As a price for the water in her well, the loathsome hag demanded a kiss from each of the brothers in turn; but only Niall overcame his revulsion and embraced her. Thereupon she was transformed into a beautiful woman: 'She was as white as the last snow in a hollow. Her arms were fully and queenly, her fingers long and slender, her legs straight and gleaming . . .'

Reading these old tales, one has the impression that the Irish of past centuries lived on easy terms with the supernatural. If we can judge by the reactions of the characters themselves, no surprise was occasioned by the intervention of folk from the Otherworld, or by spells cast and shapes shifted. The natural order of things was something vaster and more flexible than we envisage today.

D. D. R. Owen
The Evolution of the Grail Legend

National Museum of Ireland

Hunting the ferocious wild boar was a popular and dangerous pastime, for it demanded great skill, and there are many legends of supernatural boars and their adventures in early Irish and Welsh literature

sometimes allegedly the mortal mate of the tribal goddess, the Earth Mother – suggests that the Celts thought of the world of the gods as being organized in a similar way; and there are hints of this in the Irish tradition.

Over and above the numerous tribal and local divinities, we hear of such powerful shadowy beings as Anu, or Danu, mother of the gods. Anu is referred to as 'she who nurtures well the gods'. Danu, from whom the Irish gods called the Tuatha De Danann ('Tribes of the Goddess Danu') are named, has Don as her equivalent in British mythology. Danu's three sons are the gods Brian, Iuchar and Iucharba, known to tradition as *fir tri ndea*, 'men of the three gods'. Brigit the goddess is elsewhere allegedly the mother of this powerful trio, and it may be that she is in fact Danu, known by another name.

One of the most difficult factors in any attempt to get a realistic idea of the nature of Celtic deities and their individual qualities is this custom of giving a single divinity a multiplicity of names, many of them merely descriptive epithets. As a result, much that is confusing in Celtic mythology may become clear if it can be convincingly demonstrated that certain major deities, though seemingly different, are in fact a single deity with a number of names, functions and manifestations. The undoubted power of Brigantia, goddess of the Brigantes, for example, suggests a high position in some supernatural hierarchy.

At present the evidence all points to a huge number of named gods and goddesses, with a comparably large assortment of attributes and symbols, but with a markedly limited range of functions. The tribal god was an all-purpose figure and, despite the differences in his name, he was basically the same throughout the Celtic lands. He was a 'good' god, like the Dagda of Ireland, protector of the tribe, giver of all that was good and desired, their leader in war, their ultimate judge in legal matters, lord of the otherworld feast, mate of the tribal goddess.

It seems that the god himself tended to move with the tribe when it set out for new conquests and territories. But the goddess, who was much concerned with the actual geographical region over which she presided, remained behind to be overcome by the nextcomers, and to be killed or used for their own purposes, or mated with their own tribal god. Celtic gods and goddesses were not believed to be inviolable.

Over and above the basic pair, so well attested by representation in art, by inscriptions on stone and by the legends of the Celtic world, there were other gods and goddesses of lesser importance and limited but more specific functions. These deities were concerned primarily with the arts, with crafts such as that of the smith, with medicine and healing; or they presided over important local features such as sacred wells and rivers. But there must have been a good deal of overlapping, and the all-purpose god could, according to tradition, turn his hand to any skill or craft when the occasion demanded it.

The Savage Mother

Certain gods, such as Lugus (Irish Lugh, Welsh Lleu), Sucellos, Camulos, Esus, Teutates, have a fairly wide distribution in stone inscriptions and place-names, and some are known from the literary traditions. It is not clear whether these represent deities of a greater and more universal power than the local tribal gods, fathers of the gods themselves in fact, or whether their wider distribution is due to population movement and conquest. Or again, it may be that they were official gods of the Druids themselves, more concerned with 'national' than with tribal concerns.

The mother goddess of the Celts was often conceived of as a warrior, fighting with weapons and instructing the hero in superior secrets of warfare. She was also believed to be capable of influencing the outcome of battle, not by her weapons but by magic and incantation, sometimes taking the form of a sinister bird (crow or raven) and flying over the hosts, causing frenzy and confusion, foretelling the future, and rejoicing over the carnage.

The Celts believed it was undesirable and positively dangerous to name a sacred thing by its correct name. As a result the gods are often referred to in a roundabout way, as were other sacred matters. The Ulstermen, for example, do not swear by a named god but by 'the god by whom my people swear'. This is understood and sufficient to make the oath binding.

The number three was sacred to the Celts. Sometimes they portrayed their deities in groups of three, or as having three heads or three faces. In the tales the deities or semi-divine heroes are described as being one of three people of the same name and birth, or as having been born three times in succession.

The Shape-Shifters

In addition to the powerful gods and goddesses with their many names and symbols, there are other and lesser supernatural beings – spirits and guardians of certain places, godlings and nymphs, sprites and demons. There were animals and birds which were sacred to the Celts, and many of the deities are represented as having bird or animal parts, or bird or animal servants and messengers. There were sacrificial beasts, and birds of good or evil omen, the companions of the gods, and their visible form on occasion.

The boar was held in high esteem by the Celts, its flesh being their choicest food; while the boar hunt was a favourite pastime. Several of the deities have names which link them with boar cults. There are many legends of supernatural boars and their adventures in the Irish and Welsh literary traditions. The otherworld feast is alleged to be sustained by magical pigs which, no matter how often they are cooked and eaten, are whole and alive again next day, ready for the next feast.

The bull also played an important role in mythology, while the horse, the stag (attribute of the Celtic stag god Cernunnos, 'the Horned One') the dog and the ram all figure in the world of Celtic mythology. The ram-headed serpent seems to have occupied a foremost place among the sacred animals, and various other fantastic beasts are figured or referred to in different contexts.

Shape-shifting or changing of form was allegedly much indulged in by the Druids and also by the deities, and several of the semi-mythological characters in the early legends take the form of an animal, some meeting their deaths while in this shape.

Picturepoint London

Birds, too, were regarded as playing a very distinctive and individual role, the crane being sinister and ominous, an idea which has continued on into modern folk belief. The swan was invariably the form taken by benevolent deities, often when engaged in amorous exploits, and sometimes wearing chains of gold or silver, their magical badge which set them apart from other birds.

The World of Magic

The otherworld of the Celts, was a world of magic rather than a world of formal doctrine and inflexible deities; a world which mattered in everyday life rather than at religious feasts and periodical rituals alone; a world not of gloom but of gaiety. Its inhabitants were conceived to be gods and goddesses

Stonehenge was built in pre-Celtic times but was almost certainly used as a temple by the Celtic Druids: the modern Druids still hold ceremonies there on Midsummer Day

whose attitude to human beings was not always beneficent, but who could be propitiated by those who knew the correct form. It was a world which could on occasion be entered by mortals; and the deities were likewise believed to be capable of appearing at will in the world of men – not always to the benefit of mankind. It was a world whose inhabitants must always be reckoned with and appeased; a world to keep at bay, to exploit, rather than to love.

This is the basic background of Celtic religion, with all its regional variations, its

local deities and its local patterns of worship, its different cult legends based on local sacred places and their own distinctive divine associations. This homogeneous background for local expression and tribal preference enables us to speak of pagan Celtic religion as a real, if elusive, thing.

(See also CAULDRON; DRUIDS; HEAD; HORNS; MABINOGION; POETS; and articles on individual gods and heroes.)

ANNE ROSS

FURTHER READING: Anne Ross, *Pagan Celtic Britain* (Columbia University Press, 1967); T. G. E. Powell, *The Celts* (Thames and Hudson, 1980); Stuart Piggott, *Ancient Europe* (Aldine Publishing, 1966) and B. Cunliffe, *Celtic World* (McGraw-Hill, 1979).

CENTAUR

CENTAURS WERE MONSTERS in the classical sense, in that these legendary creatures combined two species in one skin. They had human heads and arms and torsos, merging into the bodies of horses. Centaurs were often savage and unbridled, according to report. Yet they had much mysterious wisdom and virtues far surpassing those of ordinary men.

The ancient Greeks regarded the centaurs as fanciful celebrants who danced in the train of Dionysus, the wine god, but also believed that their own forefathers had both befriended and fought against centaurs in the days of old. The latter conviction probably had some basis in fact, for the name centaurs signifies 'those who round up bulls' and the idea of the centaur may well have sprung from the cattle-breeders of Thessaly in northern Greece, who spent much of their time on horseback and whose manners were rough and barbarous. Alternatively, it has been suggested that the original centaurs were Cimmerian and Scythian raiders, rough-riding nomads from the north, who often invaded Thrace in the north-east.

In mythology the origin of the centaur was more poetic. It was said that a most reprehensible mortal man named Ixion had founded the race. This Ixion committed the outrageous offence of daring to attempt to seduce Hera, wife to Zeus and queen of heaven itself. To see how far Ixion's impudence would go, Zeus formed a cloud image of Hera and substituted it for the goddess. A monster, Centaurus, was born of this strange union, and when grown to maturity, himself united with the mares of Mount Pelion and so produced the centaurs.

Another, more austere legend has it that Chiron was the first centaur. Chiron had begun life as a Titan, a primeval son of Cronus (see CRONUS) and the ocean nymph Philyra. He dared make war against the young gods of Olympus but they defeated him. Apollo, the god of light and reason, punished Chiron by making him half-horse.

Caeneus, in trying to prevent the half-human, half-horse centaurs from raping the women of the Lapith tribe, was mercilessly hammered into the ground by these monsters: stone relief from Olympia

He had been educated by the gods and in turn undertook the instruction of hero after hero: Actaeon, Jason, Castor and Polydeuces, and Achilles, each served an apprenticeship with Chiron in the wilderness.

But Chiron's own fate was an unhappy one. He fell wounded by a poisoned arrow in a tragic accident. The arrow came from the quiver of a good friend, the best of men, impetuous Hercules. There was no antidote to its poison. To escape the wound's unending agony, Chiron renounced immortality in favour of his fellow-Titan, Prometheus. Zeus then generously set the kindly centaur's image in the heavens as the constellation Sagittarius, the Archer.

Feast of the Lapiths

Artists have always delighted in the challenge centaurs offer them. Arnold Bocklin, the 19th century German painter, once painted a huge centaur who stoops into a blacksmith's shop to have his shoes repaired. Rubens sketched a boyish Achilles astride Chiron's broad back; the ageless tutor turns half-way round in mid-gallop to explain some abstruse point. One of Michelangelo's first sculptures was a bas-relief *Battle of the Centaurs*. His source was the Roman poet Ovid, who vividly describes a feast held by the Lapith tribe, a legendary people of Thessaly, to celebrate the nuptials of their chieftain Peirithous.

The centaurs were invited to attend that feast as friends but they got drunk and tried to drag the Lapith women forcibly off into the bushes. A brawl ensued, with slaughter on both sides, and the centaurs were driven away as darkness fell. According to another version, the centaur Eurytion was invited to the feast but became excited with the wine, attempted to abduct the bride, and was restrained by Theseus. Eurytion then returned to the attack with a band of centaurs, who were armed with slabs of stone and trunks of pine trees. A long battle followed from which the Lapiths eventually emerged victorious. The centaurs were driven to the frontiers of Epirus and sought shelter on Mount Pindus. It was this quarrel which sadly put an end to the ancient friendship between mankind and the centaurs.

Today in Greece, the peasants will tell you of *kallikantzaroi*, 'good centaurs', who appear to be descended from the old legendary creatures. But the 'good' which has been prefixed to their names in modern times is a precaution taken out of fear, as when a superstitious northerner refers to elves or fairies as 'the good people'. The *kallikantzaroi* come up out of the ground on winter nights. They are hoofed, shaggy, swift, stupid and mischievous. In short they are 'monsters' in the modern, and not the ancient, sense.

ALEXANDER ELIOT

Mansell Collection

Andy Weir

Ceres

Roman goddess of corn and of the creative powers of the earth, the equivalent of the Greek Demeter; guardian of marriage, and associated with the dead under the earth and with the wine god; her name survives in our word 'cereal'.
See CORN; DEMETER.

Ceylon High Commission

Ceylon (Sri Lanka)

Since 1948, an independent state: some 60% of its people are Buddhists, with a substantial minority of Hindus and smaller numbers of Christians and Moslems; a tooth and a footprint of Buddha are famous relics and objects of pilgrimage.
See SINHALESE BUDDHISM.

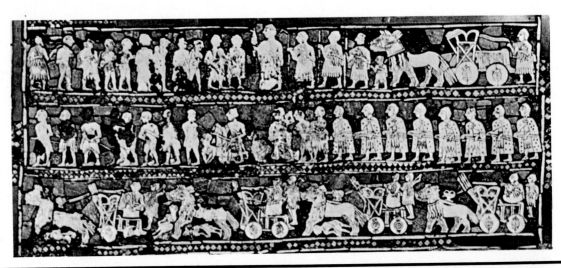

Chaldeans

A people of Mesopotamia, famed as astrologers, magicians and sages; Chaldean kings, the best known of whom are Nebuchadnezzar and Belshazzar, ruled Babylonia for close to 100 years, until overthrown by the Persians in 589 BC, and rebuilt the temples of the city of 'Ur of the Chaldees'.

CHANGELING

THE BIRTH of a deformed, moronic or exceptionally ugly child is an old tragedy. One way to make the parents feel better is to decide that the child is not their own at all but a substitute, left by the fairies in place of the child they have stolen. How much pain has been suffered by children believed to be changelings no one can measure, but early in this century in Ireland a changeling child was burned to death on a hot shovel. In 1894, near Clonmel in Ireland, a young woman was burned to death as a changeling by her husband and family. There are many stories of a child being thrown out on a dungheap to die of exposure, and a favourite way of dealing with a changeling was to whip it until the fairies came to take it back.

A changeling can also be made to reveal its true form by making it laugh or making it cross water. It is sometimes a fairy child but more often an old, even senile fairy, disguised as an infant. A typical English changeling story tells how a woman's baby never grew, was always hungry, failed to learn to walk, and lay in its cradle year after year. The woman's older son, a soldier, coming home after a long absence, saw the child's strange and hairy face, and took an empty eggshell, which he filled with malt and hops, and heated on the fire. There was a laugh from the cradle. 'I am old, old, ever so old,' said the changeling, 'but I never saw a soldier brewing beer in an eggshell before.' Now he knew for sure that it was a changeling the soldier went for it with a whip, and it vanished through the door.

A baby was likely to be snatched away by the fairies before he had been christened, that is before he had been made a Christian and before he had been officially named, and so became a person in his own right. Ways to protect him were to draw a circle of fire round him, hang a pair of open scissors over him, or put his father's trousers across the cradle.

(See also BIRTH.)

'She never had so sweet a changeling', from *A Midsummer Night's Dream*, an illustration by Arthur Rackham. Fairies were thought to steal human children and leave old, senile fairies in their places, disguised as children

Wm Heinemann Ltd/Layton-Sun

Beliefs in witchcraft and magic in the Channel Islands successfully survived the fierce persecutions of the 16th and 17th centuries, and even affected the architecture of houses

CHANNEL ISLANDS

ISLAND DEITIES are said to have something deathly about them; certainly the face of God loomed dark and menacing over the Channel Islands, during the great hunts for witches in the 16th and 17th centuries.

The most cruel tortures were applied without mercy and those sentenced to death were either hanged before being burned at the stake or, as in Guernsey, were burned without the mercy of preliminary strangulation. Mutilation and exile were among the lesser punishments imposed. In Guernsey 58 women and 20 men, mostly natives of that island, were charged with witchcraft. Four of them were burned alive and 28 were hanged before being consigned to the flames. Others were publicly mutilated or banished, and one unfortunate woman was hanged on her return from exile. The charges levelled against the accused were based in the main on rumours or on denunciations made under torture by supposed confederates.

Among the most common forms of spell for which these unfortunates were punished were the infliction of plagues of lice or maggots on their neighbours, and the drying up of the milk of some peasant's cow, a disorder which would probably be identified today with milk fever.

A Birth at the Stake

In Guernsey the witches were believed to be organized on Continental lines, with the familiar features of midnight sabbaths and Satanic orgies. As early as 1563 we find a man named Martin Tulouff confessing to having heard an old witch, his mother, cry out in the name of Lucifer, as she took flight on her broomstick.

Over half a century later an accused Guernsey witch admitted to having been approached by Satan while at the sabbath. At that very moment, she claimed, she experienced the sensation of being transformed into a bitch. Another witch, Colette du Mont, after flying to the sabbath, had copulated with Satan who had assumed for the occasion the shape of a black dog. Animal guise appears to have been common at the sabbaths, where it was not unknown for Satan to preside disguised as a cat.

A witch was often betrayed by the appearance of the 'Devil's Mark' on her body, a sign that she had associated with Satan. Respectable citizens were called on to search for the mark, by inserting pins into the most sensitive parts of the body.

The Bailiwick of Jersey, although somewhat less repressive than that of Guernsey, could also be extremely cruel, over 33 victims being hanged or burned in Jersey during the period of witch trials. In his book *The Black Art*, Rollo Ahmed has described a peculiarly gruesome recorded case in which a pregnant woman gave birth

to a child while being burned alive in the Royal Square. The child was ruthlessly cast into the flames by the frenzied mob, who were determined that no 'imp of Satan' should be allowed to live.

During the fury of the Channel Islands witch-hunt, both the malevolent witch and the good or healing witch were hunted down ferociously, whereas in England the laws against witchcraft sometimes could not be enforced because of the popularity of white witchcraft among the common people. In Jersey even the so-called victims of witchcraft, who sought relief from healing witches, were sentenced to terms of imprisonment on a diet of bread-and-water.

Witch-hunting in the islands exposed not only the witch, whether evil or good, to the rigours of the law, but also the witch's clients.

The official attitude towards witchcraft must have been modified considerably during the second half of the 17th century, if the scepticism of Philippe le Geyte, Lieutenant Bailiff of Jersey, can be taken as an example. 'How many innocent people', he wrote, 'have perished in the flames on the asserted testimony of supernatural circumstances? I cannot say there are no witches: but since the difficulty of convicting them has been recognized in the Island they all seem to have disappeared as though the evidence of time gone by had been but an illusion.' The decline of the persecutions reflected the critical mood of the thinking classes rather than any change of heart among the masses, for long after the repeal of the law against witches, in 1736, much of the popular belief in magic and witchcraft survived relatively unchanged.

Even today old people recount with conviction stories of bewitched cows either aborting or losing their milk. According to one such legend, which I was told on the island of Jersey in 1968, two families quarrelled over the qualities of their respective herds. One placed a curse on the other with the result that their best cow lost its milk. Aid was sought from the parish priest, who uttered prayers against the evil spirit but took the additional and somewhat surprising precaution of inserting quicksilver into the farmhouse walls. The cow, it is said, recovered. All this was said to have occurred in the early 1920s.

From the island of Herm, off Guernsey, comes the story of a Satanic imp which was the cause of strange noises, continually heard at midnight near an old quarry. The owner of a nearby cottage decided to face the worst and called out loudly, 'If you come from God, speak, but if from the Devil, clear out.' The demon cravenly returned to the infernal regions and was heard no more.

The Island Conjurors

White witchcraft has long remained an institution in the Channel Islands, although its practitioners always disclaim any such title, preferring instead to be regarded as healers, diviners or conjurors. To Mr Philip Ahier of Jersey I am indebted for the following anecdote describing the subtleties employed by a 'conjuror' of the last century in discovering the identity of a thief. A

young woman who had lost a ring persuaded a conjuror to assemble all the suspects in one room, where he placed a dusty old boiler over a pure white cockerel. All were then instructed to go outside the door and to return singly. The lights were put out and one by one the suspects returned, to find the room in complete darkness. Each was then told to lay his hand on the boiler and informed that at the touch of the thief the cockerel would crow three times. At the end of the ceremony the hands of all were examined for soot-marks. The only one who had clean hands, a woman, was declared guilty. She immediately made a full confession and returned the ring. The subtle conjuror had known that the guilty one would be afraid to touch the boiler, a trick that could only be successful in a community where there existed a general belief in magical powers.

These conjurors, who were supposed to be seventh sons of seventh sons, were not only diviners but also healed the sick, and have preserved their traditional reputation as psychic healers to the present day.

Visiting Jersey in 1968, I was introduced to an elderly man who had acquired a great reputation for healing by the power of touch. Born, so he said, on the seventh hour of the seventh day, he insisted that his powers were hereditary and gave as his source of inspiration the power of God. A curious feature was his insistence that during the course of his treatment of the sick there always materialized before his eyes a magic book, which was invisible to all but himself and which gave the directions for the cure. He charged no fees, relying entirely on voluntary offerings from his many grateful patients.

A story from Guernsey describes how a woman suddenly saw her sailor son walking on the road ahead of her. Thinking he had unexpectedly returned from his voyage, she hurried to catch up with him, and called his name. Suddenly she stopped abruptly, with a sense of apprehension and terror; although the figure was perfectly visible, there was no sound of footsteps. Several weeks later, she learned from the owners that the ship and all hands had been lost at sea.

A Cold Sort of Vapour

An old resident of Guernsey told me that during the German occupation she received special permission from the Commandant to take up residence in Sark, where she lived for a time alone in an isolated cottage. Almost immediately, she detected what she describes in her own words as 'a cold vapour, heavy and menacing, with the feeling also of eyes looking down on me — very evil.'

During the evenings, at about nine o'clock, she often heard the sound of a bell, ringing quite clearly from the nearby valley. Later she discovered that a previous occupier had heard the sound of chanting mingled with the tolling of the bell, and had written down the musical notation. Years afterwards while travelling abroad, the woman heard the same chant during a visit to a monastery in Italy. She showed her notes to the Abbot who was incredulous, telling her that these were associated with a small community of monks which had existed in only one other place in the past — on the island of Sark in the 6th century. It is true, in fact, that a monk named Magloire, who became patron saint of the Channel Islands, was head of a community of Celtic monks on Sark at that time and that the community later spread to Italy.

Magic and Love

Magic directed towards amorous ends was closely connected with witchcraft, though of a somewhat light-hearted character. The 'Witches' Rock' in Jersey is still pointed out as the place which used to be visited by young girls at night, to seek out their spectral lovers; and also, it is said, by tradesmen who wanted to discover by divination how to outwit their business rivals.

In a curious household rite which continued to be practised in the present century, with the object of commanding the presence of a defecting lover, a cake was baked, containing flour and soot. Half was eaten and the other half wrapped in the deserted maiden's left garter and placed beneath her pillow. This spell was supposed to bring the spectral double of the young man to her bedside at midnight.

The visitor to the Islands who is sufficiently interested in the old way of life to make the necessary inquiries will be shown curious 'witch ledges' on the chimneys.

The purpose of this peculiar feature of Channel Island houses is to provide a resting place for the witch. It was thought that if she could not find anywhere to rest on her journey, she would be angry with the householders. This custom must be seen in conjunction with another which has been observed within living memory, the custom of attaching garlic to the rooftops to keep witches from entering the house.

Occasionally the inquirer may hear the rumour that witchcraft survives in one particular parish or another, but in general the attitude to such matters today is one of half-belief. It has been truly said that the Channel Islands 'constitute a little museum of ancient habits' in the modern world.

ERIC MAPLE

Chaos

In mythology, the confusion which existed before the universe was set in order, and also the forces of confusion and disorder which still exist: frequently personified as a monster which does battle with the gods, the forces of order; they subdue it, a victory which men may have to act out periodically in rituals to keep disorder in check. See CREATION.

British Museum

Charlemagne

Great European ruler (742–814), the central character of medieval legends in which he is a super-human warrior and the champion of Christianity against Islam; said to have risen from the dead to fight in the Crusades, or to be still alive but sleeping till his people need him; connected with the constellation of the Great Bear of 'Charles's Wain'; later overshadowed in legend by his companions in arms, the 'twelve peers', who included Roland, Oliver and Ogier the Dane.

Brompton Studio

CHARON

THIS AGED and irascible boatman was believed by the Greeks to ferry the souls of the dead across the infernal river (the Acheron or Styx) which separated the land of the living from that of the dead. Charon is thus associated with Hermes Psychopompos (see HERMES), who summoned those appointed to die and led them to Hades. It has been thought that he was originally a death god, as was his Etruscan counterpart Charun. He is mentioned in Greek literature as early as the 5th century BC and is frequently depicted in art, particularly on the white-ground vases called *lecythi*.

Charon had to be paid for performing his sombre office of ferryman of the dead. It was customary to place an obolus, a silver coin, under the tongue or between the teeth of the corpse, to pay the fare. The shades of the dead who had not been properly buried, and thus equipped to cross into Hades, were refused passage by Charon and so left to haunt the living, seeking their release. The Roman poet Virgil draws a grim picture of the grisly ferryman in his *Aeneid* (book 6). 'Charon, on whose chin lies a mass of unkempt, hoary hair; his eyes are staring orbs of flame; his squalid garb hangs by a

Mary Evans Picture Library

In Greek mythology Charon, the terrifying boatman of hell, ferried the souls of the dead across the river which separated the land of the living from the land of the dead

knot from his shoulders. Unaided, he poles the boat, tends the sails, and in his murky craft convoys the dead.'

Though a pagan concept, the image of the grim boatman and his load of souls deeply affected the minds of many medieval and Renaissance Christians. Dante tells, in his *Divine Comedy*, of his encounter with Charon when he descends, with Virgil as his guide, into the Inferno. 'Charon, demonic form, with eyes of burning coal, collects them all, beckoning, and each that lingers, with his oar strikes.' And Michelangelo, in the stupendous vision of the *Last Judgement* which he painted above the altar of the Sistine Chapel, depicts Charon and his fatal boat with a realism both terrifying and unforgettable. The memory of Charon

passed into modern Greek folklore where, under the name of Charos, he carries off the young and old.

The Etruscans, that mysterious people who lived in central Italy and whose culture is known mainly from the evidence of their tombs, venerated a grisly deity called Charun. His demonic image appears on the walls of tombs, holding the hammer or mallet with which he dealt the death-blow to those whose destined time had come. This Etruscan Charun is clearly a death god; whether there was an original connection between him and the Greek Charon, as their names suggest, has not been proved.

The idea that the newly dead have to cross a river to reach the land of the dead is very ancient. It occurs in the Egyptian

Pyramid Texts (c 2400 BC) and many means of transport are devised. The most notable, in the present connection, is that of securing passage in a boat manned by one named 'He who looks behind'. The name is significant, for this Egyptian ferryman, like the Greek Charon, is a difficult character and has to be persuaded or threatened into taking the deceased to the next world. The vignette which illustrates Chapter XCIII of the Book of the Dead shows the deceased addressing a man or deity seated in a boat, whose head is turned backwards. In the ancient Mesopotamian Epic of Gilgamesh a similar idea occurs: the hero is ferried over the 'water of death' by Urshanabi, the boatman.
(See also HELL.)

Sonia Halliday

Charm

A spell: a form of words or an object believed to contain magic power, hence its broader meaning of attractiveness, fascination, allure or, as a verb, to enchant or bewitch; derived from the Latin *carmen*, 'a song'.
See IMITATIVE MAGIC; INCANTATION; TALISMAN.

ZFA

Cherub

In Jewish and Christian tradition, a type of angel, a winged being with a human head: descended from creatures with animal bodies, wings and human faces believed in ancient Mesopotamia to intercede for man with the gods; two cherubim 15 feet high stood in the Holy of Holies, the dwelling of God, in Solomon's temple at Jerusalem: later, a cherub is represented in art as a beautiful child.
See GUARDIAN SPIRITS.

Underlying the naive simplicity of many children's games are themes which are neither simple nor quaint

CHILDREN'S GAMES

TRADITIONAL CHILDREN'S games tend to consist of more or less standard movements and actions, often complicated by the accompaniment of a rhyme or chant. Older games, which today's parents and grandparents may remember from their non-televisual childhoods, generally have long roots stretching back to Britain and Europe. But, old or new, a considerable number of games have roots or antecedents that go further back – to a time when such activities were adult concerns. So most children's games can be viewed as survivals, in varying degrees, of once-important rituals or ritual dramas that involved the whole community.

In past ages, children were more closely integrated into adult life, as they still are among primitive peoples and in the more backwoods parts of civilized regions. It is not surprising, then, that the flourishing oral lore of children has perpetuated and transmitted, over the years, ritual relics that were once very serious necessities.

Take perhaps the most famous game inherited from England, *London Bridge*, traditionally played in the United States with some curious variations. Basically, two children stand facing each other, hands clasped and arms raised to form an arch. The others run under the arch, until at a signal

the arch descends and traps a child. When all players have been captured, the American game ends with a tug-of-war – which lasts until one child lets go and breaks the line. That child is then victimized in some prearranged way.

Other variations include the corruption of the original song:

London Bridge is broken down,
  Dance o'er my lady lee,
London Bridge is broken down,
  With a gay lady.

These lines have now been drastically simplified to:

London Bridge is falling down,
  Falling down, falling down,
London Bridge is falling down,
  My fair lady.

But the change is just a normal mutation, no more significant than the use in colonial Massachusetts of Charleston Bridge as the game's locale.

No, it is the act of 'trapping' players, and the final isolation of a victim, that most interests the folklorists. They see in it a reflection of the world-wide belief that some sort of sacrifice is required for successful bridge building. Often, the victim was interred alive in the foundations of the bridge. (See BRIDGES.)

Also, perhaps more imaginatively, some experts see in the tug-of-war a hint of old European games involving a symbolic contest between forces of good and evil, usually taking place on a pretended bridge. So the two

children forming the arch were demonic or angelic 'keepers of the bridge', deciding the fate hereafter of the others. It was so, certainly, in a game called *Bridge of Holland* once played by children of Pennsylvania's German immigrants.

The supernatural, on a fairy tale level, appears also in a game called *Old Witch*, at one time widely popular with American children. The child playing the witch uses standardized tricks to steal away other players from their 'mother'; the latter must find them and use similar formula tricks to rescue them. There are no winners and losers – there is merely a strong current of ritual drama, performed for its own sake, as with many other quasi-dramatic games.

The Farmer in the Dell, for instance, takes its drama from the assigning of roles – one child as farmer to begin, then 'the farmer takes a wife', 'the wife takes a child', and so on. The last player to be chosen is a cheese taken by a rat. We might see an element of victimization again here, though whether the victim is sacrifice, scapegoat, initiate or otherwise is not immediately obvious.

Elements of primitive tribal 'testing' rituals – initiations, ordeals or whatever – may be reflected not only in the rites performed by new members of present-day clubs and fraternities, but also in children's games

Following page **Many games still played can be seen in Breughel's *Children's Games*, painted in 1560. Fragments of old rituals and beliefs have survived in games which have their roots in the past**

Rev Damian Webb

Rev Damian Webb

Left The 'love games' of children may be associated with both fertility rites and with imitation of adult concern with marriage. In this popular ring game, sometimes called *Rosy Apple, Lemon or a Pear*, players in couples must dance through a symbolic wedding arch *Above* Two more ring games, *In and Out the Dusty Bluebells* (left) and the more modern *I'm Going to Kentucky* (right) both involve finding a 'fair lady' and are also enactments of grown-up courtship and marriage *Below* The tug-of-war which concludes games like *London Bridge* or *Oranges and Lemons* seems to hint at the tradition of human sacrifice, but may also be descended from ancient forms of ritual combat, mock battles between winter and summer, light and dark, good and evil

of the *Forfeits* or *Truth or Consequences* kind. In these, a player's failure to answer a question, or perform a required action correctly, makes him liable to undergo some unpleasant trial or punishment.

The initiate-victim concept also appears in games like *Tag*, or *Blind Man's Buff*, where one player stands alone against the rest, seeking to catch someone to take his place. *Blind Man's Buff* is known by many names all over the world: its initiation elements may be more apparent in an American variant where the players revolve in a ring around the blindfolded player, until the blind one raps with a staff on the floor. He then points the staff at the ring; the player singled out in this way emits some noise, in a disguised voice, and the blind one tries to

guess who it is. If he guesses correctly, the child identified must assume the blindfold.

Anyone who remembers the games of his own childhood will be able to call to mind those others which retain some hints of this testing, or initiation, 'one-against-all' ritual. We can find patterns akin to it in *Hide and Seek* or even *Thimble, Thimble* (also called *Hunt the Thimble*), both still popular among children. We can find it very clearly in that well-known test of courage and daring called *Follow the Leader*. And we can find it in a simulated war game like *King of the Castle*, where one child tries to hold the top of a rise against all besiegers.

A once popular ball game, variously called *Alley Alley Over* or *Haley Over* is equally a war game, but for two opposing groups —

Rev Damian Webb

and so is less akin to an initiation rite than to straightforward mimetic ritual. Two groups of boys stand on opposite sides of a house, and one throws a ball over the house, calling out the game's title. Whoever catches the ball then runs (or sneaks) around to the 'enemy' side and tries to hit an opponent with the ball. Anyone hit is a prisoner of war, whereupon the ball is thrown back in the opposite direction and the other side has a chance to gain a prisoner. The game ends when all one side has been captured.

Lurking prominently in the background behind many children's games is that all-inclusive category of primitive ritual, the fertility rite. The theme of celebrating fertility may lie behind the game (imitating adult work) called *Here We Go Round the Mulberry Bush*, inherited from England along with a more specifically fertile, though now less popular, game based on the song *Gathering Nuts in May*. But then practically any game like these involving a dance-like circular movement or ring can be labelled with the fertility implications, as long as all the players are included in the ring.

One old game of this sort, probably almost unknown today, was called *Oats, Pease, Beans and Barley Grows* in the United States. It held other names in Europe, where it flourished for centuries, mentioned by Froissart in the 14th century and Rabelais in the 15th. Players circle solemnly, singing or chanting lines that still hold much of the religious awe of the old 'mysteries' and true fertility rites:

Oats, pease, beans and barley grows,
How, you nor I nor nobody knows.

The game can become imitative of a marriage rite, with a boy and a girl within the circle and the children chorusing good advice.

It may be more difficult to see fertility magic in that long-lived round game for small children, *Ring Around the Rosy*, the verses of which (in some modern versions) end with a sneezing noise and then 'we all fall down'. But it seems even more fanciful to follow some modern writers in tracing the game's origin back to the Great Plague. Perhaps victims of the 'Red Death' were rosy with blood and afflicted with sneezing; certainly, in the end, they all fell down. But the game originally did not contain these precise words, on which the theory is based. Instead, older

and better forms turn out to have been sacrificial-victim games, isolating one player with a forfeit to pay – as in a famous 19th century version:

Round the ring of roses,
Pots full of posies,
The one who stoops last
Shall tell whom she loves best.

So the child who was slowest to 'fall down' had to make a blushing admission. A common variant played in more recent times also demanded a victim, but much less poetically:

Ring around the roses,
Pocket full of posies,
One, two, three – squat!

Crude as it is, this version still demanded the singling out of a victim of love – which may not be all that close to the object of fertility rituals, but is certainly a long way further from a gory death by plague.

Other games seek to draw from children an admission of love, or function as forms of love divination, and so stand perhaps at the threshold of the fertility theme. The counting game *Rich Man, Poor Man* supposedly foretells what sort of person the player will marry. A Hallowe'en game like ducking or bobbing for apples floating in a basin of water grew out of similar games for young adults; each apple bore a player's name, and you would marry the one whose apple you managed to bite. Sometimes the apple was hung from a string, and a boy or girl tried to bite into it from opposite sides – with every chance for mouth-to-mouth contact. (See ALL HALLOWS' EVE.)

And love games come into the *Forfeits* kind of play. A fairly modern game called *Spin the Bottle* requires the children to sit in a ring while a bottle on its side is spun in the centre. The player at whom the neck of the bottle points must confess whom he or she loves, and must sometimes kiss the object of affection, or else face a forfeit.

Most of the games mentioned so far have been akin, one way or another, to religious activity of older times. The links may sometimes seem rather strained, remote or unlikely – but some connections can usually be made. As a final and vivid illustration, take that universal game generally called *Hopscotch* except by the Scots, who call it *Peever*. The players mark out a specified pattern of squares on the ground, or with chalk on a city

sidewalk, and kick a marker through the squares in a fixed order, while hopping on one foot from square to square in its wake. No more than a test of agility, it seems – until it is noted that in many versions the squares are arranged in special ways, two of which are the traditional shapes of the maze and the basilica (the latter containing seven squares, roughly the plan of a church). So, it seems, the progress through the diagram – without stepping on any line or losing balance – reflects the progress of the human soul through the trials of life towards salvation, indicated by the upper square, which indeed is often rounded or domed.

This analysis may seem to be too much symbolic weight to be carried by a children's game. But remember that children and their lore are notoriously conservative, that many of these games are as old as Western civilization – and that symbol and myth and ritualization are not so alien to children's lives, even today.

The act of mythologizing can be seen to permeate even those most up-to-date games involving cops and robbers, cowboys and Indians, Batman or spacemen. Here the children are imitating the myth heroes of their imaginative world, just as primitives performed mimetic ceremonies in which their gods and heroes were portrayed (and realized). Even in those games that approach the nature of organized sport, the element of ritual has a place. In spring, when the ground is barely clear of snow in less tropical areas, it is the season for those complex and intent games of marbles, the rules and skills of which are as complex and demanding as those of a Navaho healing ceremony. Some weeks later, the time for playing marbles is over: all the children know it, by some unspoken but inflexibly binding, almost instinctual law. Perhaps this is the same instinctual process, diminished but still active, that led men in the ancient days to regulate their seasonal celebrations, evocations and ceremonial magics.
(See also NURSERY RHYMES.)

DOUGLAS HILL

FURTHER READING: Iona and Peter Opie, *Children's Games in Street and Playground* (Oxford Univ. Press, 1969); W. W. Newell *Games and Songs of American Children* (Harper, 1883).

Offspring of Typhon, a dreaded being associated with storm and tempest, and Echidna, who was part woman and part serpent, the Chimaera was a misbegotten monster of Greek mythology which belched fire as it breathed

CHIMAERA

THE CHIMAERA was a monster compounded of parts from three creatures: lion, goat and serpent. It appears in Homer's *Iliad* (books 6 and 16) as located in Lycia, in Asia Minor, where it is killed by the hero Bellerophon. Bellerophon's legend contains more than his battle with the Chimaera but these other features belong only to the background of

this article and do not concern us here.

Bellerophon was already disliked by his ruler, Proetus, the king of Ephyre in Argolis, a place usually identified with Corinth. He was also disliked by Proetus' wife, Antea, who tried to seduce him and failed. In revenge, she accused him of making advances to her. Proetus did not try to kill him directly, but sent him to Iobates of Lycia, his father-in-law. Bellerophon was at first well received by Iobates, the king of Lycia, but when the king read the calumnious letter that he brought, containing secret instructions that Bellerophon should be killed, he plotted his death by ordering him to slay the Chimaera.

The Chimaera was of divine, not human origin, being 'a lion at the front, a serpent at

the rear and in the middle a *chimaera*.' This word, which seems to leave part of its body unexplained, meant 'goat'. 'The Chimaera breathed flashing fire. But Bellerophon killed it, relying on marvels from the gods.' He then fought his way through other perils until he married the king's daughter. The Chimaera is called *amaimaketos*, an epithet which is otherwise used of fire and probably means 'raging', though some ancient writers used it to mean 'invincible'.

In Hesiod's *Theogony*, probably written in the 8th century BC, the Chimaera is mentioned as born by Echidna to Typhon with other monsters: Orthus, Geryon's hound, Cerberus and the Hydra. Typhon's origin was certainly in Lycia, so that scholars who

Chimaera

say that the Chimaera's location there is only secondary are probably wrong.

Hesiod says that the Chimaera had three heads, one belonging to each component animal, that it was killed by Pegasus and Bellerophon, and that by Orthus it was the mother of the Sphinx and the Nemean lion. A fragment of Hesiod's *Catalogue of Women* which mentions the legend of Bellerophon seems to be our earliest explicit reference to Pegasus as the name of his horse. Pindar alludes very briefly to Bellerophon's killing of the Chimaera.

Apollodorus, at the end of his history of Greek mythology, written in the 2nd century BC, once more gives the story of Bellerophon. Of the Chimaera he says that it was more than a match for many men, and

that through its middle head, that of a goat, it belched fire. It was a single creature with the power of three beasts. Bellerophon, soaring high on his winged horse, Pegasus, shot down the Chimaera from the height. Pegasus was thus a necessary means for its killing.

A celebrated representation of the Chimaera in art is the Etruscan bronze figure found at Arezzo in Tuscany, which

Famous Etruscan bronze of the Chimaera in the Archeological Museum, Florence. The name of this mythical monster, which once described a beast compounded of a lion, a goat and a serpent, has come to be used for any hybrid plant or animal or in a metaphorical sense for any imaginary fear.

shows a powerful lion's body, limbs and head, a goat's head rising from its back, and a tail consisting of a serpent's body and head.

This has an affinity with a Hittite winged lion from Carchemish on the Euphrates which has a snake for its tail and a second and human head rising from its back. The fiery breath of the Chimaera may be a mythical rendering of the flaming gas that rises from the ground here and there in the south-west of Anatolia.

Alternatively, it has been suggested that the Chimaera was a personification of the storm-cloud. Nowadays the word is used to describe any fantastic or horrible imaginary creature, and is also the term applied by biologists to plants and animals having hybrid characteristics.

CHINA

供之　俱立周倉手持偃月刀軍民人

Twin ethers encompassing the universe are known as Yin and Yang: the Yin ether is of the earth, dark, female, heavy; while that of Yang is of heaven, bright, male, light

Traditional Chinese religion, surprisingly, has something in common with Maoist ideology in that both have a strong social purpose. Long before the Communists took over, the Chinese government 'adopted' the ancient pantheon of gods and turned them into a celestial bureaucracy, with a supernatural emperor at the apex, supported by divine 'officials' of all ranks, down to the gods of the household

RELIGION IN CHINA has always been deeply embedded in the social system, and it is not possible to consider the one without the other. It is among the world's richest religions. Intermingled with the strands of Buddhism, Taoism, ancestor worship, folk religion and Confucianism is a deep concern with the fate of society. From this complex background three major interests emerge.

One interest was in man, in his individual relationship to the universe: Taoism has been its important representative. The second was in man as a being important in the future of the world, and has been represented by Buddhism. The third concern was with society rather than with man as an individual or the world at large. This 'social religion', was represented by a set of ideas which had no name of its own (although some of its parts had names) and is of central importance for understanding China.

Buddhism and Taoism are considered here largely in their role of providing social religion with some of its materials, or providing important alternative beliefs for individuals with problems in adjusting to society in different circumstances or stages of life (see also BUDDHISM; TAOISM). The period of recorded religious development in China is extremely long, going back to the Shang dynasty of the 18th to 12th centuries BC, but we are mainly concerned here with modern China.

In China today, millions of people, some speaking mutually unintelligible dialects and spread over vast areas, live under one central control. The problem of maintaining social and cultural unity is very great. This is no new problem, for it existed as early as

A 19th century Chinese screen painting of the learned god of war, Kuan Ti (seated). Being a god of heaven, as opposed to a demon, he was expected to prevent rather than encourage warfare

the Chou dynasty (12th-3rd centuries BC), when the people we call Chinese first began to expand rapidly into areas inhabited by people of different cultures.

Religion was always a major means for dealing with the problem. Even the foreign (Manchu) Ch'ing dynasty (1644-1911 AD) used Chinese religion to govern the Chinese and the peoples they had absorbed.

Religion became a means of social control by absorbing, over the centuries, most of the local cults and bringing them together under the Chinese system. This was originally the worship of heaven, of the ancestors and of a host of gods and spirits. The Former Han period (from 206 BC to 220 AD) was a time of great expansion, during which the system was given a new basis in a total theory of the universe, meaningful to all under Chinese control. Gradually, two levels for appreciating this theory developed.

One level of the system was very sophisticated and the concepts used impersonal or semi-personal. The other was 'religious' in the more conventional sense: it involved gods and other spirits. (The two levels are also present in other systems, including both Taoism and Buddhism.) The first level was meant for the scholarly and the second for the less educated, who could not read formal texts. They received their ideas from proverbs, 'good books' written in simple characters, folk stories which were told rather than read, and from pictorial materials.

This division was not completely clearcut. Certainly there was a major social gap between the mass of illiterate or semi-literate peasants and artisans, and the scholarly official classes. There were also, however, people of varied education working in occupations which were not highly regarded, in trade and commerce, in professional religious roles and in entertainment and teaching. Women, mostly illiterate or semi-literate, cut across all divisions.

In addition, the two interpretations of ideas overlapped, complementing and reinforcing each other. At the first level, a general blueprint of social relationships was authenticated by reference to ultimate 'truths' about the universe and its relation to society. Values associated with society were further underlined and acted out in rites and ceremonies. These activities were themselves seen as having a deeper cosmic significance too: they helped to balance the universe.

The second level further sanctified social relationships by reflecting them on a 'supernatural' plane. It also provided more details about specific connections between gods and the supernatural, and different social institutions. Together these sets of ideas covered the society. Some were concerned with the roles of the emperor and his officials, the form of government and territorial administration. Some were concerned with families and other kin-groups which had a high degree of political and economic control over their members, and to all other forms of association such as guilds, societies and even groups of friends. It is difficult to think of a corner into which these sets of ideas did not reach.

Because they explained everything to do with society, these ideas were even drawn upon by non-approved groups including bandits and rebellious organizations.

Yin and Yang

At the higher level, the blueprint for social relations in the traditional Chinese system was provided by a group of ideas which has been loosely and popularly termed 'Confucianism', from its connection with the teachings of Kung Fu-tze (550–480 BC). There have been many different interpretations of its precise nature. Some writers have stressed its concern with the things of this world and with ethics. Others, seeking to align it with the 'higher religions', have stressed the semi-personal nature of its concept of heaven. There has been much controversy among scholars over definitions and functions but in outline the theory is as follows.

Originally, there was a single cosmic cell containing 'ether' (*Ch'i*) which was made to pulsate by a creative force known as *Tao*. Tension set up by this activity eventually rent the cell into opposite and complementary halves; twin ethers which encompassed the universe and which are known as *Yin* and *Yang*. The Yin ether is of the earth, dark, female, heavy; while that of Yang is of heaven, bright, male, light. The continuous operation of Tao, which is a sort of natural law, causes these entities to alternate, and by this process five 'elements' are produced: water, fire, wood, metal, and earth. By various combinations of these elements, the multitude of things in this world comes into existence (see also ACUPUNCTURE).

Radio Times Hulton Picture Library

Camera Press London

Above left A new dragon boat is blessed by a Taoist priest, who brings it offerings of roast pork and vegetables. Later the boat will take part in races designed to bring rain for the spring rice planting *Above* Portrait of the powerful Empress Tzu-Hsi at her funeral in 1908. According to Chinese religious belief the earthly ruler had a counterpart in heaven, known as the Jade or Pearly Emperor *Left* Malevolent spirits were thought to be haunting the small island of Cheung Chau near Hong Kong, after the discovery there some years ago of human remains. To placate the spirits the islanders hold an annual Bun festival, at which they say prayers and light joss sticks. They also parade through the streets *(below left),* balancing their children in the air *(below).* The spirits are presented with 60ft high mountains of buns

Camera Press London

Camera Press London

The Wisdom of Confucius

From the Analects, *a collection of sayings attributed to Confucius (translated by Lin Yutang).*

Confucius said, 'I am going to remain quiet!' Tsekung remarked, 'If you remain quiet, how can we ever learn anything to teach to the others?' And Confucius said, 'Does Heaven talk? The four seasons go their way in succession and the different things are produced. Does Heaven talk?'

Confucius said, 'It is man that makes truth great, and not truth that makes man great.'

Confucius said, 'The superior man understands what is right; the inferior man understands what will sell.'

Baron Wen Chi said that he always thought three times before he acted. When Confucius heard this, he remarked, 'To think twice is quite enough.'

Confucius said, 'You can kill the general of an army, but you cannot kill the ambition in a common man.'

Confucius said, 'Truth may not depart from human nature. If what is regarded as truth departs from human nature, it may not be regarded as truth.'

Confucius said, 'The superior man is liberal towards others' opinions, but does not completely agree with them; the inferior man completely agrees with others' opinions, but is not liberal toward them'

Tsekung asked, 'Is there one single word that can serve as a principle of conduct for life?' Confucius replied, 'Perhaps the word 'reciprocity' will do. Do not do unto others what you do not want others to do unto you.'

The Yin and Yang and the elements were the basis of traditional classifications in China. Colours, parts of the empire, parts of the body, numbers and many other things, were grouped and defined in terms of them. They were thought to determine the natural forces, even the process of history and the fate of dynasties. By their continuous motion all things are formed. Death and decay is the process by which they separate into their original cosmic components. Some liken it all to the action of a gigantic pair of bellows, continually sucking in cosmic materials out of heaven and earth, forming them briefly into things as they are now, and then letting them out again to return to nothingness.

If some of this sounds obscure, the Taoist would say it is inevitable. The very adjectives used for Yin, Yang and the elements are attempts to describe the indescribable. The Taoist's task was to achieve an inward appreciation of his own nature, which is the nature of all things, for all things are governed by a single Tao. Only then could he work in true harmony with the universe.

The Harmony of Ritual

For the Confucian, however, the nature of Tao was known. It consisted of rules of conduct, etiquette and ceremonial. It was a guide for social action. Working through society, man had the important task of adjusting heaven and earth, and preserving universal balance. Heaven was seen by the Confucian as the source of morality. Earth was amoral, and man combined something of both heaven and earth. Heaven wielded the power of reward and punishment. It was approachable for knowledge of the future only by the emperor, and it was from heaven that he obtained his mandate to rule on earth. Imperial sacrifices to heaven continued until 1911, and coronations were accompanied by sacrifices, intended as 'adjustments' of heaven and earth.

All approved forms of ritual were seen as having a harmonizing function, including the cult of Confucius which took place in temples found at all administrative centres and resembling some of the temples of the gods worshipped by ordinary people. Other important cults were dedicated to the patron of literature and to the creator of writing. All these rites helped to adjust society, and to adjust further the universal order. Most important, however, was ancestor worship, in which the emperor venerated the ancestors of the whole society, and his subjects their own forbears.

The Worship of Ancestors

Confucianism did not uphold belief in the survival of the soul. In earlier times, however, the nobility practised ancestor worship at ancestral tablets and graves. These rites were related to the ancient belief that man has two souls, a superior or spiritual soul which will ascend into heaven and meet its ancestors if due ceremonies are performed, and a second soul which informs the body during life and the corpse after death, provided the correct sacrifices are made.

In later times, scholars saw such rites as caring for the living rather than the dead. Their function was to engender feelings of filial piety and therefore harmony in the family or clan. For this reason, only those involved in the continuation of the kin-group were venerated: married persons with sons. In clans, communal halls for housing ancestral tablets became also centres for trying disputes and entertaining officials and others with whom good relations were sought.

Buddhism provided an alternative conception of man after death: the idea of a soul surviving to expiate its sins against the world in purgatory before rebirth. Naturally the idea implicit here, that parents could do wrong, was abhorrent to the true Confucian. Generally speaking, Buddhist rites for the dead, performed for parents, were frowned upon except in special circumstances.

The models for correct social behaviour and attitudes were found also in the family, the basic unit of society. The young Chinese learnt that young must venerate old and that loyalty was a most important virtue. In large family households he also learnt, sometimes from bitter experience, that acquisitiveness, self-indulgence, dishonesty and lack of a ceremonial approach to relations (which were considered to be the sources of cosmic disharmony) could certainly cause tension in the group.

The values acquired in the family were extended to all other areas of life, including relations with the government, business and other forms of organization. Many institutions copied the kinship pattern for organizing themselves. Masters were like fathers to their apprentices, teachers similarly so to their pupils, and the emperor likewise to his subjects. Even religious groups, particularly the monastic orders, were organized according to pseudo-kinship principles into 'families' and 'clans'.

Balance, it was considered, could be preserved only if one acted with correct feelings. To adjust society, one had first to adjust oneself. The scholar was expected to practice self-cultivation to get an inward appreciation of the truth of the system. A non-virtuous teacher or government official could accomplish nothing good. Even epidemics, floods and other natural disasters were explained in terms of lack of virtue of the people, particularly the leaders of society.

During active social life the scholar, certainly, was expected to work entirely with Confucian assumptions. In old age, however, he was allowed to be less conventional. Some took up Buddhism as they became more concerned with physical decline and approaching death, practising meditation to assist them in their future lives. Many women were attracted to Buddhism.

Others took up Taoism, which related the individual more directly to the universe. They practised Taoist methods for prolonging life, with the object of preventing the Yin and Yang from separating. This involved exercises, such as 'Chinese boxing' and breath control, and the use of special herbs. Sometimes, although this was less approved, they employed sexual practices in order to 'nourish' Yang with Yin.

Today in Hong Kong elderly men to whom Taoism seems especially to appeal, and some women climb mountains early in the morning, or perform the careful slow movements of Chinese boxing in quiet spots of the city. Some, in order to be in tune with Nature, keep little birds in cages.

Tolerance of the eccentricities of the old had a useful function. It kept those approaching senility out of social mischief, directing them within themselves rather than outside. Such self-centred activities were less tolerated for the young, although other more social forms of Buddhism and Taoism were condoned. Business men who joined societies for performing charity (part of the Mahayana tradition of which Chinese Buddhism is part) mitigated their acquisitiveness to some extent. Those forming Taoist groups to cure disease among ordinary people were performing a social service.

Man was seen as standing between gods and demons and attempted to adjust them to his social life in orderly fashion

The Celestial Bureaucracy

The metaphysical significance of Confucianism must have been difficult for ordinary people to appreciate fully. Confucian 'results' were obtained by the use of proverbs and stories of filial piety and by a system of sermons in the rural areas; this had declined in effectiveness by the late 19th century. But a 'basis' had also to be provided. This was done by recourse to the multitude of gods and spirits of Chinese religion and the local cults it absorbed. The system was turned into an animated version of the theory of Yin and Yang.

In the ancient system, gods and spirits or demons were divided between heaven and earth respectively. Under later influence from Yin-Yang theory, gods became identified with Yang and demons with Yin. As a result of Confucian ideas the gods generally, being of heaven, were seen as the source of morality. There were a few delightfully unconventional beings, mainly of Taoist origin, however, who never quite fitted in with this scheme. Demons, being of earth, were amoral. They were greedy and impolite – like the Yin side of human nature – although like amoral people they occasionally had their uses, and sometimes destroyed each other.

In general, man was seen as standing between gods and demons and attempted to adjust them, as the scholar adjusted the Yin and Yang elements to run his social life in orderly fashion. If he showed greed and other Yin qualities, he might attract the attention of demons, and the disfavour of the gods. If he was virtuous and moral, the gods brought him the benefits of the good life.

Gods were of different kinds. Some were personified forces of Nature, while others were deified sages, buddhas and bodhisattvas, or saviours of mankind, taken from the more supernatural levels of Taoism and Buddhism. But many were former members of society: a human being contained during life both Yin and Yang or god and demon, both elements surviving as souls. It was believed that a powerful Yang soul, that of a virtuous or powerful person, might become a god; while the Yin soul of a person dying tragically and unexpectedly might be unprepared, and hence resentful, thus becoming a powerful demon.

An ingenious and rather sinister 'take-over' of the pantheon was gradually effected by the State. It took all the good, public-minded gods it could find, added to them by deifying people of noted virtue, and then placed them all in a gigantic celestial bureaucracy. This was an organization paralleling that of the worldly order but going much farther. It stretched into every institution of mankind, into areas beyond the reach of mortal officials.

Significantly, this hierarchy was not only set up but also controlled by the human bureaucracy. The head of the celestial government was the Jade or Pearly Emperor, the counterpart, of course, of the real emperor of China. Under him were boards of administration for controlling the forces of time and of Nature. There was a Ministry of Justice, comprising numerous city gods and presided over by a city god-in-chief. These gods were the counterparts of mortal officials in charge of provinces and districts of China, and individually they were based on temples in the major cities of their territories.

The origin of the city gods is said to date to the time of the Emperor Yao (2357–2255 BC) when a spirit was thought to live in the city moat and wall. They guarded their territories from spiritual enemies and influences. Ordinary people were encouraged to help in their selection and, theoretically at least, they were appointed for a limited term and could be transferred from place to place. Beneath them were the earth gods who were also of great antiquity and looked after the smaller community, such as a village or section of a village. Under them again were a multitude of anonymous officials known as 'honourable men' who acted as runners to the gods. In Hong Kong today they are pictured together with their horses, as means of transport, on charm papers used in ritual.

Gods of specific institutions sometimes shared temples with the community gods. The kitchen god was worshipped in all households. There was a goddess of the bedhead in charge of married couples and their children, who usually shared a bed, and there was often a goddess of child-rearing, who was a former midwife and powerful spirit-medium. There were various patrons of agriculture, and the crafts and trades had their gods too. Jewellers had a Minister of Works who achieved fame by making an ornament to conceal a disfigurement of an emperor's consort. Carpenters and other skilled workers had a craftsman god, said to have once made a wooden kite on which he rode. Even rogues and bandits had their patrons. This may have created 'honour among thieves' but it was largely a case of the system turned against itself.

Some gods had dual, even triple roles, which added to the complexity and size of the pantheon. The kitchen god, for instance, was also the patron of professional cooks. The Chinese goddess of mercy is thought to have been an ancient local goddess before the advent of Buddhism, in which her role was to help in the salvation of Buddhist souls. But she is also represented with a baby on her arm and in this form she helped people who desired to have children.

A 3rd century hero, seen as the embodiment of bravery, loyalty and righteousness, was known under seven names and was the patron of pawn shops, all kinds of friendly societies and sworn brotherhoods; in Hong Kong today he is even patron of the police. He was also a soldier god of wealth and, under another name, god of war. Some civic gods had a role in controlling man after death as well. The earth gods cared for graves. The city gods controlled souls in their districts and had some influence on the fate of Buddhist souls in purgatory.

Man's Right to Punish the Gods

It is difficult to assess precisely the attitude of the officials to all these gods. Certainly they were expected to venerate their celestial counterparts and consult them on community matters. As the *Book of Rites*, one of the classics of the Confucian canon, points out: 'when the scholar shows respect, the people will believe'. Folk stories show that ordinary people, at least, believed that officials could meet with supernatural punishment for lack of respect. On the other hand officials had the right to punish gods of

Although the state religion of China was remarkably successful in meeting the needs of most Chinese, some rebels and eccentrics formed secret religious societies which expected or worked for the overthrow of the established order. A priest of the Triad Society kneels before an altar in the Society's lodge. The writing above the altar calls upon members to be loyal and upright, and to burn joss sticks regularly. This society was formerly outlawed because it sought the overthrow of a foreign dynasty

Camera Press London

七殿秦山王

Michael Holford

a rank below their own for failing in civic duties: to bring rain or cure an epidemic, for example. Images might be thrashed, gods demoted and ceremonies denied them. This perhaps provided a warning to mortal officials to perform their tasks efficiently. And there were also folk stories aiming to put gods in their place, which was always below that of the Chinese emperor.

One charming story explains why the earth god is always placed on or near the ground. It appears that the emperor T'ai Tsu, who lived in the 14th century, once visited an inn on his travels and found all the tables taken except an altar table for the earth god. 'Give me your place,' he said, placing the image on the ground, and proceeded to order his dinner. After the emperor had gone the inn-keeper replaced the image but that night the god appeared to him in a dream. He told him to put him back on the ground, as he did not dare to contravene the emperor's order. And so it was from that day.

For ordinary men it would appear there was no escaping the god-officials in this life or the next and many gods were themselves former officials of the mortal world. Indeed, once a year all gods reported to the Jade Emperor on the conduct of the people in the community or institution under their control.

It was wisely recognized that some freedom, and some control of the system also, must be allowed to the common folk. It was assumed, for example, that the ordinary man, closer to the margin of subsistence than the average scholar, might find it difficult to follow the tenets of Confucianism in all circumstances. Certain gods were tolerated who sanctioned less approved aims. Gods of wealth were worshipped by ordinary people and also had an important role in business — shop owners gave annual feasts to wealth gods to which employees were invited. Some wealth gods also concerned themselves with questions of financial morality. They were deified men who had been generous with charitable donations. The jolly gods of Taoism provided entertaining if not always edifying stories, which were condoned.

It was also realized that those in desperate straits might do things which made them more vulnerable to celestial disfavour, and more easy prey for demons. Various rites for appeasing gods, obtaining their aid and defeating demons were thus tolerated,

Michael Holford

although they sometimes involved activities and words lacking in the decorum so prized by Confucians. As in life, one gave money and other gifts for favours. Paper mock 'money' in various denominations, 'gold' and 'silver' 'ingots', and paper 'clothes' were important items of paraphernalia for many rites. They were also cheaper than the real thing used in relation to mortal officials. Theoretically etiquette forbade that common folk approach high gods direct, in the same way that it forbade direct approach to mortal officials. It was correct to go through the mediation of honourable men, or lesser gods, or to use the services of a type of non-celibate Taoist priest whose major role, in the later period at least, was to serve this religion.

Since this kind of priest took the status of god on initiation into his order, and worked to gain similar powers, he could approach gods direct, and was believed to be able to defeat demons himself. Besides performing rites on behalf of those in need, he drew up 'petitions' or constructed 'edicts', 'tablets', and 'injunctions' on behalf of the gods, using yellow-faced paper and vermilion ink in imitation of bureaucratic documents. These were used by people acting on their own. Women were the main private performers, on behalf of both themselves and the members of their households. They also tended the household images daily, together with the ancestral tablets which were usually kept on the same altar-shelf.

The underworld, like the world of the gods, was thought capable of being manipulated in similar fashion to the world of men. Bribes of mock money were paid to judges at funeral performances often conducted by Taoist as well as Buddhist priests. These are still carried out with great histrionics in Singapore today. Exit permits were burnt for quick passage through the underworld by filial sons on behalf of their parents, and also for other members of the household. Even the uncomfortable notion of parental sin might be mitigated by a popular notion that souls might be wrongly imprisoned, like the living.

The State managed the supernatural system with remarkable success, allowing as it did for a certain amount of unorthodox conception and practice among the ordinary people. Those who did not fit fully into society and could not come firmly under the influence of the ideological system, the unattached and the unemployable, were often encouraged to take up some form of monasticism, which was controlled. Professional Buddhism was an approved occupation for elderly widows.

Secret Societies

But there were also those who were discontented with the arrangements, or dissatisfied with their own place, or that of certain men occupying official positions in society. They sometimes joined religious groups which confirmed their attitudes and offered solutions. A number were messianic sects inspired by faith in the coming of a saviour. They combined Chinese notions of the Yin and Yang and a predetermined universe, with elements from other sources, which included Buddhism, Taoism, and in some cases even Christianity and Islam (which has existed in China for 13 centuries). They preached a millennium, a time when perfect government would be established and ruled over by an incarnate divine. Meitreya, the 'Buddha to Come', was usually cast in this role.

Such groups recruited frustrated scholars as well as ordinary folk, and many had both sophisticated and unsophisticated levels for understanding their ideas. There were also secret societies, such as the Triad Society, which did not have their own independent ideologies but used elements from various sources and directed them not so much towards a millennium as towards the overthrow of the foreign Ch'ing dynasty and restoration of the Chinese Ming. Groups of this sort were not tolerated of course, and were often severely suppressed.

With religion so intertwined with the social system, it is clear that major social change could not be fully effected without considerable change in beliefs and practices. A new and comprehensive ideology was found in Chinese Communism — although curiously, Chinese medicine which is based on Yin-Yang theory is still positively encouraged in China today. In some ways the new system, especially in its present Maoist form resembles the old. There are striking parallels between modern and traditional methods for instilling the social ethic, for example by self-cultivation

The Ancestors Know Better

China under the Shang dynasty, c1300 BC.

In the family temples, of the imperial family as well as of the nobles, offerings of food and wine must regularly be made to each of the many ancestors, even when no especial favours are required. (When they *are*, the offerings will be supplemented by sacrifices of animals or of slaves.) The presentation to one of the ancestors of a vessel for food or wine or water is a fitting way of commemorating any auspicious event, a successful hunt or battle, or a mark of imperial favour, a grant of land or of title. After all, the ancestors' influence determines the course of events for their descendants, and they deserve a reward for their efforts. The name of the ancestor thus honoured will often be inscribed on the vessel in the pictographic script that . . . has come into use during the reign of this enlightened dynasty.

The priests are the interpreters between the dead and the living. Although they accompany the emperor on his travels in order to give him day-to-day advice from the ancestors, it is best to pose important questions within the ancestor temple in the city, where one is most likely to find the ancestors at home. Questions are submitted in writing, carved on shoulder blades of cattle or on tortoise shells, and the ancestors answer them, with a plain 'Yes' or 'No', by guiding the direction of the crack produced when the priest applies a red-hot bronze point to the back of the bone. It is a simple method, and the same bone or shell can be used over and over again. So the ancestors are asked about everything: tomorrow's weather and the best place to camp for the night, as well as the prospects for the harvest . . . The answers are not infallible, for after all even ancestors are not all-powerful. But on the whole they know better than their living descendants, and sometimes the priest will triumphantly inscribe on the bone after the event the tally of the day's hunt or the laconic remark that 'it really didn't rain'.

Geoffrey Bibby *Four Thousand Years Ago*

Shou-Lao, the god of long-life, holding a peach, a symbol of longevity and immortality, because it was thought that the peaches in the celestial orchard ripened once every 3000 years

by the reading of orthodox books and seeking strength from an inward appreciation of the contents. But the comparison between the two systems must not be pressed too far. There is much in modern China that is very different from the past.

We do not know the precise state of beliefs and customs connected with the former gods in China today. A first attempt to strip the supernatural sanctions from traditional institutions was made long before the Communists came to power. In the 20s a campaign to demolish many temples and images was launched. Among gods to be discarded, listed in a Chekiang provincial government gazette of 1928, were city gods, earth gods and the kitchen god. Many images and temple carvings have appeared in Hong Kong antique shops over the years but the last decade has seen a great increase in their numbers.

However, it should be noted that Chinese newspapers carried accounts of suppression of sectarian religious leaders right into the late 50s. They tell of 'anti-flood' campaigns in which these leaders preached that flooding was due to lack of virtue among the local establishment of officials. There are also occasional news reports filtering through which indicate the persistence of funeral and other customs.

The stronghold of Chinese religion today is undoubtedly overseas Chinese society. Confucianism is still strong in Taiwan. Singapore and Hong Kong have a multitude of temples and cults. But their practices and ideas occur against a background of social and political institutions which is very different from traditional China and have also been subject to change. The religion of overseas Chinese is traditional certainly, but it does not have quite the same relevance to society as it once did in the homeland.

MARJORIE TOPLEY

FURTHER READING: A. F. Wright, *Buddhism in Chinese History* (Stanford University Press, 1959); C. K. Yang, *Religion in Chinese Society* (University of California Press, 1961).

Michael Holford

CHRISTIANITY

CHRISTIANITY

'Other religions teach that men have become gods: Christianity that God entered into flesh and became man.' In this article the history of one of the great religions of the world is outlined

CHRISTIANITY TAKES ITS NAME from its founder, Jesus Christ. Christ is not a name but an adjective meaning 'the anointed one' and derived from the Greek *Christos* which is itself a translation of the Hebrew *Messiah*, the one chosen and anointed by God. Jesus is a Hebrew name, Jesus was a Jew, and the designation Jesus Christ points to two cardinal facts about the rise of Christianity. It sprang from Judaism, and in the early centuries it had its widest dissemination in the Hellenistic world, the Mediterranean area where Greek cultural influence was strong.

Many of the central concepts of Judaism were incorporated into Christianity: as Jesus said, he had come not to destroy the law and the prophets but to fulfil. The Old Testament, the name given by Christians to the Jewish scriptures, asserts the oneness of God: 'Hear, O Israel, the Lord thy God is one god.' An intransigent monotheism has been both the glory and the tragedy of Israel. In the ancient world this insistence set the Jews apart from their neighbours even in a political sense, as the gods of the various peoples were expected to recognize each other. In particular, Israel came into conflict with rulers who claimed to be gods themselves. This claim was made by Alexander and his successors, by the Egyptian pharaohs and by the emperors of Rome, and this claim the Jews resolutely rejected. They were the only people in antiquity who refused to place a pinch of incense on the altars of the emperors, and the only people who were tacitly granted exemption from this universal demand.

The Jewish Background

There are religions of Nature, religions of contemplation and religions of history, and Judaism was centred in history. Religions of Nature see the divine in the recurrence of the seasons, and particularly in the processes of fertility. Their rites call for the sacrifice of infants to win the favour of the god and to stimulate the fertility of the earth; sometimes also for the emasculation of men and the perpetual virginity of

women or, in reverse, for sacred prostitution. Ancient Israel met such practices in Canaan and sought ruthlessly to stamp them out.

Religions of contemplation seek the divine by turning within, until meditation is consummated in ecstatic union with the Ultimate. Judaism knew of dreams and visions but not the rapture of the mystic who loses his identity in the abyss of the godhead.

Religions of history see the divine rather in events, in the mighty acts of God as he raises up and casts down. Frequently they look forward to a great coming event, a cataclysm which will terminate the present world order and introduce a new and blessed era. For the Jews the new era was to be the restoration of Paradise, to be inaugurated by an inspired leader, the Messiah.

If the coming day of the Lord was to be light and not darkness, Israel must do God's will. Some believed that this consisted in the performance of the rites of the Temple. But when the Temple was no longer accessible, as a result of the captivity of the Jews in Babylon, in the 6th century BC, the law (called the Torah) with all its requirements of circumcision, kosher food, sabbath observance and the like, became the focus of Jewish piety. The prophets, however, deprecated formalism of this sort and thundered that God is not pleased with the blood of rams but rather when justice rolls down like waters and righteousness as a mighty stream.

By the time of Jesus the Jews, who had been an oppressed people for seven centuries, were under the yoke of Rome. Many of the peoples of the Empire rejoiced that Rome had given them security through the establishment of a universal peace but the Jews were resentful. The flower of their youth had been squandered in Rome's earlier civil wars and the Roman belief in the divinity of the emperor was contrary to Jewish belief in the sole rule of God.

There were three parties among the Jews. The Sadducees were willing to collaborate with the occupying power, the Zealots fomented rebellion, and the Pharisees would neither fraternize nor rebel but kept the law and waited for vindication at the hands of God. Those who committed themselves to political passivity in this way were all the more ready to dream of an intervention from

heaven. A deliverer would come, whether he was 'the righteous one' of the Dead Sea Scrolls, a Messiah on earth, or the Son of Man appearing on the clouds of heaven.

Did Jesus Exist?

Into this society was born Jesus the Galilean, a loyal Jew who observed the feasts by going up to Jerusalem. How much do we know about him?

There are no writings from his pen. The gospels which tell of his life and teachings were not composed until some 30 or more years after his death (commonly dated to the year 33 AD) and some portions of the Christian scriptures, called the New Testament, may date from as late as the end of the 1st century or even the beginning of the 2nd. Can we rely on the picture which they draw?

Some historians have questioned even the very existence of Jesus, despite the difficulty in that case of explaining the rise of the Christian religion. Marxists have maintained that Jesus was a myth of the proletariat, though there was no proletariat in the modern sense in that day. Some have suggested that Jesus was a Nature myth, a personification of the dying and rising of the seasons, for he rose from the dead in the spring. But the early Christians clearly did not see him in this light, and in fact they took care not to commemorate the Resurrection on the day of the spring equinox, because that was the day on which the Nature god Attis arose after the death of winter.

Other historians have said that Jesus did indeed exist but of one fact only can we be

quite sure, that he was crucified. There are variants in the accounts of all the other events of his life and, it is argued, the early Christians selected for the record only what met their own needs and hopes.

Such scepticism has diminished of late, for we are unable to account for the ways in which the early Christians differed from their Jewish forbears unless it is accepted that Jesus instituted changes. The essential picture in the New Testament is reliable, the more evidently because the authors recorded unpalatable sayings of Jesus. For example, the Church was confronted by a group stemming from John the Baptist, giving them good reason to disparage John. Yet they recorded Jesus's words, 'There is none greater born of woman than John.'

The cross itself was also a source of offence. Why revere a criminal executed by the most shameful of all deaths? Some in the early Church tried to eliminate the dilemma by denying that Jesus had a real body at all. He merely looked as if he did and on the cross he cried out 'as if in pain'. But the main body of the early Church would have none of this. Their creed asserted that 'he suffered under Pontius Pilate, was crucified, dead and buried.'

If Jesus was a Jew, loyal to the tradition of his people, and if he was not a rebel against Rome, why was he crucified? The answer is that he alienated all parties: the Sadducees because he scorned them for collaborating with the Romans; the Zealots because he would not rebel; the Pharisees

because he differed from them as to what was meant by fulfilling the law. He held that the Great Commandment was to love God and your neighbour, rather than to refrain from certain foods, or to observe the Sabbath to the neglect of human obligations. In particular, Jesus consorted with outcasts, prostitutes and tax-gatherers. Assuring them of God's forgiveness, he even undertook to forgive their sins himself. He seemed, then, to be guilty of blasphemy, by usurping the role of God. Jesus certainly spoke of God as his Father, and he appears to have thought of himself as the Messiah who would redeem Israel, not by arms but by suffering.

Jesus was conscious of standing at the pinnacle of history, about to usher in the

Christians of all denominations believe that, in Jesus, God became man, died in agony on the cross and rose from the dead, to bring all men the possibility of eternal life and happiness with God. Easter is a period of sorrow at Christ's death, repentance for human sinfulness and joy at Christ's resurrection. *Far left* Procession of the Penitents of Perpignan, in France, carrying the image of Christ crucified. The custom of doing public penance on Good Friday is a common one in many parts of the world *Left* Easter procession in Malta with the figure of Christ carrying the cross which he bore for every man *Above* The American evangelist Billy Graham, whose massive campaigns to bring the message of Christ to the people are, in their different way, as dramatically moving as the older processions and images

new Paradise of God. His challenge to the priests at Jerusalem, when he defied their authority by casting out of the Temple those who changed foreign coins into Temple currency, brought the wrath of the hierarchy upon him; but because he already enjoyed a popular following, the rulers of the people feared to lay hands on him. They were not empowered to put him to death without Roman consent, and the only charge which Rome would entertain was that of political insurrection.

Jesus could hardly be accused of committing an overt act of rebellion, and the charge finally made against him, and fixed to his cross in Hebrew, Greek and Latin, was that he had claimed to be the 'King of the Jews'. From the point of view of the Jews, therefore, his real offence was blasphemy, but to Pontius Pilate, the Roman official, he was guilty of inciting rebellion.

The Conquest of Death

After his crucifixion, Jesus was alleged by his disciples to have risen from the dead. Some historians feel that there were three stages in the growth of this tradition. First came visions of the risen Jesus, then the stories that his tomb had been found empty, and finally the belief that he had ascended bodily into heaven. But however the Resurrection may have been conceived or experienced, the followers of Jesus were convinced that their master was still alive.

This faith created the Church. Such a statement may seem too strong, for other religions have originated without a founder

who rose from the dead. But it is certain that the faith of the early Christians rested on the belief that Christ had conquered death and had broken the power of the demonic forces in the cosmos. He had given men a new power to surmount their own perverse propensities. Another vivid element in the early Christian faith was that Christ would soon return as the Son of Man upon the clouds of heaven, to set up a new order, whether on earth or in heaven.

Inspired with this faith, all the disciples became missionaries. Christianity had its first following among the Jews, to whom Peter was missionary, but Hellenist converts, who spoke Greek, soon became more numerous. As a result, the New Testament has come down to us not in Aramaic, the language of Jesus, but only in Greek. St Paul, the missionary to the Gentiles, was largely responsible for Christianity's development away from its origins in agrarian Palestine and into the urban Hellenistic world. His missionary journeys throughout Asia Minor made this region the most heavily Christianized until the time of the Emperor Constantine in the 4th century AD. He also travelled to Rome where, according to a strong tradition, he was martyred during Nero's persecution of the Christians in 64 AD.

Paul came nearer than any other New Testament writer to formulating a Christian theology. A Jew himself, he naturally accepted the Jewish picture of God as the Father. Jesus is not called God by Paul, but he is said to have been on an equality with

God and to have humbled himself, taking the form of a slave and becoming obedient even to the death on the cross. For this reason God 'has highly exalted him and bestowed on him the name which is above every name, that at the name of Jesus every knee should bow, in heaven and on earth and under the earth, and every tongue confess that Jesus Christ is Lord . . .' (Philippians, chapter 2).

Paul's statement that Christ humbled himself was taken to mean that he emptied himself of his full power and glory, a view which facilitated the later claim that he was both God and man. As man he had divested himself of some of the prerogatives of deity.

In the gospel of St John there is a more precise statement of the doctrine of the Incarnation, the doctrine that God became man. In the prologue to that gospel we read that, 'In the beginning was the Word.' The English 'Word' translates the Greek *logos*, which means the rational principle, both dormant and active, in the entire universe. This was the principle in accordance with which God created the world, and this logos became flesh in Jesus. The Latin word for 'flesh' is *carnis*, hence becoming flesh is called 'incarnation'. Other religions teach that men have become gods: Christianity that God entered into flesh and became man.

Paul was the greatest theologian among the early Christians: the greatest leader of the churches is believed to have been Peter. The Roman church looked upon Peter and Paul as the co-founders of their church and Peter, as well as Paul, is assumed to have

Christianity stressed the gentler virtues: mercy, compassion, consideration, tenderness, self-sacrifice and love, sheer love, with no consideration of recompense

suffered martyrdom under Nero. There is a tradition that Peter became the first bishop of Rome but this has not been established for certain. The bishop was at first merely the pastor of a local group of Christians. The Roman congregation soon acquired a leading position among the churches, partly because it was in the capital of the Roman Empire but even more because it was the most reliable source of the Christian tradition, since it was founded by the two martyred apostles, after whom there had been an unbroken line of succession in the bishopric.

Mercy, Pity, Peace and Love

Christian morality at that time was heroic rather than ascetic. In many respects, Christianity carried over the ethic of Judaism. But in contrast to both Judaism and paganism, Christianity stressed the gentler virtues: mercy, compassion, consideration, tenderness, self-sacrifice and love, sheer love, with no consideration of recompense.

At certain points, this early ethic was affected by the expectation that Christ would soon return. Because Paul believed that the current world order of society would only last a short time, he taught that no one should try to change his status, whether he was a slave or a free man. The early Church, therefore, sought to ameliorate the lot of the slave and Christianize the relationship of master and man, but did not call for universal emancipation.

By the same token, the married and the unmarried should remain as they were, except that marriage might be allowed to those who could not abstain from sex. This grudging concession was later given an ascetic turn and led for centuries to virginity being considered superior to marriage. The only point at which the early ethic called for a drastic change in social attitudes was with regard to war. No Christian author condoned killing in war until the time of Constantine. Various reasons were given for this pacifism, the main one being Christian love. However, some leaders of the Church allowed Christians to do military service, provided they did not kill. This was possible during the two centuries of the great Roman peace, when the army was generally engaged in what today would be police work.

Christianity seems to have emerged as a religion in its own right, recognizably distinct from Judaism, by the time of Nero's persecution in 64 AD. Once this had happened, Christians forfeited the exemption from taking part in the worship of the emperor, which was tacitly granted to the Jews. The Christians, quite as emphatically as the Jews, would give divine honour to no man. This refusal was one of the main reasons for their persecution until the time of Constantine. In addition, their rejection of all pagan gods was interpreted as atheism and the pacifism of the great majority of Christians was thought to be a danger to the state.

The First Three Centuries

During the first three centuries the Church continued to spread, especially around the shores of the Mediterranean and inland along the courses of rivers such as the Tiber, the Po and the Rhone. As Christianity expanded and the number of its adherents increased, divisions arose within the Christian body.

Reference has already been made to those who argued that Jesus did not have a real body but only the appearance of a body. The same claim was made by the Gnostics (see GNOSTICISM). They argued that, because the body is material and evil, Jesus could not have had a body and could not have been incarnated in flesh. Equally the material and therefore evil world could not have been created by God, but by a malevolent god or spirit, a 'demiurge'.

The Church strove valiantly to conserve belief in the humanity of Jesus and the creation of the world as good by God. The early Creed affirmed 'I believe in God the Father Almighty, the Maker of Heaven and Earth.'

A question of discipline caused a schism in the Church after the great persecution by the Emperor Decius in 250 AD. Many members of the congregations and even some bishops had been frightened into sacrificing to the Roman gods. When the persecution ceased they wanted to be restored to communion within the Church, for already great importance was attached to receiving the body and blood of Christ in the form of bread and wine; the rite that was later called the Mass. Most members of the Church agreed to readmit the lapsed

after suitable penance but splinter groups, who believed in the strict enforcement of rules, seceded.

The Conversion of Constantine

The conversion of Constantine in 312 AD marked the turning point in the status of the Church in the Roman world. One of the contestants in the struggle for the position of emperor – a struggle that had divided the Roman world – he overcame his rival in Rome at the battle of the Milvian Bridge outside the city.

Constantine was convinced that victory had been given him by the risen Christ. Although it seems strange that he should have looked for triumph in war from the Prince of Peace, there can be no question of his sincerity. He had nothing to gain politically by proclaiming his conversion; at that time only about 15% of the population in the West was Christian. In 323 AD he became ruler of the entire empire. When he became a Christian he had to give up being a god and the cult of the deified emperor came to an end.

Constantine declared the day on which Christ rose from the dead a public holiday and called it the Sun's Day – previously he had been a worshipper of the sun. Northern Europeans followed Constantine's lead with such names as Sunday and Sonntag.

Under Constantine there was not precisely a union of Church and State but there was a close affiliation. This became closer under the later emperors in the Byzantine East. Legislation was passed favouring orthodox Christianity and penalizing dissenters. The Jews suffered some restrictions, the pagans more, and the heretics most. The heretics were driven out, the pagans died out and the Jews alone survived, although they were treated as aliens in a Christian society.

The Arian Heresy

A doctrinal dispute which arose in Egypt is known as the Arian-Athanasian controversy from the names of the opposing leaders, Arius and Athanasius. The Arians said that Christ was a creature; he was the first of all creatures and he was associated with God in the creation of the world. But he did not have 'an eternal timeless generation' and 'there was when he was not'. The Athanasian party affirmed that Christ as

Michael Holford

the Son had been eternally present with God the Father. There had been no beginning, there would be no end. He was of one being or essence or substance with God the Father. When the Holy Spirit was included in this relationship, the doctrine of the Trinity was complete.

Supporters of this doctrine insisted that it was not tritheism (belief in three gods) as their opponents claimed. Neither was it modalism (the view that God has three modes of activity). The doctrine of the Athanasian party was adopted by the Council of Nicaea in 325 AD.

It has always been difficult to find a middle ground between Christ's separation from God, as a subordinate creature, and his full identity with God. The reconciliation

is found in the view that humanity and divinity are not incompatible. Even man can be a participant in the divine nature, and Christ participated to the full.

But if Christ was of one essence or being or substance with the Father, and if he was also human, what was the relationship of the human nature to the divine nature in him? This subject became controversial in the 5th century. The Nestorians were accused of splitting Christ into a dual personality, but denied the charge. The Monophysites (from *monos*, one and *physis*, nature) said that Christ had only one nature, the divine. The Council of Chalcedon in 451 AD affirmed that he had two natures, inseparably combined. A number of groups refused to accept this definition and the

When he was about 30, Jesus was baptized in the River Jordan by his cousin John the Baptist, according to the gospels; after the ceremony the Spirit of God descended on him in the form of a dove, and a voice from heaven declared 'This is my beloved son, with whom I am well pleased'. This illustration is from an 18th century Ethiopian manuscript in the British Museum

doctrinal difference merged with racial and linguistic divisions.

The Syrian churches divided and the Nestorian branch, driven out of the Greek empire, won a following in Persia, India and China. Another branch, the Jacobite, took the Monophysite position, as did the Armenians and the Copts in Egypt. In the

471

Daily Telegraph Colour Library

7th century Honorius, the bishop of Rome, tried to reconcile the opposing parties by giving his support to the view that Christ has only one will, a position called Monothelite (from *monos*, one and *thelema*, will). This doctrine was later rejected by the eastern and the western churches, but is still held by the Maronites, a sect found mainly in the Lebanon.

Yet another dispute which racked the Byzantine empire concerned the form of worship. The question was whether the images of Christ and the saints, and in particular the crucifix, should be allowed in churches. Iconoclasm, the breaking of images, started with the Emperor Leo the Isaurian. In Isauria, a district of Asia Minor, the bishops harked back to the days of the early church when there were no images – for even the crucifix did not appear until towards the end of the 4th century. Christians with Monophysite leanings who believed that Christ had only one divine nature, said that to portray the human was impossible, while to portray the divine was idolatry. The defenders of the images called them the books of the unlearned; they argued that if God became flesh in Christ, and Christ became present in bread and wine, there was no reason why the saints and Christ should not be depicted in art. Images were eventually restored, but only as paintings or bas relief. Rounded sculpture was excluded in the East but permitted in the West.

Ethically, the greatest change in Christian thought during and after the time of

The earliest disciples became missionaries, in particular Peter who was the chief missionary to the Jews, and Paul who preached mainly to the Gentiles. This tradition has been vigorously continued, giving Christianity a foothold in every corner of the globe
Left **The first expansion was into the Greek-speaking world of the eastern Mediterranean, where the Greek Orthodox Church continues to flourish: an Orthodox priest in the Church of the Nativity at Bethlehem, built on what was believed to be the site of Christ's birth**
Right **Christians have been working in Africa since the 15th century: a missionary with an African Christian woman who has whitened her face, apparently to make her more acceptable to a white god**

Constantine was in the Church's attitude to war. This was partly because of the martial victories of Constantine, the defender of the faith, and partly because of continuing pressure from the barbarians. Most Christians adopted a modified version of the classical theory of the just war. In the West St Augustine, at the turn of the 4th and 5th centuries, taught that the motive of the just war was love and that its objects must be the vindication of justice and the restoration of peace. Its conduct should be as humane as possible. Monks and the clergy should not fight.

After the fall of Rome in 410 AD the political unity of the Roman empire was shattered, despite a partial and temporary recovery under Justinian (c 482–565 AD).

Various Teutonic tribes established themselves within the empire, some of whom were already Christians but Arians, members of a heretical sect. Others were pagans. The conversion of both to orthodox Christianity was the work partly of the papacy, partly of the monastic orders.

Hermits in the Desert

Monasticism had developed in Egypt, especially in the time of Constantine. As the masses began to flock into the Church, the more ardent spirits withdrew to the desert. At first they were hermits who renounced the society of men, but later communities of monks were formed. From the outset celibacy was demanded of monks as it was, later, of nuns. Monasticism gradually became part of the structure of the Church. St Jerome combined monasticism and scholarship, devoting himself to the translation of the scriptures. Monks often became bishops.

Eventually, a vocational division arose. The bishops or secular clergy (from *saeculum*, the world) served the parishes, while the monks or regular clergy (from *regula*, the rule of the monasteries) engaged in contemplation and prayer, did missionary work and, later on, dispensed hospitality.

In the West the papacy, centred in Rome, became immensely powerful politically, because government had broken down and although the Byzantine emperor in the East still claimed jurisdiction over the West, he lacked the resources for dealing with the barbarians.

The Children of God

God is the God of the humble, the miserable, the oppressed and the desperate, and of those that are brought even to nothing; and his nature is to give sight to the blind, to comfort the broken-hearted, to justify sinners, to save the very desperate and damned. Now that pernicious and pestilent opinion of man's own righteousness, which will not be a sinner, unclean, miserable and damnable, but righteous and holy, suffereth not God to come to his own natural and proper work . . . But here lieth the difficulty, that when a man is terrified and cast down, he is so little able to raise himself up again and say, 'Now I am bruised and afflicted enough; now is the time of grace; now is the time to hear Christ.' The foolishness of man's heart is so great that then he rather seeketh to himself more laws to satisfy his conscience. 'If I live,' saith he, 'I will amend my life: I will do this, I will do that.' But here, except thou do the quite contrary, except thou send Moses away with his law, and in these terrors and this anguish lay hold upon Christ who died for thy sins, look for no salvation. Thy cowl, thy shaven crown, thy chastity, thy obedience, thy poverty, thy works, thy merits, what shall all these do, what shall the law of Moses avail? If I, wretched and damnable sinner, through works or merits could have loved the Son of God, and so come to him, what needed he to deliver himself for me? If I, being a wretch and damned sinner, could be redeemed by any other price, what needed the Son of God to be given? But because there was no other price, therefore he delivered neither sheep, ox, gold nor silver, but even God himself, entirely and wholly 'for me'. . . Now, therefore, I take comfort and apply this to *myself*. And this manner of applying is the very true force and power of faith. For he died *not* to justify the righteous, but the unrighteous, and to make *them* the children of God.

Martin Luther *Commentary on Galatians*

In the mid-8th century the kingdom of the Franks, to the north, recognized the bishop of Rome as the civil ruler of a strip of Italy running from Rome over the Apennines to Ravenna. Meanwhile the Benedictine monks, followed later by other orders, crossed the Alps and took over unused land. There they created self-sustaining communities and became centres from which the task of converting and educating the pagans was carried out.

The expansion of Christianity and the Church's involvement in society brought changes and corruptions. A religion cannot expand without adapting itself to the language and customs of its converts, and while this process may win converts it may at the same time pervert the religion. The pacifism of early Christianity disappeared completely in the Middle Ages, with many kingdoms, all professing Christianity, fighting between themselves. The saints were militarized. St Peter was honoured not because he had acknowledged Christ, but because he had cut off the ear of the high priest's servant. St George, St Andrew, St David and St Michael assumed the roles of the war gods of antiquity.

The Truce of God

Wealth proved corrupting. A monk described the history of western monasticism in this sequence: piety produces industry, industry creates wealth, wealth destroys piety, piety in its fall dissipates wealth. Each of the great monastic orders enjoyed at least two centuries of vitality. Enfeeblement followed, and new orders arose in an effort to recover the original spirit. The papacy, too, experienced periods of efflorescence and of decay.

The 11th century was marked by a great movement of reform, led by men from the north who had little feeling for the Mediterranean world, and who desired to cleanse the monasteries, purify the Church and give direction to society. The Western (Roman) and the Eastern (Byzantine) Churches finally separated in 1054 AD. The Cistercians supported monastic reform and restored the original Benedictine emphasis on manual labour. Priests, like monks, were required to be celibate, and the clergy were told to put away their wives. Princes were called upon to swear to observe the Truce of God, resulting in fighting being reduced to a summer sport.

This great reform, called the Gregorian after Pope Gregory VII, resulted in the papacy of the 13th century functioning as a world government more effective than any before or since. The pope was the Lord above the nations. Intellectual life flourished, universities were founded, St Thomas Aquinas brought about a new synthesis of Christian theology and Aristotelian philosophy, while Gothic architecture gave expression to piety reaching for the stars, and beyond to the very throne of God.

But reforms, if they misfire, can bring new corruptions. The Christian princes broke the vows they had made to observe the Truce of God, and the only way to reduce warfare between Christians of the West proved to be by diverting their belligerence toward the infidels in the East. The peace movement ended in the Crusades. The imposition of clerical celibacy resulted in clerical concubinage, which was rife by the time of the Reformation in the 16th century. The papacy's success in controlling Europe politically involved the popes in political machinations to such an extent that by the 15th century, the papacy was in danger of becoming a secular city-state.

So far as property was concerned, the Church in the Middle Ages had approved of rent but not of usury. However, as the Church itself became increasingly wealthy, the doctrine that a money-lender should receive compensation for the gain that would have accrued had he used the money himself, was accepted. In domestic relations the emphasis in marriage was on children and faithfulness, rather than on falling in love.

A Swarm of Sects

The Church had been without serious divisions in the West from the early 5th to the 12th centuries. Education during this period was scant and intellectual interest even scantier. But with the relative failure of universal reform, small groups arose in the 11th and 12th centuries, resolved to carry out, among themselves, the changes that had proved impracticable in the Church as a whole. Southern France and northern Italy swarmed with sects. The Cathars had views similar to those of the ancient Gnostics while the Waldenses denied the authority of the orthodox Church, appointed lay preachers, and translated large parts of the Gospels into the common speech.

To meet the threat of heresy, the Church launched the Inquisition, justified as being a work of love for saving souls from eternal damnation. The Cathars were wiped out, but the Waldenses found refuge near the timberline of the Italian Alps and survive to this day (see CATHARS; WALDENSES). The sectarian movements led by John Wyclif in England and John Huss in Bohemia were associated with the spirit of rising nationalism. Wyclif's followers, the Lollards, were largely suppressed, but those of Huss, who was burned at the stake in 1418, became so strong in Bohemia that eventually they were tolerated alongside of the Catholics. This was the first example in the Christian West of religious pluralism, the recognition of more than one religion within a given territory.

In the late Middle Ages the papacy was weakened by divisions, as a result of which there were sometimes two, or even three, popes at the same time. Church councils were called which threatened to supplant the papacy as the governing organ of the Church, but the popes regained control.

The Reformation

The opening years of the 16th century, eventually a period of vast upheaval, were characterized by an interlude of tolerance. The heretical sects of the Middle Ages had been suppressed and the Church felt sufficiently secure to suffer criticism. In fact there was much to criticize. Clerical concubinage was rife, and was tolerated to such an extent that a tax was laid on concubines. The bureaucratic machinery needed for the papacy to play its universal role had to be paid for, and the financial extortion by the Church that resulted was deeply resented, especially when the Renaissance popes spent money on wars and were so secularized as to make treaties with Turks against Christian princes. Excommunication lost its spiritual force when it was used against rulers because they had failed to make financial contributions to the papacy. Many people tried to influence God through external practices such as pilgrimages, the cult of relics, the intercession of the saints, and of the Virgin.

Then came the great reformation movement, of which one aspect was Martin Luther's attack in 1517 upon the whole

The Christian's Comfort

Heaven is glory and heaven is joy; we cannot tell which most; we cannot separate them; and this comfort is joy in the Holy Ghost. This makes all Job's states alike; as rich in the first chapter of his Book, where all is suddenly lost, as in the last, where all is abundantly restored. This consolation from the Holy Ghost makes my midnight noon, mine executioner a physician, a stake and pile of faggots a bonfire of triumph; this consolation makes a satire, and slander and libel against me, a panegyric and an eulogy in my praise . . . it makes my death-bed a marriage bed, and my passing bell an epithalamion.

John Donne *Sermons*

If Christianity were once abolished, how would the Free Thinkers, the strong reasoners and the men of profound learning, be able to find another subject so calculated in all points whereon to display their abilities? What wonderful productions of wit should we be deprived of, from those whose genius by continual practice hath been wholly turned upon raillery and invectives against religion, and would therefore never be able to shine or distinguish themselves upon any other subject. We are daily complaining of the great decline of wit among us, and would we take away the greatest, perhaps the only topic we have left?

Swift *Argument, the Abolishing of Christianity*

system of indulgences. These granted remission of penalties for sin, not only on earth but also in purgatory, and sometimes offered the forgiveness of sins. These indulgences were supposed to transfer the unused extra credits of the saints, who were better than they needed to be for their own salvation, to those whose accounts were in arrears. The recipient of the indulgence made a financial contribution to the Church.

Luther's attack was directed against the religious aspect of the system rather than the financial. He did not believe that anyone had any extra credits, as no one could ever be good enough to earn salvation. God's forgiveness of, and favour to, those who have sinned is a sheer act of grace mediated to men through the sacrificial death of Christ.

Luther took the Bible as his authority, declaring that any man guided by the spirit of God is able to interpret the Bible correctly. Papal infallibility was denied. The superiority of the clergy to the laity was denied. The sacraments, especially the Mass, were so reinterpreted that no priestly class was required for their administration. Luther believed that all laymen are spiritually priests, though not ministers by vocation.

The revolt of Luther was followed by the revolts of other reformers – Zwingli in Switzerland, Calvin in France, Knox in Scotland, Cranmer in England. Christendom, in the sense of a unified Christian society, was shattered. The new divisions were to some extent national, becoming more so when the population became religiously unified as a result of the expulsion of minorities. Eventually, Protestantism was strongest in the north, and Catholicism in the south, a pattern that has led to the generalization that Protestantism was the religion of the Teutonic peoples and Catholicism of the Latin. But France for a time had an enormous Protestant element and France was a Latin country. Ireland was Roman Catholic but not Latin. Bavaria and the Rhineland were Teutonic but remained Catholic.

The result of this growing nationalism was a weakening of the papacy even in Catholic countries. There was a strong movement in France, the Gallican movement, that maintained the independence of the French Church against Rome, while the Catholic Church in Spain has often gone its own way regardless of papal pronouncements.

The main effect on the Roman Catholic Church was to tighten the dogma, the discipline and the bureaucratic structure of the Church. The secularized papacy of the Renaissance came to an end. The popes became as austere as the Puritans. Clerical celibacy was enforced and dogma was more rigidly formulated. This was the work of the Council of Trent, in the years between 1545 and 1563.

The Problem of Freedom

The violent conflicts of Roman Catholics and Protestants in the 16th and 17th centuries brought to the fore the problems of Church and State and the problem of religious liberty. In effect, the solution was a system of religious liberty on a territorial basis, which carried with it the right of emigration. One region was to have only one religion and those who could not in conscience subscribe to it were not sent to the stake or the dungeons of the Inquisition but were free to emigrate.

This was not an ideal solution, and only lasted for a short time. As France learnt through the expulsion of the Huguenots, it is disastrous for a country to lose many of its finest citizens.

There are various reasons why religious pluralism within the single state was eventually tolerated. One was sheer weariness of war. The Thirty Years' War in Germany in the 17th century left cities with inhabitants dead of starvation in the streets with grass in their mouths. Another factor was trade. Holland was particularly sensitive to this consideration as she was the market-place of the world, and if she restricted her commerce because of religious beliefs, her prosperity would suffer.

The deepest considerations were religious. The champions of religious liberty pointed out that faith cannot be constrained, that sincerity cannot be forced. Compulsion may make men into martyrs or hypocrites. It cannot make them into genuine converts. To burn a man because he refuses to save his life by renouncing his convictions is to burn him for telling the truth, that is, what he believes to be the truth. Sincerity does not necessarily make a man right, but insincerity makes him necessarily wrong.

England in the 17th century made the greatest progress towards religious liberty.

This was partly because the Puritan struggle was between various Protestant groups, who were less bitter towards each other than they were towards the Church of Rome. Oliver Cromwell believed that the differences between Presbyterians, Congregationalists and Baptists were unimportant, though Catholics, Anglicans and Quakers presented more of a problem. He did not want to suppress any religious group, although he was severe with Roman Catholics in Ireland on political grounds. He did not believe in the separation of Church and State but in an establishment based on the beliefs of three religious groups, Presbyterian, Congregational and Baptist. Although his regime did not last long, it proved that religious pluralism and religious stability are compatible. The American system is basically the same. Although Church and State are separated, the State relies heavily on the three pillars of Protestantism, Catholicism and Judaism for moral sanction.

Genesis and Geology

Since the 18th century, Christianity has gradually been moving towards overcoming its own divisions. At the same time it has been wrestling with new scientific and social developments. Until recently this was more true of Protestants than of Roman Catholics. After the Council of Trent, the Catholics continued to enhance rather than diminish their claims on behalf of the papacy, and at the same time felt a greater alienation from the contemporary world of thought. Protestants were more open to new ideas, even at the risk of making so many concessions as to depart radically from the Christian tradition.

One area of controversy has been natural science. The Catholic Church suppressed Galileo; and Luther and Calvin rejected the views of Copernicus on biblical grounds. However, many Protestants accepted his views and his writings were allowed to circulate. The theories of Newton and Galileo did not trouble the Protestants, and they accepted the new astronomy as an impressive commentary on the text 'the heavens declare the glory of God'. Serious conflict began only in the 19th century when geological discoveries cast doubt on the biblical account of the creation of the world in six days. Some scientists attempted to

reconcile the two points of view by assuming that a day meant 1,000 years or even longer, and that God created the world in six of these periods. But biblical scholars retorted that the word 'day' in the book of Genesis meant 24 hours. Genesis conflicted with geology, and geology won. Liberal Protestants came to regard the book of Genesis as inspired mythology, not as a scientific treatise.

The doctrine of organic evolution was more disconcerting because it affected the understanding of man. If man is biologically descended from lower forms of life, among whom Nature is red in tooth and claw, is man ineradicably predatory and warlike by nature? If animals are mortal and man immortal, when in the scale of ascent did

The early Christians expected that their master would soon return in glory on the clouds of heaven to set up the kingdom of God on earth, and his coming was awaited with joyous expectancy: 19th century painting on a ceiling of the Rila monastery in Bulgaria

man become immortal? Some theologians have suggested conditional immortality, asserting that not all men are immortal but only those who are capable of living in the atmosphere of the spirit.

The application of historical techniques to the Bible raised the problems of uncertainties as to the texts and discrepancies between various accounts. These problems were passionately pursued from the 18th

century onwards, especially in Germany and mainly by Protestants. Catholics were not granted freedom in the field of biblical study until the time of Pope John XXIII and the Second Vatican Council, which opened in 1962.

Politically, Protestantism has been hospitable to, and has contributed toward, political democracy, largely as a result of the Puritan revolution in England and America. The Catholic Church, which is organized as a hierarchy, has preferred on the whole to deal with highly centralized governments. This situation has been modified in the United States where Catholics have recognized that both democracy and the separation of the Church and State might be advantageous to the Church. Had

475

there been an autocratic government and an established Church in the United States, neither would have been Catholic.

Modern Christian Theology

Modern theology is centred on the doctrine of the Trinity: the Father, the Son and the Spirit. In the case of God the Father, some schools of thought emphasize his immanence, as a being who pervades the universe. This was true of Protestant Liberalism. Others stress transcendence, the belief that God exists beyond and apart from the universe.

Mystics, on the one hand, who are stupefied by the overwhelmingness of God, and scientists on the other, who are aghast at the immeasurable universe, shy away from all concrete language about God, especially from all personal adjectives. Many theologians turn to Christ as the focus of their piety because they 'can walk with Him and talk with Him'. In Pietist movements there has been a saccharine Jesus cult. Yet others emphasize the Spirit which lies at the heart of all rules and structures and doctrines. Believing this, they may sever themselves from any organized church and be led beyond Christianity to a combination of all religions.

Christianity expanded phenomenally during the 19th century, its greatest numerical gains having been among primitive peoples. Although it has made no serious inroads into the ranks of the world's other great religions, Christianity has influenced other faiths, which have adopted Christian attitudes without acknowledging formal adherence to the faith.

(See also JESUS; MARY; MASS; PAUL; and many other articles on Christian beliefs and practices.)

ROLAND H. BAINTON

FURTHER READING: The literature of the subject is vast, of course, but good modern books include R. H. Bainton, *The Horizon History of Christianity* (American Heritage Publ., 1964) and the volumes in the 'Pelican History of the Church' series; F. C. Copleston, *Medieval Philosophy* (Harper and Row, 1961); J. N. D. Kelly, *Early Christian Doctrines* (Harper and Row, 1978); Basil Willey, *Christianity Past and Present* (Hyperion, 1980).

Two views, by an outsider and a Christian Scientist, of a movement which has aroused intense controversy ever since its foundation. The founder was one of the most remarkable women of the last 100 years

CHRISTIAN SCIENCE

IN 1875 the 'discoverer and founder' of Christian Science, Mary Baker Eddy (1821–1910), published her book *Science and Health*. Frequently and extensively revised, a definitive edition appeared towards the end of Mrs Eddy's life, as *Science and Health with Key to the Scriptures*, the authoritative textbook of the movement. Mrs Eddy's other writings are regarded as valuable supplements to it. Formal doctrine has remained unchanged since the founder's death and none of the many commentaries on Christian Science by loyal members of the movement are regarded as authoritative. Mrs Eddy decreed that her textbook and the Bible were the movement's only 'preachers', and she swept away at one stroke the numerous pastors who initially occupied the pulpits of Christian Science churches.

Christian Science is both an interpretation of Scripture and the basis of a system of healing. It rejects the conventional doctrine of the Trinity. Jesus is said to have been a man, a Way-shower, who 'demonstrated' the truth by healing the sick, casting out demons and raising the dead. Christian Science claims to teach all men how to make the same type of 'demonstrations', which are not miracles, but rather the consequences of a true understanding of God. Healings are wrought by assertions of the truth – the allness of God, good, and the nothingness of error, evil. Man is held to be entirely spiritual, a reflection of God: physical man, the man known to the senses, is a 'counterfeit', and it is only this false, material man who can suffer.

Christian Science teaches that when men grasp this truth, they overcome the flesh and all the ills to which it is heir, and that ultimately man will overcome death itself, by knowing that there is no matter to die, but only spirit to enjoy eternal life. Man is enslaved to the body, when he should realize that he has all the attributes of God, whose character is expressed in seven synonyms: Principle, Mind, Soul, Spirit, Life, Truth, Love. All testimony of the senses is to be rejected, and only pure metaphysical ideas are to be entertained.

This endeavour to entertain only pure thoughts and to assert metaphysical truths, is seen as both divine worship and scientific achievement. But the truth of Christian Science is to be tested pragmatically, in the healing of sickness and the elimination of all disharmony which, it is claimed, are achieved by its application. There is a certain paradox in this, since it is maintained that by denying the existence of matter, and by affirming the absoluteness of spirit, so man's experience of the material world is improved and evil eliminated. The material world is an illusion, but it is an illusion the improved experience of which is necessary to prove its illusory character. Man is healed by learning that there is nothing to heal, but in practice it is to improved physical effects that Christian Science must point for proof of its claim.

This metaphysical theory is supported by reference to the Bible, and scriptural texts are used to establish that this teaching is the substance of what Jesus taught. His revelation is demonstrated as what Mrs Eddy referred to as a 'science' in her own writings. Sin, like sickness, is an illusion, stemming from man's failure to realize his divine son-ship. Christian Science has no doctrine of soul: since man is said to have no body, he is therefore all soul, the reflection of God, who is called Soul. Conventional ideas of heaven and hell have never been accepted. They are mere conditions of mind. The afterlife is little emphasized, but it is believed that man must progress into Christian Science, either in this stage of his existence or in the next.

Malicious Animal Magnetism

What man must do is to overcome the false claims of his mortal mind, from which all evil stems. This mortal mind has power over men only because they credit it with power. Its most specific form is 'malicious animal magnetism', on which Mrs Eddy laid the utmost stress, and which means conscious or unconscious evil thought, the source of all sin, sickness and death.

This concept is the most original and distinctive feature of Christian Science theology. In the early years of Christian Science, Mrs Eddy tended to identify malicious animal magnetism with individuals, particularly with her apostate students. Later she dealt with it as a more impersonal agency, sometimes attributable to other systems of thought (particularly to Theosophy, Spiritualism and Roman Catholicism) but always to be discounted by Christian Scientists, who were taught appropriate defensive work to protect their own thinking.

To the general public, Christian Science is best known for its rejection of medicine. Instead, it declares that real healing occurs only through its own agency. It has often been the boast of Christian Scientists that their ranks have been recruited from hospitals and almost from the cemeteries. Accredited Christian Science practitioners undertake no other gainful employment but charge fees for their services. Any Christian Scientist who has undergone a week's course of instruction may, without charge, undertake mental work for others. A treatment consists in the practitioner 'knowing the truth' for his patient, praying for him by affirming scientific thoughts relevant to the case, and by passing on to the patient particular thoughts to 'hold on to'. These are usually texts from the Bible, extracts from Mrs Eddy's writings, or sometimes the words of Christian Science hymns.

Christian Science declares that real healings are not achieved by orthodox medicine but only through Christian Science. Where medicine appears to heal, this occurs only because the patient's thought is changed by receiving treatment. It is the mental operation, not the physical effect of drugs or medicine, which produces health. Christian Science treatment can be sought and administered by telephone.

The organization of the Christian Science movement underwent a number of radical changes in its early days, particularly in the period of its rapid growth in the 1880s and 1890s. At first, Christian Science was taught as a therapeutic system in institutes, and it was only gradually that the 'church organization, which Mrs Eddy also established, became predominant.

Mrs Eddy had originally, so it is said,

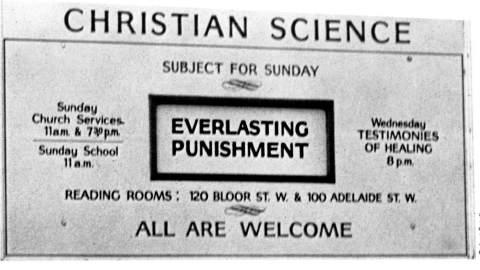

expected Christianity to embrace her new teaching. When this did not occur, she provided her movement with its own ecclesiastical organization, with a permanent, highly centralized structure. She founded the First Church of Christ, Scientist, at Boston, Massachusetts, as the Mother Church of the movement, of which all other Christian Science churches were to be branches. The Directors of the Mother Church were established as the ultimate authorities in the movement, subject always to Mrs Eddy's will as long as she lived.

Her intention with regard to local churches was clear; they were to have no independent preachers, and indeed no professionals involved in their operation. They were allowed some autonomy in their local business affairs but in religious matters were completely controlled from Boston. Sunday lesson-sermons were to be read, without comment, by readers elected from the congregation. These sermons were to consist, as they still consist, of set readings from the Bible and from *Science and Health*. The 'First Reader' reads from the textbook and it is he (or she) who conducts the service; the 'Second Reader' reads from the Bible. A good Christian Scientist reads the quotations which constitute Sunday's sermon every day in the week preceding the Sunday on which the sermon is publicly read. The evening service is always a repetition of the morning service in any given church, not one word or one note being changed, and the sermon is identical in all Christian Science churches.

In most churches a 'testimony' meeting is held once a week, and on this occasion adherents describe their appreciation of Christian Science and recount its healing powers. The testimonies at these meetings tend to be highly stereotyped. Christian Science services lack the expressive qualities of most religious gatherings. Liturgical embellishments are eschewed: there are no special vestments; there is no choir, but often there is a soloist who performs once in each Sunday service. Musical expression and church decor are in restrained, impersonal taste. There are no intrinsically significant rituals. The communion service, held twice a year, is marked by a slight variation of ritual in which the congregation is, exceptionally, invited to kneel. Christian Science churches do not normally have a warm community life.

Growth and Division
The movement grew rapidly in America in its early years. Its optimism, emphasis on the benevolence of the Deity, and its novelty gave it a certain congruity with a rapidly expanding society. Its apparent reconciliation of Christianity and science, at a time when the two appeared to be in profound conflict, was undoubtedly an important factor in its early growth. Though the movement has not placed much emphasis on missionary work, Christian Science spread to Britain and other English-speaking countries before the end of the 19th century. In continental Europe, success was generally confined to Protestant countries, particularly Germany and Switzerland.

In the early 1950s there were some 10,000 Christian Science practitioners in the world, about 80% of them in the United States. Almost 90% of all practitioners were women at that time. The movement has always had far more women members than men, but the very high ratio of women to men among practitioners probably reflects the fact that women, many of whom have other means of support, are much more likely than men to be able to forgo other gainful employment.

Especially in its early years, the movement was criticized and ridiculed by churchmen, doctors and sometimes by legislators. Christian Science healing has not been generally accepted outside the movement, and the medical profession has remained unconvinced by its claims.

The early days of the movement were also marked by internal disputes. Many of Mrs Eddy's early students quarrelled with her, and some established rival systems of metaphysical healing. After her reorganization of the government of the church, many local schisms were resolved by the system of duplicate membership of the church, by which the individual was more firmly attached to the Mother Church in Boston than to his branch church. Schismatics could join another branch, or found one, without having to lose their standing in the movement.

Even so, expulsions from the movement have been relatively frequent over the years, many of those expelled being teachers and practitioners who have challenged the authority of the Directors of the Mother Church. Others have been excommunicated for teaching Christian Science by unapproved methods. Most of the dissentients from the practice of government in the movement, and even those considered heretical in their statement of Christian Science, continued to affirm their loyalty to Mrs Eddy after their excommunication.

Divisions and struggles to gain control at the top were particularly marked during the decade after Mrs Eddy's death.

In 1936, at the last census of religious bodies in the United States, some 238,000 people were recorded as Christian Scientists in that country, and this certainly constituted the great majority of adherents in the world at the time. No more recent membership figures are available but the

Above Notice board in front of a Christian Science church in Canada *Below* 'Mrs Mary Baker Eddy, founder of the Christian Science Movement: she emphasized that 'healing physical sickness is the smallest part of Christian Science. It is only the bugle-call to thought and action, in the higher range of infinite goodness'. Formal doctrine has remained unchanged since her death

number of practitioners declined in most American states and in Great Britain between 1953 and 1968. Obviously, numbers of practitioners are at best an indirect guide to the fortunes of the movement but except in California, Florida and Texas few new churches have been established in the last two decades and this suggests that Christian Science has now passed its period of growth and that it is likely to decline in the future.

(See also EDDY; NEW THOUGHT.)

A Way of Life
For its adherents, Christian Science is above all a way of life. Its radical reinterpretation of traditional Christianity has kept it, until recently, under fire from the religious establishments of the countries in which it has flourished. Its audacious pioneering in the field of religious therapeutics has, for the most part, won only

reluctant acknowledgement from the medical profession. Little serious scholarship has been devoted to it during the century of its existence, but this is now changing.

The period in which it appeared seethed with occultism, spiritism, 'animal magnetism' and all kinds of forays into the supernatural. From the outset, Mary Baker Eddy took sharp issue with these popular manifestations, as she also did with traditional Christian beliefs in special miracles. There was no such thing as a miraculous infraction of law, she held; the seeming miracle must be the natural result of a not yet apprehended law. As early as the 1870s she described the current spiritistic phenomena as the result of either trickery or autosuggestion, and in the still pre-Freudian 1880s she wrote in *Christian Healing*: 'When I learned how mind produces disease on the body, I learned how it produces the manifestations ignorantly imputed to spirits . . . The belief that produces this result may be wholly unknown to the individual, because it is lying back in the unconscious thought, a latent cause producing the effect we see.'

The phenomenon of Christian healing she put in an entirely different category. Genuine spiritual cures, in her view, came from a rational understanding of the nature and laws of the realm of being which is revealed through Christian experience. This wholly spiritual order, described in the New Testament as 'the kingdom of God . . . within you', constituted the inner structure of reality, the essential nature of man as the child of God. The New Testament healings, instead of being blindly accepted as miracles or summarily rejected as myths, were to be understood as evidence of the transforming power of ontological insight energized by Christian love. 'The miracle,' she wrote in *Science and Health with Key to the Scriptures*, 'introduces no disorder, but unfolds the primal order, establishing the Science of God's unchangeable law.'

To the deeply Christian Mrs Eddy the virgin birth, healing ministry, resurrection and ascension of Jesus represented the quintessential example of the power of Spirit over matter and of Life over death. His words, 'He that hath seen me hath seen the Father', were the guarantee not of a God made in the image of human personality but of a divine, inexhaustible, creative Love at the heart of existence, a Love that was made manifest in the compassionate power of the Christ.

Mrs Eddy's definition of God as the Principle of being was entirely compatible, in her view, with the concept of conscious purpose, care and creativity usually associated with belief in God as a personality: it simply united these with the idea of universal order and law. 'As the words *person* and *personal* are commonly and ignorantly employed,' she wrote in *Science and Health*, 'they often lead, when applied to Deity, to confused and erroneous conceptions of divinity and its distinction from humanity.' God is Person, she explained, only in the sense of being infinite Mind, Spirit and Soul.

In reducing matter to a limited and fallacious kind of thinking — a mistaken 'mode of consciousness', in her own words — Mrs Eddy indicated that it must yield its tyranny over appearances in proportion as human experience was brought under the laws of spiritual being. This differed basically from the philosophical idealism that would make matter an idea in the mind of God. It also conflicted with 19th century physics, which believed in an irreducible matter-stuff. In effect, she was proposing a mind-matter continuum, with matter described as the lowest stratum of 'mortal mind' and that mind described in turn as 'matter's highest stratum'.

In her system a new dualism between mortal mind (the matter-mind continuum) and divine Mind (God expressing Himself through spiritual ideas) replaced the old one between mind and matter. This represented the absolute metaphysical distinction between error and truth, belief and understanding, appearance and reality.

Mrs Eddy's quarrel with hypnotism (animal magnetism) as a therapeutic agent was directed at its reliance on the energies of the human mind, on the power of suggestion (belief). Christian Science, like traditional Christianity, called for a surrender of the human mind to the divine, but not in terms of blind faith or a special esoteric knowledge, any more than in terms of directed suggestion or willed belief. It was rather a matter of exchanging belief for understanding.

The Importance of Healing

The central importance of healing to the Christian Scientist is that this is the area in which he feels that he can most concretely test his understanding of God and of man's relationship to God. What looks to many observers like a fixation on physical health may perhaps be better understood as a commitment to make religion practical. If quick relief from bodily pain were the Christian Scientist's major aim, a pill might be more attractive than study and prayer aimed at drawing him closer to God as the source of his true being. The emphasis on physical healing in the public 'testimonies' relate to the New Testament emphasis on healing as one of the major signs testifying to the coming of 'the kingdom'.

The concept of healing has been broadening among rank and file Christian Scientists over the years. In the foreword to a 1966 compilation entitled *A Century of Christian Science Healing*, published to commemorate the centenary of Mrs Eddy's 'discovery', the Christian Science Board of Directors brings this out and quotes her words from *Rudimental Divine Science*: 'Healing physical sickness is the smallest part of Christian Science. It is only the bugle-call to thought and action, in the higher range of infinite goodness.' Christian Scientists, the foreword continues, apply the word 'healing' to 'the demonstration of spiritual wholeness in all the aspects of human living', and to the 'rectification of all the ills and evils of the human condition.'

This states the sweeping ideal. A final chapter of assessment in the same book relates the ideal to the actuality. 'Whether a Christian Scientist participates in the social battles of our day as a liberal or a conservative, a fighter or a reconciler, a partisan or an independent, a private or a general, his ultimate purpose is to *heal*. Yet most Christian Scientists would probably agree that up to now only a small fraction of the healing dynamic of their religion has been utilized in relation to the urgent collective problems facing the world.'

Involvement in the World

Mrs Eddy's own concern in this direction is illustrated by her founding in 1908, when she was 87 years old, of the soon famous international daily newspaper *The Christian Science Monitor*. Generally accounted an outstanding achievement in secular journalism, the *Monitor* was also an integral part of the healing programme she envisaged for the Church of Christ, Scientist, and in her own estimate was her most important undertaking since the writing of *Science and Health*. As a unique form of social outreach by a church, it has aimed through the years to report the problems of the world in a balanced and realistic way.

While many signs point to a developing social awareness within the Christian Science Church, discussions with representatives of traditional Protestantism have led to a lessening of old tensions and suggest a closer integration of interest, if not of organization and doctrine, with the Christian community as a whole. The growth of a vigorous spiritual healing movement in the traditional churches, coupled with the social impact of psychotherapy in general and psychosomatic medicine in particular, have also left Christian Science less isolated in the contemporary scene.

The chief problem for Christian Scientists now may be to maintain the spiritual radicalism which has constituted both their uniqueness and their reason for being. As with other 'errors' of the human condition, however, they see this as no real danger so long as they hold fast to the essential guide-lines laid down for them in the Bible and in Mrs Eddy's works. The Christian Science way of life is inevitably oriented toward healing, whether of the body physical or of the body politic, and Mrs Eddy put the issue briskly to her followers when she wrote in her *Miscellaneous Writings*: 'If Christian Science lacked the proof of its goodness and utility, it would destroy itself; for it rests alone on demonstration.'

FURTHER READING: Mrs Eddy's own works can be consulted at Christian Science reading rooms; see also Norman Beasley, *The Cross and the Crown* (Duell, 1952); John Dewitt, *Christian Science Way of Life* (Christian Science, 1971); H. A. S. Kennedy, *Mrs Eddy* (Mitre Press, London, 1947); B. R. Wilson, *Sects and Society* (University of California Press, 1961).

Illustration attacking the growth of the Movement, published in the *Illustrated London News* in 1906 when Mrs Eddy was reported to be dying: in fact she died in 1910

MRS. MARY BAKER EDDY, FOUNDER OF CHRISTIAN SCIENCE.

THE CHRISTIAN SCIENCE CHURCH AT CONCORD.

THE FIRST CHURCH OF THE CHRISTIAN SCIENTISTS IN NEW YORK CITY.

A SHRINE OF CHRISTIAN SCIENCE: LYNN HOUSE, WHERE MRS. EDDY WROTE "SCIENCE AND HEALTH."

THE MOTHER CHURCH OF CHRISTIAN SCIENCE, BOSTON.

THE HIGH PRIESTESS'S ABODE: MRS. EDDY'S HOME AT CONCORD.

THE INSCRIPTION ON THE FIRST CHURCH OF CHRISTIAN SCIENCE, BOSTON.

WAITING THE ARRIVAL OF MRS. EDDY AT THE CONCORD CHURCH.

VISIT OF CHRISTIAN SCIENTISTS TO MRS. EDDY'S HOME AT CONCORD.

Christian Science has been much talked of lately, owing to the reported incurable illness of its founder, Mrs. Eddy, and also a recent case in the English Courts, where a Christian Scientist Mr. Justice Grantham said the ways of the Hottentot witch-doctor were more enlightened.

Despite many attempts in the past to suppress Christmas, this ancient midwinter feast has survived, but has undergone many changes. Starting as a pagan festival and later adopted by the Church, today Christmas has come full circle. The religious aspects no longer predominate and it has become, as it was originally, a time of feasting and revelry

CHRISTMAS

CHRISTMAS HAS ITS ORIGIN in two ancient pagan festivals, the great Yule-feast of the Norsemen and the Roman Saturnalia. Extending from Advent, which begins on 30 November or the Sunday nearest to it, to Candlemas Day on 2 February, it was close enough to the winter solstice to acquire many of the associations of the Norse ceremony: the Yule-log, the evergreen decorations in houses and churches, even the Christmas feast itself. These elements were combined with the Saturnalia of the Romans to provide the basis for the early Christian festival.

During the Saturnalia, gifts were made by the wealthy to the poor in honour of the golden age of liberty when Saturn ruled the known world, and slaves were allowed to change places and clothing with their masters. They even elected their own mock king who, for the period of the festival, ruled as a despot. The Saturnalia involved the wildest debauchery, and was a festival worthy of Pan himself.

Naturally it came under heavy censure from the early Church and despite the fact that Jesus Christ and the saints gradually replaced the pagan deities it was long considered completely out of character with the Christian ideal. However, the festival was far too strongly entrenched in popular favour to be abolished, and the Church finally granted the necessary recognition, believing that if Christmas could not be suppressed it should be preserved in honour of the Christian God.

Once given a Christian basis the festival became fully established in Europe with many of its pagan elements undisturbed.

It was only in the 4th century that 25 December was officially decreed to be the birthday of Christ, and it was another 500 years before the term Midwinter Feast was abandoned in favour of the word Christmas. Even then on the Continent the festival continued to show many features inherited from the Saturnalia. In particular, the Feast of Fools was a wild debauch reminiscent of the pagan past. The Normans when they invaded England in 1066, introduced a Master of Ceremonies into the English Christmas. Known as the Lord of Misrule, his counterpart in Scotland was called the Abbot of Unreason. A mock king, he ensured that Christmas was conducted along traditionally pagan lines. The custom of electing boy bishops, youths chosen from the cathedral choirs and accorded the honours due to bishops, also started at this time.

The main contributions of the medieval period to the Christmas ceremony were the carol and the nativity drama. During the 15th century Father Christmas was already known by that name, although he was then merely a background figure to the Christmas season.

The coming of the Reformation at first had little effect upon the pagan content of Christmas. The number of saints was reduced drastically and the boy bishops were abolished but on the whole Christmas continued to be celebrated as it had always been. The newly discovered turkey appeared on the Christmas table before 1573, in addition to the boar's head, once symbol of the Scandinavian Sun Boar. The favourite drink at this time was a concoction of hot ale, eggs, apples and spices known as lamb's wool. A century later, this was replaced by punch.

The undisguised pagan element in Christmas had often provoked criticism from extreme Protestants but the festival was not really affected by their beliefs until the Puritans came to power in the 17th century. Christmas was attacked as 'the old heathens' feasting day to Saturn their God' and carols were forbidden.

Father Christmas's importance in the festivities of Christmas is a comparatively modern phenomenon. Long ago he was a minor character in mumming plays, with no connection with either children or presents. He still has a role in the procession and dance of the mummers of Marshfield in Gloucestershire on Boxing Day

Finally, 25 December was proclaimed a fast day in 1644. The new rule was enforced by the army, which spent much of its time pulling down the greenery that festive 'pagans' had attached to their doors. In Scotland the prohibition was enforced with great rigour. This anti-Christmas attitude spread to Puritan territories in America. The Church established special services for Christmas in Boston during the 1690s, but many civil authorities strongly opposed this move. And it was not until some 150 years later that Christmas first became a legal holiday in the United States, in Alabama in 1836.

The First Christmas Trees

In Britain during the 18th century the popularity of the Christmas festival and revelling began to decline, and during the first quarter of the 19th century the decline continued — to such an extent that William Sandys, the antiquary, began to record old Christmas customs before they were forgotten. Unknown to Sandys, however, social conditions were laying the foundations for a glorious revival of the Christmas spirit, as a reaction to the wretchedness and drab poverty that was a by-product of the Victorian age. The festival we know today, colourful, sentimental, extravagant, and very much centred on the family, is a typical product of that period, not least in its vague compassion for the infant Jesus and his parents, pictured (incorrectly) as homeless outcasts. As early as 1841 *Punch* suggested

that the Christmas season should be a time for helping the poor and hungry, a sentiment that was given tremendous impetus by Charles Dickens in his *Christmas Carol* two years later. So the custom arose of a special benevolent Christmas dinner for the poor, gushingly described in the song 'Christmas Day in the Workhouse' by George Sims, where

> . . . with clean washed hands and faces
> In a long and hungry line
> The poor sit at the table
> For this is the hour they dine.

Many authorities have claimed that Martin Luther first introduced the idea of the Christmas tree to 16th century Germany; but it is more likely that the use of the tree has roots in the old worship of trees by the tribesmen of northern Europe. Certainly the Germans first brought the tree into Christmas before other peoples. And they took it to America: German mercenaries, fighting on the British side in the War of Independence, raised Christmas trees in their camps, and German settlers in Pennsylvania also set up their trees. It was a longer time coming to Britain, but its popularity there was ensured when Queen Caroline erected a tree at a royal Christmas celebration in 1821, and when in 1841 Prince Albert provided one for a children's party at Windsor.

Christmas soon became popular once again, although in Scotland it was a long time before religious prejudice could be overcome. Some customs, such as Twelfth Night

mumming and wassailing, vanished but others rapidly took their place. The Christmas greeting card first appeared in 1844, and by the 1870s had become firmly entrenched in Britain and the United States. In the 1850s the paper hat had become a feature of Christmas parties, where games very similar to the frolics of the medieval Feast of Fools were played. Kissing under the mistletoe also became a popular custom in England and America, and is a reflection of the festival's ancient Scandinavian origins (see MISTLETOE).

Americans soon added much more greenery to their Christmas decorations, including holly wreaths on front doors, and illuminated the trees growing in front gardens. The United States also instituted the 'communal' tree: the first was put up by the people of Pasadena, on Mount Wilson in 1909, and the next went up in 1912 in Madison Square Garden, for the people of New York. In Colorado in the 1930s, the people of Palmer Lake began a communal Yule-log ceremony, where the log was ritually found, and burned in a special fireplace made in the town hall.

Feast of Light

Christmas has always been a Feast of Light, and so candles and special fires have had major roles in the festive traditions. Today the candles have been replaced, on inflammable evergreen trees, with special electric lights, but the symbol is the same. In Spanish-American parts of the southwestern United States, small fires are lit

Radio Times Hulton Picture Library

F.O.T.

Left The strong pagan elements in Christmas reflect the influence on it of the ancient Yule-feast of the Norsemen and the Roman Saturnalia. They include the tree, feasting, drinking and gaiety, the mummers in animal masks who have now turned into pantomime companies, and the use of evergreens for decoration
Above Santa Claus on ice: one of the most popular symbols of Christmas, he is also one of the most commercialized

The immense Christmas tree outside New York's Rockefeller Center *(facing page)* and the Regent Street decorations *(right)* contrast sharply with carol singers *(above)* and the traditional 19th century pastime of 'snapdragon', snatching at raisins alight with brandy

outside houses, and lighted candles set into bags of sand illuminate roofs and walls.

Santa Claus, probably the most widely accepted of all the symbols of Christmas, arrived in Britain sometime during the 1880s from America, where he had long reigned as the gift-bringing St Nicholas of the German and Dutch settlers. As St Nicholas he had become famous as a result of Clarke Moore's poem 'The Night Before Christmas', published in 1823. By the 1890s the English Father Christmas, originally a minor character in a mummer's play, had been absorbed into the personality of his American counterpart, and become the jovial figure that he is today.

Holiday for Ghosts

St Nicholas was only one of a number of legendary personalities who traditionally bring gifts during the Christmas season, and who invariably come from some unknown land to which they return after the ceremony. Others are the Knight Rupprecht of north Germany, who is possibly identified with Odin, and the Three Kings who, at Epiphany (January 6) bring gifts to the children of Spain. Occasionally the bearer of gifts is a woman, as in Alsace where she appears wearing a crown of candles, or as in Italy where the good fairy Befana fills children's stockings with toys when they go to bed on the eve of Epiphany.

In Holland St Nicholas is accompanied by a forbidding black companion, and in other lands the Christmas scene is not without its ghosts and demons, supporting the old

tradition that it is the time of year when spirits and trolls make high holiday. Only in Britain has Father Christmas shed his forbidding aspects, although here, as elsewhere, children are solemnly warned that only if they are very good will they receive their presents.

Scarlet Flowers

There is a combination of both old and new in the many pleasing customs that grace the Christmas season. Old holly and ivy together with ancient mistletoe have now been joined by the scarlet flower of the poinsettia, which has become a common motif on greeting cards and wrapping paper. The elevation of this wild flower to a place of honour began in the United States. It is said that a little Mexican boy made his offering of humble wild flowers to the infant Jesus and that when they were placed under the altar the flowers turned scarlet.

Boxing Day, which falls on St Stephen's Day, 26 December, was originally the time when donations were made in the Church, or to the apprentices of local tradesmen. It survives in modern times as little more than a sporting holiday.

Many minor customs reflect the pagan traditions of the season. The sergeant-major serving tea to privates on Christmas morning is an echo of the Saturnalian custom in which master and slave exchanged roles; similarly the pantomime tradition that the principal boy is played by a girl and the 'dame' by a male comic. Telling ghost stories by the fireside is a relic of the

belief that at this particular time of year the family ghosts return to their old homes. Some quite ordinary actions can be of symbolic importance, as is illustrated by the superstition that for every mince pie eaten there will be a happy month in the year to come.

Other traditions have a solemn content as, for example, 'a green Christmas means a full churchyard', which is countered by 'a white Christmas means a happy New Year'. At midnight on Christmas Eve cattle in the barns are said to turn to the east and bow, while horses reverently kneel.

The Christmas season popularly ends with Twelfth Night on 5 January, and this is generally accepted as being the date on which all evergreen decorations must be taken down if the luck of the year is to last. Twelfth Night was once a time for eating Twelfth Cakes, but this custom is now almost extinct.

In the Church, however, the Christmas season lasts until Candlemas Day, 2 February, the feast of the Purification of the Virgin Mary, held in honour of the occasion when she presented Christ in the Temple. During the Candlemas ceremony lighted candles are blessed, and carried in procession, celebrating the fact that Jesus Christ was called 'the light of the world'.

ERIC MAPLE

FURTHER READING: G. Buday, *The History of the Christmas Card* (Gale, 1972); T. G. Crippen, *Christmas and Christmas Lore* (Gale, 1976).

Chthonian

Underground deity or spirit, from the Greek word for 'earth', *chthon;* the term includes the gods and powers of the underworld, the earth goddess herself in some of her aspects, and frequently the spirits of the dead, believed to live on under the earth in which they lie buried.
See EARTH.

Cicatrization

Practice of cutting the skin and causing permanent scars to form; widespread among primitive peoples, partly as an aid to beauty and partly for magical and religious reasons.
See AFRICA; AUSTRALIA; TATTOOING.

Leni Riefenstahl

Between 400 and 500 versions of the Cinderella story have been recorded in Europe alone. The one most widely accepted in Britain derives from a 17th century French rendering, but the earliest known version appeared in 9th century China

CINDERELLA

IN ESSENCE, CINDERELLA is the story of a poor and ill-treated girl, victim of a cruel stepmother, who appears before a prince in a gorgeous disguise provided by a supernatural helper. She wins his admiration, and later marries him after she has passed a test of recognition. Some authorities on folk tales reduce even this outline to a more fundamental type of story which they call 'the unpromising hero'. The leading character may even be a boy who, though dirty and apparently even lazy, astounds everyone with his beauty and prowess after receiving supernatural aid, and wins a desirable girl. The story occurs even among polygamous peoples, where the child of a first wife is victimized by his father's later wife or wives. In a Bantu version, for example, the hero is a boy and the supernatural helper is an ox.

In Europe alone between 400 and 500 versions – with the stepmother, disguise and recognition themes included – have been recorded. It is not known where the story originated, and even Andrew Lang's half-humorous assertion that 'a naked and shoeless race could not have invented Cinderella' is not necessarily true, because in some variations of the story the heroine is recognized by means of a ring or a lock of hair. The earliest known version appears to be Chinese, of the 9th century.

The Glass Slipper

The version now best known in the British Isles derives not from folk tradition, but from a comparatively sophisticated rendering by the French author Charles Perrault in his collection of fairy tales, published in 1697. Perrault added some details of his own to the story and these are now some of its most familiar features. Indeed, they have even entered folk tradition in some parts of the world. The pumpkin that turned magically into a golden coach, and the mice who became dapple-grey horses to pull it, were

invented by Perrault. He also introduced the notion of Cinderella having to leave the dance by midnight, when her magic finery would revert to rags. Perrault is also responsible for the glass slipper. But it is not clear whether this confusion had already arisen in the sources Perrault used for the story, or whether he (presumably deliberately) introduced it himself.

Perrault not only embellished the story with inventions of his own, he also omitted some of the important points found in the folk tale versions. In these the heroine is usually helped by her dead mother, or by agents sent by her mother, and the prince carries off a false bride, who is denounced by a bird. Perrault also transformed some of the more archaic elements in the story. In most of the folk tale versions, the heroine receives supernatural help from a domesticated animal – a cow, or a sheep, for example – who is often her dead mother reincarnated. Perrault changed this animal agent into a fairy godmother, a curious half-pagan, half-Christian conception. At the end of Perrault's story, Cinderella shows a Christian forgiveness towards her stepsisters, and even marries them off to 'two grand noblemen of the Court'. This is in striking contrast to the end of the story as it is told by the brothers Grimm. In their version, which was based on German oral tradition, the stepsisters' eyes are pecked out by pigeons, and 'for their wickedness and falsehood, they were punished with blindness as long as they lived.' Christian, too, are the morals Perrault drew from the tale: the only true gift is grace, and whatever gifts you may have, they are useless without a godfather or a godmother.

The Red Calf

No specifically English folk tale of the Cinderella type appears to have survived. About a century ago, however, two versions were recorded in the Scottish counties of Morayshire and Aberdeenshire, under the title of 'The Red Calf' or 'Rashin Coatie', the heroine taking this name from a coat of rushes that she wore. In these Scottish versions the heroine, who is ill-treated and fed on porridge and whey, while her ugly and ill-natured elder sister is the favourite, is helped by a red calf among the cattle she is sent to herd. The red calf is guided by her dead mother, and in one variant of the story

is slain by the cruel stepmother. However, a magic power resides in its bones and the dead calf speaks to her:

> Tak me up, bane by bane
> And pit me aneth yon grey stane

Whatever she wants, if she comes and asks him for it, he will give it to her. In the other version, the heroine herself is ordered to slay the calf, but the calf instructs her to kill the wicked stepsister instead, and to jump on its back and escape.

On their travels, they make a coat of rushes for the heroine, and Rashin Coatie, as she is now called, goes to the palace, where she is set to work as a kitchen maid. At Yuletide, Rashin Coatie is supposed to stay at home and get the dinner ready, while everyone else goes to church. The red calf, however, procures fine clothes and slippers for Rashin Coatie, and undertakes to cook the dinner, so that she can go too. Rashin Coatie goes to church, where the Prince sees her and falls in love with her, and tries to stop her when she leaves. He succeeds in keeping the slipper which she leaves behind.

The Prince tries to find the owner of the slipper, but no woman has a foot dainty enough to fit it. The henwife's daughter clips her toes and pares her foot until the slipper fits, but a bird warns the Prince as he is carrying off this false bride. The Prince returns to his palace, where Rashin Coatie is working. He recognizes her, finds the slipper fits, and marries her.

The first meeting between the heroine and the Prince, and the incident of the dropped slipper, also occur in church in a modern Greek version of the story. In this the role of the red calf (or Perrault's fairy godmother) is played by the carefully tended bones of the dead mother. In a Russian version, the heroine's dead mother again appears as the supernatural helper, first in the form of a sheep, and later as a birch tree. Here the mother actually assumes the form of a beast herself, instead of merely sending one to help. This is midway between the Scottish versions and the most primitive version of all, in which the mother actually *is* an animal in the first place. The motif of a helpful tree – usually one that has grown up on the mother's grave – is widespread in the Cinderella stories. In the version recorded by the brothers Grimm

Cinderella plants a branch at her mother's grave, and waters it with her tears until it becomes a beautiful tree. Cinderella sits under it three times a day, and a little white bird – representing, no doubt, the dead mother's soul in early belief – always perches on the tree. If the heroine expresses a wish, the bird throws down at her feet whatever she has wished for.

The Mutilated Foot

From these various versions it can be seen that there are a number of elements and motifs associated with the story, and any folk tale that includes a minimum number of these features can be recognized as belonging to the Cinderella type. The name Cinderella itself, which derives from

Perrault's *Cendrillon*, is not an essential feature of the story. In one Italian folk tale on this theme, the heroine is called *Vaccarella*, or the cowherd; in a Russian version, she appears as Pigskin Hood.

Marian Roalfe Cox, who published a study of 345 versions of the Cinderella story in 1893, considered the ill-treatment of the heroine, and her final recognition by means of the shoe or other personal token,

The magical pumpkin *(left)* and the glass slipper *(right)*, two of the most familiar features of the story of Cinderella, were introduced by Charles Perrault the French author, who in 1697 published the definitive version of the fairy tale: illustrations by the 19th century painter and illustrator, Gustave Doré

as the two essential elements. She lists, however, some 27 motifs which are associated with it in one place or another. An enormous variety of treatment can obviously be obtained by mixing these motifs in various ways and story-tellers all over the world have allowed themselves a great deal of freedom in this mixing. In a Moravian version, when the Prince has set off to church with the false bride the heroine transforms *herself* into the bird, whose usual function is to direct attention to the mutilated foot. It is interesting that not one of these motifs, the false bride, the bird or the mutilated foot, occurs in Perrault's version, by now the classic rendering of the tale for most of the world.

DAVID PHILLIPS

Mary Evans Picture Library

CIRCE

THE FAIR-HAIRED SORCERESS Circe is described in the *Odyssey* as a goddess, although her reputation throughout mythology is rather that of a witch. She was the daughter of Helios, the sun god, and sister of Aeetes, the divine wizard and King of Colchis. Another celebrated witch, Medea, was her niece.

Circe was banished to the isle of Aeaea, after she had poisoned her husband, the King of the Sarmatians, a nomadic people of Persia. Circe's island has been sited as lying at the head of the Adriatic; not far from the mouth of the river Po; according to Hesiod, however, Aeaea lay off the

coast of Latium, now a part of Italy, in the promontory called Circaeum, which was once an island.

Circe lived in a marble palace surrounded by woods, practising her magic arts and singing as she sat by her loom. She was attended by nymphs and a troop of wild beasts, whom she had transformed from men she had ensnared. When Odysseus's men landed on her island, they cast lots to decide who should stay to guard the ship and who should go to reconnoitre the land. Odysseus's friend Eurylochus set out with a band of men and, attracted by Circe's singing, they were drawn to the palace. Wild beasts came out to meet them, but instead of attacking the men, they fawned on them and made them welcome. Circe invited them

to dine at her table and all entered unsuspecting, except Eurylochus who stayed behind, fearing a trap.

As soon as the sailors had drunk the goddess's drugged wine, she struck them with her wand and turned them into hogs. Eurylochus escaped and told Odysseus what had happened. He set off to rescue his friends and on the way he met the god Hermes who gave him a magic herb named moly, to protect him against Circe's magic. When Circe attempted to transform Odysseus, she found that her magic was useless. Odysseus forced her to restore his men to human shape.

Circe, who had become enamoured of Odysseus, by her wiles persuaded him to remain for a year on her island. At length

Odysseus became restive and was determined to be on his way again. Circe advised him how to navigate the River of Ocean and descend into Hades, and how to deal with the ghosts. When Odysseus returned to Aeaea, having been advised about his own future by the ghost of Tiresias, Circe sent him off on his homeward voyage to Ithaca. She warned him against the Sirens and against Scylla and Charybdis; also of the fatal consequences that would follow if any of his men were to kill and eat the cattle of the Sun on the island of Thrinacia. Circe is an important figure in the *Odyssey* and it is due to her warnings and advice that Odysseus finally reaches home.

She appears from time to time in later literature, always in connection with Odysseus. She bears him a son, Telegonus, according to the *Telegonia*, the lost poem by the epic poet Eugammon of Cyrene, which has survived only in a prose summary. Telegonus comes to Ithaca, seeking his father. Arriving at night, he is mistakenly attacked as a raider and mortally wounds Odysseus, with his poisoned spear. He then carries off Odysseus's body and also Penelope, Odysseus's wife and their son Telemachus to Circe, who makes them immortal with her magic powers. Telemachus marries Circe and Penelope marries Circe's son, Telegonus.

In folk tales told from western Europe to Mongolia, Circe's story has many counterparts. It has been suggested that such folk tales spread from the Near East and originated in the Babylonian myth of Ishtar, who killed her lovers when she became tired of them. During the progress from myth to folklore, the slaughter of the goddess's lover became changed into transformation into beasts.

Circe, it has also been suggested, may be related to the powerful ancient Mediterranean goddess known as the 'Lady of the Beasts'. Her image has been found engraved upon Minoan gems a millennium before Homer's day. Flanked by lions, she crowned the main gate of Mycenae at the time of the Trojan War. Around the year 1200BC, invading Dorians drove the goddess's ancient worship from the shores of Greece, but it lingered for centuries in Italy and places further west.

From ancient rites to astrology, alchemy and magic, the circle is one of the most powerful and most widely used of all symbols

CIRCLE

IF YOU WANT TO DEPICT a group of things, linked together, complete in itself and separated from everything outside the group, the shape which most effectively expresses completeness and separateness at the same time is the circle. A group of people linked by a common aim or interest which for the moment sets them apart from others may call themselves a 'circle', the old-fashioned 'ladies' sewing circle', for instance, or the Rotarians, and your friends and acquaintances constitute your social 'circle'.

These ideas of completeness and apartness lie behind the confusingly paradoxical uses of one of the most powerful and most widely employed of all symbols. Sometimes it stands for the sun, or for the sun's course through the year, or for time in general. The zodiac is the circle of the sun's apparent progress through the stars in a year, and astrological horoscopes are now almost always circular. Clock faces are usually circular too, showing the remorseless, ever-repeated round of the hours.

As a symbol of time and of the ups and downs of fortune which time brings to every man, the circle often takes the form of

In ancient times a circle often marked the boundary of a sacred area, and protected it against evil influences: passage grave in County Meath, Ireland

a wheel (see WHEEL). But if the circle is a symbol of time and its divisions, it is also a symbol of eternity, because it consists of an endless line. Standing for sun, the stars in their courses, time and eternity, it can also mean heaven and perfection. Some of the Greek philosophers said that the circle is the perfect figure and circular motion the perfect motion, and in the 13th century the great theologian Thomas Aquinas agreed, on the ground that in a circle a return is made to the beginning. Here is the circle as a complete whole.

Whole and Hole

The circle is a symbol of 'all things' because it can be imagined as a line drawn round everything but at the same time it is a symbol of 'one thing', because it is a single figure. It is therefore an emblem of the proposition that 'All is One', that all the various phenomena of the universe are linked together in a unity. The alchemical symbol called the *ourobouros* is a demonstration of this. It is a circle formed by a snake or a dragon swallowing its own tail, and sometimes bearing the Greek phrase *En To Pan*, 'all is one'. This phrase is made of three words having seven letters, and 3 + 7 = 10. Again, ten means 'all things' because it completes the series of the primary numbers, of whose combinations all other numbers are constructed, but ten also means 'the One', because it is made of 1 and 0, and 1 + 0 = 1.

The circle is a whole but also a hole. It is the symbol of nought, 0, and so it stands for emptiness, non-existence, nothing. But it is the Nothing which contains the potential existence of everything, the primeval chaos from which God made the world, the 'abyss' or 'ground' or 'womb' of all being (see BREATH; CABALA).

The Magic Circle

The use of a circle to mark the boundary of an area which is sacred, set apart from everyday life and to be protected against worldly or evil influences, is very ancient. The stone circles of Stonehenge, Avebury and many other prehistoric sites are examples. The Babylonians drew a circle of flour round the bed of a sick man to keep demons away from him. A Roman ambassador to a foreign potentate would draw a circle round himself with his staff, to show that he should be safe from attack. Medieval German Jews drew a circle round the bed of a woman in childbirth to ward off demonic attack, and the words 'Sanvi, Sansanvi, Semangelaf, Adam and Eve, barring Lilith' were chalked on the door or the walls for additional protection.

In medieval and modern European textbooks of ritual magic the circle is of great importance. The magician and his assistants stand inside a circle to protect themselves from the spirits, demons or forces they intend to conjure up. But the circle is not only intended to keep something out

Magic circle from *Le Veritable Dragon Rouge*, a 16th century magical textbook: the magician and his assistants stand in the triangle, with wax candles on either side and a brazier of charcoal in front; the inscription JHS stands for Jesus

but also to keep something in – the magical energy which the magicians will summon up from within themselves in the course of the ceremony. It is this energy which will force the spirit to appear and if it were not for the circle the energy would flow off in all directions and be dissipated. The circle keeps it inside a small area and so concentrates it. The same motive lies behind the circle of people who link their hands at a seance.

The magic circle should be nine feet in diameter, drawn on the floor or the ground with a sword or a knife, or with charcoal or chalk. Inside this circle is drawn a slightly smaller one, eight feet in diameter. In the narrow rim between the two circles are bowls of water, crosses, names of power (see NAMES) and plants like vervain, which demons are said to dislike, to reinforce the barrier against hostile forces. There must be no gap or break in the circle, through which an evil influence could get into it and take possession of the magician, and when the magician has entered the circle he must close it carefully behind him.

The 18th century French *Grand Grimoire*, introducing a grislier note, says that the circle should be made of the skin of a young goat, cut into strips and fastened down

with four nails from a dead baby's coffin. The magician stands in a triangle, drawn inside the circle, with a wax candle placed in a circlet of vervain on either side.

A modern formula for drawing the magic circle is given in Dion Fortune's book *Psychic Self-Defence*. The magician begins by facing east and making the sign of the cross, touching his forehead, shoulders and solar plexus. This is not the Christian cross but the equal-armed cross, standing for the four elements and the four cardinal points, and so for mastery of all things (see CROSS). Next, he imagines that he is holding a great cross-handled sword in his right hand, point upwards. He says, 'In the Name of God I take in hand the Sword of Power for defence against evil and aggression.' He imagines himself as a 'tremendous armed and mailed figure, vibrating with the force of the Power of God.' He draws the circle on the floor with the point of the imaginary sword, in a line of imagined golden flame. Facing east and clasping his hands above his head, he says, 'May the mighty archangel Raphael protect me from all evil approaching from the east.' He repeats the same formula facing south, west and north in turn, naming Michael, Gabriel and Uriel respectively.

This circle has been drawn 'deosil' or clockwise, moving to the right, which is the side of good. In black magic the circle would be drawn the opposite way, moving to the left or 'widdershins', a word derived from an Anglo-Saxon phrase meaning 'to walk against', and which means moving against the direction of the sun and therefore in an unnatural and evil manner.

Circumambulation, moving round something in a circle, is a very old magical and religious rite, and circular dances are known from all over the world (see CAROLE: DANCE). In eastern Europe, at least until recently, at a Jewish wedding it was the custom for the bride to walk round her husband three or seven times under the wedding canopy. The original purpose was probably to keep the pair and their marriage safe from evil by drawing a protective circle round them.
(See also RING.)

FURTHER READING: Richard Cavendish, *The Black Arts* (Routledge & Kegan Paul, 1967).

Circumcision

Removal of all or part of the foreskin: the underlying motives for its use in a religious context are uncertain but it is usually a form of initiation; occurring at puberty, as among many African peoples, it is part of the initiation into adulthood; sometimes, as in Jewish practice, it is connected with the naming of a child, which makes him a real person and so initiates him into human life.
See AFRICA; INITIATION.

Clairvoyance

Mysterious ability to see what is not present to ordinary sight, including objects or happenings at a great distance, and things in the future; clairaudience refers to hearing instead of seeing; distinguished from telepathy, which is the ability to sense other people's thoughts and mental states, or to convey your own to other people, without the use of speech, gesture or the other normal methods of communication.
See DIVINATION; EXTRA-SENSORY PERCEPTION.

The churchyard of a ruined church was the sinister setting for a series of events at Clophill in Bedfordshire. Tombs were discovered broken open and the skeleton of a young woman who died two centuries ago was disinterred

CLOPHILL

A DERELICT CHURCH on the slopes of Dead Man's Hill at Clophill in Bedfordshire, has twice been the scene of incidents apparently connected with the practice of ritual magic.

On the first occasion, in March 1963, seven tombs in the churchyard were seriously damaged and the coffin of a girl who had been dead for 200 years was removed from one of them. Her bones were found inside the church. In 1969, on Midsummer Night, a tomb was smashed to pieces and attempts were made to dig the body from beneath it.

The first desecration is thought to have taken place at full moon. It was discovered, according to a newspaper report, when a visitor to the churchyard saw a child carrying a human skull. Arranged in a circle inside the church were the thigh, shin and arm bones, and part of the pelvis; an earlier visitor claimed to have seen the skull impaled upon a spike in the centre. The feathers of a cockerel were scattered nearby. The bones were those of Jenny Humberstone, the young wife of an apothecary, who had died in 1770 at the age of 22.

At first the affair was regarded as a hoax,

possibly carried out by students. This was not unlikely considering the large number of graveyard desecrations that had taken place in the previous year. At Knutsford, Cheshire, the grave of a man buried in 1682 had been opened, while many of the stone crosses in Eltham churchyard, near London, had been damaged by vandals. Nevertheless there was a strong suggestion that other, more sinister, agencies had been at work. Westham church in Sussex had been invaded by black magicians who spat upon the crucifix in broad daylight. In Haydale Wood, Derbyshire, a girl had been found tied to a tree after being scourged with whips by Satanists. Only a few miles from Clophill itself the mutilated heads of a number of cattle were found in a bluebell wood, outside Luton.

Commonplace as these incidents were becoming, the Clophill affair seemed to suggest that some kind of organization might be involved. For one thing it was evident from the damage inflicted upon the tombs that a great deal of effort had been put into the attempt to break them open, which seemed to discount a mere students' frolic. They were table-top tombs and each was surmounted by an extremely heavy slab of stone. Prising this masonry from its base must have involved intensive effort with crowbars, and the attendant risks of detection and imprisonment were considerable. The entrances to six of the tombs had been securely sealed with layers of bricks, and only Jenny Humberstone's grave permitted entry. The raiders had smashed open the

coffin and removed the skeleton. It seemed unlikely that this was merely a sick practical joke. Certainly the police believed that the evidence suggested that a Black Mass had been celebrated.

The incident was widely publicized and the suspicion that one of the modern English witch covens might be involved soon arose. This was strenuously denied by the then spokesman for British witchcraft, the late Dr Gerald Gardner, who insisted, 'It is nothing to do with us. We are as puzzled as everybody else. English witches don't do things like this.' He was undoubtedly right. The Clophill affair had nothing in common with modern witchcraft which is concerned with white or good magic. A more pertinent theory was that Satanism or necromancy was involved.

One national newspaper claimed to have interviewed a prominent Satanist who was reported as saying that a Black Mass had indeed taken place in the church. 'The ideal arrangement,' he had said, 'is to use a naked woman as an altar for the ceremony but it was too cold that night. So it was decided to use a woman's bones. This was part of the cult's worship of the mother figure as represented by the goddess Diana.'

Shreds of a Shroud

It is far more likely, however, that the ceremony performed that night involved necromancy, the art of making the spirits of the dead return and speak. It was a common practice among black magicians during the Middle Ages and even today is well known

Tombs in the graveyard of the church on the slopes of Dead Man's Hill at Clophill have twice been desecrated in what seem to have been preliminaries to necromantic rites: on one occasion the bones of a 200-year-old corpse were arranged in a circle inside the church *Facing page* Clophill church: a notice on its walls reads 'Keep away. This church is dangerous' *Right* The remains of one of the tombs

in Africa and in Haiti, the land of Voodoo. A corpse is essential for necromancy, but is not necessary for Satanic rites.

Another incident, not generally reported, added to the mystery of the Clophill affair. The Rector had told the press that he intended to re-inter the skeleton and fill in the grave as soon as possible. Meanwhile, he locked the bones away for safety in another building. The tomb robbers returned to search for the skull and other objects that had played such a prominent role in their sinister rites. On discovering the grave to be empty, they vented their rage upon what was left of the coffin, smashing it into fragments which were left scattered about the church and churchyard.

Jenny Humberstone was finally laid to rest in her old grave by the church porch, with eight tons of earth over her coffin.

Six years later, yet another tomb was smashed and attempts made to disinter the corpse. The Rector was horrified, and spent the following two nights in a lonely vigil by the gutted church. On the third night he went home to bed, thinking that the danger

was over. The following morning, two more graves were found destroyed and opened.

Understandably, the villagers of Clophill are reluctant to discuss the strange happenings; they refer to them as 'the troubles up in the church'. Meanwhile no one knows when more 'troubles' may occur. On the red tiled floor of the ruined church lie shattered

pieces of Jenny Humberstone's coffin, with ragged pieces of her shroud still attached. Everyone in Clophill hopes the remaining coffins on Dead Man's Hill will continue to stay underground.

FURTHER READING: *Ghosts,* edited by W. Mayne (Elsevier-Nelson, 1971).

Little is known of one of the greatest mystical writers, the author of the Cloud of Unknowing, *yet thousands of Christians have gained help and solace from this 14th century work, which argues that the dark cloud which shuts us off from God, can be penetrated with God's aid, not by the intellect but only by a sharp dart of love*

CLOUD OF UNKNOWING

THE AUTHOR of the *Cloud of Unknowing,* one of the most famous of all mystical works, is himself unknown. Even the date when it was written is still uncertain, although its style and other evidence place it in the late 14th century. The author belonged to a group of mystical writers which included Richard Rolle of Hampole, Walter Hilton and Julian of Norwich, and which arose at the same time as the Rhineland and Flemish mystical school, among whose members were Eckhart, Tauler, Suso and Ruysbroek.

The two groups, however, appear to have developed independently, although along parallel lines. They were both products of a similar intellectual climate which seems to have fostered the search for an experimental form of religion. Both groups drew their inspiration from a writer known to us as Pseudo-Dionysius, whose works were first heard of in Constantinople in the 6th century

AD (see DIONYSIUS THE AREOPAGITE).

The teaching of the *Cloud,* insists throughout on the impossibility of knowing God by human reason. Right at the beginning occurs the passage:

For of all other creatures and their works — yea, and of the works of God himself — may a man through grace have fullness of knowing, and well can he think of them; but of God himself can no man think.

And towards the end, appealing to Dionysius, the author says, 'The most godly knowing of God is that which is known by unknowing.' The 'cloud of unknowing', in fact, which lies between God and man, is pierced not by the intellect but only by a sharp dart of love.

A Beam of Ghostly Light

The people for whom he is writing, the author says, are those who aim at being perfect followers of Christ, not merely by the practice of good works but through contemplation. Like Hilton and the other English mystics mentioned above, he uses what was then a new approach to religion, the cult of contemplation. The word contemplation, in this its technical, mystical sense, means a mental prayer based on intuition rather than on reason, and is distinct from meditation. In the *Cloud* contemplation is seen, according to the principles laid down by Dionysius, as being beyond the intellect. The working of the intellect can only hinder it, and so it must consist in concentrating the mind on the

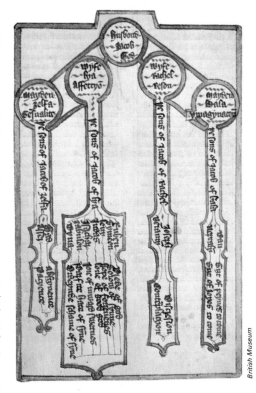

Illustration from the *Cloud of Unknowing* showing the twelve sons and one daughter born to Jacob, later called Israel, by his two wives and their handmaidens: the sons' descendants became the twelve tribes of Israel, the chosen people of God, and each of them is here linked with one of the qualities of the faithful worshipper of God

simplest idea of God, with all created things rigidly excluded.

> This darkness and this cloud . . . is betwixt thee and thy God, and hindereth thee, so that thou mayest neither see him clearly by light of understanding in thy reason, nor feel him in sweetness of love in thine affection. And therefore shape thee to bide in this darkness as long as thou mayest, evermore crying after him whom thou lovest. For if ever thou shalt see him or feel him, as it may be here, it must always be in this cloud and in this darkness. And if thou wilt busily travail as I bid thee, I trust in his mercy that thou shalt thereto come

But this initial effort is not contemplation, though the writer believes that to one in the proper frame of mind God will bestow this formless knowledge. He makes it very clear that it is God who must be sought, not an experience, but he does say that it is possible that of his goodness God will sometimes grant a mystical experience:

> Then will he (God) sometimes peradventure send out a beam of ghostly light, piercing this *cloud of unknowing* that is betwixt thee and him, and show thee some of his secrets, the which man may not and cannot speak . . .

Much research and speculation has gone into the attempt to identify the author of the *Cloud*. At one time it was suggested that Walter Hilton (see HILTON) may have been responsible, but this theory has now been abandoned. It seems likely, however, that Walter Hilton knew the author, who was himself acquainted with the work of Richard Rolle. The language of the *Cloud* suggests that the author lived in the north-east Midlands. Some scholars have suggested that he was a Carthusian monk, others that he was a secular priest, but his identity remains an unsolved mystery.

LANCELOT SHEPPARD

FURTHER READING: *Cloud of Unknowing and Other Works* translated by Clifton Wolters (Penguin, 1978); J. McCann ed., *The Cloud of Unknowing* (Burns, Oates, London, 1952); for general historical background, *The Waning of the Middle Ages* (St. Martin, 1924).

Clover

A three-leafed clover is a symbol of the Trinity and a protection against evil and witchcraft; the four-leafed variety is also lucky, provided it is not given away, and is supposed to give its owner clairvoyant powers; five-leafed clovers are unlucky unless given away.

Coal

A rock which burns, a paradoxical quality which suggests that it contains powerful magic: it is lucky to find a piece in the street; coal brings good luck if carried in the pocket and there are cases of burglars using it in this way, of schoolchildren carrying it with them to examinations, and of prisoners taking it with them to their trials; in Scotland and the north of England coal should be the first thing to be brought into the house on New Year's Day.

Timekeeper, scarer of demons and giver of health, the cock is connected with dawn and the sun. Its pugnacious nature has caused it to be one of the oldest symbols of the fighting spirit

COCK

THE PROUD STRUTTING, aggressiveness and sexual ardour of the cock, together with its striking appearance and loud crowing, are the reasons for this bird's particularly widespread involvement in folk customs and traditions. It has retained its association with ancient lore, and has also tended to accumulate new beliefs and practices wherever it has been introduced.

The cock appeared in southern Europe in post-Homeric times, probably about the 5th or 6th century BC. Early in the 5th century a cock was depicted on a Sicilian coin. The Persian wars were fought during this period and there can be little doubt that the bird's introduction was due to this Asian incursion. The cock was sacred in Persia and to kill one of these birds was regarded as a serious sin. Its Persian name indicates that it was considered oracular. Aristophanes, in *The Birds,* called it 'the Persian bird' and compared its crest to the head-dress of the Persian king.

The Persians, in their turn, called the Carians, who came from a region in Asia Minor, 'cocks' because they wore crested helmets. A Greek writer compared the cock's adornments to the magnificent robes of Croesus, the proverbially wealthy king of Lydia. Pliny, too, commented on the remarkable comb. Because of the bird's pugnacity and courage, a cock was placed on the head of the statue of Athene on the Acropolis, as symbol of battle.

The crowing of the cock attracted special attention among the Greeks because it occurred about dawn, although the bird does, of course, crow at other times. There was a Greek story that when Mars chose to spend a night with Venus in the absence of

The cock is part of folklore and tradition in many parts of the world; in both Asia and Europe the crowing of a cock was believed to drive away ghosts and demons: mosaic at Misis, Turkey

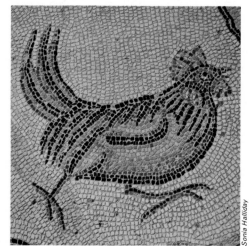

her husband, Vulcan, he commissioned Alektraon (the Greek for 'cock') to watch at the door. He fell asleep and Mars, surprised by the returning husband, punished Alektraon by transforming him into a cock. He has been vigilant at dawn ever since.

Because evil spirits, 'the powers of darkness' have always been believed to be particularly active at night, the dawn crowing of the cock was usually a welcome sign, and the belief arose that the bird itself was effective in exorcizing evil. In the Persian sacred books it was stated that the cock's crow awakens the dawn, arouses mankind to praise the perfect Holiness and drives away spectres and demons. This tradition persisted in Europe.

The belief arose that a bird that could frighten devils must be able to scare wild animals, and travellers in Libya carried a cock with them to frighten lions and basilisks. The basilisk was a fabulous monster, hatched by a serpent from a cock's egg, and alleged to be able to kill with a glance. The Greek writer Aelian, who died in about 222AD, remarked that the basilisk dies in convulsions on hearing the crowing of a cock. It is widely believed that a crowing hen is a sinister omen.

The Healing Bird

Another Greek author, Heliodorus, writing in the 3rd to 4th centuries AD, stated that the cock crows because of its affinity with the sun. The bird's solar connection dates from ancient times in Europe as well as in

Asia, and we may assume that this association was introduced at the same time as the bird itself. The Greeks believed that the cock was sacred to Apollo, god of the sun, and it became associated with Asclepius, the god of healing, Apollo's son by the nymph Coronis. This association with Asclepius and healing is an outcome of the bird's connection with the sun and the life-giving powers, and its opposition to the powers of darkness. In the *Phaedo* Plato records Socrates's request before drinking the hemlock that a cock should be offered to Asclepius on his behalf, although this request was not connected with any desire to escape the effects of the poison.

The practice of sacrificing cocks has been widespread. Cocks were sacrificed to the sun in Mexico, and elsewhere served as ritual sacrifices after the erection of a building or bridge (probably instead of human victims). In the East a cock may be killed over an invalid's bed and the

Below left The cock is renowned for its courage and pugnacity, and cock-fighting is an ancient entertainment that still survives in some parts of the world: cock-fight in Haiti *Below right* 'Saviour of the World': the cock was a sacred bird in Persia and India, and this figure with a man's body and the head of the bird which daily saves the world from darkness, by crowing to bring the dawn, was often found on amulets used by members of the Gnostic sects which flourished in western Asia and the eastern Mediterranean area. Late 18th century gilt statuette, in the Gerald Yorke collection

blood sprinkled on the sufferer. It is, or was, a custom in Ceylon for a red cock to be dedicated to a sick person and sacrificed if he recovered. In Scotland, the blood of a red cock was administered in a flour cake to the invalid. There were places in Germany where it was believed that illness and bad luck could be warded off by hiding the head, heart and right foot of a cock in the house. In both Germany and Ireland a cock was sacrificed on 11 November, St Martin's Day (or Eve, in Ireland). In Athlone in Ireland the blood was sprinkled on the threshold and the four corners of the house. D'Arcy Thompson in *A Glossary of Greek Birds* (1936) states that he himself remembers a cock being sacrificed to St Nicholas to cure a sick cow. Cocks are sacrificed among the Arabs and in North Africa, although in some African regions it is considered wrong to kill these birds.

Denial before Cock-Crow
The cock's symbolism is important in Christian traditions. Its crowing gained additional significance because of its role in St Peter's repudiation of Christ (Matthew, chapter 26) and it naturally became symbolic of the Christian's duty to remain alert against temptation and 'the wiles of the devil'. As such it became customary to place a weathercock on church towers and steeples.

A tradition dating from the 4th century tells how the cock announced Christ's birth by calling out *Christus natus est*, 'Christ is born'. Shakespeare embroidered tradition

when he made Marcellus comment on the disappearance of the ghost in *Hamlet*:

It faded on the crowing of the cock.
Some say, that ever 'gainst that season comes
Wherein our Saviour's birth is celebrated,
The bird of dawning singeth all night long;
And then, they say, no spirit dare stir abroad;
The nights are wholesome; then no planets strike,
No fairy takes, nor witch hath power to charm;
So hallowed and so gracious is the time.

Many ideas concerning good and bad luck involve the cock. American lore says if a cock crows on a porch, visitors will come; if in the rain, the rain will stop. A cock crowing facing a house, at the front door, on a banister, or inside the house, is an omen of death. In Germany it was an ill omen if a wedding procession met cocks fighting while on its way to church.

Cock-fighting is an ancient amusement, popular in some eastern countries and all over Central and South America, also still carried on illegally in certain regions of Europe and the United States. As early as the 3rd century AD the Christian writer Lactantius had declared cock-fighting an unsuitable spectacle for Christian people, but the compassion for animals shown by many saints had little effect in encouraging humane treatment.

EDWARD A. ARMSTRONG

491

Cockle-Shell

Or scallop-shell, the heart-shaped shell worn in the hats of pilgrims to the shrine of St James of Compostela in Spain; the polished side of the shell was engraved with a drawing of the Virgin Mary or the Crucifixion, and the shell was blessed by a priest to protect the pilgrim from spiritual harm; hence Sir Walter Raleigh's famous lines, 'Give me my scallop-shell of quiet, my staff of peace to walk upon. . .'

Kress Collection, Seattle Art Museum

Cockroach

Large beetle-like insect infesting many old houses, dark-coloured and nocturnal, so acquiring supernatural attributions: in the Old American South, it was believed that a witch could be caught by leaving a jar in the hearth ashes overnight; a cockroach found in the jar was the trapped witch: folk medicine used cockroaches to treat urinary ailments, epilepsy and worms in children: United States lore suggests ridding your house of roaches forever by sweeping them out on Good Friday.

Giving up all entertainment was demanded of anyone who joined the Cokelers, a small 19th century Nonconformist sect which survives today

COKELERS

THE STRICT PURITANICAL sect of the Society of Dependants, or Cokelers as they were known popularly, was founded in 1850 and still has a small following today. It is exclusive to the West Sussex area and parts of south-west Surrey. The origin of the strange name Cokelers is not certain, although it has been suggested that it refers to the members' custom of drinking cocoa at their meetings, as part of the simple refreshments which were provided on these occasions. Another possible explanation is that it derived from a place called Cokkeg, in the village of Loxwood in Sussex, where the sect was formed.

The Cokelers were founded by a London shoemaker named John Sirgood, who was born at Avening, Gloucestershire, in 1820. As a young man, living in the Clapham area of South London, Sirgood became a member of a small sect named the Plumstead Peculiars, which had been founded by the evangelist William Bridges in 1838 (see PECULIAR PEOPLE).

At first Sirgood preached in Clapham, but he soon discovered that the further he journeyed from London the more genuine the response became. Closing his shop, he and his wife set out, with their belongings packed into a hand-cart, and walked into Surrey and West Sussex. They decided to settle in Loxwood, a small village about eight miles from Horsham. Here John Sirgood started to preach in the fields and behind the cottages. Informal prayer-meetings were held, and his fame as a preacher soon spread around the countryside. He was reputed to possess remarkable powers as a faith healer and even to have raised someone from the dead.

Forbidden Flowers

In 1850 Sirgood decided that the time had come to form his own sect. The principles which he prescribed for his followers were that they should lead a life of simple Puritan austerity. 'We believe that man must have a second birth,' he preached, 'he must realise Christ in his own life.' Those who joined him were expected to renounce the world. They must accept that they had become possessed of part of the body of Christ and therefore free from sin; the sect was first known, in fact, as the 'Body'.

The demands which he made on his followers were rigid in the extreme. Villagers and labourers who had once enjoyed their ale in the local inn found that, once they had joined the Society of Dependants they were expected to scorn all intoxicants and other pleasures. The Bible was their only literature, and whole passages had to be learned by heart and quoted in conversation. No flowers were allowed in the cottages, which had to be austerely furnished, with the minimum of decoration. Entertainment and music were forbidden, and pictures and photographs were destroyed. Sport, literature, drama and most of the relaxations of the average man and woman were denied to the Dependants. Furthermore, the Society did not advocate marriage. Anyone wishing to marry was at liberty to do so, but no marriage service could be solemnized by the followers of John Sirgood. They believed that marriage interfered with one's relationship with God, and that it was impossible for God to permit a marriage service in one of their chapels. This severe mortification of the flesh attracted many sincere, but often simple, followers and half the farm labourers in the district were soon Dependants.

As Sirgood's doctrine spread further afield, many new Dependant communities sprang up in neighbouring towns and villages, and the Cokelers still use their chapels today. Large provision shops were opened by the Society wherever a colony was formed, and were owned by the members on co-operative lines. At Loxwood there still is a large store with a meeting-house, steam bakery and laundry, and with every kind of article for sale, from provisions to bicycles, haberdashery, kitchen utensils, gardening equipment and furniture. These shops have paid big dividends over the years, and only the ale houses have been the poorer for the coming of John Sirgood. For generations the Cokeler farmers have sold their produce to the Dependant dairies, and families in the various districts have invested their savings in the shops, with whom they have dealt exclusively. John Sirgood's system meant that labourers in this part of the country have always been comparatively well-off and better dressed than those in other parts of Surrey and Sussex.

Joyful Funerals

But although the Cokelers prospered, they have not multiplied. Their doctrines were sterile and their membership dwindled, out of touch with the world beyond their little kingdom. In 1885, the year of Sirgood's death, membership in the district totalled 1,500. At the beginning of this century the members formed almost a third of the population of Wisborough and Northchapel, and there were many other villages under their influence. By 1904 there were only about 900 members regularly attending their chapels, dressed in black. Today a few of the meeting-houses remain open, but only a few Cokelers attend the services. Many of the stores and communal farms have been sold. It is not a religion likely to attract young people, in a world where the internal combustion engine, television, pop music, the cinema and alcohol are worshipped.

Visitors nevertheless are welcomed to the Loxwood meeting-house and are warmly received by this friendly sect. They will observe that members of the congregation spend the interval between the morning and afternoon services in a small back room where refreshments are served free of charge. At their gatherings, when prayers have been said and hymns sung without music, the meeting is thrown open. Any member can stand up and give testimony to God's goodness.

When John Sirgood was buried in the field behind the Loxwood chapel which he had built, the interment was attended by many hundreds of followers, farm hands and labourers. A Cokeler funeral is impressive and lasts for several hours. Death is not considered fearful, but is regarded as a happy release from a world where there is much sin and misery.

The whole of a Cokeler's life is devoted to attempting to reduce sin and unhappiness to a minimum. The funeral, with its feasting and singing, is therefore more a celebration than an occasion for mourning. Instead of the usual gravestone, the Cokeler's grave is marked simply with a number on a metal plate.

COLERIDGE

THE MIND OF COLERIDGE (1772–1834) has been described as an ocean. This image is apt for many reasons — for its all-embracing scope, its profundity, unity, movement, and mystery. As the supreme literary critic not only of the Romantic movement and of his friend Wordsworth, but of English poetry in its entirety, Coleridge stands alone; his lectures on Shakespeare are unsurpassed in their kind. His *Aids to Reflection* remains a living contribution to Anglican and Protestant theology. Coleridge has been seen as an early Existentialist philosopher. He was a declared Platonist, and the names of two of

his sons, Hartley and Berkeley, declare his affinities in English philosophic thought. 'Every man', he wrote, 'is born an Aristotelian or a Platonist. I do not think it possible that anyone born an Aristotelian can become a Platonist; and I am sure no born Platonist can ever change into an Aristotelian. They are the two classes of man, beside which it is next to impossible to conceive a third. The one considers reason a quality, or attribute; the other considers it a power. I believe that Aristotle could never get to understand what Plato meant by an idea.'

As a young man Coleridge visited Germany in order to study the language and philosophy of Kant and Schelling, with whom he has many affinities. He was among

Illustration by J. Noel Paton to Coleridge's *Ancient Mariner:* the belief that it is unlucky to shoot an albatross was largely invented by Coleridge

the last minds to attempt that universality of knowledge which characterizes Renaissance thinkers, but which has scarcely been possible since. 'I am, and ever have been, a great reader, and have read almost everything — a library cormorant. I am *deep* in all out-of-the-way books, whether of the monkish times, or of the puritanical era. I have read and digested most of the historical writers; but I do not *like* history. Metaphysics and poetry and "facts of mind", that is, accounts of all the strange phantoms that ever possessed "your philosophy"; dreamers, from Thoth the Egyptian to Taylor the English pagan, are my darling studies.' From childhood, when his father first showed him the starry sky, his mind had been 'habituated *to the vast*'. His favourite reading as a child was *The Arabian Nights*, for its marvels. A fine classical scholar, he read the Greek philosophers in the original.

In its immense scope, Coleridge's mind embraced all that European civilization had to offer. He corresponded with Humphry Davy on scientific subjects. At the same time he was one of the first to attempt that kind of introspective observation which has since laid the foundation of modern psychology. He held a very low opinion of Locke and the materialists; his own thought was given its unity and coherence by his unwavering view of man as a spiritual being. For Coleridge, both as Christian and Platonist and as transcendentalist, mind is primary. As against Locke's view that nothing is in the mind that was not first in the senses, he considered Imagination to be 'the living Power and prime Agent of all human Perception, and as a repetition in the finite mind of the eternal act of creation in the infinite I AM. The secondary Imagination I consider as an echo of the former, co-existing with the conscious will, yet still as identical with the primary in the *kind* of its agency, and differing only in *degree*, and in the *mode* of its operation. It dissolves, diffuses, dissipates, in order to re-create; or where this process is rendered impossible, yet still at all

events it struggles to idealize and to unify. It is essentially *vital*, even as objects (*as objects*) are essentially fixed and dead.' This view of imagination differs in its dynamic character from Plato's more static presentation of the world of ideas.

Pleasure-Dome in Xanadu

It is well known that Coleridge wrote the poem *Kubla Khan* from the vivid recollection of an opium-dream. He was perhaps the first poet to draw upon the unconscious images of dream, uncensored by rational understanding and without reference to any theological or mythological system. 'Dreams with me are no Shadows, but the very Existences and foot-thick Calamities of my Life.' His immense learning, his knowledge of traditional mythology and its symbolism, is interwoven with archetypal dream-figures luminous with the aura of mystery which belongs to our dreams.

Coleridge insisted upon the distinction between Reason and Understanding; the former being an immediate perception, the latter the discursive faculty of the mind. 'Understanding is the Faculty of *Reflection*. Reason of Contemplation. Reason indeed is much nearer to SENSE than to Understanding; for Reason . . . is a direct aspect of Truth, an inward Beholding, having a similar relation to the Intelligible or Spiritual as SENSE has to the Material or Phenomenal.' He writes elsewhere, 'For to us, self-consciousness is not a kind of *being*, but a kind of *knowing*, and that too the highest that exists in us.' In the *sum*,

or I AM, 'object and subject, being and knowing are identical, each involving and supposing the other.'

Coleridge never completed the great work for which he felt, to the end of his life, that all his writings and studies had been only a preparation. His thought is to be discovered throughout his letters, note-books, lecture-notes and table-talk recorded by his friends and the hearers of his inimitable extempore lectures on literature; and in the political and literary journalism to which he devoted so much time and energy; to the detriment, it may be, of his incomparable poetic genius. It is impossible to dip into Coleridge anywhere without discovering some rich treasure; and yet the whole is greater than the parts, for perhaps no other man has ever left such a record of all that passed through his mind and senses.

His profound intellect notwithstanding, Coleridge was a man of deep feeling, capable of great love and great suffering. If knowledge be a fourfold experience, as Jung has explained, embracing intellection, feeling, sensation and intuition, Coleridge was, in this respect also, a complete man to a degree seldom achieved. 'My opinion is this,' he wrote, 'that deep thinking is attainable only by a man of deep feeling, and that all truth is a species of revelation. The more I understand Sir Isaac Newton's works, the more boldly I dare utter to my own mind . . . that I believe the souls of five hundred Sir Isaac Newtons would go to the making up of a Shakespeare or a Milton.'

KATHLEEN RAINE

Daily Telegraph Colour Library

Druids at the investiture of the Prince of Wales in 1969, wearing robes of colours which indicate their rank: white for the chief Druids, green for the bards, and blue for recent initiates

COLOURS

THE RUSSIAN PAINTER Vasily Kandinsky, one of the founders of the modern movement in art, believed that colours have 'a corresponding spiritual vibration' and that 'colour harmony must rest only on a corresponding vibration in the human soul'. The experiments conducted by B. J. Kouwer and reported in his book *Colours and Their Character* (1949) suggest that people react to colours in ways which match their traditional significance, whether because each colour has some innate quality of its own or because of the association of similar ideas with them for centuries.

The traditions are embedded deep in myth. The Aztecs spoke of four main colours — red, yellow, white and black — which were the four main types of corn, the four cardinal directions, and the gods associated with them. The Pueblo Indians, Cherokee and other American tribes also assign special colours and myth qualities to the four directions.

A colour's meaning may vary considerably in different parts of the world. Black is generally the colour of mourning in Europe but in China mourners wear white. Even in Europe, the ideas associated with a colour vary. Black is the hue of death but the typical flower of death is the white lily, and white birds are usually considered ominous, because of their rarity. But broadly speaking, there is a rough general agreement in the European tradition on the significance of the principal colours.

Black is naturally linked with night and darkness, and by extension with death, the night that ends a man's days, with mourning and sorrow, and with evil, the Devil and the 'powers of darkness'. Black magic is evil magic, a black day is one of disaster, a black sheep is the one that goes astray, the black flag marks the pirate, the lawless rebel, and the arch-rebel himself, the Devil, frequently appeared to witches as a black animal, or as a 'black' (dark-complexioned) man, often in black clothes.

Black is also the colour of the earth, in which the dead lie buried. In Greece and Rome black animals were connected with the earth goddess, the powers below and the ghosts of the dead in the underworld.

Standing for both death and earth, in alchemy black means death and putrefaction but also germination, new life burgeoning in the depths. Renewed life comes to the surface in the 'white' stage of the alchemical work (see ALCHEMY).

The contrast of black and white is fundamental to European colour symbolism. In churches the black trappings of Good Friday are replaced on Easter Sunday by white for Christ's resurrection. Black and white knights do battle in legends and also on chessboards. Where the Devil and his legions are black, the angels and the righteous wear white in heaven.

White means cleanliness, and therefore purity and innocence. A bride wears white for purity. White magic is good magic. The sacred horses of the Greek, Roman, Celtic and Germanic peoples were white. White is the moonlight that shines in the blackness of night, and so it may stand for inspiration and insight, light in the darkness of the mind. Black is ruthless, as in the black shirts of Fascists, white is meek, or sometimes even cowardly, the white feather and the white flag.

Red For Danger

Red is pre-eminently the colour of blood, and the words for 'red' in English, French, German and Latin all stem from a root which probably meant 'blood'. As a result red means physical life and energy, and in prehistoric burials the body was often sprinkled with red ochre, apparently to give the corpse life in the underworld. In American superstition, red occurs in many folk cures: a red silk handkerchief for neuralgia, red yarn around the thumb to stop a nosebleed. But red also means bloodshed, and is the colour of the planet and war god Mars. When a victorious general rode in triumph through the streets of Rome, his

Above Buddhist monks at a theological college in Bangkok. In the East saffron robes, varying in shade from yellow to orange or red, are a symbol of spiritual greatness *Below* Spanish Cardinals wearing red vestments, in the Christian Church a symbol of divine love

Colours

face was painted red. In Irish legend, the fiercest of all warriors were the Red Branch, the guards of Conchobar mac Nessa, King of Ulster in the 1st century AD. In a wider sense, red means violence in general, danger (as in traffic lights) and all fierce and passionate emotions, including revolutionary enthusiasm and lust, the red flag of Communism and the red light that marks the brothel. Kouwer found that the ideas people principally associate with red are passion, emotion, temperament, action, mutinousness, force, sexuality.

Green is the colour of vegetation, and our words 'green', 'grass' and 'grow' all come from the same root. Green is the peaceful bounty of Nature and most people find it a soothing and restful colour. Its connection with fertility appears in The Green George of Slav countries, a young man covered from head to foot in branches and flowers, the centre of a joyful procession in April, or the Jack o' the Green in England, wearing green boughs and ivy on May Day.

The symbolism of blue is less clear. It is the colour of the unclouded sky, and so the blue in the United States flag means vigilance (the white is for purity and the red for courage). It is linked with supreme gods, ruling from the sky, and perhaps as a result with aristocracy and conservatism, blue blood and true-blue: though in France and Russia white has been the symbol of the old order. The Virgin Mary's robe is usually blue, perhaps because of her role as the queen of heaven. On the other hand, blue is sometimes connected with the sea and water, with tears and sadness, 'the blues', and with the murky depths of pornography, as in blue films.

Yellow is also ambivalent. As the colour of the sun and gold, it means perfection, wealth, glory, power. But in early times saffron-yellow vestments were worn in churches on Good Friday, as a reminder of the Jews' vindictiveness in crucifying Christ, and Judas was given reddish-yellow hair in medieval paintings, because yellow meant jealousy and hate.

(See also CORRESPONDENCES; GREEN; RED; WHITE.)

A colour's meaning varies considerably in different parts of the world. In the West the colour of death and mourning is black *(above)* but in China mourners wear white *(below)*

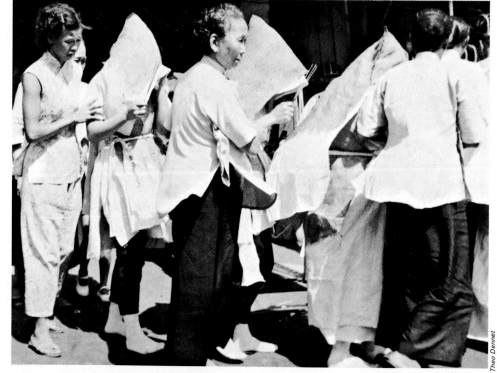

Comets

The appearance of a comet was long believed to mean that some cataclysmic disaster was likely to occur — war, famine, plague, the downfall of kings or even the end of the world: presumably because the comet's swift and unexpected passage through the sky was seen as a disruption of the orderly regularity of the heavens, heralding a parallel disruption on earth: a comet was seen before the Norman invasion of England in 1066, and comets accompanied both the birth and the death of Julius Caesar. See OMENS.

'They did not seek profits but they did what they had to do with pleasure and creativity.' Some religious Utopias in which all property is held in common have been extremely successful, not only financially but in giving their members a happy and constructive life: in some cases, even with what to most people would be an impossible ban on all sexual relations

COMMUNISTIC RELIGIOUS MOVEMENTS

HOLDING ALL PROPERTY IN COMMON has never been a widespread practice among religious movements. It is an interesting variant of the much more frequently found monastic arrangement, in which the monk abandons all his goods on entering the order. Orders of monks, nuns and friars, as they are found in Christianity and Buddhism, differ from communistic religious movements principally in being constituted of members of only one sex; in accepting a hierarchic system of authority; and in emphasizing personal poverty rather than communism of possessions. Most important of all, these orders are part of a wider religious organization and tradition. By contrast, communistic movements are total social systems, which usually do not admit those outside the commune to any place in their religious scheme of things.

Communistic movements are necessarily communitarian, that is, they establish communities, in which the principles of communism are applied. Without the total control of the activities of everyday life possible in a separate community, communistic principles would be difficult, if not impossible, to implement. The initial aim of many of these sects has been to create a community, rather than to establish communism, and the principle of common ownership has often been adopted only after the life of a separated community has been established.

Although many Christian communities have existed which have not been communistic, when sects set up separated communities, their basic principles of brotherhood, equality in the love of God, and the shared prospect of salvation, predispose them to communistic arrangements. When a group has drawn together as a fellowship, any disparities of wealth among them are irrelevant to their new hopes, a hindrance to their common purpose, and a symbol of the vain and corrupt values of the world.

So communism may be adopted as a matter of expediency, as an outgrowth of the movement's new circumstances once it has established a separated colony. In this case, the new system may be justified by inspiration or revelation, as among the Community of the Truly Inspired (the Amana Society), who adopted communism of goods after they had emigrated to America and whose new practice was made legitimate, after some members had challenged it, by revelation of the Holy Spirit to their leader.

Common beliefs and interests have led members of the Amish sect, an offshoot of the Mennonites, to set up segregated communities in the United States, where they pool their resources for the welfare of the group

In other cases, as among the Oneida Community, or the Tolstoyans, communism is prescribed as part of the way of life of the saints and is a basic principle, to be realized by the establishment of a colony. Sometimes there is explicit reference to the early Church at Jerusalem, as described in the Acts of the Apostles, which provides scriptural justification for communism.

Politics and Persecution

Religious communism differs from the communism of political Utopians, such as the followers of Robert Owen at New Harmony or the disciples of Fourier, who set up many colonies in the United States during the 19th century. Religious groups are not necessarily, and not usually, attempting to provide a model of social organization for other men to imitate — at least not until other men learn the spiritual truths which they know. In the event, political communities have always failed, usually very soon after being founded. Religious communistic colonies have had more varied fortunes and some have flourished for decades.

One of the necessary conditions for the establishment of sectarian communism is the possibility of finding a place in which the sect can be sufficiently isolated from the

Mary Evans Picture Library

Communistic sects have sought isolation from the rest of society to enable them to safeguard their beliefs *Left* In Paraguay Mennonite communities often recruit new members from the local Indians; communal baptism of Lengua Indians *Below* The Shakers, who got their name from the ecstatic trembling which took place at their religious meetings, fled to America in the 18th century to escape persecution; there they organized themselves into strictly disciplined celibate communities *Right* In the 16th century, Protestant revolutionaries known as Anabaptists established a 'kingdom of the saints' at Münster in Germany; they were accused of all manner of atrocities

rest of the world. This is essential, to prevent the contamination of the group by outside influences and to provide a stable context in which children can be brought up in the values of the sect. Since such groups come out of the wider society, the colony is both a place of refuge and a heavenly community.

It is not every society that allows men to congregate in this way. The Levellers and Diggers of 17th century England were seen as a threat to the social order, and when this is the response of the political authorities such groups are not permitted to establish themselves. Only where royal or aristocratic patronage was gained, as the Hutterian Brethren gained it successfully in Moravia, Hungary and Russia (see HUTTERIAN BRETHREN), were European sects able to practise communism, at least until late in the 18th century. More often, the sects fled from persecution, usually to North America where land was abundant and diligent settlers were welcomed.

The principal religious communistic sects have come from central Europe and have usually been German-speaking. Some semi-communistic sects have arisen in England but the groups like the Girlingites in the New Forest met with opposition.

An important factor aiding the success of communistic sects has been their isolation from the wider society, and one of the most important insulating mechanisms has been the use of a language differing from that of the surrounding people. The Mennonites in Brazil, who were not always communists though they always lived in segregated communities, were well aware of the importance of retaining their native German as a defence against assimilation to the society outside. In those communistic groups which have permitted sexual relations and have raised children, difference of language has been of great importance in preventing young people from learning too quickly about the attractions of the world outside.

Shaking with Joy

The Shakers are perhaps the most celebrated of all the communistic sects. This sect owes its origin to the preaching of refugee French Camisards (see CAMISARDS) in 18th century England. They converted some Quakers in Lancashire to belief in the imminent return of Christ, with the unusual feature that the returning Christ was expected to appear as a woman. The Shakers got their name from

the ecstatic shaking that occurred in their noisy religious meetings.

In 1770 a woman named Ann Lee became their leader, after she had experienced a vision in which she clearly saw that sexual intercourse was the source of all the evil in the world. Her preoccupation with this subject may no doubt be explained by the fact that she had had several stillborn children. She now saw that redemption was to be gained by renouncing sex and reproduction. Although scarcely literate and given to shaking and speaking in tongues, Ann Lee was undoubtedly an impressive leader of considerable intelligence. She declared that to escape persecution the sect should go to the New World, where they expected to make converts in what they thought of as the last days of the existing order of things. Eight Shakers made the journey to America in 1774.

In the following years Shakers came into being in various places, scattered over several states. Perhaps as a defensive measure, and as a way of establishing the appropriate control of the godly life, the leading Shakers, after Ann Lee's death in 1782, decided to organize themselves in segregated communities. From 1787 Shaker communities were set up. Within them were organized large groups known as 'families', each with its male and female head. Celibacy was the absolute rule and each man was provided with a 'sister' who undertook a variety of household tasks for him. Care was taken never to leave individuals of opposite sex alone with each other, and there is no record of scandal in any of the 18 Shaker communities that were eventually established.

To become a Shaker was no light undertaking. New members, on entering a community, gave up all their possessions for the good of the fellowship. Thereafter they received a share of what was termed 'just and equal rights and privileges, according to their needs.' Should anyone leave the community – and inevitably some did – he received an agreed sum on discharge.

Practicality was a much prized Shaker virtue, their organization was a model of efficiency, and although agricultural work was the basis of their economy they were from the outset interested in a wide range of craft and industrial activities. Since no wages were paid, and each received simply what he needed according to the modest assessments that their religious dispositions dictated, the Shakers could devote all their

energy and ingenuity to the work that they saw as the testimony to their faith. Among the many useful devices that they produced were a new type of circular saw, a much improved washing machine (this in the early 19th century), a tilting chair, and new designs in sewing machines and brooms.

Industry and inventiveness were principal outlets for Shaker enterprise, facilitated by the fact that they were a celibate community, in which no one had family problems or sexual distractions. Visitors were generally impressed by the spirit of harmony that prevailed among the Shakers. This harmony, and their successful economy, have been attributed to the simple principles of faith on which they based their way of life, and the intensity with which these were inculcated. Order, neatness, cleanliness, frugality and sobriety were the pervasive demands.

The discipline of the daily lives of the Shakers was informed by the joy that they expressed most fully in their worship, particularly in their ecstatic dancing, which in time was organized along a wide variety of set patterns. They believed in communications from spirits (though they found nothing in common with Spiritualism when that movement arose), in direct revelation from God, in faith healing and in speaking in tongues. They gave a good deal of time to religious exercises and, like other communistic sects, they did not have to give too much time to labour, because their needs were very limited.

Despite celibacy, the Shakers recruited sufficiently from the outside world to continue through the 19th century and into the 20th. They can rarely have numbered more than 3000 at any one time and there probably cannot have been more than about 16,500 of them altogether during the movement's entire life. By the mid-1960s only a few old ladies remained, still living together in the last surviving Shaker community. Shaking as such had ceased to be practised and so had the dancing, which had been so fully developed in the 19th century. (See also SHAKERS.)

Living in Harmony

A strong injunction to celibacy and community of goods were the distinguishing features of another sect that flourished in 19th century America, the Harmonists, or Rappites. This sect built successively, at ten-year intervals, three substantial villages in the states of Pennsylvania and Indiana. Initially the sect was composed of the personal following of its remarkable, autocratic and impressive leader George Rapp, a weaver, who in the 1780s began to conduct his own religious meetings in his native village in Württemberg, Germany, expressing severe disapproval of the outward show and ritual of the Lutheran Church. Württemberg was a strong centre of sectarianism at this time, and Rapp soon acquired a significant following from his own and neighbouring villages. His separatism and the emptying of the Lutheran churches caused the Lutheran authorities to seek the intervention of the state to discourage Rapp, and periodically he was called to account for his teachings and activities.

Of One Heart and Soul

Many religious communists have cited the book of Acts in the New Testament as their scriptural justification:

Now the company of those who believed were of one heart and soul, and no one said that any of the things which he possessed was his own, but they had everything in common. And with great power the apostles gave their testimony to the resurrection of the Lord Jesus, and great grace was upon them all. There was not a needy person among them, for as many as were possessors of lands or houses sold them, and brought the proceeds of what was sold and laid it at the apostles' feet; and distribution was made to each as any had need . . .

But a man named Ananias with his wife Sapphira sold a piece of property, and with his wife's knowledge he kept back some of the proceeds, and brought only a part and laid it at the apostles' feet. But Peter said, 'Ananias, why has Satan filled your heart to lie to the Holy Spirit and to keep back part of the proceeds of the land? While it remained unsold, did it not remain your own? And after it was sold, was it not at your disposal? How is it that you have contrived this deed in your heart? You have not lied to men but to God.' When Ananias heard these words, he fell down and died. And great fear came upon all who heard of it. The young men rose and wrapped him up and carried him out and buried him.

After an interval of about three hours his wife came in, not knowing what had happened. And Peter said to her, 'Tell me whether you sold the land for so much.' And she said, 'Yes, for so much.' But Peter said to her, 'How is it that you have agreed together to tempt the Spirit of the Lord? Hark, the feet of those that have buried your husband are at the door, and they will carry you out.' Immediately she fell down at his feet and died. When the young men came in they found her dead, and they carried her out and buried her beside her husband. And great fear came upon the whole church, and upon all who heard of these things.

Acts, chapters 4 and 5

In the earliest known formulations of Rapp's beliefs there was no explicit demand for celibacy among his followers, although he himself — in spite of being married — was known to be leading a celibate life. Nor, in the first two decades of his movement, was there any direct assertion that there should be community of goods among the faithful. Perhaps, however, in those circumstances, such a demand would have been scarcely practicable for the farmers and artisans who were among his following. They believed that withdrawal from the world was necessary, in preparation for Christ's reappearance, which they believed to be imminent — as indeed did many quite orthodox Protestants in Europe and America at the time of the Napoleonic wars.

It was after the keenest members of the sect had emigrated to America, in 1804, that communism proper was adopted by them. Migration itself tested the faith of the Rappites, since they all gave what they had to support the costs of the journey for themselves and others, and for their initial expenses in America. The Harmony Society, as the sect called itself, bought land and, after considerable hardship in the early days built a model village on the Connoquenessing Creek, near Pittsburg in Pennsylvania. The community regarded itself as a Church, in which all members surrendered their property to the society and pledged themselves to its laws. In return, they were ensured all the necessities of life, education and religious instruction, and insurance for their dependants.

The Harmonists soon achieved a reputation for industry and good husbandry, despite financial difficulties, dissensions, disappointments about the land they had purchased, and, above all, despite their intense expectation of the early second coming of Christ. Celibacy was instituted in the very early days, but some marriages took place. Rapp held that the imitation of Christ, which was the aim of the community, was incomplete without celibacy. He permitted marriages only for those who were insufficiently spiritually advanced to accept the full rigours of the wholly dedicated life, although he did so less readily and with more impatience over the years. Since the Harmonists, like the Shakers, were sure that they lived in the last days their failure to reproduce did not trouble them.

Visitors from outside were eager to see the way of life of the Harmonists and were impressed by their simple dedication, their complete security, their indifference to profits and to entertainments, and their certainty about their heavenly reward. Yet within ten years of first settling in Pennsylvania, the Harmonists, disturbed by the close encroachments of the world around their land, seeking water power and a milder climate better suited to the vine, and despite all the labour involved in beginning again the work of creating a settlement, put up the town of Harmony for sale, and moved to the banks of the River Wabash in Indiana Territory.

Wonder of the West

In the new location, the Harmonists were less surrounded by German-speaking immigrants, but they were more immediately involved in political affairs, being a sizeable community with opportunity to influence political decisions in their county. As a frontier society, their achievement in Indiana was all the more remarkable, and New Harmony was regarded as 'a wonder of the West'. Robert Owen, the English socialist manufacturer heard of it: he visited the community, and eventually bought the settlement, when the Harmonists again moved on. But Robert Owen's secular communists, who permitted freedom of religious belief, preached emancipation of women, and who lacked the community discipline that characterized the religious society of George Rapp, failed within a year or two to make the ready-made colony function. The Harmonists, meanwhile, set up a third prosperous colony, named Economy, on the Ohio River in Pennsylvania. Again, they established a town that was a model of neatness and order.

Celibacy was, however, a severe test. The community ceased to recruit by new immigration from Württemberg, and indeed came increasingly to regard itself as the completely gathered remnant of the faithful, enjoying wisdom quite different from that available to men in the world whom it now had no interest in recruiting. As a result the average age of its members rose and its numbers began to decline. A schism occurred in 1831, when an impressive imposter arrived at Economy, presenting himself as His Royal Highness Maximilian of Este,

Ambassador of Christ. The Harmonists were undergoing an internal crisis at the time and were anxious for the coming of Christ. Expectant and gullible as they were, a number seceded with Count Leon, as he was also known, and continued to practise communism in other parts of America; this reduced the community even further.

Throughout the 1830s and 40s the Society continued to prosper but, having completely closed its ranks, ensured its own decline. Its reserves of wealth were considerable, and became the subject of prolonged litigation in the 20th century. That they had accumulated so impressively, was largely due to the competence of Frederick Rapp, adopted son of George, who died in 1834, and to the spiritual control of George Rapp himself, who died at the age of 90 in 1847. In its day, the Harmony Society had been a pioneer of the oil industry and had built the first oil pipelines.

The Truly Inspired Ones

The productivity, inventiveness and social usefulness of the communistic religious societies is again illustrated in the history of the Amana Society, the Society of the Truly Inspired, which eventually settled in Iowa. The Amana Society which numbered some 1500 people at the height of its success also came from south Germany. It had originally arisen early in the 18th century, at the instigation of two inspired preachers, Rock and Gruber, who had travelled to various places at the bidding of the Spirit, preaching the word. The sect which they founded was pacifist and committed to the view that God still inspired men through the Holy Spirit, whose instruments some men were called to be.

After Rock's death, no new 'instrument' appeared for some time, but a number of prophets arose in the sect at the beginning of the 19th century in various parts of Germany. In 1842, under the leadership of Christian Metz, it was revealed that they should emigrate to America. Initially, the sect settled near the city of Buffalo and called their community Ebenezer. They were not, at this stage, communists: their intention had been to find a place where they could live the life of faith in peace.

Trouble with the Seneca Indians and fear of encroachments on their withdrawn way of life from the growing city of Buffalo, induced them in the late 1850s to sell their land and move to Iowa, where they settled in seven villages. They took the name Amana from the Song of Solomon (chapter 4, verse 8). Force of circumstances caused them to become communists, and this was an understandable development for a group that had already committed itself to a common destiny in this world and the next. Their adoption of the communistic principle was conveniently reinforced and made legitimate by the inspiration of the Holy Spirit, speaking through Metz, the leader of the community. The regulations concerning the entitlements of individuals and the responsibility of the community were similar to those of the Harmonists. They ate as a community, in common dining halls, the two sexes being separated.

Low Status of Marriage

The Amana Society did not impose celibacy. It was approved, but was not so strongly enjoined as among the Harmonists and the Shakers. Even as children, the sexes were kept apart, and marriage was permitted only when a man reached the age of 24: ideally, however, the faithful should not marry. This had been an early injunction, long before the sect became communistic but, of course, the virtual elimination of the family unit predisposes a sect to communism of goods and mutual help.

The sect had three orders of piety, and those who married revealed by so doing that they were of the lowest order. Only by leading a conscientious life could a couple who married rise again in spiritual status. Families did, however, dwell in individual homes in Amana, which suggests that marriage continued to be a common, if disapproved arrangement. In contrast with the Shakers, whose way of life allowed for considerable elements of recreation, the Amana Society frowned on entertainments and all levity.

The Amana Society was governed by trustees under the inspired instruments of the Holy Spirit. After Metz died, Barbara Landmann was the leader of the community, but she was the last of the 'instruments' and long before the end of the 19th century the Society ceased to have a spiritual head with inspired power. The villages were organized by elders, who were not necessarily old, but who were recognized as spiritually advanced. They were in charge of industrial and agricultural activities. In their dealings with the outside world, the Amana Society gained a reputation for honesty and shrewdness, neither cheating others nor letting themselves be cheated.

The religious beliefs of the sect were simple. They accepted the Bible in a literal

Above The pacifist Russian Doukhobors, who emigrated to Canada at the beginning of the century, practised communism for a time; they caused embarrassment by parading in the nude as a protest against government interference *Below* Drop-Out City in America is a haven of refuge for hippies, and others who feel themselves at odds with the highly organized world around them; they share their goods in common and practise free love

Keystone Press Agency

Eve Arnold – Magnum

way, believed in the Trinity and in the resurrection of the dead, but not in eternal punishment, since hell would purify even the most wicked in time. They sought to avoid the world in every way, and to lead retired, withdrawn lives in humility and simplicity, eschewing anger, impatience, criticism, levity and idleness. They were exhorted neither to desire nor to grieve. The men were to 'fly from the society of womenkind'.

Without an inspired leader, the Amana Society continued, although in decline, until in 1932 they decided to abandon their communistic organization. They reconstituted themselves, abandoning the old restrictions on dress and in other matters. In time their settlements became tourist attractions.

Promiscuous but Perfect

Perhaps the most thorough-going of all communistic religious societies was that founded by John Humphrey Noyes, which was eventually established at Oneida, in the state of New York. Its thoroughness consisted in its adoption not of celibacy, or preferred celibacy, but of communism of sexual relations.

The Oneida Community were known as Perfectionists, because they taught the possibility of perfection in this world. This was an extreme version of the Holiness teachings that had developed among some Methodists, Presbyterians and Congregationalists in the eastern United States in the second quarter of the 19th century. The principal idea of Holiness teachings was that men might, after their conversion, experience a second blessing of sanctification; the more extreme advocates held that sanctification might be instantaneous. Although the majority of Holiness believers took the doctrine to mean that the converted person who was 'born again' should lead an exemplary life, others believed that, being sanctified, they could no longer sin, no matter what they did. In consequence, promiscuity occurred among some as a 'proof' of perfection, and theories of 'spiritual wivery' opened the way to considerable sexual licence (see SPIRITUAL WIVES). The Oneida Community were frequently condemned on this score and their intentions misunderstood.

After a false start in 1846 at Putney, Vermont, where local hostility drove them out, the Perfectionists who had gathered around Noyes set up a community at Oneida. The farmers who joined Noyes sold their property and settled for life in common. They engaged in agriculture, trapping, silk-manufacture, satchel-making and the production of a variety of other consumer-goods. They justified their experiment by a distinctive theology. Noyes believed that the second coming of Christ, which so many Americans were then awaiting, had in fact occurred in 70 AD. Catholics had perverted the consequence of the advent, but now his own community were to restore the perfection of the 1st century Christians.

The early Church at Jerusalem, with its communistic organization, was the obvious model. To avoid the sexual excesses current among Holiness extremists, many of whom he knew, Noyes taught that it was evident that when God's will was done on earth there would be no more marriage, just as there was none in heaven. But abolition was possible only when men were perfected. Thereafter, two individuals would not be bound, either in marriage or outside it. Possessiveness and its accompanying selfishness would be put aside. At Oneida, a man was not permitted to claim a woman as his wife, and neither could a woman claim a child as 'hers'. Sexual relations were a matter for the community, not just for the individuals involved. Cohabitation had to be planned. Noyes enjoined a high degree of continence, in favour of intelligent, well-ordered procreation. Children were detached from their mothers as soon as possible, and put under the care of others.

Defeat by Public Opinion

Noyes was both the theological architect and the administrator of Oneida. In some ways he was undoubtedly a genius, as the remarkable success of his experiment in religious communism indicates. The community was seen as the social state of heaven governed by God – a community in which personal sanctification preceded social reconstruction. While the Bible was the foundation of their faith, they were, as a sanctified community, people who had passed beyond the literal interpretation of the scriptures. What they sought was absolute love among men: they were still growing in spiritual grace, even though they regarded themselves as already sinless.

One of the ways in which this grace was developed was through the practice of mutual criticism within the community. The community assembled to hear the self-criticism of one of its members, and then to engage in comments on his shortcomings; finally Noyes himself would offer an exhortation to the member concerned, usually with some words of commendation included. Such a process may have done much to sustain allegiance to the community. Members, as William James put it, 'externalized their rottenness', and publicly re-dedicated themselves to the life of the community.

Oneida flourished, and was still flourishing, when in the 1870s the propagation of its views led to considerable misrepresentation and brought public pressure to bear against it. Eventually, in 1879, the community was constrained to abandon its way of life in deference to public opinion, and its substantial property was converted into a joint stock company for the 280 members. The industrial activities were continued.

A number of other communistic religious sects have flourished, some of them, such as the Russian Doukhobors, who settled in Canada at the turn of this century, espoused communism in part and for a period, but without particular success. An outstanding case from Africa is the Aiyetoro Community in Nigeria. This sect was constituted by seceders from the revivalist movement known as Cherubim and Seraphim. They established themselves on the coast, and organized a communist system of production. Within a few years, their fishing enterprise had produced considerable profit, and the plain uniforms of the early days were abandoned for dress of individual choice. The community is essentially religious, and although it has a living standard far higher than the Nigerian average, it has maintained its collective services and its community structure.

BRYAN WILSON

FURTHER READING: E. D. Andrews, *The People Called Shakers* (Peter Smith); K. J. R. Arndt, *George Rapp's Harmony Society, 1785–1847* (University of Pennsylvania Press, 1965); Mark Holloway, *Heavens on Earth* (Smithers, 1951); C. Nordhoff, *The Communistic Societies of the United States* (Peter Smith).

Comparative Religion

The systematic study of religions, concerned to analyse, compare and classify them, and to trace their history and their relationships to the societies in which they exist, rather than to evaluate the truth of their beliefs.
See RELIGION.

Confucius

Kung Fu-tze (550 – 480 BC), Chinese sage: much of the traditional Chinese view of the universe, the gods and human morality and conduct was based on his teaching: Confucius himself had a cult in temples found in all administrative centres: the *Analects* of Confucius is a collection of his sayings.
See CHINA.

Mary Evans Picture Library

CONGO

Macabre stories of idol-worship, witchcraft, human sacrifice and ritual cannibalism which have at one time or another been told about the tribes of the Congo, reflect their deep abiding fear of the supernatural

ITS RELIGION, MYTH AND MAGIC make the Congo the most striking region of Africa, for here black men lived for thousands of years completely out of touch with outside civilizations. The Congo has always been the heart of Africa both geographically and, to some extent, culturally. Most of the aboriginal population of 15 million people are pure Negroes, racially different from the Semites of North Africa and the Bushmen and Hottentots of South Africa.

It was not until the 15th century that Portuguese explorers, looking for a new route to India, landed on the west coast and penetrated into the interior of Equatorial Africa. They found a country of immense rivers and impenetrable forests, peopled by black men who lived in a state of semi-barbarism. Portuguese missionaries made strenuous efforts to Christianize these pagans, and we read of 1500 of them being baptized with a hose by a Jesuit priest on his rounds of the villages. The conversion of the Congolese, however, was short-lived; it is estimated that there was not a single Christian in Central Africa by the end of the 18th century.

When the European merchants and missionaries returned to the Congo a century later, they found the natives living very much as they had done when the Portuguese first saw them 400 years before. They lived by hunting and primitive agriculture and, as far as their religious life was concerned, were accounted 'heathen who bowed down to wood and stone'.

In fact, some observers maintained that these Negroes had no concept of God whatsoever and only worshipped idols called ju-jus and fetishes. They were said to be under the domination of witch-doctors, depicted as masked wizards who performed unmentionable rites, including the sacrifice

Witch-doctor in the Congo with wooden arrows thrust through his cheeks: feats of this kind contribute to the awe in which he is held

Federico and Aldo Patellani

503

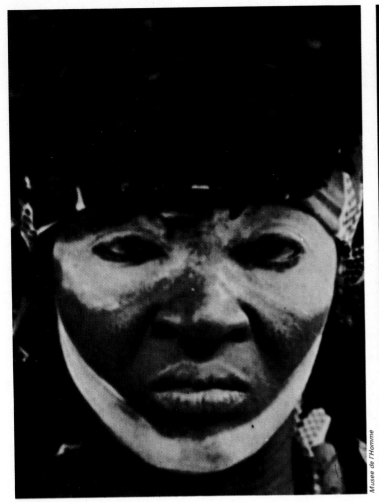

Musee de l'Homme

God is depicted as something of a tyrant who drove both men and animals from a pleasant land to a harsh life here below

of living infants. In addition, the Congolese were described as having such a low view of the value of human life that they strangled several of a dead chief's wives and buried them with their feet pointing towards their deceased husband. Cannibalism, too, was rife among certain tribes. Idols, witchcraft, human sacrifice and ritual cannibalism — these were thought to be the sum of Congolese religious beliefs and practices.

It is now known that this picture is only half-true, and is partly due to the difficulties encountered by white men in trying to discover the truth about African myths and magic. It is inevitable that a subject people should be wary of revealing their secrets to their alien masters. This is especially the case where ritual murder,

With so many ghosts and spirits to contend with it is natural that the pagan Negro should turn for help to experts in the supernatural. Two witch-doctors from Stanleyville; Congolese witch-doctors, called *Mganga* or *Mfumu* are a combination of soothsayer, herbalist philosopher and psychiatrist

trial by ordeal and similar savage practices are involved, since the European authorities immediately made such customs illegal. Whether the colonial governments were ever able to eradicate such ancient tribal rites in remote areas of the Congo is doubtful.

It is, however, generally agreed that the Congolese have some idea of what civilized people call God, though the principal difference is that whereas Christians,

Jews and Moslems believe in a *personal* deity, the African regards God as a vague figure with no particular interest in him as an individual. Yet most natives would readily admit that there must have been a Creator, or Lord of the Universe, a sort of super-king who rules the whole world. They have various proper names for this mysterious and remote deity — Maweja, Mulopo, Nzambi, Kalunga, Akongo and so forth; and various honorific titles such as 'Elephant in Strength', 'Tortoise in Patience' and even 'Tomato in Sweetness'.

More specific is a god-chief called Lyangombe, a combination of a folk-hero and a supernatural being of great power. In general, Lyangombe is a beneficent god who is prepared to help his devotees,

Federico and Aldo Patellani

provided he is well treated. As he can protect his worshippers against sickness and calamities, he has a special cult and priests. Lyangombe enters into his chosen people and controls their actions, even deigning to allow his women followers to bear his children. In consequence, missionaries have found him an obstacle to Christian teaching, for his cult is said to lead to considerable licence and promiscuity.

But whatever the Congolese call God, their attitude towards him is inclined to be unceremonious for they neither love nor fear him as Christians are supposed to love and fear their God. This indifference is reflected in the lack of any kind of temple or even of a representation of the Almighty. Congolese folktales which embody a great

Armed with weapons and dressed to kill, the Watusi of the former Ruanda province dance themselves to a frenzied pitch of excitement before going to war

deal of their religious and social history emphasize the distant, almost hostile attitude towards the Supreme Creator.

At the same time, there is a close, almost personal relationship between men and animals. The legend of why the dog has no hands, for instance, is typical of the animal myths. God denied the dog hands, but told him he could always live close to man, who would be his hands. Thus the dog is the servant of man, and vice-versa. God, however, is depicted as something of a tyrant who drove both men and animals

from a pleasant land to a harsh life here below. No particular reason is given for man's expulsion from paradise, except that God was angry over some small misdemeanour. Alternatively, woman is blamed as the prime cause of men's troubles, as in Hebrew and Greek myths (see WOMAN).

The Drumming of the Dead

Despite the impersonal attitude towards the deity, the Congolese are conscious of the supernatural at every turn: 'every breath that the native draws is tempered and controlled by his awareness of the supernatural.' This means that the black man in the forests of Central Africa believes the world around him to be peopled with a multitude of spirits and ghosts, some

The Burning of Shakespeare

The famous explorer H. M. Stanley set out to cross the largely unknown territory of Central Africa in 1874. During this expedition, while encamped on the banks of the River Congo, his party was surrounded by hostile native warriors

'What is the matter, my friends?' I asked, 'Why do you come with guns in your hands in such numbers, as though you were coming to fight? Fight! Fight us, your friends! Tut! this is some great mistake, surely.'

'Mundele,' replied one of them . . . 'our people saw you yesterday make marks on some tara-tara' (paper). 'This is very bad. Our country will waste, our goats will die, our bananas will rot, and our women will dry up. What have we done to you that you should wish to kill us? We have sold you food, and we have brought you wine, each day. Your people are allowed to wander where they please, without trouble. Why is the Mundele so wicked? We have gathered together to fight you if you do not burn that tara-tara now before our eyes. If you burn it we go away, and shall be friends as heretofore . . .'

My note-book contained a vast number of valuable notes, plans of falls, creeks, villages, sketches of localities, ethnological and philological details, sufficient to fill two octavo volumes – everything was of general interest to the public. I could not sacrifice it to the childish caprice of savages. As I was rummaging my book box, I came across a volume of Shakespeare (Chandos edition), much worn and well thumbed, and which was of the same size as my field-book; its cover was similar also, and it might be passed for the note-book provided that no one remembered its appearance too well. I took it to them.

'Is this the tara-tara, friends, that you wish burnt?'

'Yes, yes, that is it!' . . .

We walked to the nearest fire. I breathed a regretful farewell to my genial companion, which during many weary hours of night had assisted to relieve my mind when oppressed by almost intolerable woes, and then gravely assigned the innocent Shakespeare to the flames, heaping the brush-fuel over it with ceremonious care.

H. M. Stanley *Through the Dark Continent*

---

benevolent, but many more malevolent. Further, he is concerned more with the spirits than he is with gods, because the former affect his life more obviously and are much closer to his own material world. Thus, even the members of his family, once they are dead, are still not far away; they retain the power to harm as well as to help him.

The African spends a great deal of time and energy in placating these *mizumu*, or spirits of the departed. In a sense, he believes in an afterlife much more fervently than many Christians, since no one 'dies' in the course of Nature. He is spirited away. And when the departed leaves his village, he continues to exist very much as he did on earth, needing to be fed, talked to, and even housed. Of course, life is more pleasant in this afterworld, because there is more time to drink beer and to dance.

Proof of the existence of the mizumu is easy enough to obtain, say the Congolese. Put your ear to the ground and you will hear their drums. And since they obviously exist, they must be treated with respect. It may even be necessary to offer them a human sacrifice in order to placate them; otherwise they will harm the living. One can see their handiwork all around – in the suicide of this person, or the death in childbirth of another.

This obsession with the ghosts of the dead should not be compared with ancestor worship. The Congolese do not properly worship anybody or anything. Their religion is based on a fear of the unknown. Their chants, dances, drum-beating, sacrifices, food offerings, and the wearing of all manner of ju-jus are nearly always intended to ward off evil. When the Congolese address their ancestors, they assume a tone half-wheedling, half-hectoring. A typical 'prayer' would go, 'O Father! O Mother! Can you hear me, old ones? Why don't you come and drink this good beer? And isn't it time you brought us good hunting?'

Casting the Bones

With so many ghosts and spirits to contend with it is natural that the pagan Negro should turn for help to experts in the supernatural. For the black man believes just as firmly in magic as we believe in science, his whole attitude to life is based on the mystery of Nature, as ours is based on a rational explanation. Two men are swimming a river. One man is devoured by a crocodile, another escapes. Why, the Congolese ask, is one spared, the other taken? The answer is that malevolent spirits are responsible, where we attribute it to chance.

The experts in magic and the supernatural are the witch-doctors whose religious and social functions have been greatly misunderstood by Western observers. The genuine witch-doctor called *Mganga* or *Mufumu* in the Congo – is a combination of soothsayer, herbalist, philosopher, and psychologist. He undertakes to predict the future, cure the sick, administer the tribal laws, and cast out evil spirits. He must not be confused with the sorcerers, or *Mlozi*, who work in the dark against their fellow-men and are hated by all.

One of his primary functions, as tribal medicine-man, is to treat the sick. Like all African pagans, he starts with the premise that sickness is caused by magic – in some cases by a sorcerer who has to be rooted out; in others by a malign spirit in the form of some animal hostile to man, such as a snake or a lion. The witch-doctor's job is to compound an even stronger 'medicine' than the magic spell under which his patient is suffering. Perhaps he will try to transfer the disease to the sick man's enemy. Or he will impregnate his potions and salves with secret incantations. To this extent, the witch-doctor relies more on psychology than physiology, and most of his cures would fall in the category of faith healing.

Another important function of the witch-doctor is to predict the future, and no Congolese would undertake an enterprise of any significance without first consulting him in his role of soothsayer. Divination is usually effected with the aid of 'the bones' – traditionally the leg bones of goats, highly polished and shaped to resemble the heads of various animals. The witch-doctor, after falling into a self-induced trance, casts his bones. There are reports from reliable witnesses that certain of these objects actually stand up and remain standing on end, while others lie flat on the ground. The soothsayer interprets them accordingly. If the bones signifying a crocodile or lion stand erect, he predicts danger, while if those representing a friendly animal remain standing, he forecasts a successful journey.

The witch-doctor is also responsible for the general welfare of the community and is called upon in times of drought to make rain. For this ceremony he organizes an impressive spectacle, decking himself out in a mask, feathers and animal skins, and leading a ritual dance to the accompaniment of drums. If he is a good weather forecaster, he will time the ceremony to coincide with the gathering of the storm-clouds; and if he fails to make rain, he can always fall back on the excuse that some evil spirit or some undiscovered wizard is opposing him. It follows, then, that his most important function is to 'smell out' sorcerers.

He has numerous ways of achieving this object, the most common being 'trial by ordeal'. The method most used is the poison test, based on the belief that the innocent will not be affected by the medicine while the guilty will succumb to it. Accordingly, all those members of the community who are under suspicion will be required to drink a poisoned brew. The witch-doctor will then interpret their degree of guilt from their reaction. Some Western observers maintain that the potion the witch-doctor administers is not poisoned at all, but the guilty assume that it is and thus reveal their guilt. In any case, the idea is not to kill the witch outright, since first a confession must be extorted, by torture if necessary.

The Secret Societies

And so it is that despite the complete irrationality of these Central African methods of 'smelling out' witches and despite the cruelty of the punishments – poisoning, drowning, feeding the victims to crocodiles, and even burning alive – the natives of the vast forests of the Congo accept without

Previous page **During the painful initiation ceremony performed by the Mongongi secret society, members emerge from the forest in line, forming a giant snake, and encircle the new initiates, who are tested by being beaten and trampled underfoot**
Above **The ceremonial dress of the natives of the Kasai region, once worn by their ancestors for rites of human sacrifice and cannibalism, is now used during circumcision rituals**
Below **Among the Bapende the annual dance, known as *Nioka*, in which the men are painted to look like snakes, harks back to an old myth which tells how woman tempted man in the form of a serpent, and man turned into a serpent to possess her**

Federico and Aldo Patellani

question the necessity of eliminating sorcerers by any means. They are absolutely convinced that at night, crouched in their hovels, wizards make wax images of their enemies and slowly destroy them by tearing off their limbs one by one. In order to identify himself with the powers of evil, the sorcerer sacrifices infants and drinks their blood. Among his paraphernalia will be found human teeth, bones, cocks' feathers, and magic pebbles. And, to distinguish him even further, the sorcerer is said to have a special sullen appearance and to be noticeably antisocial in his behaviour. Hence, anthropologists trace the origin of the pagan Negro's obsession with sorcery to the primitive fear of the 'outsider', of the member of the tribe who in some way or other does not

The wise and serene chief of a tribe may, after his death, attain the status of a god-chief, with the power to help and protect his people

conform to the conventions of the group.

This obsession with witches and sorcerers often leads to the formation of secret societies whose professed aim is the smelling out of the Mlozi, but who, in the natural course of events, turn into gangs who terrorize the weak and innocent. Members of these societies, like the Bamucapi and the Atinga, who have been known to operate in the Congo, disguise themselves in animal masks and skins and travel from village to village intimidating and robbing the inhabitants. Such organizations were never wholly controlled by the white colonists. With the

departure of the Europeans, it is probable that they have strengthened their hold on a helpless and superstitious population.

The general impression the European is bound to get from a study of the Congo is that the natives are self-condemned to a life of considerable wretchedness, caused on the one hand by their obsessive fear of the unknown and on the other by the severity of their tribal law. These factors account for their outbursts of violence as well as their indifference to cruelty, their love of dancing, feasting, and drinking, as well as their acceptance of drudgery and boredom.

JAMES WELLARD

FURTHER READING: E. G. Parrinder, *African Traditional Religion* (S. P. C. K., 1962).

CONJURE MAGIC

ONE NAME for the magical beliefs and practice among Negroes in America's Old South; also called 'hoodoo' or 'voodoo' though only vaguely resembling the complex Voodoo religion. Elements of religious worship were perhaps more evident in some areas, as in New Orleans in the last century, but now the idea of 'conjure' means simply magic-working. In this it seems to have retained much of the African way of magic.

Practitioners – called many names, including 'hoodoo doctors' – were employed to cast spells on clients' enemies, or to take off spells cast on clients. Thousands of charms designed to kill or afflict illness have been recorded, using ingredients like graveyard dirt, bat's blood, chicken bones and feathers, salt and ashes, usually tied up in red flannel. Every conjure man had his own recipes.

The charms were not always harmful, but were used to cure ailments like barrenness, impotence, ill temper, anything (as the saying goes) from a bald head to a broken heart. The powerful New Orleans 'gris-gris' went into action for gamblers' luck and lovers' success. And these magics can still be found in parts of the South, even in northern ghettoes, wherever the credulity remains.

In the Old South a black cat's whiskers were often used in 'conjure' magic

Barnaby's Picture Library

This holy man, who predicted that the world would end in 1900, aroused the hostility of both the government and the Church in Brazil but his followers regarded him with reverence and fought to the last man for his beliefs

ANTONIO CONSELHEIRO

THE MOST SPECTACULAR of the various leaders of millennial movements that have arisen in Brazil, Antonio Vicente Mendes Maciel, called Conselheiro, 'the Counsellor', was born in 1835. He was the child of a family of impoverished landowners in northeast Brazil.

Millennial movements expect a cataclysmic end of the world and the coming of a better one. The migrations of some Brazilian Indians, sometimes extending across the whole continent, are explained in terms of a search for a 'land without evil' before the present earth is destroyed. A similar influence came to Brazil from Portugal, centring around the young King Sebastian who disappeared mysteriously at the battle of Kassr-el-Kebir, fought by the Portuguese in North Africa in 1578. Stories of the imminent return of Sebastian periodically agitated Portuguese and, later, Brazilian society, just as myths of the return of Arthur or of Frederick Barbarossa circulated in England and Germany.

The many wandering monks, friars, holy men and vagabonds who roamed about Brazil in the 19th century often speculated about the returning hero who would save the people from their distress. These penitents were often herbalists and prophets, and in regions without very many priests they catered for the religious needs of the illiterate peasantry. Some were held in much greater respect than the priesthood.

As a young man, Maciel worked as a clerk in various places. His marriage was unsuccessful and after his wife had left him he drifted into the life of a wandering preacher. He quickly gained the respect of the superstitious peasants, and acquired his name of 'Counsellor' because of a reputation he gained for wisdom and as an arbitrator in local disputes.

Maciel's appearance was striking, and his strange way of speaking in short, unconnected phrases won him the reputation of being a prophet and a holy man. He lived on alms, but very sparingly, and his fasts, ascetic habits and mysterious manner, made him an object of superstitious awe. Unsolicited by him, mendicants and others began to follow him from place to place, reciting beads and litanies.

In time, his fame had spread through all the great cities of the country, although he kept himself to the backwoods areas. In 1876 he was arrested on a false charge, and to his asceticism was now added a note of martyrdom. His followers, and the ignorant peasantry, were even more devoted to him on his release, and he moved about the country as before.

The End of the World

Conselheiro's influence was generally beneficial, and he was able to command local people to a variety of good works – repairing buildings, mending walls, building chapels – which otherwise would have been neglected. As a result, local priests were prepared to tolerate the descent into their parishes of the prophet and his rabble of followers. Such was his influence that just as he could persuade the poor to work, he could also persuade the rich to supply the materials for various undertakings. Civic authorities could not interfere, and the ordinary life of the villages and small towns of the backlands ceased when Antonio arrived to preach and prophesy. Healings and miracles were claimed.

After the establishment of the Republic of Brazil in 1889, Conselheiro's prophetic utterances came to have a clear anti-republican character. As long as he had been only the object of clerical censure, on the grounds that he over-excited the consciences of men and preached an 'over-rigorous morality', the civil authorities had done nothing to stop the prophet and his entourage of several hundreds. The accusation that he sought to convince men that he was the Holy Ghost, whether true or not, had not induced the government to confine him to an asylum. His preaching against the new and highly insecure Republic, however, led to a skirmish with the police but his followers, who were often vagabonds of dubious character, were too numerous and too ferocious to be routed, and inflicted severe casualties on the police.

Conselheiro's preaching began to take up the millennial strain that had reappeared at various times in Brazilian history. He prophesied the return of Sebastian, who would arise with an army from the sea to free men from the yoke of the Republic. He promised the end of the world in 1900, and saw his own movement as the gathering of the flock under the one shepherd. Many of his sayings appear meaningless, but they had that dark mystery well calculated to impress the simple people who listened to him.

Now in open conflict with the authorities, Conselheiro led his following north into the arid backlands and settled in the village of Canudos, remote from civilization. There he was joined by people from villages around, and then from farther afield, until a sizeable community grew up around the old village and in the hills round about. Bandits joined the new settlement and from there foraged the surrounding countryside.

Conselheiro preached austerity and privation, and set aside normal marriage, as the community prepared for a siege. He was hostile to the Republic, and his own society was run as an independent state at war with the outside world. But in 1895 he permitted a Capuchin friar to undertake a mission, to marry a number of couples, and to baptize over 100 children, even though many members of the settlement were opposed to the friar's being allowed to stay. The community remained a religious society, however, and in its own way was very devout, engaging in a great deal of prayer and the kissing of images.

The Siege of Canudos

Endemic banditry and the general inefficiency of the civic authorities in dealing with these numerous local manifestations of disorder perhaps accounted for the long lapse of time before any attempt was made to disperse the rebellious settlement at Canudos. Trouble arose after Conselheiro's followers came into conflict with the authorities of Joazeiro, a town some 125 miles from Canudos. Troops were called to deal with the millennialists, who lost many killed and wounded in the ensuing action, but managed to stop the offensive.

In 1896 a new force of over 500 men was sent against the settlement. This body was also repelled, and as a result of this victory many new recruits set out for Canudos, which now became an effective

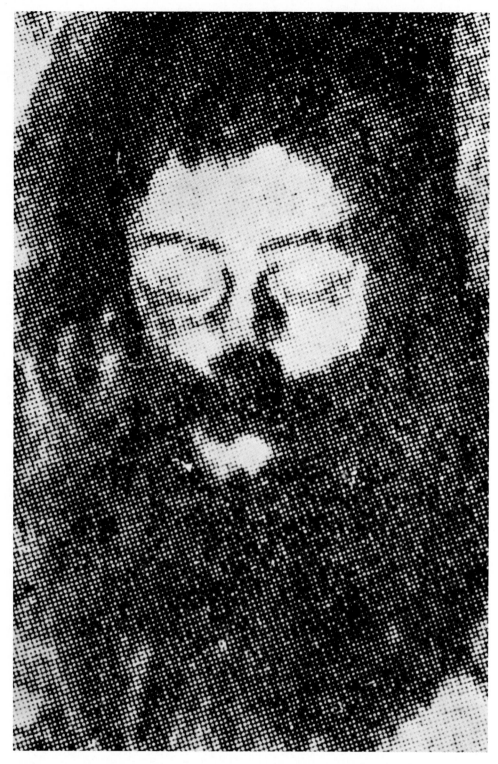

The exhumed body of Antonio Conselheiro. This holy man prophesied that a saviour would arise with an army from the sea to free the Republic of Brazil

military camp. A third military campaign, with 1300 troops involved, was no more successful and the military were again put to flight. Eventually, a force of over 5000 was dispatched by an alarmed government which feared a major insurrection. A long campaign ensued, in which the troops suffered more than 2000 casualties in dead and wounded, and which required more recruits for the final assault on the stronghold. The difficulties of the terrain, the inexperience of the army officers and the guerilla tactics of the rebels were all factors which lengthened the struggle.

The millennialists were prepared for just such a siege; they viewed it as part of the events leading to the end of the world, when salvation would be vouchsafed only to those at Canudos, whereas the Republic would everywhere be damned. Only at Canudos would there be a promised land, in which men would enjoy the earth's abundance. A church with walls as thick as a fort had been built at Conselheiro's direction, where the long services of the community were conducted, and the ceremonies performed in which images were kissed.

Fortified with elaborate rituals such as these, which often ended in hysteria, the followers of the Counsellor fought with extraordinary tenacity. Time and again, they cut off the troops' supplies, and only when a regular supply line was established, and larger cannon brought into the difficult positions around Canudos, was there a prospect of victory for the government. The cannon destroyed the towers of the new church and soon afterwards, in 1897, Conselheiro fell ill, apparently of dysentery, and died.

The situation in the encampment was now desperate, with the military closing in around the centre. Conselheiro's followers continued to hold out, believing that their leader had gone to heaven to summon the assistance of angels. Two weeks later, the troops succeeded in forcing the millennialists to raise a white flag, but only the elderly and the children came out. The grown men remained, and fought for a few more days to the very last man.

Antonio Maciel himself was undoubtedly a deluded fanatic, of whom the principal commentator has written: 'The multitude created him, refashioning him in its own image . . . The people needed someone to translate for them their own vague idealizations, someone to guide them in the mysterious paths of heaven . . . He drew the people of the backlands after him not because he dominated them, but because their aberrations dominated him.' This is to see Conselheiro as the personification of the aspirations of a disoriented and disorganized people, whose way of life had never been provided with stability and settled customs, and whose grasp of religious ideas was tenuous and permeated with superstition.

Personification of a Dream

Maciel was a curious and magnetic figure, whose contribution to events, in providing the dreams in which his followers sought their salvation, became significant only after the end of monarchy in Brazil. He did not envisage himself as outside the Christian tradition, but rather as a special emissary of God, holier and more inspired than priests, but deprived of the priest's right to officiate at Mass. He had been infuriated when, on occasion, he had sought the right to preach in churches and had been refused by priests. These experiences may have hardened his teaching, and led him to make some dire predictions about the fate of the Church. Despite these prophecies, he had remained essentially in the Roman tradition of liturgy, and had encouraged its more superstitious and fetishistic aspects.

The overthrow of the Empire may have fitted into his hazy conceptions of the time of the end. Equally his change of attitude may simply have reflected a more serious turn in the mental derangement from which he was evidently suffering. There is nothing to suggest that his militancy stemmed directly from the aspirations of his followers, although, since many were vagabonds, his willingness to lead them as a hostile religious movement admirably fitted their aspirations and their pent-up and otherwise frustrated hostility to the authorities.

BRYAN WILSON

FURTHER READING: E. Da Cunha, *Rebellion in the Backlands* (Chicago Univ. Press, 1944).

Conversion, whether of an individual or a crowd, involves a fundamental change of belief. The methods by which people can be induced to change their beliefs are strikingly similar, whether employed by the preacher, the psycho-analyst or the political indoctrinator

CONVERSION

THE CHANGING OF BELIEF to an extent that substantially affects an individual's outlook and personality is the sense in which the word 'conversion' is used in this article. This change brings with it, at least temporarily, a change from 'a self hitherto divided, and consciously wrong, inferior and unhappy,' to a self 'unified and consciously right, superior and happy', in the words of William James (in *The Varieties of Religious Experience*).

The restriction of the term to those changes in belief that *substantially* affect the individual's outlook and personality means that changes on this scale are likely to relate to religious outlook; indeed, in the past, when conversion in this sense was spoken of, it was always religious conversion that was intended. But conversion may be not only *to* religion but equally *from* religion, and in so far as the change in belief relates to those needs which religion exists to satisfy, such a change may fairly be called a religious conversion. Moreover, nowadays the conversion process may as readily be seen in changes of political belief, and in those major changes in an individual's outlook that may be brought about by psycho-analysis or other psychiatric treatment; and Walter de la Mare has spoken of falling in love as 'a conversion of the heart'. The processes of conversion are similar, whatever the change in belief effected.

Such changes can be divided into two basic categories: the conversion of people in groups; and the conversion of individuals. The classic example of the conversion of

The conversion of a person to a new religious belief is often confirmed by a ceremony after which the convert feels cleansed, purified and regenerated. Communal baptism, by Canadian Baptist missionaries, in a stream near Lake Titicaca in Bolivia

Most scholars agree that conversion is a gradual process, often culminating in a sudden and dramatic climax. The climax may come at the traditional revival meeting with a spell-binding preacher like the Rev Billy Graham *(left)* and an outburst of group emotion, or at a mass political rally like those held by Adolf Hitler *(above)*, or in solitude like the conversion of St Paul *(below)*, who saw a blinding flash of light and a vision of Jesus saying, 'Saul, Saul, why do you persecute me?'

people in groups is the revival meeting in its traditional form. With a spell-binding preacher, making full use of such aids to arousing feeling as lights or fire, and music – often of a strongly percussive kind – and expounding graphically the terrible alternatives to acceptance of belief, members of the congregation will lose their individualities in group emotion. They may sing and shout, groan and wail. Some may 'speak in tongues', usually in an uncontrollable and incoherent babble. Others may be stricken by convulsions and roll on the ground in apparent agony. The revival reaches its climax with complete breakdown of rationality in all or most of the congregation. On recovering their calm, they will announce that they have undergone conversion. Accepting the new belief, they feel cleansed and purified, remade and newly regenerated.

Famous examples of religious conversions by this process are those effected by John Wesley in the 18th century, by Billy Sunday in the early years of the 20th century and by Dr Billy Graham today. There are also the early Salvationist meetings, and the many camp meetings, so called, of revivalists of one creed, or another in the rural districts of the United States. In the political field, such mass rallies as those held by Adolf Hitler in the 1930s clearly fall into the same pattern.

In the religious field it is not only the Holy Spirit who is believed to move the congregation. The notorious convulsionists of Loudun in France in the 17th century (see GRANDIER) were believed to be possessed by the Devil; and John Wesley, who had originally believed that the peculiar manifestations at his own meetings were the work of God, came to believe that they were sent by the Devil to bring discredit to his work.

The mental processes that result in the dramatic if short-lived conversions of this kind are believed to be understood and have been extensively discussed, notably by Dr William Sargant (in *Battle for the Mind*). What apparently happens, briefly and figuratively, is that the individual is brought to a point of emotional stress whose only relief is breakdown, at which point acceptance of the new belief proffered is felt to be remedial and therapeutic. In the revival meeting, the stress is applied to people who may have been in a state of comparative equilibrium shortly before; their need for breakdown, release, new belief, is artificially induced. As the need is not long or deeply felt, the remedy is not long-lasting.

The Discovery of Unease
It is rather in the conversion of individuals that the process can be studied in greater detail. To start with, the often dramatic instances of instantaneous or lightning conversions sometimes adduced as proof of the miraculous workings of Grace can be dismissed. As the Catholic writer, R. C. De Sanctis has shown (in *Religious Conversion*), no conversions are in fact sudden and unprepared, although many converts like to believe them so. Conversion is the end of a long process of 'mutation', although much of this process may take place at an unconscious level of the mind; as it obviously did in the most famous convert of all, St Paul.

Its beginning may perhaps be defined as 'the discovery of unease'. The individual finds himself, as William James put it, divided and wrong, inferior and unhappy, in what concerns a major part of his outlook. Consciously or unconsciously he begins to seek an outlook that offers greater prospects of harmony and happiness. He may even decide what outlook it is that will suit him, and then seek to believe it. This was the case, for instance, with St Augustine of Hippo; originally a Manichean, he had made an intellectual decision for Christianity some time before he was able emotionally to accept it. But it is equally usual for potential converts not to know what it is they are seeking. If, however, they are eventually to emerge from the disturbed self through conversion, they will gradually become more inclined to one possible answer than another. Evidence that suggests that *this* is the right answer will be consciously or unconsciously accepted, and other evidence rejected.

During this period of seeking an answer whether it is consciously known early on or not, the subject is likely to become increasingly disturbed and unhappy. He will probably show, to a greater or lesser degree, many symptoms of the depressive stage of manic depression. He may feel himself to be lonely, isolated, unwanted; guilty and soiled; incapable of creative thinking; devoid of any capacity for happiness. He may reach that extreme state known to Catholics as 'aridity' or the dark night of the soul.

Sometimes the conversion — we might almost call it a cure, and such it is felt to be by the subject — is gradual. Gradually the loneliness, unhappiness, guilt, pass away and are replaced by more positive attitudes. Gradually the subject realizes that he is possessed of new and (for the time being, at least) satisfying beliefs. But sometimes the

actual moment of conversion is sudden and dramatic, and these, not surprisingly, are the conversions we hear most about.

It seems clear that such a moment occurs when the subject is ready for it, but what constitutes readiness we do not know. Certainly the pattern of the new belief has been more or less established and is awaiting emergence. Almost certainly, in some sense stress has been increased to the point of breakdown. What seems usually to happen is that breakdown is triggered by encounter with some potent object, event or idea, a breakdown often accompanied by ecstatic happiness and followed by almost immediate acceptance of the new belief.

The 'triggers' themselves are various. For St Augustine it was the reading of a verse in the Bible that suddenly took on powerful significance. Often it is encounter with Nature. St Ignatius Loyola, the founder of the Jesuits, was by a river at the moment of his conversion; the American missionary, David Brainerd, in a wood at night. It may be a meeting with another person of inspiring ideas, though this is more often an early point in the mutation process than the actual moment of conversion. The trigger may be a religious service or edifice or image: Paul Claudel, the French writer, had his moment of conversion in Nôtre Dame. But the trigger may be comparatively trivial and only the sudden change perceived.

Calculated Stress
In psycho-analysis the moment of breakdown known as 'abreaction' is clearly similar to that of conventional conversion. It follows a long period of usually painful self-examination and probing. It is followed by the characteristically joyful release, the feeling of being 'made new'; in this state such hypotheses as the Freudian ones are accepted as true because they *feel* true. Political conversions, forceful or willed, can be brought about by similar means, as Dr Sargant has shown. For most individuals to be, as it is now called, *brainwashed,* all that is needed is a sufficiently long period of enforced stress, during which the subject is reduced to a state of confusion, guilt, isolation and misery; while he is presented, as an alternative, with the political ideas to which it is desired to convert him. The point of breakdown is reached, often expedited by a sudden show of kindness, a promise that guilt, isolation and misery will be replaced by happy purged 'belonging' once the change of heart is achieved. The breakdown occurs: the promised change is effected, though how long it will last again depends, in most cases, on continuous follow-up and indoctrination. Nearly all the American soldiers brainwashed in Korea reverted to their former beliefs soon after they had returned to their former environment.

Many of these were, however, processed in small groups. This is an increasing tendency, whether used openly for religious or political conversion or indoctrination, or for psychiatric therapy. The method is both more economical than individual treatment and more likely to be effective with people of higher intelligence than would respond to the revival or mass meeting.

It is believed that some kinds of people are more susceptible to conversion techniques than others, though there is disagreement as to what types are most likely to resist or succumb; and there may well be differences according to whether individual or group techniques are in question. Hysterics, for instance, may respond to the more dramatic manifestations of group conversion, but are unlikely to hold any beliefs stoutly or lengthily. Psychopaths do not in general respond. It is variously said that people already holding strong beliefs are likely to resist conversion techniques or to accept them. It is generally agreed that the apparently normal healthy extrovert is the most vulnerable.

Renewal Through Exhaustion
The general physical process of conversion has obvious similarities to various others where change of belief may be less in question than mere release from tension. Native dancing is often adduced as an example, where a strong state of tension can be built up to the point of exhaustion and collapse, with subsequent feelings of release and renewal. The dancing manias of the European Middle Ages have clear likenesses to this pattern (see DANCING MANIA).

Since the important outward manifestation of conversion is the adoption of new belief, felt, at least for the time being, to be satisfactory, the possible worth of the new belief must come into question. For the person concerned, this is not in doubt: the new belief is validated by the satisfaction it gives and its ultimate truth is certain. A dispassionate judgement, however, must accept that *feeling* a belief to be true is no proof that it *is* true. As we have seen, all kinds of beliefs may be acquired through conversion processes, but some at least outsiders will judge to be of doubtful truth and dubious moral value, whatever immediate benefit they may confer on the person concerned.

As to the scope and durability of conversions, it would appear that the conversion of an individual by his own efforts and as the result of a personally-directed search is likely to be the longest lasting and most deeply held. This holds good whether it is brought about by gradual processes or by a final 'lightning flash' experience — except in the cases of those few people who apparently need more or less frequent changes of beliefs. The kind of conversions effected by group pressures are likely to be only temporary unless reinforced by constant indoctrination. Conversion may, as we have seen, be to any kind of belief substantially affecting the individual's outlook, and, whether belief it may be, to be properly called *conversion*, its adoption will change the individual, temporarily or permanently, from 'a self hitherto divided, and consciously wrong, inferior and unhappy,' to a self 'unified and consciously right, superior and happy.'

MARGHANITA LASKI

FURTHER READING: William James, *The Varieties of Religious Experience* (Collier-Macmillan, 1961) and by the same author *The Will to Believe* (Harvard University Press, 1979).

The extravagant manifestations of the Convulsionaries included violent agitation of the body and cataleptic trances, during which they were insensitive even to the pain of crucifixion

CONVULSIONARIES

THE TOMB of an obscure deacon, François de Pâris, in the little Parisian cemetery of St Médard, was the scene of a series of extraordinary events in the early 18th century. Not only were miraculous cures of the afflicted reported to have taken place after touching the tomb, but some of the visitors began to be seized with convulsions similar to those of epilepsy. These events attracted considerable notoriety; they were events which had their roots far back in the past and which were to have far-reaching religious and political consequences.

François de Pâris was born in 1690, the son of a wealthy member of the Parlement. A man of heroic humility, he declined to be ordained priest, although conscious of the call to serve God. His ascetic and charitable practices were legendary; so much so that in self-mortification he went without communion for almost two years. Worn out by his asceticism and his labours for the poor, he died in 1727, at the early age of 37.

On the day of the funeral, an old woman whose arm had been paralysed for 25 years was cured on touching the bier. Other miraculous cures were reported from time to time during the next four years. But it was in the early months of 1731 that a new and disturbing element began to manifest itself. Visitors to the tomb at St Médard began to be seized with convulsions and in extreme cases to pass into cataleptic trances, evidently as a result of contagious hysteria.

The Church of St Médard had Jansenist connections, situated as it was near Port-Royal which was a renowned centre of Jansenist scholars. When the cult of François de Pâris grew, the adherents who became known as Convulsionaries were a group of Jansenists, a sect named after a heretical Flemish bishop Cornelius Jansenius (1585–1638). The Vatican had issued a series of Bulls condemning Jansenius's teachings, the latest of which was the Bull *Unigenitus* of 1713. A Jansenist heretic was therefore anyone who refused to accept this Bull.

Strange Things at St Médard
Jansenism had already been associated with spiritual healing before the events at St Médard. The first link was forged in March 1656, at Port-Royal, when a young girl named Marguerite Périer was cured of a terrible ulcer. She was the niece of the theologian Pascal, who had written in defence of the Jansenists. The second link came much later, in 1725, when a certain Anne Charlier was cured of a haemorrhage. This took place in the course of a religious procession, but the priest who had celebrated Mass and was carrying the host, was against *Unigenitus*, and therefore a heretic. The third and fourth links followed in 1727, with the deaths of Gerard

In violently ecstatic trance states, the Convulsionaries were completely insensitive to pain: from Collin de Plancy's *Dictionnaire Infernal*

Rousse, a priest of Avenay, and François de Pâris. Cures were effected on both tombs, but the greatest wonders took place on the tomb of Deacon de Pâris.

The fame of St Médard spread and the number of visitors multiplied. However, not all those who came did so for worthy reasons; on 7 August 1731 a certain widow Delorme came to the cemetery to scoff, and was paralysed for her impudence. Insult was added to injury when she was thrown into jail. Public opinion was still further roused, for political issues were involved; near-riots ensued, and in January 1732 the cemetery was closed by royal decree. This action provoked some unknown wit to write:

De par le roi, défense à Dieu
De faire miracle en ce lieu

which we might paraphrase as: 'God is forbidden to work miracles here by order of the King.'

But although the focus of the convulsionary movement was thus removed, neither the healings nor the convulsions were thereby brought to an end. Evidently the connection with the tomb of François de Pâris was incidental, rather than essential. The movement spread into the provinces. Significantly, it found support among the aristocracy, and even Voltaire's brother, Armand Arouet, counted himself among its adherents.

The most celebrated of the Convulsionaries was a member of the Parlement, Louis-Baptiste Carré de Montgeron (1686–1754). Montgeron, whose early life had been far from exemplary, went out of sheer curiosity to St Médard in September 1731, and addressed to Deacon de Pâris a typical sceptic's prayer, beginning, 'If it is true that you exist and that you can hear me . . .' After four hours at the tomb, he emerged from the cemetery a believer, and the rest of his life was devoted to working out the implications of what must be reckoned as a classical conversion experience. He at once began the work of attempting to persuade the world that the events at St Médard were both true and significant. Although for political reasons he was in exile from

Paris, he returned in 1737 to present to Louis XV in person the first volume of his massive book *La Vérité des Miracles*, in which he defended the authenticity of the cures of St Médard. Predictably, he was arrested and thrown into the Bastille.

Montgeron's book (the first volume of which had been ordered to be burned on his arrest) was not only a defence of the Convulsionaries; it was equally an attack on the French Church, the Pope and the Bull *Unigenitus*. He paid the price; the last 17 years of his life were spent in captivity, and when he died in 1754 Montgeron was buried in a pauper's grave. But he gave the world a disciple's picture of a movement which even the doctors of the Sorbonne who were against *Unigenitus* felt to imply 'reprehensible things', and urged should be 'rejected in its entirety as an object of horror and mistrust.'

Crucified in a Trance
If we ask what the Convulsionaries actually did to provoke these extreme judgements, the account of an interview which took place in 1758 between Lieutenant Bertin of the French Police and a certain Dr Dubourg of Paris is illuminating. Dubourg's testimony was restrained and factual. He was privately convinced that although the practices of the Convulsionaries were odd and indeed repugnant, there was no question of imposture or trickery; nor was there anything in them to offend against public decency. He reported that the convulsions led to five classes of apparent maltreatment, varying from kicks and blows to the dropping of weights on the abdomen, the driving of nails into the flesh and, in extreme cases, actual crucifixion – all in a state of trance. Women were particularly desirous of undergoing such tortures, which in their own private jargon they called *secours* (aids); those responsible for providing them, usually young men, were known as *secouristes*. The sexual implications are obvious. Other contemporary accounts tell of similar manifestations: for instance, the case of one Marie Sonnet, who was said to have remained suspended over a fire for 36 minutes, supported only by the head and feet.

Clearly what was involved was spontaneous or induced catalepsy, more common in primitive and Oriental religions than in Christianity but not unknown, either before or since, in the West. The body's rigidity and insensitivity to pain when in such a state are well-known symptoms, attested from many religions and many parts of the world. The ultimate object is usually to demonstrate the relative worthlessness of the body, and the triumph of the spirit over the flesh. In this respect the Convulsionaries have their place in the history of religious asceticism. But in this case the Jansenist origins of the movement introduced a political element into the picture, and as a result the authorities adopted repressive measures. Thousands of Convulsionaries were imprisoned. This had the effect of driving the movement underground, where it later gave rise to competing sects before disappearing completely.

Since the prosperity of a community and indeed its very life hung on the success or failure of the corn crop, our ancestors wove many superstitions around the harvest

CORN

WHEAT WAS GROWN in the Middle East some 7000 years ago and was known in Northern Europe as early as 1000 BC. With its cultivation grew up the concept of a spirit or goddess living within the corn plant who must be kept alive from harvest time until next year's sowing to guarantee the renewal of the crop.

In ancient Greece the goddess was called Demeter, the 'Giver of Wheat', and her Roman equivalent was Ceres, the goddess of grain crops and the harvest (see DEMETER). Not even the advent of Christianity substantially affected the essentials of this pagan belief, except to effect a transformation in the nature of the object venerated. Thus in France, the Virgin became known as 'Our Lady the Bread Giver', while in Ireland St Vulgan was appointed the patron saint of sowing and the harvest.

Any intrusion into the domain of the Earth Mother by the plough was surrounded by taboos and superstitions. In the ancient world a new plough could not be manufactured from the wood of an old one that had been struck by lightning, while hair was plucked from the hides of the oxen that pulled the plough as a protection against the assaults of the sky gods.

The Plough of Death
The plough alone became the focal point of many superstitions. If a man omitted a furrow while ploughing it was taken as an omen that one of his household would die, while even to dream of a plough, with its undertones of newly-turned earth for a grave, could be a portent of death. As a means of protecting the community from the assaults of malignant spirits a plough-share was ritually drawn in a circle around the village by naked women at dead of night.

To ensure an auspicious sowing a hen's egg or a loaf from the previous year's harvest was sometimes placed under the plough before the first furrow was cut, and in Prussia the ploughman and sowers were doused with water in the hope that there would be a plentiful supply of rain. Some American farmers invariably sowed their corn in the dark of the moon, believing that this prevented the growth of over-tall, spindly stalks. (But South Carolinians preferred the light of the moon.) American superstition also tells farmers to plant corn when the leaves on hardwood trees are as large as squirrels' ears; and never finish cutting your corn before sunset. A corn stalk hung over a mirror brings good luck.

The Irish farmer tries to encourage the growth of his corn by placing a sickle in its

Plaited corn dolly from Montenegro, Yugoslavia, made from the last ears of the harvest; throughout Europe corn dollies were kept in the farm to ensure the success of future harvests

midst, to remind the crop of its destiny. In Europe it was a favourable omen if poppies grew in cornfields, since this flower was originally associated with the Roman corn goddess Ceres.

For American Indians who grew corn, the ceremonies and festivals associated with the crop took a paramount place in their worship. Most Indian mythology personifies the corn as a corn mother, or perhaps two corn maidens (though the corn deity of the Hopi was the male god of the underworld – rather as if Hades supplanted Persephone). Many origin myths among Indians depict the disappearance and return, or resurrection, of the corn deity; and the corn plant is important in charms and prayer sticks used in ceremonies.

But the corn's dominant role is a central

feature of the year's biggest ritual, the spring Corn Dance. The Pueblos have a secret and gorgeous Green Corn Dance in spring, really a series of complex rites, addressed to the corn maidens, the rain and the clouds. The Shawnee, Cherokee and some eastern tribes like the Iroquois have similar corn ceremonies: the Iroquois Corn Festival is a harvest rite, in September, with many circle dances and other fertility motifs, and women taking the major parts.

Corn was supposed to be particularly vulnerable to adverse psychic influences, and had to be carefully protected from contamination by the presence of the sick or by death. Those who were seriously ill were kept well away from the cornfield, and under no circumstances was a funeral procession

permitted to pass through it. A vindictive extension of this theme was the custom among jealous Irish peasants of magically transferring their own misfortunes to a neighbour by secretly burying a dead animal or a piece of meat in his field.

Rain, one of the primary essentials for growth, could be secured by the farmer in a number of ways. Primitive communities usually employed for this purpose a rainmaker whose rites varied from scattering water from a hut roof as an intimation to the rain spirits to follow suit, to those of the Omaha Indians who spurted water into the air to make a fine mist. Among the Macedonian Greeks, it was customary for a procession of children to visit every spring and well in times of drought, led by a girl adorned with flowers, singing:

> Send Thou us a still small rain
> That the fields may fruitful be
> And vines in blossom we may see
> That the grain be full and sound
> And wealthy grow the folks around.

In the United States farmers of the old school in the Ozark hills tried to ensure plentiful rain by soaking cobs from the seed corn in water. Only when the new crop was thought secure would the cobs be buried or cast into a running stream.

The Last Sheaf
When the corn was ripe for harvesting the first sheaves were sometimes gathered and taken into the church. The people of Lillers in France celebrated a Mass for the crop and blessed the wheat and fruit. At Valenciennes, following the feast of St Veronica, dancers were led by a girl dressed in white who presented grain to the onlookers in return for money which was spent on wine. In a similar custom taking place annually at Richmond, Yorkshire, the first farmer to offer the Mayor a substantial specimen of the new crop is ceremonially given a bottle of wine at the Market Cross.

In the British Isles the gathering of the harvest was generally supervised in the old days by a workman called 'The Lord of the Harvest', assisted by another known as 'The Lady'. During the reaping the farmer generally remained well in the background. In Ireland it was the custom to attach a small box containing insects to the scythe handle in the belief that it would intensify its cutting

Italian bread baked to represent the local goddess of crops and fertility

power. The most significant of the former rituals enacted by the reapers were associated with the last sheaf, once believed to contain the spirit of the corn. Sometimes a few ears of corn were left standing in the field but more often these were plaited as they stood into a 'corn dolly' and then severed by the sharp blades of sickles hurled by the reapers. The 'dolly' was kept in the farm until the beginning of the new season's ploughing, thus ensuring continuity.

The last sheaf of the harvest might symbolize either a human being or an animal. In parts of Germany the sheaf was referred to as a pig, he-goat, wolf, straw cock or rye sow, and in the Kiel district as the corn cat. In Scotland it was called the maiden, the old wife, or the clyack chief, while in England it was variously known as the mare, the maiden, kern baby, or kern doll.

Trespassers Will Be Sacrificed
In Cornwall the last handful of corn, called 'the neck', was always ceremoniously cut by the oldest reaper who cried out at the same time: 'I havet! I havet! I havet!' When asked what he had, he replied, 'A neck! A neck! A neck!' The sheaf was cut and carried to the farm with much merriment, decked with ribbons and then left until the following year. Sometimes it might be set up near the gate of the cornfield as a magical charm against unfavourable weather.

In Central Europe the 'corn mother' wandered the fields in spirit at night, dressed in a linen robe with cornstalks for hair. During summer when the wind blew through the corn, sending great waves from one end of the field to the other, German peasants would mutter 'the corn mother is going through the corn' and children were warned to keep well away lest the corn mother should catch them. Behind this mysterious belief lie certain dark traditions of human and animal sacrifice, as suggested by the saying in parts of Bavaria that he who gives the last stroke at threshing has 'killed the corn man'. In ancient times any stranger passing through the cornfield might be sacrificed as the ritual representative of the corn spirit, and it was long accepted that a forfeit might be demanded from any stranger venturing among the harvesters.

Among the other rites which have gone the way of sickle and scythe has been a ritual associated with gleaning, in which there was a garlanded Queen of Gleaners: this was once as important a rite of the corn harvest as the dolly. Yet although mechanization has gradually displaced the age-old rites, man stubbornly refuses to abandon ideas that are as old as the cultivation of corn itself. But the ceremonial side is today mainly confined to the revived agricultural festivals of the Church and in particular the Harvest Festival.

Most interesting, however, is the survival of a tradition that originated with ancient rites of the cornfield and which forms part of the wedding ceremony. It is not generally realized that the wedding cake is a relic of the symbolic corn ears worn by the bride in the pagan past to ensure fertility. These, in the course of time, were replaced by cakes and were scattered over the newly-married couple as they left the church. The pleasing custom of sending pieces of cake to guests and friends is a modern expression of an ancient desire to share with one's friends the magic of the corn spirit.

ERIC MAPLE

FURTHER READING: G. E. Evans, *Ask the Fellows who Cut the Hay* (Faber, London, 1966); J. G. Frazer, *The Golden Bough* (St. Martin's Press, 1980); R. Sheppard and E. Newton, *The Story of Bread* (Fernhill, 1957).

Cornucopia
Literally in Latin, 'horn of plenty': generally a twisted horn overflowing with fruit and flowers, a symbol of abundance and prosperity; often shown in the hands of Plutus, god of wealth, Fortuna, goddess of fortune, and other deities: in Greek mythology it was originally the horn of Amaltheia, the goat which suckled the infant Zeus; he rewarded her by putting her in the sky as the constellation Capricorn.

Fairies of one sort or another were once commonly seen in Cornwall — and not only by imaginative children. Grown men and women had a healthy respect for the 'little people' and preferred to keep on the right side of these touchy and capricious spirits

CORNWALL

A CENTURY AGO the Cornish 'piskey', now surviving merely as a banal motif on innumerable brass toasting forks and other souvenirs for tourists, was alive in the imagination of thousands of Cornishmen. He was only one of a number of supernatural beings which were believed to people the countryside, both above and below ground.

Because of its isolation, geographical and linguistic, Cornwall has a strongly individual tradition of legend. Folk tales, or 'drolls' as they are called, are of giants, of saints not known in England, and of holy wells. Superstitions sometimes centre around the great standing stones, the cromlechs, the *men scryfa* left in Cornwall by the contemporaries of the men who put up Stonehenge. There are also the stories and beliefs of those who follow the traditional occupations of the Cornishman: mining tin and catching fish.

The Little People

In the 19th century, belief in the 'little people' was widespread, as illustrated in two stories quoted in A. K. Hamilton Jenkin's book *Cornwall and its People*. Mrs Rebecca Noall of St Ives, who died in 1927, told the author how she had seen the little people in her youth. One evening after working late at her trade as a dressmaker, she was walking home escorted by her father when an extraordinary sight appeared: on each side of them they saw a procession of the little people, walking in orderly fashion, arm-in-arm, with the greatest decorum and dignity. The old lady used to describe them as being the neatest little creatures imaginable, and beautifully dressed in scarlet cloaks and black steeple-crowned hats. Her father had evidently seen them as clearly as herself for, in a whisper, he bade her keep strict silence and avoid attracting attention by any exclamation of surprise. Thus they reached home in safety, none the worse for their strange encounter.

The fairies were mischief-makers and took a naughty delight in 'mazing' walkers in the country, so that they lost their way on familiar paths. The only way to break the spell was to turn some garment inside out. Jenkin had such an incident described to him by a man whose wife had recently suffered from the fairies' attentions. The small people could be aggressive: William Bottrell, in a 19th century collection of Cornish folklore, tells how a smuggler who planned to land some goods on Penzance's Eastern Green, went to spy out the land. Climbing a hillock, he came across hundreds of the piskeys dancing. 'Tom noted that the little men were all rigged in green,' says Bottrell, 'except for their scarlet caps (small people are so fond of that coloured headgear,

The mischievous and sometimes malevolent piskeys, reputed to have caused so much havoc in 19th century Cornwall, have now become familiar figures in the Cornish tourist trade

that they used to be nick-named "redcaps"). But what struck his fancy and tickled him most was to see the little, old, grave-looking pipers with their long beards wagging. For the life of him, Tom could not forbear shouting "Will 'e be shaved . . . will 'e be shaved old redcaps?"' At once hundreds of the dancers lined up, armed in an instant with bows, spears and slings. 'Tom made off to the boat, and his comrades followed close on his heels; but on the way, a shower of pebbles fell on them, and burned like coals of fire wherever they hit them.'

Miniature Miners

The 'knackers' or 'knockers' are mine fairies. They haunt only the richest lodes, so to hear them at work was a good sign; many a lode of good ore has been discovered by hearing them singing and knocking. The miners would leave a small piece of their dinner on the floor for the knackers; if they did not, then the little creatures would find some way of punishing this meanness. This was called leaving a 'didjan' (a small piece) for 'bucca'. Originally a bucca was a spirit that must be propitiated and fishermen would leave a fish on the sands for him; at harvest time they left bread and beer. There were two buccas, 'Bucca Gwidden', the good or white one, and 'Bucca Dhu', the bad or black one. Many miners have recounted

suddenly breaking through into a lode and finding the knackers all at work in a cavity, with miniature picks and other equipment.

Other small inhabitants of the West Cornwall peninsula were the spriggans, spiteful creatures forever carrying off babies from their cradles, and popping their own ugly brats inside instead. One way of getting rid of the changeling was for the robbed mother to take the creature and dip it in a holy well on the first three Wednesdays in May. Another was to make a smoky fire with green ferns in the hearth; when the house was full of smoke, the unfortunate changeling would be thrown down on the hearthstone, and the injured mother would rush out of doors and run three times around the house. When she returned, her own child should have been put in the changeling's place.

Spriggans, like the buccas, were watchful of old pieties. They guarded the vast treasures that were buried by the old kings. Anyone digging for treasure was likely to find himself surrounded by hundreds of spriggans, who would so scare him that he would be forced to rush off; after this experience he would be so ill that he must spend several days in bed. If he dared to return to the place he had tried to desecrate, he would find the hole filled in, so that no trace of it could be found.

Cornwall is famous for its logans or rocking stones, the best known example being at Treryn Dinas on the western peninsula. Logan Rock was most delicately balanced, though enormous. Like all others of its kind, it had magical associations, and for thousands of years the Cornish had regarded the stone respectfully. Early in the 19th century a lieutenant in the Royal Navy for a wager sent the great stone crashing to the bottom of the cliff with a single push. Local opinion was outraged and the Admiralty ordered the officer to replace the stone at his own expense. The operation was duly carried out with block and tackle, but the logan never rocked as well again.

All the great rocks have some association. In connection with Merlin's Chair, a square formation of rock, situated opposite Mouse-hole, there was a saying:

> There are those who shall land on the
> rock of Merlyn
> Who shall burn Penzance, Paul and Newlyn

This prophecy was fulfilled in 1595, when a force of Spaniards landed and did just that.

Logans and 'chairs' are natural forma-tions, but the prehistoric standing stones were put there by the hand of man. The most potent magically was the *Men-an-Tol*, the holed or 'crick stone'. The most famous of them is at Madron, near Penzance. Here there are three standing stones, the middle larger one pierced with a hole in its centre. Until this century, the country people used to crawl through this hole for the cure of lumbago, sciatica and cricks in the back. It also possessed curative powers for rickets. Children afflicted with this defect were passed nine times through the hole. A man stood on one side of the stone, a woman on the other; the child was passed with the sun

from east to west, and from right to left, a boy from the woman to the man, and a girl from the man to the woman. The order had to be very strictly observed.

There are many other holed stones too in this neighbourhood, called 'Quoits'. According to local legend the giants who inhabited the district used these stones to play quoits. One of these was the giant who lived on Carn Galva, who used them to play with a human friend and also with neigh-bouring giants. The rocks scattered all over West Cornwall are the result of the giants bombarding each other when vexed.

Cursing and Ill-Wishing

There are many Cornish ghost stories associated with the sea. A seaman's appari-tion will appear to his wife or sweetheart at the moment of his drowning; sometimes a great ghost ship in full sail appears off the coast. The most gripping story concerns the wreck of Sir Cloudesley Shovel's flag-ship, the *Association*, on the Gilstone in the Scillies. This has recently been discovered by underwater divers, who have recovered considerable amounts of treasure from the bottom. It is said that a local man in the crew warned Sir Cloudesley that he was steering too close for safety. Incensed, the Admiral ordered him to be hanged. Before he was launched off the yardarm, the con-demned man requested that a psalm be read, and chose the 109th, known as the 'cursing psalm'. The execution was duly carried out but not before he had sworn that the ship would sink. No sooner had the

sailor's body been heaved overboard than the sky grew dark, and a tempest blew. The ghost of the hanged man appeared in the water, and followed the ship till she struck.

The cursing psalm was often used by witches. Powers of sorcery ran in certain of the oldest families, in the seventh son of a seventh son, or daughter of daughter. Touching a logan stone nine times at mid-night also turned a person into a witch; another method involved the feeding of a toad with consecrated bread. Witches often transformed themselves into hares and would ride about in the night on ragwort stems, usually to a meeting at a logan stone.

Witches could cure complaints, and they could also 'ill-wish'. It is still believed by quite a few people throughout the county that power to bring ill-luck by cursing does in fact reside with certain persons, and that they use it. The idea is very much alive: anyone looking pale and wan is likely to hear the comment 'Es, me'andsome, yor lookin' brer ill-wished. Was the matter?' ('Yes, my handsome, you are looking very ill-wished. What's the matter?') This common expres-sion does not in fact mean that the speaker believes that ill-wishing has taken place, but it does show the survival of the idiom.

As well as verbal charms, there were actual objects. The most interesting was the 'milpreve' (from the Cornish *myl pref*, 'a thousand snakes'). This was a type of pre-historic bead, blue with sometimes a yellow wriggly line (a 'snake'). Boiling water with this bead, which is also known as an 'adder stone', makes an effective draught for those stung by adders. This is a living link between Cornwall and the Druids, for Pliny describes how among the Druids a bead known as the *ovum anguinum*, the 'snake's egg' was worn as a badge of office, and how it was formed from the breath of a mass of snakes.

These milpreves were often worn in rings by white witches or 'pellars', who used to provide written charms for placing under pillows to work against ill-wishing. They often charged a handsome fee for this service. Numerous omens predicted death: the sudden appearance of rats or mice in a house, the perching of a bird on the window-sill of a sick person's room, a blackbird seen through glass or the appearance of a robin. The hand of a dead man used to be passed over sore eyes or facial disfigure-ments. A wedding ring taken from the hand of a dead woman was supposed to be effec-tive in curing a stye on the eye, if the eye is stroked with it.

Although many of the superstitions recorded by folklorists at the end of the 19th century have disappeared, there are still many curious survivals in the county, among fishermen and in children's talk. There are still families which get up at dawn on May Day and go for a long country walk – a tame survival of the elaborate 'Maying' ceremony of former times, but a real one nevertheless.

GRAHAM NORTON

The *Men-an-Tol* or holed stone at Madron near Penzance. Until this century people would crawl through it for the cure of lumbago, sciatica and cricks in the back

CORRESPONDENCES

CORRESPONDENCES

THE LION, THE SPARROWHAWK and the phoenix, the colour yellow and the number six, the heliotrope and the sunflower, gold, the god Apollo, a child, the zodiac sign of Leo, cloves, cinnamon and myrrh, a cock, a sceptre: the link which connects the items on this list together is the fact that they are all associated with the sun in ritual magic. These chains of association are part of what is called a 'system of correspondences'.

The most familiar correspondences are those between the days of the week and the planetary gods: Sunday is the day of the sun, Monday of the moon, and so on. European magicians use this set of links as a guide to the best time for performing different types of magical operation. For example, the *Key of Solomon*, the most famous of European magical textbooks, says that Sunday, the day of the sun (or one of the traditional hours of the sun — see DAYS) is the right time for a ritual intended to gain money or attract the support of influential people. A magician performing a ceremony for this purpose will use as many of the things which correspond to the sun as he can. He will light six candles on his altar, he will wear a gold ring on his finger, he may drape the room in which he is working with yellow hangings, he may wear a yellow robe adorned with hexagrams, six-pointed stars. He will burn cloves, cinnamon or myrrh in a brazier, and he may perhaps sacrifice a cockerel. He uses these things because he believes that they are secretly linked with a powerful force or current of energy operating in the universe, and that by using them he attracts this force and brings it to bear on the object of his ceremony.

This idea is part of one of the basic beliefs underlying European magic, the conviction that the universe is not a disorderly collection of stray bits and pieces but an ordered whole, a design or a pattern. The main strands in the pattern are the correspondences. They are the magical equivalent of a scientist's classification of the phenomena he studies into orderly groups, and they go back to men's attempts to make sense of the world by classifying things in terms of the gods who controlled them. The modern magician has substituted for the gods the mysterious currents or forces, at work both in himself and in the universe outside him (see FORCES), but many of the correspondences are drawn from the ancient world and are based, not on any principles known to science but on a symbolic or poetic logic which links together things that outwardly and rationally do not appear to be connected.

The dove and the sparrow, for instance, are still said to correspond to Venus, the force of love, just as they were sacred to Aphrodite in Greece, because they are noticeably amorous birds.

Planets, Metals, Colours

Similarly, the traditional connections between planets, metals and colours have a certain logic behind them.

Planets	Metals	Colours
Sun	Gold	Yellow
Moon	Silver	White
Mercury	Quicksilver	Grey
Venus	Copper	Green
Mars	Iron	Red
Jupiter	Tin	Blue
Saturn	Lead	Black

Gold and silver belong to sun and moon respectively, partly because of their colour and partly because it was natural to connect the two most valuable metals with the most valuable planets, the ones which gave light. The sun's link with gold explains the *Key of Solomon's* recommendation of Sunday as the right day for a magical operation to make money.

Quicksilver belongs to Mercury because it is the most mobile of the metals and Mercury is the fastest-moving planet. Green is the colour of Venus or Aphrodite as ruler of Nature, the force behind the green growth of vegetation, and copper is probably her metal because Cyprus was both the place of Aphrodite's birth and also the classical world's principal source of copper.

Iron is the metal of Mars because of its use in weapons of war and red is the colour of blood and bloodshed: also the planet Mars sometimes has a reddish look. Blue belongs to Jupiter as lord of the sky but his connection with tin is obscure though very old, for the Sumerian term for tin was 'metal of heaven'. Lead, the darkest and heaviest of the metals, and black as the colour of death were naturally associated with Saturn as the dimmest and slowest-moving of the planets known in antiquity (see also COLOURS).

The same type of thinking lies behind the other sun correspondences listed earlier. The cock, for example, is here because it greets the sun at dawn, and the sparrowhawk because it soars towards the sun. Cloves and cinnamon correspond to the sun, as the preserver and sustainer of all life on earth, because they were used as preservatives, and do in fact have powerful bacteria-killing properties. Myrrh is also a preservative, used by the Egyptians in embalming corpses and offered at midday to the Egyptian sun god.

Magicians influenced by the Cabala relate their correspondences not only to the planets but to the ten *sefiroth*, the aspects of God or parts of the divine being in the cabalistic Tree of Life, and also to the 22 Paths which link the sefiroth together on the Tree, and to the 22 letters of the Hebrew alphabet and the 22 major trumps of the Tarot pack (see CABALA; TAROT). A detailed system of cabalistic correspondences was published by Aleister Crowley in his book *Magick in Theory and Practice.* It was based on the work of Crowley's one-time master and later bitter enemy Macgregor Mathers, head of the Order of the Golden Dawn (see GOLDEN DAWN).

One of the uses of this system is to provide the aspiring occultist with a set of signposts on the 22 Paths, along which he tries to 'rise through the spheres' or climb towards God, a hazardous undertaking in which he may easily stray from the true way (see CABALA). For example, the path from Malkhuth up to Yesod, the first path which he must follow, belongs to Saturn and emblems of death are assigned to it, including the colour black and the yew and the cypress, which are graveyard trees. If he sees a figure in red on the path, or a horse, which is a beast of Mars, or an almond tree, which belongs to the moon, he knows he has strayed from the true path. Similarly, if he believes he is in the region of Netsah, the sphere of Venus, he would expect to see doves or sparrows, or a swan, or a spotted beast like a leopard or a lynx, which are creatures of Venus.

FURTHER READING: R. Cavendish, *The Black Arts* (Routledge & Kegan Paul, 1967).

CORYBANTES

THE WHIRLPOOL of Greek mythology not only mingled together a myriad of conflicting tales but sucked into itself many elements of foreign belief, especially from Asia Minor. The result, more often than not, is confused. The Corybantes provide a good example of this confusion. Their very name probably means 'whirlers', although even this is uncertain. In their various guises they usually appear as supernatural beings devoted to noisy, orgiastic dancing. But who they danced for and why is disputed — not only by modern scholars but also in the Greek stories themselves, where the Corybantes are frequently confused with another band of loud leapers, the Curetes (youths) of Crete.

The reason for this confusion is the interaction between Greek and Asiatic myths. Apart from their similar behaviour, both Corybantes and Curetes are presented as attendants on the Great Mother of the gods: Rhea in the Greek stories, Cybele in the Asiatic. As the cultures intermingled between the two sides of the Aegean Sea, Rhea and Cybele became identified with each other and so did their attendants.

Some authorities, attempting to make the matter clearer, tell us that the Corybantes are not Greek at all but purely Asiatic. They are ecstatic dancers in the train of the 'mountain mother' Cybele, playing the piercing instruments of the uplands. These were cymbals, rattles and 'bull-roarers' or stones with a hole in them which, when whirled round on a thong, made a noise like a rushing wind; they were believed to invoke rain. As well as being dancers, the Corybantes are associated with magical cures, especially of mental disorders. They seem, in fact, to be an example of the ancient and still surviving concept of the medicine-man, whipping his followers into a trance-like dance, purging them of evil and controlling the elements.

Such a precise attribution cannot get rid of the fact that the Greeks themselves muddled up the Corybantes and the Curetes and when they were describing the Cretan Curetes quite often called them Corybantes.

Yet another element arises in that the Corybantes, or Curetes, appear to be connected with the Dactyls, who also served Rhea, the Great Mother. Rhea's husband, Cronus, had the habit of devouring their children. After she had given birth to three daughters (Hera, Demeter and Hestia), Rhea found that she was again with child. In order to cheat her husband, she decided to bear the infant secretly and went into hiding in a mountain cave in Crete. In which mountain the cave lay is, again, disputed: some say Aegeon, others Dicte, yet others Ida. It is interesting incidentally that Cybele was connected with another Mount Ida, in Phrygian Asia Minor. When her labour began, Rhea pressed on the ground with her hands. From each of her fingerprints, spirits or divinities sprang up to assist at the birth and protect the infant Zeus. These beings are generally called the 'Idaean Dactyls', *dactyl* being the Greek for 'finger'. There are various accounts of their nature and characteristics but they are all, in a sense, children of the Great Mother.

The Corybantes (or Curetes) are sometimes identified with the Dactyls and sometimes said to be the latter's offspring.

The Corybantes were frenzied armed dancers who guarded the infant Zeus. These strange nurses, who frightened away enemies by the clanging of metal, were believed to have magical powers of healing

Whatever their name and parentage, they were armed with sword and shield which they clashed together as they danced round Zeus's cradle to prevent his father hearing his cries. (No scholar has yet suggested that the great god's later predilection for thunder dates from his earliest aural experiences.) The number of Corybantes or Curetes varies from account to account but they are often said to be three and it is thus that they are usually represented in art.

In other versions of the birth of Zeus, Hera persuaded her mother Rhea to allow her to take the new-born infant to the Cretan fastnesses, where she cared for her baby brother until he was old enough to marry her. In these accounts the Curetes are local youths assembled by Hera to dance and clash their weapons when the child cried. From a hymn discovered in Crete, it is evident that the Curetes were the object of a cult and were revered as attendants of 'Zeus Curos', the adolescent Zeus. The hymn is of the Hellenistic period but it has been plausibly suggested that the rite itself has far more ancient origins and that historical Curetes existed. These were Cretan youths who, in Minoan times, worshipped Zeus as a god of their own age.

In all these stories, whether they be of Greek or Asiatic origin, the same elements occur. In each there is a connection with the Mother of the gods, wild dancing, the warding-off of harm and the clashing of metal on metal. The last point leads to further ramifications. Many of the ancient tales present the Dactyls as the earliest workers in metal and also as magicians, weavers of spells both good and bad. The same qualities are also attributed to the other beings associated with the Dactyls, including the Corybantes, the Telchines, semi-divine beings of Rhodes, and the Cabiri, Phrygian deities associated with Samothrace and also with Asia Minor. In many versions there are dark stories of male fertility and mutilation, of three brothers, one of whom is murdered or revoltingly maimed by the other two.

This strand of fratricidal strife runs through all the accounts of the sons of the Great Mother. These artisan beings seem often to be thought of as dwarfs, echoing quite foreign myths such as that of the Niebelungen, the Teutonic smith-dwarfs who dwelt in caves beneath the earth.

Alinari

Harald Schultz

Cosmetics

Preparations designed to beautify the skin: body painting, cicatrizing or tattooing are common in many parts of the world, for ornamental and also for magical and religious reasons: the Old Testament writers generally disapproved of cosmetics and the elaborate beauty aids of ancient Egypt, Greece and Rome were condemned as pagan and immoral by the early Christians.
See COSTUME; TATTOOING.

Axel Poignant

Cosmogony

Theory of how the universe was created: 'cosmos' means the universe as an ordered whole: the great variety of creation myths can be divided into two groups; aetiological myths were speculative accounts of how things came to be; ritual creation myths were an essential element of ceremonies meant to ensure that human society, prosperity, order and the universe itself would continue.
See CREATION MYTHS.

COSTUME

Clothes can be the distinguishing mark of the specialist, whether he is a medicine-man, a monarch or a monk. Their purpose is less to protect the wearer from the bitter winds and burning sun than from hostile magical attack

WHY HUMAN BEINGS took to wearing clothes is still not agreed upon by anthropologists. A hundred years ago such a question would have produced the inevitable response that the answer was to be found in the Bible, in the first chapter of the Book of Genesis. When Adam and Eve had eaten of the fruit of the Forbidden Tree they 'knew that they were naked' and hastily sewed fig leaves together to cover their bodies. In more secular language, human beings were alleged to have an innate sense of modesty.

This theory has fared badly as anthropological knowledge has increased. It has been pointed out that notions of modesty vary widely at different times and in different places. An Arab woman caught with her veil off will raise her skirts over her head, thereby causing what Europeans would regard as a much more indecent exposure. Chinese women used to think it improper to expose the foot, and Japanese women the nape of the neck. Even among Europeans the parts of the body — especially the female body — which could be exposed without impropriety have varied from age to age.

Another reason which is often given for the wearing of clothes, that human beings clothed themselves as a protection against

Above The costume of medicine-men and shamans reflects the belief that wearing ornaments or clothes made from feathers or skins will transfer the qualities attributed to the bird or animal to the wearer: a North American Indian, wearing wings made from eagle feathers, performs the Eagle Dance to bring prosperity to his tribe

the cold, does not bear examination either. The early civilizations arose in comparatively hot climates, in the valleys of great rivers such as the Nile and the Euphrates. But while the Egyptians wore little or even, in the case of the lower classes, no clothing, the Assyrians and Babylonians were enveloped in layers of fringed shawls. Even today the Arabs in some of the hottest

Even in Europe, the parts of the body, especially the female body, which could be exposed without impropriety have varied from age to age

regions on earth wear voluminous clothing, while the inhabitants of Tierra del Fuego, in South America, where the climate is bitterly cold, wear no clothes in the proper sense of the word. They merely hang from their necks a kind of leather shield which they turn around in accordance with the direction of the wind.

According to yet another theory, clothes were invented as a protection against the bites of insects: this would explain the concentration of clothing around the middle of the body to protect the vulnerable sexual organs. The modern view, however, is that primitive man was not trying to protect his sexual parts from insect bites – although such a subsidiary motive may have existed – but from hostile magic.

Primitive man had a horror of sterility, for a tribe which did not breed doomed itself to extinction. This horror was reinforced by his belief in magic. The 'evil eye' of an enemy could, he believed, rob him of the power of begetting offspring. He therefore sought to to protect his sexual organs either by concealing them or by the more primitive method of hanging near them some kind of fertility amulet. From the earliest times the most potent of such amulets was thought

Priestly clothes in both primitive and advanced societies often show strong feminine elements *Left* **North American Indian priest, painted in 16th century by John White: British Museum** *Right* **Archbishop Albert Gori, Latin Patriarch of Jerusalem**

to be the cowrie shell; specimens have been found all over the world in burial mounds, even many hundred of miles from the sea. This shell was chosen on the magical principle of 'like to like'. To those who believe in it, everything that *resembles* something else *is* that something else, by a kind of mystical affinity. Therefore since the cowrie shell bears a certain resemblance to the female sexual organs, it is believed to have the power of promoting fertility.

In the same way, if a powerful animal such as a bear can be killed and its teeth made into a necklace, then the wearer's own vigour will be reinforced. There were other motives, of course, in wearing such a necklace for, in addition to being an amulet, it was a trophy and a decoration. The history

Modern body-painting *(above)* is a striking throwback to the tattooing or painting of patterns with special magical or social meanings, common in many primitive societies *Right* Brazilian Indian: the pattern painted on his body represents a jaguar, an animal that figures largely in South American mythology

of clothes, apart from their utilitarian and protective qualities, is largely a matter of interaction of these three motives. They are still exemplified in a modern woman wearing a valuable necklace. It is at once a decoration and a proof of her husband's wealth and social status; men having transferred such proofs to their womenfolk.

In any developing civilization the secular and the sacred gradually become separated. Protective magic is more and more left to a specialist: the shaman or medicine-man. Cave paintings of the Ice Age show that such persons were already distinguished from what we would call the laity by their costume. As Lawrence Langner puts it (in *The Importance of Wearing Clothes*), 'The ornaments and clothes of the medicine-man, sorcerer or magician of present-day primitive religions are intended to indicate his special relationship to the spirits or gods and his control or power over them. Thus feathers, horns or antlers, amulets in the form of shells, claws and teeth of animals, and complex systems of painting or tattooing having special magical meanings, and symbols of the totems, form part of the medicine-man's or shaman's stock-in-trade.'

We do not nowadays regard tattooing as 'costume' but to the primitive mind there was not much distinction between them, especially if both shared the same magical purpose. The earliest tattoos of which we have any record are those on the skins of Egyptian mummies, some of which date back to 2000 BC (see TATTOOING).

Why Priests Wear Skirts

Anthropologists have long noted the curious fact that the costume of the shaman or his equivalent in primitive societies has strong feminine elements. Some scholars have suggested that the wizard wears women's clothes because 'he stole them from a witch'. In other words, the first channels of communication with gods or spirits were ecstatic women whose functions were gradually taken over by men. It is remarkable that priestly

Above left Ornaments and masks symbolizing the animals and birds associated with gods and spirits are often worn by primitive peoples during ritual ceremonies: woman of the Umutina tribe in South America wearing a feather head-dress, and necklaces made from the teeth of animals, addresses the souls of the dead which are believed to be incarnated in the animals of the forest *Below left* A member of the Umutina tribe is threatened by assailants made anonymous by enormous straw masks, during the Hatori mask ritual *Above* Because a tribe that does not breed will eventually become extinct, sexual potency is recognized as vital by primitive tribes: tribesman of the Sepik River area of New Guinea

clothes are still 'women's clothes' even in the most advanced of world religions.

A curious paradox in early representations of gods and goddesses is that sometimes they are shown elaborately clothed and sometimes completely naked. The reason would seem to be that sometimes it is desired to protect the *mana* or mysterious spiritual power of the deity in question from too rapid an evaporation. Sometimes, on the other hand, it is desired that the *mana* should flow out freely, as in the case of fertility goddesses. Hence the exposed breasts of the snake goddesses of Crete, or even complete nudity and the exposure of the sexual parts.

In classical Greece participants in sacred rites wore, in general, a longer version of ordinary dress. The Romans did the same

For Glory and Beauty

Part of God's instructions to Moses for making the garment of the high priest:

'And you shall make a plate of pure gold, and engrave on it, like the engraving of a signet, "Holy to the Lord." And you shall fasten it on the turban by a lace of blue; it shall be on the front of the turban. It shall be upon Aaron's forehead, and Aaron shall take upon himself any guilt incurred in the holy offering which the people of Israel hallow as their holy gifts; it shall always be upon his forehead, that they may be accepted before the Lord.

'And you shall weave the coat in chequer work of fine linen, and you shall make a turban of fine linen, and shall make a girdle embroidered with needlework.

'And for Aaron's sons you shall make coats and girdles and caps; you shall make them for glory and beauty. And you shall put them upon Aaron your brother, and upon his sons with him, and shall anoint them and ordain them and consecrate them, that they may serve me as priests. And you shall make for them linen breeches to cover their naked flesh; from the loins to the thighs they shall reach; and they shall be upon Aaron and upon his sons, when they go into the tent of meeting, or when they come near the altar to minister in the holy place . . .'

Exodus, chapter 28

with the difference that while the Greeks sacrificed bare-headed, the Romans always covered the head with a fold of the toga. The vestal virgins wore a white robe with a border which could be drawn over the head and fastened under the chin. The priests of some cults wore the high conical bonnet called a *tutulus*.

We have no pictorial representations of the religious garb of the Jews, owing to their horror of 'graven images', but there is an elaborate description of the high priest's vestments which Moses was instructed to make for Aaron (Exodus, chapter 28).

There is some difficulty in distinguishing between priestly vestments and royal robes. In the early days of monarchy, the king was a priest-king. Even when the two functions separated, the priestly character of the king's office persisted, even if only vestigially, in his ceremonial robes. Certain ecclesiastical garments are assumed to this day by the English monarch at a coronation, and in earlier times the resemblances were much more obvious.

When Constantine, the first Christian emperor, moved his capital from Rome to Constantinople he abandoned the austerity of his predecessors and clothed himself in oriental splendour, wearing a robe of gold tissue embroidered with flowers. Byzantine costume reached the height of its splendour in the 6th century, as can be seen in the splendid mosaics in the Church of San Vitale in Ravenna. In these it is impossible not to be struck by the ecclesiastical look of the imperial costume. The emperor was indeed a priest-king, the Viceroy of Christ on Earth, and if he did not actually say Mass he scattered incense on the altar and presided over Councils.

The vestments of the Roman Catholic Church followed a somewhat different line of evolution, their starting-point being sometimes purely utilitarian. The maniple, for instance, was a simple strip of linen worn over the arm and used, in the hot climate of Italy, to wipe the brow of the officiant. It later became more elaborate and was invested with all kinds of symbolic meanings. The same might be said of the cope, the chasuble, the stole, the cincture, and the dalmatic, a wide-sleeved, long loose robe slit at the sides. All these garments were originally worn by all persons above a certain social level but, from the 5th century onward, clerical garments became more and more different from the costume of the laity.

Frock-Coat and Top Hat

Liturgical costume — as opposed to the everyday dress of priests and monks — had become almost entirely stereotyped by the end of the 12th century. The only important modification was in the form of the mitre which began to be worn with the two peaks back and front instead of sideways and gradually increased in size. During the last two centuries of the medieval period, the Church grew richer and richer, and even the ordinary dress of the higher clergy reflected this affluence. For religious ceremonies, elaborate vestments, glittering with gold, jewels and embroidery were worn. Then, in the 16th century came the Reformation, one aspect of which was a deliberate attempt to return to the simplicity of the primitive Church.

With most of the Reformers this meant an abandonment of vestments altogether. The Mass was abolished or reduced to a communion service requiring no special garments. Preaching became the most important part of worship, and the Calvinist preachers wore for the purpose what was known as the 'Geneva gown'. This was simply the professional dress of the day, such as worn by doctors, lawyers and academic persons, and, like their costume, was black. In the pulpit ministers continued to wear a gown, usually of academic origin. For ordinary wear the cassock persisted until the 18th century, one of the last Anglican clergymen to wear it being John Wesley. By the end of this century the costume of a clergyman was no different from that of any gentleman, except, of course, that it was invariably black.

The Anglo-Catholic movement of the mid-19th century brought back the use of vestments for the service of the altar, but in ordinary life most clergymen wore the frock-coat and top hat of their lay contemporaries. Their neckwear, however, was white, but varied in form from the 'Pusey collar' of the High Churchman to the white tie of the Evangelical. Up to the early years of the 20th century it was often possible to tell a clergyman's religious convictions at a glance by this exterior sign.

It is only within recent years that psychologists and anthropologists have begun to give serious attention to the

British Travel Association

Above The wigs and impressive robes worn by judges and other members of the legal profession in Britain do much to emphasize the majesty of the law
Right Stylized flowers, symbols of fertility, and elephants, one of the most powerful of animals, form a pattern on the brightly coloured fabrics worn by masked Nigerian dancers

basic meaning and derivation of religious dress. Some of its elements undoubtedly go back to very primitive times, and have a significance which would horrify their pious wearers today. It has been suggested, for example, that the mitre is ultimately derived from the open-mouthed fish's head worn by the priests of Dagon. The form of the chasuble with the hole in the middle has been thought to have had, originally, a phallic significance, since all primitive religions were heavily concerned with fertility.

This may be speculation, but what seems certain is that religions which have retained a magical element have also retained their gorgeous and symbolic vestments. Those that have become, or are in process of becoming, ethical societies and social service organizations, have shed their splendour and conduct their services in ordinary dress. Some clergymen even decline to wear the clerical collar or any kind of distinctive dress on the grounds that it imposes a barrier between themselves and the laity. The magical apparatus of the medicine-man has thus been completely laid aside. (See also HEAD-DRESS.)

JAMES LAVER

FURTHER READING: R. H. Kemper, *Costume* (Newsweek, 1978); L. A. Liddell, *Clothes and Your Appearance* (Goodheart, 1981).

Camera Press London

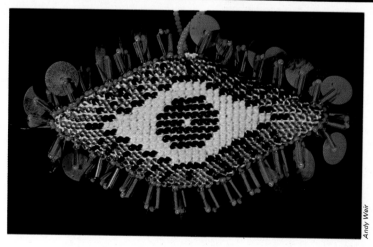

Andy Weir

Counter-Charm

A spell intended to counteract hostile magic: examples are the gesture of defence against the Evil Eye, making the sign of the cross for protection against evil, or the hex signs, still seen on farmers' barns in the United States, which traditionally keep witches at bay.

529

The gentle cow plays an important part in mythology and nowhere more than in India, where in recent times she has become the symbol of the Indian nation

COW

THE COW FOR CENTURIES has been looked upon as a tangible symbol of life and fertility by nomadic and pastoral peoples, who depend on this uncomplaining beast for nourishment and prosperity. In mythology the cow has come to be associated in particular with the divine givers of life, the mother goddesses, either of the sky or of the earth.

In ancient Egypt the goddess Hathor, mother of the sun god, was frequently represented either as a cow, or as having a human face, with cow's horns and ears. It was believed that every night she engulfed the sun god, only to give birth to him afresh every morning. Similarly Nut, another Egyptian sky goddess, was depicted as a cow, supported by the other gods, and with the stars on her underbelly.

In many ancient religions, however, the cow as a source of fecundity took second place as an object of worship to the bull as a source of generative power. The male symbol thus took precedence over the female. This is true of ancient Near Eastern religion generally. In Greece and Crete, too, the bull-cult of Minoan-Mycenean religion was far more important than any corresponding veneration of the cow, though in some traditions the sky god Zeus was said to have been nursed by a cow. His consort, Hera, is described by Homer as *boopis*, 'cow-eyed'.

This idea of divine nourishment is also to be found in ancient Scandinavian mythology. Snorri's *Edda* tells of the primeval giant, Ymir, who was nourished by four rivers of milk from a cow. The beast, Audumulla, was herself created out of condensing frost. Being thirsty, she licked the blocks of salty ice around her and as the ice melted under her warm tongue, the head and then the body of a man appeared. This was Buri, grandfather of Odin, greatest of the gods.

Accept the Cow

It is in India and in Hinduism that the cow plays the most striking role, both in mythology and in the day-to-day practice of religion. In practice, Indian cow-worship is restricted to one species of the animal, the East Indian humped zebu. The roots of this worship are certainly Indo-European, and have much in common with features already mentioned. The cow is thought of as a symbol of the divine bounty of the earth, and as the 'mother' of gods and men. The high god Varuna is called 'son of Aditi' in the oldest of the four chief Hindu collections of prayers and hymns, the *Rig Veda*, while the goddess Aditi is called 'the Cow, the sinless'.

The myth of the earth taking the form of a cow receives its first detailed expression in the *Vishnu Purana*, an ancient Sanskrit collection of legendary lore. In this, Prithu, the monarch of all, approached the earth in order to make her yield plants. The earth assumed the form of a cow and ran away, but was finally caught and persuaded to nourish the earth with her milk. Then Prithu milked the earth into his own hand, and there grew up all manner of corn and vegetables for man's food.

Although there was no express prohibition of cow-killing or the eating of beef in early Indian history, by the time of the great epic, the *Mahabharata*, of the 3rd century BC, it was stated categorically that the killing of a cow was the greatest of all crimes: 'All that kill, eat, and permit the slaughter of cows, rot in hell for as many years as there are hairs on the body of a cow so slain.' The *Laws of Manu*, the greatest of the Hindu codes of law, are less extreme. They lay down that slaying cows is a 'minor offence'. Provided the killer lives in a cow-house, bathes in urine, and follows the cows all day, standing when they stand and sitting when they lie down, he may expiate his crime in three months. It may also be noted that Zoroastrianism knew of similar prohibitions: Ahura Mazdah is the lord of all cattle, and therefore 'all robbery and violence against the (sacred) Kine' is forbidden.

The cow, by reason of her sacredness, is also a practical means towards the expiation of other sins. Again according to *Manu*: 'He who unhesitatingly abandons life for the

The Egyptian goddess Hathor, mother of the sun god and guardian of the dead, was often represented as a cow: statue of Hathor protecting the Pharaoh Psammetichus II

Brahmanas (the priestly caste) or cows, is freed from the guilt of the murder of a Brahmana, and so is he who saves the life of a cow, or of a Brahmana.' Similarly, he who has committed a mortal sin can be purified by attending cows for over a year. On a somewhat different level, a birth at an inauspicious time can be remedied by passing the infant beneath the body of a cow – thus bringing about a symbolic rebirth from the source of holiness.

Death Clutching a Cow's Tail

Not only the cow itself, but also its products, are powerful sacred instruments in Hinduism. They are especially effective in purifying a person from the stain of sin. There are five of these products: milk, curds, clarified butter, dung and urine; none must be wasted. All were important in the sacrificial rituals of early Hinduism, and have increased in significance down the ages.

Of the many reasons for the tenacity of the cow-cult within Hinduism, special mention must be made of the association of Krishna, the most popular of Hindu gods, with the cow. A legend told of Krishna's youth depicts him as a cowherd, devoted to their care, and yet dallying with the maidens who shared his responsibilities. Their devotion to him is a pattern of human devotion to God; but the setting, amid the cows, is also significant. Cow-worship was further strengthened in opposition to the Moslem invaders who had no compunction about the slaughtering of cattle. Again, it received fresh impetus with the development of the doctrine of *ahimsa* (harmlessness), with its implicit reverence for all forms of life, animal as well as human. A more modern development has been the symbolical identification of the cow with India as a nation – a localization of the original identification of the cow with the earth.

At present, the cow plays a variety of roles in the religious life of Hindu India. In some Hindu temples, a cow is brought in every morning, placed with her back to the image

'All that kill, eat, and permit the slaughter of, cows, rot in hell for as many years as there are hairs on the body of a cow so slain', according to the *Mahabharata*, written in the 3rd century BC: even today in India the cow is a sacred animal, and its protection was described by Gandhi as being Hinduism's gift to the world

of deity and solemnly milked. In Hindu rituals generally, every part of the cow – as well as the five products mentioned earlier – has significance.

At an annual festival, the Gopastami (cow holiday), women attend an adorned cow, placed in the temple courtyard. They move round it four times, each time pouring water on the tail from a jug, and then lifting the tail to their eyes and head. Finally each woman kisses the cow, whispering, 'Truth belongs to you, and it is our duty to keep our promises.'

It is widely believed among Hindus that the cow is able to act as a pathfinder in the world beyond the grave, and that it is highly auspicious to be able to die clutching a cow's tail. For the lower castes, often forbidden

direct access to temples, a cow-shed has come to fill the function of a temple in their daily lives.

The protection of cows in India because of their sacredness has led, ironically, to the neglect of their welfare, partly because controlled breeding and the exercise of ownership and restraint is virtually impossible. The traditional Hindu attitude, however, is summed up in Gandhi's well-known words: '"Cow Protection" to me is one of the most wonderful phenomena in all human evolution; for it takes the human being beyond his species . . . Man through the cow is enjoined to realize his identity with all that lives . . . "Cow Protection" is the gift of Hinduism to the world; and Hinduism will live as long as there are Hindus to protect the cow.'

Richard & Sally Greenhill

Coyote

Major Trickster figure in myths of Plains Indians and other tribes, including Californian; sometimes described as taking human form in a mythic past when animals lived like men; a creator and a central culture hero, he appears in many origin myths, teaching basic skills, bringing fire and so on, but his dual nature also places him in tales of entertainment where he appears mischievous, violent, erotic or merely foolish.
See TRICKSTER.

Michael Holford

Crab

Sometimes a symbol of the union of opposites, because it is at home both on land and in the water: in the Tarot card called the Moon a crab crawls up onto land from a pool, a symbol of the depths of the mind revealing themselves: in some of the Pacific islands crabs are gods, or the shadows or messengers of gods: the fourth sign of the zodiac is Cancer, the Crab.
See CANCER.

CRANE

CRANES FLYING IN LARGE, clamorous flocks attracted much attention in ancient times. The Greeks noted that the cranes travel in a wedge formation, which reminded them of the triangular shape of their letter D (△); and so a connection arose between cranes and the alphabet.

There was also a mythological or symbolic association between cranes and trees. On a Celtic altar of the 1st century AD, found in Paris, the god Tarvos Trigaranus is shown felling a willow tree in company with three cranes and a bull. In Eastern symbolism the crane and the pine tree, signifying long life, are often depicted together. In Irish legends there are indications that the crane was once regarded as having supernatural qualities. St Columba, who was called 'crane cleric' was said to have turned some women into cranes. In the West the lofty 'alphabetical' flight of the birds connected them with Apollo, the god of sun and poetry, and with Hermes, the patron of communications. But the association between long-necked birds and the sun is very ancient. Such birds appear frequently as a design on early pottery in the Middle East and it seems that not only cranes but other long-necked birds such as geese, egrets and even flamingoes were associated with the sun.

The migrations of cranes and geese have been connected with the coming of spring, and with increasing warmth and fertility, since time out of mind. Even today, when the numbers of cranes breeding in Europe are much reduced, the migrating flocks arouse excitement as they pass noisily overhead.

As happened not infrequently in the bird lore of antiquity, accurate observation merged into myth. Aristotle noted that cranes when sleeping stand first on one leg, then on the other. Aelian, the Roman writer of the 3rd century AD, improved on this; he stated that they posted sentinels and that these birds held a stone in the raised foot to help themselves to stay awake. Horapollo, a Greek grammarian living in the 4th century AD, referred to the crane as a symbol of vigilance. Thus the stone-grasping belief is probably an addition to much earlier tradition, based on the fact that the crane is indeed a wary bird.

Dancers Entombed Alive

During the mating season, cranes perform an elaborate and impressive type of dance, and this was interpreted by some ancient peoples as a form of magical ceremonial. The crane's curious movements during its 'dance' were imitated in human dances in Crete, China and elsewhere. Describing

The complicated and impressive dance performed by cranes during their mating season was at one time believed to be a magic ritual, and its movements were imitated in human dances: the sinister climax to an ancient Chinese crane dance was the burying alive of the dancers. Chinese watercolour in the Victoria and Albert Museum

the courtship display of the American whooping crane, now a rare species, Margaret Rawlings wrote (in *The Yearling*): 'The cranes were dancing a cotillion . . . two stood apart, erect and white, making a strange music that was part cry and part singing. The rhythm was irregular like the dance. The other birds were in a circle. In the heart of the circle, several moved counter-clockwise . . . The outer circle shuffled around and around. The group in the centre attained a slow frenzy . . .' A crane dance was performed by human dancers in ancient Crete in connection with the labyrinth, the home of the Minotaur. The lay-out was circular and apparently the performance was enacted on an arena of swastika pattern. The circle and the swastika are both symbols of the sun so we may assume that the dance was a solar ritual, which is in agreement with evidence that the crane was a bird of the sun.

In ancient times crane dances were also performed in China. According to historical records Ho-lu, king of the ancient kingdom of Wu in the Yangtze Valley, offered his daughter a fish of which he had already eaten a portion, thereby breaking a taboo. She committed suicide, whereupon the king in order to propitiate her spirit and avert evil, sacrificed dancers by burying them alive. He constructed a magnificent tomb, furnished with objects of priceless value, for her remains. An underground passage led to the sepulchral chamber. The dance of the white cranes was enacted in the market-place of the capital. The crowd was ordered to follow the funeral cortege and boys and girls were instructed to enter the passage following the crane dancers. Then a machine was set in motion to close the passage and bury the dancers alive.

In the Far East crane dancers were associated with a group of ideas – thunder, rain, fertility and reincarnation. In Chinese records it is stated that black cranes and demons danced during times of drought. A picture of a crane is placed on the catafalque when coffins are carried to the grave in parts of China; a crane fashioned from paper is sometimes harnessed to the sedan chair containing an image of the deceased. Such a paper crane may be suspended from the window of the dead man's house during Taoist funeral ceremonies. The patriarch of Taoism, Lao-tze, is shown wearing a red robe embroidered with white cranes and riding a one-horned monster, not unlike a water buffalo. Thus in China, as in Crete and Gaul, there is an association between a supernatural being, a horned beast and the crane.

The crane figures in a number of fables. The story of a war between cranes and pygmies goes back to Homer's reference in the *Iliad* and is mentioned, among others, by Aristotle and, in English literature, by Milton. It was constantly repeated by Greek and Latin writers. It even travelled to India, where a tradition became current that dwarfs fought the monstrous mythical eagle of Hindu mythology, Garuda.

FURTHER READING: W. Harter, *Birds: In Fact and Legend* (Sterling, 1979).

Michael Holford

CREATION MYTHS

The phenomenon of birth, and artistic creativity, lie behind many of the world's myths of how the world began; this article deals with the creation myths of the ancient world, including the stories in the early chapters of Genesis

THE CREATION OF THE WORLD and the origin of mankind are the themes of many myths. They are found among the primitive peoples of most lands and they can be traced back into remote antiquity. Creation myths are of two kinds: aetiological myths which concern the beginnings of things, and stem from primitive speculation about their origins; and ritual myths, which were essentially connected with various periodic ceremonies, particularly at the New Year, designed to ensure the continuation and well-being of the state or even of the world.

It is interesting to consider how the idea that the world had a beginning or had been created arose in the first place. Although the idea is a familiar one to us, it is not self-evident. The earliest members of our race obviously could not have witnessed the creation of the world – indeed, to them in their brief lives, their physical environment must have seemed eternal, supposing that their minds were sufficiently developed to have reflected on the fact. However, two factors in the experience of the Paleolithic peoples doubtless gave them some idea both of the beginning of life and of creativity. The remains of Paleolithic culture reveal a great concern with the phenomenon of birth, both of humans and animals. The emergence of the child from the womb of its mother must surely have been a most impressive demonstration of the beginning of a new creature, whether human or animal. The earliest creation myths, indeed, instinctively used the imagery of biological birth.

The idea of creativity can also be traced back to the Paleolithic era. As the evidence of their art shows, the Paleolithic peoples must have been aware of the mysterious power of creation when they drew the image of an animal on the blank wall of a cave, or fashioned a piece of stone into the figure of a woman. When pottery was invented in Neolithic times, further stimulus was given to the conception of creativity. In several myths the creator-god is imagined as a divine potter who fashions men out of clay.

It is accordingly not surprising that in the earliest written cosmogonies, or creation myths, we find a mixture of thought and imagery about the beginnings of things which derives both from the new needs of civilized society, and from the cruder concepts of the pre-literary past. Egypt and Sumer provide our earliest examples of creation myths, the texts concerned dating in each instance from about the middle of the 3rd millennium BC.

Birth of the Earth and Sky

The earliest evidence of ancient Egyptian thought about the beginnings of things occurs incidentally in the Pyramid Texts. The fact is significant, because these texts are not concerned with the creation of the world but with the destiny after death of the kings of Egypt (see BOOK OF THE DEAD). The priests of Heliopolis, who composed the texts about 2480–2137 BC, drew upon traditions about their god Atum, whose temple at Heliopolis was one of the oldest cult-centres in the land. Atum was a mysterious deity, whose name could mean 'the not-yet-Completed One, who will attain (completion)'. He was identified with the sun god Re, under the composite title of Atum-Re. Various passages in the Pyramid Texts reveal that the priests of Heliopolis believed that originally there had been only a primordial waste of water, without shape or order, called Nun. The 'first time' started when Atum emerged from this primeval deep and began the work of creation. In order to begin this work, Atum needed a firm place on which to stand, and reference is made in the texts to a primeval hill which also emerged with Atum out of Nun. This primeval hill was identified with the site of Atum's temple at Heliopolis, thus making it the most ancient and sacred place in Egypt, since it was there that the creation of the world began.

God created the world in six days, according to the book of Genesis, and rested on the seventh day. Section of an initial letter in a 13th century illuminated manuscript in the British Museum, showing, from top to bottom, the acts of God on the seven days of Creation: the separation of light from darkness; the creation of Heaven; and of the Earth, the seas and vegetation; the stars, moon and sun; birds and creatures of the sea; animals and 'everything that creeps upon the ground', man and woman. On the seventh day God rested

Creation Myths

The sky goddess Nut and her brother Geb, the earth god, were originally locked in a close embrace according to Egyptian belief; their separation, by Shu the personification of air, gave the universe its shape: scene from the papyrus of Tamenill (c 1000 BC) in the British Museum, showing Nut, her body forming the vault of heaven, arched over her brother the earth

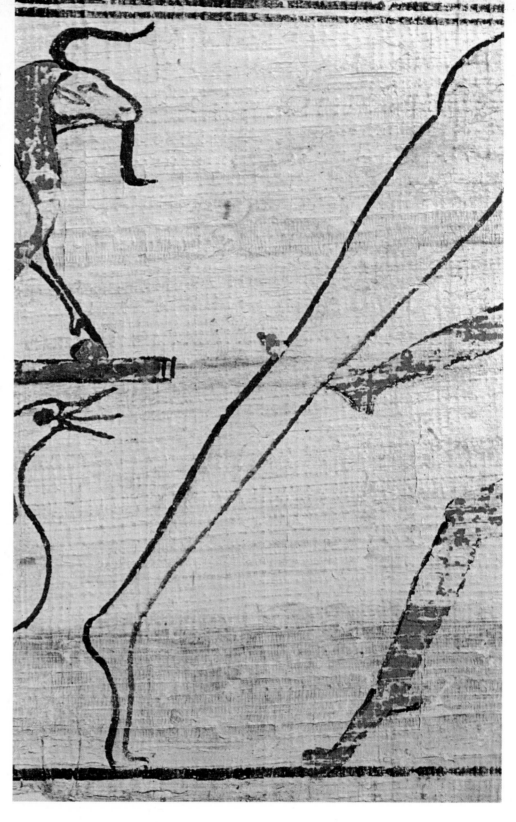

The idea of a waste of waters existing from the beginning, called Nun, from which the first land emerged, doubtless reflects the conditions of the Nile Valley. Each year the Egyptians witnessed the inundation of their land by the mysterious rising of the river Nile; then, as the flood subsided, the higher points of land began to emerge from the water. Beyond the delta of the Nile lay the Mediterranean Sea, the 'Great Green', which seemed a limitless expanse of water. Hence came the imagery of Nun and of the primeval hill.

Having conceived of the emergence of their god Atum, the priests of Heliopolis had next to imagine how he could have created the universe. Since they instinctively thought in terms of biological generation, they were, consequently, faced with the problem of accounting for the process of creation from a sole male deity. Their solution was crudely primitive. According to one passage in the Pyramid Texts, Atum produced two deities, Shu and Tefnut, by masturbation; in another passage, by spitting. These deities were, respectively, personifications of air and moisture.

Since Shu and Tefnut were male and female, the next stage in cosmic creation could be described as an action of procreation. From the union of Shu and Tefnut were born Geb, 'earth', and Nut, 'sky'. In later Egyptian art, Shu, as the personification of air, is represented as lifting up the sky goddess Nut from the recumbent body of the earth god Geb. Evidently the earth and sky were imagined as being at first in close embrace, and thus had to be separated in order to give the universe its shape. In art Nut is generally depicted as a gigantic woman, whose body over-arches the earth. The sun, moon and stars are shown as passing over her body, which forms the vault of heaven. It is interesting to note that Egyptian cosmogony differs from most other cosmogonies in making the earth male and the sky female.

The Heliopolitan priests, having thus accounted for the four chief constituents of the cosmic universe, namely air and moisture, earth and sky, did not go on to describe the origin of vegetation, animals or mankind. Instead, they told how from the union of Geb and Nut were born two pairs of deities: Osiris and Isis, Set and Nephthys. This fact significantly reveals the real motive behind their myth of creation. The four deities mentioned were ancient and important deities who originated from other parts of Egypt. By making these deities the great-grandchildren of Atum, the Heliopolitan priests asserted the precedence of their own god. In other words, this earliest example of a creation myth was designed to exalt Atum as the supreme creator, to whom other gods owed their existence, and his temple at Heliopolis as the most ancient and holy place in the Egyptian world.

The Cosmic Egg
This Heliopolitan cosmogony seems to have provided a stimulus to the priesthoods of other great temples in Egypt. At Memphis, as we learn from the famous Shabaka Stone, now in the British Museum, the priests of the local god Ptah neatly rebutted the claims of Heliopolis by claiming that Ptah was the original creator and that he used Atum as his agent. This Memphite cosmogony is more sophisticated in its imagery, and Ptah is represented as creating by the power of his magical word.

Hermopolis in Upper Egypt was distinguished by the peculiar form of its creation story. There, it was related, eight original beings, represented as frogs or serpents, deposited on an island an egg, out of which the sun god emerged to begin the work of creation. According to the tomb-inscription of a priest of Hermopolis in the 3rd century BC, pilgrims were still being shown the shell of this cosmic egg.

When Thebes became the political capital, about 1580 BC, and its god Amun the chief state god of Egypt, the priests composed a cosmogony which represented Amun as a life-giving wind moving over the inert waters of Nun; this initiated the process of cosmic creation. Thebes, too, claimed to be the first of cities – 'the water and the land were in her at the First Time'. Other temples each had its creation myth, notable examples being those of Esna and Edfu.

One remarkable feature of the ancient Egyptian creation myths is that they show no concern to explain the origin of mankind. They are literally 'cosmogonies', in that they deal with the beginning of the 'cosmos' or world and the relations of the

gods. There are passing references to the creation of men in various other texts; but the Egyptians were not so much concerned with the origin and purpose of the human race as were the Mesopotamians and Hebrews. There is evidence, however, of the manner in which the Egyptians believed that human beings were created, as for example in a bas-relief commemorating the birth of the pharaoh Amenhotep III (1405–1370 BC) at Luxor. In this the ram-headed fertility god Khnum is depicted as fashioning the infant king and his *ka* or double on a potter's wheel, while the goddess Hathor endows them with life. According to a text of the 7th century BC, 'man is clay and straw'.

In the creation myths of ancient Sumer

attention was focused more upon the beginnings of civilization and mankind than on the origin of the world. The goddess Nammu, the personification of the sea, is called 'the mother, the ancestress, who gave birth to all the gods'. But it is Enki, the god associated with the fresh waters, who figures most as the creator in the early Sumerian texts. He is depicted as arriving by sea in Sumer, in a kind of golden age at the dawn of time, and impregnating Ninhursag, 'the mother of the land'. Enki's fertilizing activity produces the plants necessary for food. He also invents the pickaxe and brick mould, the two essential implements of Mesopotamian economy.

In one notable Sumerian myth the creation of mankind is described. To relieve the

'So God created man in his own image, in the image of God he created him' *Left* 16th century tapestry in the Accademia del' Arte, Florence, depicting the sixth day of creation *Below left* Adam and Eve, tempted by the serpent in the garden of Eden: 15th century painting by Hugo van der Goes
Facing page The first living being of Scandinavian mythology was the giant Ymir, born from melting ice and nourished by the cow Audumulla who came from the same source. While licking the blocks of ice in order to obtain salt for herself, Audumulla released the bodies of Buri and his son Bor, the first men. After Ymir's death his body became land, his blood the seas and his skull the heavens: painting of Ymir and Audumulla from the Statens Museum fur Kunst, Copenhagen

gods from the toil of providing their own food, Enki causes human beings to be fashioned out of clay to act as servants of the gods. At a feast given by the gods to celebrate the creation of their new servants, the goddess Ninmah challenges Enki to deal with two freaks which she has made. These freaks are a eunuch and a barren woman. Enki adroitly finds a place for them in the Mesopotamian social system. He then challenges Ninmah to find a purpose for the two freaks which he himself has made, a diseased and an aged man. Ninmah can do nothing with them, and she curses Enki because what he has made cannot be unmade. This addition to the myth of the creation of mankind is significant; for it reveals that the Sumerians were concerned with the problems of disease and old age, and that they attributed these ills to the sport of the gods.

The most famous of the Mesopotamian creation myths is the Babylonian *Enuma elish*. This cosmogony is similar in motive to the Egyptian cosmogonies, in that it was designed to exalt the god of Babylon, Marduk. This deity was not reckoned among the most ancient of the gods of Mesopotamia; in fact, he was regarded as the son of Enki. But when Babylon rose to political supremacy, it was evidently felt by the Babylonian priests that the status of their god had to be raised.

This was done in the *Enuma elish* by telling how Marduk became the leader of the gods and the creator of the world. A primordial chaos is described, when there existed only Tiamat, the personification of the sea, and Apsu, who personified the fresh waters. From the mingling of these two entities the first generation of the gods was born, among whom was Enki, who slew Apsu. Tiamat, imagined as a great monster, sought to avenge Apsu by destroying the gods. Her horrific appearance, and the monsters she creates to aid her, so terrify the older gods that they readily accept the offer of the younger god Marduk to save them on condition that his supremacy is recognized. Marduk meets Tiamat in battle and kills her. He then slices up her body and fashions the universe from it. From the blood of Kingu, leader of Tiamat's monstrous host, Marduk makes mankind to serve the gods. The poem ends with an account of how the gods, in gratitude, build

The Babylonian god Marduk killed Tiamat, personification of the sea ... he fashioned the universe from her body; and from the blood of the leader of her monstrous host he made mankind to serve the gods

Ole Woldbye

for Marduk his great temple at Babylon.

The Hebrew creation myths, though later in date than the Egyptian and Mesopotamian, are better known and have exercised a profound influence upon Western thought and culture. They are contained in the first three chapters of the Book of Genesis. Although these chapters in their present form have the appearance of a continuous narrative, careful analysis of the text reveals two distinctive cosmogonies.

Be Fruitful and Multiply

The first (Genesis, 1. 1 to 2. 4a) contains an account of the creation of the world in six days, the creation of mankind being the last episode. Scholars generally agree that this cosmogony dates from the 5th century BC, and represents what is known as the Priestly tradition. This account of creation reveals traces of Mesopotamian influence, particularly in the picture of the original watery chaos: 'And the earth was waste and void; and darkness was upon the face of the deep.' The Hebrew word *tehom* 'deep' is akin to the Babylonian Tiamat. What is especially notable about this Priestly cosmogony is that God does not create the world out of nothing, as later theologians maintained; a watery chaos existed before God's acts of creation. Mankind is represented as being created 'in the image of God' and commanded to 'be fruitful, and multiply, and replenish the earth, and subdue it'. God finishes his work of creation in six days and rests on the

seventh, thus providing, according to the Priestly writer, the divine example and authority for the Sabbath.

The other Hebrew creation myth (which starts at Genesis 2. 4b) is recognized by scholars as an older tradition. They designate it the 'Yahwist' tradition, dating it about 900–750 BC. This version does not deal with the creation of the world but concentrates on the creation of mankind, which precedes the creation of the animals, contrary to the Priestly account. God (who is here given his characteristic Hebrew name of Yahweh) fashions Adam out of the earth (*adamah*) as the Egyptian god Khnum and the Mesopotamian deities made men out of clay. Having animated Adam with the 'breath of life', Yahweh places him in the

537

British Museum

garden of Eden, imagined as a kind of oasis. In the narrative that follows, the Yahwist writer was primarily concerned to show how mankind became subject to death through Adam's original act of disobedience to his divine creator. This episode involves the mysterious 'Tree of the Knowledge of Good and Evil' and the 'Tree of Life'. The writer's second motive, to account for the beginning of things, also finds expression in these chapters. He explains the origin of the names of animals, the creation of woman, the wearing of clothes, why the serpent 'goes upon his belly', the origin of the pain of childbirth and the toil of agriculture.

Egypt, Mesopotamia and Israel provide the earliest and most striking creation myths of the ancient world. Fragments of such myths have been found among Hittite records, and they seem to have exercised some influence on Greek mythology. In ancient Greece, however, there was no established tradition of creation myths. Certain vague references in Homer suggest some belief that Oceanus was the source of life. The Greek writer Hesiod devoted a whole work, the *Theogony*, to explaining the beginnings of things; but the composition is a strange mixture of mythical imagery and primitive rationalization. Traces of creation myths are found in other Greek writings. But the naturalistic explanations of the origin of the world advanced by the early Greek philosophers are, doubtless, more characteristic of the Greek mind here; and it is significant that Zeus was not

Above Tloque Nahuaque, the god-above-all of the Mixtecs in Central America, and the original giver of all life including his own: illustration from the Codex Zouche-Nuttal *Below* Daylight is created as the morning star is wafted into the heavens by the east wind: Australian bark painting

Axel Poignant

regarded as the creator of the world.

The earliest forms of Iranian cosmogony are difficult to determine. Under the influence of Zoroastrianism a cosmogony recognizing two independent principles was later formulated, in which Ahura Mazdah was responsible for the good aspects of creation, and Ahriman for the evil (see AHRIMAN). Ancient Indian literature contains brief references to speculation about creation but no mythological tradition concerning the origin of the world. China also produced no established creation myth; the alternating cosmic forces of *yin* and *yang* characterize Chinese cosmogony (see CHINA).

In the myths of more primitive peoples, tales of the origin of life on earth often seem to take precedence over cosmogonies. Among American Indians, only tribes of the south-west, and some in California, have true creation myths – on the lines of the Zuni myth of the god-being Awonawilona, who existed before 'the Beginning', and who created Sky and Earth from whom all life came. Otherwise, Indian accounts of the origin of things concern, for instance, some culture hero like the Earth Diver bringing up sand from some primal sea, and making the earth out of that sand – not as a creation from chaos or nothingness.
(See also FIRST MAN.)

S. G. F. BRANDON

FURTHER READING: S. G. F. Brandon, *Creation Legends of the Ancient Near East* (Verry, Lawrence, 1963) with full bibliographies.

¶ *Then ſhall be ſaid or ſung the Apoſtles Creed by the Miniſter, and the People, ſtanding.*

I Believe in God the Father Almighty, Maker of Heaven and Earth :

Creed

A system of belief: in Christianity, a statement of the principal Christian doctrines; the creed recited during Mattins and Evensong in Anglican and Roman Catholic churches is the Apostles' Creed, dating from the 3rd century or earlier; the creed recited during the Communion service is the Nicene Creed, dating from the 4th century and containing formulae directed against the Arian heresy.

A notable 19th century advocate of cremation was an eccentric doctor who cremated his own son, at the risk of being arrested. The rapid increase in cremation over the last century is largely due to the efforts of a few individuals

CREMATION

IN MODERN BRITAIN, more people are cremated than are buried. In America, high pressure funeral salesmanship combines with organized religion to keep the figures down; still, cremation is growing more popular every year, so that now in California and other Pacific states one out of five dead bodies is cremated. Yet it is less than a century ago that cremation became legal. A long and heated battle for the right to dispose of the dead by burning was waged from early in the 19th century until the practice gained official sanction when England's Cremation Act was passed in 1902.

The earliest way of disposing of the dead was by burial. Cremation was very rare until the appearance of agricultural peasant-village communities from about 8,000 years ago. These communities spread through Europe from the 4th millennium BC, and while they mainly disposed of their dead by burial, cremation occurred as a variant rite. Thus in the long barrows of England and the chambered megalithic passage graves of Ireland and Brittany cremation took place, though not as the principal burial custom.

In the 2nd millennium BC in Europe cremation became more and more common, and from the 15th century BC was the main method of disposing of the dead. In Britain, cremation had completely displaced burial by the Middle Bronze Age and the dead throughout much of Europe were interred cremated in Urnfields, or cremation cemeteries, by the Late Bronze Age. Previously, cremated remains in bags or urns had been put in barrows. The prehistoric Iron Age saw mixed rites of burial and cremation. It seems clear that the change from burial to cremation in the 2nd millennium was one which took place within society and did not involve the incursion of new people.

Burning on the funeral pyre was the custom in Rome from the end of the Republic in the 1st century BC to the end of the 4th century AD. In Hindu India, cremation has always been widely practised and the burning ghats are a feature of many Indian cities today. Here the dead, not in coffins, are burned in public on funeral pyres. In the past, it was the custom for a widow to jump on to her husband's funeral pyre and be consumed by the same flames that burnt his body. This custom was made illegal in India in the 19th century under British administration but one still hears of isolated cases of such suicides by widows on the funeral pyre (see SUTTEE).

In some societies there have been objections to cremation because burning the dead was thought to be polluting the sacred principle of fire. This was not the objection of Christianity. The Christian religion

In many cultures burning the body of a dead hero or warrior was thought to be a fitting and spectacular way of speeding him on his journey to the otherworld, a romantic belief that retained its appeal even when cremation was rejected by the Christian church: illustration from a 16th century manuscript

objected to burning the dead because it seemed to violate and invalidate the doctrine of the resurrection of the body. In Christian countries cremation was forbidden for centuries although in the 19th century even clergymen advocated it.

Support from Science

The main defence of cremation in Europe came from people horrified by the insanitary conditions caused in towns by the custom of burial. The problems caused by drainage from churchyards and cemeteries and the waste of land in and around towns and villages were set out in a book by Edwin Chadwick, *A Special Inquiry into the Practice of Interment in Towns*, published in 1843. In the second half of the 19th century many physicians and chemists, especially in Italy and Switzerland, recommended the adoption of cremation. A congress at Milan in 1874 petitioned the Chamber of Deputies for a clause permitting cremation. In the same year the Cremation Society of England was founded to promote the practice of cremation. 'We disapprove

British Museum

"A weleisty Dominus Fortis—?
Darogan dwin Dominus?
Budyant Uffern?
Hic nemor i por progenii?
Ef a dilhyngys ei thwrf—
Dominus Virtictum!
Kaeth nawt kyn hulhwys, estis, iste—est,
(Est) *o chyn*, buasswn, as im sei.
Rwyf derwin, y Duw diheu!
A chyn mynnwyf derfyn creu,
A chyn del, ewyn friw, ar vyggenen,
A chyn vyg kyf alle, ar y latheu pren,
Poet ym heneit yd a kyfadeu.
Abreid, om dyweit, ilythyr llyfreu,
Kystud dygyn, gwedy, gwely agheu,
Ar sawl a gigleu vy mardh Lyfreu,
Ky bryn hwynt wlat Nef, adef goreu,
Ky prynhwynt wlat Nef, adef goreu!"

Gwr ych Echen Neu Maur Llyndau

of the present custom of burying the dead,' it declared, 'and desire to substitute some mode which shall rapidly resolve the body into its component elements by a process which cannot offend the living, and shall render the remains absolutely innocuous. Until some better method is devised, we desire to adopt that usually known as cremation.'

Four Pounds of Lime Dust

The founder of the society was Sir Henry Thompson who had for years brought the question of cremation to the attention of the English public. He used to say that the problem was a simple one: 'Given a dead body, to resolve it into carbonic acid, water and ammonia, rapidly, safely and not unpleasantly.' He himself experimented with a furnace in which a body weighing 144 pounds was reduced in 50 minutes to about four pounds of lime dust.

Great difficulties were placed in the way of all who wanted to bring back the ancient rite of burning the dead. The Council of the Cremation Society of England was unable to purchase a freehold until 1878, when an acre of land was obtained at Woking not far from the cemetery there. In 1882 the Council received an application to undertake the cremation of two deceased persons who had left express instructions that their bodies were to be burnt. The Home Secretary was approached but refused permission. The bodies were therefore preserved. A member of the Society thereupon erected a crematorium on his estate in Dorset, and the cremation of these two persons took place. A year later he himself died and was also cremated: the cremations were supervised by an official of the Cremation Society.

Police Protection

No comment, for or against, was made by the Home Office, who seemed nonplussed by the situation. In 1884, however, they took action when a Dr William Price of Llantrisant in Glamorgan, announced publicly that he intended to cremate the body of his infant son and proceeded to do so. William Price is justly described in *The Dictionary of Welsh Biography* as 'eccentric'. A practising doctor, he claimed to be an arch-druid, practised free love and opposed vivisection and vaccination. He carried out rites dressed in a white tunic with a huge fox skin on his head, and constantly advocated cremation. The dead boy had been born to him at the age of 83 and christened Jesus Christ.

At first the police did not know what to do but eventually Price was arrested. His trial took place at Cardiff Assizes, where Mr Justice Stephen ruled that no offence

had taken place and that cremation was legal, provided that it was carried out without nuisance to others. A year later, in 1885, the first publicly organized and controlled cremation in Britain took place, at Woking. Price himself was cremated when he died in 1893.

There was still much opposition and prejudice in the early days and police protection was required at some cremations. Now all this has changed. Today 51% of those who die in Britain are cremated, and there are already more than 200 crematoria in the country. The ban on Roman Catholic cremations was lifted in 1964. Orthodox Jews, however, still continue to object to cremation.

The ashes from cremated bodies are disposed of in various ways. The remains of a Hindu funeral pyre are put in the river — usually the sacred river Ganges. The Digger Indians smear the ashes with gum onto the heads of the mourners. In Europe and America the ashes are stored in urns, buried in the earth or in graves inside a church, thrown to the winds, or scattered in a garden of remembrance. Cremation has dealt with the sanitary problem that worried the 19th century reformers; the scattering of ashes deals with the problem of storage and grave-space, but its widespread adoption brings to an end the tombs and monuments for the dead which were a feature of western European Christian civilization for so many hundreds of years.

GLYN DANIEL

Left Dr William Price, an eccentric who cremated his own son, whom he had christened Jesus Christ: he was tried at Cardiff Assizes and his acquittal in 1884 cleared the way for Britain's first 'official' cremation in 1885 **Right** In Bali, the body of a king is placed on a tower together with effigies of bulls and a dragon, and burnt: cremation of Chokorda Sukawati, the last king of Bali

Transworld Feature Syndicate

Giraudon

Crescent

The shape of the waxing moon, and so a symbol of increasing power, hence its adoption as the badge of the Ottoman Turks: it became an emblem of Islam: often an attribute of deities connected with the moon: a horned moon stands for growth and fertility, both because it is waxing and because horns are symbols of fertility (see HORNS): a crescent and star together stand for paradise.

'For the Cretans the supreme embodiment of the divine power in the world was feminine.' In her many roles the Great Goddess dominated the Minoan civilization, so named from the title of the Cretan king, Minos

CRETE

AN EXTRAORDINARY CIVILIZATION flowered in Crete after 2000 BC. Its geographical position made Crete a natural meeting-point for many of the cultural currents of the Mediterranean. It belonged to the Aegean world, making a link between Asia Minor and Greece, yet at the same time commanded sea routes southward to Egypt and eastward to the rich trading ports of the Levant. The influence of such widespread contacts is particularly evident in the religious ideas by which Minoan civilization was so largely inspired.

Crete seems to have remained uninhabited until early Neolithic times when the beautiful and fertile island attracted settlers, presumably from the adjacent region of Asia Minor. The Anatolian peninsula is now recognized as one of the earliest centres of the development of the new farming economy and then of urban life. Already by 6000 BC a large settlement such as Catal Hüyük had many shrines devoted to fertility cults. A supreme goddess, a lesser male divinity, birds, lions and bulls were represented in art. Actual bulls' horns were mounted as cult objects, while much later, in the Bronze Age of Beycesultan, in south-west Anatolia, these were architecturally formalized into horned altars − in one instance associated with a sacred wooden pillar.

These forms are strikingly similar to what was to emerge in Crete. Whether an important element of Cretan religion was directly derived from Anatolia, or whether it was only that both shared in a common inheritance is open to question. In spite of chronological and cultural difficulties, it is likely that there was a direct relationship. The initial settlement of Crete was followed by further immigration from the peninsula, and during Minoan times the two territories remained linked by ties of trade, and probably of language and of social custom as well.

Fashionably Dressed Goddess

For the Cretans the supreme embodiment of the divine power in the world was feminine. The Great Goddess or Mother Goddess, whose worship was common to the early agricultural peoples of the Mediterranean and south-west Asia, was probably immediately introduced into Crete by the Anatolian settlers. She kept her supremacy, although in appropriately changing forms, with the rise of high civilization. She was at once the one and the many. In the words that Apuleius put into the mouth of Isis herself in *The Golden Ass*, she was one 'whose godhead, single in essence but of many forms, with varied rites and under many names, the whole earth reveres'. In Minoan times the emphasis on pregnancy, maternal amplitude and nakedness found in the prehistoric idols was left behind and the goddess was usually portrayed in the same elegant fashion as the ladies of the court.

Among the 'many forms' of the Great Goddess some, indeed, were domestic. One was as guardian of the house, and particularly of the royal palace, where the prince may have ruled as her servitor and consort. At the same time her wilder aspects, more directly related to the old fertility cults, were no less important. She was the divinity of vegetation, mistress of animals, at home in forest, cave and mountain peak. In rites concerned with the death and rebirth of vegetation and seed, the goddess was associated with a young male divinity, probably both son and consort. She represented the continuity of the vegetation cycle, he its discontinuity. He died and was born again.

The various aspects of the goddess can be seen emerging in the divinities of historic times. As guardian she is best represented by Athene − already worshipped at Cnossus in late Minoan times. Demeter, with her other-self Persephone, was recognized as Cretan, as also was Hera. An association with doves seems to evoke Aphrodite, while Artemis best expresses her role as mistress of animals and virgin goddess of the wild places. Artemis was identified with Britomartis (the name means 'sweet virgin') who was worshipped in eastern and central Crete, and with Diktynna (Lady of Dikte), who was her western counterpart.

As for the young god, he too has local Cretan manifestations in Hyacinthus and probably also in the leader, or single embodiment, of the Curetes. Under the influence of the Achaean Greeks, the Indo-European Zeus was identified with the Cretan god, and the story of his concealment (or birth) in a Cretan cave, of the Curetes dancing and beating their shields to save the infant from his devouring father, was an accepted part of Greek mythology (see CORYBANTES). While the Greeks thus allowed their supreme god to have been born in Crete, they denied the inevitable Cretan heresy that he also died there.

Frenzied Dancing

The rites centred on the household goddess of the palaces and involving the princely families must have been formally ceremonious. Those enacted out of doors in the fertility and vegetation cults were ecstatic and mystic. The Greeks came to associate the island with mystical religion, and the Cretans themselves claimed, probably with justification, that they had enacted in public those Mysteries which at Eleusis were veiled in utter secrecy (see ELEUSIS).

Scenes engraved on gold signet rings and seal stones may represent rites celebrating the cycle of the seasons. The goddess is shown sitting below a tree, dancing in flowery meadows or occasionally perhaps lamenting at a shrine or over ritual jars. In these scenes the goddess is attended by female votaries, including young girls. In others, especially where boughs and trees are being plucked, she is accompanied by the young god. In these vegetation rites the dancing, especially of the god, is often ecstatic or frenzied.

Ritual meaning was expressed in positions of the arms. The goddess is often shown with arms bent and raised above the head, or extended before her. A common position of worship was with the right hand clenched and pressed against the forehead. Conch shells were blown, perhaps in order to summon the goddess.

The supreme deity of Crete was feminine, 'single in essence, but of many forms', one of which was guardian of the royal palace: the prince may have ruled as her consort. 'Prince of the Lilies', wall painting from the Palace of Minos at Cnossus; the lily was the most sacred flower in Crete

Funerary rites were related to the general conception of rebirth through the goddess. The elite were buried in unpretentious chamber tombs, dressed, ornamented and accompanied by pots, bronze vessels or other grave goods. It can be supposed that a happy Cretan view of the afterworld survived in the Elysian Fields of Greek mythology, associated as they were with the Cretan Prince Rhadamanthus, who was renowned as a just ruler. Frescoes on a sarcophagus from Hagia Triada in southern Crete illustrate funerary rites of the late Minoan period, c 14th century BC. They include the pouring of a libation, to the accompaniment of a lyre; the dedication of what look like fruits and wine at an altar; the blood sacrifice of a bull, to the accompaniment of a double flute, and apparently the carrying of offerings to the dead noble's tomb. The principal officiants are women wearing skirts of fur or fleece that may be priestly garments. Others, however, wear ordinary courtly dress and may have been royal ladies who were also priestesses. It seems to have been a princess of this kind who had been buried at Arkhanes near Cnossus. Among her rich grave furniture were gold amulets and a gold ring engraved with a ritual scene. She had been buried in a dress similar to that worn by the goddess on her ring.

The number and richness of ritual vessels are proof of the important place of libations and perhaps of ceremonial purificatory sprinkling in Minoan ritual. These vessels were often in the shape of the heads

'Snake Goddess', her hands raised in a ritual gesture: the snake was generally attributed to the Great Goddess of Crete in her role as guardian of the household, although this symbol may also have been associated with fertility. Faience statuette in the Heraklion Museum, Crete

of sacred animals, particularly of the bull and lion. In one of the Hagia Triada funerary scenes libations are being poured from a large two-handled vase into another vessel that may have carried them into the earth. On a seal stone strange composite figures referred to as 'demons' are represented bearing elegant beakers, the contents of which are to be poured into a conical vessel held by the enthroned goddess. Little narrow-necked jars of exquisite workmanship may have served to sprinkle holy water.

Serious Play

Minoan society had reached a stage of sophistication at which activities which were originally religious had become partly secularized. For the peaceful, conservative island society this led to a kind of serious playing characteristic of Minoan culture. Crete was later said to be the home of the dance, and dancing — sometimes graceful, sometimes frenzied — was among the rites of the goddess. Less purely religious dancing formed an important part of both court and country life, probably often associated with seasonal festivals. The sacred nature of some ring dances appears in a model where naked dancers, arms clasped, are circling

within an area enclosed by horns of consecration (formalized horns, indicating sacredness). Dancing in line in an altogether more stately fashion was practised by court ladies (see DANCE).

The most remarkable manifestation of serious play was in the famous Cretan bull games. Young men and girls, both wearing men's dress of tight-fitting belt and loincloth, performed athletic feats with the beasts, including vaults and somersaults between the horns (see BULL). The bull, symbol of male potency in relation to the goddess, was here encountered in actuality, possibly to celebrate life's renewal, or as an initiatory test of skill and courage. These games were, however, watched by lighthearted audiences. The palaces were provided with sacred ways and theatres that must have made a setting for processions and other performances.

Snakes in the Palace

The goddess of many names was also identified by a variety of symbols and manifestations. The most used were the horns, the pillar, the double axe, the tree, the dove and other birds, the snake and the shield. Horns of consecration were placed on palace buildings, on shrines, on the head of the goddess and in many other settings. Freestanding or sculptured pillars were part of the sacred furnishings of palaces, villas, shrines and tombs. They were anointed and offerings were made on, or to, them. Their primary meaning was probably phallic, but some authorities believe that they stood for the Great Goddess herself. In 'pillar crypts' such as the one in the palace of Cnossus, functional pillars seem also to have been anointed and held sacred.

The double axe, perhaps originally a sacrificial symbol like the cross, came to represent the goddess. It may often, as in the scenes on the Hagia Triada sarcophagus, have been set on the apex of the sacred pillar; it was represented between the horns of a sculptured motif representing an ox's skull or within horns of consecration. For votive use, double axes were made in gold or bronze and in a variety of sizes (see also AXE). Trees appear in many ritual scenes, often growing in shrines or small enclosures. They were not formalized in the usual manner of symbols, but shown naturalistically, usually in leaf but occasionally bare.

The snake was principally an attribute of the goddess in her role as guardian of the household, although it may also have had chthonic and sexual meanings. The two 'snake goddesses' of Cnossus are well known. In the town shrine at Gournia nearby, a crude goddess figure was twined with a snake, and there were snake tubes among the utensils; these were terra cotta cylinders with snakes represented twining round them, the purpose of which is not known. Real snakes were probably kept in the palaces, and rooms were set aside for them in private houses.

The goddess was sometimes portrayed between a pair of lions (as long before in Anatolia) or between birds and fabulous griffins, of oriental origin. The god was similarly shown as a master of beasts. Among the least understood figures of Minoan art are those known as demons — strange hybrid creatures, which often have the head of a lion or an ass. They attended upon the goddess, sometimes in procession and bearing libation ewers; demons appear to have been particularly concerned with the growth of crops.

A figure-of-eight oxhide shield, a recurring motif, gave rise to a religious symbol. It was occasionally personified in male or female form, presumably god and goddess. Its significance may partly have derived from the shields of the Curetes, but it must also have stood for the protective power of the goddess. Not only the shield but also the snake, the bird and the tree

all survived as attributes of the Athene of the classical world.

Spirals, including linked and running forms, were among the most popular motifs in Minoan art. They were often used decoratively, but possessed symbolic meaning, perhaps of eternal continuance. They appear on altars, shrines and ritual vessels. Among minor symbols were a sacred knot and a human ear and eye. The lily was the most sacred flower of Crete, and three poppy seeds might be worn or carried by the goddess.

Ecstasy in the Open Air

Unlike most of their contemporaries in the Bronze Age world, the Cretans had no large temples or temple figures. There were shrines of modest size in the palaces. At Cnossus there was a pillar shrine in the main court, and nearby the low, dimly lit throne room with stone basins and a sunken tank, suggesting use for purification ceremonies. The throne, with its flanking griffins, may have seated a divine prince, a high priestess or even a queen. Houses had their small shrines for private worship, and probably most towns and villages, like Gournia, had public shrines where little images and symbols of the goddess were ranged on a shelf in an inner sanctum.

More characteristic of Minoan Nature worship were sanctuaries in the countryside. Caves, probably often associated with the birthplace of the god, were among

The embodiment of strength and sexuality, the bull was the symbol of masculinity in relation to the Great Goddess: pot in the form of a bull, from Mesara, Crete

C. M. Dixon

the most ancient and most popular. Some were walled and provided with chapels, altars and offering-tables. Very many generations of islanders visited them to worship and leave their offerings. The counterpart of the caves were the peak sanctuaries, of which there were about a dozen in the island.

The more ecstatic rites of the goddess were celebrated out of doors, in localities where there might be shrines for a sacred tree, or an enclosure with a sacred grove.

Minoan influence on the Mycenean culture of the Achaeans in the late Bronze Age is nowhere more dominant than in its religious forms. The goddess appeared on the mainland with all her familiar attributes. The pillar between lions stood above the great gate of Mycene itself. Yet even by this time nearly all of the gods of the Olympian pantheon were already being worshipped. Dionysus also had his place, and at Cnossus there was a shrine to the legendary craftsman Daedalus. The goddess still held a high place but the male divinities, and particularly Poseidon, were now perhaps held in at least equal honour.

Directly, and through Mycenean civilization, Minoan religion gave much to that of Hellenic Greece. In addition to the relationship between the Cretan goddess and her classical descendants, there was the powerful Cretan element in the Eleusinian Mysteries, and a traditional Cretan founder at Delphi, later to be presided over by Apollo. All the main centres of Greek mythology were of Mycenean origin. The connection between the cult of Dionysus and the ecstatic rituals of the goddess is evident. In their stories of Theseus and the Minotaur, the Greeks embodied their sense of the strangeness of ancient Crete and memories of its former power.
(See also GREECE.)

JACQUETTA HAWKES

FURTHER READING: J. Hawkes, *Dawn of the Gods* (Random House, 1968); R. F. Willetts, *Cretan Cults and Festivals* (Greenwood, 1980); G. R. Levy, *The Gate of Horn* (Humanities, 1968); Arthur Cotterell, *Minoan World* (Scribner, 1980); A. C. Vaughan, *The House of the Double Axe* (Doubleday, 1959); T. B. L. Webster, *From Mycenae to Homer* (Praeger, 1959).

The Bull-King

Theseus and the Athenians at Cnossus:

Picture to yourself all the kings' palaces you ever saw, set side by side and piled on one another. That will be a little house beside the House of the Axe. It was a palace within whose bounds you could have set a town. It crowned the ridge and clung to its downward slopes, terrace after terrace, tier after tier of painted columns, deep glowing red, tapering in toward the base, and ringed at head and foot with that dark brilliant blue the Cretans love. Behind them in the noonday shadow were porticoes and balconies gay with pictured walls, which glowed in the shade like beds of flowers. The tops of tall cypresses hardly

showed above the roofs of the courts they grew in. Over the highest roof-edge, sharp-cut against the deep-blue Cretan sky, a mighty pair of horns reared toward heaven . . .

We entered the Palace precinct by the great West Gate. On either side there were staring people. Before us was the great red lintel-column, the painted shadows beyond . . . Once more we waited, but this time in deep decorum. The people peeped discreetly, and murmured together. To pass the time, I raised my eyes to the walls; and then I forgot my resolve to stare at nothing new. For pictured there was the bull-dance, from the taking of the bull to the very end: beauty and pain, skill and glory, fleetness and fear and grace

and blood, all that fierce music . . .

The guards' spears rattled. King Minos entered, and went up the side of the dais, and sat upon his carved white throne, resting hands on knees like the gods of Egypt. He wore a long red belted robe, and he looked tall; but that might have been his horns. The light from the portico gleamed dimly back from his gold face and crystal eyes.

In the quiet, I heard from the Cranes' soft indrawn breaths. But that was all. Old Cretans say we were the first band of victims, seeing Minos in his bull-mask, of whom not one cried aloud for fear.

Mary Renault *The King Must Die*

CRONUS

MORE IMPORTANT in myth than in cult, Cronus was chief among the Titans, the 12 'former gods', according to the Greek writer Hesiod (c 700 BC). The Titans were the children of Heaven and Earth, together with the Cyclopes and the hundred-handed monsters, but they were not able to reach the light until Cronus, the youngest Titan, castrated his father with a sickle and so separated heaven from earth. As king of the gods, Cronus married his sister Rhea, who bore him six children: Hestia, Demeter, Hera, Hades, Poseidon and Zeus. Earth and Heaven had prophesied that one of Cronus's children would overthrow him, and he tried to prevent this by swallowing them as they were born. But Rhea smuggled the last child away to Crete, delivering to Cronus a swaddled stone, which he duly swallowed. Zeus grew up safely, and somehow made Cronus regurgitate his other children; after a ten-year was between the older and younger gods, Zeus defeated Cronus and the other Titans and fettered them in Tartarus, where they remain.

It was formerly assumed that the myth reflected a historical displacement by the worship of Zeus of an earlier, no doubt pre-Greek cult of Cronus. Hittite tablets, however, have revealed that a curiously similar story was current in Asia Minor before 1200 BC. The counterpart of Cronus is Kumarbi, who becomes ruler of the gods by biting off and swallowing the genitals of Heaven (a combination of the castration and swallowing motifs). As a result, Kumarbi conceives a son, who becomes the weather god (the chief deity, corresponding to the Greek Zeus). Like Cronus, Kumarbi wishes to destroy his offspring, and probably swallows a stone in an attempt at abortion – the same action as in the Greek myth, but differently motivated. The attempt fails; the weather god is born,

Cronus castrated his father Uranus, 'Heaven', in order to free himself and his brothers and sisters from their prison in the depths of the earth *Above* 16th century painting on the ceiling of the Palazzo Vecchio, Florence, showing the infant Cronus mutilating his father *Below* Another version of Uranus's castration: Gaea, wife and mother of Uranus, and mother of Cronus, looks on with approval

POLIDORO DA CARAVAGGIO
INVENTORE

he fights a battle, and emerges triumphant.

It was probably in the period before 1200 BC, when eastern contacts were strong, that the Greeks took over the Asiatic myth, though some scholars put it shortly before Hesiod. We should like to know what Cronus was before he had oriental castrations and swallowings foisted on him, and why he was chosen for that role. Possibly he was already the father of Zeus, though his name indicates non-Greek (possibly pre-Greek) origin and the relationship cannot go back to Indo-European times. If he had special functions, they are obscure. For the Greeks of the historical period, he is fettered in the underworld, in other words, he plays no part in the world of men and has no influence there. (In 5th century Athens his name was used to mock the old, the stupid and the passé.)

There is, however, an alternative version which says that Cronus's reign was the Golden Age and that he now rules over the fortunate heroes in the Isles of the Blessed (see GOLDEN AGE). It was Zeus's accession that brought hardship and the necessity of tilling the soil. This may be connected with the annual Cronia, or Feast of Cronus, celebrated at Athens and certain other towns. Its date differed in different places, but so far as we can tell, it always fell in the idle period between harvest (May) and ploughing (October), and slaves joined their masters in merriment. If Cronus was a seasonal figure who played a part only at this celebration, the myth can be understood as a construction to go with it.

'We enjoy this feast and this leisure as a legacy from the time when Cronus ruled all the year round; but now Zeus is king, and we shall need our ploughs again.' This relationship between Cronus and Zeus would make a suitable basis for the adoption of the more complex oriental myth.

Child Sacrifice

Other traces of Cronus in cult or myth are scanty and of uncertain significance. Adopting the form of a horse, he mated with the nymph Philyra and became the father of the centaur Chiron. At Olympia there was a Cronus Hill, at the top of which priests known as the Kings made an annual sacrifice to Cronus at about the spring equinox; this may be a pre-Greek survival. Here,

before the foundation of the Olympic Games, Cronus and Zeus were said to have wrestled.

Cronus Hills existed also in Laconia in Greece, and in Sicily. Carthaginian influence had been strong in Sicily and it has been suspected that there 'Cronus' may represent the Phoenician El or Moloch. Cronus was identified with this god at least as early as the 5th century BC, probably because of the Phoenician reputation for sacrificing children to him. The identification affected interpretation of the myth of Zeus's birth, child sacrifice becoming attributed to the early Cretans. The Romans identified Cronus with their Saturn for a different but equally superficial reason: the Saturnalia, though held at a

different season (December) from the Cronia, had the same character of egalitarian merrymaking.

Like all the main Greek gods, Cronus was affected by attempts at etymology. From at least the 5th century BC the obvious (but false) equation was made with *chronos*, meaning 'time'. This fused with the idea of Time as a divine progenitor, which reached Greece independently from Iran, to give an allegorical sense to the story that he swallowed his children: Time consumes us all, his progeny.

FURTHER READING: *Hesiod & Theognis* tr. by D. Wender (Penguin, 1976) where the Hesiodic myth and its oriental counterparts are fully discussed.

Mansell Collection

Crook

The hooked staff of a shepherd, and so a symbol of the loving care of a pastor for his flock: a crozier, the hooked staff of a bishop or abbot, may be derived from the shepherd's crook or from the staff of a Roman augur: crozier is also used for an archbishop's cross.

WILLIAM CROOKES

EMINENT AMONG A GROUP of distinguished Victorian scientists who interested themselves in Spiritualist phenomena, Sir William Crookes (1832–1919) was a meticulous and penetrating experimentalist. He was elected to the Royal Society at the early age of 31, following his discovery of a new element, thallium. He was President of a number of learned societies, ranging from the Chemical Society to the Society for Psychical Research, and was President of the Royal Society itself from 1913 to 1915. His extraordinary versatility was reflected in the stream of papers reporting his work published between 1851 and 1918.

The group of scientists who concerned themselves with the fantastic phenomena claimed to take place at the Spiritualist seances which were so common at this time included the physicist Lord Rayleigh, the astronomer Sir William Huggins and the anthropologist Sir Francis Galton. Crookes's investigations, however, went far beyond anything attempted by his contemporaries. His energy was prodigious, and between 1869 and 1875 he undoubtedly attended more seances for physical manifestations than any scientifically qualified investigator before or since.

As a result of his investigations he reported the occurrence of a variety of phenomena in a series of papers published during 1870–1874 in his own magazine, the *Quarterly Journal of Science*. They

included levitations of objects and of human beings, paranormal sounds, and the materialisation of hands and complete human forms.

Almost all of Crookes's records of his psychical experiments seem to have fallen into irresponsible hands and been destroyed after his death, so his work must be judged almost entirely from his published reports and the accounts of a few eyewitnesses. His contemporary papers were collected and published in book form: *Researches in the Phenomena of Spiritualism* (1874).

Best documented of all are his seances with D. D. Home, the renowned physical medium (see HOME). Home first arrived in England in 1855 from America, where he had already made his mark. He was at this time a tubercular young man of 22. It has been said that there was hardly a person of note in London who had not attended his seances or who could not consult a friend who had, although most scientific men, including the great Michael Faraday, preferred to keep away. Home's mediumship was unique in that he always sat as one of the 'circle' and not hidden within a cabinet, and his phenomena were normally produced in light rather than in the more usual total darkness so conducive to fraud.

Controversy continued, however, between those acclaiming Home and those denouncing him as a charlatan — albeit without any convincing evidence of fraud being produced. Into the arena of argument sprang Crookes, already an established Fellow of the Royal Society. In a paper

published in the *Quarterly Journal of Science* in 1871, he announced that his experiments with Home's mediumship, which he described in detail, and which had been conducted in his own laboratory, appeared 'conclusively to establish the existence of a new force, in some unknown manner connected with the human organisation, which for convenience may be called the Psychic Force.' Before publishing this account he had submitted essentially the same paper to the Royal Society, only to have it rejected. In correspondence with one of the secretaries, Professor G. G. Stokes, he stated: 'I consider it my duty to send first to the Royal Society, for by so doing I deliberately stake my reputation on the truth of what I send.'

He invited the two secretaries of the Royal Society, Professors Stokes and Sharpey, to visit his home to witness the phenomena for themselves — an invitation which neither of them accepted.

Darwin Much Perplexed

There was much consternation in the scientific world over the appearance of Crookes's papers reporting his research with Home, Kate Fox and other mediums. Charles Darwin, writing to the anthropologist Sir Francis Galton on 23 January 1872, said: 'Have you seen Mr Crookes? I hope to heaven you have, as I for one should feel entire confidence in your conclusion.' In 1874 after reading Crookes's *Notes of an Enquiry into the Phenomena called Spiritual*, Darwin remarked in a letter to Lady Derby, 'If you had called here after I had read the article you would have found me a much perplexed man. I cannot disbelieve Mr Crookes' statements, nor can I believe his results.'

Galton did indeed call on Crookes, and he was soon able to report to Darwin, in a letter dated 28 March 1872: 'Crookes is working deliberately and well.' Three weeks later Galton wrote: 'Crookes, I am sure, so far as it is just for me to give an opinion, is thoroughly scientific in his procedure. I am convinced, the affair is no matter of vulgar legerdemain . . .'

There were, however, critics of a virulent kind, notable among whom was Dr W. B. Carpenter, F.R.S., who made an anonymous and viciously personal attack on

Crookes in the *Quarterly Review*. Crookes's reply (included in his *Researches*) was both crushing and devastatingly witty.

The most controversial of all the spiritualistic phenomena vouched for by Crookes were the fully-materialized spirit-forms which walked and talked in the Victorian seance rooms. Crookes described his experiences with 'Katie King', the form materialized by the medium Florence Cook, in three letters to the journal *The Spiritualist*. The fantastic nature of his reports on 'Katie' has led one recent critic, Trevor H. Hall, to conjecture that Crookes and Miss Cook were lovers, and that his published championship of her phenomena resulted from this relationship and a desire to protect her reputation. However,

it is known that he also vouched for the authenticity of an equally solid 'phantom' known as 'John King'. materialized by another medium, Charles Edward Williams, and it would be going rather far to attribute a similar motivation in this case!

Nothing to Retract

Much of the difficulty in assessing the work of Crookes and his contemporaries stems from the fraud that undoubtedly flourished in the darkness of the Victorian seance rooms. Crookes's comment on this was: 'I have myself frequently detected fraud of various kinds, and I have always made it a rule in weighing Spiritualistic evidence to assume that fraud may have been attempted, and ingeniously attempted, either by seen or unseen agents.' In addition he emphasized that the occurrences he described took place in nearly every instance *in the light*'.

Crookes finally withdrew from participation in the Spiritualist scene, due to the pressure of his work in the physical sciences, and what he described as the 'calumny, slander, backbiting and abuse from Spiritualists'. as well as from fellow scientists, that he suffered during his investigations. Whenever the opportunity presented itself, however, he continued to sit with both physical and mental mediums.

'I have nothing to retract,' he declared in his Presidential Address to the British Association in 1898, 'I adhere to my already published statements . . . I regret only a certain crudity in those early expositions which, no doubt justly, militated against their acceptance by the scientific world.'

Crookes's records of his experiments fall far short (as he himself admitted) of the standards the subject demands. His great scientific achievements may have engendered a certain assumption of omnipotence, for in 1871 he was able to say without embarrassment: 'Others . . . have gone so far as to question my veracity: "Mr Crookes must get better witnesses before he can be believed!" Accustomed as I am to have my word believed without witnesses, this is an argument which I cannot condescend to answer.'

Most present-day parapsychologists are sceptical of at least the more extreme phenomena accepted by Crookes and would consider him deluded. We cannot do better, perhaps, than sum up in the words of his friend Sir Oliver Lodge: 'It is almost as difficult to resist the testimony as it is to accept the things testified.'

K. M. GOLDNEY, R. G. MEDHURST

FURTHER READING: R. G. Medhurst and K. M. Goldney, *William Crookes and the Physical Phenomena of Mediumship* (Proceedings of the Society for Psychical Research, Vol 54, 1964); E. J. Dingwall, *The Critics' Dilemma* (privately published, London, 1966); T. H. Hall, *The Spiritualists* (Duckworth, 1962).

Sir William Crookes: physicist and chemist, and a President of the Royal Society, he claimed to have seen materialized spirit forms walking and talking during seances

Layton-Sun

CROSS

'Life is but the shadow thrown by the cross of Christ': to Christians everywhere the cross is the supreme emblem of their faith. Ethiopian Christian carrying an ornate cross

Older than Christianity, the cross has been used as a symbol of the world, the sun, fire and life. The Christian cross is an emblem of the triumph of life over death, of good over evil

CROSS

ALTHOUGH THE CROSS is best known as the supreme emblem of the Christian faith, cross symbolism is much older than Christianity. The simplest form of cross, the equal-armed or Greek cross (*crux quadrata*), has been used since prehistoric times. The oldest examples are those found engraved or painted on flat pebbles, dating from c 10,000 BC, at Le Mas d'Azil, a cave in the French Pyrenees. Other pebbles found there have lines, circles and rudimentary human figures on them, and it is possible that they were 'ancestor stones', believed to contain the spirits of the dead.

In pre-Christian uses of the cross its meaning is usually uncertain. Sometimes it seems to stand for the four directions, or the four directions plus the centre, in which case it can mean 'the world' or 'everything'. Sometimes it is a symbol of the sun, apparently as the four spokes of the wheel which is a common symbol of the sun (see WHEEL). Both meanings reappear in early Christian symbolism, in which Christ is frequently associated with the sun and in which the cross is a symbol of his rule of all things, the arms of the cross stretching out to bring under his sway the uttermost length and breadth, the uttermost height and depth.

The Nazi Cross

The swastika, an equal-armed cross with a line projecting from each arm, has been found drawn on prehistoric clay figures of animals. It was revered as a symbol of the rain god in Central and South America, and the Aztec goddess of rain is depicted carrying a cross. The Aztecs and Mayans linked the cross symbol with the Tree of Life, erecting sizeable crosses in temples which greatly excited the conquistadors. In North America also certain Athapascan Indians used the cross symbol in their rites praising the new moon; New Mexican Indian grave mounds have yielded shells marked with crosses and swastikas; the Dakotas, Creeks, Blackfoot and other tribes brought crosses into rain-making magic; the Pueblos and others used crosses of many shapes as religious decoration, and some Californian tribes at times depict their great mother goddess with her arms and legs splayed on a cross or swastika.

The swastika has also been found in the Greek fortress of Mycenae and among the Etruscans in Italy, on early Christian tombs and on pagan tombs in northern Europe. There are swastikas on sword hilts of the 3rd century AD which were recovered from peat bogs in Denmark, and a fine 7th century scabbard fished out of the Seine has a cross and a swastika side by side.

The swastika usually seems to stand for the sun or fire, and so for life and vigour, perhaps because it originally represented

the whirling round of a fire-drill, an apparatus for making fire by revolving a wheel at the base of an upright stick. (It has also been suggested, less plausibly, that the equal-armed cross originally represented the two sticks which primitive man rubbed together to make fire.) The Nazi party in Germany adopted the *Hakenkreuz* or 'hooked cross' as its official emblem, under the mistaken impression that it was a purely Germanic symbol (see SWASTIKA).

The *crux ansata*, shaped like a T with a loop on top of it, is also very old and was originally the Egyptian *ankh*, a symbol of 'life' which appears frequently in Egyptian art, held in the hand of a god or applied to the nose of a dead man to give him life in the afterworld. The Egyptians wore it, usually as the pendant of a necklace, as a charm to prolong life and they buried it with the dead to ensure their resurrection. The ankh looks like a key and may be connected with the symbolism of the key as the instrument which unlocks the gates of death and opens the road to immortality. It is found in some early Christian tombs and was adopted by the Coptic Christians of Egypt.

By This, Conquer

Besides the Greek cross, the principal types of Christian cross are the T-shaped cross (*crux commissa*), the X-shaped or St Andrew's cross (*crux decussata*) and, most important of all, the Latin cross (*crux immissa*) in which the base arm is longer than the others, and which is generally shown in representations of Christ crucified.

When a man was crucified, his hands were tied or nailed to the cross-piece, and there was often a projection from the upright beam which helped to support the body. It might take days to die on the cross and it was not only a cruel death but an ignominious one, reserved for slaves and criminals of inferior social status.

It was probably as much the fear of ridicule, of the sneer that they worshipped

a common criminal, as the fear of persecution or the dislike of seeming to ape the pagan veneration of idols, which made the early Christians reluctant to use the symbol of the cross openly. But they evidently regarded it as an important emblem, for they marked their burying-places and tombs with disguised crosses – an X, an anchor or an axe, for example. They also made the sign of the cross frequently, as a mark of their faith and for protection against evil. The 2nd century theologian Tertullian, who had a flair for exaggeration, said that a Christian traced the sign of the cross on his forehead in all the actions of daily life, at every forward step or movement, whenever he went in or out, when he put on his clothes, when he sat down or lit the lamps or went to bed.

The symbol of the cross naturally began to be used much more openly after Christianity had become the official religion of the Roman Empire in the 4th century and crucifixion had been abolished. It was said that the Emperor Constantine the Great was converted to Christianity in the year 312, when he was marching on Rome to deal with a rival claimant to the throne. He saw a towering cross of light in the sky, with the words *In hoc vinces* (By this, conquer). He defeated his rival in battle and attributed his victory to the Christian god. The initial letters of the Latin words, IHV, or later IHSV or IHS, when the phrase was expanded to *In hoc signo vinces* (By this sign, conquer) frequently appear in Christian art, partly because in Greek the capitals IHS are the first three letters of the name 'Jesus'.

Constantine used the cross as a symbol on his coins and statues, on armour and on the walls of his palaces. He was also fond of the chi-rho monogram, an X impaled by a P, being the Greek letters for the 'Chr' of *Christos*. Both symbols were very popular with his Christian subjects.

Finding the True Cross

'Life is but the shadow thrown by the cross of Christ,' wrote an anonymous medieval author, 'outside that shadow is death.' Once the instrument of an ignominious death, the cross became the symbol of eternal life, the emblem of a triumphant death which had brought to all men the promise of immortality in heaven. Suitably enough in view of its shape, the cross became one of the great symbols of the reconciliation of opposites, the opposites of death and life, of punishment and self-sacrifice, of shame and glory, of earth and heaven, of agony and joy.

By c 350 it was believed that the true cross, the cross on which Christ died, had been found. St Cyril, a bishop and lecturer at Jerusalem, said that pieces of its wood had been distributed all over the world. By the end of the century Christian writers in Italy knew the story that Constantine's mother, the Empress Helena, had discovered the true cross at Jerusalem in 326. Directing excavations on the site of Christ's execution, she uncovered three crosses, the nails which had pierced Christ, and the mocking inscription 'This is the King of the Jews'

To Each His Cross

Foreign crosses, other men's merits are not mine; spontaneous and voluntary crosses, contracted by mine own sins, are not mine; neither are devious and remote and unnecessary crosses, my crosses. Since I am bound to take up my cross, there must be a cross that is mine to take up; that is, a cross prepared for me by God, and laid in my way, which is temptations or tribulations in my calling; and I must not go out of my way to seek a cross; for, so it is not mine, nor laid for my taking up. I am not bound to hunt after a persecution, nor to stand it and not fly, nor to affront a plague and not remove, nor to open myself to an injury and not defend. I am not bound to starve myself by inordinate fasting, nor to tear my flesh by inhuman whippings and flagellations. I am bound to take up my cross; and that is only mine which the hand of God hath laid for me, that is, in the way of my calling, temptations and tribulations incident to that.

John Donne *Sermons*

Besides its Christian associations forms of the cross have been used as potent symbols of many other beliefs. In ancient times it could mean universality, representing 'the world' or 'everything' *Left* This carved Pictish swastika from Perthshire, symbolizing life and vigour is formed by human bodies *Above* 'Jews are not welcome here'; the Nazis adopted the *Hakenkreuz* or swastika in the mistaken belief that it was a purely Germanic symbol *Below left* Egyptian animal-headed gods holding looped crosses or *ankhs*. As a life-giving symbol the ankh customarily accompanied the dead to ensure everlasting life in the afterworld *Below right* Human bodies reappear in this curious cross, once owned by Montague Summers, an authority on witchcraft and demonology: now in the Witches' Mill, Isle of Man

which had been fastened to his cross. There was no way of telling which was Christ's cross and which were those of the two thieves crucified with him, until the crosses were taken to the bedside of a dying woman and the true cross revealed itself by miraculously healing her.

The inscription and a piece of the cross are preserved at the church of the Holy Cross in Rome, which was built on the site of one of Helena's palaces. One of the nails is said to form the inner circlet of the famous Iron Crown of Lombardy, at Monza. Pieces of the true cross were indeed distributed all over the world, in such quantities as to arouse cynicism.

In 884 the Pope sent a piece of the wood of the true cross to King Alfred in England, an event which inspired poets to write expanded versions of an earlier Anglo-Saxon poem called 'The Dream of the Rood' (rood is an old English word for cross). The earliest surviving version of the poem is carved in runes on the 8th century cross at Ruthwell in Dumfriesshire.

The Glory-Tree

In the poem the true cross, 'the glory-tree', describes how it was hewn down and made into a scaffold, how it was set up on a high hill and how 'mankind's brave King' mounted it. And the cross goes on to tell how, when Christ's body had been taken down, it and its two companions were buried in a deep pit where 'friends found me', a reference to the legend of Helena.

Christian missionaries in northern Europe carved crosses on standing stones already venerated by pagans, to Christianize them. The eventual result was the Celtic standing cross, a stone pillar which sometimes has no cross-piece at all. When it does, there is often a circle round the point where the four arms join, the circle possibly standing for eternity and immortality (see CIRCLE).

Some early crosses in northern Europe dramatically combine Christian and pagan motifs. One side of the Gosforth Cross in Cumberland shows the Crucifixion but on the other side are scenes from pagan mythology of the destruction of the gods at the end of the world. This was evidently to show that in his death and resurrection Christ had overthrown the powers of hell,

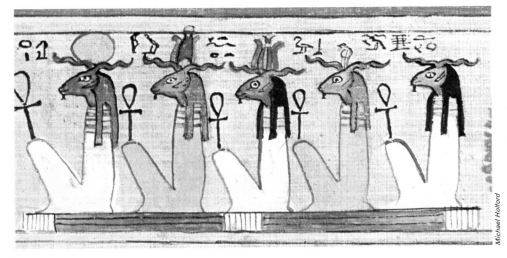

the false gods of the heathen who were regarded by Christians as devils.

Similarly, the Scandinavian world-tree which stood at the centre of the universe (see ASH) was replaced by the 'glory-tree', the cross on which the Saviour hung in death and in triumph at the exact centre of the world. In medieval art the cross is often shown as a tree. An example is a 16th century engraving showing Christ crucified on a tree whose branches are heavy with fruit, which men and women are picking, a symbol of the fecundity of Christ's sacrifice, the hope of immortality which his death brought to all men.

Christian artists and story-tellers frequently identified the cross with either the tree of life or the tree of knowledge in the story of Adam and Eve (see FIRST MAN). One widely accepted story was that when Adam lay dying, he sent his son Seth to Eden. The angel who guarded the gate of paradise gave Seth three seeds of the fruit of the forbidden tree. Seth placed them on Adam's tongue and Adam died happy, knowing that mankind would be saved from the consequence of his crime in Eden. The three seeds grew into a great tree, from which the cross was fashioned. Christ was

Once the instrument of an ignominious death, usually reserved for common criminals, the cross became the symbol of eternal life, the emblem of a triumphant death which had brought to all men the promise of immortality in heaven. Raphael's *Crucifixion*

crucified on it at the centre of the earth, the place where Adam had been created and where he had been buried. And Christ's blood falling onto Adam's skull redeemed him too at last.

The T For Protection

The figures shown beside the cross in medieval representations of the Crucifixion were used to point the moral that in founding the Church, Christ had abolished the authority of the Jewish Synagogue. Sometimes the Church is shown as a figure on Christ's right, catching in a bowl the flow of blood and water from his wounded side, the blood and water standing for the Mass and Christian baptism. On the other side is the Synagogue, a blindfolded figure holding a broken staff. Or the Church may be represented by the Roman centurion, who pierced Christ's side with a lance but then recognized him as the son of God, while the Synagogue is the man who held a sponge filled with vinegar to Christ's lips, the sour vinegar being the outmoded doctrines of the Jews. Or the penitent thief may be the Church and the impenitent one the Synagogue.

Even when the Virgin Mary and St John are shown beneath the cross, the Virgin may stand for the Church, the second Eve, born of the second Adam, and St John for the Synagogue. The oddity of this was explained by pointing to the story in St John's own gospel (chapter 20) of how he arrived at Christ's tomb before St Peter, but then hung back and let the impetuous Peter go in first. This showed, it was said, that the Synagogue must give place to Peter, to the Church.

Making the sign of the cross is naturally a common Christian defence against evil and the Devil, and magicians conjuring up evil spirits drew crosses inside the magic circle for protection. They also used the T-shaped cross for the same purpose. The origin of this is a passage in Ezekiel (chapter 9). The prophet saw a vision in which God ordered a mark to be made on the foreheads of the righteous inhabitants of Jerusalem. Those who had this mark would be spared when the city was destroyed and its people slaughtered.

The Jews believed that this mark was a T, the last letter of the Hebrew alphabet and so a fitting symbol of 'the end', 'the last days' when the world would be destroyed and made anew. Many Jewish burial urns of the 1st century AD in Palestine have T-crosses carved or scrawled on them in charcoal (though some authorities believe that these were Christian burials). The tradition that the letter T is a mark of protection became firmly entrenched in European magic.

RICHARD CAVENDISH

FURTHER READING: For medieval cross symbolism, see E. Male, *The Gothic Image* (Harper and Row, 1973); for 'The Dream of the Rood', see *The Earliest English Poems*, tr. M. Alexander (Penguin). See also J. E. Cirlot, *A Dictionary of Symbols* (Philosophical Library, 1972).

·I·N·R·I·

Michael Holford

Fragments of messages purporting to come from beyond the grave from several distinguished psychic research investigators were received by a group of eminent people who were interested in automatism at the turn of the century

CROSS CORRESPONDENCES

THE AUTOMATIST, Mrs Verrall, invented this term early in the present century to describe any concordance between the automatic scripts or trance utterances of two or more automatists operating independently (see AUTOMATIC ART).

The idea that such concordances might occur or might be experimentally induced was not entirely new but favourable conditions for testing it arose only after the death in 1901 of F. W. H. Myers of the Society for Psychical Research and the posthumous publication of his famous book, *Human Personality and its Survival of Bodily Death*. At that time a number of people who had been impressed by Myers began to produce automatic scripts purporting to come from Myers himself or from his friends and collaborators Edmund Gurney and Professor Henry Sidgwick, and comparison of their scripts soon began to reveal apparent concordances. The most important of these automatists were Mrs Verrall, a Lecturer in Classics at Newnham; her daughter Helen Verrall, afterwards Mrs W. H. Salter; Mrs Holland, pseudonym of Mrs Fleming, a sister of Rudyard Kipling; and from 1908 onwards Mrs Willett, pseudonym of Mrs Coombe-Tennant, who was a prominent public figure and a British delegate to the Assembly of the League of Nations.

All these were amateurs of the highest standing. The only professional 'medium' concerned was the famous American, Mrs Piper, who played a leading part in some of the earlier cross-correspondences. Later on, other amateur automatists were drawn into the group, which continued to function down to about 1930. By that date it is said to have produced over 2000 scripts — by far the largest body of 'automatic' material now in existence anywhere. These scripts were carefully transcribed, compared and annotated by a number of experienced investigators, of whom the most active were Alice Johnson, an official of the Society for Psychical Research, J. G. Piddington, President of the Society 1924–5 and Gerald Balfour, afterwards the 2nd Earl of Balfour. Many scripts showing cross-correspondences have been published and discussed in the *Proceedings* of the Society.

Spheres of Influence

Cross-correspondences can be classified in various ways. Most of them occurred spontaneously, without any prompting by the investigators; but there are one or two experimental cases in which the 'script-intelligence' of one automatist was asked to introduce a specified topic into the script

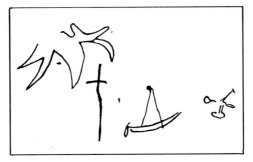

Society for Psychical Research

Three individual examples of automatic scripts, believed to be communications from the dead, which were received early this century by Mrs Verrall, a lecturer in Classics at Newnham College, Cambridge. On their own they were virtually meaningless, but when compared with messages and incidents encountered by other psychical researchers, they seemed to form a pattern. *Above* Message received on 11 March 1902, advising Mrs Verrall that there is no information today, but that she should watch for further communication *Centre* On 28 August 1901, Mrs Verrall produced an automatic script in Latin which made specific reference to fir trees in a garden; the script, signed with a scrawl, also included sketches of a sword, a bugle suspended by a nail and a pair of scissors. Unknown to Mrs Verrall, another researcher, Mrs Forbes, was at the same time receiving messages from her dead son, Talbot, a soldier killed in the Boer War. When the two subsequently met and compared notes, it was found that Mrs Forbes had several fir trees planted from seeds sent by Talbot. A further link was Talbot Forbes's regimental badge, a suspended bugle surmounted by a crown *Below* Between April 1903 and March 1906, Mrs Verrall received several messages alluding to a cross mounted on five stone steps, with a fresh green wreath, bearing the inscription AJC. Later at the home of another experimenter, Miss Curtois, Mrs Verrall's attention was drawn to a photograph which resembled in detail the cross of the scripts. She was told that it was a memorial to Miss Curtois's mother, whose initials were AHC

of another and more-or-less successfully complied. The following is a curious instance.

On 28 January 1902, Mrs Piper's script-intelligence, which called itself 'Rector', was asked to show itself to Helen Verrall with a spear in its hand. 'Why a sphere?' asked 'Rector'. The mishearing was corrected, but the confusion apparently persisted, for on 4 February 'Rector' claimed to have shown himself to Helen Verrall with a 'sphear' (so spelt). The claim was unsubstantiated so far as Miss Verrall was concerned; but on 31 January Mrs Verrall was seized by an impulse to write automatically and produced a brief script in a mixture of Greek and Latin which was only in part intelligible but contained *both* the word 'sphere' (in its original Greek form *sphaira*) *and* a Latin phrase descriptive of a spear (*volatile ferrum pro telo impinget*). This looks pretty much like a successful experiment in telepathy between the living, save that the telepathic 'message' was picked up by the mother instead of the daughter. That it emerged in a mixture of Greek and Latin is not particularly surprising: Mrs Verrall was conversant with both languages, and her earlier scripts were mostly written in dog-Latin and Greek.

Another distinction is that between 'simple' and 'complementary' cross-correspondences. The most obvious kind of simple correspondence is one in which the same thought is independently expressed, preferably in the same words and at about

the same date, in the scripts of two or more automatists. Examples of this have occurred occasionally. A good instance is the 'Thanatos' correspondence, where within a fortnight the key idea 'death' was independently expressed in three different languages by three different automatists — Mrs 'Holland', Mrs Piper and Mrs Verrall (see AUTOMATIC WRITING). The weakness of this case is that in a series of communications purporting to come from the dead the theme of death is, to say the least, a pretty obvious one. It does raise an interesting question: how did Mrs Piper, who knew no Greek, get hold of *thanatos*, the Greek word for death, which seems to have conveyed nothing to her conscious mind?

Psychic Jigsaw

More frequent and more important, is the complementary type; indeed, some writers recognize only this type as constituting a true cross-correspondence. The ideal complementary case would be one in which a coherent and significant message was split into several fragments, each meaningless by itself, with each being successively communicated through as many different automatists; the sense of the whole appearing only when their contributions were put together, forming a kind of jigsaw puzzle. It must be admitted that no actual cross-correspondence fully conforms to this ideal model. The 'complementary' fragments are usually found interspersed with irrelevant matter; the interval of time between one such fragment and the next is often rather

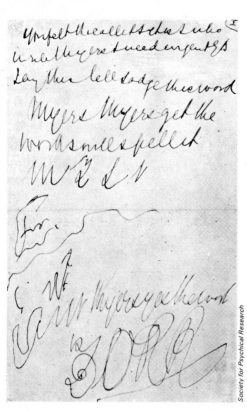

Society for Psychical Research

'You felt the call it I it is I who write Myers.' Automatic script produced by Mrs Willett, containing a message from F. W. H. Myers to the eminent psychical researcher Sir Oliver Lodge

long; and the 'message' when finally deciphered is not always so meaningful as could be wished. There are, however, a large number of cases which approximate in varying degrees to the ideal type. Most of them are highly complicated, turning as a rule on obscure literary allusions. For that reason they can be appreciated only by intensive study and are virtually impossible to summarize. All that can be done here is to quote briefly a single, relatively straightforward, example.

On 16 January 1907, Piddington asked Mrs Piper's 'Myers' intelligence to mark attempts at cross-correspondences in some way, say by drawing a circle with a triangle inside it.

On 28 January Mrs Verrall's script opened with the word *aster* (Greek for 'star'), followed by a number of what seem to be free associations with the word. Then came the following passage (the words italicized are partly quotations from, partly garbled reminiscences of, Browning's poem *Abt Vogler*): 'the hope *that leaves the earth for the sky* — Abt Vogler *for earth too hard that found itself or lost itself — in the sky.* That is what I want. *On earth the broken sounds — threads — In the sky, the perfect arc. The C major of this life.* But your recollection is at fault.' After this came two drawings of a triangle inside a circle, with a further reference to 'the part that unseen completes the arc'.

On 3 February Miss Verrall's script included drawings of a star and a crescent moon, with the words 'the crescent moon, remember that, and the star'.

On 11 February 'Myers', writing through Mrs Piper, claimed to have referred through Mrs Verrall to 'Hope and Browning' and also 'Star'.

On 17 February Miss Verrall's script contained another drawing of a star and the words 'the mystic three(?) and a star above it all'. (This has been taken as an allusion to the line in *Abt Vogler*, 'That out of three sounds he frame, not a fourth sound, but a star', which is an apt analogy to a complementary cross-correspondence.) Finally, on 8 April 'Myers', writing through Mrs Piper, stated that through one of the other automatists he had drawn a star and a crescent.

Voices from the Grave

The question of how such complementary correspondences are to be explained, is one of the most difficult and disputed questions in the whole field of psychical research. Four different explanations are theoretically possible: fraud, chance, telepathy from (or possession by) the dead, and telepathy between the living. The first of these, however, can be discarded with confidence. That a large number of persons of high intelligence and high moral standing should without apparent motive have conspired together to deceive the world and should have kept up the deception for some 30 years is psychologically incredible. The very ambiguity and vagueness of even the best cross-correspondences is the surest proof of the automatist's honesty.

The hypothesis of sheer chance has a different status. No exact limit can ever be set to the possibility of chance coincidence, and the sceptic can argue a number of considerations which suggest that chance may have played a greater part in the production of correspondences than the investigators have been willing to admit. But the fact remains that very few who have made a careful study of the complete evidence have found it possible to regard the correspondences as *purely* accidental.

There remains the alternative choice either of postulating a rather unusual kind of telepathy between the living or of accepting in some form the actual agency of the dead. Most of the original investigators came to prefer the second view for three main reasons. There was, first, the testimony of the scripts themselves: if the true agents were the subconscious minds of the automatists, why did they persist in calling themselves 'Myers', 'Gurney', and so on? Would not this have been a joint 'conspiracy to deceive' such as we have already rejected? Second, and more important, there was the argument from design. 'Simple' correspondences might indeed be explained by telepathy between the automatists, but how could this apply to 'complementary' cases, where the overall design was not understood by any of the automatists until their scripts were put together and compared? If none of them knew the design, none of them could have invented it. And thirdly, if one of the automatists was nevertheless the designer, how did she collect the materials for her design, some of which were outside her normal knowledge? Are we to picture her subconscious mind rummaging in the minds of her colleagues, until she came on precisely the items required for building up the correspondence? Such *selective* telepathy, it was urged, was unexampled and hard to conceive.

Unsolved Problem

To these arguments tentative answers have been offered by a number of critics. (1) To the argument from the consensus of the scripts their reply is that such dramatization is characteristic of all subconscious products, including ordinary dreams, and that at this level no real distinction can be drawn between believing and make-believing. Since it was Myers's death which set the whole movement going, 'Myers' naturally becomes the hero of the drama; and a dissociated fragment of Mrs Verrall's mind groping after an identity, may declare 'I am Myers' with a confidence as innocent (and perhaps as temporary) as that of the small child who states 'I am a steam engine'. (2) The argument from design has been countered by pointing out that 'complementariness' does not in itself prove intention. Ordinary telepathic impressions often emerge undesignedly in just the same fragmentary and enigmatic way: the famous Gilbert Murray experiments furnish good examples. (3) If, however, we concede that some correspondences do involve deliberate planning, the critic may urge that it is still unnecessary to attribute the planning to the dead. We do not know how telepathy works, in this case or in any other, but we need not imagine it in terms of picking out bits of the jigsaw from someone else's mind; we are equally free to think of an automatist subconsciously constructing the puzzle out of material already available to her, some of it familiar to her conscious self, some of it once familiar but now dropped out of conscious memory, and some which has drifted in on the accidental winds of telepathy. And if we ask 'What automatist?', a case can be made for replying 'Mrs Verrall'. She had known Myers well; she was the first of the group in the field and the first to hint at correspondences in her script; she possessed most of the classical learning needed for the construction of certain recondite puzzles; she had reported cases of spontaneous telepathy from her husband and her daughter long before she took to automatic writing; and, finally, after her death in 1916 there was a marked falling off both in the quantity and the quality of alleged correspondences.

There for the present the discussion rests, and there it is perhaps likely to remain until the complete body of script material is made available for study and analysis.

E. R. DODDS

FURTHER READING: The cross-correspondences have been published in Britain in a long series of articles in the *Proceedings of the Society for Psychical Research* from vol. XX (1906) onwards. A detailed list will be found in H. F. Saltmarsh's *Evidence of Personal Survival from Cross Correspondences* (Arno, 1975); E. D. Mitchell's, *Psychic Exploration* (Paragon, 1979) is also well worth reading.

CROSSROADS

THE PHRASE 'dirty work at the crossroads' sums up the ominous significance of places where roads meet. In Russia vampires lurked at crossroads and attacked travellers at night. In Japan phallic symbols used to be set up at road junctions to protect passers by, and in India offerings were made at crossroads to Rudra, the god who ruled ghosts and evil powers. A crossroads is an uneasy and uncanny place, perhaps because it imposes a choice of routes or symbolically of paths through life, with dangerous possibilities of choosing the wrong way and with the threat of the nightmare childhood experience of being lost.

In classical Europe offerings of food called 'Hecate's suppers' were placed at crossroads for this sinister goddess (see HECATE), whose image was often to be seen there, frequently in triple form – a statue with three faces looking three ways, or three wooden masks on a pole.

The 'suppers', which sometimes included cakes set with candles like our modern birthday cakes, also placated the malevolent ghosts which were believed to follow the goddess, ghosts which could not stay quiet in their graves but which roamed the earth hunting human prey.

It was an old custom to bury at a crossroads the body of a suicide, whose ghost could be expected to be restless and vengeful, with a stake driven through the corpse's heart to prevent it from walking. Criminals, whose ghosts would also be vengeful, were often executed at crossroads. On the other hand, some American Indians buried dead babies at crossroads, intending that the ghosts would 'enter' passing women and so be reincarnated.

The connection of crossroads with evil powers and ghosts made them suitable places for witches' meetings, for making a pact with the Devil and for operations of black magic – and sometimes white magic, as in many United States folk cures and marriage divinations that are required to be performed at crossroads.

Caxton Gibbet which is still to be seen at a crossroads in Huntingdonshire

Michael Busselle

The sinister crow in its rusty black plumage is associated with death and disaster. In ancient times it had the reputation of being wily and knowing, the confidant of the gods and the messenger of man

CROW

THE CROW FAMILY form a group of conspicuous, large birds with a wide distribution throughout the world from the arctic to the tropics. In particular the raven and crows proper, of Europe and Asia, have attracted man's attention, and much folklore is connected with them. These associations arose primarily from their carrion-feeding behaviour; hunters in ancient times, aware that the presence of the birds provided clues to the whereabouts of game, and often of carcasses, would regard them as endowed with knowledge and insight surpassing their own. As death has long been a mystery to mankind the observed close association between carrion-feeding birds and corpses meant that they aroused disquieting responses.

The raven's habit of picking out the eyes from a corpse before eating the flesh was commented on by Aristophanes in *The Birds*. In the Bible, in Proverbs (chapter 30) it is said: 'The eye that mocks a father and scorns to obey a mother, will be picked out by ravens of the valley.' In Bohemia it used to be said that crows picked out the eyes of St Lawrence. One of the crows in

According to one legend, the downfall of Britain will follow swiftly if the ravens in the Tower of London are harmed in any way

the Scottish ballad 'The Twa Corbies' says of the fallen knight, 'I'll pike out his bonny blue e'en.' By the odd kind of inversion which sometimes occurs in folklore it was said in Wales that blind people who showed kindness to ravens would regain their sight. In Czechoslovakia there was a tradition that a man who ate three ravens' hearts reduced to ashes would become a crack shot. The notion that by partaking of the heart or flesh of a creature one could acquire some of its qualities was extremely widespread and in this instance it was evidently supposed that the raven's farsightedness could be acquired. According to the Greek writer Porphyry (3rd century AD), by eating the hearts of crows one might acquire the birds' prophetic powers.

Why the Raven Croaks

Black, the colour of the crow, has long been associated with death and disaster; and because large birds of this colouring are relatively uncommon, a need was felt to explain their dark hue. A number of legends purport to explain how they acquired it. Thus, according to the Greek geographer Pausanias (2nd century AD) and other writers, when Apollo became the lover of Coronis, the mother of Asclepius, he commissioned a snow-white crow to mount guard while he went to Delphi; despite this, Coronis although already pregnant by him, became unfaithful with Ischys. Before the crow set out with the news Apollo divined what had happened and, infuriated that the crow had not picked out Ischys's eyes, turned the bird black.

Another story relates that the gods were sacrificing and the raven was sent to bring water from a fountain for a libation but he dallied, waiting until some figs were ripe. So the bird was condemned to suffer from thirst in summer – and that is why the raven croaks so hoarsely.

The frequent allusions in folklore to the association between the raven or crow and water might seem unaccountable, for these birds are not especially partial to damp habitats and, indeed, sometimes frequent rocky outcrops and ruins in desert country. The association has apparently arisen through ravens being frequently seen circling among black storm clouds. Thus the species was credited with some of the qualities of a storm bird such as were attributed to large high-flying, and sometimes mythical, birds in Asia and elsewhere. Among the Greeks and Romans the crow was likewise considered to be a weather prophet. Many Greek writers refer to the raven as presaging tempests, though some characteristics of its behaviour were interpreted as prognosticating good weather. The raven's association with clouds and rain meant that it was often regarded as a thunderbird.

Perhaps the most familiar episode in which the raven is associated with water is the account in Genesis of the sending forth of a raven by Noah from the Ark to search for land. This is derived from an older myth

of the Deluge originating in the ancient city of Acre in Israel, in which the dove, swallow and raven are sent forth in turn to discover whether the waters had subsided. It is recorded that at Krannon in Thessaly there were two ravens and never more – a detail perhaps based on observations that the birds pair for life – but at Krannon the ravens were connected with a magical rain-making ceremony. Coins of the 4th century BC depict two ravens on a small wagon containing a jar of water with pieces of metal suspended from it. By jolting this contrivance the jangling sounds and splashing water simulated a miniature thunderstorm. It was believed that in this manner rain could be induced.

Messenger and Guide

In common with the eagle and some other conspicuous, large birds the raven was regarded as being in contact with higher powers; and in this capacity it was regarded as entrusted with carrying information, water or fire, or performing other missions. In what seems to be a variation of the Deluge story the culture hero of a Siberian tribe, the Koryak, comes to the rescue during a period of incessant rain by flying up to heaven and stopping the leak. The mythical association with water was apparently carried to the New World where we find an American Indian culture hero Yetl transforming himself into the form of a raven in order to obtain and escape with fresh water. He was surprised in the act and was turned from white to black. However, he succeeded in flying to earth and disgorging the water to become streams, rivers and lakes.

The mythological figure Raven is of course the major culture hero and trickster of all tribes of the North Pacific coast. (Crow is a lesser figure in Indian myth, being a minor trickster of the Canadian Chipewyan and some Plains tribes.) For the Kwakiutl, Haida and other North Pacific tribes, he is the transformer who brought mankind into being (out of a clamshell), gave them fire, water, game and the wealth of Nature. As a trickster, he is a great stealer of food, usually thwarted laughably (see TRICKSTER). Raven appears too in Jicarilla Apache myths, where he is responsible for making man mortal; while in Iroquois and other woodland Indian ceremonials Raven is often evoked for curing rituals.

Death is a Hooded Crow

As a wise bird flying hither and thither and at times reputedly in touch with the gods the raven was said to act as messenger, informant and guide. Ravens led the Boeotians to where they founded a new city and they guided Alexander to the shrine of Jupiter Ammon in the oasis of Siwah in Egypt and later foretold his death. It was said that when the people from the island of Thera in the Aegean emigrated to Libya ravens flew alongside their ships to guide them. The Emperor Jimmu of Japan marched to war in the 7th century with a golden raven as guide. Pausanius recorded that a crow indicated the grave of the Greek writer Hesiod; according to Aelian a crow carried messages for King Marres of Egypt. Odin's two ravens, Huginn and Muninn, went forth each day prying into what was happening in the world and returning to perch on his shoulder and whisper their news into his ear.

In Celtic areas the importance of the raven and crow was once great though it is uncertain to what extent we are justified in speaking of a raven divinity or crow god. Various supernatural female figures appeared in the form of ravens or crows. Odin was called Hrafna-gud, god of the raven. The goddess of slaughter who came to the Celtic hero Cu Chulainn when he was mortally wounded appeared with her sisters as hooded crows and perched on his shoulders as he was dying.

Scottish folklore still holds reminiscences of these ferocious beings in the person of the dread Cailleach, a female who can appear as a raven, hooded crow or other birds. In Anglo-Saxon poetry the raven is constantly associated with battles. The similarities between Germanic and Celtic raven and crow traditions are such that we may assume with some confidence that their origin dates from the period when the peoples concerned lived in close proximity to one another. According to the *Prose Edda*, while his body lay sleeping, Odin could take the shape of various creatures, including that of a wild beast or bird. Odin's ravens were not fierce flesh-eating birds; Huginn and Muninn represented Thought and Memory — the mind's ability to go roving as in a shaman's trance. On a 7th century helmet from Sweden he is shown on horseback with two birds presumably ravens flying round his head.

In Christian Europe the raven had sinister significance, derived from Roman ideas concerning augury, dim recollections of the raven's connection with pagan gods, and from its dark plumage and deep croaking. Shakespeare refers several times to the ominous raven, and its association with death and fortune. In 1650 Dr Nathaniel Hone wrote: 'By the flying and crying of Ravens over their houses, especially in the dusk of evening and where one is sick, they conclude death.'

Apparently there has been a transference of oracular beliefs from the crow to the magpie, another member of the family, and the sayings and rhymes, and even minor ritual, such as taking off one's hat to it in Wales, seem to be derived from Roman crow augury.

The raven and grey (hooded) crow still retain in parts of the British Isles something of their reputation as oracles. There is an Irish phrase 'raven's knowledge' meaning to see and know all. It is also said in Ireland that the raven and grey crow 'tell the truth'.

The references in the Bible to Elijah being fed by ravens and to ravens being fed by God predisposed Christians to regard the bird as benevolent but, on the principle that the gods of a defeated faith may become the evil spirits of its successor the raven was sometimes viewed with suspicion — not surprisingly in view of its many heathen associations. St Ambrose wrote at length on the bird's impiety in not returning to the Ark. Jewish, Moslem and Christian legends regarded it as blameworthy for remaining to eat carrion and it was said that henceforth it was condemned to eat carrion. In the Koran the raven is sent by God to show Cain where to bury Abel but this is a version of an older Jewish legend. We hear of desert saints being assailed by devils in the form of 'black stinking ravens'. In Germany witches were said to ride on them. When St Vincent was thrown to the beasts at Saragossa his body was defended by ravens and when at length it was buried at Cape St Vincent ravens kept guard. Shakespeare makes use of both traditions malevolent and benevolent. In a single scene of *Titus Andronicus* (Act II Sc. 3) he mentions the 'fatal raven' and quotes 'ravens foster forlorn children' — an extension of the story of Elijah's ravens.

The ravens at the Tower of London remind those who are interested in ancient traditions of the significance which these birds have possessed in the British Isles and elsewhere for many centuries. It is said that disaster to these ravens would presage Britain's downfall. At one point in the Second World War, people were disquieted by the rumour that the Tower ravens had not croaked for five whole days.

Sun-Crow of China

The most interesting of the many fables concerning ravens and crows is the War of the Owls and Crows which appears in Indian as well as classical sources. It seems to embody reminiscences of very ancient beliefs with regard to the heavenly bodies, the owl representing the moon and the crow the sun. In China the three-legged sun-crow is an important symbol. The tradition that a crow never enters the Acropolis at Athens appears to be based on the tradition of the enmity between Athene, whose symbol was an owl, and the crow.

The raven and crow have been the subjects of a number of heterogeneous beliefs. Parts of the raven were used in medicine, according to Pliny, and raven's eggs were used by the Greeks in homoeopathic magic. Ovid, in *Metamorphoses*, refers to the witch Medea infusing into the veins of the elderly Jason a decoction of an aged deer and the head of a crow that had outlived nine generations of men. Folklore attributes a very long life to birds of the crow family. Aelian states that raven's eggs dye the hair black but unless you filled your mouth with oil while you applied this remedy for grey hair you would find that your teeth also had become indelibly black.

EDWARD A. ARMSTRONG

FURTHER READING: E. A. Armstrong, *The Folklore of Birds* (Dover, 1969).

Despite its widespread reputation as a bird of ill omen, Christians were generally more kindly disposed towards the raven: for according to the Bible the prophet Elijah, while in hiding, was kept alive with bread and meat brought to him by ravens. A painting by the Italian artist Giovanni Givolano Savoldo

An air of unsavoury mystery still surrounds the life and teachings of Aleister Crowley nearly a quarter of a century after his death. Violently hostile to Christianity and its God, he saw himself as the Messiah of a new religion

ALEISTER CROWLEY

POET, NOVELIST, WRITER of books on magic, eccentric – Crowley (1875–1947) was all this and more. He strove hard to assume the mantle of magician, and long before he died he knew that he had succeeded. He is thus in direct line of descent from Sir Edward Kelley, Cagliostro, the Comte de Saint-Germain, Eliphas Levi and Madame Blavatsky, all of whom were credited with remarkable, if not miraculous powers. Crowley's father was a successful brewer, the manufacturer of Crowley's Ales, but whose main interest by the time Aleister was born was that of travelling about the English countryside preaching the doctrines of the Plymouth Brethren and trying to gain converts to his sectarian views. The first important fact, therefore, about Aleister Crowley is that he was brought up amid the mysteries of the Christian religion; at the age of 11, however, when his father died, he grew to detest the faith in which he had been brought up and, without knowing why, went over to the side of Satan. While still a Christian and subjected to daily Bible readings in the Crowley household, he had taken a fancy to the 'False Prophet', 'the Beast whose number is 666', and the 'Scarlet Woman', characters or archetypes which were to play a prominent and decisive part in his later life.

Educated at Malvern and Tonbridge schools, and later at Trinity College, Cambridge, as a young man Crowley began to write verses after the manner of Swinburne. His real seat of learning, however, which suited his peculiar talents, was the magical society known as the Hermetic Order of the Golden Dawn, the leading light of which was a man of considerable magical potential, Samuel Liddell Mathers, known as MacGregor Mathers.

The Secret Chiefs
The Golden Dawn, which had about 100 members spread among several lodges, taught the use of magical weapons, how to consecrate talismans, set up magic circles, travel astrally and so on. It also gave instruction in the use of that ground plan of Western magic, the Cabala. In a word, it taught and practised ceremonial magic as opposed to magic which used other aids such as drugs or sex (see also GOLDEN DAWN).

Although one member at that time, 1900, described the Golden Dawn to the present writer as 'a kind of club, like any other club', it was quite unlike any other

Portrait of Aleister Crowley, the 'Great Beast', the most famous – and infamous – magician of modern times; he reviled the Christian God and sought by magical means to set himself up in his place

club in one respect: its constitution was not derived from its governing body but from superior beings or intelligences called (following Madame Blavatsky) Secret Chiefs. Mathers, it was said, had met the Secret Chiefs one night in the Bois de Boulogne in Paris. Crowley joined the Golden Dawn in 1898. Accepting all the vows and obligations, he took the magical title of Perdurabo (I will endure to the end).

At this time, Crowley was living in a flat in London's Chancery Lane and describing himself as Count Svareff, a Russian nobleman. Under this and other names, he published at his own expense several books of verse and, anonymously, a work of pornography entitled *White Stains* (1898).

Mathers was also a scholar, and translated and edited three important works: *The Kabbalah Unveiled*, *The Key of Solomon* and *The Book of the Sacred Magic of Abra-Melin the Mage*, 'as delivered by Abraham the Jew unto his son Lamech, AD 1458'. *Abra-Melin* inflamed Crowley's spirit; he described the book as one which is in marked contrast with all the puerile nonsense written on the subject. The technique of this magic has something in common with yoga; a secluded spot and a long period of purification are necessary before one's Holy Guardian Angel or Higher Intelligence can be invoked. Crowley searched the Lake District and Scotland and found what he wanted in Boleskine House, near the village of Foyers, in Inverness. He dropped the title of Count Svareff, assumed that of Lord Boleskine, constructed his oratory and began the operation. But instead of his Holy Guardian Angel appearing, he merely attracted a host of evil spirits.

He quarrelled with Mathers and was expelled from the Golden Dawn. Crowley retaliated by denying that Mathers had met the Secret Chiefs in the Bois de Boulogne and been confirmed by them as Head of the Order. Mathers, he said, had only bumped into some evil demons. He continued to pour out a torrent of verse and to climb mountains, in Mexico and in the Himalayas. He acquired a wife, Rose, and wrote for her the pornographic *Snowdrops from a Curate's Garden*. His greatest need was to make his own link with the Secret Chiefs or Mahatmas; without such a link he was a negligible force.

This uncertain state of affairs did not last long. Towards the end of 1903, when Crowley was 28, he went with his wife on a trip to Ceylon. In the new year, he decided to return home, and on the way back stopped for a while in Cairo. Wearing a turban with a diamond aigrette, a silken robe and a coat of cloth of gold, he gave out that he was Prince Chioa Khan. He was driven with Princess Khan (formerly Rose Kelly, the daughter of the Vicar of Camberwell) about the Cairo streets, with 'two gorgeous runners to clear the way for my carriage'. Despite his style of living, Crowley was undecided about his future and growing short of money. Then an event occurred which put at last some magical ground under his feet. This was 'the Great Revelation in Cairo'. The old world of Christianity came to an end for Crowley

and a new world, of which he was prophet, was born.

Aiwass, also spelt *Aiwaz*, the name of his Holy Guardian Angel whom he had tried with only partial success to invoke at Boleskine House, appeared to him in his Cairo flat and commanded him to take down a message for mankind. After an hour's dictation, Aiwass disappeared, but he was back again the following day at the same time, noon. Aiwass described himself as the minister of Hoor-Paar-Kraat (the Graeco-Egyptian god Harpakrad or Harpokrates), that is 'a messenger from the forces ruling this earth at present'. Aiwass came on three occasions and each time dictated a chapter of *The Book of the Law*, as the work is called. In other words, a new era, or rather aeon, in the world's history had begun, one which will last for 2000 years. The heart of Crowley's magic is derived from this work; it is the text behind his magic and his philosophy which he summed up in the phrase *Do what thou wilt shall be the whole of the Law*.

The Number of the Beast
Just before Aiwass appeared in Crowley's Cairo flat, a curious incident occurred in the Boulak Museum (now the National Museum). Rose had been in a strange, dazed state of mind and in this condition she had been mumbling something about Horus. 'Who is Horus?' asked Crowley, who was not aware that his wife knew anything about Egyptian religion. 'There', said Rose, pointing, 'there he is'. She was indicating an ancient Egyptian stele on which was painted Horus in the form of the hawk-headed Ra-Hoor-Khuit (Ra-Harakhte). Crowley went forward, then fell back in amazement. The exhibit bore the number 666, the number of the Beast, his number!

Many years later, in 1946, I asked Crowley, 'Why do you call yourself the Beast?'

'My mother called me the Beast,' he replied briefly, presumably not wishing to go into the deeper aspects of the subject. Crowley's mother was a pious woman and the behaviour of her son reminded her of the Beast of the book of Revelation that came out of the depths of the sea, with horns on his head, blaspheming God.

The cosmology of *The Book of the Law* is explained by Crowley thus: there have been as far as we know, two aeons in the history of the world. The first, the aeon of Isis, was the age of the domination of the woman, of matriarchy. The choice of Egyptian names for these aeons is purely arbitrary and does not imply that they are confined to Egypt. The second aeon, that of Osiris, was the aeon of the man, the father; it coincides with the Christian period, also with that of Judaism, Buddhism, Mohammedanism. It was superseded in 1904 by the aeon of Horus, the child. He explained that the emphasis for this present period, that of Horus, is on the will *(thelema)* or true self in man as opposed to external authority, priests and gods. 'Be strong, o man! lust, enjoy all things of sense and rapture: fear not that any God shall deny thee for this.'

The Silver Star

On his return to Europe in the spring of 1904, Crowley wrote to Mathers informing him that the Secret Chiefs had appointed him the head of the Order and declared a new magical formula – thelema. 'I did not expect or receive an answer,' said Crowley, 'and I declared war on Mathers accordingly.'

The following year Crowley led a disastrous climbing expedition to Kanchenjunga and added to his evil reputation by deserting his comrades on the mountain. In 1910, he published the curious and obscene *Bagh-I-Muattar* or 'The Scented Garden of Abdullah the Satirist of Shiraz'. This was a volume of homosexual love poems, supposedly translated from the medieval Persian.

But all this was marginal activity; his work was to spread the good tidings. A new world had been born and a new aeon had arisen. To this end, he founded his own magical association, the A∴ A∴ (*Argenteum Astrum*, the Silver Star) which constituted the Inner Order of the Great White Brotherhood; the Outer Order was the Golden Dawn. And he brought out his own publicity organ, *The Equinox*. This was issued for several years at the rate of two bulky volumes a year. Its articles and reviews were mainly written by Crowley under a variety of names. The series entitled 'The Temple of Solomon the King' contains details of Perdurabo's ascent in the Great White Brotherhood. No 7 contains *The Book of the Law* with his first brief comment; he thought it time to give it out to the world, but it caused no stir whatsoever. Between whiles he went off on any magical adventure which offered itself, during which he probed the gods for further guidance.

One night during 1912 Crowley received an unexpected visit at his flat in Victoria Street, London, from Theodor Reuss, a high ranking German Freemason. They were strangers to each other and Reuss had apparently come over from Germany for the express purpose of meeting Crowley. Without beating about the bush, he accused Crowley of giving away magical secrets. Reuss wore a handle-bar moustache and pince-nez; he was alleged to be a member of the German Secret Service. Crowley denied the accusation. Reuss replied by going to the book-shelf and taking out Crowley's *Liber CCCXXXIII: the Book of Lies*. He opened it at the page which begins, 'Let the Adept be armed with his Magical Rood and provided with his Mystic Rose,' and showed it to Crowley.

The secret that Crowley had been giving out to all the world was that sex can be used ritually or magically; but as he had been expressing it in veiled language, as in this extract, Reuss's point is difficult to see. The previous head of the order to which Reuss belonged, a wealthy German ironmaster called Karl Kellner, had learned this so-called secret from Tantric yogins in India during the last decade of the 19th century. He had been introduced to the ritual of *maithuna* (sexual union), in which the mind, the breath and the semen are held still. And on his return to Germany, he had expounded the delicate subject to his fellow Freemasons, among whom was Franz Hartmann, one of the companions of Madame

'Be strong, O man! lust, enjoy all things of sense and rapture: fear not that any God shall deny thee for this.' In 1904 Crowley proclaimed the advent of a new era in which the emphasis would be on man's true inner self, as opposed to the external authority of gods and priests *Above* Crowley in Arab dress: he loved aliases, disguises and exotic costumes. In Cairo, calling himself Prince Chioa Khan, he received the communications from his Holy Guardian Angel which marked the opening of the new era *Above left* Drawing by Crowley, who was a painter, mountaineer and chess-player as well as a magician *Far left* Top of his Janus-headed magical wand *Left* The Australian violinist Leila Waddell, 'Laylah' or 'Sister Cybele', one of Crowley's many mistresses and magical assistants, with the mark of the Beast between her breasts *Right* A 1930s poster, attacking Crowley as 'The Beast 666', a title bestowed on him by his mother

John Symonds

Michael Holford/Gerald Yorke Collection

Blavatsky, and proposed that they should start a new magical society to embody these sex and yoga teachings. Thus in 1902 the *Ordo Templi Orientis*, or Order of the Templars of the East, was founded. It claimed that it could communicate in nine degrees the secrets not only of Freemasonry but of the Rosicrucians, the Illuminati, the Order of the Hidden Church of the Holy Graal, the Knights of the Holy Ghost, and those of St John, of Malta, and of the Holy Sepulchre – in fact, of every mystic order that they could think of. 'Our Order possesses the KEY which opens up all Masonic and Hermetic secrets, namely, the teaching of *sexual magic*, and this teaching explains, without exception, all the secrets of Nature, all the *symbolism* of FREE-MASONRY and all systems of religion.'

Sexual Magic

Crowley and Reuss talked long into the night. 'Since you know our hidden sex teachings,' said Brother Merlin (Herr Reuss's magical name), 'you'd better come into our Order and be its Head for Great Britain.' Crowley, who never declined a dinner, an adventure or a title, readily agreed. After a journey to Berlin, he was transformed with due ceremony into 'the Supreme and Holy King of Ireland, Iona, and all the Britains that are in the Sanctuary of the Gnosis.' And with that keenness and audacity of mind which sees and seizes the main point, he gave himself the magical name in this secret society of Baphomet; this was the name of the idol which the original poor Knights of the Temple were accused of worshipping (see BAPHOMET).

One could not join the Order and start attempting to perform maithuna. The aspirant had to work his way diligently up to the IX°. One more degree was added by Crowley, the XI°, that of homosexual workings (or IX° inverted). In Paris during 1914 he worked this XI° O.T.O. with his pupil Victor Neuburg on 24 different occasions, the whole being known as The Paris Working. The X° was of an honorary character to distinguish the 'Supreme and Holy King' of the Order in each country where the Order was established.

The Ordo Templi Orientis claimed that the teachings of the Knights Templars (whose Order was disbanded amid a great scandal at the beginning of the 14th century) were known and continued by them, but this is wishful thinking. And the prostitutes whom Crowley frequently took as partners in his practice of sexual magic, apart from their not being trained in this form of worship, were completely ignorant of what he had in mind. His descriptions in *The Magical Record of the Beast* of these activities are quite out of keeping with the tone and elaborations of maithuna.

At the outbreak of the First World War, Crowley transferred his activities to America. The one important magical event which happened to him at this time, apart from his meeting with Leah Hirsig, the Scarlet Woman who outdid all other Scarlet Women in the Beast's Life, was his assumption during 1916 of the Grade of Magus.

Since 1909, he had been a Master of the

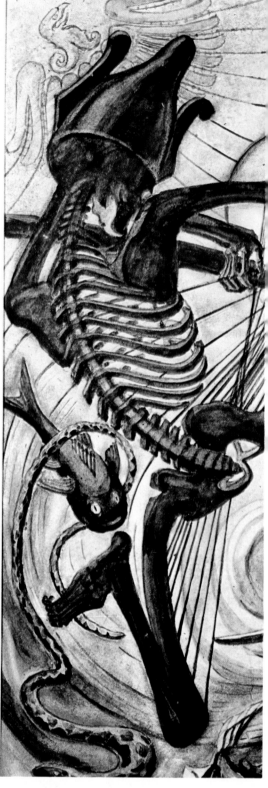

Temple, an exalted grade which enabled him to join the Secret Sanctuary of the Saints or the abode of the Secret Chiefs; now he went one higher. These upper stages in his career were implied in the Great Revelation in Cairo, that is to say in his being the vehicle of *The Book of the Law*. At last, he was ready to assume the throne and proclaim his word, thelema or 'do what thou wilt,' which ushers in the new aeon of liberty, as opposed to the old aeon of suffering (Christianity and other slave religions). The words of the ceremony which he performed, and during which he crucified a frog, make this clear.

'Night being fallen, thou shalt arrest the frog, and accuse him of blasphemy, sedition and so forth, in these words: *Do what thou wilt shall be the whole of the Law*. Lo, Jesus of Nazareth, how thou art taken in my snare. All my life long thou hast plagued me and affronted me. In thy name – with all other free souls in Christendom – I have been tortured in my boyhood; all delights have been forbidden unto me; all that I had has been taken from me, and that which is owed to me they pay not – in thy name. Now at last I have thee; the Slave-God is in the power of the Lord of Freedom. Thine hour is come; as I blot thee out from this earth, so surely shall the eclipse pass; and Light, Life, Love and Liberty be once more the law of Earth. Give thou place to me, O Jesus; thine aeon is passed; the Age of Horus is arisen by the Magick of the Master the Great Beast.' And so on and so forth.

Do What Thou Wilt

With the end of the war, Crowley returned to England; he did not stay in England for long but departed with small means and two mistresses, one of whom was his Scarlet Woman, Leah Hirsig, for Sicily. At Cefalu, he rented a villa, consecrated a temple to the New Aeon in one of the rooms, and painted on the front door the words DO WHAT THOU WILT. This was his famous 'abbey', his Collegium ad Spiritum Sanctum; here, during three years, he had time to add copious details to his diary, to paint pictures which reveal his remorseless vision, and to try to fuse together the bits and pieces of his life. His aim at Cefalu was to create a world centre for the study of occultism, but few availed themselves

Cards from a Tarot pack designed by Crowley and painted by Frieda Hariss *Left* The Magician or Juggler: Mercury with the ape of Thoth, his Egyptian counterpart, the whole symbolizing the creative will of God and man *Centre* Death, the skeleton and scythe, performing the whirlwind dance of change *Right* The Hierophant or Pope who holds the key of heaven and hell: the pentagram which contains the dancing child symbolizes Crowley's belief in the new age of Horus

of the opportunity of going there. Furthermore, the Beast's increasing dependence on heroin undermined his driving-force and the discipline of the abbey. However, during this period, he was revived by a commission from Collins, the publisher, to produce a novel about the drug traffic and to write his confessions; he set to work with unexpected vigour. The good produces the bad: *The Diary of a Drug Fiend*, 1922, was the initial cause of his expulsion from his abbey following the review of the novel, and a general attack on Crowley and his creed in a Sunday paper.

But Crowley had uttered his word, thelema, and done his work; it remained only for him, the Logos (word) of the New Aeon, to publish some more magical writings and attend to the affairs of the Order. The turn of the wheel of fortune produced new followers in Germany, and the Mandrake Press which brought out during 1929 two of the projected six volumes of his *Confessions* which Collins had dropped. He also published about this time his magnum opus, *Magick in Theory and Practice.*

Crowley, who behaved as if the world was only an exhalation of his own being, wound the vast subject of magic round himself and the petty incidents of his life, with the result that *Magick* is a city within a city. Whoever penetrates into the inner city will find there Perdurabo, the false god, choking with guilt from having set himself up in God's place.

JOHN SYMONDS

FURTHER READING: J. Symonds and K. Grant ed., *The Confessions of Aleister Crowley* (Hill & Wang, 1970); J. Symonds, *The Great Beast* (Roy Publishers, 1952) and K. Grant, *Aleister Crowley and the Hidden God* (Weiser, 1974).

CROWN

A CROWN is an object placed on the head, and so it is a symbol of pre-eminence, of having reached the top. We call the top of the head itself the crown, and we use the same word for the top of a hill.

The custom of placing an object on a person's head as a visible sign of success, of having reached the summit, as it were, is very old. The Greeks gave wreaths of wild olive to victorious athletes at the Olympic games. A Roman general celebrating a formal triumph wore a wreath of laurel or bay leaves, and wreaths were presented to soldiers for bravery, and to poets or artists for excellence. We still call the greatest

success of a man's life his 'crowning achievement' and if his work bears fruit we say it is 'crowned with success'.

Something placed on the head could also be meant to protect the part of the body which contains the intelligence and also the breath, and hence the life and soul of a person. In Rome suicides or people who knew they were about to die veiled their heads: when Julius Caesar was confronted with the daggers of his assassins, he drew the top of his gown up over his face. The same idea may be behind the old custom of

The Investiture of the Prince of Wales at Carnarvon Castle in 1969. The widespread custom of placing a crown on a person's head signifies triumph and pre-eminent authority

putting a wreath on the head of a dead man before his burial, to keep his soul from harm. We continue this custom, though we now put the wreath on top of the coffin. It is circular and made of evergreen leaves, both as symbols of hoped-for immortality.

Another old custom, still continued, is for a bride to wear a veil and a circlet of flowers, which again may have been meant to protect her against evil. Guests at Greek and Roman banquets wore wreaths of flowers, apparently to keep their heads clear and prevent them from getting drunk.

Crown Royal

Gods and kings wear crowns to show their pre-eminent authority. Kings are 'crowned heads' and the ceremony in which a man is acknowledged as a king is called a coronation, or literally 'a crowning'. In Mesopotamia deities and kings were shown wearing a high conical head-dress rising from between pairs of horns, apparently as a symbol of fertile vigour and of rising upwards, the top, the summit. The royal head-dress of Egypt, which was itself regarded as divine, was a curiously shaped high cap. Persian kings also wore high caps, studded with jewels. The Byzantine emperors followed suit and the high cap with one, two and eventually three bands round it became the tiara of the popes.

In the early Christian centuries small crowns, circlets of gold or some other metal, were hung up in churches as offerings to God. It is likely that the celebrated Iron Crown of Lombardy, probably dating from the 9th century, was originally one of these. Only six inches wide, it is a circle of six rectangular gold plates with a narrow band of iron on the inside, believed to be made of a nail from Christ's cross (see CROSS). Napoleon set it on his own head when he was crowned King of Italy in 1805.

As a symbol, almost an incarnation, of kingship, the old royal crown of England, St Edward's crown, was destroyed in the time of the Commonwealth. A new one, as nearly as possible a copy of the old, had to be made for Charles II. A special crown was made when George V was crowned Emperor of India at Delhi in 1911, because by British law the royal crowns could not be taken abroad, a striking example of the intimate connection between the crown, the king and his country.

Daily Telegraph Colour Library

Crusade

Christian term for a holy war, first applied to the armed expeditions to recover the Holy Land from the Mohammedans, later to other wars officially approved by the Church, including the Albigensian Crusade against heretics in southern France: more generally, any aggressive campaign against an evil; derived from the same root as 'cross'.
See CATHARS; KNIGHTS TEMPLAR; WAR.

British Museum

Crystal-Gazing

Or scrying: divination by looking into a ball of rock-crystal, a mirror, a pool of ink or other liquid: events at a distance or in the future may show themselves in the crystal as pictures or symbolic images: also used to communicate with spirits, as by John Dee and Edward Kelley in the 16th century.
See DEE; SCRYING.

Barnaby's

CU CHULAINN

THE CENTRAL CHARACTER in a group of early Irish stories known as the *Ulster Cycle,* Cu Chulainn is the supreme example of the ideal Celtic hero. The pagan Celts venerated god and hero alike; the hero possessed many of the qualities of the tribal god — bravery and near-invincibility in conflict, for example — but both were capable of surrendering to superior forces, natural or supernatural. Both hero and god had strong intellectual capacities, and a quickness of wit which resulted in martial success as frequently as did mere brute force and the clever handling of weapons. Both were often in possession of some especially potent weapon, in Cu Chulainn's case the mysterious *gae bolga,* the spear he had obtained from a warrior goddess, once it penetrated the body it could not be withdrawn without inflicting fatal wounds from its barbed sides. This concept of the hero, like the Celtic concept of deity, allowed of no unintelligent, handsome brute, blundering along and succeeding only by means of his phenomenal strength. Beauty the hero must have, and great physical stamina, but he must also be intelligent, and educated according to the standards of his time. He must be able to outwit the hostile forces, not only of this world but of the supernatural, by his superior knowledge and by his quick wit.

A Law unto Himself

The stories of the *Ulster Cycle* were written down in the form in which we now have them c 1100 AD, but their manuscript origins were much earlier. They are concerned with the *Ulaid,* the people of Ulster, in northern Ireland, about the turn of the Christian era. The main story in the cycle is that of the cattle raid of Cualnge (*Tain Bo Cualnge*), the splendid epic which deals with the rivalry between the provinces of Connaught and Ulster, and with Cu Chulainn's heroic defence of the Ulstermen.

Cu Chulainn knew the secret language of the poets, for the great *fili* or poet, Amairgin, had been his foster-father, and had instructed him in the poetic and juridical arts. He first outraged, then pacified, the society into which he entered, in true heroic fashion. He had physical beauty of a kind that was extraordinary because it differed from the physical ideal of his tribal background and yet it was striking enough to impress favourably all who saw him. He was small, in a society in which height was revered; dark, where fairness was in vogue; a beardless boy, not a mature bearded warrior. He was called a *sirite,* 'sprite', a law unto himself, nevertheless upholding the honour of his people against impossible odds. He was known as *siabartha,* 'distorted one', because of the terrible change in his appearance when his battle ardour was

Statue of the Irish hero Cu Chulainn in Dublin's General Post Office. His legendary exploits, aggressiveness and great physical beauty commanded the highest respect in pagan Celtic society

Irish Tourist Board

aroused. He was the fear of every warrior, the beloved of all women who looked upon him in his full beauty. He was the son of the great god Lugh, the lover and subjugator of the goddesses, arousing the desire even of the terrible Morrigan, the war goddess, with her dark bird-form and her terrifying magical and prognostic powers.

The *Ulster Cycle* contains some historical material, but the main characters and episodes are of a manifestly mythological nature. It reflects a society which is strikingly similar to that described by the classical commentators on the continental Celts, and suggested by archeological evidence and Roman writings for parts of Britain. It was an intensely aristocratic society, and Cu Chulainn was a youth of noble birth and connection. His mother was Dechtire, sister of the high king Conchobar mac Nessa, the wife of the warrior Sualtaim, who is then Cu Chulainn's earthly father. According to one version of the conception of the hero, his birth is the result of an incestuous union between Dechtire and her brother the king. By the time Cu Chulainn is seven years of age he has left childhood far behind him, being the equal of a 14 year-old youth and clamouring for action.

The Heat of Battle
While still a small boy, Cu Chulainn sets out for Emain Macha, the court of Conchobar; he is equipped only with his toy weapons. He bursts into the precincts of the royal residence and attacks and overcomes the 150 youths who are practising games on the playing field there. The *Tain Bo Cualnge* contains the fascinating account of the young hero's progress, describing the various ordeals he undergoes in his journey from childhood to the status of a hero. His great boyhood feat is that of killing the monstrous hound of the smith Culann. The smith bewails his loss, and the boy promises to act as watch dog for him until another beast shall have been reared. He is then known as Cu Chulainn, Culann's Hound, and so acquires his name.

Next, he gains weapons by treachery. He has heard the Druid Cathbad saying to his pupils that 'a boy who would take up arms (on that day) would be splendid and famous, but would be short-lived and transient'. Cu Chulainn goes to the high king and

demands weapons, leading his uncle to believe that Cathbad has sent him. He breaks all the weapons which are given to him, only those of the high king himself enduring. Against all advice, he goes off to try his luck as a warrior and has phenomenal success against great odds.

He returns to Emain Macha in a great state of triumph and exhilaration. The watchers at the fort are disturbed when they see him approaching, because they recognize that his dreaded battle ardour which distorts his appearance has come upon him; he is berserk. They try various ruses to calm him. Naked women are brought before him, and when he hides his face he is seized and placed in a vat of cold water, which boils and bursts open. A second vat is brought, and this also he heats in the same way. A third calms him, and he is then restored to his normal appearance. He is dressed and brought before the king.

A dramatic description from the same story demonstrates the non-normal appearance of this supreme Celtic hero. 'His comely appearance was restored, and he blushed crimson from head to foot. He had seven toes on each of his feet, and seven fingers on each of his hands. He had seven pupils in each of his royal eyes, and seven gems sparkling in each pupil. Four dimples in each cheek, a blue dimple, a purple, a green and a yellow. Fifty tresses of hair he had between one ear and the other, bright yellow like the top of a birch-tree or like brooches of pale gold shining in the sun. He had a high crest of hair, bright fair as if a cow had licked it. He wore a green mantle in which was a silver pin, and a tunic of thread of gold. The boy was placed between Conchobar's knees, and the king began to stroke his hair.'

Cu Chulainn epitomizes the concept of the Hero for Ireland. We must suppose it to have been a concept common to the early Celtic world, where magical powers and superhuman battle feats were believed to be accompanied by fierce physical distortions and strange emanations such as the 'hero's light'. In the *Tain* it is said of Cu Chulainn: 'The hero's light rose from his forehead, so that it was as long and as thick as a hero's whetstone. As high, as thick, as strong, as powerful and as long as the mast of a great ship was the straight beam of dark blood which rose up from the very top of his head

and became a dark magical mist, like the smoke of a palace when a king comes to be attended in the evening of a wintry day.'

Kiss for a Severed Head
The epic of the *Tain* is concerned with the hero's single-handed defence of the province of Ulster, when the rest of the male population were suffering from a debility that rendered them utterly incapable of physical effort. Cu Chulainn is immune from this affliction, perhaps another indication of his foreign origin. He engages in a series of triumphant single combats, which are described in detail.

He has various taboos, and the violation of these must inevitably lead to destruction. He is named after a dog, and so must never taste the flesh of this animal. But the hostile forces of the otherworld combine to destroy him. He is tricked into tasting canine flesh, thus violating his taboo, and from then on his end approaches swiftly. He dies, fighting against his enemies to the last. His head is struck off and, when placed on a rock, splits it with its enduring battle-heat. His wife Emer, whom he had won in true heroic fashion from her father by violence, kisses the lips of the severed head and dies with her husband.

The character of Cu Chulainn, then, epitomizes all that pagan Celtic society venerated and desired. His skills, his intellectual powers, his chariot feats; his harnessing the powers of the otherworld, his acceptance of fate and the choice of a brief, violent, glorious career rather than a long, safe, mundane existence; his colourfulness and his aggressiveness; his aristocratic nature and his great physical beauty. All these qualities are those we know the early Celts to have desired in their gods and in their heroes alike. Such stories must have been told in the crude houses of the rich Celtic chieftains throughout the pagan Celtic world and, although the names of the hero and the deities concerned must have differed, the basic concept must have been recognizably similar. And so enduring that it has persisted, and come down the ages to survive today in vestigial form in the hero tales told in the humble homes of the Celtic-speaking survivors of this pagan Celtic past, on the fringes of the western world.

ANNE ROSS

CUCKOO

THE LOUD CALL of the cuckoo, heralding the arrival of spring, is of greater importance in folklore than its other well-known habit of laying its eggs in the nests of other birds. None of the familiar birds visiting Europe announces the advent of spring with so loud, reiterative, and distinctive a call — a call whose pitch and other characteristics make it easily imitated by the human voice. Other birds with call-notes having some resemblance to the human voice, such as the great northern diver and some owls, are commonly regarded as mysterious and have also achieved prominence in folklore.

The 13th century song 'Sumer is icumen in, Lhude sing cuccu' reminds us that to our forefathers, as to us, the cuckoo was a welcome harbinger of increasing sunshine, warmth and growth. Its arrival was a notable date in the calendar, as is indicated by local traditions in the English counties that the cuckoo arrives for the local fair — for example, in Hertfordshire, where it is said to come to Sawbridgeworth fair. In Siberia some of the tribes timed their spring ceremonies by its call.

It was a small step from noting correlations between birds' calls, weather and farming operations to assuming that correspondences between the cuckoo's calling and human affairs were such that personal

fortunes could be predicted by noting the bird's behaviour. Thus, in England, Scotland and on the Continent it was said that a person could tell how long he had to live by noting how often the cuckoo called. All was well if, as often in spring, the cuckoo called incessantly — but probably such sayings were never taken very seriously. It was also said that a girl could ascertain how long she would remain unmarried by counting the calls; but in Germany, if the cuckoo called more than ten times in such circumstances, it was generally regarded as bewitched and unreliable. In the United States it is said that a cuckoo's call, especially if from low-lying lands, is a forewarning of rain. And another American

Radio Times Hulton Picture Library

superstition states that, whatever you are doing when you hear the first cuckoo of spring, that activity will predominate in your life for the rest of the year.

A belief dating from the time of Aristotle or earlier, and still lingering in the countryside today, is that the cuckoo turns into a hawk in winter; this arose, no doubt, to explain the bird's disappearance. Plausibility was given to the notion by the similarity between the cuckoo and the merlin, a kind of falcon, together with the disappearance of the merlin from much of its winter range to its breeding haunts about the time the cuckoo arrives.

There was a widespread belief in Europe and North America that on hearing the first cuckoo of the year one should wish, and there are still people who make a ritual event of the occasion by turning the coins in a pocket, for luck. It is said that if you have money in your pocket on hearing the bird, you will not want for it throughout the year. In parts of Germany it was the custom for rustics to roll on the grass when the bird was first heard, claiming that by so doing they could avoid suffering from lumbago. In Norfolk and Sussex it was unlucky to hear the first cuckoo while in bed, as this was a warning that someone in the family would become ill. In the Scottish islands and in France it was undesirable to hear the cuckoo before having broken one's fast. The Scots expected bad luck to follow, but the French said that the person who heard the cuckoo while fasting would suffer from numbed limbs

The similarity of the cuckoo's two syllable call to words in various languages has led some people to regard it as a bird endowed with the gift of prophecy: from the title page of Andrew Borde's *Merry Tales of the Madmen of Gotam*

or become a good-for-nothing idler.

There appeared in print as far back as 1685 a procedure for obtaining a clue to one's future spouse. It was said that if a man looked under his left shoe on first hearing the cuckoo he would find a hair of a similar colour to that of his future wife; a woman could discover her future husband in the same way. There were various other somewhat similar procedures.

Prophetic Bird

Augury and ornithomancy are based on notions that bird behaviour has ulterior and sometimes supernatural significance. Thus in Cornwall to hear the cuckoo on the right presaged good fortune, while to hear it on the left boded ill. In Norway more elaborate prognostications were made according to the point of the compass from which the bird was heard calling. As bird augury was practised on a considerable scale by the Romans, some of the associated notions may have been carried north and have influenced regard for the cuckoo. They must also have been carried to the New World, for an old rural American belief reads similar meanings into the location of the bird – especially the first of the year. If it calls from the south, a good harvest is presaged; if from the north, death or other tragedy;

from the east, luck in love; from the west, general good luck.

The similarity of the cuckoo's two syllable call to words in various languages has formed a basis for some traditions. A Bohemian legend relates that the cuckoo is a metamorphosed girl calling for her lost brother or, alternatively, if the words are interpreted differently, announcing that he has been found. The theme of a Serbian song is that the spirit of a dead man could not find release because his sister wept so incessantly at his grave. So she transformed herself into a cuckoo and cries continually, 'Ku ku, Ku ku,' meaning 'Where are you?' There may be some connection between these two stories and a belief that the cuckoo goes to a mysterious realm, the land of the dead, in winter. This is supported by an odd Estonian legend according to which Christ came to a cottage after a wicked stepmother had murdered two children and told the father that they would appear in spring as two living creatures. They emerged as a cuckoo and a swallow.

The cuckoo has often been associated in the past with cuckoldry: Shakespeare speaks of the cuckoo who 'mocks married men'. In the *Asinaria* of the Latin dramatist Plautus (c 250–189 BC), a man's wife, finding him in adultery, shouts at him: 'What? is the cuckoo lying there? Get up, gallant, and go home.' The connection between the cuckoo and cuckoldry appears to have arisen from its nesting behaviour and its consequent reputation as a usurper.

EDWARD A. ARMSTRONG

CULT OF THE DEAD

Baschieri Salvadori

568

Man, in contrast to other animals, treats his dead with love, hatred, awe or sorrow: he rarely ignores them completely. Behind this is the hope that they live on after death, and very often the belief that they will help those who survive

Left Papuan natives blow through tubes into figures which represent their ancestors, perhaps to keep them alive with breath
Right Among the Kraho Indians of Brazil women weep for their dead relatives by the special logs made to receive the souls of the dead

The appeasing of ancestors by human sacrifice is a far cry from Poets' Corner in Westminster Abbey or the Lenin mausoleum in Moscow. But the basis for these is the same – the impulse to forge a link between the living and the dead

IN THE GUATTARI CAVE on Monte Circeo, on the Italian coast north of Naples, there was found in 1939 a solitary skull, lying on a platform of earth and stones. Round the skull was a circle of stones, and strewn about the floor were the bones of deer, buffalo and horses, and also the lower jaw of another human being. The skull belonged to a man aged 40 or 50, who had been killed by a blow on the right temple with a sharp weapon. There were indications that the brain had been extracted, perhaps to be eaten. The skull may originally have been set up on a stake, the ring of stones suggests a magic circle and the animal bones may be the remains of offerings to the skull or of meals eaten in its presence.

Since prehistoric men left no written explanation of themselves, much of what can be said of them is highly speculative but it looks as if this skull was worshipped in some fashion, though it is not certain that its owner was murdered: he may have been killed in battle or by accident. What is certain is that one of the most striking differences between men and other animals is that animals ignore their dead and men do not. Men treat their dead with love, hatred, awe, sorrow, or even with appetite, but rarely with casual disregard.

Lying behind this is an even more important distinction. Unlike the other animals, a man is aware that he himself will eventually die. The effects of this realization on human behaviour have been incalculably great. It is the root of the hope for a life beyond death and it is probably one of the roots of belief in supernatural beings which do not die, which create and maintain the order of Nature, on which each man depends for his brief earthly existence.

The Dear Departed

The men or man-like creatures who lived in the Choukoutien caves near Peking about 500,000 years ago already used fire and made rough tools. They may also have been cannibals who ate the brains and the marrow of the bones of their dead. Perhaps they did this (if they did it at all) merely because they liked the taste, but if they believed that in eating the dead they acquired their strength and skill, or that the dead lived on in the bodies of their eaters, this is the earliest trace of a cult of the dead, in the sense of a belief that something survives death and that what survives has power and requires special treatment.

Later, though still very early, burials suggest concern for the dead and possibly fear of their power. In the Teshik-Tash cave in Uzbekistan, in central Asia, a child had been buried in the middle of a circle of ibex skulls. In a cave on Mount Carmel in Palestine the bodies of five men, two women and three children had been trussed up with their knees drawn up to their bodies. This may have been done to save space and so make grave-digging less taxing. Or it may have been a magical attempt to help the dead to be reborn, by arranging them in the position of a foetus in the womb. Or it may have been meant to stop the dead from getting out of their graves and attacking the living. Or death may have been seen as a kind of sleep and the bodies arranged in a sleeping position, in which case our euphemism 'laid to rest' is an extraordinarily old one.

Later still, though before true man had emerged, Neanderthal burials in Europe show care and respect for the dead, possibly tinged with fear. Of six skeletons discovered near La Ferrassie in central France, all except one had been buried facing west. The west is the direction of the dying sun in the evening, and it was later widely believed that the far west was the home of the dead. The single exception was a body which faced east and had been trussed before burial with the legs drawn up. Perhaps this elderly woman had been feared in life and was still feared in death.

But Neanderthal burials generally suggest an affection for the dead. They were buried under the floors of the caves in which the people lived, sometimes near the hearth, presumably to give the cold corpse warmth and perhaps with the feeling that the departed was still one of the family and should keep his accustomed place by the fire. The fact that tools and joints of meat were buried with the dead suggests that they were thought to be still alive somehow, somewhere, and that it was the duty of the survivors to help them.

The Place of Skulls

In the Upper Paleolithic period (c 30,000 to 10,000 BC) *homo sapiens* himself, with a brain markedly larger than that of the average modern man, spread from Asia into central and western Europe, and across northern Africa into Spain. He again buried his dead with care, close to the living, and often sprinkled red ochre on them, apparently to give them the blood-red colour of renewed vitality. The dead were dressed in their best, hung with valuable ornaments, and generously equipped with food and weapons, which means that the

C. M. Dixon

Picturepoint London

living made real sacrifices, in the literal sense of the term, for their dead.

Dating from the Mesolithic period in Europe (c 10,000 to 3500 BC) are the 33 human skulls found in the Great Ofnet cave near Nördlingen in Bavaria. All of them faced west and were covered with red ochre. At least five, and possibly 21 of these people had been killed by hatchet blows. This collection of relics may have belonged to headhunters, who thought that by taking their victims' heads they acquired an extra supply of human energy. Or the heads may have been buried with ceremony to pacify the angry ghosts of the murdered.

These heads, like the Monte Circeo skull and the human skulls found at Catal Hüyük in Turkey, resting on what was apparently an altar of the great mother goddess (see ALTAR), suggest that the head was already regarded with particular awe, as it certainly was later. The head is the part of the body with which a man breathes, sees, hears, eats, talks and thinks. It is the part which you think of as pre-eminently *you*, the home of your personality, and it was perhaps already believed to contain the essence of a person's life-energy and character (see also HEAD; SKULL).

The earliest surviving realistic portraits of human beings were found at Jericho in Palestine, dating from not later than 6250 BC. They are human skulls covered with plaster, in which the features were modelled, with eyes made of shells. They probably come from a family portrait gallery and

represent ancestors who were venerated by their descendants. The practice was apparently fairly common at Jericho, because quite a number of decapitated skeletons were found buried under the floors of houses.

The Panoply of Death

The Neolithic period (from c 3500 BC) saw the spread of the techniques of breeding cattle, as distinct from hunting them, and growing crops instead of merely gathering them. Presumably these changes would have strengthened the feeling that a man's land and herds were his because his forbears had owned them, that they were the gifts of his ancestors and belonged to his family — past, present and future — a feeling which lies at the root of ancestor worship (see below). This period has left plentiful evidence of human attention to the dead, especially to those who had been powerful in this life.

At Alaca Hüyük in Turkey the stone-lined graves of chieftains who ruled from c 2400 to 2200 BC contained astonishing quantities of gold, silver and copper objects — daggers, maces, battle-axes, cups and jugs, ornate pins and mirrors. At the same period in Mesopotamia the royal graves at Ur were magnificently equipped, and there courtiers, soldiers and servants had been killed with their masters, no doubt to continue serving them in the afterworld. At Maikop in southern Russia a man was buried under a canopy which was partly supported by golden figures of bulls, and he

The commemoration of our dead predecessors is an explicit recognition of our indebtedness to them *Above left* The Celts paid particular attention to their dead, especially to those who had been powerful in this life. Celtic chieftains were often buried with chariots and their regalia. Central Court Grave in Co Sligo, Ireland *Above right* Arlington Cemetery, Washington, reserved for those who have given distinguished service to their country *Opposite* Skulls of monks sharing a single anonymous grave, as they shared all things during life. Down the centuries the remains of monks have been preserved in the monastery garden on Mt Sinai *Left* Mourners pay their last respects by the deceased's open coffin *Right* The Karaja Indians of Brazil leave food on the top of ceramic urns, containing the remains of the dead, to sustain them in the afterworld

wore a robe on which were 87 gold plaques representing bulls and lions.

For the living to spend so much on the dead suggests a mixture of affection for them, an obligation to equip them fittingly for the life to come, and a healthy respect for the help and protection which they could give to those who survived them. The earliest written records in human history are concerned with securing a happy immortality for the kings of Egypt (see BOOK OF THE DEAD). In the 14th century BC in China, the rulers of the Shang dynasty were interred with what has been described as 'extravagant pomp'. The king was buried in a wooden room at the bottom of a pit 45 feet deep and 65 feet square.

Even secular societies such as the Soviet Union inter their illustrious sons with pomp and circumstance, and provide for the cult of the dead

Other human beings might be killed and buried with him and in some cases he was given chariots and horses as well.

In the 5th century BC the great traveller Herodotus wrote a famous account of the burial of a Scythian king (in his *Histories*, book 4). The Scythians lived to the north of the Black Sea. When a king died, they slit open the corpse's belly and filled it with pleasant-smelling substances, sewed it up again and buried the body, lying comfortably on a mattress, in a great square pit. They strangled one of the king's concubines and several other members of his household and buried them with him. They also buried horses, golden cups and a selection of his other treasures with him. Then they piled up a mound of earth over the grave and waited for a year.

After a year, they strangled 50 of the king's remaining servants, whose bodies were gutted and filled with straw, and similarly 50 of his finest horses. Then the men and the horses were impaled on spikes and placed round the tomb, each horse with its rider, and left there.

Herodotus also remarked that when an ordinary Scythian died, the body was taken by his family on a round of visits to friends. The friends provided meals, serving the corpse with food just like the rest.

The Megaliths

Meanwhile in the eastern Mediterranean area, burying the dead underground had begun to be accompanied by the building of structures above ground. These structures were sometimes far more imposing than the homes the dead had inhabited in life, like the colossal pyramids built to tower over the mummified corpses of Egyptian pharaohs. Before 2000 BC in Crete, for example, the dead were being buried in caves, or in underground chambers resembling the rooms of houses, or in chambers above ground.

This fashion in burials spread westwards to Malta, Spain, Portugal and southern France. Large stones (megaliths) began to be used for the walls and roofs of the tombs, an architectural style which spread to the rest of France and into northern Europe. Some of the tombs and the stones used were of huge size. Near Seville in Spain there is a tomb close to 70 feet long with a block of granite at the front of it which

is 11 feet high, weighs 21 tons and had been fetched from a quarry more than 20 miles away. At New Grange in Ireland, a burial chamber, with a passage 62 feet long leading to its entrance, was covered with a circular mound of earth 265 feet across and about 45 feet high.

Not all megalithic tombs were anything like as big as this but even the smaller ones required human sweat and toil far in excess of what would have been needed merely to tuck the dead neatly away out of sight. The monuments imply a powerful sense of awe and respect for the dead, and possibly an urge to keep them tethered to their graves, close to their kinsmen and descendants for the help they could give.

Many of these tombs seem to have been the burying places of a family, or a larger group of people, used over a long period of time. When a man died, apparently, his corpse was left in the tomb with food, weapons and other equipment, and the door of the burial chamber was walled up, to keep him inside. When the next corpse was to be buried, the door was broken down again and offerings were burned to honour the spirit of the first occupant. This would go on until too many bodies had accumulated, and to make room for newcomers the skeletons already inside were pushed out of the way and piled up in disorderly heaps at the sides of the burial chamber. The apparent disregard of these elderly bones suggests that, not unnaturally, when a person had been long forgotten his remains were no longer treated with great respect.

In Brittany, there is often a menhir (a single upright stone) at the head of a grave and the entrance of the burial chamber inside points towards the menhir. It has been suggested that the people who built these graves believed that the souls of the dead liked to come out to take the air, and that the menhir was both a perch on which the soul could rest and also a marker which would help it find its way back.

The Dead and the Goddess

It is possible that the use of large stones and mounds of earth to wall in and roof over the dead was a development from the older tradition of cave burial, and was connected with the belief that burial under a weight of earth was the right way to put the dead where they belonged, in the

domain of the earth goddess. Some megalithic tombs in Europe contain paintings and idols of a goddess, pottery decorated with a face or a pair of eyes, and geometrical patterns which may be symbols or stylized pictures of the goddess. These representations are almost certainly derived from figures of goddesses in Asia Minor and the eastern Mediterranean.

Both in Europe and elsewhere, many of the representations of a prehistoric mother and earth goddess have been found in burying places. Her connection with the dead was a natural one, for the dead were buried in the earth and it was the earth from which the crops sprouted. Perhaps to be committed to the womb of the earth carried with it the hope of a new life, just as the plants which die drop their seeds into the earth and are reborn again in due season.
(See also PREHISTORIC RELIGION.)

RICHARD CAVENDISH

Ancestor Worship

The basis of ancestor worship lies in a feature found in all human societies, the commemoration of the dead. There are obvious reasons why the dead live on in the memory of the living. The greater part of man's behaviour, as well as the material surroundings within which he works, is transmitted to him from his forbears. This body of customs and artefacts that we call culture includes his language, his buildings, his art and his social organization. None of these stand still; each generation makes its own contribution; but each does so in a cumulative way on the basis of the achievements of earlier generations.

This is especially true of simpler societies. There a man is often exploiting the same productive resources as his immediate predecessors. In Australia the territory of a band of hunters is usually one that has been passed down from earlier generations. In agricultural societies, men are yet more dependent upon their forbears. Among the Ashanti of West Africa, for example, land was regarded as belonging to the Earth, a female principle, but it also belonged to the ancestors. When a farmer began to cultivate his land, he sacrificed a fowl upon some mashed yam and said, 'Grandfather, you once came and hoed here and then you left it to me.' It was because his ancestor had hoed the

In the Belly of the Earth

Then Fa and the old woman laid Mal gently on his side. They pushed the great gaunt bones of his knees against his chest, tucked in his feet, lifted his head off the earth and put his two hands under it . . . Mal's fingers were moving aimlessly and his mouth was opening and closing. Fa and the old woman lifted the upper part of his body and held his head. The old woman spoke softly in his ear.

'Oa is warm. Sleep.'

The movements of his body became spasmodic. His head rolled sideways on the old woman's breast and stayed there.

Nil began to keen. The sound filled the overhang, pushed out across the water towards the island. The old woman lowered Mal on his side and folded his knees to his chest. She and Fa lifted him and lowered him into the hole. The old woman put his hands under his face and saw that his limbs lay low. She stood up and they saw no expression in her face. She went to a shelf of rock and chose one of the haunches of meat. She knelt and put it in the hole by his face.

'Eat, Mal, when you are hungry.'

. . . The old woman took handfuls of water and the others dipped their hands too. She came back and poured the water over Mal's face.

'Drink when you are thirsty.'

. . . At a sign from the old woman, Lok began to sweep the pyramid of earth into the hole. It fell with a soft swishing sound and soon Mal was blurred out of shape. Lok pressed the earth down with his hands and feet . . .

The old woman squatted down by the freshly stamped earth and waited till they were all looking at her.

She spoke:

'Oa has taken Mal into her belly.'

William Golding *The Inheritors*

land before him that he himself had the right to farm there.

The commemoration of our dead predecessors in an explicit recognition of our indebtedness to them, whether they are Christian saints, the benefactors of an Oxbridge college or our more immediate forbears. It is as appropriate to secular as to religious practice, and the visits of Soviet leaders to London are regularly marked with excursions to the grave of Karl Marx at the Highgate cemetery. Even secular societies such as the Soviet Union inter their illustrious sons with pomp and circumstance, and provide for the cult of the dead (while rejecting their continued existence in the afterlife). Both the Lenin mausoleum and Westminster Abbey celebrate not only the major political figures of the country, but also 'cultural' heroes like the astronaut Yuri Gagarin and the poet William Wordsworth.

An Influence after Death

It is useful to distinguish ancestor worship proper from the cult of the dead and from forms of memorialization. The interment of Yuri Gagarin does not imply any idea of personal continuity after death, and yet it is difficult to disentangle personal continuity from social continuity, that is, from the influence a man continues to have after his death. The cult of the dead implies a belief in an afterlife of some sort; the worship of ancestors recognizes their participation in everyday affairs; by appeasing the dead, or more often by failing to do so, we bring about their intervention in the world of the living.

But ancestors are not just any dead; they are a man's specific forbears, his lineal kin, those who have socially and physically brought him into being. Hence there is a close association between the kind of kinship groups which a society possesses and the custodianship of the ancestral shrines. In Chinese society, where men belonged to their father's clan, custodianship followed the paternal line; it was the sons that looked after their father's shrine. Indeed, here, as among the Hindus and the ancient Romans and Greeks, a childless man might adopt a son to ensure that he had worshippers at his shrine (and an heir to his property). Even a widow might adopt a son in her husband's name and so preserve, as the

Chinese say, the continuity of the incense smoke, which is burnt at the ancestral tablets.

Incense is burnt daily; other offerings, such as fruit, preserves, sweets, rice sprouts, fragrant wood, lotus flowers and cooked food are made on festive occasions. At the same time the richer families employ a priest to read from the scriptures and perform certain rituals before the shrines. His function is to report the names of the dead (he has a complete family genealogy) to superior deities and to uplift them by reading the scriptures so that they are able to proceed to the Western Heaven of Happiness as soon as possible. (See also CHINA.)

The Hell Named Kalasutra

In India the ancient Hindu Law of Manu recognized the obligation of a man's sons, by birth or adoption, to provide food for the dead. 'The ancestors of men are satisfied a whole month with sesame, rice, barley, black lentils or vetches, water, roots and fruit, given with prescribed ceremony; two months with fish, three months with venison, four with mutton, five with the flesh of such birds as the twice-born may eat . . .' Such offerings are made mainly at the *Sraddha* or mind-rite of the orthodox Hindu, when offerings to the ancestors can be made indirectly through the priests. 'Whatever mouthfuls . . . are eaten by the Brahmins are eaten by the ancestors,' writes another lawgiver. The food may be given to a cow, a kid or burned but 'that fool . . . that gives the residue . . . to a man of servile class, falls headlong down to the hell named Kalasutra.'

In societies such as Ashanti in West Africa, where a man belonged to the kin group of his mother and her brother, then the matrilineal descendants, the sister's sons, looked after the shrines. This did not mean that a man could not sacrifice to his father, but he had to do so through a member of his father's clan.

The Watchful Dead

Worship of the dead (of which ancestor worship is one form) varies between simply warding off the dead with gifts lest they should intervene, and asking for their positive blessing in the way the Ashanti did. In the Eurasian continent, ancestor worship often seems to be of the placatory kind. 'Death and life' wrote Sir Edward Tylor, 'dwell but

ill together, and from savagery onwards there is recorded many a device by which the survivors have sought to rid themselves of household ghosts.' Funeral ceremonies are full of examples of customs whereby the ghosts are set apart from the living, particularly from their nearest and dearest, the widows and the orphans, who are seen to be in the greatest danger from their loved ones. In more generalized form, such sentiments seem to be associated with many offerings to the tombs of the dead. In China, India and in the classical world, the dead appear actively to intervene if they do not receive their due. When they are treated properly, they are benevolent. But if the Hindu dead do not receive their due, then they wander around as ghosts; if neglected, the Chinese ancestors apparently turn into demons and bring trouble upon the world.

There seems to be a division in Europe and Asia between good, appeased ancestors and bad, rejected ghosts or demons. In Africa such ghosts exist, persons who have not yet reached the Land of the Dead. But the ancestors, as ancestors, seem to play a more positive role, both good and bad, in the affairs of men; translation of their immaterial forms into masks, figures, shrines, is more developed. These differences are partly related to the wider distribution of literate, universal religions in the Eurasian continent. Islam, for example, forbids the representation of the human image; and the worship of the One God allows little room for the propitiation of ancestors. Nevertheless, just as Christianity took over some local shrines and turned ancestors into saints, capable of acting as intermediaries between man and God, so too the Moslems of North Africa turned the graves of ancestors into the tombs of saints.

In addition to these religious influences, there were also some differences in the organization of kin groups and in systems of inheritance which may have affected the worship of ancestors. It is clear that attitudes towards parental figures must affect the attitude towards the ancestors, the dead parents. In China it has been suggested that because a man often took over his share of the patrimonial property during his father's lifetime, his relationship with his parents was less hostile as a result; his advancement no longer depended upon their death. In Africa it is generally those ancestors

Picturepoint London

from whom one inherits that one has most to fear; 'guilt' feelings apart, it is to them that one has a particular debt which needs to be repaid in offerings.

The Shrines of Ancestors

At death the dead make their journey to the other world. But communication with them has to continue from this world. Even the memorialization.of the dead inevitably tends to take on material forms; the appropriate behaviour is directed towards and focused upon a grave, or an object associated with the dead man or an effigy, such as a statue or painting. In this context, great stress is placed upon the actual burial, the actual dwelling-place, the actual representation of the dead. It has been argued that drama began with the acts and scenes of burial ceremonies, which incorporated drama and mime. However this may be, many forms of representative art are rooted in ancestor worship and memorialization of the dead. For the living individual, the portrait on the walls of the ancestral home ensures one's survival after death: and the greater the artist, the greater the hope of immortality. For the survivors, the creation of an image provides a point of contact, a living and enduring memorial.

Such memorials and shrines range from the abstract to the representational, these different forms often being found side by side in the same region, though in general it is true that the simpler the society the more abstract the style. In West Africa, the poorer agriculturalists have shrines of mud

mounds or earthenware pots, or even of selected stones. Among the Ashanti, with their elaborate state system and richer resources, the ancestor shrine is a carved stool, which is blackened on a man's death.

The Ashanti stool is an example of the complexity of such ancestral shrines. In the first place, it is an outward and visible sign of an individual's status. A child will be presented with a small stool when, after seven days, he goes through the 'out-dooring' ceremony and acquires a real human personality. Different chiefships and different clans have their own stools, carved in a traditional way and often illustrating some appropriate proverb.

On such a stool only the office-holder himself may sit; when he rises it is placed on its side. For someone else to sit there would be a direct challenge, not only to a man's office but to his very existence. For so closely is the stool identified with the individual, impregnated as it is with the 'dirt' of his body, that his life itself is threatened by such an act.

The stool is at once chair and throne, the symbol of authority. The Ashanti believe that at the birth of their nation a golden stool descended from the heavens and became the most valued part of their regalia, the symbol of their new-found unity, the 'soul of the nation'. In 1900 when the British Governor of the Gold Coast, Sir Frederick Hodgson, tried to take possession of it in the name of Queen Victoria, the result was insurrection.

The stool represents not only the spirit

of the nation, but also the spirit of the individual. At death a man's stool is seized and the white wood blackened with soot. It is then placed in the 'stool-house' of the lineage to which the dead man belonged, normally just a room in the elder's compound. Here it rests among the shrines of earlier dead, receiving offerings of food and flesh from the living members of the lineage. (See also ASHANTI.)

Shrines and memorials may be collective or individual, the former tending to be abstract, the latter representational. Among the Ashanti only the stools of important members of the lineage are placed in the shrine-room. To the north, in the savannah lands of Ghana, each individual Tallensi has a shrine, but only when he has been survived by two generations of descendants and therefore established his own 'house'. Among the nearby LoDagaa every man who leaves behind him a son (or whose widow produces a son to his name by marrying his brother) has an ancestor shrine carved for him during the long course of the various funeral ceremonies.

Few systems of ancestor worship are as elaborate or as specific as these, nor yet so closely linked with organizing the relationships between living men; for to sacrifice together to common ancestors is clearly a unifying bond of the greatest importance. In most societies, it is the more immediate dead that are man's primary concern. But here too the tombs, relics and shrines, both abstract and representational, provide a thread of continuity between the

574

Camera Press London

Shrines, portraits, images and graves are important because they provide a point of contact between the living and the dead
Left Entrance to Forest Lawn Cemetery in Los Angeles, California. In America the corpse is often embalmed and made to look as lifelike as possible, the emphasis being on 'eternal preservation'
Above Ancestor worship is still a powerful force in China: in Hong Kong joss sticks and candles are burnt, with prayers for the spirits of the dead

Lop-Sided into Paradise

A Chinese girl goes to the grave of her mother:

. . . I would return to this place, this being the eighth year of her tenancy, and draw her forth. With a Taoist priest of Macau I would come, which would pay tribute to my mother, and a labourer. I would expose the coffin and lift the lid. One by one I would take out her bones, first hiding the skull under my coat away from eyes. Then I would polish the bones with sand, the little bones of her feet I would polish first and place them at the bottom of the Canton urn. Next the leg bones I would take, and these I would perfume, and lay them next in the urn, then the rib cage, the arms, the tiny bones of the fingers — all these I would place most carefully in the urn lest I bring her lopsided into Paradise. On these, amid the incantations of the priest, I would lay the skull and cover the mouth of the urn away from flies.

Alexander Cordell
The Bright Cantonese

living and the dead; not only do they represent a continuation of the same personality but they provide a focus for communication between a man and his descendants.

Food for the Dead

Ancestor worship is simply a form of communication between the living and the dead. The forms of the communication vary, though all fall within the range of normal human intercourse. There are verbal forms — prayer, oaths, written formulae. There are visual forms — gesture (usually gestures of obeisance), painting, sculpture, the temple itself, then dance and more extensive types of movement such as the procession and the pilgrimage. Finally there are the offerings of flesh and food which form so important a part of ancestor worship. The worshippers pay homage to a 'divinity' that was once a man, a 'god' who was once a producer and consumer, and in many cases owner of the very means by which the living continue to produce — the land, the oxen or the ploughshare. So the dead continue to be offered the basic food and drink of the country, the bread and the wine, the yam and palm sap, the porridge and the beer.

But service to the dead cannot be the simple duplication of service to the living; the things of this world have a different meaning for those who can no longer enjoy them in the same way. With food the ancestors receive only a part of the whole; with livestock, the whole is offered in sacrifice,

but the biggest portion is in fact consumed by those who remain behind. As far as the ancestors are concerned, a major element in the transaction would seem to be not so much giving as repaying; one is in perpetual debt to the forefathers, just as one is to parents who have raised one from infancy; one can repay this debt only by continual piety in the shape of sacrifice.

Human Sacrifice

Sacrifice is of two general kinds. The regular offerings to the dead are made on festivals like the three day period (the period of moon's rebirth, the period of Christ's resurrection) of Hallowe'en, All Saints and All Souls. Then there are the occasional sacrifices made at times of affliction, when one's child is ill and a diviner has pointed to an ancestor as the cause. For the dead, while beneficent to their descendants, can also punish. Indeed recent ghosts and others who have not been properly settled in the land of the true dead, are often plain vindictive, sometimes so that the living will be forced to undertake the correct rituals on their behalf, or to right a wrong that has been done them. Whereas the regular transactions approximate to the payment of debt, to the fulfilment of an obligation, the latter smack more of a gift that tries to repair some damage done. But often the damage has itself been caused by failing to give the ancestors their due, thereby incurring their wrath.

Sacrifice is not, of course, confined to the ancestors: it is a way of communicating with supernatural agencies of all kinds. But there is one kind of offering of living beings that is often directed towards the dead – human sacrifice. The ritual immolation of human beings was widely practised; it was found among practically all the Indo-European peoples; in early Israel, Samuel 'hewed Agag in pieces before the Lord'; it occurred in India and Japan, among the Aztecs of Central America and in the forest states of West Africa.

But human beings (often criminals, slaves or war captives) were also sacrificed to accompany the dead on their journey to the other world. They were used, as in the West African kingdom of Dahomey, to convey messages from the living to the dead, especially to dead kings. As the 19th century explorer Richard Burton wrote, 'They periodically · supply the departed monarch with fresh attendants in the shadowy world. For unhappily these murderous scenes are an expression, lamentably mistaken but perfectly sincere, of the liveliest filial piety . . . Whatever action, however trivial, is performed by the king, it must dutifully be reported to his sire in the shadowy realm. A victim, almost always a war-captive, is chosen; the message is delivered to him, an intoxicating draught of rum follows it and he is despatched to Hades in the best of humours.'

In the United States, Plains Indians went to war after a death so they would not 'grieve alone'. The Natchez of the lower Mississippi, alone among American tribes, practised wholesale sacrifice at important funerals, killing wives, relatives, friends, all to accompany the dead – and others not connected with the dead man often volunteered for the same honour, while parents killed their children as extra sacrifices and thereby gained great status.

Human sacrifice, or 'ceremonial murder', is akin to ceremonial suicide. Again the act is often associated with the cult of the dead. In earlier times Hindu widows were expected to sacrifice themselves upon their husband's funeral pyre (see SUTTEE). So too the Japanese *hara-kiri*, when committed at the funeral of a dead person, is in the nature of an offering to the soul of the dead.

Human sacrifice also lies close to cannibalism. For just as animal sacrifices are

Memorial to Karl Marx in Highgate Cemetery, London, frequently visited by foreign Communist officials paying their respects to the dead philosopher

consumed by both god and man, so too man may be expected to consume part at least of the fellow humans he has offered. This practice was not very common, except as a ritual gesture. Indeed many societies, especially those following the major world religions, disapproved of the sacrifice of animals, let alone humans.

Royal Ancestor Worship

While the ancestors of ordinary men continue to communicate with their descendants, guarding over them and receiving their due, so the royal ancestors continue to be involved in the affairs of the state.

Indeed one of the strengths of dynasties like that of Egypt or of Ashanti, one of the sources of their legitimacy and a discouragement to their overthrow, was their role as intermediaries between their subjects and their ancestors, the earlier kings.

In Ashanti one can see royal ancestor worship as a simple extension of what occurred among the commoners. But in the Middle East and the Eurasian continent, ancestor worship in the full sense seems largely confined to the royal dynasty. At death in Egypt every dead man became the god Osiris, who was the king of the dead, associated with the idea of resurrection and the annual life and death of the cereal crops. There was no specific worship

directed towards the individual, though the relatives of the dead often commemorated them. The worship of individual ancestors was largely confined to the burning of incense for the royal dead who were installed in their monumental stone pyramids in the valley of the Nile.

Crime and Punishment

A belief in the continued influence of the ancestors on human life is often an important factor in maintaining the laws and customs on which social life rests. In Rome, the man who sold his wife was given over to the ancestors for punishment; so too was a child who struck his father and the violator of graves. It is over the most serious offences against one's fellow men, such as fratricide and incest, that the ancestors are often the main instruments of social control, more important than the judges who administer the earthly punishments.

The ancestors are never completely cut off from this world. Often they are seen as returning to the world in the shape of their own descendants, either by the process of reincarnation or by other kinds of spiritual identification. Among the Murngin, a hunting tribe of Northern Australia, the soul of a dying man goes back to the 'totemic well' on the territory of his clan; it is from here too that the spirits of the unborn emerge to find a home in the womb of a wife of a clan member. When a man dies, it is his father's father or other grandparent that escorts him back again. Thus there is a continuous chain of being.

JACK GOODY

FURTHER READING: For the general background to the prehistoric cult of the dead, see G. Clark and S. Piggott, *Prehistoric Societies* (Knopf, 1965) and for more detail see J. Maringer, *The Gods of Prehistoric Man* (Knopf, 1960); Glyn Daniel, *The Megalith Builders of Western Europe* (Penguin, 1963); E. O. James, *The Ancient Gods* (Putnam, 1964). For ancestor worship, see also Jack Goody, *Death, Property and the Ancestors* (Stanford Univ. Press, 1962); John Middleton, *Lugbara Religion* (Oxford Univ. Press, 1960); M. Fortes and G. Dieterlen, *African Systems of Thought* (Oxford Univ. Press, 1960); Francis Hsu, *Under the Ancestors' Shadow* (Routledge, London, 1948).

Cup

Symbol of woman, of abundance, of spiritual sustenance: the cup of the Mass or Holy Communion which holds the consecrated wine is called a chalice: in Christian legend the Holy Grail was the cup used by Christ at the Last Supper, preserved by Joseph of Arimathea.
See GRAIL; MASS.

Cupid

The Roman god of love, identified with the Greek Eros: son of Venus or Aphrodite, the love goddess; frequently depicted as a beautiful winged boy with his bow and arrows, which arouse love in those they strike: like love itself, he is erratic and mischievous: the delightful story of how Cupid woos the mortal Psyche is told in *The Golden Ass* of Apuleius.
See EROS.

Un père de famille est rendue à la santé par ses prières.

Il rend la parole à un enfant muet.

Il rend l'usage des jambes à un boiteux.

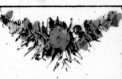

Faites, Seigneur que nous soyons toujours animés de la crainte et de l'amour de votre saint nom, puisque vous ne cessez jamais de protéger ceux que vous avez établis dans la solidité de votre amour.

VÉRITABLE PORTRAIT DU CURÉ D'ARS, Né à Dardilly en 1786.

JEAN-MARIE-BAPTISTE VIANNAY

Il distribue du pain aux pauvres.

Il convertit beaucoup de personnes en prêchant

Il prie Dieu d'éclairer ses ouailles.

Dieu de bonté accordez à notre faiblesse les secours de votre grâce; et comme nous honorons la mémoire de la Ste Mere de Dieu, faites que par le secours de son intercession nous puissions nous relever de nos iniquités. Amen

CURÉ OF ARS

THE LIFE OF St Jean-Marie-Baptiste Vianney, patron saint of parish priests, is of great interest from the viewpoints both of mystical theology and psychical research.

Born in 1786, the second son of a small farmer in the village of Dardilly, near Lyons, he proved exceptionally responsive to his mother's religious teaching. A sensitive and nervous child, he was also robust, lively and vivacious but occupied his mind with religious topics while assisting in the fields. The French Revolution entailed persecution of those Catholics who repudiated the state organized church. Vianney therefore had little schooling and attended secret Masses.

Jean-Marie's sense of religious vocation, the desire to 'win many souls to God', crystallized about 1798 when he was sent to work on his uncle's farm at Ecully, about four miles south of Dardilly. Ecully sheltered several priests including Abbé Charles Bellay who prepared Jean-Marie for his first Communion, administered secretly. In 1805, when religion was restored, his father let him return to Ecully to study at Abbé Bellay's presbytery school. He found Latin agonizingly difficult and only a 60-mile pilgrimage on foot to the tomb of St John Francis Régis at Lalouvesc in the mountains

Editions du Chalet

of Ardèche saved him from despair. As an intending priest registered under the Archbishop of Lyons (Napoleon's uncle), he was exempt from military service, but in 1809 was called up in error.

Falling ill of a 'slow fever', he was sent on to rejoin his regiment. Exhausted he was picked up on the road by a military defaulter who conveyed him to Les Noës in the shelter of the Bois Noirs hills. The Mayor, a confirmed anti-Bonapartist, advised him to stay in hiding.

In consequence of an amnesty he returned to Eculiy in 1811 and from 1812 to 1814 he studied at seminaries in Verrières and Lyons. He failed the examinations (conducted in Latin) but was allowed to take them in French. He was ordained priest (deacon) at the age of 29.

In 1818 Vianney was appointed to the tiny parish of Ars, across the Saône about 16 miles from Lyons. One small church of primitive design and four large taverns ministered to the needs of the 230 inhabitants who tended to be indifferent to religion. But the Abbé could not reconcile himself to a single soul eluding Heaven.

The Conversion of Ars

By calling at mealtimes, though himself refusing refreshment, he came to know every family. He spoke to them as peasant to peasant, but never failed gently to insist on the claims of religion. Soon the villagers learned of his fasting and prayers for sinners late into the night and before dawn. In the pulpit he declared innkeepers to be the source of sin and poverty, incapable of salvation. As the church filled the taverns emptied. The innkeepers went out of business, the last one being bought out by the Curé.

An able strategist, Vianney first converted the women, who prevailed on their menfolk to attend church and not work on Sundays. In the confessional the little Abbé ruthlessly withheld absolution until convinced that contrition was genuine and sin renounced. The most prolonged of his struggles was against communal dancing, rustic drunken revelries tending to promiscuity. But by 1824 he had effectively won his battles.

His parishioners soon discovered his remarkable talent as a confessor. He had a wonderful ability to penetrate their secret thoughts, it seemed. His words were few but always perfectly aimed. In time the faithful flocked to confession from Ars, Dardilly, Eculiy and Les Noës, and eventually from all France.

His was an incredibly exhausting regime. He became so thin that he seemed but a flame glowing through skin and bone. His

large bright eyes, radiant in a shrunken and wraithlike face, gave him the semblance of a saint on earth, and it was not surprising that broadsheets extolled him as if he were already enthroned in glory.

His sermons were as famous as his confessional. He depicted the horror of damnation; but it was not mere 'hell-fire' preaching or 'bible-punching'. Spontaneously he shed tears, as did his congregation, at the plight of souls separated from God and spoke with moving simplicity of the joy of those who perpetually saw God face to face. Bishops and dignitaries came from all France to hear him, as well as writing to him for advice on dealing with moral and pastoral problems.

In later years the Curé was constantly exposed to the temptation to retreat from Ars to a monastic and contemplative existence. He tried to leave the village three times but always returned. At his last attempt, in 1852, he was apprehended by his parishioners. He died in Ars after a brief illness, in 1859 at the age of 73.

The Making of a Saint

In his last years he reluctantly accepted the ribbon of the Legion of Honour. By this time 100,000 pilgrims, it is estimated, visited Ars annually. Consequently the first papal Process for inquiry into Vianney's merits began as soon as 1862. He was declared Venerable in 1872, Blessed in 1905 and canonized as a Saint in 1925, on the basis of two cures effected at his tomb.

The Curé's remains were exhumed in 1904 preparatory to his beatification. The flesh was dried and darkened but intact except for the face which, though recognizable, had suffered damage.

For many of the pilgrims Ars and its Curé had a mystic lustre, and many came in the hope of physical cure as well as spiritual healing. As in all pilgrimages a proportion of the suppliants were cured of bodily ailments. Few of the accounts extant are sufficiently detailed medically for us to decide whether they were natural or supernatural. Since such cures can and do occur outside of a religious setting, we cannot affirm them to be patently supernatural. But, whatever the cause, Ars was as productive of faith-cures as any of the world's famous shrines.

Vianney was a fine intuitive psychologist. His remarks, often humorous and always gentle though firm, revealed a penetrating simplicity. Some of the qualities of G. K. Chesterton's character Father Brown were inspired by the Curé. Numerous testimonies suggest that he had an insight superior to the normal, as if he was literally capable of reading thoughts. In modern terms, we should describe him as a 'sensitive' with a marked capacity for telepathy. From a crowd of pilgrims Vianney would pick out a total stranger and tell him the problem that had brought him to Ars and intimate facts of his life. These stories are based on written testimonies with circumstantial detail. It is possible that the Abbé was also clairvoyant and precognitive.

We are in no position to decide whether he had these powers by nature or by God's

A visionary and mystic, the Curé of Ars was also a penetrating and intuitive psychologist; in addition various testimonies suggest that he was capable of reading thoughts *Previous page* **Portrait of the Curé: the scenes surrounding his picture illustrate events in his life, including miracles that he is believed to have performed** *Left* **Statue, in wood, of the Curé of Ars: canonized in 1925, he is the patron saint of parish priests**

Michael Holford

grace as a token of sanctity. Such abilities are not manifested by all saints. Modern sensitives tell us that response to human need is a factor very conducive to the operation of paranormal powers, a suggestion supported by other evidence from psychical research. Also the Curé's austerities rivalled those of any oriental yogi, though whether paranormal powers can in fact be reinforced by asceticism is not yet certainly known.

Ecstasies and Visions

Those who lead lives of spiritual intensity are often visionaries. The Curé would sometimes pass into the state of calm and joyful contemplation, known technically as 'ecstasy'. In ecstasy numerous mystics have believed themselves to be in direct spiritual union with God. The Curé was most guarded about his experiences, but phrases he let slip suggest that at times he felt the close presence of John the Baptist, the Blessed Virgin and St Philomena, as well as Christ himself.

Some witnesses testify that they themselves had visions in the Abbé's presence. In 1840 a Mlle Durié heard a gentle voice talking to the Curé. Entering the room she saw a lady of ordinary stature, in a robe of dazzling white bearing golden roses and with a wreath of stars about her head. Addressing the lady as Mother, Mlle Durié, who believed herself to have cancer, asked to be taken to Heaven. 'Later', said the lady who then vanished. Mlle Durié aroused the Curé from what appeared to be an ecstasy, 'his countenance radiant and his gaze fixed'. When Mlle Durié referred to the presence of 'our Lady', the Curé told her she was not mistaken but must never speak of it again. It appears that Mlle Durié was cured of her presumed cancer after a lapse of three and a half months.

Attacks of the Devil

The Curé's life corresponded to saintly prototypes in a further respect. From 1824 to 1858 he suffered sporadically what he believed to be persecutions by the Devil. At night he heard noises as of rats gnawing or scratching, or of blows on the doors of the presbytery, or of hammering or drumming. Sometimes the Curé would hear the sound of footsteps and a coarse rough voice mocking him as 'a potato eater' and growling abuse and obscenities. A picture of the Annunciation was found smeared with filth. The Curé's bed was shaken and pulled across the room while he lay on it. The testimony of contemporaries suggests that on some occasions only the Curé heard the diabolical speech and noises, and it is natural to suppose that sometimes they were only hallucinatory. The act of vandalism could, in theory at least, be attributed to the Abbé himself in a condition akin to sleep-walking, as with Father John of Castille, of whom it was said that the Devil compelled him to use his own hands to deface pictures of the Blessed Virgin. But there was also testimony from Ars which suggests that some of the happenings, including the voice, were actual objective physical events. And there is no evidence positively to support the sleep-walking theory.

The haunting of the Curé bears a strong resemblance to poltergeist outbreaks, many of which are objective phenomena. Many features common to poltergeist disturbances suggest that a goodly proportion of them are due to obscure natural causes and related to emotional tension in the person on whom they centre. We know that the Curé's heroic virtue in his pastoral office was maintained in the face of a longing for solitude and contemplation, and it is arguable that the internal struggle was externalized in the drama of the Satanic persecution.

The mysterious happenings attendant on the Abbé cannot be surely interpreted as either natural or supernatural by considering his life in isolation from the data of psychical research on the one hand, or the phenomena of the mystics on the other. As a person at first he repels as a reactionary puritan, but in the end the most agnostic of readers is liable to be vanquished by Vianney's strange and improbable charm.

A. R. G. OWEN

FURTHER READING: René Fourrey, *The Curé D'Ars* (P. J. Kenedy, 1959); L. C. Sheppard, *Portrait of a Parish Priest* (Newman Press, 1958); Francis Trochu, *The Curé D'Ars* (Tan Books, 1977); Margaret Trouncer, *St Jean-Marie Vianney: Curé of Ars* (Sheed & Ward, 1959).

CURSE

SWEARING IS NOT TAKEN very seriously in our society but its old religious and magical connotations linger on. The word 'oath' usually means a careless imprecation but it can also mean a solemn statement, backed by a man's honour or by an appeal to God. To swear is generally to use 'bad language', a socially incorrect and ill-mannered activity, but to swear on the Bible in a court of law is a socially correct action, still likely in practice to make a witness more reluctant to tell lies than he might be otherwise.

Old-fashioned people object to swearing not only because they consider it vulgar but because it is blasphemy (a word whose meaning is now commonly restricted to swearing, in fact). The old phrase for it is 'taking the Lord's name in vain' or, in other words, trying to use God's powers for your own trivial or wicked purposes.

A curse is still the product of inner tension, which it still relieves. It still frequently achieves its basic object of bullying others into compliance, even though few of us any longer expect the curse to do physical damage to its victims. In societies which do expect a curse to

Because Adam and Eve surrendered to the serpent's tempting, and ate the fruit of the tree of the knowledge of good and evil, they were cursed by God, and expelled from the Garden of Eden: 14th century Bible Historiale

Bodleian Library Colour Filmstrip

ራሔል፡እን፡ዘ፡ቱበ፡ባ፡ሰደቂ፡ቃ።

Michael Holford

harm its victim, it is part of the accustomed armoury of the magician and its effects can be damaging and sometimes even lethal. In 1956 an Australian aborigine was taken to hospital in Darwin, apparently dying because he knew that a death-spell had been cast against him. Placed in an oxygen tent and fed intravenously, he gradually recovered because he believed that the white man's magic was stronger than the aborigine sorcerer's.

Claude Lévi-Strauss has described the deadly effects on a man who knows he is the victim of hostile magic, in a society which believes and has conditioned him to believe that sorcery will kill him. The man himself is certain that he will die. His family and friends are equally certain, and treat him as if he was already dead. The victim's fear and his rejection by everyone around him may in practice prove fatal.

In this light, the effectiveness of excommunication, the solemn Christian ritual of cursing, in the Middle Ages is less surprising than it might seem at first sight. In his *History of the Inquisition* H. C. Lea described the plight of a man who had been excommunicated, in terms very like those of Lévi-Strauss. 'To the public law of the period he was an outlaw, without even the right of self-defence against the first-comer, for his very self-defence was rated among his crimes; in the popular faith of the age he was an accursed thing, without hope, here or hereafter. The only way of readmission into human fellowship, the only hope of salvation, lay in reconciliation with the Church through the removal of the awful ban.' And the *Catholic Encyclopaedia* echoes the same theme in saying of the excommunicated outcast that he can be 'considered as an exile from Christian

society and as non-existent, for a time at least, in the sight of ecclesiastical authority.'

In most cases a curse is not meant to be either fatal or permanent. It punishes an enemy until he makes amends, when the curse is formally removed. Nor need a curse always be spoken aloud. For instance, there is an Eskimo belief that you can injure a person by spitting on the ground in front of him, meanwhile formulating a malevolent wish against him in your mind. In Europe and the United States witches have long been thought capable of harming people by 'ill wishing' them, usually by means of some magical action that may be as simple as spitting, pointing a finger, or a mere glance of the eye. And this is no dead and forgotten folk belief: it still prevails in civilized times. In 1906, a farmer in Pennsylvania paid a woman a large sum of money to remove her curse or spell on his livestock, which had been inexplicably dying one by one for a year. More recently, in 1953, an Arizona rancher shot and killed a woman whom he (and everyone in the area) thought was putting a curse on his wife. In Limoges, France, in 1963 an old woman was investigated by police for alleged 'witchcraft' activity, though she claimed to be a lifter of spells, not a caster. And in southern Germany, where the witch belief is especially strong, a farmer in 1964 accused his wife of having cursed his cattle, so that cows went dry and calves died.

But cursing need not always be malevolent. In writing about the Lugbara people on the northern borders of Uganda, John Middleton has explained how the head of a family invokes the ghosts of his ancestors to punish with sickness any of his relatives who need to be disciplined. He does this by sitting near the shrines of the ancestors and thinking the words of the curse in his mind. If he says the words aloud, if he 'whispers into the shrine', the effect will be so drastic that the victim is likely to die. 'Silence in the face of offence, or merely the words "you will see me later" from an elder or kinsman of the same family cluster, are ominous and tantamount to a threat to invoke the ghosts.'

This is an example of the curse as a support of authority and established order, a threat which ensures good behaviour. In an essay on 'Zande Blood-Brotherhood' E. E. Evans-Pritchard has described the Azande ritual in which two men (or two groups) form an alliance by drinking each other's blood. The blood each man has swallowed will take vengeance on him if he betrays the alliance. 'If you see someone struggling with your blood-brother and you run and attack him also and strike him violently, may you not recover from the vengeance of the blood. If a child of mine is in danger of the law and hides in your hut and you give him away so that he gets into trouble, may you die from the blood . . .'

Often the speaker takes a piece of cord, holds it in his blood-brother's hair and twists it round and round on top of his head while the spell is pronounced. The twisted cord stands for the grip which the blood will take on the other's vitals if he breaks the alliance.

If one of the men is false to his blood-brother, the blood in his stomach is expected to take vengeance by itself but sometimes the injured partner will take the cord which he used during the ritual and wind it into a ball, meanwhile calling on the blood to exterminate the offender and his family, to bring upon them leopards, lions, snakes, thunder, dysentery, leprosy and other evils. He wraps the ball in leaves and hides it in the roof of his hut. If the offender comes to make amends, the ball is taken down and unwound, and the blood is ordered to release the man from its grip.

The Well of St Elian

This type of curse, which is to strike someone only under certain stated conditions, is known from many parts of the world as a way of ensuring that obligations which have been undertaken will be met, and so of preserving social harmony. According to

Death by Magic

An individual who is aware that he is the object of sorcery is thoroughly convinced that he is doomed according to the most solemn traditions of his group. His friends and relatives share this certainty. From then on the community withdraws. Standing aloof from the accursed, it treats him not only as though he were already dead, but as though he were a source of danger to the entire group. On every occasion and by every action, the social body suggests death to the unfortunate victim, who no longer hopes to escape what he considers to be his ineluctable fate. Shortly thereafter, sacred rites are held to dispatch him to the realm of shadows. First brutally torn from all of his family and social ties and excluded from all functions and activities through which he experienced self-awareness, then banished by the same forces from the world of the living, the victim yields to the combined effect of intense terror, the sudden total withdrawal of the multiple reference systems provided by the support of the group, and, finally, to the group's decisive reversal in proclaiming him – once a living man, with rights and obligations – dead and an object of fear, ritual and taboo. Physical integrity cannot withstand the dissolution of the social personality.

Claude Lévi-Strauss
Structural Anthropology

the Roman historian Livy, when the Romans made a treaty with their neighbours the Albans, the Roman spokesman prayed to Jupiter: 'If the Roman people shall knowingly and of set purpose depart from the terms of this treaty, then smite thou them, O Jupiter, as I smite this boar-pig today.' And he killed the pig with a flint knife.

The use of the cord in the Azande blood-brotherhood ritual recalls the prominence of the idea of 'binding' in curses from the ancient world. In the *Republic* Plato condemns magicians who, 'if anyone wishes to injure an enemy, for a small fee they say they will bring harm on good or bad alike, binding the gods to serve their purposes by spells and curses (*katadesmoi*).' The Greek word means literally 'bindings' and refers to curses scratched on lead tablets or bits of pottery and placed in tombs or buried in the ground. Sometimes

Facing page After the birth of Jesus, Herod ordered the massacre of all male infants in Bethlehem, in an attempt to kill the child who was destined to become 'King of the Jews': according to St Matthew's Gospel, this fulfilled one of the prophecies of Jeremiah through whom God had declared a curse against the Hebrews 'for all their wickedness in forsaking me'. 17th century Ethiopian manuscript in the British Museum, depicting the Massacre of the Innocents *Below* The ancient belief that a curse would prevent a grave from being disturbed survived into Elizabethan times: epitaph on Shakespeare's tomb at Stratford-on-Avon

British Travel Association/Vicar & Churchwarden of Holy Trinity, Stratford

the lead tablet was tied round with wire, to 'bind' the victim more effectively. A curse scrawled on a piece of pottery and dating from c 400 BC says, 'I put quartan fever on Aristion to the death'.

These curses were frequently intended to disable opponents in a legal action. A late 4th century example from Athens says, 'I bind Theagenes in tongue and soul, and the speech that he is preparing. I bind also the hands and feet of Pyrrhias the cook, his tongue and his soul and the speech that he is preparing.' Two other hostile witnesses are similarly 'bound' and the curse ends, 'All this I bind, obliterate, bury, impale'. In some cases the curse was believed to be effective by itself but sometimes the spirits of the dead or the underworld deities were also called upon.

This method of cursing is not as far from us in the modern West as we might like to think. The cursing well of St Elian at Llanelian-yn-Rhos, near Colwyn Bay in Wales, was doing a flourishing trade in the mid-19th century. The procedure was to write the name of your enemy on a piece of paper, put it in a lead box and tie it to a slate on which you wrote your initials. You took it to the keeper of the well and paid him a fee. Your curse against your victim was then recited and the lead box was thrown into the well.

The keeper would probably also receive a fee from the victim, who would hurry to pay for the curse to be removed. The keeper would read two psalms to him and make him walk round the well three times. Then he would draw up the curse in its lead box from the well and give it to the victim.

Another long-lived use of a curse was to deter robbers from violating graves. Many curses of this sort have been found in funeral inscriptions from the ancient world, especially in Asia Minor, and in northern Europe curses were written in runes on gravestones (see ALPHABET). The fear of being disturbed in the grave and the use of a curse to prevent it survived into Shakespeare's time. The epitaph which he chose for his tomb at Stratford says:

> Good friend, for Jesu's sake forbear
> To dig the dust enclosed here.
> Blest be the man that spares these stones
> And curst be he that moves my bones.

The idea is still by no means dead, as the

stories of curses alleged to have overtaken those who have disturbed the rest of Egyptian mummies show.

A curse may also overtake a man as the result of some crime which not he but his ancestors committed. The hereditary curse which haunted the house of Atreus, kings of the Greek city of Argos, played a part in the murder of Agamemnon, leader of the Greeks in the siege of Troy, by his wife Clytemnestra, as told in the *Agamemnon* of Aeschylus.

Bell, Book and Candle

In Greece an official curse could be pronounced by magistrates or priests against an enemy of the state or an offender against the laws, and evidently had a terrifying effect on the victim. In the Old Testament, chapter 28 of Deuteronomy contains a catalogue of maledictions against those who do not obey the voice of the Lord God, so comprehensive and so drastic that Jewish congregations were frightened of hearing it read at all, in case it brought the curses down upon them.

These official curses are the predecessors of the Christian ritual of excommunication, in which the notion of 'binding' appears again, for the Church based its right to curse, with effects reaching even beyond the grave, on Matthew 18.18, where Jesus tells his disciples that 'whatever you bind on earth shall be bound in heaven, and whatever you loose on earth shall be loosed in heaven.'

The most ceremonious form of the rite of

Left A magical method of causing death or injury is to curse a doll made in the image of the intended victim: witch doll, with photograph of the subject of the curse attached **Right** A protection against curses is a 'witch bottle': the nails, and heart made of felt and pierced with pins, were originally inside the bottle, which would disable a witch before she could cause harm **Below** The ceremony of excommunication is popularly known as bell, book and candle: the book from which the curse was read was closed, a bell was tolled as for a dead man, and candles were extinguished, symbolising the removal of the offender's soul from the sight of God: detail from an encyclopedia of canon law and theology compiled in the 14th century: British Museum

excommunication is popularly known as bell, book and candle because the officiating cleric closes the book from which he has read the curse, a bell is tolled as for a dead man, and candles are extinguished as a sign that the soul of the offender has been removed from the sight of God. Of course, the excommunication can be lifted if the offender repents.

In the 8th century Pope Zachary devised a formula for popes to use in pronouncing anathema (another word for ceremonious excommunication). The pope was to wear violet vestments and his mitre, and to be assisted by 12 priests carrying lighted candles. He formally deprived the offender of the Mass and separated him from the society of all Christians: 'we exclude him from the bosom of our Holy Mother the Church in heaven and on earth . . . and we judge him condemned to eternal fire with Satan and his angels and all the reprobate, so long as he will not burst the fetters of the demon, do penance and satisfy the Church.' Finally the pope and the 12 priests threw their lighted candles to the ground.
(See also INCANTATION; OATH.)

FURTHER READING: E. E. Evans-Pritchard, *Essays in Social Anthropology* (Free Press, 1963); W. K. C. Guthrie, *The Greeks and their Gods* (Beacon Press, 1968) for the Greek curses and the well of St Elian; J. Middleton ed, *Magic, Witchcraft and Cursing* (Natural History Press, 1967) contains the essays by Lévi-Strauss and Middleton mentioned in the article.

CYBELE

THE GREAT GODDESS of Nature and her young lover or son, well-known deities in the Near East, appear in Anatolia (now Turkey) as Cybele and Attis. As figures of classical mythology they are best known from literature of Roman times, both Greek and Latin, but they have a previous history, which this literature reveals in part. They were always known to be foreign to Greece and Rome.

The cult and myth of Cybele as known in the classical world originated with the Phrygians who entered Anatolia from Thrace in the 13th century BC. It contained elements taken over from the native population, among which was perhaps the figure of Attis. Even in ancient times Attis was sometimes identified with the Syrian Adonis, so closely did they resemble each other. But Cybele, though she is akin to such other forms of the Great Goddess as Astarte in Syria and Ishtar in Babylonia, Ma in Anatolia and Rhea in Greece, is a distinctive figure because of her special connection with mountains and with wild beasts.

According to some scholars Cybele is the same as Cybebe of the Lydians (who lived in what is now southern Turkey) and certainly little distinction between them is found in classical literature. Cybebe originates from the South Anatolian and North Mesopotamian nature-goddess Kubaba, 'mistress of doves'. But the name Cybele is likely to be Phrygian, since Cybela or Cybelus was a name of her sacred mountain and apparently meant a place of caves or chambers where she dwelt and had her image. In some Phrygian inscriptions from 700 BC onward she is called *matar Kubile* and Attis *Atte papa*, which suggests that Attis was a male consort.

The original centre of her cult was Pessinus near Ankara in Phrygia (now central Turkey) at the foot of Mount Dindyma or Dindymum. The mountain is now called Gunusu Dagh.

During the 7th century her cult appears to have spread through Anatolia to Lydia and the coast of the Black Sea. From Lydia it reached Greece, where it was little favoured and usually left to Phrygian slaves. In 205 BC at the crisis of the Hannibalic war it was brought direct from Pessinus to Rome. Cybele was accepted there as a goddess who protected cities and maintained life, was established in a temple on the Capitol, and was later honoured with a festival, the *Megalensia*, the Great Mother's Games. Fortune began to favour the Roman armies, and there was even an unprecedented harvest in Italy which repaired the ravages of war. But in spite of its magical efficacy the cult with its rites was found scandalous at Rome, so that it was insulated by special rules. No Roman was permitted to join directly in its rites, still less to serve as a priest. From Rome in the imperial age, when in its train other oriental cults were introduced, it spread to the provinces and lasted until the triumph of Christianity.

The original character of Cybele may be gathered best from the scornful description

Attis, the consort of Cybele: bronze statue in the Louvre, Paris

Giraudon

of the Christian apologist Arnobius who touches on it in a tract written about 300 AD; some of the same details appear in the writings of Pausanias, the Greek geographer of the 2nd century AD, and elsewhere. Cybele was born of the rock Agdus from the seed of Zeus; hence her name Agdistis used in this story. She was at first a bisexual monster of great strength and ferocity. The monster devastated the country and terrified gods and men until Bacchus tricked it by pouring into its favourite drinking fountain a great quantity of the strongest neat wine as a soporific. As it slept, Bacchus tied its male organs firmly to a tree with a rope of twisted bristles, so that when it woke and sprang up, these organs were torn off with a great flow of blood, and it lost its male sex. From the blood the first almond tree grew. One of the almonds was picked for its beauty and put in her lap by Nana, daughter of the river Sangarius. It disappeared, but Nana became pregnant. She was shut up without food by her father, but fed by the Great Mother until she bore her child Attis. By order of Sangarius, Attis was exposed in the open and left to die, but he was fed by a wild goat.

The Black Stone

As he grew up, his beauty attracted the love of Agdistis who hunted with him in the woods and presented him with the game. Midas, King of Pessinus, wishing to deliver Attis from this disgraceful attachment, arranged for him to marry his own daughter, closing the town's gates for the ceremony. But Agdistis burst in, raising the town walls on her head, because she knew that danger threatened Attis if he should marry. Thereupon Attis went mad and castrated himself under a pine tree; scornfully making a gift of his severed organs to Agdistis, who gathered them up and preserved them. Violets grew from them, with which the pine was decorated. But Attis himself died from his wounds. In spite of Agdistis's prayers, Zeus would not restore him to life, but merely preserved his body from corruption and kept its little finger in perpetual motion. Agdistis installed the body in a tomb at Pessinus with castrated priests to maintain a cult.

The childish and dream-like grossness of this form of the myth is surely a sign that it is the original one. Its savagery persists in all later forms. Primitive too is the black stone of Pessinus, the uncarved fetish which was specially identified with Cybele and was later taken to Rome. The high, flat-sided crown that her images wore, explained in this myth as the walls of Pessinus raised on her gigantic head, is a feature which suggests that she was originally conceived as a living mountain or rock, as well as an anthropomorphic goddess. This is borne out by the account of her origin. The myth was toned down and even allegorized by later writers, such as the Emperor Julian (331–363 AD), the last powerful defender of paganism.

The poet Lucretius (c94–55 BC) recognized Cybele as the Great Mother, wearing her 'mural' crown and riding in her chariot drawn by lions, and described her cult. Catullus (c84–54 BC) again describes the cult. The hero of his story is a young Greek, not the mythological Attis. He visits the mountainous area in the north-west of Phrygia to hunt on Mount Ida, is seized by madness, castrates himself and joins Cybele's followers, and when he wishes to escape is driven back into the forest by one of her lions. The versions in which Attis dies by the wound of a boar's tusk are affected by the myth of Adonis. But in some versions of the myth, and evidently in the cult, Attis is said or assumed to rise again from the dead. As a spirit of vegetation, which renews itself every year, he would naturally do so, and it was the purpose of Cybele's cult to maintain life. The castration, which persists in the myth and cult, had the nature of a sacrifice to Cybele. Sacrifices of bulls and rams were also customary.

The cult was unique in the Greek and Roman world for its noise and frenzy. It was psychologically akin to the cult of Dionysus, which was likewise by origin Thracian and Anatolian but much better known to the Greeks, having been long ago adopted by them and controlled. Cybele's procession of eunuch priests marched, danced and whirled through the streets to the scream of flutes, the throbbing of drums, the clatter of castanets and the clash of cymbals. Where this was allowed, devotees who joined it wounded and sometimes castrated themselves. The priests wore long robes like women. The cult had regular beggars, the *metragyrtae*, and municipal officials, carriers of the sacred pine, to administer it. In spite of the decorous statues of Cybele known in classical art, her cult always showed her underlying nature. Traces of the same originally hermaphrodite character are found in other goddesses.

E. D. PHILLIPS

FURTHER READING: Sir James Frazer, *The Golden Bough* (St. Martin's Press, 1980 reprint).

Cyclops

Or 'circle-eye' (plural Cyclopes), name given to the one-eyed giants of Greek myth; divine craftsmen, they were the forgers of Zeus's thunderbolt: best known is Polyphemus who, in Homer's *Odyssey* imprisons Odysseus and his men, but is outwitted by the hero: generally depicted in classical literature as a figure of burlesque and fun

Michael Holford

Cypress

A graveyard tree, symbolic of death and, because it is evergreen, of resurrection: associated with powers of the underworld by the Greeks and Romans: according to various stories, the cross on which Christ was crucified, the pillars of Solomon's Temple, the club of Hercules and the arrows of Cupid were made of cypress wood.

Jim Bamber

Spirit possession is a characteristic feature of the traditional religion of southern Dahomey. A devotee who wishes to be 'captured' by a particular spirit has to undergo a long period of seclusion, during which his body is marked with ritual scars

DAHOMEY

FROM THE BEGINNING of the 18th century down to the 19th, Dahomey formed one of the most important kingdoms on the old Slave Coast of West Africa. In the complex Dahomean religion, the term *vodun* (from which is derived, through the slave trade, the West Indian 'Voodoo') was a key word in the religious vocabulary of several West African tribes, notably the Fon. Although in European accounts the vodun have often been described as gods or deities organized in a pantheon and constituting a system of polytheism, it would be more accurate to describe them as spirits. A characteristic feature of the religion of Dahomey is spirit possession.

A spirit or group of spirits usually has at least one 'temple', which may be a simple mud hut or a much more elaborate structure. If it is believed to be especially powerful, it may have many temples in different parts of the country. Each temple has its priests, who may be male or female, and whose position tends to be hereditary, although new cults and temples are constantly being founded by persons who become possessed

by spirits. The priests minister to the devotees, *vodunsi*, who are attached to their temple and who have been initiated by them into the cult of that spirit. Often the devotees, the majority of whom tend to be women, have sought initiation in gratitude for, or in anticipation of, benefits conferred by the spirit, such as good health, fertility and prosperity. Membership in a cult may also be inherited.

The normal initiation ceremony can be very elaborate and expensive for the initiate and his kin who must pay the priest and sacrifice frequently to the spirit. It often includes a long period of seclusion at the temple, during which the initiate is said to have been 'killed' by the spirit and then to have been 'revived' or 'reborn'. While he is in seclusion, an initiate is marked with the body scars peculiar to the cult, is taught the language (often that of another tribe) associated with it, and rehearses its special songs and dances. Towards the end of his seclusion, he is 'captured' by the particular spirit which has 'declared war' on him and which 'enters his head' to take temporary possession of him. This condition is indicated by a trance-like state which normally occurs during dances in which the devotee is dressed in a costume special to that spirit and in which he imitates behaviour said to be characteristic of the spirit. Since the devotee acts in this way as a vehicle for the spirit, he hopes to derive benefits from it. After his initiation is completed, the devotee is expected to continue supporting the temple and its priest; to observe days

dedicated to the spirit by abstaining from work and sexual intercourse; and to join in the dances which bring on possession and which are held periodically for the spirit. When he eventually dies, his fellows, led by the priest, conduct special ceremonies for him.

Shades of the Ancestors

This brief summary of the complex cult organization may give the impression that all spirits are much the same but in fact there is an extraordinary variety. One important class comprises the ancestral spirits who are called *tovodun*. The Fon and the other tribes in the area are divided into clans and lineages, membership of which is normally transmitted in the male line, and the ancestors of these groups can influence the fortunes of their living members. Each lineage confirms its identity as a separate branch of the clan to which it belongs partly by building and consecrating a shrine to its own ancestors. The shrines of the senior lineage include some which are used on behalf of the clan as a whole. Each lineage makes annual sacrifices to its dead and at less frequent intervals they are honoured with more lavish ceremonies. Periodically, too, the more recent dead have to be properly 'established' as ancestors. In other words, they do not become tovodun merely by dying, but are given this status in rituals performed by their descendants who hope for some return from them. Many of these ceremonies can only be performed by a 'priest of the ancestors' whose training and appointment is (or was) partly controlled by the monarchy. A prominent feature of the ceremonies is the possession of lineage members by the spirits of their ancestors.

Within the general category of tovodun, some receive special attention. Each clan, with one or two exceptions, is said to stem from the mating of a woman with an animal or vegetable, which is regarded as the embodiment of a spirit. The first son born of this miraculous union is known as the clan-founder, *tohwiyo*. It is he who transmits to his descendants the special observances laid down for them by his non-human parent. These include prohibitions on eating certain foods and the use of particular tattoos. The tohwiyo is believed to concern himself with the affairs of the living, such as births, marriages, divorces

and deaths, and should be informed or consulted about them at the shrine which each lineage of the clan has dedicated to him. At the annual ceremonies for the ancestors, one dancer impersonates and is possessed by him.

The beliefs about the clan-founder and his parents represent the notion that the origin and persistence of the clan depend on the conjunction of the human and non-human — the vodun, in fact. The tohwiyo is appropriately the intermediary between the two spheres, because he is the product of their conjunction and is therefore both

Dahomey fetish: dominated by a multitude of spirits, Dahomeans worship inanimate objects which they believe to have magical powers

human and spirit. He and his father also signify which practices are peculiar to that clan and distinguish it from the others.

Some tohwiyo acquire such a reputation that they attract devotees from outside their own clans. A conspicuous example is the founder of the royal clan, supposed to be the son of a princess and a leopard. The kings of Dahomey encouraged commoners to participate in this cult, and at the same time prohibited members of their own clan from joining the cults of other vodun — a striking case of the political uses of religion.

These vodun are commonly associated with a few clans which trace their origins, not to partial but to complete human beings who came down from the sky or out of holes in the ground. These clans are therefore

Almasy

William Sargant

The Smallpox God

One unpleasant way in which Sagbata manifests himself to human beings is by afflicting them with smallpox or other eruptive diseases, and Europeans have therefore often called him the 'smallpox god', just as they have called Sogbo the 'thunder god'. They and Mawu-Lisa are in fact vodun which have been especially successful in competing with others to attract devotees. Some legends say that, like the tohwiyo, they were originally ancestral spirits and that their cults have only become more general in relatively recent times. Why they spread is not very clear, but they could hardly have done so if they had not appealed to human desires for security and well-being. Even so, they did not satisfy these desires completely for there are other successful vodun, several of which are especially concerned with the personal fate or destiny of individuals. The most well known of these are Legba, Dan and Fa.

Legba is a spirit for whom a common material representation is a figure with an exaggerated, erect penis, which symbolizes his inordinate demands for attention and his freedom from normal constraints. He has this character because he is a 'messenger' between all the other vodun who cannot communicate directly, since they 'speak different languages', and between them and mankind. Therefore, if he is not given the sacrifices he constantly requires, he may disrupt communications and thereby bring about natural calamities and individual misfortunes. The idea of Legba thus provides an explanation for those disasters which occur even when men have apparently discharged their obligations to other spirits.

Dan, who is commonly figured as a snake holding its tail in its mouth, is associated with the rainbow, with water and with smoke, and in general is said to represent the idea of motion. Primarily though, he is envisaged as a source of individual success or failure in gaining wealth. Therefore, he has to be treated carefully because, like Legba, he is notoriously fickle and can withdraw his favours if insufficient attention is paid to him. Both Legba and Dan are connected by Dahomeans with their most elaborate system of divination, which they probably acquired from the Yoruba. Its vernacular name is Fa and, besides revealing what good or ill the future may hold for an individual, it offers him the means of securing or evading it. Therefore, as well as being a technique of divination, Fa is a cult with its own metaphysical doctrine of man and nature, which some of its practitioners can expound in great detail. Indeed, Fa is often spoken of as a vodun. That this should be so may serve as a fitting final comment on the complex religion of Dahomey, which provides individuals with so many alternative ways of trying to interpret experience and to control it.

W. J. ARGYLE

FURTHER READING: W. J. Argyle, *The Fon of Dahomey* (Oxford Univ. Press, 1966); D. Ronen, *Dahomey: Between Tradition and Modernity* (Cornell University Press, 1975).

sometimes said to have no tohwiyo, their place being taken by the so-called 'gods', the most famous of whom are called Mawu-Lisa, Sogbo and Sagbata. There is evidence that these vodun and the clans associated with them originated amongst the Yoruba peoples who live mainly in western Nigeria, but are also found in Dahomey.

There is certainly a close correspondence between the spirits known to the Fon as Mawu-Lisa and to the Yoruba as Odudua-Orishala (Obatala). These spirits form a composite being, described sometimes as a hermaphrodite, sometimes as a pair of twins. They clearly symbolize an idea of duality in the world, since Mawu is female and is also the earth, the moon, the west and the night, whereas Lisa is male, the sky, the sun, the east and the day. At the same time, they express the unity achieved through the interaction of these dual elements and are commonly represented by the two halves of a gourd which are carefully joined together, suggesting the junction of the earth and the sky. In some myths, they are credited with having created the world, and they are then supposed to have divided the various features of it amongst their 'children', who are other vodun, born of their union. This multiplication of spirits within one cult is common in Dahomey.

Somewhat similar ideas are held about the group of spirits led by Sogbo, who is very like the Yoruba Shango. Sogbo is another hermaphrodite, supposedly living in the sky, who, like Mawu-Lisa, produced a number of 'children' to whom control over

Priests, either men or women, are attached to the temples dedicated to each of the many spirits or groups of spirits in Dahomey: their position is usually hereditary, although new cults and temples are founded by people possessed by spirits

different natural phenomena was given. Considered together, these 'children' represent a dual division of the world, in which the sky again stands for everything above, but it is the sea, and not the earth, which represents everything below. This feature is perhaps explained by the fact that the cult, in this form, originated at a village near the coast. Certainly, the beliefs about these vodun reflect a preoccupation with water, whether as the sea, the rivers, the lagoons or the rain. The 'sky spirits' in this group are also associated with thunder and lightning, which is one means by which they may attack human beings, who therefore have to placate them.

The third group of vodun is dominated by Sagbata (Yoruba – Soponna), who is called 'king of the earth'. He too is sometimes a single being, sometimes a pair of twins. and propagates 'children' who are the spirits of different aspects of the earth. The notion of duality is not very evident in the cult itself but there are myths in which Sagbata and Sogbo agree, after a quarrel, to divide the universe between them, the one taking the earth and the other the sky. These are clearly attempts to explain the overlapping and often contradictory claims of the cults.

DANCE

Initiates have learned the secrets, they have symbolically died and have awakened to a new status

Man has always expressed his feelings in movement, and dancing is one of the oldest arts. But it is also a means of marking the crises of life, or encouraging the crops or healing the sick soul and body. Behind many ritual dances is the belief that it is through the dance that man speaks directly to his gods

WHILE WESTERN MAN generally regards the dance as a pastime, many other people, especially in non-literate societies, still dance as a form of prayer or magic, directed to a variety of practical ends. Ritual dances of today serve many functions, particularly as celebrations of life's crises, for healing or as efforts to promote the fertility of crops.

Puberty rites survive among aborigines in various parts of the world. The *waiang-arree*, for example, is the circumcision rite of the tribes of Broome on the west coast of Australia. After initiations and a climactic group dance by men and boys in a double circle, the novices become fully fledged members of tribal society. They have learned the secrets, they have symbolically died and have awakened to a new status.

Women may hold their own rites for pubescent girls. Choroti and Lengua women of South America danced for a month, circling the girl with slow steps, and striking the ground with bamboo staffs topped by deerhoof rattles. In this rite for demon exorcism they had the aid of four singing medicine-men. In the Maipure tribe of Venezuela the older women chase away

Although dancing, in the West, is generally regarded as a social pastime, or entertainment, dances in Africa still retain their ritual character *Previous page* **Nigerian stilt dance, a test of skill** *Above* **Basuto girls, their faces symbolically concealed behind masks made from beads, perform an initiation dance**

demons, who are really masked men miming wild beasts. An Apache girl of New Mexico joins in a circle dance with attendants. For four days four men, the masked *gahe*, impersonate horned mountain spirits with pointed swords and angular gestures. During the ceremony the girl practises her future tasks as a woman. Such instruction is an important function of these rites.

Therapeutic dances may also take the form

The Dance of Life

In the ecstasy of the dance man bridges the chasm between this and the other world, to the realm of demons, spirits and God. Captivated and entranced he bursts his earthly chains and trembling feels himself in tune with all the world . . . The dance, inherited from savage ancestors as an ordered expression in motion of the exhilaration of the soul, develops and broadens into the search for God, into a conscious effort to become part of those powers beyond the might of man which control our destinies. The dance becomes a sacrificial rite, a charm, a prayer, and a prophetic vision. It summons and dispels the forces of nature, heals the sick, links the dead to the chain of their descendants; it assures sustenance, luck in the chase, victory in battle; it blesses the fields and the tribe. It is creator, preserver, steward and guardian.

From its deep and far-reaching influence it will be apparent that in the life of primitive peoples and of ancient civilizations scarcely anything approaches the dance in importance. It is no art that disregards bread; on the contrary it provides bread and everything else that is needed to sustain life. It is not a sin, proscribed by the priest or at best merely accepted by him, but rather a sacred act and priestly office; not a pastime to be tolerated only, but a very serious activity of the entire tribe. On no occasion in the life of primitive peoples could the dance be dispensed with. Birth, circumcision, and the consecration of maidens, marriage and death, planting and harvest, the celebrations of chieftains, hunting, war and feasts, the changes of the moon and sickness — for all of these the dance is needed . . . the dance in its essence is simply life on a higher level.

C. Sachs *World History of the Dance*

of circling or demon impersonations. They may show startling, individualistic whirls or spasms, depending on the purpose and location. They achieve therapy by inducing ecstasy, by curing a disease, or both. Ecstatic dances bring worshippers into communion with supernatural beings, by means of regulated movements, hypnotic musical accompaniment and sometimes with the aid of narcotics. The most spectacular mystic cult is that of the Turkish dervishes. Rufai or howling dervishes stamp and spring in a double circle, swaying and jerking their bodies. Mevlevi dervishes whirl individually, faster and faster, while the upraised right hand receives supernatural power and carries it to earth through the lowered left hand. (See DERVISH.)

Balinese men dance themselves into a near-suicidal trance, as they direct their kris daggers against their own breasts. The frenzy of the Asiatics brings to mind medieval dance manias — the St Vitus tremors which are now extinct, and the self-flagellant ecstasy of Penitentes, who still celebrate their Easter rites in New Mexico and the Philippines, to atone for their sins.

Asiatic shamans whirl themselves into a trance not only for mystic experience, but also for the cure of illness. Siberian shamans of the Tungus and Yakut tribes commune with the spirits of ancestors or animals and they effect cures by means of a revelation. Noisy exorcisms are the aims of the masked Devil Dancers of Ceylon and the Nalke and Paraiyan castes of India. These inspired men (rarely women) have their counterparts in the New World, especially among the Eskimo and the tribes in the jungles of the Amazon. They restore sick patients by bringing their souls back from the spirit land.

The New World received other ecstatic cults from Africa, under various names. Negro slaves brought the *vodun* cult (from which the word Voodoo is derived) to Haiti from Dahomey. The Bantu perpetuated their Macumba in Brazil, making many adaptations to the new environment. For instance, they know their ancestral gods by the names of Catholic saints as well as by the tribal names but they have preserved the essence, the traditional movements, songs and drums, and retain the strict ritual organization, with male and female priests. The worshippers impersonate deities in traditional movements, such as undulations for the snake god. As the deity 'rides' a worshipper, he or she may lose consciousness or become violent. Priests, who remain conscious, must often restrain ecstatic individuals, and help them regain consciousness. Though these rituals appeared malevolent to missionaries, they actually benefited the participants by relieving psychic tensions and by effecting better rapport with fellow human beings.

Masks with Staring Eyes

Missionaries saw such ecstasy arising within the groups of Christian converts. The Shouters and the Holy Rollers are among the sects which seek communion with Jesus in a semi-trance. Any member of a congregation can start a gospel song. A pianist and steel guitarist pick out counter rhythms; then the entire assembly syncopates the melody with hand-clapping, tambourine or triangle. As the worshippers rise from their chairs, some flex their knees rhythmically; some shuffle their feet; some skip in the aisles with spasmodic foot twists. They jerk their torsos or sway with upraised arms, shouting 'Halleluia', 'Thank you, Jesus!'.

In the New World, medicine dances of native origin cure mental and physical ailments. The Iroquois of New York State and Canada hold many medicine dances with traditional songs. At midwinter the Society of Maskers represents disease spirits and exorcises spirits which have afflicted members of the traditional native religion. In wry, wooden masks with staring eyes and long hair, they enter the sanctuary, the specially sacred area of their meeting place, crawling, whinnying and knocking turtle-shell rattles on floor and door. They hop about grotesquely, causing mingled awe and mirth. From a fireplace they collect ashes and rub them on the hair and arms of patients who are suffering from toothache or some other ailment. Finally everyone joins in a circle dance and a subsequent feast of corn mush. The Iroquois hold equally jolly medicine dances to propitiate the spirit of an animal that has taken offence at some ritual misdemeanour and has afflicted a man or woman. If a shaman decides that a bear spirit has caused cramps, for instance, he recommends a ritual for the bear. After a prayer and a tobacco offering, ritual conductors lead a circle dance, imitating bears with waddling and growling. Then the spectators join in a mimetic counter-clockwise circuit. They stamp, kick, eat nuts and berries, the bear's favourite food, and end by greatly cheering the patient.

Other tribes, like the Navaho of Arizona, hold long curative ceremonies, with singing and sometimes with masked spirit impersonations. They have special success with emotional ailments, by virtue of the musical and dance rhythms. They do not try to cure ailments brought by the white man from Europe.

To encourage a plentiful supply of food dances are performed to honour animal spirits in hunting rites, and plant spirits in agricultural rites. They vary greatly in accordance with the environment, fauna and flora. Animal dances, which are usually imitative, please animal spirits before a hunting expedition and appease them after a successful kill. Early man and some groups of modern men have held beasts in awe, not only because of their food value but also because of their agility and power. These animists endow all creatures with souls. Their animal mimicry is often very realistic. Boys of the Australian Kemmirai tribe imitate kangaroos by jumping, holding up their hands before their chests, or scratching themselves. African mimes can be great comics, such as the monkey men near Odienne of the Ivory Coast of West Africa. Tewa Indian men of New Mexico act like deer in some animal ceremonies; they gallop lightly or stand and tremble, nervously turning their antlered heads from side to side. In another version, however, they have stylized the mime; they stand erect as they sing and tread the ground.

Many animal dances survive as entertainments. Japanese folk festivals include realistic masked deer, bears, dragons, herons, cocks, and a comic lion imported from China. Turkish festivals enliven begging processions with camels and foxes in skins. England's prehistoric dramas survive in the Mummers, with real skins or shaggy imitations made of newspaper. The stylized reindeer of Abbots Bromley are six men who hold antlers in front of their heads as they face each other in two files, cross over and interweave sedately (see HORNS).

Agricultural dancers of today rarely impersonate plant deities. The Aztecs appointed elaborately garbed priests or

Gerald Cubitt

Popperfoto

Spanish National Tourist Office

Israeli Government Press Office

Caroles, or ring and chain dances, spring from ritual practices thousands of years old. Two variations are the Sardana of Spain *(left)* and the Israeli Hora *(below)*
Facing page Dances honouring animal or plant spirits to ensure success in hunting and a plentiful harvest are found all over the world
Top left Coconut dancers of Bacup in Lancashire in a version of the Morris Dance hold floral hoops above their heads
Top right The stylized reindeer heads carried by the dancers at Abbots Bromley in Staffordshire are probably a survival from prehistoric hunting rituals
Right The Morris Dance was originally a vital part of the ritual that ushered in the summer: detail from painting of the Old Palace at Richmond

priestesses for the impersonation of deities like Cinteotl, god of maize, in their seasonal ceremonial dances. The ancient Egyptians and Greeks also visualized their agricultural deities, like Dionysus, god of wine and seasonal rejuvenation. Iroquois women, however, merely symbolize the spirits of corn, beans and squash, without imitative attributes. Tewa women represent corn in great communal dances for the harvest, huge circuits and intricate lines danced by hundreds of men, women and children.

As in the case of animal mimicry, some agricultural dances are losing their religious significance but retain their ancient patterns. Balkan peasants still celebrate the harvest with circle dances by men and women – *kolos* of Serbia, *horas* of Rumania, Greece and Palestine, descendants of the ancient Greek *choros*, yet even more complex in steps and rhythms. The Tarascan Indians of Mexico still perform a sowing dance for women.

Folk dances and singing games preserve the forms of other occupational dances besides the hunt and agriculture. The Spanish *Filada* mimes spinning; the German *Webertanz* represents weaving; the Danish Shoemaker's and Tinker's Dance, the English Sailor's Hornpipe and Cobbler's Jig indicate these occupations.

Dancing Class Distinctions

The various classifications of people within a society, by birthright, occupation, age and sex, affect dance participation. In Western society such classifications are not rigid, but in many parts of the world social status determines a person's rights as a dancer.

Social organization, which may involve ritual organization, has evolved an infinity of patterns and restrictions. India's caste system is probably the world's most rigid division of people into gradations of prestige and occupations (see CASTE). The lowcaste, the Paraiyans, clatter in masked, shamanistic trance movement, the purpose of which is curative. Peasants of Maharashtra in south-west India perform calendric festive dances, such as the *kolattam* stick dances. The Devadassis (female temple dancers) excel in the fine art of Hindu *Bharata Natyam*. Hilltribes like the Todas cling to ancient round dances.

Past civilizations have similarly, though less rigidly, divided people into social and

choreographic classes. Europe's medieval feudal system separated people by location and simultaneously by occupation. Aristocrats in their castles held lavish festivals with comic dances by professional clowns and paired dances by the elegant men and women, including *caroles* and later on *pavanes* and *gaillardes*. Burghers in the cities tried to emulate the aristocrats, but they also took over dances from the peasants like the rough *weller*, which they eventually developed into the waltz. The peasants or serfs were the custodians of ancient, pagan ritual dances. Partly as tradition, partly as release from an arduous life, they continued to impersonate the awesome animal maskers at Twelfth Night and Carnival. In many parts of Europe, the descendants of these

peasants perform folk dances for harvests, for weddings and for tourist shows.

In Mexico the Aztecs developed a similar class system between the 12th century and the 15th. They expressed their social-ritual divisions during huge seasonal ceremonies. Priests and war captives, who were also sacrificial victims, impersonated deities. Warriors held ritual combats, not unlike the sword dances of northern Europe. Nobles held special dignified dances, in double file. Women had special roles, as priestesses. In some serpentine dances harlots were the partners of warriors; in other serpentines respectable virgins of the merchant class joined youths of their class. Serfs never participated; they watched the ceremonies, or were drafted as sacrificial victims.

Telling the Men from the Boys

The Aztec caste system was exceptional in the New World. Most native tribes had a comparatively democratic organization, based on clans, and some still do. Iroquois society is divided into hereditary clans, which are traced through the women. All social and ritual activities hinge on the interaction of two groups of clans, termed moieties by anthropologists. Members of each moiety have their assigned places in the sanctuary and in the dance line. They must sit at opposite sides of the sanctuary. Generally they participate in the same ceremonies. In New Mexico, however, the members of the two moieties often have separate ceremonies. The summer moiety manages the summer dances for crops,

The devil dances of Liberia, West Africa, are performed on occasions such as the death of a king or at harvest time. The dancers *(right* and *facing page, below),* made anonymous by their costumes and usually wearing terror-inspiring masks, represent malignant supernatural powers or devils: by imitating these evil spirits they hope to propitiate them *Facing page above* War dances, in preparation for battle or to celebrate a victory, also attract attention to the masculinity of the participants: Chuka dancers in Kenya

Popperfoto

while the winter moiety is in charge of winter ceremonies for animals.

Age grades nowadays have little effect on dance arrangements, except that in Europe and America children keep up singing games. In some aboriginal esoteric rites children are not admitted. In puberty rites they are the leading performers. In the now obsolete war societies of the Indians of the American Great Plains the boys were members of certain societies according to their particular age grade. Today in most American Indian and other folk dances, children participate, usually at the end of a dance line, copying their elders. While aboriginal dances involve elders as vigorous as their grandchildren, Western man tends to assume that energy is a prerogative of youth. The idea that modern dancing is for the youngsters has a long history. In the Middle Ages it was customary for the older couples to march slowly through the *branle double,* for younger couples to engage in the *branle gai,* and for youngsters to leap through the lively steps of the *branle de Bourgogne.*

Another form of segregation, according to sex, has deep-seated biological and sociological motivation. Men dance for war and the hunt, but women for peace and horticulture. The sexes may dance alone in their special rites, or they may occupy separate parts of a dance line, perhaps with different steps. Rarely are women the partners of men. That is a recent development in the social and stage dances of Europe and America.

The Geometry of Dance

The dance functions, organization and inter-personal relationships find expression in visible and audible patterns. The ingredients of the visible pattern are posture, arm gestures, footwork and geometric formations. They are usually synchronized with sound effects. Some rituals call for imitative body postures or special gestures. Other rites, as for harvests and most sociable dances, emphasize steps that carry the dancers over the ground in simple or elaborate formations. Local factors also determine the kind of ingredient. That is, different peoples emphasize certain ingredients in special ways called style. Many African tribes and their New World descendants move the whole body expressively, even acrobatically. India's art dancers emphasize arm gestures. European peoples like footwork – small, intricate steps in the Balkans, high leaps and kicks in the Basque Provinces. In southern Spain the men and women of Andalusia excel in sinuous torso and arm movements as well as in intricate footwork. Peasants of northern Spain prefer circle dances or interweaving 'longways'; this term is used for dances performed by two rows of dancers standing opposite each other in parallel lines. Ireland's folk dancers are masters of every kind of geometric floor pattern.

Postures have certain universal connotations. Dirges and other sad dances produce flexed bodies, while in gay moods the torso is thrown out and the head raised. Heavy animals like bears or buffalo suggest a bowed position in mime; while birds suggest light, upward imitation of flight. At the same time, every tribe and national group shows local posture tendencies. West African Negroes and Spanish flamenco dancers exaggeratedly extend their backs; English Morris dancers tilt backwards; Basques hold themselves erect; Serbians and Indians of North America tilt forwards or even flex their bodies. Within these regional postures, age grades cause variations. American Indian war dancers remain fairly erect, if the men are old; they flex and extend to extremes if they are young.

Speaking with Their Hands

Sex also has an effect on traditional postures. In many parts of the world, from America to Russia, women are supposed to dance with a meek posture, head bowed, feet close together, while men may expand and stretch. In Chinese theatre, male characters often assume a straddling posture, but female characters hold legs and arms closed in. Within these conventions there are also individual variations. Even in stylized group dances some individuals move joyously and others meekly. In mime some experts have more extreme interpretations of flexion and extension than others. Also – a more elusive constituent – some dancers use more force than others, in their more emphatic exhibition.

Gestures of the arms and hands similarly express universal moods and thoughts, and also regional and individual variations.

Dance gestures, which ultimately derive from daily gestures, are always stylized; they may be simple and intelligible or elaborate and obscure. The gestures of European folk dancers are simple compared to the code of India. Everywhere gestures can be imitative or symbolic, involving the whole arm or just the fingers, executed with or without props. They can be realistic, expressive of emotions, or decorative. In ancient and modern India *nritya* signifies narrative, stylized gestures, while *nritta* is decorative. Both types contrast with the forthright, realistic gestures of European dances such as the Swedish flax-reaping. For an understanding of nritya and of Katha-Kali folk dramas, the spectator must know the sacred myths, the tales of Krishna, Shiva and legendary heroes. He must also know the meaning of the hundreds of finger positions and arm positions. The gesture code has been simplified in the ritual dances of Manipur in north-east India, the Indonesian enactments of the *Ramayana* and *Mahabharata*, in the narrative gesture dances of Samoa and the Hawaiian *hula*.

The only American Indians with a gesture code are the tribes of British Columbia, though the Aztecs and Maya apparently had ritual codes. Their manuscripts show gestures similar to those of Balinese priests lowering their hands to the earth or raising them to the sky. These codes of Asia and native America have had little or no effect on art dances of Europe and America. Ballet dancers persevere in a set of conventionalized positions for love and sorrow; followers

of the American pioneer, Isadora Duncan, invent their own gestures; followers of the German pioneer, Mary Wigman, show the influence of Indonesia's decorative hand positions with overstretched fingers. In general, dancers of the Western world neglect gesture in favour of footwork. (See also GESTURE.)

Focus on the Feet

Footwork or steps may be the basis of a dance, a rhythmic background to gestures, or a means of progression. The leaps of Basque men, the intricate crossing of the feet of the Scottish dancer, the brushes and flaps of an American tap dancer take the full attention of performer and audience, perhaps formerly as ritual, certainly now as exhibition. The high leaps of the Basques and the similar leaps of the men of the Ukraine and Georgia may hark back to ancient vegetation rites to promote the leaping of plants into life. The jumps and turns of Balkan folk dancers and of England's Morris men may also have ancient roots in supplications to the earth and the seeds.

On the other hand, the footbeats of India and southern Spain appear as rhythmic backgrounds to the filigrees of arms and hands. In contrast with such virtuoso uses of feet and legs, the simpler steps of most folk dances serve as a means of progression. In their forward, backward or sideways movements European groups and couples may use the polka or waltz steps. More frequently they run through

Spear dance by the Wogogo tribesmen of East Africa: one of the many versions of the war dance, performed throughout the world with sword or shield, spear, sticks or bow and arrow

their formations as do people in other parts of the world.

Closed or open circuits are the most commonly found ground patterns of dance. In closed circuits the participants may move in the direction of progression or they may face the centre and then step sideways. They can move clockwise, as commonly in hunting cultures and in north-west Europe, or counter-clockwise, as in agricultural rites of south-east Europe and Africa. Some peoples regard the latter direction as sinister and evil, as the Algonquins of America's Great Lakes and the medieval English, who considered 'widdershins', meaning against the sun, as the witches' direction. The closed circle, single or double (in couples) has its limitations. The open circle is really a follow-my-leader line and offers many possibilities of serpentining, winding into a spiral, and so on. It is known among the Bambuti Pygmies of Africa, the French Provencale *farandole* dancers, and agricultural American Indians.

Straight lines are less common than circling patterns. They take many forms. Simplest are the multiple stationary lines of the Maori in New Zealand, and of Africans such as the Watusi, who lay more stress on gestures and leaps than on formations. Two parallel lines offer more artistic possibilities,

Maze, Snake and Goddess

Among later Greek writers there is a persistent tradition of a maze or labyrinth dance in Crete, in which the dancers pursued a winding course suggestive of the devious passages of a maze. The fact that the palace at Knossos . . . is complex in plan and suggests the Labyrinth of legend, perhaps lends some support to this tradition. Dances of the maze type are common to many early peoples in various parts of the world, whether they have Labyrinthine buildings or not. Some historians trace them all to a very primitive dance form which is really an imitation of the crawling of a serpent. The importance of the snake in Minoan religion is well attested, and it is possible that in primitive times a python or other large snake . . . was kept as an embodiment of the goddess. Some students think that a snake-line dance was performed in the gloom of the many caves in the mountains near Knossos, and that it was climaxed by the exhibition of a living python. Such a performance would have been weird and spectacular in the highest degree.

Certain figurines indicate also that there were in Crete snake-handling rituals, in which woman votaries carried small living snakes in their hands. Earlier, such figurines were interpreted as 'snake goddesses', but recent studies have shown that they portray worshippers, dancers, or priestesses. Snake-handling rituals in the United States and in other parts of the world are usually accompanied with shouts and hymns, and with a shuffling sort of dance.

Lillian B. Lawler *The Dance in Ancient Greece*

Camera Press London

Couple dances, with women partnering men, are rare in many parts of the world: men traditionally dance for victory in war, women for peace. 18th century Turkish miniature from the Topkapi Library, Istanbul

and have greater scope for dramatic expression. The facing lines may be two groups of warriors, or two lines of men and women in a mime of courtship repulsion and magnetism. The former type has shown most elaborate developments in the sword dances of Europe. The latter type persists in various parts of Africa, in simple patterns; it has evolved into the intricacies of the 'longways sets' of Scottish and New England country dancing and also into the patterns of Pueblo Indian harvest dancers. In many of these longways the approach-and-recede pattern is combined with the serpentine motif of the open circle, as in the Virginia Reel. In this and many other longways the arch pattern introduces an ancient tree symbolism into geometric formations: successively, partners hold up their joined hands and other 'couples run through the arch. American Indians have adopted this ornamental pattern, Yucatan Indians with the aid of actual flower arches, and Great Lakes Indians by holding hands.

Group formations may combine with couple patterns in European folk dances, from Palestine to Finland. In Moravian dances the couples circle counter-clockwise. At the same time they change from parallel progression with joined hands to separation, reunion, pivoting, and so forth. In the French quadrilles and American square dances all circle and then the four couples successively cross over, break up into small circles, finally spinning by twos in the swing. In these folk dances couples and individuals conform to regulations, unlike the undisciplined dancing that takes place in the modern ballroom.

Patterns in Time and Space

The various ingredients of the dance are combined into structures by patterns in tempo or variations of steps. Quadrille types open with the circling, continue with a 'body' of distinctive formations, and close with a promenade and swing. The original French quadrilles were suites, with precise, named sections, like the Morris dances with their five successive dances. Many dances have simpler forms. Some, like the Palestinian *hora*, continue with the same step and formation of an open circle, but they build up excitement by a crescendo in speed and intensity. Others use the simple device of contraction, like the German *Siebenschritt*, with its ever shorter and shorter series of steps. A common device is the two-part set of slow and fast dance, like the Renaissance *Pavana* and *Gaillarda*, the later Minuet and Rondeau, the present Hungarian *Lassu* and *Gyors*, the Norwegian *Gangar* and *Springar*, and the Tewa Harvest slow and fast dance. Each part has distinctive steps, first processional, then lively and leaping; and special music.

Dances often combine with other activities into traditional dramas, with preparations, intensifying action, and aftermath. African possession cults and the corresponding Holiness Church services start with prayer and solemn music; work up to a climax of frenzied solo and circle dancing, with interludes for speeches; and they calm down into a benediction and song, with in Africa a concluding feast. This is the structure of the Greek Dionysian rites and the resultant Greek dramas and medieval Passion Plays. While these dramas last only a few hours, some rituals occupy many days, like the 27-day Midwinter rites of British Columbia tribes. (See also DRAMA.)

Dance Music

Over thousands of years dances have developed an infinite variety of musical accompaniments, costumes and settings. Musical accompaniment may involve separate musicians, single or grouped. Drums of many sizes and shapes are almost ubiquitous; they are most advanced in Africa. Stringed instruments have spread from the Near East to most of Asia and Europe, and thence to the Americas. Gongs characterize Southeast Asia. Flutes and other wind instruments are sporadic, varying from the tiny flute of the one-man flute-and-tabor music in England, Spain and Mexico, to the enormous horns of Tibet and native Chile. Europe has evolved the most complex instruments and ensembles of strings, accordions, pianos and other instruments. The most elaborate ensembles, the orchestras of the modern world, have the least significance, while the drum-and-voice combinations are closest to the original magical intentions.

These separate accompaniments generally conform to the mood, tempo and metre of the dances, and they have the same structure. They may thus be in triple or double time; or in irregular metres. They may synchronize with the footwork of the dancers and with each other, or they may be in syncopation or antiphony. The relationship is closest when the dancers produce their own accompaniment, as the sole musicians, or as enrichments of the background music. Dancers may manipulate their instruments, as they sing or chant, or move them automatically as part of their clothing, or create rhythmic sounds with parts of the body.

Sometimes drummers dance, kneel, leap, as they beat the rhythms. Small drums are used by tribesmen of New Guinea; the Santals and Oraons of Bihar in India have more cumbersome ones slung around their shoulders; gypsy men of Turkey and Macedonia perform remarkable feats with huge, double-headed instruments. The tambourine players in the Italian *tarantella* have a relatively lightweight instrument with a simple playing technique. Almost as impressive as the gypsy drumming is the self-accompaniment of Mexico's Concheros, who strum rhythmic chords on a lute-like instrument, made of an armadillo shell, as they stamp out their dance steps. In the New World such music may be a substitute for ancient native rattles. Iroquois men shake horn or turtle-shell rattles. Many tribes shake tortoise rattles for rain. The Siouans of North America and the Yaqui of Mexico use deer-hoofs, on sticks or on their belts. Yaqui clowns, who play an important role in the dance, strike a rattle with brass discs on the palm of the left hand. At the same

595

The shift from faith to fun has not destroyed all native ritual, and even in urban society serious artists are seeking a return to faith or to a deep, almost ritualistic dedication

time they wear bells dangling from their belts, and rustle anklets of butterfly cocoons filled with gravel. Many dancers wear such jinglers on their belts, hems or ankles.

More skill is involved in the manipulation of castanets, held in the hands, with different timbre for the right and left hands. The castanets of Spain are descendants of ancient finger-cymbals; Andalusian women often have the same poses as the cymbal players of Egypt and Greece. At the same time they and their partners stamp out intricate sounds with their hard-heeled shoes. Flamenco dancers also stamp *zapateados* but they clap their hands or snap their fingers. They belong to a widespread cult of stamping either with or without shoes and of handclapping in counter-rhythms.

Dressing for the Dance

Costumes sometimes add such sound effects to the visual designs. Morris men jingle the bell pads on their shins as they leap and simultaneously wave kerchiefs or strike sticks. Nautch dancers of India jingle ankle bells and stamp while they pirouette and whirl voluminous skirts. But many props are soundless, like the fans of Japanese geishas or the long sleeve extensions of Chinese theatre dancers. The manipulations of the fans are symbolic and represent falling leaves, waterfalls, and many other things. Some props are realistic or descriptive, or simply decorative. Tewa men manipulate feathered wings to simulate eagles. An American stage dancer, Loie Fuller, whirled hundreds of yards of cloth as flames under red lights. Isadora Duncan's disciples wafted silk scarfs merely for an effect of lightness.

Masks similarly serve many purposes, most importantly symbolic or imitative purposes. The Iroquois False-Face masks and the Tewa eagle half-masks with beaks represent supernatural beings without impeding dance movements. But many ritual masks are so huge as to preclude any dance movement except for a walk, such as the huge disc worn by impersonators of the Inca sun god and the towering demon masks of Melanesian and West African dancers. Some masks require special manipulation. Thunderbirds in British Columbian dances move their beaks on hinges. Other masks heighten character

acting, like the demons, heroes and court ladies of Japanese theatre, and the comic Old Men of the Tarascan people of Mexico.

Special garments are prescribed for the effectiveness of the masks. The dancers may be completely covered in bulky grasses or in stiff and decorative kimonos. At the other extreme, they may be nude but for painted stripes. Without masks, costumes rely on other devices for their effect. Tewa Indians decorate their tunics or kilts with magical designs, zigzags for lightning, terraces for clouds and rain. Folk dancers of many lands emphasize their femininity and masculinity by costume patterns and rich ornaments. Women wear layers of full skirts which they whirl as they turn and sometimes flip with their hands. Men exaggerate their strong chests with bouffant sleeves. (See also COSTUME; MASKS.)

Settings enhance the meaning and effectiveness of dance movements and props. Maypole dancers belong on a village green. Tewa dancers belong in their sunny semi-desert, against a horizon of snow-capped mountains, their turquoise, red, black and white costumes brilliant against the beige adobe of the homes around the dance plaza. British Columbian maskers appear more weird than ever in the dimly lit dance house, by a flickering fire. But Melanesian and Polynesian dances are set against the background of jungle or sea, the sun, and the fragrance of exotic flowers.

Environments have often changed for dances, as people have migrated to new lands, have conquered or visited other peoples. Such

---

The Joy of Dancing

How can I describe the joy of dancing . . . Voluminous, vast, swelling like sails in the wind, the movements of my dance carry me onward — onward and upward, and I feel the presence of a mighty power within me which listens to the music and then reaches out through all my body, trying to find an outlet for this listening. Sometimes this power grew furious, sometimes it raged and shook me until my heart nearly burst from its passion, and I thought my last moments on earth had surely arrived. At other times it brooded heavily, and I would suddenly feel such anguish that, through my arms stretched to the Heavens; I implored help from where no help came.

Isadora Duncan *My Life*

---

migrations have resulted in the diffusion of dance forms, with adaptations to their new homes, and in mixtures. Other changes such as secularization and professionalization have taken place locally and also through migrations.

Recent dance importations to North America followed the immigrations of the 19th century. Some of the immigrants have tried to re-create their seasonal festivals in the new environment. In settlements like Heightstown, New Jersey, Slovaks and Moravians attempted processionals through the streets of the village, imitating their native harvest festivals. In big cities, like New York and Detroit, they have tried to stage fragments of their dance rituals or have invented plays representing their custom.

Mixtures generally result in the course of transfers. Some of the mixtures are among the world's most picturesque dances, such as a dance representing the battles of Moors and Christians, with a Spanish libretto and Aztec movement styles. America's most accessible mixtures are the square dances, which started as diversions of British immigrants, then added Scottish motifs, later on, Danish and Norwegian motifs in the Middlewest, and, in the Southwest, figures from Spanish *cuadrillas*. Such mixture has affected art dance, too, but in a more self-conscious manner. Americans such as Fred Astaire and Paul Draper have combined European ballet with American tap dancing.

Dance in the Modern World

Professionalization has had an increasing effect on the forms and settings of dances. Certain gifted individuals in every culture become so expert that they elaborate the traditional forms, or create new routines. In ancient times, as in Pharaonic funerals, and still today, as in India's Katha-Kali dramas, experts who became professional by virtue of their excellence were as dedicated to the gods as to their art. African virtuosi, like the Watusi men, do not expect remuneration. Today in the Western world, however, the supreme performers serve both art and mammon.

Secularization has resulted from professionalization, but the process is not identical. Some professionals, like Japanese Shinto priests, still serve religion. Most secular dancers, as in the ballroom, are

Right In the modern world the dance has become increasingly secularized, as in ball-room dancing, but folk dancing even as a stage or tourist attraction retains many of the characteristics and much of the appeal of its ritual past, when it was a vital part of the community's life: Russian dancers in traditional costume *Centre* The symbolism of a dance is heightened, and it comes closest to its original magical function, when music or rhythm is provided by only one type of instrument: children at Kabul, Afghanistan, dance to the sound of tambourines *Below* According to Hindu belief the god Shiva set the world in motion with a dance, and dancing is an intrinsic and highly formalized part of life in India: Orissa dancers in Delhi

amateurs. The process of secularization has certainly been going on for untold centuries. In many parts of the world rituals survive side by side with pleasure dances, as among the Iroquois and the Basques. For centuries special 'social' dances have been created, like the minuet, polka and waltz; these dances emphasize communications between the sexes instead of communication with deities.

The shift from faith to fun has followed in the wake of Euro-American industrialization and urbanization. Yet it has not destroyed all native ritual, and even in urban society, serious artists are seeking a return to faith, or to a deep, almost ritualistic dedication. The devotees, be they performers, producers, or scholars, believe that the dance plays a role in modern society, even though it is no longer integrated with beliefs and activities.

Ritual dances are taking on new forms, suited to modern Christianity. While ancient dance rituals persist in Africa's Coptic churches and in Spain's cathedrals; while stage performers enact Stravinsky's *Rite of Spring* as a spectacle, a few devotees have tried to reinstate dancing in Christian churches, particularly in the United States where a number of Sacred Dance Guilds have interpreted biblical themes in dignified movements.

Therapeutic dances survive here and there within urban culture. Inside the industrial pattern they may help the mentally ill, the problem child, and the worker on an assembly line. Many experts believe that this ancient healing function of dance has considerable potentialities for exploitation in the future.

(See also CAROLE; CORYBANTES; HOBBY HORSE; MORRIS DANCES; SWORD DANCES.)

GERTRUDE KURATH

FURTHER READING: Good introductions to this enormous subject include V. Alford and R. Gallop, *The Traditional Dance* (Methuen, London, 1935); M. Huet, *Dance, Art and Ritual of Africa* (Pantheon, 1978); D. Kennedy, *England's Dances* (Clarke, Irwin, 1949); L. B. Lawler, *The Dance in Ancient Greece* (Columbia University Press, 1978); C. Sachs, *World History of the Dance* (Norton, 1937); for an interesting sociological survey, see F. Ruse, *Dance in Society* (Routledge & Kegan Paul, London, 1969).

DANCE OF DEATH

IN DANCES OF DEATH, people reflect their attitude towards this final, catastrophic crisis in human life. Some people have regarded death with horror and they have feared the ghosts of the dead. Some express their grief in mournful ceremonies. Others try to cheer each other and the departed spirit by dance and song. Others again consider death a transfiguration, a door to another, better life. Similarly, the celebrations take many forms: impersonations of the image of death, imageless homage to the deceased, or joyous folk dancing.

Death was often personified as a grotesque skeleton, as in the medieval European Dance of Death. This is best known through frescoes and woodcuts, but it had a foundation in actual miming dances. Death in the form of a skeleton capered in turn with sinners of all classes and ages, cardinal, labourer, child. This dance was an expression of the medieval horror of death, despite the Church's promises of a better afterlife. Clown-skeletons still cavort in ecclesiastical celebrations descended from the Middle Ages. In Catalonia, Spain, skeleton figures dance during religious holidays, notably Carnival and Holy Week, sometimes at Corpus Christi. In the *danza macabra* or *bal de la mort* of the Ampurdàn area of Spain, a quadrille of skeletons carries a scythe, clock and banner. In Mexican *carnavales* Death is a horrid clown, armed with a pitchfork,

descended from the Spanish impersonations.

The burial wake is another common manifestation. A motif of cheer and consolation pervades Spanish wakes. The mourners dance a lively *jota* or *canario*. Catholicism has introduced the word 'angelitos' (little angels) for the spirits of recently deceased children. Mourners celebrate wakes with a *baraban* or *lucia* in Sicily and Tuscany, and with a jig in Ireland. Negro wakes in South Carolina work up to a frenzied pitch of dance and song. Food and liquor contribute to the festivity of these wakes.

Banishing the Dead

Another form which the celebration may take is the release or exorcism of the spirits, motivated by fear of their evil potentialities as well as by affection. American Indians of many tribes perform a series of funerary and anniversary rites. The California Luiseno banished the spirit from his familiar haunts with the *tuvish* and *chuchamish* (wake), and in memorials for all the dead of the past year or several years. They imitated the character of the dead persons in the *yunish matackish*. They burned images in the *tauchanish*. Similarly, until recently, the Yuma tribe in the Mohave desert burned rush images in a circular dance and a cremation ritual termed *keruk*. The Tarahumara Indians of Chihuahua, Mexico, perform a *rutuburi* circle dance and a special death dance around their belongings, during a three-week fiesta. After a year they perform other dances – the

The *Dance of Death*, an allegorical representation of Death leading all men and women inevitably to the grave was a popular theme in late medieval art: these illustrations from Holbein's series of woodcuts on the subject show Death as a grotesque skeleton who appears to various people and is finally himself engulfed by men and women who have already died

yumari and *pascol*. The Yaqui tribe of Sonora, Mexico holds a fiesta and dance at the wake of a child, similar to a Catalan wake. They hold a special *matachina* dance or a *chapayekas* dance for members of these ceremonial societies. Another ritual finally releases the spirit.

Though ghosts are not feared quite as much among the Iroquois of New York State and Canada, these people do believe in them and make efforts to allay them. In case of a violent death, they dispatch a priest for prayers at the site of the murder. After four nights they sing for the release of the spirit and to aid its trip to the other world. After ten days they reinforce this supplication through song and dance. In the winter women chant and circle in the *ohgiwe* for their ancestors, with drum accompaniment. The assembly concludes with a feast and gay round dances.

Chinese and Japanese Buddhists celebrate the Feast of Lanterns as memorials to their ancestors. Japanese villagers, especially in Asage, circle counter-clockwise in the *Bon Odori*, during mid-July or in August, in connection with harvest celebrations. Men

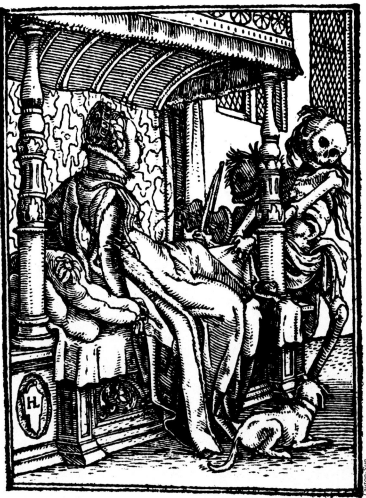

and women sing as they gesture or clap their hands; sometimes they also have a musical accompaniment.

In some instances there may be a fusion of the concept of death and resurrection. Boys' puberty rites may enact the symbolic death of the initiates and their rebirth to a new status (see DANCE). Funeral rites of antiquity often included the hope of resurrection. The high kicks of Egyptian female mourners symbolized new life. The Egyptian Osiris rituals and the Greek spring festival for Dionysus mimed the death and final resurrection of the deity. Babylonians and Romans had similar customs. In the Middle Ages funeral dances symbolized resurrection by a kiss between male and female performers, with the anticipation of new life. The Hungarian *Gyas Tanc* perpetuates this concept.

Relics in modern children's games of many countries form yet another manifestation. English and American children preserve the actions and song words of ancient funeral rites, as in *Old Roger is Dead*, *Jenny Jones* and *Green Gravel* (see CHILDREN'S GAMES). In their Hallowe'en masks and pranks small children perpetuate All Soul's ceremonies for the return of the spirits and propitiatory food offerings.

Impersonations of death are also found in modern art dances. Two German choreographers visualized death as an ugly thing: In *Totenmahl* or *Feast for the Dead* (1929), Mary Wigman masked her group in white, cadaverous faces, as homage to the dead of the First World War. In his *Green Table* (1933), Kurt Jooss envisaged the figure of death in wartime as a skeleton resembling the great reaper of the Middle Ages. A few years later, in 1937, the American, José Limon, created his *Danza de la Muerte* and Andrée Howard produced *Death and the Maiden* to Schubert's music for the English Ballet Rambert. These modern spectacles echo the anxieties of folk laments.

FURTHER READING: A. Strindberg (translated by A. Paulson), *Dance of Death* (Norton, 1976).

DANCING MANIA

THERE APPEARED ON THE STREETS of Aachen (Aix-la-Chapelle) in Germany, in July 1374, a body of men and women, belonging almost entirely to the poorer classes, who began to exhibit the signs of an alarming disorder. Its symptoms were convulsive running, leaping and dancing, frequently accompanied by elaborate hallucinations, and those so affected seemed powerless to stop themselves; indeed, attacks could be terminated only by forcible binding, or by the onset of utter physical exhaustion. No one seemed to know how the outbreak started, though we hear of the 'dancers' as having come 'out of Germany' and that they were popularly known as 'St John's Dancers'.

It is this name which provides a clue to the possible origins of the phenomenon. Already in the early Church, the Feast of St John the Baptist had been placed at Midsummer – incidentally, the only example in the Church Calendar of a saint celebrated on the day of his birth, rather than of his death; according to St Luke he was born six months before Jesus. It is common knowledge that in pre-Christian Europe, and elsewhere, Midsummer was a time of celebration, in which dancing, processions and the lighting of fires played their part. These elements were, it seems, transferred bodily to the Festival of St John the Baptist – a measure of which the Saint is unlikely to have approved. It is not known for certain but it appears at least likely that the dancing mania began with the celebration of a semi-Christian Midsummer in 1374. Memories of the Black Death were still strong; there was a widespread sense of fear and insecurity; and the result was a form of mass hysteria which spread with startling rapidity. Within a very short time dancing mania was reported from the streets and churches of Liege in Belgium, from Utrecht in Holland and many other towns and cities.

Predictably the phenomenon was officially attributed to evil spirits, and recourse was made to chapels of St John for the purposes of exorcism; this strengthened the connection with the saint under whose auspices the dancing had begun, though occasionally the issue became confused by the introduction of St John the Apostle in his place. The common people, too, were convinced that demons were at work but accounted for this by the theory that the persons affected had been invalidly baptized by priests living in concubinage, which added an unpleasant moral and theological dimension to the problem.

Although each separate outbreak came to an end in a few weeks, sporadic instances of the dancing mania continued for the remainder of the 14th century. The next serious wave occurred at Strasbourg in 1418. By this time the original link with St John the Baptist had been forgotten, and those afflicted were taken instead to the chapels of St Vitus (an obscure 4th century Christian saint who had long been thought, for no apparent reason, to protect sufferers from convulsive diseases) to be cured. Again, the saint's day was closely connected with the celebration of Midsummer. The name 'St Vitus's Dance', *Veitstanz*, was applied to this new outbreak, the symptoms of which were identical with previous epidemics; this name has survived to this day as a popular name for convulsive chorea.

Below This ecstatic dancer in a Los Angeles nightclub is a throwback to the medieval men and women who danced compulsively in the streets of Europe in the 14th century, a phenomenon that was attributed to possession by evil spirits

Camera Press London

Dance of the Spider

These outbreaks of dancing mania in 1374 and 1418 are the best-known, but there is ample evidence to show that the disease itself had appeared earlier; there are records of similar visitations in 1237 at Erfurt in Germany and in 1278 at Utrecht, for example. It continued, though on a smaller scale, well on into the 17th century. In Italy, for instance, an almost identical disease, known as Tarantism, was popularly believed to be caused by the bite of the tarantula spider. The main symptom in this case was extreme lassitude, out of which the patient could be brought by means of music (giving rise to the dance-form the *tarantella*); this induced a convulsive crisis and finally exhaustion, after which the sufferer was regarded as cured. Tarantism was known intermittently from the 14th to the 18th centuries.

In Scotland, three men and four women were burned at the stake at Paisley on 10 June 1697 for the crime of witchcraft, and it seems from the evidence that they were sufferers from some form of chorea. Many of the symptoms exhibited by the Convulsionaries of 18th century France, and in connection with Methodist and other Christian revival movements in Britain and America in the 18th and 19th centuries, were substantially those of the dancing mania, though not known by that name. Other parallel manifestations, ranging from the medieval Flagellants to the more recent Holy Rollers, might also be cited.

Dancing mania was basically a contagious form of hysteria, brought on in a situation of peculiar stress. It was largely psychological in origin, though it was not without its physical causes, such as undernourishment. As an expression of European life in the Middle Ages, its imagery was that of popular Christianity, though pathologically distorted. It is therefore without theological significance, though it has considerable interest for the student of the psychology of religion, not least as evidence of what can happen within the framework of organized religion when individuals and communities are subjected to severe mental strain. In this sense, both the disease and its cure are significant religious facts.
(See also CONVULSIONARIES; HOLY ROLLERS.)

DANIEL

THE BOOK OF DANIEL in the Old Testament is named after its central personality, a noble young Jew taken, with three of his friends, from Judea to the court of the Babylonian king. The book recounts the life, piety and wisdom of Daniel, as well as his visions of the future. The name Daniel seems to be that of an ancient Semitic legendary figure.

The book is written partly in Hebrew and partly in Aramaic, and presents many problems. The first, more biographical part of it tells how Daniel and his friends lived as exiles at court, remaining faithful to their ancestral faith in spite of trials, tribulations and temptations. The best known incident in this connection is that of Daniel's being cast into the lion's den for refusing to give divine worship to King Darius the Mede. An example of Daniel's god-given wisdom was his ability to interpret dreams and to read the writing on the wall in Belshazzar's banqueting hall.

The second – and in later periods more influential – part of the book reports a series of dreams and visions. The symbolism of these – the four beasts, the beast with the horns, the visions of the 70 weeks, the 'son of man' seated on a throne, the final revelations of the angel – refers to the course of history, that is, to the destruction of the four successive world empires and their wicked and idolatrous rule by the kingdom of God and his saints (the 'fifth monarchy').

Although the book purports to date from the period of the Babylonian exile, from the reign of Nebuchadnezzar (605–562 BC) to that of Darius the Mede (521–486 BC), this dating is accepted by few scholars and the general consensus of critical scholarship ascribes the composition of its main part to the time of the persecution of the Jewish religion under Antiochus IV Epiphanes, and the period of the Maccabean revolt (c 165 BC). This would account for many of the

A visionary whose writings form the basis for the millenarian beliefs of some present-day Christian sects, Daniel is probably best known for surviving a night spent in a den of lions: painting from the Ailsa Mellon Bruce Fund

peculiarities of the book as well as for many of its dominant motifs: persecution and martyrdom, the rule of the wicked, the hope for a divinely operated *dénouement* and for the imminent establishment of the rule of the saints. If this dating is correct, then the 'four kingdoms' are the Babylonian, (unhistorical) Median, Persian and Greek (Seleucid dynasty) empires. When Rome became the dominant power symbolizing the rule of the wicked (the 'great whore of Babylon' in the symbolism of the Revelation of St John), the four kingdoms were interpreted to refer to Babylonia, Persia, Greece and Rome. In later periods other identifications were offered: the later medieval *Book of a Hundred Chapters* took them to refer to France, England, Spain and Italy. During the Civil War in England, a radical Puritan sect which was strongly represented in Cromwell's army were known as the 'Fifth Monarchy Men', because of their expectation to establish the rule of the saints.

The original purpose of the book was no doubt to strengthen the faith and the hearts of the persecuted Jews, making them persevere in their uncompromising opposition to the policy of hellenization ('idolatry') enforced by the Greek government and embraced by certain Jewish circles, and holding out hope of imminent salvation by revealing the divinely predestined course of history. The cryptic and symbolic character of the book's visions lent itself to reinterpretation in other analogous historical situations, whenever severe crises and tribulations generated fervent hopes and expectations of a coming end of the world.

The significance and historical influence of the book derive from its powerful apocalyptic character: history is conceived on a wide canvas as the succession of pre-ordained world empires, their turning against God, the triumph of wickedness and idolatry, the ultimate punishment and destruction of the evildoers, and the establishment, in power and glory, of the kingdom of God and his saints. The book consequently became a favourite with many mystics and millenarian enthusiasts, who looked forward to a blessed time to come. Some of the visionary motifs of the book, such as the 'son of man' and the 'Ancient of Days' (both in chapter 7) played a considerable role in subsequent eschatology (doctrines of death, judgement, heaven and hell) including that of the early Church; Jesus refers to himself, in the New Testament, as the 'Son of Man' rather than as the Messiah; and in the mysticism of the Jewish Merkabah visionaries (see CABALA).

The notion of four successive world empires and the cryptic references to the deliverance of the saints after 'a time, two times, and half a time' (chapter 12) and other symbolic details and numbers have frequently stimulated the imagination of millenarian enthusiasts and provided prooftexts for apocalyptic speculations. Throughout the Middle Ages Jewish mystical interpreters of the Bible computed the date of the coming of the Messiah on the basis of the Book of Daniel. Among Christians in the Middle Ages, the Book of Daniel combined with the Book of Revelation and its prophecies of a rule of the saints for one thousand years (the 'millennium') to nourish millenarian speculations.

The Book of Daniel contains certain innovations in angelology, such as the idea that each nation has its guardian angel, Michael being the guardian of Israel (12.1 — see also ANGELS). It also provides the first biblical reference to a belief in a resurrection and afterlife (12.2).

R. J. ZWI WERBLOWSKY

The Great Vision

In those days I, Daniel, was mourning for three weeks. I ate no delicacies, no meat or wine entered my mouth, nor did I anoint myself at all, for the full three weeks. On the twenty-fourth day of the first month, as I was standing on the bank of the great river, that is. the Tigris, I lifted up my eyes and looked, and behold, a man clothed in linen, whose loins were girded with gold of Uphaz. His body was like beryl, his face like the appearance of lightning, his eyes like flaming torches, his arms and legs like the gleam of burnished bronze, and the sound of his words like the noise of a multitude. And I, Daniel, alone saw the vision, for the men who were with me did not see the vision, but a great trembling fell upon them, and they fled to hide themselves. So I was left alone and saw this great vision, and no strength was left in me; my radiant appearance was fearfully changed, and I retained no strength. Then I heard the sound of his words; and . . . I fell on my face in a deep sleep with my face to the ground.

Daniel, chapter 10

Dante's vision encompassed the whole range of human life and destiny; a vision which is as relevant today when man is steadily conquering space as it was in the day of the medieval astronomer

DANTE

DANTE ALIGHIERI'S *Divine Comedy*, as his *Commedia* is generally known, is one of the rare and great works of literature that give a comprehensive vision of the place of man in the universe. It sets in a tremendous panorama the past, present and future; combines poetry and prophecy; and is profoundly concerned with the problems and prospects of human life and destiny. Since it was written, in the early years of the 14th century, this poem in three parts, *Inferno*, *Purgatorio* and *Paradiso*, has made a constant impression, not only in the Florentine poet's own land but on readers in any country — or language. There are beauties of phrase and expression that essentially belong to the Italian original but nothing is lost in translation of the universal meaning inherent in the subject.

The full significance appears when the poem is considered as a whole. To confine attention to the first part, the *Inferno*, which has been a popular tendency, is to miss the point. It is a misconception to think of Dante as a grim sadist who rejoiced in describing the tortures he wished his personal enemies to suffer in hell. The word 'Comedy' of the title has of course no implication of humour but suggests rather a series of events that may lead to a happy conclusion. With Dante one ascends by many stages from the depths to the region of supreme bliss.

The inferno was not merely the place of punishment for those who had done wrong in life. Here it is first necessary to consider the parallel that is maintained throughout between the material inventions of the story and the spiritual condition for which they stand. Hell in the material sense is imagined as an inverted cone extending into the bowels of the earth, in which persons known and named, as well as an anonymous multitude, undergo a variety of torments according to the nature of their wrong doing. But all this has an allegorical meaning as an analysis of the individual or also, if one so chooses to interpret it, the kind of society, that in the exercise of free will has elected to be governed by evil motives and desires and suffers in consequence an inevitable corruption.

The implacable inscription over the gate of hell — 'All hope abandon, ye who enter here' — refers to the impenitent, thus self-condemned. But purgatory for those who had not obstinately and irrevocably persisted in self-ruinous courses represented the dawn of hope and the possibility of redemption. This was to be achieved by active effort to throw off the burden of sin and guilt. Purgatory was not simply an annex of hell, a place of penalty for minor offenders or a kind of waiting-room before admittance into heaven. It is imagined as a vast mountain in the southern hemisphere, to climb which was an expiatory labour.

Virgil, whom Dante so greatly admired and whom he represents as his guide, made the often-quoted remark in the *Aeneid* on the easiness of the descent to Avernus; possibly less often remembered is the observation that followed on the toil of regaining the upper air. Dante likewise, emphasizes the labour involved in getting rid of every taint of error by the ascent of the seven encircling cornices of the mountain, each marking a stage of purification. There was still a progression to be made after the Earthly Paradise was reached at the summit. Above the region and condition of primal purity which it represented, like the Garden of Eden before the fall, there were the heavens to be ascended. The soul was launched radiantly into space and beyond it to its final union with the Divine Will.

The Dual Image of Beatrice

Dante himself was the pilgrim of this visionary journey. It occupied a week at Easter in the year 1300, he being then 35, 'midway on life's road'. It contains much that related to his own experience. Lost in a dark wood (having strayed, this implies, from the strait and narrow path), distracted by wild beasts (symbolic of temptations), he is relieved and delighted to find he has the shade of the great Latin poet, Virgil, to act as his guide. The appearance of a pagan writer in a context of essentially Christian character may seem surprising. But apart from the respect in which Virgil was held in medieval Italy as supposedly foretelling the coming of Christ and as being a kind of benevolent magician, he had the admiration of Dante as the genius of Rome's imperial order. The city founded by Aeneas, the 'pious' instrument of divine powers, which grew into an all-powerful and all-embracing empire, was the more admirable to Dante in contrast with the disorders and strife of cities and parties in his own time. He favoured the so-called Holy Roman Empire as a continuance of the ancient Roman Empire and his support for the 'new Caesar', Henry of Luxembourg, in his designs on the city of Florence, perpetuated the decree of exile against Dante for his part in the Florentine contentions of Guelf and Ghibelline.

Virgil in the *Aeneid* had also described a visit to the underworld. His Hades provided various suggestions of setting and nomenclature for the *Inferno*. Dante (the author) allows Virgil to be for a while a companion to Dante (the character in the poem) on his journey. He is a guide through the depths of the inferno and an escort up the Mountain of Purgatory but takes his leave as they approach the Earthly Paradise. That Virgil should have accompanied him is explained in the poem as at the request of Beatrice, a haunting presence in Dante's mind and art.

She was Beatrice Portinari, the daughter of a wealthy Florentine. Dante first met her when both were children and Beatrice a year younger than he. Her beauty of feature and character inspired in him an adoration that the years had strengthened. Though they went their separate ways, Beatrice becoming the wife of Simone dei Bardi and Dante taken up with poetry, soldiering and diplomacy, her image remained with him. She died at the age of 24 but for Dante lived on, as he describes in the sonnet-sequence of 'The New Life' (*La Vita Nuova*), the mystically passionate work that long preceded the *Commedia*. He was then already married to Gemma Donati by whom he had several children. In time the image of the Florentine girl he had first loved gained a strange duality or multiplicity; she was at once human and a personification of qualities in the abstract – of love, conscience, maternal tenderness, goodness, religious feeling; even, in an ultimate abstraction, of Christian beatitude. It is thus that she appears in the *Divine Comedy*. Dante creates a complexity of allegorical subtleties, though one may read into them the trace of her actual impact on his life and character. The thought of Beatrice seems in fact to have weaned him from moral lapses, he admits, and given him the hope of salvation.

Thus at the beginning of the *Inferno*, Virgil explains that it is at Beatrice's plea that he has come to rescue Dante from the 'dark wood' of his own moral confusion. Allegorically, she might be thought of as Christian piety enlisting in the person of Virgil the aid of philosophy and reason. But in the *Purgatorio* there is a direct confrontation in which in a very human fashion Beatrice sharply reproaches Dante for his sins. It may be noted that the Pre-Raphaelite image of Beatrice, conveyed by the paintings of Dante Gabriel Rossetti as that of mournful and languorous suffering, departs considerably from the plain-speaking and vital creature whom Dante portrays. It is she and not Virgil the excellent pagan, who must lead him upwards in the *Paradiso* through the heavens, though there comes a point when, having delivered her Christian admonitions and heard his contrition, she at last takes her departure. The soul of Dante goes on to the supreme revelation of the light eternal and divine.

The Ten Circles of Hell

In working out his design, Dante makes use of the classifications by number in which the Middle Ages found a mystical virtue. But in his sense of structure and mathematical proportion he showed also a bent of the Florentine genius that had other expression in painting and sculpture. There were ten main divisions of hell, as also ten heavens. Even the terrifying landscape of hell had its order. Dante clearly thought of the earth as a globe, oriented by Jerusalem. At surface level was the brink of the vast pit and there the ditherers, unable to make up their minds between good and evil, aimlessly ran after banners whirling to and fro.

Across the river Acheron and below was the dizzy descent of circle after circle. Five of them formed the outworks of the infernal city of Dis. The first was the Limbo where dwelt the Unbaptized and Virtuous pagans whose unconscious fault it was to be ignorant of Christianity and to be confined by the material or erroneous nature of their own beliefs. The second was that where the Lustful were driven before a gale that signalized their own tempestuous passions; in the third, the Gluttonous wallowed in the mire; in the fourth and fifth the Hoarders, the Spendthrifts and the Wrathful carried on their futile battles. A nether hell was contained within city walls, with a growing terror of descent into the sixth circle of the Heretics and the seventh of Violence where tyrants boiled in a river of blood, profligates were pursued and torn by hounds, suicides turned into withered trees pecked by harpies and sodomites scorched in a sterile desert under a constant rain of fire. Lower still in the eighth and ninth circles the many variations of Fraud and Malice were contained in the pits of Malbolge; the word means 'evil pouches' and Dante describes the area as an inverted hollow cone intersected with ten concentric valleys. The tenth circle was the frozen lake of Cocytus where icy figures

Dante Alighieri: in the *Divine Comedy* the reader ascends with him 'from the depths (of hell) to the region of supreme bliss'. In this allegorical portrait, of the Florentine School, the poet is shown gazing across a river, probably Acheron, to the Mountain of Purgatory

symbolized the final extinction of all feeling in wrongdoers and Lucifer was a frosty monster, different in every way from the active Satan, defiantly heroic in nonconformity, of Milton's *Paradise Lost*.

A hidden path took Dante and Virgil from this underground lair at earth's centre to the Antipodes and the healthier atmosphere of the Mountain of Purgatory. The inferno was an unchanging spectacle, purgatory an active process of improvement. The inferno recalled the specific offences of sinners, purgatory was the place of strengthening and purifying, for getting rid of sin. After the quarantine of ante-purgatory (for the excommunicated and the belatedly repentant) and the passage all must take through Peter's Gate, there followed the arduous but salutary regime nicely adapted to the nature of each of the 'Seven Deadly Sins'; in appropriate and modern fashion the taint of gluttony is removed by starvation. Passing through a final wall of flame the pilgrim reached at last the flowery meads and peaceful pinewoods of the Earthly Paradise. There is a beauty that recalls the paintings of Botticelli in the verses describing the setting of a religious pageantry in which Dante again met and was reconciled with Beatrice. His imagination rises grandly to the supreme test of describing the passage through the heavens; his encounters with the souls of many famous persons; his ascent to the highest of the revolving spheres, the *Primum Mobile* that gives motion to the rest; and thence to the

Empyrean where in a flash of intuitive vision Dante perceives the human will in the encirclement of the Divine Will.

Dante's thought and purpose in the *Divine Comedy* have several aspects. He gave a version of the Christian story, in the general outline of which orthodox Catholicism could find nothing to object to. In another aspect it was his personal confession as one who had erred but at last found redemption. Then again, it was in part a criticism of his times, his countrymen and native city: a rebuke and exhortation. In the struggle between Pope and Emperor that gave their partisans the names respectively of Guelf and Ghibelline he was on the imperial or Ghibelline side; in the split of the rival party into two, the Black Guelfs and White Guelfs, however, he sympathized with the latter and was exiled when they were. The papal supporter of the Black Guelfs, Boniface VIII, is pilloried in the *Divine Comedy* for many misdeeds including simony (the buying or selling of ecclesiastical preferments), avarice, and greed for temporal power.

The Italy of Dante's time is vivid in the poem and so also are the many incidental stories like the sad tale of Paolo and

In the *Inferno*, the first part of the *Divine Comedy*, Dante describes his journey through the ten circles of hell with the Latin poet Virgil as his guide: detail from Signorelli's *Last Judgement* in Orvieto Cathedral, showing the damned tormented by the winged, horned demons of hell

Francesa and the horrifying confession of Count Ugolino. A question that remains is how far the poem has a significance for the present time, apart from its manifest splendour as a work of art and the interest of its historical associations. The progress of science in modern times has strengthened a materialistic view of the universe far removed from Dante's scheme of things. The present mapping out and proposed 'conquest' of space might seem to make the heavens he wrote of no more than a naive reflection of medieval astronomy. Yet is there any reason why his conception of a spiritual dimension is less valid now than at any other time? In the last canto of the *Paradiso* he leaves no artificial picture of heaven but the feeling of a wonder remaining, the transcendent source of the good which is the soul's objective. The intense feeling, he says (of the glory intuitively perceived for a moment) stayed with him on his return to his earthly life. Without detailed memory of his greatest experience Dante retained the comfort of the love 'that moves the sun and all the stars'. His great 'allegory of the soul' can be fortifying amid the confused welter of today's thought.

WILLIAM GAUNT

FURTHER READING: Among translations which can be recommended are those by L. Binyon, *Inferno* (1933), *Purgatory* (1938) and *Paradise* (1943), published by St. Martin's Press; C. H. Sisson, *The Divine Comedy* (Regnery Gateway, 1981); D. L. Sayers, *Hell, Purgatory* (Penguin, London, 1962, 2 vols).